Nonverbal Communication In Human Interaction

Ninth Edition

Mark L. Knapp
The University of Texas at Austin

Judith A. Hall
Northeastern University

Terrence G. Horgan
University of Michigan, Flint

Kendall Hunt
publishing company

Kendall Hunt
publishing company

www.kendallhunt.com
Send all inquiries to:
4050 Westmark Drive
Dubuque, IA 52004-1840

Published in the United States of America

BRIEF CONTENTS

DETAILED CONTENTS

PREFACE

You do not have to be a researcher to know that an enormous amount of daily interaction takes place through the infinitely complex nonverbal medium. Furthermore, people's expertise in using and understanding nonverbal communication is extraordinary: every person reading this book is already an expert. It is our job, however, as textbook authors to break it down, analyze it, and look at it from every angle so that you will have an intellectual and not just an intuitive grasp of this endlessly fascinating subject.

In undertaking the 9th edition of this book that we love, we were humbled once again by the mountain of wonderful research available to summarize, with more coming out every day. We had a terrific time reading and rereading, and deciding what research would be most important and interesting to our readers. The decisions were often hard. Our goal was to respect the scientific literature while keeping the attention and enthusiasm of our readers. This book serves, we believe, two noncompeting goals. The first is to offer the best and soundest presentation on nonverbal communication available in any textbook. The second goal is to provide the scholarly resources that any interested person—from an undergraduate to a professional researcher—can find of value. This is why you will find such a long reference list at the back of the book. Those references are intended to help you when you want them. The *Instructor's Manual* for this book also provides the information and imagination necessary for effective classroom learning in nonverbal communication.

The fact that this book is coauthored is worth noting. One of us represents the field of communication and the other two social psychology. This collaboration, which requires the blending of two distinct perspectives, is symbolic of the nonverbal literature we report in this volume. The theory and research addressing nonverbal phenomena come from scholars with a wide variety of academic backgrounds and perspectives—communication, counseling, psychology, psychiatry, linguistics, sociology, neuroscience, management, speech, and others. Understanding the nature of nonverbal communication is truly an interdisciplinary enterprise.

In revising this book, we retained the features that students and instructors valued from the previous editions while adding and changing other things that we believe will improve the book. This edition deals with many social, sexual, and political issues of our time, as they relate to the broad discipline of nonverbal communication. For some chapters, we highlight an area of nonverbal communication that is in need of research attention. Our goal is to encourage current and future researchers to explore nonverbal phenomena that are poorly understood at this time.

One change that we hope students like is the inclusion of more text boxes in each chapter. These text boxes cover important, interesting, or current topics relevant to the field of nonverbal communication. Sometimes they are teasers designed to introduce a novel issue to the reader, and sometimes they summarize timely and important research. This edition also includes a suggested activity at the end of each chapter, to help nonverbal communication come to life for the reader, along with a set of discussion questions. In addition, because we recognize how important photographs and drawings are in a book like this, we have continued to use visual representations to aid comprehension of certain nonverbal actions, including a great many new ones not seen in previous editions. Because an increasing amount of communication is mediated by some form of technology, we have also incorporated new research findings and topics in that area that are relevant to the lives of students and teachers, such as Facebook, online dating, and text messaging, to name a few. Another change is in the use of pronouns. In line with the American Psychological Association's new guidelines, we use the singular "they" throughout our book. The singular "they" is not only more gender-inclusive, it also is easier to read than "he or she."

In every new edition, we incorporate the most recent theory and research while retaining definitive studies from the past. Readers will find that some areas of study have fewer recent references than others. This simply means that there has not been a lot of recent research in that area or that the recent work, in our judgment, does not substantially change the conclusions from earlier studies. If something we know about human behavior today was first revealed in a study from 1958, we want readers to know that, and we will maintain the 1958 reference. Research on a particular topic often has an ebb and flow to it. During the 1960s and 1970s, the fear that a worldwide population boom would create terrible problems spawned a lot of research on space, territory, and crowding. In recent years, far less research has been done in this area. The study of gestures, on the other hand, has gone from an area of relatively little research activity during the 1960s and 1970s to an area that is of primary interest to numerous scholars today. Therefore, in this book we honor the entire history of nonverbal communication studies.

The book is divided into five parts. Part I introduces the reader to some fundamental ideas and addresses the following questions: What is nonverbal communication? How do verbal and nonverbal communication interrelate? What difference does knowledge of nonverbal communication make to your everyday life? Are some people more skilled than others at communicating nonverbally? How did they get that way? With this general perspective in mind, Parts II, III, and IV take the reader through the nonverbal elements involved in any interaction: the environment within which the interaction occurs, the physical features of the interactants themselves, and their behavior—gestures, touching, facial expressions, eye gazing, and vocal sounds. Part V begins with a chapter focused on how all the separate parts of an interaction combine as we seek to accomplish very common goals in daily life—for example, communicating who we are, communicating closeness and distance, communicating varying degrees of status and power, deceiving others, and effectively managing the back-and-forth flow of conversation. Chapter 13 examines nonverbal communication in the context of advertising, therapy, the classroom, politics, culture, and technology. Throughout the book, we repeatedly point out how all interactants involved are likely to play a role in whatever behavior is displayed by a single individual—even though this perspective is not always adequately developed in the research we review.

There are many people to thank for the success of this book. First and foremost are the many thousands of students and instructors who have used this book and provided feedback to us during its nearly 50 years of existence. More than anyone else, you readers are responsible for the longevity of this book. With this in mind, we undertook this 9th edition by putting what we believe to be instructor and student needs at the forefront of our writing. As with previous editions, we encourage you to let us know whether we have succeeded.

This revision of our book took place during the global COVID-19 pandemic. We would like to sincerely thank all the folks at KendallHunt who helped make this edition of the book possible during a challenging time in our nation's history in which many people's personal lives and work environments were dramatically and negatively impacted.

We have individuals to thank as well. Angela Willenbring of the Kendall Hunt Publishing Company was supportive and helpful at every step. We also thank Kimberly Fillah-Horgan for her drawings in the book, Alyssa Petruski for her work on the references, and Morgan Stosic for updating our instructor materials. We extend a special thanks to Melissa Grey. We greatly appreciate her reviews, edits, and suggestions for improving some of our textboxes. We also thank her for the textbox on the objectification of women. Finally (and this is the second and third authors speaking), we wish to thank Mark Knapp for inviting us to join him as authors—Judith Hall on the 3rd edition and Terrence Horgan on the 8th edition. Mark has been a generous mentor to both of us and we extend our deepest thanks to him. We are honored to be coauthors with Mark.

ABOUT THE AUTHORS

Mark L. Knapp (PhD, Pennsylvania State University) is the Jesse H. Jones Centennial Professor Emeritus in Communication and Distinguished Teaching Professor Emeritus at The University of Texas at Austin. He co-edited the *Handbook of Interpersonal Communication* and *The Interplay of Truth and Deception*. He authored, then co-authored *Lying and Deception in Human Interaction*, *Nonverbal Communication in Human Interaction*, and *Interpersonal Communication in Human Relationships*. He is past president and fellow of the International Communication Association and past president and distinguished scholar of the National Communication Association.

© M. Knapp

Judith A. Hall is University Distinguished Professor of Psychology, Emerita, at Northeastern University in Boston, MA. She is a social psychologist who studies interpersonal interaction, with a focus on person perception and nonverbal communication in daily life and in medical interactions. She co-authored *Doctors Talking with Patients/Patients Talking with Doctors: Improving Communication in Medical Care* and co-edited *Emotion in the Clinical Encounter*. Other books include *Nonverbal Sex Differences: Communication Accuracy and Expressive Style*, *Interpersonal Sensitivity: Theory and Measurement*, and *The Social Psychology of Perceiving Others Accurately*.

© J. Hall

Terrence G. Horgan is Myron and Margaret Winegarden Professor of Psychology at the University of Michigan, Flint. He also is one of the Associate Editors of the *Journal of Nonverbal Behavior*. He is a social psychologist who studies person perception, factors that impact person memory, and the verbal and nonverbal cues people use to signal romantic interest during courtship.

© T. Horgan

AN INTRODUCTION TO THE STUDY OF NONVERBAL COMMUNICATION

What is nonverbal communication? How does nonverbal behavior function in relation to verbal behavior? How does nonverbal communication affect people's everyday lives? Does a person learn how to perform body language, or is it instinctive? Are some people more skilled at communicating with these face, voice, and body signals? The answers to these fundamental questions are the focus of Part I of this book.

CHAPTER 1

NONVERBAL COMMUNICATION: BASIC PERSPECTIVES

Those of us who keep our eyes open can read volumes into what we see going on around us.

—E. T. Hall

It may come as no surprise to you that, in everyday life, you are an expert in nonverbal communication even though you have yet to read a page of this book. Consider the following questions:

- Have you ever looked at another person in such a way as to communicate your sexual interest in them?
- When you enter an elevator full of strangers, do you take a sudden interest in how those buttons light up as the cage moves from floor to floor?
- Do you know when a baby is hungry as opposed to tired, just from hearing how he cries?
- If you cut someone off in traffic, would you have a problem understanding the other driver's reaction if they showed you an upright middle finger?
- How would you use your right hand when you are introduced to a potential boss during an interview?
- Can you tell when a loved one might be mad, sad, or happy by looking at their face?
- Imagine entering a dorm room and seeing two men. One is wearing athletic shorts and a tank top over a heavily muscled body, and he has posters of football stars on the wall near his bed and his clothes litter his side of the room. The other man—thin and bespectacled—appears to be neat as a pin, with stacks of math and engineering books around his desk. Would you suspect potential conflict between these two?

Chances are you had no problem answering these questions. That is because everyone possesses a wealth of knowledge, beliefs, and experiences regarding nonverbal communication. These questions bring to mind three aspects of nonverbal communication that you make use of during your day-to-day interactions with others. One concerns the sending of nonverbal messages; the second, receiving them; and the last, the complex interplay between the first two. First, you send (or encode) nonverbal messages to others—sometimes deliberately, sometimes not. When the message is deliberate, your goal is for the other person to understand a particular message that you have sent in one or more nonverbal cue channels, such as your tone of voice, posture, and facial expression ("She could tell I was mad at her"). Sometimes you succeed. If you do not, it could be because your message was unclear, contradictory, or ambiguous or because the other person missed, ignored, or misread your nonverbal message. You also may send nonverbal messages to others that are not deliberate or even intended by you. For example, you likely communicate your gender to others via a series of static nonverbal cues that include your body shape and facial features, or you might burst into tears when sad. You have sent a powerful nonverbal message to others in each case, even though your goal was not necessarily to do so. There are times in which important information about your emotional state, attitudes, and intentions leaks out of you nonverbally. Your bitterness toward a rival's remarks might be revealed in a flash of anger across your face despite your best efforts to conceal it. Such facial cues are dynamic in nature because they change during an interaction.

As you might have guessed already, you live in a sea of static and dynamic nonverbal messages. These messages surround you when you are interacting with others, and even when you are alone you emit nonverbal cues ("I start to shake when I think about my date tonight"). Nonverbal cues come to you from other people, such as strangers, acquaintances, neighbors, coworkers, friends, and loved ones. They even come to you from animals, such as the neighbor's dog that wags its tail every time it sees you. They also come to you from the physical structure of, and objects contained within, the environments that you move in and out of during your day. These environments are real in a physical sense because you can make physical contact with them. However, one such environment is not physical in this sense: cyberspace. While in cyberspace, you can hear and see nonverbal messages, such as those delivered by others' profile "pics" and emoticons or avatars. These computer-generated nonverbal messages are probably becoming increasingly important to you in a world where online interactions are taking the place of some face-to-face interactions. Indeed, some students might take a nonverbal communication class online. And some of you may be using FaceTime to get to know another person.

Elbow bumps, remote working/learning, face masks, and social distancing are part of the new realities of life during the COVID-19 pandemic, as of this writing. The long-term applicability of these protective measures to worldwide society is not known. Their relevance to nonverbal communication is obvious, however. People struggle to understand others' expressions when only the eyes show. People wonder if others will think they are rude for not shaking hands. After the crisis is over, will people continue to be wary of touching or standing close to others? Will educational and business institutions rely less on face-to-face interactions and does it matter? Any change could impact what is seen as acceptable nonverbal behavior. For example, Dr. Anthony Fauci, leading public health expert on COVID-19, advised that the practice of shaking hands should stop for health and safety reasons.

https://abcnews.go.com/Politics/fauci-perfect-world-americans-stop-shaking-hands/story?id=70062797

Verbal messages are meaningless unless someone is there to interpret them. Nonverbal communication is no different. The process of receiving nonverbal messages, including your own ("Why is my fist clenched when he's around?"), includes giving meaning to or interpreting those messages. (This process will be defined later as *decoding* a nonverbal message.) As a receiver of nonverbal messages, you may focus on one particular nonverbal cue or several in an attempt to understand the message that another person has sent to you. For example, in an effort to understand the emotional state of your friend James, you might focus on his facial expression , his posture, and/or his tone of voice. Whether you are successful at interpreting that emotional message is another matter. You might have missed or ignored that nonverbal message. Or, depending on your skill level at reading others' emotion states, you might have misinterpreted his nonverbal message. Finally, you might have correctly interpreted his message but still do not understand how he truly feels because he used nonverbal behavior to feign a feeling or conceal a particular emotional state from you.

It is obvious that words can be combined in an infinite number of ways and that the meaning of a sentence may depend upon contextual information, word choice, and the arrangement of the selected words. For example, take the following sentence fragment: "Mia learned about … She drove to … Charity … with a … in her hand." It is unclear what is going on in this situation. Let us see what happens when we add different contextual information and words to these sentences. (1) Mia learned about the plight of the children. She drove to the Charity with a checkbook in her hand. (2) Mia learned about her husband's infidelity. She drove to the house where Charity lives with a gun in her hand. In a similar fashion, the meaning of nonverbal communication is not as simple as knowing what specific nonverbal

CAN PEOPLE READ OTHERS LIKE A BOOK?

It depends on your definition of *like a book*. There became book titles that tell a lot about what is inside (e.g., *How to Taste: A Guide to Enjoying Wine*). Similarly, there are nonverbal displays that can tell a lot about what a person is feeling inside (e.g., red face, eyebrows lowered and drawn together, shaking fists). Book covers and titles can also be categorized (e.g., nonfiction, history, civil war battles). And so can people—their age, gender, and personality traits—by looking at their head and facial characteristics (see Chapter 6).

However, understanding books and people is generally a far more complicated matter than just categorizing. If you read Stephenie Meyer's *Twilight* series, you had to learn about the characters, the events, the setting, and the plot to grasp the story. Understanding people is no different. If you were observing another person, you would want to take into consideration their characteristics (physical, social, psychological), their nonverbal and verbal behavior, the setting they are in, whom they are interacting with and why, and so on. More important, people's nonverbal cues are only one clue—the meaning of which is dependent upon a host of other factors—to understanding who they are.

© Jure Divich/Shutterstock.com

© Billion Photos/Shutterstock.com

behavior, say touching, is seen by you. It depends upon contextual information, the sender (encoder) of the nonverbal behavior, the receiver (decoder) of that behavior, the relationship between the sender and the receiver, the arrangement of other nonverbal cues, as well as any words being exchanged by the two.

Let us consider an example to illustrate the complexity of nonverbal communication. You see two people hug. What does that hug mean? Now what comes to your mind when additional information is added?

- There are other people around dressed in black standing near an open casket at a funeral.
- The people are at a restaurant celebrating their baseball team's victory earlier that evening.
- The people are at work. One person is the boss. The other is their subordinate.
- What if the two people are leaning toward each other from a distance, touching shoulders only briefly? What if they are instead pressing their bodies together and resting their heads on each other's shoulders? What if the person being hugged stiffened their body before receiving the hug?
- Historical and cultural factors likely play a role in your perception of that simple hug as well. If you had lived around the turn of the 20th century, you would have looked askance at the two people if you knew that they had just ended their first date, whereas nowadays such behavior would not even raise one of your eyebrows. If the two were Eastern European men, you would not be surprised if they began cheek-kissing as well, whereas you would be if they were from the United States.
- Last, you would take into consideration any words exchanged between the two people, as this could significantly alter the meaning of their hug to you. For instance, in the funeral setting mentioned earlier, it would matter if, during the hug, one person said to the other, "Sorry for your loss," as opposed to "We can now finally get our hands on our inheritance money!"

FIGURE 1-1 What will this hug mean?

Being an expert in using and understanding nonverbal cues, you probably had no problem understanding how the meaning of that hug changed in these scenarios. On the basis of the hugging scenarios (see FIGURE 1-1), it might be clear to you that a particular nonverbal cue has multiple meanings (or maybe even no apparent meaning at all) and that the particular meaning you settle on depends on a host of other factors, including the presence and absence of other nonverbal cues.

Therefore, as a sender and receiver of nonverbal cues, you have to make decisions about the cues you transmit to and pick up from others, which suggests that there must be rules that you follow. Some of these rules may be very clear to you, such as knowing that you should not sniff a person you have just met. Other rules that you follow are completely unknown to you, operating outside your conscious awareness. Do you know the array of cues that you send and receive that allow you and a friend to smoothly and effortlessly take turns while talking to each other? Probably not, but you do know how to use them. Finally, other rules occupy the middle ground between the two; they can be brought to your conscious awareness at times, to some extent at least. One such rule concerns not standing too close to others when talking with them. Although you are aware of this rule, you probably do not think about it much during day-to-day interactions. However, although the exact distance of your personal comfort zone may be unknown to you, you certainly know when it has been violated by someone.

Despite being an expert in the everyday use of nonverbal cues, you are new to the scientific study of nonverbal communication. The need to formally investigate what people do in everyday life becomes quickly apparent when you think about the specifics of nonverbal behavior. The purpose of this book is to introduce the scientific study of nonverbal communication to you, which includes an examination of how nonverbal cues are used—whether intentionally or spontaneously, consciously or not—in human interaction. Of importance, understanding of nonverbal communication comes from many different disciplines, including anthropology, biology, communication, gender studies, psychology, and sociology, which will become apparent in the chapters that follow.

Before we get to that, there is a need to discuss five basic perspectives through which we can view these chapters:

1. As with other scientific disciplines, there is a need for a common language for discussing the topic at hand. Thus, nonverbal communication will be *defined*.
2. Nonverbal behavior will be classified (e.g., territoriality, gestures, touching, eye behavior). By classifying nonverbal behaviors, we will be able to review the relevant research in each area in an organized fashion.
3. Nonverbal behavior that has been defined and classified (e.g., touching behavior) should not be thought of as occurring in isolation from nonverbal behavior that is part of another category (e.g., eye behavior) or, for that

matter, from verbal behavior. Indeed, consideration of the interplay between nonverbal cues and verbal cues is a vital part of understanding the *total communication process* that occurs between people in daily life and even on social networking sites.

4. The scientific roots and *historical trends* in nonverbal communication research will be reviewed, as they provide the foundation and framework, respectively, for exploring contemporary research.

5. The potential relevance of this scientific endeavor to *everyday lives* will be discussed, as many of its findings have implications for people's personal lives and can be applied to various real-life settings.

Each of these basic perspectives will be covered in greater detail in the remainder of this chapter.

PERSPECTIVE 1: DEFINING NONVERBAL COMMUNICATION

To most people, the phrase *nonverbal communication* refers to communication effected by means other than words, assuming words are the verbal element. This definition is generally useful, but it does not account adequately for the complexity of this phenomenon. This broad definition should serve us well, though, as long as we observe some important points.

First, however, the distinction between *communication* and *behavior* needs discussion. Readers should know that we use the terms "nonverbal communication" and "nonverbal behavior" more or less interchangeably. We acknowledge that some authors would distinguish between communication—which is more deliberate and involves a shared code between two people—and behavior, which might be inadvertent. To illustrate, it would be communication if you displayed your delight in getting a gift from your friend using nonverbal cues, whereas if your professor inferred you were impatient by seeing your feet jiggling under the desk, we would not say that you were "communicating" your impatience to the professor. Although this distinction is a valid one, it is a very difficult one to make in real life where others' intentions are often not known.

Now for the needed additional points. One needs to understand that separating verbal and nonverbal behavior into two separate and distinct categories is virtually impossible. Consider, for example, the hand movements that make up American Sign Language, a language of the deaf. These gesticulations are mostly linguistic (verbal), yet hand gestures are often considered behavior that is "other than words." And for those who can hear, their own hand gestures may be used to retrieve the words they wish to speak to others (Hadar, Wenkert-Olenik, Krauss, & Soroker, 1998). McNeill (1992) demonstrated the linguistic qualities of some gestures by noting that different kinds of gestures disappear with different kinds of aphasia—the impairment of the ability to use or comprehend words—namely, those gestures with linguistic functions similar to the specific verbal loss. Conversely, not all spoken words are clearly or singularly verbal, for example, onomatopoeic words, such as *buzz* or *murmur*.

Also, one needs to understand that our definition does not indicate whether the phrase "by means other than words" refers to the behavior produced—that is, its *encoding*—or to the perceiver's interpretation of it—its *decoding*. Decoding involves attributing meaning to the cues that have been perceived. A first step toward understanding the process of attributing meaning to nonverbal behavior is to understand how the brain processes nonverbal stimuli.

PROCESSING NONVERBAL INFORMATION

Currently, many brain researchers believe that the two hemispheres of the brain process different types of information, but each hemisphere does not process each type exclusively. Nonverbal messages may be processed by either hemisphere, even though the bulk of the work is probably done by the right side. The left hemisphere processes mainly sequentially ordered, digital, verbal, and linguistic information. Nonverbal messages processed by the left hemisphere may involve symbolic gestures and facial expressions that have a closely linked verbal translation, for example, speech-independent gestures that have a direct verbal translation, such as thumbs-up. The right hemisphere of the brain is normally credited with processing visual/spatial relationships and analogic or Gestalt information. And it seems to be the main processing area for some types of gestures as well as spontaneous, expressive displays of emotion in the face and voice (Buck & VanLear, 2002; Kelly & Goldsmith, 2004). It is important to note, however, that few scientists currently believe that either side of the brain deals *exclusively* with a particular kind of information. In fact, the following case illustrates how adaptable the brain can be.

Bruce Lipstadt had the left hemisphere of his brain removed when he was 5 years old (Koutlak, 1976). Few physicians thought that his verbal skills would develop, and most thought his body would be paralyzed after the operation. Twenty-six years later, Bruce had an IQ of 126—better than 9 out of 10 people. He swam, rode his bike, and got an A in a statistics course. Because his speech was normal, the right hemisphere must have taken over many of the functions formerly conducted mainly by the left hemisphere. Obviously, this does not always happen as a result of operations of this type, especially after puberty. But it does suggest that, although the right and left hemispheres seem to specialize in processing certain types of information, they are by no means limited to processing only one.

Even when information is being processed primarily by one hemisphere, it is unlikely that the other hemisphere is totally inactive. While someone is reading a story, the right hemisphere may be playing a specialized role in understanding a metaphor or appreciating emotional content, whereas the left hemisphere is simultaneously trying to derive meaning from the complex relations among word concepts and syntax. Despite the apparent complexity and adaptability of the brain, much of what is processed by the right hemisphere seems to be what we call *nonverbal phenomena*, whereas much of what is processed by the left hemisphere is what we categorize as *verbal phenomena*. However, because some nonverbal behavior is more closely aligned with verbal behavior than others (e.g., speech-independent gestures), we might expect to see more left-hemispheric activity in such cases.

AWARENESS AND CONTROL

Nonverbal behavior, like verbal behavior, is encoded with varying degrees of control and awareness (Lakin, 2006; also see FIGURE 1-2). Sometimes people have time to plan their responses, but sometimes it is important to respond rapidly when a great deal of information is impinging on their senses. When this occurs, people are unaware, or only dimly aware, of why they responded as they did. These responses are linked to a cognitive program that takes place immediately and automatically following the perception of a particular stimulus (Choi, Gray, & Ambady, 2005).

When people use speech-independent gestures such as the "A-ok" or thumbs up gesture, pose for photographs, or select attire, a high level of awareness and control is usually present. In contrast, nervous mannerisms, pupil dilation, and mimicking the behavior of an interaction partner are examples of behavior that is often enacted outside of awareness and control (e.g., Bargh & Chartrand, 1999). Also, a given behavior may be enacted without much awareness on some occasions but with a great deal of awareness at other times. For example, a person may not be aware that their tone of voice is signaling dislike for someone, but might be very much aware of using their voice to communicate a sarcastic message.

Decoding nonverbal behavior also may be performed with varying degrees of awareness. Seeing a man who looks elderly might automatically trigger the perception that the man is also walking slowly—whether he is or not. When people say they think a person is lying but cannot explain what behaviors led them to believe that, it may mean there is an out-of-awareness program in their brain that is associated with detecting deception and triggered by the perception of certain behaviors.

More important, responses that are out of awareness and control need not always be that way. Feedback on the accuracy or utility of an automatic process may lead to changing the program or eliminating it. Reading this book may also make you more aware of certain behaviors you have been encoding and decoding.

PERSPECTIVE 2: CLASSIFYING NONVERBAL BEHAVIOR

Another way of defining nonverbal communication is to look at the things people study. The theory and research associated with nonverbal communication focus on three primary domains: the environmental structures and conditions *within which* communication takes place, the physical characteristics of the communicators themselves, and the various behaviors manifested by the communicators. A detailed breakdown of these three features follows.

THE COMMUNICATION ENVIRONMENT

Although most of the emphasis in nonverbal research is on the appearance and behavior of the people communicating, increasing attention is being given to the influence of nonhuman factors on human transactions. People change environments to help them accomplish their communicative goals; conversely, environments can affect moods, choices of

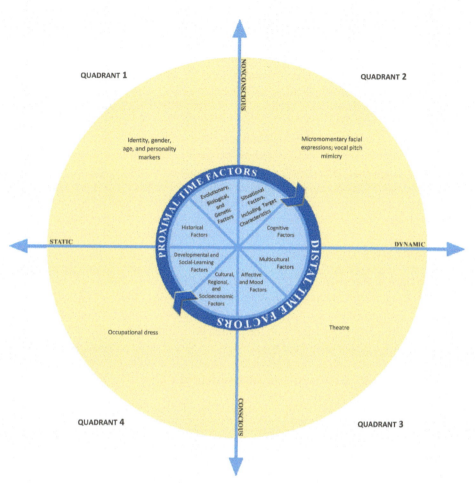

FIGURE 1-2 Hall, Horgan, and Murphy (2019) have provided a new model for how people encode nonverbal information. The horizontal axis shows that encoding covers a continuum anchored by static and dynamic cues, and the vertical axis covers a continuum anchored by nonconscious and conscious encoding processes. Static refers to encoded behavior that is relatively typical for a person across different contexts. The center circle depicts how proximal (e.g., situational factors) and distal (i.e., the process begins in the past, for example, a person's developmental history) time factors may impact the relative location of specific cues—and thus their potential informational value to perceivers—along the two axes.

Let's examine the utility of this model in terms of describing static versus dynamic cues that are not under the conscious control of people. Your biological sex appears static to others during an interaction, and it is not something that you consciously control (see Quadrant 1). Obviously, you cannot change your face from male to female at will. If the person you are interacting with makes you mad, your facial expression may change (dynamic, proximal) with a flash of anger, although you did not consciously initiate the process (micromomentary facial expressions of emotion; see Quadrant 2).

Now consider how a distal factor, such as a person's developmental history, might influence the informational value of their facial cues to perceivers. The person's personality traits may impact how they respond emotionally and facially to situational factors. These facial expressions, although dynamic and proximal in the moment, may over time lead to changes in their facial appearance. These facial cues now appear static and not under the person's control and may then be used by perceivers as potential markers of their social or personality traits (Adams, Garrido, Albohn, Hess, & Kleck, 2016; Bjornsdottir & Rule, 2017).

words, and actions. Thus, this category concerns those elements that impinge on the human relationship but are not directly a part of it.

Environmental factors include the furniture, architectural style, interior decorating, lighting conditions, colors, temperature, additional noises or music, and so on amid which the interaction occurs. Variations in arrangements, materials, shapes, or surfaces of objects in the interacting environment can be extremely influential on the outcome of an interpersonal interaction.

This category also includes *traces of action*. For instance, as you observe cigarette butts, orange peels, and waste-paper left by the person you will soon interact with, you could form an impression that influences your meeting with them. Perceptions of time and timing make up another important part of the communicative environment. When something occurs, how frequently it occurs, and the tempos or rhythms of actions are clearly a part of the communicative world even though they are not a part of the physical environment per se.

Spatial Environment

Proxemics is the study of the use and perception of social and personal space. Under this heading is a body of work called *small group ecology*, which concerns itself with how people use and respond to spatial relationships in formal and informal group settings. Such studies deal with seating and spatial arrangements as related to leadership, communication flow, and the task at hand. On an even broader level, attention has been given to spatial relationships in crowds and densely populated situations. *Personal space* is sometimes studied in the context of conversation distance and how it varies according to the gender, status, roles, cultural orientation, and so on of the interactants. The term *territoriality* is also used frequently in the study of proxemics to denote the human tendency to stake out personal territory, much as other animals and birds do in the wild.

THE COMMUNICATORS' PHYSICAL CHARACTERISTICS

This category covers things that remain relatively unchanged during a typical human interaction. These static nonverbal cues include a person's physique or body shape, general attractiveness, height, weight, hair, overall skin color or tone, and so on. Body or breath odors associated with the person are normally considered part of physical appearance as well. Furthermore, objects associated with interactants may be part of their physical appearance. These are called *artifacts* and include things such as clothes, eyeglasses, hairpieces, false eyelashes, jewelry, and accessories (e.g., a briefcase). Last, physical appearance includes the various ways people choose to decorate their skin. These include tattoos, piercings, cosmetics, and face and body paint.

BODY MOVEMENT AND POSITION

Dynamic body movement and positioning typically include gestures; movements of the limbs, hands, head, feet, and legs; facial expressions, such as smiles; eye behavior, including blinking, direction and length of gaze, and pupil dilation; touching behavior; vocalics; and posture. The furrow of the brow, the slump of a shoulder, the tilt of the head, and changes in vocal pitch are all examples of body movements and positions.

Gestures

There are many types of gestures, and many variations of these types, but the most frequently studied are the following:

1. **Speech independent.** Some gestures can stand alone, without speech, because they have a well-known verbal translation in their usage community, usually consisting of a word or two or a phrase. The gestures used to represent "okay" or "peace" (also the "V-for-victory" sign) are examples of speech-independent gestures for large segments of U.S. culture.
2. **Speech related.** These gestures are directly tied to, or accompany, speech and often serve to illustrate what is being said. These movements may accent or emphasize a word or phrase, sketch a path of thought, point to objects, depict a spatial relationship, depict the rhythm or pacing of an event, draw a picture of a referent, depict a bodily action, or serve as commentary on the regulation and organization of the interactive process.

Posture

Posture is normally studied in conjunction with other nonverbal signals to determine the degree of people's attention or involvement, the degree of status relative to the other interactive partner, or the degree of liking for the other interactant. A forward-leaning posture, for example, has been associated with higher involvement and more liking in studies where interactants did not know each other very well. Posture is also a key indicator of the intensity of some emotional states. Examples include the drooping posture sometimes associated with great sadness and the rigid, tense posture linked to intense anger. The extent to which communicators mirror each other's posture may indicate the degree of their conversational involvement, which sometimes results in greater rapport between them.

Touching Behavior

Touching may be self-focused or other-focused. Self-focused manipulations, not usually made for purposes of communicating messages to others, may reflect a person's particular state or habit. Many are commonly called *nervous mannerisms* or *self-adaptors*. Some of these actions are relics from an earlier time of life, when a person first learned how to manage emotions, develop social contacts, or perform some instructional task. Self-adaptors may involve various manipulations of one's own body, such as licking, picking, holding, pinching, and scratching. Object adaptors are manipulations practiced in conjunction with an object, as when a former cigarette smoker reaches toward their breast pocket for the nonexistent package of cigarettes.

One of the most potent forms of nonverbal communication occurs when two people touch each other. Touch can be practical, ritualized/formal, comforting, sexually arousing, or hurtful in nature. As you will see later, touch is a highly ambiguous form of behavior because its meaning often depends more on the context, the nature of the relationship, and the manner of execution than on the configuration of the touch per se. Some researchers are concerned with touching behavior as an important factor in a child's early development, whereas others are interested in the impact of touching behavior in adults' relationships.

Facial Expressions

Most studies in this domain are concerned with facial configurations that display various emotional states. Anger, sadness, surprise, happiness, fear, and disgust are the most studied facial expressions of emotion. Facial expressions also can function as regulatory gestures, provide feedback and commentary, and manage the flow of interactions.

Eye Behavior

Where, when, and how long people look during an interaction are the primary foci for studies of gazing. *Gaze* refers to the eye movement we make in the general direction of another's face. Mutual gaze occurs when interactants look into each other's eye area. The dilation and constriction of the pupils can indicate interest, attention/involvement, or deception.

HURTFUL TOUCHING

Sexual harassment is a serious problem for women. News outlets have shared numerous polls documenting the disturbing frequency of its occurrence. According to reports, 35% of women have been sexually harassed or abused at work (Nation, 11/2017 [https://www.thenation.com/article/sexual-harassment-has-not-changed-so-much-since-the-1970s/]), 62% of women have been sexually harassed at university (K12 academics, 10/2019 [https://www.k12academics.com/education-issues/sexual-harassment/statistics]), and 51% of women have experienced unwelcome sexual touching (NPR, February, 2018 [https://www.npr.org/sections/thetwo-way/2018/02/21/587671849/a-new-survey-finds-eighty-percent-of-women-have-experienced-sexual-harassment]).

©Yakobchuk Viacheslav/Shutterscock.com

At the societal level, the *Me Too Movement* has been instrumental in addressing and redressing one form of sexual harassment: inappropriate sexual touching.

At the institutional level, a university may have a link on its homepage where students, faculty, and staff can report sexual misconduct confidentially.

Online and face-to-face training programs are available for individuals to learn how they can, as bystanders, stop the sexual harassment of others.

Vocal Behavior

Vocal behavior deals with how something is said, not what is said, as well as some sounds made without concurrent speech. A distinction is typically made between two types of sounds:

1. The sound variations made with the vocal cords during speech that produce changes in a person's pitch, duration, and loudness.
2. Sounds that result primarily from physiological mechanisms other than the vocal cords, for example, the pharyngeal, oral, or nasal cavities.

Most of the research on vocal behavior and its effects on human interaction has focused on pitch level and variability; the duration of sounds, whether they are clipped or drawn out; pauses within the speech stream and the latency of response when switching speaking turns; loudness level and variability; resonance; precise or slurred articulation; rate; rhythm; and intruding sounds during speech, such as "uh" or "um." The study of vocal signals encompasses a broad range of topics, from stereotypes associated with certain voices to the effects of vocal behavior on comprehension and persuasion. Even specialized sounds such as laughing, belching, yawning, swallowing, and moaning may be of interest to researchers because they can affect the outcome of an interaction.

PERSPECTIVE 3: NONVERBAL COMMUNICATION IN THE TOTAL COMMUNICATION PROCESS

Even though this book emphasizes nonverbal communication, it is important not to forget the inseparable nature of verbal and nonverbal signals. Ray Birdwhistell, a pioneer in nonverbal research, reportedly said that studying only nonverbal communication is like studying noncardiac physiology. His point is well-taken. The verbal dimension is so intimately woven and subtly represented in so much of what has been previously labeled *nonverbal* that the term "nonverbal" does not always adequately describe the behavior under study. Some of the most noteworthy scholars associated with nonverbal study refuse to segregate words from gestures; these scholars work under the broader terms of *communication* or *face-to-face interaction* (Bavelas & Chovil, 2006). Kendon put it this way:

> It is a common observation that, when a person speaks, muscular systems besides those of the lips, tongue, and jaws often become active.... Gesticulation is organized as part of the same overall unit of action by which speech is also organized.... Gesture and speech are available as two separate modes of representation and are coordinated because both are being guided by the same overall aim. That aim is to produce a pattern of action that will accomplish the representation of a meaning. (1983, pp. 17, 20)

Because verbal and nonverbal systems operate together as part of the larger communication process, efforts to distinguish clearly between the two have not been very successful. One common misconception assumes that nonverbal behavior is used solely to communicate emotional messages, whereas verbal behavior is for conveying ideas. But words transmit emotional information—one can talk explicitly about emotions, and also communicate emotion with verbal nuances. Conversely, nonverbal cues are often used for purposes other than showing emotion; for example, people in conversation use eye movements to help each other know when it is time to switch speaking turns, and people commonly use hand gestures while talking to help convey their ideas (McNeill, 2000). Hall and Schmid Mast (2007) showed that people turn relatively more to nonverbal cues when they want to know how a person is feeling and more to verbal cues when they want to know what a person is thinking, but that does not mean the desired information is necessarily in those communication channels.

The ways meaning is attached to verbal and nonverbal behavior are not all that different, either. Nonverbal actions, like verbal ones, may communicate more than one message at a time. For example, the way you nonverbally make it clear to another person that you want to keep talking may simultaneously express your need for dominance over that person as well as your current emotional state. When you grip a child's shoulder during a reprimand, you may increase their comprehension and recall, but you may also elicit such a negative reaction that the child refuses to obey you. A smile can be a part of an emotional expression, an attitudinal message, a self-presentation, or a listener response to manage the interaction. And, like verbal behavior, the meanings attributed to nonverbal behavior may be stereotyped, idiomatic, or ambiguous. Furthermore, the same nonverbal behavior performed in different contexts may, like words, receive different attributions of meaning. For example, looking down at the floor may suggest sadness in one situation and submissiveness or lack of involvement in another.

To identify the fundamental categories of meaning associated with nonverbal behavior, Mehrabian (1970, 1981) identified a threefold perspective:

1. **Immediacy.** Sometimes people react to things by evaluating them as positive or negative, good or bad.
2. **Status.** Sometimes people enact or perceive behaviors that indicate various aspects of status to us, such as strong or weak, superior or subordinate.
3. **Responsiveness.** This third category refers to perceptions of activity as being slow or fast, active or passive.

In other verbal and nonverbal studies, dimensions similar to Mehrabian's have been reported consistently by investigators studying a range of phenomena. It is reasonable to conclude, therefore, that these three dimensions are basic responses to the environment and are reflected in the way meaning is assigned to both verbal *and* nonverbal behavior. Most of this work, however, depends on people translating their reactions to a nonverbal act into verbal descriptors. In general, then, like words, nonverbal signals can and do have multiple uses and meanings; like words, nonverbal signals have denotative and connotative meanings; and like words, nonverbal signals play an active role in communicating liking, power, and responsiveness. With these in mind, we can now examine some of the important ways verbal and nonverbal behaviors interrelate during human interaction. Ekman (1965) identified the following: repeating, conflicting, complementing, substituting, accenting/moderating, and regulating.

REPEATING

Nonverbal cues can simply repeat what was said verbally. For instance, if you told a person they had to go north to find a parking place and then pointed in the proper direction, this would be repetition.

CONFLICTING

Verbal and nonverbal signals can be at variance with one another in a variety of ways. They may communicate two contradictory or incongruous messages (see FIGURE 1-3). It is quite common, and probably functional, to have mixed feelings about some things. As a result, incongruous verbal and nonverbal messages may be more common than we realize. But it is the more dramatic contradictions that draw attention. Perhaps it is the parent who yells to their child in an angry voice, "Of course I love you!" Or the public speaker who, with trembling hands and visible beads of perspiration, claims, "I'm not nervous."

Why do these conflicting messages occur? In some cases, it is a natural response to a situation in which communicators perceive themselves to be in a bind. They do not want to tell the truth, and they do not want to lie. As a result, their ambivalence and frustration produce a discrepant message (Bavelas, Black, Chovil, & Mullett, 1990). In other situations, conflicting messages occur because people do an imperfect job of lying. Suppose you have just given a terrible presentation, and you ask me how you did. I may say you did fine, but my voice, face, and body do not reinforce my words.

© Prostock studio/Shutterstock.com

FIGURE 1-3 Is this an aggressive or playful situation? What observations influenced your decision?

On still other occasions, conflicting messages may actually combine to form a new message that neither conveys by itself. Sarcasm and joking are both like this: saying one thing with words and the opposite with vocal tone and/or facial expression. Another meaning that emerges from contradictory messages is *coyness*, which involves the display of signals that invite friendly contact along with signals of rejection or withdrawal.

How do people react when confronted with conflicting messages *that matter to them*? Leathers (1979) identified a common three-step process:

1. The first reaction is confusion and uncertainty.
2. Next, a person searches for additional information that will clarify the situation.
3. If clarification is not forthcoming, one will probably react with displeasure, hostility, or even withdrawal.

We do not wish to give the impression that all forms of discrepant messages are harmful. Some discrepancies may actually be helpful. In an experiment, teachers used mixed messages while teaching a lesson to sixth-grade pupils. When the teachers combined positive words with a negative nonverbal demeanor, pupils learned more than with any other combination (Woolfolk, 1978). Similarly, a study of doctors talking with patients found that the combination of positive words said in a negative tone of voice was associated with the highest levels of patient satisfaction with the visit (Hall, Roter, & Rand, 1981). Possibly, the positive verbal/negative nonverbal combination is perceived in classrooms and doctors' offices as "serious and concerned," and therefore it makes a better impression on students and patients alike.

Some research has questioned whether we trust and believe nonverbal signals more than verbal ones when we are confronted with conflicting messages (Bugental, 1974; Burgoon, 1980; Mehrabian, 1972a; Stiff, Hale, Garlick, & Rogan, 1990). People often assume that nonverbal signals are more spontaneous, harder to fake, less likely to be manipulated, and hence more believable than a person's words. It is probably more accurate to say, though, that *some* nonverbal behaviors are more spontaneous and harder to fake than others and that some people are more proficient than others at nonverbal deception or manipulation.

With two conflicting cues, both of which are nonverbal, people predictably place reliance on the cues considered harder to fake. The credibility of information in conflicting messages is also an important factor in determining which cues to believe. If the information being communicated in one channel lacks credibility, a perceiver is likely to discount it and look to other channels for the "real" message (Bugental, 1974). We do not know all the conditions that influence which signals people look to for valid information. As a general rule, people tend to rely on those signals they perceive harder to fake, but this will most likely vary with the situation; so the ultimate impact of verbal, visual, and vocal signals is best determined by a close examination of the people involved in a specific communication context.

COMPLEMENTING

Nonverbal behavior can modify or elaborate on (i.e., complement) verbal messages. When the verbal and nonverbal channels are complementary, rather than conflicting, the messages are usually decoded more accurately. Some evidence suggests that complementary nonverbal signals also may be helpful when attempting to remember the verbal message. A student who reflects an attitude of embarrassment when talking to a professor about their poor performance is exhibiting nonverbal behavior that complements their verbal statements. When clarity is of utmost importance, as in a job interview or when making up with a loved one after a fight, people should be especially concerned with making the meanings of verbal and nonverbal behavior complement each other.

SUBSTITUTING

Nonverbal behavior can also substitute for verbal messages. It may indicate more permanent characteristics (gender, age), moderately long-lasting features (personality, attitudes, social group), and relatively short-term states of a person such as emotions. As an example of the latter, a dejected and downtrodden executive might walk into their house after work with a facial expression that substitutes for declaring "I've had a rotten day."

Sometimes, when substituting nonverbal behavior does not get the desired response, the communicator tries to verbally clarify the message. Consider someone who uses distancing cues such as sitting rigidly or staring straight ahead in order to get their date to stop trying to become physically intimate. If the other person still does not stop, a verbal reprimand would have to follow.

ACCENTING/MODERATING

Nonverbal behavior may accent (amplify) or moderate (tone down) parts of the verbal message. Accenting is much like underlining or *italicizing* written words to emphasize them. Movements of the head and hands are frequently used to accent the verbal message. When a parent scolds a teenager for staying out too late, a particular phrase may be accented with a firm grip on the shoulder and an accompanying frown. In some instances, one set of nonverbal cues can accent or moderate other nonverbal cues. For example, by observing other parts of a person's body (e.g., a clenched fist), the full intensity of their facial expression of anger is realized.

REGULATING

Nonverbal behavior is also used to regulate verbal behavior. This happens in two ways:

1. By coordinating verbal and nonverbal behavior in the production of one's own message
2. By coordinating verbal and nonverbal behavior with those of interaction partners

People regulate the production of their messages in a variety of ways. Sometimes, nonverbal signs will segment units of interaction. Posture changes may demarcate a topic change; a gesture may forecast the verbalization of a particular idea; pauses may help organize spoken information into units. When people speak of a series of things, they may communicate discreteness by linear, staccato movements of the arm and hand; for instance, "We must consider A, B, and C." A chopping gesture inserted after each letter suggests a separate consideration of each. The flow of verbal and nonverbal behavior is also regulated between interactants. This may manifest itself in the dramatic (e.g., every time one person gets mad and yells, the other behaves in a solicitous manner) or less obvious (e.g., the signals of initiation, continuation, and termination of interaction) types of behavior that two interactants elicit from each other. The way one person stops talking and another starts in a smooth, synchronized manner may be as important to a satisfactory interaction as the content of their conversation. After all, people do make judgments about others based on their regulatory skills; consider the familiar descriptions "Talking to Jessica is like talking to a wall" or "You can't get a word in edgewise with Pete." When another person frequently interrupts or is inattentive, they may seem to be making a statement about the relationship, perhaps one of disrespect. There are rules for regulating conversations, but they are generally implicit. It is not written down, but most people know that two people should not generally talk at the same time, that each person might want an equal number of turns at talking, that a question should be answered, and so on. Wiemann's (1977) research found that relatively minute changes in these regulatory behaviors—interruptions, pauses longer than 3 seconds, unilateral topic changes, and so on—resulted in sizable variations in how competent a communicator was perceived to be. Listeners attend to and evaluate a host of fleeting, subtle, and habitual features of a speaker's conversational behavior. Attention is heightened, of course, when things do not go in the "normal" way. Conversational regulators involve several kinds of nonverbal cues. When Person A wants to indicate that they are finished speaking and Person B can start, Person A may increase eye contact with Person B. This is often accompanied by the vocal cues associated with ending declarative or interrogative statements. If Person B still does not figuratively "pick up the conversational ball," Person A might extend silence or interject a "trailer" such as "you know" or "so, ah." To keep another person from speaking in a conversation, one might avoid long pauses, decrease eye contact, and perhaps speak louder. Chapter 12 gives more complete attention to nonverbal behavior in the regulation of behavior.

PERSPECTIVE 4: HISTORICAL TRENDS IN NONVERBAL RESEARCH

The scientific study of nonverbal communication is primarily a post–World War II activity. This does not mean we cannot find important early tributaries of knowledge; even ancient Chinese, Greek, and Roman scholars commented on nonverbal behavior. Quintilian's *Institutio Oratoria*, for example, is an important source of information on gestures written in the first century. If we were to trace the history of fields of study—such as animal behavior, anthropology, dance, linguistics, philosophy, psychiatry, psychology, sociology, and speech—we would no doubt find important antecedents of today's work (Asendorpf & Wallbott, 1982; Davis, 1979; DePaulo & Friedman, 1998; Hecht & Ambady, 1999). Nonverbal studies never have been the province of any one particular discipline. In the last half of the 19th century, Delsarte, among others, attempted to codify and set forth rules for managing both "voice culture" and body movements or gestures (Shawn, 1954). Although Delsarte's "science of applied esthetics" and the elocutionary movement gave way to a less formal, less stylized manner in the 20th century, it represents one of several early attempts to identify various forms of bodily expression. One of the most influential pre–20th-century works was Darwin's *The Expression of the Emotions in Man and Animals* in 1872. This work influenced the modern study of facial expressions, and many of Darwin's observations and ideas have been validated by other researchers (Ekman, 1973).

During the first half of the 20th century, there were isolated studies of the voice, physical appearance and dress, and the face, as well as studies of accuracy in sending and receiving nonverbal messages. Studies of proxemics, the environment, and body movement received even less attention, and the least attention was given to the investigation of eye behavior and touching. Two distinct but noteworthy events occurred during this period: The first involved some controversial scholarship and a scandal; the second concerned a work of extraordinary influence in the study of nonverbal behavior.

In 1925, Kretschmer authored a book, *Physique and Character*. This was followed in 1940 by Sheldon's *The Varieties of Human Physique*. These works were based on the idea that if we precisely measure and analyze a person's body, we can learn much about their intelligence, temperament, moral worth, and future achievement. Sheldon's belief that certain characteristics are associated with certain body types—the thin ectomorph, the muscular mesomorph, and the fatty endomorph—is still debated (see Chapter 6). His work was featured on the cover of the popular magazine *Life* in 1951. To develop a catalogue of body types, Sheldon was permitted to photograph freshman students in the nude at Yale, Wellesley, Vassar, Princeton, Smith, Mt. Holyoke, and other colleges (Rosenbaum, 1995). The students were told it was a project involving posture, and thousands complied—including future president George H. W. Bush and future Secretary of State Hillary Rodham Clinton. The photos have reportedly been destroyed, and Sheldon's personal notes indicate that he drew racial conclusions from his work. People continue to associate certain characteristics with different body types, but the validity of these perceptions was not proven by Sheldon or any researchers since.

In contrast, Efron's *Gesture and Environment* (1941) has become a classic because it made three important contributions. Efron's innovative and detailed methods of studying gesture and body language, along with his framework for classifying nonverbal behavior, influenced future generations of scholars. In addition, Efron's work documented the important role of culture in the nature of gestures and body movement, which at the time was contrary to the belief of many—including Adolf Hitler—who thought that people's behavior was not subject to much modification by changing contexts and environments.

The 1950s showed a significant increase in the number of research efforts that delved into nonverbal communication. Some of the milestones included the following:

1. Birdwhistell's *Introduction to Kinesics* appeared in 1952, and E. T. Hall's *The Silent Language* in 1959. These anthropologists were responsible for taking some of the principles of linguistics and applying them to nonverbal phenomena, providing new labels for the study of body movement (kinesics) and space (proxemics), and launching a program of research in each area.
2. Trager's 1958 delineation of the components of "paralanguage" (see Chapter 11) greatly enhanced the precision with which researchers classify and study vocal cues.
3. Psychiatrist Jurgen Ruesch and photographer Weldon Kees combined their efforts to produce a popular book titled *Nonverbal Communication: Notes on the Visual Perception of Human Relations* in 1956. This was probably the first book to use the term "nonverbal communication" in its title. Therapists, including Freud, had been interested in nonverbal cues prior to the 1950s. Ruesch and Kees provided additional theoretical insights into the origins, usage, and coding of nonverbal behavior; they also provided extensive visual documentation for the communicative role of environments.
4. Also in 1956, Maslow and Mintz's study of the environmental effects of a "beautiful" room and an "ugly" room was published. This oft-cited study is a highlight in the study of environmental forces impinging on human communication.
5. Frank's comprehensive article "Tactile Communication" appeared in 1957. He offered a number of testable hypotheses about touching in human interaction.

If the 1950s witnessed an increase in the number of nonverbal studies, the 1960s must be classified as a nuclear explosion of the topic. Specific areas of the body were the subject of extensive programs of research: Exline's work on eye behavior; Davitz's work on vocal expressions of emotion, which culminated in *The Communication of Emotional Meaning* in 1964; Hess's work on pupil dilation; Sommer's continued exploration of personal space and design; Goldman-Eisler's study of pauses and hesitations in spontaneous speech; and the study of a wide range of body activity by Dittmann, Argyle, Kendon, Scheflen, and Mehrabian. During this time, psychologist Robert Rosenthal and his colleagues brought vividly to our attention the potential impact of nonverbal subtleties when they showed how experimenters can affect the outcome of experiments—and teachers can affect the intellectual growth of their students—through their nonverbal behavior (Rosenthal, 1966; Rosenthal & Jacobson, 1968). Perhaps the classic theoretical piece of the 1960s is Ekman and Friesen's article on the origins, usage, and coding of nonverbal behavior (Ekman & Friesen, 1969b). This article distinguished five areas of nonverbal study that served as a guide for their own research and ultimately that of many other researchers. These areas were emblems, illustrators, affect displays, regulators, and adaptors.

The 1970s began with a journalist's account of the study of nonverbal communication from the perspective of a handful of researchers. Fast's *Body Language* (1970), a best seller, was followed by a steady stream of books that attempted to make nonverbal findings understandable and usable to the American public. These books, in the interest of simplification and readability, often misrepresented findings when recounting how to make a sale, detect deception, assert one's dominance, and obtain a sexual partner.

Although popular books aroused the public's interest in nonverbal communication, they incurred criticism. Readers were too often left with the idea that reading nonverbal cues was the key to success in any human encounter. Some of these books implied that single cues (legs apart) had single meanings (sexual invitation). Modern-day researchers understood that not only is it important to look at nonverbal *clusters* of behavior, it also is crucial to appreciate that nonverbal cues, like verbal ones, rarely have a single denotative meaning. Some of these popularized accounts did not sufficiently remind readers that the meaning of a particular behavior is often understood by looking at the context in which the behavior occurs; for example, looking into someone's eyes may reflect affection in one situation and aggression in another.

Another common reaction to such books was the concern that once the nonverbal code was broken, people would be totally transparent; everyone would know everything about you because you could not control your nonverbal signals. As noted earlier, people actually have varying degrees of conscious control over their nonverbal behavior. Some behavior is very much under your control; other behavior is not, but it may be once awareness is increased. Furthermore, it may be that as soon as someone exhibits an understanding of your body language, you will modify it and make adaptations.

The 1970s were also a time of summarizing and synthesizing research findings. Ekman's research on the human face (*Emotion in the Human Face*, 1972, with Friesen and Ellsworth); Mehrabian's research on the meaning of nonverbal cues of immediacy, status, and responsiveness (*Nonverbal Communication*, 1972b); Scheflen's kinesic research in the framework of general systems theory (*Body Language and the Social Order*, 1972); Hess's study of pupil size (*The Tell-Tale Eye*, 1975b); Argyle's study of body movement and eye behavior (*Bodily Communication*, 1975; and *Gaze and Mutual Gaze*, with Cook, 1976); Montagu's *Touching* (1971); and Birdwhistell's *Kinesics and Context* (1970) were all attempts to bring together the growing literature, or a particular research program, in a single volume.

The 1970s also marked researchers' formal interest in measuring people's accuracy in understanding nonverbal cues (Rosenthal, Hall, DiMatteo, Rogers, & Archer, 1979). The development and validation of tests of skill in decoding the meanings of cues indicative of emotion, personality, and other states and traits, and using such tests to study the determinants and correlates of this skill, became and continue to be a major endeavor of nonverbal communication researchers.

During the 1980s, some scholars continued to specialize, but others focused on identifying the ways in which a variety of nonverbal signals work together to accomplish common communicative goals, such as showing affection, deceiving someone, or getting a person to do something for you (Patterson, 1983). It became clear that we could not fully understand the role of nonverbal behavior in accomplishing these goals unless we also looked at the role of co-occurring verbal behavior and tried to develop theories about how various verbal and nonverbal cues interact in the process (Bavelas & Chovil, 2006; Kendon, 1983; Streeck & Knapp, 1992). Thus, we are gradually beginning to learn how to put the pieces back together after several decades of separating them and examining them microscopically. This trend is a manifestation of a larger movement to bring research more in line with the way we know human communication occurs in life's laboratory (Archer, Akert, & Costanzo, 1993; Patterson, 1984).

The following list conveys some of the ways in which nonverbal research continues to change in the modern day:

- From studying noninteractive situations to studying interactive ones
- From studying one person to studying both interactants
- From studying a single point in time to studying changes over time
- From studying single behaviors to studying multiple behaviors
- From the view that people perceive everything that occurs to acknowledging that we need to know more about how people perceive signals during interaction
- From single-meaning and single-intent perspectives to acknowledging that often multiple meanings occur and multiple goals exist
- From a measurement perspective focused almost exclusively on frequency and duration to one that also includes issues related to when and how a behavior occurs
- From attempting to control and understand context by eliminating important and influential elements to attempting to account for such effects
- From studying only face-to-face interaction to examining the role of nonverbal messages in mediated communication settings (e.g., Facebook, instant messages, texting, email)
- From an overemphasis on studying how strangers interact to one equally concerned about how intimates interact
- From studying only culture or only biology as possible explanations of behavior to examining the roles both play

Such a brief historical view inevitably leaves out many important contributions (see Knapp, 2006). The preceding discussion is simply an attempt to highlight some important developments and depict a general background for our current perspectives. The future of nonverbal research holds breakthroughs in neuropsychology (how the brain processes cues and creates behavior), cue elicitation (virtual reality), measurement (automated recordings, eye tracking devices), and scale (large data sets collected from many locations).

PERSPECTIVE 5: NONVERBAL COMMUNICATION IN EVERYDAY LIFE

Clearly, nonverbal signals are a critical part of all communicative endeavors. Sometimes, nonverbal signals are the most important part of a message. Understanding and effectively using nonverbal cues are crucial to success in virtually every social encounter (Horgan, 2020).

First impressions often have a strong impact on any given social interaction and can affect subsequent interactions (Ambady & Skowronski, 2008). We also know that people can make some valid inferences about others based on their initial reading of the other's nonverbal cues (Hall, Andrzejewski, & Yopchick, 2009; Horgan, 2020). Thus, each interaction begins with both interactants trying to draw accurate inferences about the other and simultaneously trying to manifest the verbal and nonverbal behavior that will give them the best shot at accomplishing their communicative goals. This process continues as the interaction unfolds.

Nonverbal cues such as attire, eye gaze, smiling, posture, distance, and listener responses are just as important as choosing the right words—sometimes more so. Nonverbal behavior can have profound real-life impacts, as Lieutenant General David McKiernan found out. In June 2003, the *Boston Globe* reported that he was taken off the list of possible candidates for the top leadership position of Army Chief of Staff because Pentagon officials observed "bad body language" from him. Apparently, McKiernan was standing with his arms crossed and did not respond in positive ways during "applause lines" while listening to a speech given by then-Secretary of State Donald Rumsfeld in Iraq ("Next Army Chief," 2003). Another example is the "taking a knee" gesture of pro football player Colin Kaepernick during the playing of the national anthem at a football game to protest the inequality and injustice directed at African Americans. His gesture effectively ended his NFL career. We could add that, in the wake of the killing of George Floyd, the NFL commissioner has apologized for the treatment of players who kneeled in protest before games and has encouraged teams to sign Kaepernick.

Nonverbal messages are no less important in formal job interviews or in ongoing performance on the job, whether it involves public relations, customer service, marketing, advertising, supervision, or leadership (DePaulo, 1992; Hecker & Stewart, 1988; Riggio, 2005). Some occupations and leadership positions require establishing or implementing policies involving nonverbal messages. Some schools and businesses have rules about hair length, facial hair, or appropriate clothing and artifacts; sexual harassment cases may hinge on determining the type of touching that occurred;

and some airlines, broadcasters, and others have been involved in lawsuits dealing with physical-appearance-based discrimination. The San Francisco City Council was reportedly discussing a ban on certain nonverbal expressions—smirks, raised eyebrows, or loud guffaws—in an effort to restore civility to council debates ("Proposed Smirking Ban," 2003). Reporters are increasingly discussing whether touching—even handshakes—should be permitted in the workplace at all or how it can be minimized (Chong, 2019—Life; Gray, 2020—The Blog).

The consequences of work-related problems in the use or misuse of nonverbal behavior/cues are unquestionably important. Sometimes, they can even be life-threatening. Effective nonverbal communication between nurses and physicians during surgical procedures can literally make the difference between life and death for their patients.

Courtrooms are also places where nonverbal cues play a consequential role. Once a person has been charged with a crime and the trial process begins, we can see several important and influential sources of nonverbal cues (Peskin, 1980; Pryor & Buchanan, 1984). Because of the important implications of decisions made in courtrooms and the desire to maintain impartial communication, almost every facet of the courtroom process is being analyzed (Searcy, Duck, & Blanck, 2005). Judges are cautioned to minimize possible signs of partiality in their voice and positioning. In one study, mock jurors were very much aware of judges whose nonverbal behavior suggested a lack of involvement in the proceedings and perceived this behavior negatively (Burnett & Badzinski, 2005). Other studies confirm the belief that the attitudes and nonverbal cues enacted by judges do in fact influence the outcome of a trial (Blanck & Rosenthal, 1992; Hart, 1995). The study of nonverbal behavior is also important to the process of jury selection. Although this attention to nonverbal signals emanating from prospective jurors may indicate a degree of sensitivity that did not previously exist, we need not worry that attorneys or social scientists will become so skilled that they can rig juries (Saks, 1976).

TAKING A KNEE FOR ONE'S BELIEFS AND VALUES

World-class athletes sometimes use the playing field to protest or make political statements. In the photos above, super-star Megan Rapinoe in soccer and Colin Kaepernick in football are shown kneeling during the national anthem.

U.S. citizens are expected to at least stand during the National Anthem out of respect for the flag and what it represents to our country.

For Kaepernick, what the flag is supposed to symbolize does not apply to all of our country's citizens equally. Rapinoe believes that the Trump administration did not promote the values embodied in our country's flag.

Firestorms of criticism followed each athlete's refusal to perform the expected gesture of standing during the national anthem. Kaepernick lost his job as a quarterback in the National Football League.

Yet the kneeling behavior of Rapinoe and Kaepernick also energized political movements designed to address the causes that these two athletes were attempting to draw viewers' attention to at their respective sporting events.

In the end, this debate demonstrates the impact of some gestures, especially those that are not performed when people are expecting to see them, on people's personal, political, and professional lives.

A list of all the situations in which nonverbal communication plays a significant role would be almost endless and would include areas such as dance, theater, music, film, and photography. The nonverbal symbolism of various ceremonies and rituals—the trappings of the marriage ceremony, holiday decorations, religious rituals, funerals, and so on—provide stimuli that guide the responses of those involved.

From this broad array of situations in which nonverbal communication plays a central role, we have selected some areas that we feel are particularly meaningful and discuss them further in the book. In Chapter 12, we examine nonverbal behavior used in communicating intimacy, dominance or status, identity, deception, and interaction management. Chapter 13 is devoted to an analysis of nonverbal signals in advertising, politics, education, culture, health care, and technology.

SUMMARY

The term *nonverbal* is commonly used to describe all human communication events that transcend spoken or written words. However, any classification scheme that separates these phenomena into two discrete categories—verbal/nonverbal—will not be able to account for behaviors that do not seem to fit either category.

Nonverbal behavior is encoded and decoded with varying degrees of awareness and control. There are times when responses are carefully planned, and a person is very much aware of what they are doing. There are other times when responses occur more automatically, with little conscious planning and awareness.

In our book, the theoretical writings and research on nonverbal communication are broken down into the following three areas:

1. The communication environment (physical and spatial)
2. The communicator's physical characteristics
3. Body movement and position (gestures, posture, touching, facial expressions, eye behavior, and vocal behavior)

Aside from describing and documenting the nature and purposes of nonverbal communication, researchers also study the processes and outcomes of individuals' ability to decode its meanings.

Nonverbal communication should not be studied as an isolated phenomenon but as an inseparable part of the total communication process. The relationship between verbal and nonverbal behavior was illustrated in our discussion of how nonverbal behavior functions in repeating, conflicting with, substituting for, complementing, accenting/moderating, and regulating verbal communication. Nonverbal communication is important because of its role in the total communication system, the tremendous quantity of informational cues it gives in any particular situation, and its use in many crucial areas of daily life.

This chapter also reviewed some of the historical highlights of this field, noting the current influence of the works of Darwin, Efron, Birdwhistell, E. T. Hall, Ruesch and Kees, Mehrabian, Rosenthal, Ekman and Friesen, and others. We reviewed the important roles and shortcomings of the popular literature. The chapter concluded with an account of the prevalence and importance of nonverbal signals in selected areas of daily life.

QUESTIONS FOR DISCUSSION

1. Identify a situation in which you believe verbal behavior was clearly more important to the outcome of an interaction than nonverbal behavior. Explain why.

2. Identify a situation in which you would give more credibility to a person's verbal behavior when verbal and nonverbal behavior convey different messages.

3. Discuss the most unusual or subtle nonverbal signal or signals you have observed in an interaction partner. What helped you assess their meaning?

4. If you could get an instant and true answer to any question about nonverbal communication, what would your question be?

NONVERBAL COMMUNICATION IN ACTION: TRY THIS

In addition to learning about nonverbal communication through reading about it, you can learn by your own experiences. In each chapter, we will suggest a simple exercise or activity you can try. For Chapter 1, try this:

> Seat yourself in a busy public place and watch the people there for 20 minutes; take as many notes as you wish. Describe the nonverbal behaviors you see, and what you think they mean. How does the setting, and the likely relationships among the people you see (e.g., strangers vs. friends/lovers), influence their behavior? Can you see any regularities in how people behave in this location? What are the norms for appropriate nonverbal behavior in this setting?

READING RESOURCES

Because our concern is the scientific study of nonverbal communication, we include many scholarly citations in this book's chapters. In addition to these specific research works, the following are good general resources for the student of nonverbal communication:

Hall, J. A., & Bernieri, F. J. (Eds.). (2001). *Interpersonal sensitivity*: *Theory and measurement*. Mahwah, NJ: Lawrence Erlbaum.

Hall, J. A., & Knapp, M. L. (Eds.). (2013). *Nonverbal communication* (Vol. 2, *Handbooks of communication science*). Berlin, Germany: deGruyter Mouton.

Hall, J. A., Schmid Mast, M., & West, T. V. (Eds.). (2016). *The social psychology of perceiving others accurately*. Cambridge, UK: Cambridge University Press.

Harrigan, J. A., Rosenthal, R., & Scherer, K. R. (Eds.). (2005). *The new handbook of methods in nonverbal behavior research*. Oxford, UK: Oxford University Press.

Manusov, V. (Ed.). (2004). *The sourcebook of nonverbal measures: Going beyond words*. Mahwah, NJ: Lawrence Erlbaum.

Manusov, V. L., & Patterson, M. L. (Eds.). (2006). *The SAGE handbook of nonverbal communication*. Thousand Oaks, CA: Sage.

Matsumoto, D., Hwang, H. C., & Frank, M. G. (Eds.). (2016). *APA handbooks in psychology*®. *APA handbook of nonverbal communication*. Washington, DC: American Psychological Association.

CHAPTER 2

THE ROOTS OF NONVERBAL BEHAVIOR

As we look back on a long phylogenetic history, which has determined our present day anatomical, physiological, and biochemical status, it would be simply astounding if it were found not to affect our behavior also.

—T. K. Pitcairn and I. Eibl-Eibesfeldt

In 1967, when David Reimer was 8 months old, his genitals were accidentally mutilated when he was being circumcised. Subsequently, on the advice of physicians, David's parents agreed to a surgical sex change and set about raising David as a girl. Nurture, it was believed, would triumph over nature, and David would become "Brenda." Despite 12 years of social, mental, and hormonal conditioning, David never felt he was a girl. His parents gave him dolls, dressed him as a girl, and tried in every way to reinforce his identity as Brenda. But his twin brother expressed what others observed as well: "I recognized Brenda as my sister, but she never, ever acted the part … when I say there was nothing feminine about Brenda … I mean there was *nothing* feminine. She walked like a guy. Sat with her legs apart. She talked about guy things … she played with *my* toys" (Colapinto, 2000, p. 57). It was not that Brenda did not learn what others were teaching her about how to behave like a girl. Nurture played its part. But what surprised everyone involved in this real-life nature/nurture experiment was the powerful influence that genetics, or hardwiring, can play in behavior and identity.

During the 20th century, the question of whether human behavior is influenced more by nature or nurture was hotly debated. For many years the prevailing view was that all human behavior was the result of learning. The behaviorists believed that any differences between individuals could be erased if they experienced the same environmental stimuli. In short, genetic heritage was presumed to be highly malleable. Today, scientists tend to reject the either/or approach to the debate. Instead of trying to argue that all of human behavior is primarily guided by nature or nurture, most believe it is wise to assume that there may be nature and nurture components associated with any given behavior pattern. No doubt nonverbal behavior has both innate and learned, including imitative, aspects to it.

Ekman and Friesen (1969), whose work in this area is detailed later, outlined three primary sources of nonverbal behavior:

1. Inherited neurological programs
2. Experience common to all members of the species (e.g., regardless of culture, the hands are used to place food in the mouth)
3. Experience that varies with culture, class, family, or the individual

Biological and cultural forces overlap in many important ways. Some common biological processes can be used to communicate; for example, breathing becomes a sigh of relief, grief, or boredom; a hiccup becomes an imitation of a drunk's behavior; audible blowing through one's nose may be interpreted as a snort of scorn; and coughing becomes "ahem." Later in this chapter, we discuss studies that suggest that some aspects of facial expressions of emotion are inherited and common to members of the human species. These studies, however, do not negate the importance of cultural learning in manifesting these expressions. The neurological program for any given facial expression can be altered or modified by learned "display rules" specific to a culture, such as "men should not cry in public." Different stimuli may trigger a given facial expression, again depending on one's cultural training. A snake may evoke an expression of fear in one culture and bring out an expression of joy in another if it is an important food source. The society one grows up in is also largely responsible for the way two or more emotional expressions can be blended on the face, such as showing features of surprise and anger at the same time.

Studies of birds show clearly the joint impact of biology and environment on behavior. The European male robin attacks strange robins that enter his territory during the breeding season. Research using stuffed models has shown that the red breast alone triggers this attack mechanism. The female robin who shares the nest, however, also has a red breast and is not attacked. Thus, the aggressive behavior, which is believed to be innate, is modified by certain conditions in the environment or by the situation that calls forth the response. As another example, some birds instinctively sing a song common to their own species without ever having heard another bird sing the song. These birds may, on hearing the songs of their particular group, develop a variation on the melody that reflects a local dialect. It has also been noted that without exposure to mature songs, the young bird's song remains rudimentary and imperfect. And even when a bird is born with its basic song, it may have to learn to whom the call should be addressed, and under what circumstances, and how to recognize signals from other birds.

Many of the inherited components of human behavior can be modified similarly. It is like the human predisposition for, or capacity to learn, verbal language (Lenneberg, 1969; Pinker, 1994). Although everyone is born with the capacity to learn language, it is not learned without cultural training. Children isolated from human contact do not develop linguistic competence. Some nonverbal signals probably depend primarily on inherited neurological programs; others probably depend primarily on environmental learning; and, of course, many behaviors are influenced by both.

Finally, the answer to the nature/nurture issue concerning nonverbal behavior varies with the behavior under consideration. As you will learn in Chapter 9, there may be multiple origins of facial expressions of emotion. Certain nervous mannerisms or self-touching gestures may be learned primarily as a person learns to perform certain tasks and cope with various interpersonal experiences. Some behaviors may be primarily the product of imitating others. Some hand gestures, such as the thumbs-up gesture, are primarily culture specific, but certain patterns of eye gaze seem to have a strong genetic component. The stronger the learned component of nonverbal behavior, the more we would expect to find variations across cultural, class, and ethnic lines. Note, however, that a behavior that varies from group to group may still have a common biological base, after cultural teachings are stripped away.

THE DEVELOPMENT OF NONVERBAL BEHAVIOR ACROSS EVOLUTIONARY TIME

Human beings, like other species, have evolved through a process of adaptation to changing conditions (Barkow, Cosmides, & Tooby, 1992). Which nonverbal behaviors have ancient roots in human history? On what basis do social scientists conclude that a behavior or behavioral pattern includes an inherited component? It is not an easy task. Some patterns may represent a grouping of inborn nonverbal communicative behaviors; for example, the Moro reflex in infants (which includes the sudden spreading of the arms and fingers, as though grasping) seems to convey a newborn's need to be picked up, which has obvious survival value (Rousseau, Matton, Lecuyer, & Lahaye, 2017). Other behavioral displays may be only fragments of larger patterns no longer enacted in their entirety. Some behaviors now embedded in rituals have little to do with their original function. And, last, a behavior that seems to serve one function may be associated with something completely different (e.g., self-grooming may be the result of confusion or frustration in achieving a goal rather than a behavior enacted for self-preservation, courtship, or cleanliness goals).

The fossil record of our species is not much help in understanding the biological roots of human behavior. The best evidence for inferences about whether a behavior has been inherited and is genetically transmitted to every member of the human species is derived from as many of the following five research perspectives as possible. If we can compile strong evidence in all five of these perspectives, confidence in a phylogenetic dimension—that is, biological roots—reaches its highest level.

- Evidence from sensory deprivation—noting the manifestation of a behavior in blind and/or deaf people who could not have learned it through visual or auditory channels.

- Evidence from infants—observing behaviors displayed within minutes or hours after birth.
- Evidence from identical twins reared in different environments—identifying the behavioral similarities of people whose gene structure is known to be virtually identical and whose learning environment is known to be very different.
- Evidence from other animals—showing an evolutionary continuity of a behavior up to and including our closest relatives, nonhuman primates.
- Evidence from multicultural studies—observing the manifestation of similar behaviors used for similar purposes in other cultures around the world, both literate and preliterate.

Research from each of these perspectives makes up the remainder of this chapter. The nonverbal behavior that has received the most scrutiny in each perspective is the facial expression of emotion. You should first keep in mind, though, that evolved facial expressions may serve more than one function. A facial expression of anger might have evolved to communicate a person's feelings of anger as well as the expression of strength to rivals (Sell, Cosmides, & Tooby, 2014). Second, as Buck and Powers (2006) remind us, the origin of any behavioral display by an individual communicator is only part of the story. Evolution may also be responsible for "preattunements" that structure a person's *perceptions* of these behavioral displays. For example, physical attractiveness is perceived with a high degree of consistency, and certain facial expressions of emotion have been decoded accurately in a variety of cultures around the world. According to Buck and Powers, this interplay between biologically structured displays and preattunements "creates the basis for the social organization of the species" (p. 120).

EVIDENCE FROM SENSORY DEPRIVATION

Many have observed the early appearance of nonverbal behavior in children. Perhaps the behaviors are learned quickly. To verify such a hypothesis, we need to examine children who, because of being blind and deaf at birth, could not learn such behaviors from visual or auditory cues. Eibl-Eibesfeldt (1973, 1975; Pitcairn & Eibl-Eibesfeldt, 1976) filmed several blind/deaf children between the ages of 2 and 10 and reached conclusions similar to those of others who have systematically compared the behavior of blind/deaf children with sighted/hearing children. His conclusion was that the spontaneous expressions of sadness, crying, laughing, smiling, pouting, anger, surprise, and fear are not significantly different in blind/deaf children.

Some might argue that such expressions could be learned by blind/deaf children by touching or through a slow reinforcement program. Eibl-Eibesfeldt points out, however, that even babies born with no arms or other severe birth defects, as well as children who could hardly be taught to raise a spoon to their mouths, showed similar expressions.

Galati and colleagues (Galati, Miceli, & Sini, 2001; Galati, Scherer, & Ricci-Bitti, 1997; Galati, Sini, Schmidt, & Tinti, 2003) found similar results with sighted and congenitally blind children between the ages of 6 months and 5 years. Spontaneous expressions of sadness, anger, joy, fear, disgust, surprise, and interest were filmed and coded with Ekman and Friesen's Facial Action Coding System (see Chapter 9). There were few differences between the expressions of the sighted and blind children, and observers who looked at the faces were able to accurately identify the situations that triggered the expressions for both. A more recent summary of the literature published from 1932 to 2015 came to a similar conclusion: Blind individuals produce some spontaneous facial expressions of emotion the same way that sighted individuals do, even though the former group has never had the opportunity to see those expressions on the faces of others (Valente, Theurel, & Gentaz, 2018). In sum, being able to see the facial expressions of others does not seem to provide a significant advantage in being able to make basic facial displays of emotion.

In addition to facial expressions, the deaf/blind children studied by Eibl-Eibesfeldt also showed other patterns of movement exhibited by sighted children. They sought contact with others by stretching out one or both hands, wanted to be embraced and caressed when distressed, and showed a remarkably familiar sequence of refusal gestures.

Eibl-Eibesfeldt also reported some interesting eye patterns of blind children. When he complimented a 10-year-old girl on her piano playing, she looked at him, coyly looked down and away, and then looked at him again. A similar sequence was recorded for an 11-year-old boy when asked about his girlfriend. This sequence of turning toward and away is also seen in sighted children under similar circumstances. Magnusson (2006) observed some similarities in the way sighted and blind communicators managed conversational turn-taking and displayed turn exchange and regula-tion, like nodding and smiling, but fewer similarities were observed with the congenitally blind than with those whose blindness was the result of an accident.

However, the facial expressions of blind/deaf children and blind children may be different in some ways when compared with those of sighted and hearing children. These differences are particularly evident as the children grow older and learn certain display rules by looking at the way others perform expressions. For example, subtle gradations in the onset and offset of expressions were not observed as often in the blind/deaf children; their expressions seemed to quickly appear and suddenly disappear, leaving the face blank. Display rules about the suitable intensity of expressions is another lesson blind/deaf children appear to be less familiar with; for example, how intense crying and laughing should be in various situations. Sighted children also seemed more likely than blind children to learn a display rule for masking negative emotions (Galati, Miceli, & Sini, 2001; Galati, Sini, Schmidt, & Tinti, 2003). The general absence of facial blends among the blind/deaf suggests that this may also depend on learning. Making voluntary expressions—that is, deliberately mimicking another's facial expressions—is also a learned behavior, and young deaf children do not perform this skill very well. Individuals who are blind also have more difficulties posing facial expressions of emotions (Valente et al., 2018). But at least one study suggests that congenital blindness does not prevent adults from producing expressions that are as accurately decoded as those of sighted adults (Galati, Scherer, & Ricci-Bitti, 1997). All of these findings point to a joint role for innate predispositions and social learning via visual exposure to others' facial expressions of emotion.

Thus far, the focus has been on the encoding (i.e., production) of nonverbal information among the blind/deaf. Regarding decoding nonverbal cues, children who have been blind/deaf since birth obviously have not had the op-portunity to see other people's facial expressions / hear people speak. However, recent technological advances—with more surely to come—may afford these children the opportunity to decode such nonverbal information for the first time. Cochlear implants (CI), for example, permit deaf children to perceive sound. Research with children who had been deaf since infancy and later equipped with a CI in their right ear found that, although these children could identify the emotional meaning of facial expressions, they had difficulty recognizing emotion in voices (Hopyan-Misakyan, Gordon, Dennis, & Papsin, 2009). This difficulty might stem from shortcomings in the CI design or suggest that there is a critical period for learning how to decode emotion cues from voices.

Last, we have focused on only infants or children with sensory deficits. But it is also the case that infants without any deficits have parents who do. For example, what happens when infants who can see are raised by parents who cannot? One study showed that at the neurological level these infants did not seem to differentiate between shifts in the eye gaze of a face that looked either toward or away from them, whereas infants with parents who could see did (Vernetti, Ganea, Tucker, Charman, Johnson, & Senju, 2018). Thus, the specific nonverbal experiences that infants have with their parents may impact how their brains learn to process specific nonverbal cues.

EVIDENCE FROM INFANTS

Children learn from adults, and their nonverbal and verbal cues help them along the way. For example, a toddler may look at an adult, shrug, and say that they "don't know" as a way of communicating ignorance (Harris, Bartz, & Rowe, 2017). This is in part how children acquire the knowledge they need from adults to function in the world. In this sec-tion, however, we are concerned with the question of whether humans come into the world prepared to receive specific nonverbal cues from their parents.

At the neurological level, newborns appear to respond differently to their mother's breast milk than they do to for-mula, showing greater oxygenated blood flow to the orbitofrontal region of their brain to the former than to the latter (Aoyama et al., 2010). At the behavioral level, newborns show less distress in response to heel sticks when they are exposed to the odor of their own mother's breast milk as opposed to that of another woman or formula (Nishitani et al., 2009). These results do not imply that newborns do not learn maternal odors outside the womb. Indeed, there is evi-dence that newborns have a sensitive period for learning new odors (minutes after birth; Romantshik, Porter, Tillmann, & Varendi, 2007). However, particularly important maternal nonverbal cues, such as those linked to sustenance, may be learned in utero, due to their importance in ensuring the survival of the newborn.

DID YOU MAKE SCENTS TO YOUR MOTHER EVEN AT BIRTH?

Yes!

Your signature communicates your uniqueness as an individual to others. As adults, others recognize who you are by how you write your name. At birth, mothers can recognize their own babies by how they *smell*. It appears people have an "olfactory signature" (see Chapter 6). As evidence of this, postpartum women are able to quickly tell by scent alone which clothes were worn by their baby as opposed to another woman's baby.

A human mother's ability to recognize her offspring by scent would be an example of evolutionary conservation. That ability is there because, presumably, it has been an effective

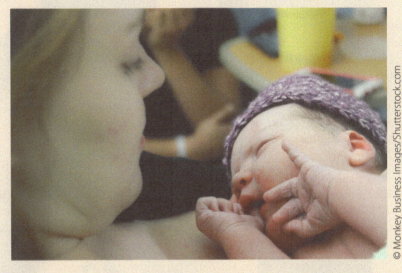

© Monkey Business Images/Shutterstock.com

means of offspring recognition among animals over a great span of time. Offspring recognition is important because it is needed for the establishment and maintenance of the parent–child bond. Without that bond, an offspring—and thus the parents' genes—might not survive. Therefore, being able to recognize an offspring's olfactory signature must have worked (in an evolutionary sense) for mothers, whether she is an ewe or a human. Whether fathers are equally capable of identifying their infants from smell alone remains inconclusive, according to research.

Human mothers can identify their offspring using other nonverbal cues as well, including the cry of their baby, the tactile characteristics of their baby's hand, and the visual features of their baby's face. Thus, infant recognition among human mothers likely involves the integration of multiple nonverbal cues, which they quickly associate with *their* baby. This ability distinguishes humans from ungulates in which infant recognition depends more heavily on offspring odor and is likely due to the greatly expanded neocortex in humans.

Newborn babies are born ready to process certain nonverbal cues that they could not have learned in utero, such as the human face (Pascalis & Kelly, 2009), as well as the jointly occurring gaze and voice of an adult (Guellai & Streri, 2011), as they presumably begin the task of identifying others. They also show indications of being naturally upset when a person's face suddenly becomes nonresponsive to them (i.e., the "Still-Face"); they avert their eyes, become distressed, and cry more in this situation (Nagy, Pilling, Watt, Pal, & Orvos, 2017).

Newborn babies also seem to have the facial muscle actions necessary to express virtually all the basic affect displays of adults (Oster & Ekman, 1978). The questions of interest in the remainder of this section are whether newborns show affect displays resembling those of adults, and if so, do those displays convey the same emotions as they do in adults? Here the evidence is mixed, partly because of intrinsic difficulties in determining what emotion a baby is experiencing.

Researchers disagree on this important question: Does an infant's facial repertoire consist of undifferentiated expressions of arousal and distress, which are then shaped by experience, or is a baby born with a biologically based predisposition to display the full repertoire of emotional expressions identified in adults? Much research has been inspired by the latter view, which is embodied in what has become known as *differential emotions theory* (Izard, 1977; Izard & Malatesta, 1987). This proposes a strong genetic basis for emotional facial expressions, and thus, emotions would produce the same distinctive facial patterns in both infants and adults.

Infants only a few months old do display some expressions consistent with prototypical emotion displays in adults—specifically expressions for joy, surprise, and interest (Oster, Hegley, & Nagel, 1992). These expressions are also easily recognizable by untrained observers as representing those emotions. This does not mean, of course, that the infants were actually experiencing those emotions, only that the facial configurations match the adult prototypes (Camras, 1994). For the negative emotions, however, evidence indicates that discrete expressions corresponding to adults' expressions of emotions such as fear, anger, disgust, and sadness do not exist in young infants (Camras, Sullivan, & Michel, 1993; Oster, Hegley, & Nagel, 1992). Stenberg, Campos, and Emde (1983), though, found the capacity to express anger to be well developed in infants by 7 months of age and that the associated facial expression was reliably detected in the absence of contextual information.

To date, the data from infant studies do not provide complete support for a biological root to discrete facial expressions of emotion. Moreover, it has been pointed out that too much emphasis on finding adults' expressions in infants might lead researchers to make several errors, including the following:

1. Researchers may reach erroneous conclusions about what emotions are actually being felt; just because an infant and an adult show the same expression, they may not be feeling the same emotion.
2. Researchers may fail to observe distinctive infant emotional expressions that do not happen to match up with adult expressions (Barrett, 1993; Oster, Hegley, & Nagel, 1992). Such difficulties are not restricted to emotion expressions; adults also have problems recognizing the meaning of infants' gestures (Boundy, Cameron-Faulkner, & Theakston, 2016).

All researchers seem to agree, however, that infants' faces convey information about their states, that more research is needed to uncover exactly what is being conveyed and what regularities exist in the developmental unfolding of emotional expression, and that socialization plays a crucial role.

The study of pain expression in infants and adults also yields information on the biological basis of expression and seems a less debatable topic than the expression of basic emotions. It is easy to argue that the adaptive advantage of being able to engage adult care from the earliest moments of life would lead to the evolution of an innate program for displaying pain (Prkachin & Craig, 1995). Expressions of pain in infants, even in newborns, are highly similar to those observed in adults. These are the five most consistently seen facial movements:

1. A lowered brow
2. Eyes squeezed tightly shut
3. Vertical wrinkles at the side of the nose (the nasolabial furrow)
4. Open lips and mouth
5. A taut, cupped tongue (Grunau & Craig, 1990)

Computer-based technology has been used to measure how a neonate's face changes in expression after being exposed to a painful stimulus, such as a heel stick. These changes include mouth opening, drawing in of the eyebrows, and closing of the eyes (Schiavenato et al., 2008). Moreover, when a male neonate is experiencing more pain (e.g., from a circumcision without analgesia), he opens his mouth vertically wider than does a male neonate feeling less pain (e.g., from a heel stick; Schiavenato, Butler-O'Hara, & Scovanner, 2011). A wider mouth may be an important pain cue to know about, especially given that, although adults routinely recognize facial signs of pain, there is evidence that observers also tend to underestimate the extent of pain in infants (and adults for that matter; Prkachin & Craig, 1995).

Research on imitation highlights the complex intertwining of biology and socialization in the development of expression. The early ability to imitate others' expressions may be inherited and may ultimately play a role in the development of various facial displays. Meltzoff and Moore (1977, 1983a, 1983b) demonstrated that 12- to 21-day-old infants imitated adults who performed four actions: tongue protrusion, mouth opening, lip protrusion, and sequential finger movement. Subsequent research replicated the findings for tongue protrusion and mouth opening for neonates 0.7 to 71 hours old. The experiments seem to negate explanations for such behavior based on innate releasing mechanisms similar to those found in many animals as well as on learning processes linked to caregiver behavior. Instead, they argue that infants are born with the ability to use what they call *intermodal equivalencies*, which means the infant is able to use the "equivalence between the act seen and the act done as the fundamental basis for generating the behavioral match." Perception and production, then, are closely linked and mediated by a common representational system from birth (see Bargh & Chartrand, 1999).

The Meltzoff and Moore research is complemented by other studies (Field, Woodson, Greenberg, & Cohen, 1982) that examined the imitation of specific facial displays of emotion by 2-day-old infants. These findings support those of Meltzoff and Moore and indicate that the ability to discriminate and imitate happy, sad, and surprised facial expressions is one with which infants enter their social world. (See FIGURE 2-1).

Perhaps even more significant for understanding the early processes of learning and socialization is the finding that 9-month-old infants can imitate behavior from memory after a 24-hour delay (Meltzoff, 1985, 1988a; Meltzoff & Gopnik, 1989), and 14-month-olds can accurately imitate a sequence of acts after a week's delay (Meltzoff, 1988b). The early integration of cognitive, linguistic, and communicative development is also demonstrated by the infant's ability to process visually the connection between mouth shape and sound, for example, that the "ah" sound comes

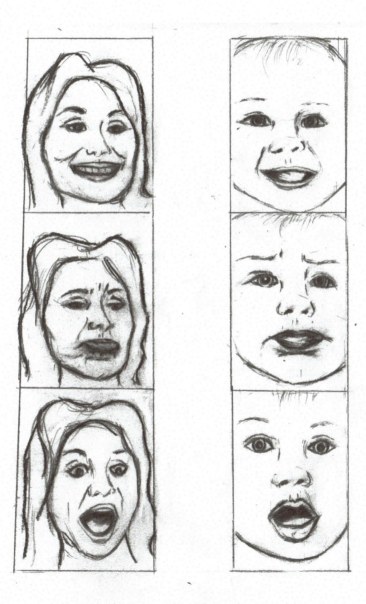

© Kimberly Fillah-Horgan

FIGURE 2-1 Sample drawings of model's happy, sad, and surprised expressions and infant's corresponding expressions. Drawings were based on photos of these expressions found in the work of Field, Woodson, Greenberg, and Cohen (1982).

from a mouth with the lips wide open and the "ee" sound comes from a mouth with corners pulled back (Kuhl & Meltzoff, 1982).

EVIDENCE FROM TWIN STUDIES

Monozygotic (i.e., identical) twins are sometimes separated at birth and reared in very different environments. Because their genetic similarity is known, it is possible to compare and contrast their abilities and behavior to determine how much nature and nurture contribute to each.

Plomin (1989) provided an extensive review of the research using identical and fraternal twins as well as adopted children. This research shows a substantial hereditary influence—usually about 50% for identical twins—on the following items: job satisfaction; religious interests, attitudes, and values; IQ; vocational interests; reading disability; intellectual disability; extraversion; emotionality; sociability; alcoholism; and delinquency and criminal behavior. Extensive studies at the University of Minnesota of identical twins reared apart indicate the amount of genetic influence on a behavior can be high, but it varies with the behavior in question.

The genetic influence on behaviors can be substantial, but nongenetic factors such as family and nonfamily environment are responsible for at least half of the variance in most complex behaviors. Even though genes may account for half of the variance associated with a particular behavior, note that this is almost never a highly deterministic, single-gene influence. And just because we have a genetically based predisposition to behave in a particular way does not mean that these behaviors are unalterable or that they will even be displayed.

Despite the intriguing results from a variety of behavioral areas, there is very little systematic research that bears specifically on nonverbal behavior. Pairs of monozygotic (MZ) and dizygotic (DZ) twins from the Minnesota Study of Twins Reared Apart project had their facial expressions coded as they watched emotion-inducing films (Kendler et al., 2008). MZ twins showed greater similarity in their facial expressions than did DZ twins, suggesting the heritability of facial displays of emotion. In another analysis of identical twins reared apart, some statistical evidence showed striking similarities between twins in vocal pitch, tone, and talkativeness (Farber, 1981). Other mannerisms such as posture, laughter, style of walking, head turning, and wrist flicking were also observed as "more alike than any quantifiable trait the observers were able to measure." Farber went on to say, "Possibly the most interesting observation over the years was that many sets had identical 'body languages'—that is, they unconsciously moved and gestured in the same way, even when they had not had an opportunity for mutual identification" (p. 90).

Researchers at the University of Minnesota Center for Twin and Adoption Research echo these observations (Bouchard, 1984, 1987; Segal, 1999). For example, Segal said,

> One of my favorite tasks was faithfully capturing hand gestures, head positions, foot tapping and energy level in one-hour videotaped sessions of each twin alone, followed by half-hour videotaped sessions of the twins together. Distinctive physical expressions co-occurring in identical twins reared apart suggest that genetic factors are involved. Jerry Levey and Mark Newman, identical [twin] volunteer firemen, held pinky fingers under cans of Budweiser beer long before they met. Other pairs were notorious for swaying side-to-side while walking, accenting long slender fingers with abundant jewelry, and belting out warm, rich laughter. (pp. 143–144)

When asked to stand against a wall for a series of photographs, identical twins in the University of Minnesota studies frequently assumed the same posture and hand positions; this happened only occasionally with fraternal twins reared apart. One pair of identical male twins reared apart had grown similar beards, had their hair cut similarly, and wore similar shirts and wire-rimmed glasses. Their photo shows them both with thumbs hooked into their pants tops. Another pair of female twins both started crying at the slightest provocation, and it was later learned that each had behaved in this manner since childhood. These unsystematic observations do not prove anything about heredity and nonverbal behavior; they only suggest intriguing avenues for research.

Most of the studies comparing twins reared apart have emphasized responses to paper-and-pencil tests. But it seems reasonable to assume that detailed observational studies will indicate a hereditary influence associated with behavior as well. For example, studies of twins show an inherited component to the trait of extraversion (Pedersen, Plomin, McClearn, & Friberg, 1988; Viken, Rose, Kaprio, & Koskenvuo, 1994), and we know that certain nonverbal behaviors, such as faster speech, are associated with the trait of extraversion. Therefore, it is possible that these and other nonverbal cues related to extraversion are common between identical twins.

Researchers have begun to look for genetic factors that might lead to strengths or deficits in twins' abilities to send or interpret nonverbal cues. As one example, Petitclerc and colleagues (2019) pointed to a possible genetic link in the relationship between twins' (mean of age of 7) poor recognition of facial expressions of fear and their "callous-unemotional behavior" at school (e.g., lack of empathy, disregard for others).

Brain imaging studies should offer one intriguing avenue of insight into the possible role of genes in individual differences in the processing of nonverbal behavior. Anokhin, Golosheykin, and Heath (2010), for example, recorded the brain activity (specifically, event-related brain potentials [ERPs]) of MZ and DZ twins who watched a face change in expression between neutral, happy, and fearful. The authors noted that 36% to 64% of the individual variation in the ERPs to these changes in facial expression could be attributed to genetic factors.

EVIDENCE FROM NONHUMAN PRIMATES

Human beings are primates, as are apes and monkeys. If we observe our nonhuman primate relatives manifesting behaviors similar to ours in similar situations, we are more confident that such behavior might have phylogenetic origins. Parr, Micheletta, and Waller (2016) provide an extensive review of research on primate communication.

For Charles Darwin, evidence of similarities in expressive behavior across different species constituted important support for his theory of evolution. For Darwin, the increasing use of the face, voice, and body for emotional and communicative purposes demonstrated the process of evolutionary advancement. Darwin wrote:

> With mankind some expressions, such as the bristling of the hair under the influence of extreme terror, or the uncovering of the teeth under that of furious rage, can hardly be understood, except on the belief that man once existed in a much lower and animal-like condition. The community of certain expressions in distinct, though allied species, as in the movements of the same facial muscles during laughter by man and by various monkeys, is rendered somewhat more intelligible if we believe in their descent from a common progenitor. (1872/1998, p. 19)

Among vertebrates, the functionality of a rich repertoire of expressive and signaling behaviors is clearly related to the complexity of a species' social organization. We need only compare the differing number of facial muscles possessed by a lizard to those of a monkey to understand why Darwin considered expression a critical link in the argument for evolution.

Before we begin emphasizing similarities, we should acknowledge some important differences in human and nonhuman primates. Human beings make little use of changes in body color, but we do have an extensive repertoire of gestures that attend verbal language. Apes, monkeys, and chimpanzees use almost no referential gestures with each other (Pika, Liebal, Call, & Tomasello, 2005; Pika & Mitani, 2006). We also seem to have a greater variety of facial blends, and our response repertoire is not nearly as limited to immediate and direct stimuli. And although other animals are capable of complex acts, the level of complexity, control, and modification shown by the human animal may be hard to match.

Behavioral similarities are often linked to common biological and social problems that confront human and nonhuman primates: for example, mating, grooming, avoiding pain, expressing emotional states, rearing offspring, cooperating in groups, developing leadership hierarchies, defending, establishing contact, and maintaining relationships. Chimpanzees, like humans, form political alliances to gain power, show empathy for those in distress, do favors for others, and reconcile after a fight with a touch or embrace (de Waal, 2002). FIGURE 2-2 shows some of these similarities in grooming and bodily contact. Of the many behaviors that might be explored for evolutionary roots (Altmann, 1968; Thorpe, 1972; van Hooff, 1973), we focus on three: facial expressions, perception of the color red on conspecifics, and eye behavior during greetings.

Studies comparing the facial displays of nonhuman primates and human beings find that the "tense-mouth display" of nonhuman primates shows social and morphological kinship to anger on human faces. When circumstances trigger a combination of anger and fear, nonhuman primates manifest a threat display (see Figures 2-3). In human beings, this most closely resembles a blend of anger in the mouth—an open-mouthed anger expression—and fear in the eye area (Redican, 1982).

FIGURE 2-2 Some similarities between humans and other primates in bodily contact and grooming.

Chevalier-Skolnikoff has proposed similar phylogenetic chains for expressions of happiness, such as smiling and laughter, and sadness with and without crying (Chevalier-Skolnikoff, 1973; van Hooff, 1972). Figure 2-5 provides both written and visual descriptions of probable evolutionary paths for facial displays of anger in three living primates. It shows evolutionary dead ends for some expressions and continuity for others.

Extensive studies of different species of macaques also demonstrate a wide variety in the social functions served by particular facial expressions. Thus, even within these closely related monkey species, the same facial expression can be used with different overall frequencies and can have different meanings. For example, there are "remarkable species differences with respect to the exact social meaning of the "silent bared-teeth display" or fear grimace (Preuschoft, 1995, p. 201) (see Figure 2-7). This grimace usually signifies submissiveness and appeasement in species marked by rigid status hierarchies. However, in species in which status differences are weakly expressed, the expression has converged with other expressions—for example, the "play face" shown in Figure 2-6 and the "open-mouthed bared-teeth display," a more extreme version of the grimace—to signify genuinely affiliative and reciprocal social interaction, such as during greeting, grooming, embracing, or huddling, and also to reassure a lower-ranking partner. The likely relation to human smiling has long been noted by primate researchers (van Hooff, 1972). Thus, in species marked by a reduction of power asymmetry and an increased overlap of interests among interactants, there has occurred an "evolutionary emancipation of silent bared-teeth display from its originally fearful motivation" (Preuschoft, 1995, p. 209). Such evidence that the same expression can have a diversity of meanings and functions among macaques should caution researchers of human expressions not to leap to simplistic conclusions about what human expressions mean based on the primate evidence.

Many human facial expressions have evolved from noncommunicative behaviors such as attacking, moving toward or away from things, self-protective movements, and movements associated with respiration and vision. Chevalier-Skolnikoff argued, for instance, that

> threat postures of most primates contain elements derived from attack (mouth open and ready for biting) and locomotion toward (body musculature tense and ready to advance), while the submissive postures contain elements derived from protective responses (retraction of lips and ears) and locomotion away from the sender. (1973, p. 30)

Thus, a behavior such as flight from an enemy, which was originally critical to survival, may eventually become associated with feelings of fear and/or anger. It is possible, then, that an expression of fear and/or anger may appear even if the original behavior (fleeing) is unnecessary, for example, a male monkey that feels fearful when approaching a female to copulate. The facial display has, over time, become associated with a particular feeling state and appears when that feeling state is aroused. It is likely that those animals that substituted facial expressions of threat for actual attack and fighting had a higher survival rate and, in turn, passed on this tendency to succeeding generations. Similarly, humans' greater dependence on signals received visually—rather than through smell, for instance—may have been especially adaptive as our ancestors moved into open areas and grew in physical size.

Humans and nonhuman primates need to be able to not only encode emotional information on the face but also interpret facial cues and expressions, as they both live in group settings in which others communicate emotional information to them. Here are a few examples of this involving nonhuman primates:

- Lemurs follow the gaze of other lemurs as they move about in naturalistic settings (Shepherd & Platt, 2008).

© Kimberly Fillah-Horgan

FIGURES 2-3A A tense-mouth display by an adult female rhesus monkey. Ears are flattened, brows are raised, the gaze is fixed and staring, jaws are close together, and lips are compressed. Teeth are not prominently exposed, although this animal is highly disposed toward attack. Angry humans display a similar configuration.

© Kimberly Fillah-Horgan

FIGURES 2-3B An adult female rhesus macaque (Macaca mulatta) displaying a facial threat. Notice that the teeth are not prominently exposed. Ears are flattened against the head, the brow is raised, the gaze is fixed and staring, nostrils are flared, and the upper lip is rounded over the teeth.

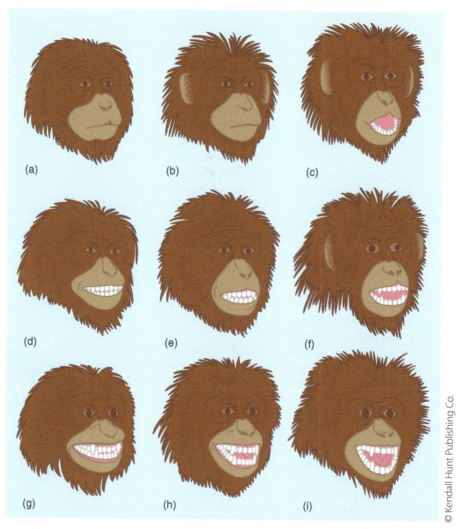

FIGURE 2-4 Facial expressions of *Macaca arctoides* according to intensity and emotion. Note that on the anger axis (top row, left to right) as the monkey becomes increasingly angry, the stare intensifies, the ears are brought forward, the hair is raised over the head and neck, the lips are tightened and contracted, and the mouth is opened. On the fear axis (left column, top to bottom) as the animal's fear increases, the gaze is averted; the ears are drawn back against the head, where they do not show; and the lips are retracted horizontally and vertically, baring the teeth.

Reading left to right, and from top to bottom, these are the expressions: (a) Neutral face. (b) "Stare": mild, confident threat. (c) "Round-mouthed stare": intense, confident threat. (d) Slight "grimace": slight fear. (e) A mild fear–anger blend. (f) "Open-mouthed stare": moderately confident, intense threat. (g) Extreme "grimace": extreme fear. (h) Mild "bared-teeth stare": extreme fear blended with anger. (i) "Bared-teeth stare": intense fear–anger blend.

- Rhesus monkeys and chimpanzees can discriminate between the facial expressions of conspecifics (Parr & Heintz, 2009; Parr, Waller, & Heintz, 2008).
- Great apes (chimpanzees, gorillas, orangutans) might be able to use facial expressions to infer behavior. Buttelmann, Call, and Tomasello (2009) had great apes observe a male human reacting happily to what was inside one container and in a disgusted fashion to what was inside another container. Afterward, the apes saw the human eating food. When given the opportunity, the apes were more likely to choose the container that the human had shown disgust toward, presumably inferring that there was still food in there (i.e., the human had eaten the food in the

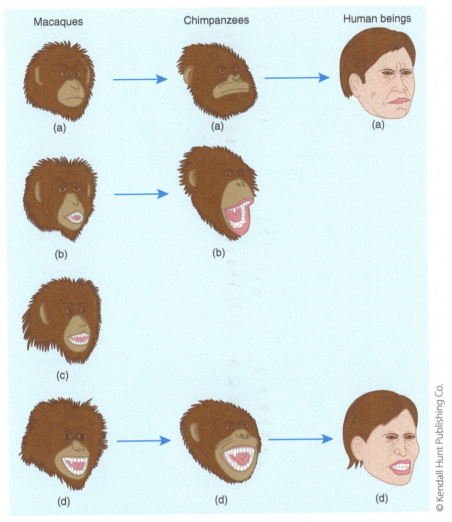

FIGURE 2-5 A between-species analysis and probable evolutionary paths for facial expressions of anger. (a) The closed mouth, Type I Angry Face in humans has an equivalent in both macaques and chimpanzees. In all species, the mouth is closed, the eye gaze is direct, and brows are either pulled down and together or raised and lowered. (b) This anger display has no equivalent in human beings. In macaques and chimpanzees, the mouth is partly opened with lips covering teeth. The macaques' mouth is rounded. The gaze is direct and accompanied by a roar or bark. (c) This anger display is found only in macaques. The common elements are direct gaze, jaws slightly to moderately open, accompanied by a roar or bark. Macaques will raise and lower their brows, and sometimes the lips will not cover the lower teeth. (d) An equivalent of this open mouth, Type II Angry Face in humans is found in all the nonhuman primates identified here. Direct gaze; lower eyelids tensed, often producing a squint; brows lowered and pulled together; jaws moderately open in a rectangular form with teeth showing are all part of the human display. Words often accompany this display, as do screams and shrieks in other species. Source: Adapted from Chevalier-Skolnikoff, 1973, p. 27

other container). This finding suggests that great apes can infer how a human had behaved toward two containers of hidden food based on the human's prior emotional reactions to each.

We also can look at psychological reactions to color as a stimulus, as well as entire sequences of behavior that may have some genetic components and evolutionary origins. For example, there appear to be parallels in how humans and nonhuman primates react to seeing the color red on a conspecific in particular settings. Human males and male rhesus macaques seem to perceive dominance in opponents wearing or displaying red in competitive situations (Hill & Barton,

© Kimberly Fillah-Horgan

FIGURE 2-6 A playful chimpanzee (Pan troglodytes) displaying the primate equivalent to the human laugh and pleasurable smile.

© Kimberly Fillah-Horgan

FIGURE 2-7 A grimace by an adult female rhesus macaque. Teeth receive a prominent frontal exposure in this and related compound displays.

2005; Khan, Levine, Dobson, & Kralik, 2011), and human males and male chacma baboons appear to perceive greater "sexiness" in their respective female counterparts when those females are displaying red on their body or, in the case of humans, appearing in a red background or wearing red clothing (Bielert, Girolami, & Jowell, 1989; Elliot & Niesta, 2008; Roberts, Owen, & Havlicek, 2010; cf. Peperkoorn, Roberts, & Pollet, 2016). Similarly, human females and female rhesus macaques appear to be more sexually attracted to males wearing red clothes or displaying reddened faces, respectively (Roberts, Owen, & Havlicek, 2010; Waitt, Lane, & Head, 2003). The color red on the body may signal sexual maturation or receptiveness in male and female humans and nonhuman primates alike, resulting in similarities in how each responds to conspecifics displaying that color in specific settings (e.g., mating).

Many factors affect the way greetings are handled: place, time, relationship between the greeters, and so on. With so many sources of potential variation, it is noteworthy when seemingly invariant patterns are found. Pitcairn and Eibl-Eibesfeldt (1976) observed the eye behavior of adult human beings, human infants and children, blind persons, and nonhuman primates in greeting rituals and found some remarkable similarities. In each case there was a pattern of looking at the anticipated interaction partner from a distance and looking at them during the greeting at a closer range and as interaction began; then there was a period of looking away prior to reestablishing gaze for interaction. They believe this behavior is a "stream of activity which, once started, must continue to the end" and that there is a strong possibility of a genetic or inherited program behind it.

Eibl-Eibesfeldt's studies of what he calls *basic interaction strategies* in several different cultures led him to conclude that rules related to dominance, bonding, and affiliation are at the root of both verbal and nonverbal human behavioral displays, whether in greeting, trying to block aggression, getting the focus of attention, or persuading a partner to give you something. But he acknowledges that cultural teachings and environmental factors may play an enormous role in making these strategies seem very different from one culture to another. Still, his observations of children in various cultures led him to state,

> We can assume there exists a system of universal rules that structure social interactions, verbal and nonverbal alike. These rules could be rooted in certain panhuman dispositions that channel the acquisition of norms, and some norms may even be encoded in reference patterns given to us as phylogenetic adaptations. (1988, p. 114)

Although Eibl-Eibesfeldt's view may be perceived as overstated or radically deterministic (given the evidence he provides for behavioral universality), his observations do open the door for consideration of specific behaviors or entire chains or sequences of behavior involved in relating to our fellow human beings that may be rooted in our biological makeup. One example is that both nonhuman primates and people are less likely to gaze at a conspecific who is displaying a dominant versus submissive body posture (Holland, Wolf, Looser, & Cuddy, 2017). In each case, looking less at the face of a powerful-acting conspecific could be protective in nature—specifically, a way of not triggering the perception that you are adopting a challenging stance toward them.

EVIDENCE FROM MULTICULTURAL STUDIES

Human beings the world over have two basic adaptive problems to solve: how to stay alive and how to raise their offspring to a reproductive age. Solutions to these problems might have evolved because they were successful in dealing with these two problems, and thus are part of the human heritage. Such solutions would be biological (e.g., the configuration of facial muscles; the ability to run), psychological (e.g., the ability to experience emotion states), and social (e.g., the ability to communicate with others verbally and nonverbally). To use an overly simplified example, when confronted by a predator, those humans who could experience fear or could display that emotion on their face or could understand the emotional meaning of that expression in others might have been more likely to survive, assuming those abilities were also associated with the motivational behavior of fleeing the situation. To the extent that nonverbal communication aided survival and the ability to reproduce, it would not be surprising to find cross-cultural similarities in how humans communicate emotional and social information to one another.

If we observe human beings in different environments with different cultural guidelines similarly encoding and/or decoding particular nonverbal behaviors, we will develop increasing confidence that inherited components of the species may be responsible. Nonetheless, even though multicultural similarities may be attributable to a common human inheritance, such observations are not absolute proof of innateness. It only means that the cause of similarities across cultures is due to something people have in common and thus makes a genetic explanation a possible one to explore.

Some of these cross-cultural similarities concern the perception of discrete emotions or socially relevant state information in people, whereas others concern the enactment of specific behaviors. In terms of emotion states, Sauter, Eisner, Ekman, and Scott (2010) demonstrated that negative emotion states, such as fear and anger, have specific vocal qualities that are decoded similarly by people from different cultures. A considerable amount of research has been conducted examining similarities in the cross-cultural recognition of facial expressions of emotion, a topic we will cover shortly. Other research suggests that individuals from different cultures may also recognize others' emotion states (e.g., anger, fear, happiness, sadness, pride) from their body movements alone (when the face is not visible) because each emotion is signaled by similar body movements in people across cultures (Parkinson, Walker, Memmi, & Wheatley, 2017).

Regarding socially relevant information, it appears that both people from industrialized Western cultures and those from a preliterate African tribe recognize the nonverbal expression of pride (Tracy & Robins, 2008). The combination of nonverbal cues that signal pride includes a head tilted backward slightly, postural expansion, a low-intensity smile with the mouth, and arms akimbo with hands on the hips.

Eibl-Eibesfeldt (1988) suggests we might find entire sequences of behavior manifesting cross-cultural similarities, for example, coyness, flirting, embarrassment, open-handed greetings, and a lowered posture for communicating submission. In fact, Schiefenhövel (1997) believes his own work and that of Eibl-Eibesfeldt have "clearly proven the existence of universal facial, proxemic, and to a lesser extent, gestural behaviors" (p. 65). Although others may not share the unequivocality of Schiefenhövel's claim, he reminds us of the extensive body of research ethologists and psychologists have accumulated around the globe that speaks to a common behavioral heritage.

Cultural *differences* in nonverbal communication are also observed. For example, if you want to draw someone's attention to something by pointing, say to person X, you will likely use your index finger to point to person X. Cooperrider, Slotta, and Núñez (2018) have challenged the assumption that this type of manual pointing behavior is universal. They found that the Yupno of Papua New Guinea were more likely to point to something using their nose or head, whereas U.S. participants overwhelmingly favored manual pointing (as would people in many other countries, we can assume).

This example demonstrates that the question of universality is not all-or-nothing; against a backdrop of similarity, there can be differences. Thus, even if cross-cultural similarities are found, we should not overlook how social or cultural factors might lead to differences in the expression of that nonverbal behavior, whether those expressions concern

LAUGHABLE RESEARCH

Research on laughing is now a serious matter. If you travel to any place on this planet, you will observe people laughing. Laughing, like smiling, is a panhuman phenomenon. It signals positive feelings in a person as well as positive relationships with others, among other functions. Researchers have examined the differences between what are called true enjoyment smiles ("Duchenne") and merely social smiles ("Non-Duchenne"), noting that people can distinguish between the two types. Recently, researchers have examined whether people can distinguish between genuine (spontaneous) and deliberate laughter. People from various cultures could tell the difference between spontaneous/genuine laughter and volitional/fake laughter because the two types have different vocal features (Bryant et al., 2018). Moreover, listeners could distinguish between the laughter of friends and the laughter of strangers, again because of vocal differences in the two types of laughter (Bryant et al., 2016).

basic emotions (see Hwang & Matsumoto, 2015); nonbasic emotions, such as triumph (Hwang, Matsumoto, Yamada, Kostić, & Granskaya, 2016); or other nonverbal cues or sequences. Several examples illustrate this point:

- There have been claims that, in the area of seeking a mate, a common "courtship dance" among humans and non-humans exists, and that cross-cultural similarities can be observed in the nonverbal behaviors used by humans when flirting with members of the other gender (Birdwhistell, 1970; Eibl-Eibesfeldt, 1971). Yet how that process unfolds within a culture may be impacted by other factors, such as the presence or absence of fathers in a family. Van Brummen-Girigori and Buunk (2016) found that, relative to teenage girls who grew up with a father, those who did not employed more direct cues of flirtation around males.

- Muzard, Kwon, Espinosa, Vallotton, and Farkas (2017) observed that 1-year-old children from the United States displayed more intense bodily gestures of pleasure and discomfort than did their counterparts from Chile. In a comparative study involving U.S. and Chilean women, those from the United States more intensely showed the emotion states of happiness and anger with their bodies, whereas those from Chile more intensely showed the emotion states of happiness and pride with their faces (Muñoz & Farkas, 2017).

- Vocal expressions of anger and triumph from Japanese speakers are easier for Japanese than Dutch listeners to categorize (Yoshie & Sauter, 2020). It seems that these "socially disengaging" emotion expressions from Japanese speakers are perceived as less intense among Dutch than Japanese listeners.

- In terms of the smile intensity of 8-year-old Dutch and Chinese children while they were playing a game, it was greater for only Chinese children who played with someone else as opposed to alone (Mui, Goudbeek, Swerts, & Hovasapian, 2017).

Next, we detail two behaviors with widespread documentation in a variety of cultures—findings that urge us to look for the possibility of phylogenetic origins: (1) the eyebrow flash and (2) facial expressions of emotion.

Eibl-Eibesfeldt (1972) has identified what he calls the *eyebrow flash*. He has observed this rapid raising of the eyebrows—maintained for about one-sixth of a second before lowering—among Europeans, Balinese, Papuans, Samoans, South American Indians, Bushmen, and others. Although the eyebrow flash often can be seen in friendly greeting behavior, it has also been seen when people are giving approval or agreeing, seeking confirmation, flirting, thanking, and when beginning and/or emphasizing a statement. The common denominator seems to be a "yes" to social contact, or requesting or approving such contact. Smiles and nods sometimes accompany this gesture. The Japanese, however, are reported to suppress it as an indecent behavior. However, other instances of reported eyebrow raising seem to indicate disapproval, indignation, or admonishment. These "no" eyebrow signals are often accompanied by a stare and/or head lift with lowering of the eyelids, signaling a cutting off of contact. Because Eibl-Eibesfeldt observed eyebrow lifting in some Old World monkeys, he began speculating on their possible evolutionary development. He reasoned that in both the "yes" and "no" displays, a similar purpose was being served: calling attention to someone or letting someone know for sure that they were being looked at. When we display the expression of surprise, for instance, we raise our eyebrows and call attention to the object of our surprise. It may be a friendly surprise or an annoyed surprise. The evolutionary chain hypothesized by Eibl-Eibesfeldt is presented in FIGURE 2-8.

Perhaps the most conclusive evidence supporting the universality of facial expressions is found in the work of Ekman and his colleagues (Fridlund, Ekman, & Oster, 1987). Photos of 30 faces expressing happiness, fear, surprise, sadness, anger, and disgust/contempt were presented to people in five diverse, literate cultures. Faces were selected on the basis of meeting specific criteria for facial musculature associated with such expressions. There was generally high agreement among the respondents regarding which faces fit which emotions. Other studies have found results supporting the accuracy of decoding of the posed facial expressions of emotion. These studies tested people from 21 different countries, ranging from Kyrgyzstan to Malaysia and from Ethiopia to Estonia (Boucher & Carlson, 1980; Ekman, 1972, 1998; Izard, 1971; Niit & Valsiner, 1977; Shimoda, Argyle, & Ricci-Bitti, 1978).

Because these people were exposed to the mass media and travelers, we might argue that they learned to recognize aspects of faces in other cultures from these sources. However, Ekman and Friesen's (1971) research with the South Fore in Papua New Guinea and Heider's (1974) work with the Dani in western New Guinea show that these isolated, preliterate peoples—who were not exposed to the mass media and travelers—decoded the posed expressions

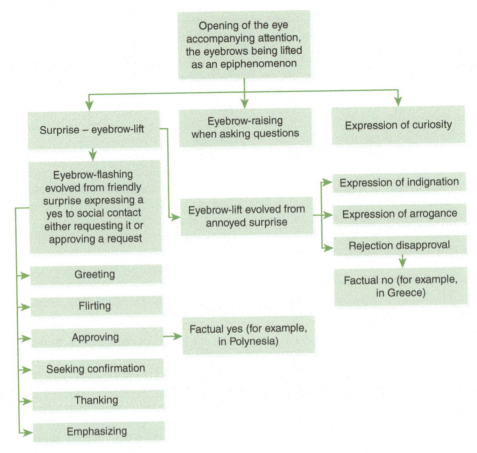

FIGURE 2-8 Eibl-Eibesfeldt's hypothesized evolution of eyebrow movements.
Adapted from Eibl-Eibesfeldt

comparably to the people from literate Eastern and Western cultures. In Ekman's work with the South Fore, stories were told to the subjects who were then asked to select one of three facial photos that reflected the emotion of the story. Distinguishing fear from surprise was the most difficult discrimination to make. Perhaps, as Ekman says, fearful events in this culture are often surprising, too. Interestingly, when Ekman obtained photos of expressions made by these New Guineans and asked Americans to judge them, the Americans accurately decoded all the expressions with high levels of accuracy, with the exception of fear, which was often judged as surprise and vice versa.

Physiological reactions associated with facial expressions have also been established. Ekman, Levenson, and Friesen (1983) found that greater heart rate acceleration and increased skin conductance occurred when people in the United States made negative facial expressions displaying fear, disgust, and anger. Levenson, Ekman, Heider, and Friesen (1992) found the same physiological reactions in the Minangkabau of Sumatra.

Although Ekman's program of research is perhaps the most complete, other studies of other cultures support his findings. There does seem to be a universal association between particular facial muscular patterns and discrete emotions. Note that this is only a specific element of universality and does not suggest all aspects of facial affect displays are universal, as Ekman and Friesen (1969) testify:

> [W]e believe that, while the facial muscles which move when a particular affect is aroused are the same across cultures, the evoking stimuli, the linked effects, the display rules and the behavioral consequences all can vary enormously from one culture to another.

Do these cultural display rules follow a pattern too? Matsumoto (1991) believes two important dimensions of culture will help us predict the display rules for facial expressions in any given culture:

1. *Power distance*, or the extent to which a culture maintains hierarchical, status, and/or power differences among its members
2. *Individualism versus collectivism*, or the degree to which a culture encourages individual needs, wishes, desires, and values versus group and collective ones

Matsumoto hypothesizes that members of power-distance cultures will display more emotions in public that preserve status differences. Cultures that stress individualism, according to this theory, will manifest greater differences in public emotional displays between in-groups and out-groups (relative to collective cultures).

Although the evidence seems to point toward universal recognition of certain emotions from facial expressions, it is important to note that the only facial expression that received close to or above 90% accuracy by those tested in Japan, Brazil, Chile, Argentina, and the United States was happiness (Ekman, 1973, 1994). The smile, surely the most salient feature of the happy expressions, may indeed have nearly universal meaning. But even here, we should exercise caution because studies like those conducted by Ekman ask people to judge "pure" expressions and they are often out of context. The social and emotional context of a smile, and the exact combination of facial muscles used, can add many new and even contradictory meanings, as we will discuss in Chapter 9. The claim of universality is not, therefore, that *all* smiles will always be interpreted as happy but that the prototypical happy expression, involving movements of certain facial muscles, will have a common meaning across most cultures.

The possibility of great variation in the meanings attributed to facial expressions is made even clearer when we examine the judgments made about smiles as well as facial expressions of negative emotion states (e.g., fear, surprise, anger, disgust/contempt, and sadness). In terms of judgments about smiling people, viewers appear to attribute different qualities to them, such as how trustworthy they seem to be, as a function of the extent to which corruption exists in their society (Krys et al., 2016). For expressions of negative emotion states, even the prototypical ones, the accuracy rate across the cultures Ekman studied was noticeably less than it was for happiness. Perhaps, for these emotional expressions, the biological determinants are weaker or have been overridden more by cultural norms. Furthermore, Russell (1994) demonstrated that recognition scores for people from non-Western cultures are significantly lower than Western respondents for expressions of fear, disgust, and anger.

As you learn in later chapters, there is also evidence that cultures can differ widely in the overall frequency with which specific gestures or expressions are used, as well as in the meanings attributed to those cues. So even though some facial displays of emotion may have a neurologically hardwired component to them, they are also modified by local norms, values, and customs. As a result, these emotional displays can be accurately recognized around the world. However, due to local emotion expression "dialects," cultures are *most* accurate when judging expressions made by people from their own culture (Elfenbein & Ambady, 2002).

Thus, again, the debate over universality versus cultural specificity cannot be viewed as either/or any more than the nature-versus-nurture debate can be. To illustrate, two cultures might engage in different *amounts* of interpersonal touch, but the meanings *attributed* to various kinds of touches—sexual, friendly, dominant, aggressive, and so on—may be the same in both. Thus, we would see cultural specificity in terms of usage but universality in terms of meaning. Or different cultures might use the very same hand gesture with the same frequency but may use it to convey very different messages. In this case there would be universality of usage, but there would also be cultural specificity on meaning.

We have ended this chapter by introducing the idea of differences among cultures in emotional displays and recognition. In Chapter 3, we will expand on the "difference" concept to examine differences among individuals in the ability to send and understand nonverbal cues.

SUMMARY

In this chapter, we examined five different ways researchers accumulate data relevant to questions of genetic and learned behavior. If we had data from each area for a particular behavior, the evidence would be strong. Instead, we have fragments and tantalizing possibilities. The evidence that facial expressions of emotion have an inherited component is, to date, the strongest data we have on any nonverbal behavior. Facial expressions of emotion seem to manifest themselves in children deprived of sight and hearing, in infants, in nonhuman primates, and in literate and preliterate cultures around the world. A genetic component passed on to members of the human species seems probable for this behavior. The innate capacity to perceive various kinds of behaviors and imitate them also has important implications for nonverbal study. And even though little detailed and systematic evidence is available, the possibility that entire sequences of behavior may have a link to inheritance is most intriguing.

We take the point of view that neither nature nor nurture is sufficient to explain the origin of many nonverbal behaviors. In many instances, we inherit a neurological program that gives us the capacity to perform a particular act or sequence of acts. Our environment and cultural training, however, may be responsible for when the behavior appears, the frequency of its appearance, and the display rules accompanying it as well as its intended meaning.

QUESTIONS FOR DISCUSSION

1. What do you think it means to say that nonverbal behavior is universal? State evidence supporting and not supporting such a claim. What exceptions can you think of?

2. Darwin thought there were many similarities between the nonverbal expressions of humans and those of lower animals. Discuss communication in the animal world. Do you think animals send the same messages via nonverbal behavior that we do?

3. Why, in your opinion, do infants imitate adults' facial movements? Do you think they know what different expressions mean? Why do babies have such expressive faces and voices?

4. The eyebrow flash is seen in cultures around the world. Reflect on your own use of this gesture. Do you use it? If so, when do you use it and with what meanings?

NONVERBAL COMMUNICATION IN ACTION: TRY THIS

Depending on your location and individual circumstances, you may choose which kind of stimuli you want to observe in this exercise. Go to a zoo or spend time with one or more human babies (under 6 months)—or, if neither is available, look at many photographs of animals or babies on the Internet. At the zoo, look at different kinds of animals, and if you are watching babies be sure to watch them in a variety of circumstances. Make your own catalogue of their nonverbal behavior and your interpretations. Keep careful notes so that you can make a systematic statement describing what you saw. After this exercise, where do you stand in terms of the theory that human nonverbal behavior has roots in biology?

CHAPTER 3

THE ABILITY TO RECEIVE AND SEND NONVERBAL SIGNALS

The study of nonverbal communication as an interpersonal skill represents a significant shift in the investigation of human social behavior.

—**H.S. Friedman**

As you look around, you will readily note that some people seem more socially wise than others. Some people can "get along with anybody"; some we call savvy, tactful, shrewd, or poised. In contrast, some people seem insensitive, awkward, obtuse, or just tuned out. All of these qualities fit into the concept of *social competence*. Social competence is not easy to define, but it has long interested researchers, and *social intelligence* is considered a basic intellectual capacity distinct from other cognitive abilities (Rosenthal, Hall, DiMatteo, Rogers, & Archer, 1979; Sternberg & Kostic, 2020). *Emotional intelligence* is a related concept that includes the ability to judge emotional messages, to regulate one's own emotions, and to use emotions wisely to guide thought and action (Matthews, Zeidner, & Roberts, 2002; Salovey & Mayer, 1989). Even though it may seem that social and emotional intelligence are distinct—one cognitive, the other emotional—a person's success in daily living may depend on their ability to tie their emotions to their thinking (Damasio, 1994).

We definitely know that skill in nonverbal communication is part of social competence. Some people are comparatively more alert to nonverbal cues and better able to identify what these cues mean, and some people are more capable than others in expressing their feelings and attitudes nonverbally. Some people try, using nonverbal as well as verbal cues, to project an image of themselves; for example, they want to be seen as cool, reckless, intellectual, sincere, or competent, but they just cannot pull it off convincingly; their performances seem fake or flawed. Others do an excellent job of projecting exactly the image they desire. The social competence that comprises such skill is often referred to as *impression management*, and it is essential in daily life, both personal and professional. While impression management can involve portraying oneself in misleading or deceptive ways, much of the time people manage others' impressions in ways that are authentic or at least consistent with legitimate social goals (Wang & Hall, 2020). A trial lawyer must act convinced of the defendant's (perhaps doubtful) innocence. A psychotherapist needs to convey interest and acceptance to their client. A manager has to, at times, cover their own bad mood with a smile and a cheerful greeting for subordinates. And a parent may use nonverbal communication constantly and deliberately to reinforce and direct a child's behavior in socially acceptable ways. Everyone has a multitude of roles to play in life, and a skilled understanding of the nonverbal cues relevant to each role is important for the smooth functioning of society and can serve to keep a person in good standing with others.

In this chapter, we focus on the receiving and sending of nonverbal messages, using the terms *skill*, *ability*, and *accuracy* more or less interchangeably. Although nonverbal communication skills are often talked about with reference to judging and expressing emotions, people actually judge and express many other kinds of nonverbal messages, states, and traits as well. People make such inferences and expressions so often in daily life that they are barely aware of doing it.

A person needs to *notice* characteristics of others in order to interpret them correctly. Such noticing does not have to be fully conscious; much of what we see and mentally process in the social environment is "beneath the radar" of conscious awareness. These cues include aspects of physical appearance such as a person's facial structure, clothing, and hairstyle, as well as their nonverbal behaviors. Sometimes the noticing by itself is the important thing, independent of whatever interpretations might be made (Hall, Murphy, & Schmid Mast, 2006; Horgan, McGrath, Bastien, & Wegman, 2017; Horgan, Schmid Mast, Hall, & Carter, 2004). For example, you might notice and remember that your friend wears silver more than gold earrings, that they often wear blue, or that they might be a bit too thick in the middle for the sweater you are thinking of buying for them. Other times, there is an immediate interpretation ("She is jumping up and down at the news—she must be really excited" or "Whoops, that ring tells me she's married"). Sometimes, you grasp its meaning later, as in "Oh, you didn't get your promotion. No wonder you were so quiet at dinner."

Social communication skill relies on more than just noticing the cues, however. People also need to grasp verbal meanings—literal, metaphoric, and shades of innuendo—and to integrate verbal and nonverbal cues; sarcasm and joking, for example, are expressed through combinations of verbal and nonverbal cues. The ability to connect a name with a face is yet another skill required in daily life, as is the ability to know whether you have heard a certain voice (see Chapter 11) or seen a certain face before (Leeland, 2008).

People also need to understand social contexts and roles: what is and is not expected in a given social situation; how people in particular roles—for example, professors and students—are expected to behave; and what consequences might ensue from violating others' expectations (Bernieri, 2001). The sociologist Kurt Danziger (1976) argued that social interaction is impossible without a subtle and unspoken—in other words, nonverbal—negotiation of the respective roles to be played by the two parties in an interaction. Usually one person lays claim to a particular role or definition of the relationship, and the other has to go along or else counter with a different role definition. Until the two people tacitly agree on a common understanding, they cannot successfully interact, because they cannot effectively enact the interlocking roles such as friend-friend, teacher-student, salesperson-customer, doctor-patient, interrogator-suspect, or mother-child. People generally know how to play these roles very well, and they do so without having to think about it consciously; furthermore, people are sensitive to whether roles are being enacted appropriately by others. This subtle negotiation over roles usually goes unnoticed until one person acts "out of role" or inappropriately to the other's unspoken expectations. Then people are likely to become aware that the interaction has become problematic, although they still may not know why. Clearly, the ability to read and send the subtle cues required for role negotiation, and to know when roles are being fulfilled appropriately, is an important social skill.

Although much research has been done on nonverbal abilities, many questions remain less than fully answered. These include the origins of nonverbal abilities; the role that both positive and negative motivations play in accurate judgment and expression; whether skill in receiving and sending are part of one larger skill or are separate skills; and, within the receiving modality, whether there are many distinct sub-skills—such as skill in judging emotion, skill in judging personality, and skill in judging deception—or whether all these can be subsumed under the general concept of judgment accuracy. There are also unresolved methodological issues in this domain (Hall, Bernieri, & Carney, 2005), some of which we will touch upon in this chapter.

DEVELOPMENT AND IMPROVEMENT OF NONVERBAL SKILLS

No one knows how much individual variation in nonverbal skills is inborn or due to experience, but most of what we know suggests an important role for experience. Most of people's ability to send and receive nonverbal signals is derived from "on-the-job training," the job being the process of daily living. In short, people learn nonverbal skills, not always consciously, by imitating and modeling others and by adapting their responses to the coaching, feedback, and advice of others. This process starts in infancy with babies' mimicry of adult facial expressions. Even within the first few days of life, infants can imitate mouth opening and tongue protrusion; within the first few months, imitation extends to lip protrusion, finger movements, brow movements, and even different emotional expressions on the face. By 9 months, a mother's facial expressions are not only reciprocated by her baby but also have a clear influence on the baby's affect and play behavior (Field, 1982; Field, Woodson, Greenberg, & Cohen, 1982; Meltzoff & Moore, 1983a, 1983b; Termine & Izard, 1988). Experts believe that an innate repertoire of facial expressions, innate imitative ability, and selective reinforcement by caretakers combine to give the child an understanding of the socially agreed-on meanings of different nonverbal cues and that these processes enable people to label emotions in themselves and others (Lewis & Rosenblum, 1978).

That nonverbal and other social skills are strongly rooted in learning seems apparent enough and provides insight into why individuals differ so much in these skills. Among many animals, social interaction is also essential to developing appropriate social behavior later in life. Harlow's famous studies of rhesus macaque monkeys showed that monkeys raised in complete isolation for 6 months and then tested at 2 to 3.5 years of age "displayed aggression even to 1-year-old infants, as no self-respecting socially raised rhesus would" (Harlow & Mears, 1978, p. 272). Even specific communication skills in monkeys have been linked to social experience early in life. Miller, Caul, and Mirsky (1967) found that rhesus monkeys reared in isolation were deficient in facial expression and judgment ability. In an experiment, two monkeys could each avoid an electric shock if one could communicate to the other through facial cues that the shock was imminent (indicated to the expressor monkey by a colored light) so that the other monkey could press a bar in time to cancel the shock for both of them. Monkeys reared in isolation were incapable of producing the necessary expressions and, when put in the role of receiver monkey, proved deficient at reading the fearful facial expressions of the other monkey.

Feedback from others as you grow up does not have to refer to your behavior explicitly; it can be a *response* to your behavior. Such feedback may be another person treating you like you are an unhappy person because they noticed how you were behaving. Through feedback people increase awareness of themselves and others, learning what behaviors to enact and also how they are performed, with whom, when, where, and with what consequences. You can practice nonverbal sending and receiving frequently, but without regular, accurate feedback, you may not improve your ability. Feedback in the form of telling participants when their nonverbal judgments are right or wrong is one of the more successful methods of improving nonverbal abilities (Ambady, Bernieri, & Richeson, 2000; Blanch-Hartigan, Andrzejewski, & Hill, 2012).

THE TRUTH ABOUT DECEPTION

"Hey, I just lied to you!" How many times have you heard that right after someone has just lied to your face? If you ever learn about another's deceit, it is likely well after the fact. Not knowing that you are being lied to when you are being lied to gives little opportunity to detect associations between the nonverbal cues of the liar and the lie itself.

Moreover, even when you suspect deception, the liar is not likely to admit that they lied, depriving you of the feedback needed to hone your deception-detecting skills. How often have you heard the following? "You're right, I am lying to you. What gave me away?" For these reasons, the learning environment for decoders is rather impoverished when deception is involved. Skill at decoding deception is consequently not all that good.

People might not be aware that their skill at detecting deception is not all that good for the same reasons they are not good at distinguishing between a lie and the truth. In general, people learn that another person has lied only after the fact. The recipient is thus required to search their memory banks for clues about what the liar did or did not do. Such recollections could be misleading because what sticks out in memory will likely be salient nonverbal cues that do not signal deception per se (e.g., "I remember she got angry when I accused her of pilfering money from the company's petty cash fund"). One might also remember seeing cues that were not actually present during the lie because these cues fit with the faulty stereotypic information we have about the nonverbal behavior of liars (e.g., "I recall his eyes became shifty when I confronted him about flirting with our neighbor"). Last, when suspecting deception, a person might ignore the feedback from the other person—"I'm not lying about this!"—that would lead one to understand that the person is actually telling the truth. Ironically, people cannot be good lie detectors without understanding the nonverbal behaviors associated with telling the truth.

The truth about deception is that, in general, people do not fully appreciate the fact that they are not all that good at detecting it.

Overall, structured programs to improve accuracy in understanding nonverbal cues have produced positive results. Studies have incorporated a variety of approaches, including teaching the meanings of cues and providing discussion, practice, and feedback as mentioned earlier. Although the evidence is positive, most studies do not test for the generality of the gains resulting from training because they test the impact of the training on audiovisual materials that are similar or identical to the ones used in the training. Also, most studies do not attempt to evaluate how long such improvements last or how they impact social functioning (Beck & Feldman, 1989; Costanzo, 1992; Ekman & Friesen, 1975; Elfenbein, 2006; Grinspan, Hemphill, & Nowicki, 2003). Both of these shortcomings were overcome with a recently developed computerized program called Training Emotion Recognition Ability (TERA; Schlegel, Vicaria, Isaacowitz, & Hall, 2017), a brief, self-administered training for 14 different emotions expressed through face, body, and voice. Gains in accuracy from the training persisted for as long as four weeks and extended to several different tests of emotion recognition. The capacity to improve people's emotion recognition ability through a brief training offers many new avenues for research. The pragmatic impact of training could be large, as well. For example, men at high risk for physically abusing their children could benefit from training in emotion recognition, as they appear to have deficits in this area (Asla, de Paúl, & Pérez-Albéniz, 2011), and physicians could benefit from improving their understanding of patients' emotions (Blanch-Hartigan & Ruben, 2013).

Some everyday experiences that are not formal training in interpersonal perception may also contribute to a person's skill in this domain. For example, parents, especially mothers, of toddler-age children were shown to be more accurate in judging nonverbal cues on a standard test than were similar married people without children (Rosenthal et al., 1979). Also, training in dance or extended athletic experience (Pitterman & Nowicki, 2004) are associated with greater ability to decode nonverbal cues, perhaps because those activities often require a person to be very aware of other people's expressions and movements (other dancers, teammates, or opponents).

There have also been efforts to train people's abilities in sending—not just decoding—nonverbal cues, especially using the social skills model developed by Argyle (1988). According to this model, socially skilled behavior is analogous to skilled motor behavior, such as driving a car. In both kinds of skills, a person makes moves; observes their effect, including others' reactions to them; and takes corrective action, all with the purpose of obtaining a goal. The different elements of social behavior are seen as hierarchical. The finer, lower-level elements are automatic and habitual; the higher levels are more strategic in nature and, therefore, under more direct cognitive control. This kind of training involves more active role-playing and practice than the research described previously. Social skills training based on this model has been used to train people of low social competence in the effective use of nonverbal cues to make friends; it is also aimed at helping distressed married couples, psychiatric patients, children with learning disabilities, and professionals who need social skills for their occupations (Argyle, Trower, & Bryant, 1974; Hargie, 2006).

A major category of behavior emphasized in social skills training is reinforcement, which involves the provision of encouragement and reward to others in the course of an interaction. Reinforcers can be verbal and nonverbal. Verbal reinforcers include acknowledgment, agreement, and praise. Nonverbal reinforcers include the positive use of smiles, head nods, looking at the other, touching, body proximity, certain gestures (e.g., thumbs-up), and an encouraging voice quality. A particularly well-developed form of reinforcement training using nonverbal communication (among other modalities) is Applied Behavior Analysis (ABA), which is used for addressing many kinds of behavioral problems, including those seen in children on the autism spectrum.

HISTORICAL HOOFNOTE

You might wonder what a story about a horse has to do with interpersonal accuracy, but you will soon find out. Herr von Osten purchased a horse in Berlin in 1900. When von Osten began training his horse, Hans, to count by tapping his front hoof, he had no idea that Hans would soon become one of the most celebrated horses in history. Hans was a rapid learner and soon progressed from counting to adding, multiplying, dividing, subtracting, and eventually to solving problems involving factors and fractions. Even more startling, when von Osten exhibited Hans to public audiences, Hans could count the size of the crowd and the number of people wearing eyeglasses. Responding only with taps, Hans could tell time, use a calendar, recall musical pitch, and perform numerous other seemingly fantastic feats. It seemed that Hans, a common horse, had complete comprehension of the German language (because he was always asked the questions that way), the ability to produce the equivalent of words and numerals, and an intelligence beyond that of many human beings.

Even without promotion by the mass media, the word spread quickly, and Hans became known throughout the world. He was soon dubbed *Clever Hans*. Because of the profound implications for several scientific fields, and because some skeptics thought a gimmick was involved, an investigative commission was established to decide whether deceit tainted Hans's performances. Professors of psychology and physiology, the director of the Berlin Zoological Garden, a director of a circus, veterinarians, and cavalry officers were appointed. An experiment with Hans, in which von Osten was absent, demonstrated no change in the apparent intelligence of the horse. This was sufficient proof for the commission to announce that no trickery was involved.

But the appointment of a second commission was the beginning of the end for Clever Hans. Von Osten was asked to whisper a number in the horse's left ear while another experimenter whispered a number in the horse's right ear. Hans was told to add the two numbers—an answer none of the onlookers, von Osten, or the experimenter knew. Hans failed. And with further tests, he continued to fail. The experimenter, Pfungst (1911/1965), had discovered that Hans could answer a question only if someone in his visual field knew the answer and was attentive to the situation.

When Hans was given a question, onlookers who knew the answer assumed an expectant posture, increased their body tension, and bent their heads slightly forward (even barely perceptibly). When Hans reached the correct number of taps, the onlookers would relax and make a slight upward movement of their heads, which Hans used as the signal to stop tapping. Hans could detect head movements as slight as one-fifth of a millimeter. Subsequent experiments found that Hans also would cease tapping when a knowledgeable onlooker raised their eyebrows or even showed a dilation of the nostrils.

Hans's cleverness was obviously not in his ability to understand verbal commands but in his ability to notice and respond to barely noticeable and unconscious nonverbal movements by those surrounding him (Spitz, 1997). Hans could not answer questions correctly unless the questioner or some other onlooker knew the correct response and emitted some tiny cue that Hans could then use. The story of Clever Hans makes a foundational point for understanding the amazing interpersonal perceptivity of both animals (such as dogs) and humans. Whether you know it or not, you are emitting cues and responding to other people's cues that are just as tiny as those Hans was noticing.

IS IT GOOD TO HAVE MORE ACCURATE KNOWLEDGE OF NONVERBAL COMMUNICATION?

Students frequently ask whether attempts to learn about and develop skills in nonverbal communication might have negative consequences. They wonder whether a person can "know too much" about others for their own good, and whether those who have this information might use it to manipulate others for self-serving ends. Or they worry that being expert in reading nonverbal cues will make a person unhappy or unpopular because that person is able to see through others' lies and insincerity. Although all of these could happen in specific circumstances, there is, thus far, little overall evidence of these negative consequences. In general, we believe that increasing people's knowledge of nonverbal cues is a good thing and that both individuals and society benefit when everyone's communication skills are better.

Greater knowledge of cues and more developed skills may also make people less vulnerable to manipulation. But even tactics that work do not work all the time. A good analogy can be drawn from the study of verbal persuasion. People have been studying the art of persuasion for over 2,000 years, yet it does not appear that persuaders have become so sophisticated that they invariably succeed. Furthermore, it is the nature of human adaptation to change behavior when it becomes unproductive. Whenever people who know more about nonverbal behavior are suspected of using it against others, we soon see attempts to expose or counteract the attempted influence. It also goes without saying that each person has the ethical responsibility not to use knowledge to harm others.

MEASURING THE ACCURACY OF DECODING AND ENCODING NONVERBAL CUES

Interest in measuring receiving (decoding) and sending (encoding) accuracy goes back to the early decades of the 20th century. Sometimes, the purpose has been to study the decoding and encoding process itself: Can emotions be recognized from nonverbal cues? What cues do people rely on most when making their judgments? Sometimes, the goal is to compare accuracy in different communication channels or among different emotions: Is it easier to decode the face than the voice? Which are the hardest messages to send via nonverbal cues? And sometimes, the purpose is to compare the accuracy of individuals and groups. It is the accuracy of individuals and groups that we emphasize in this chapter. Other chapters take up some of the other questions.

Most research on nonverbal communication skill has focused on emotions. However, emotions are only one of many different states and traits people communicate nonverbally. Also, there is variation in how the skill is measured (Hall & Bernieri, 2001; Hall, Schmid Mast, & West, 2016). The following list shows some of the variety and richness of the information that is sent and received in daily life.

- Interpersonal orientation: "That person was trying to dominate me," or "He didn't seem very threatening."
- Attitudes: "I really like you," or "I could tell that you didn't like that movie."
- Intentions or needs: "She wants to leave," or "She wants attention."
- Physical states: "I'm in pain," or "You look really tired."
- Personality: "She was the most extraverted person I've ever met," or "He is so neurotic."
- Personal characteristics: "You don't look a day over 30," or "I think he's gay."
- Intelligence: "I have to seem really smart to get this job," or "He's not as dumb as he looks."
- Deception and insincerity: "I like this present, I really do," or "I thought she was a big phony."
- Appearance and behavior: "Remember Jenny? She's the one who smiles a lot," or "You've worn the same thing three days in a row!"

The following examples will give you a taste of actual research. Bernieri, Gillis, Davis, and Grahe (1996) have studied *rapport*, which is defined as how much positivity, attentiveness, and coordination are experienced by people toward each other when they interact (Tickle-Degnen & Rosenthal, 1990). Bernieri measured observers' accuracy in rating the degree of rapport felt by two people having a conversation by comparing these ratings to the degree of rapport reported by the people themselves. Observers' accuracy was better than the guessing level but was impeded by their reliance on some cues that were not, in fact, indicators of actual rapport. For example, they thought more smiling was a sign of rapport, when in fact it was not.

On the opposite side of rapport, adults and children may pick up on nonverbal cues linked to interracial disharmony. Using 20-second clips of white undergraduates speaking with black or white experimenters, Richeson and Shelton (2005) found that the speaker's prejudice against blacks was detectable by other undergraduates who rated how positively toned the speaker's behavior was. Accuracy in predicting prejudice was especially high when the rater was black, and the video clip showed a white student speaking with a black experimenter. In other words, the black student raters seemed especially able to discern how the more prejudiced whites spoke to a black person.

Yet another kind of accuracy was studied by Carter and Hall (2008), who measured how well people could notice *covariations* between characteristics of people and how they behave. People use this skill when, for example, they become aware that women typically smile more than men or that students tend to sit with others sharing their ethnicity in school cafeterias. In everyday life, people notice social covariations so often they don't usually think of it as an aspect of social perception ability, but it is. Carter and Hall tested the skill experimentally by forming small groups of strangers and instructing some of group members to behave in a certain way, after which the authors tested whether observers could identify the covariations. For example, when observing a group of people talking about living on campus versus living off campus, did the observer notice that those who lived on campus talked more than those who did not? Women's accuracy on this test was higher than men's, and accuracy was higher for observers who had more extraverted and less neurotic personalities.

Other kinds of interpersonal accuracy include the ability to recognize what social groups people belong to as well as their sexual orientation. Kraus and Keltner (2009) noted that observers could distinguish between individuals of upper and lower socioeconomic status (SES), and that a person's SES might be signaled by their nonverbal cues of disengagement (e.g., doodling, shown more by upper SES individuals) and engagement (e.g., head nodding, shown more by lower SES individuals) during interactions. Ambady, Hallahan, and Conner (1999) measured the accuracy with which people could identify the sexual orientation (gay/lesbian vs. heterosexual) of people shown speaking for only a few seconds. Accuracy was higher than would be expected by chance, and when there was less information available to perceivers on which to base a judgment, the more accurate gay and lesbian observers were relative to heterosexual observers. Rule and Ambady (2008b) further demonstrated that college students had an accuracy rate higher than guessing when shown gay and straight men's faces for only a 20th of a second.

As one final example, accuracy in judging personality traits can be measured not only from how people behave but also from their *social footprint*. This footprint can include their tastes in music and recreation, their self-representation on personal websites, their clothing choices, and the manner in which they decorate and maintain their living or working spaces. Accuracy in judging personality from such footprint cues has been shown to be surprisingly good, as documented in studies of music tastes, dress, and living/working spaces, among others (Borkenau & Liebler, 1993a, 1995; Gosling, Ko, Mannarelli, & Morris, 2002; Zweigenhaft, 2008). Social footprint information also seems to help in detecting the trait of narcissism. Observers appear to be aware of the flashy dress and neat appearance of narcissists (Vazire, Naumann, Rentfrow, & Gosling, 2008).

The most common method for testing both sending and receiving skills is to present perceivers (decoders) with excerpts of the senders' behavior as captured in videotapes, photographs, or audio recordings. The stimuli might show all of the information, as one would see and hear in a video recording, or the researcher might present the nonverbal cues in different modalities such as silent video, face only, or voice only. A receiver's perception accuracy is defined as their success in judging the senders' cues, and a sender's communication accuracy is typically defined in terms of the accuracy achieved by a group of perceivers (receivers) who guess what the senders were expressing. As an example, Koerner and Fitzpatrick (2003) had spouses deliberately send emotional messages to each other and then scored encoding accuracy by showing the videotapes to a group of new perceivers who had to guess what emotion was being conveyed. The proportion of judges whose guesses matched the original affective intention of the spouses was used as the operational definition of encoding accuracy.

Naturally, any test requires a "correct answer" for each test item. Sometimes, the correct answer can be hard to determine, and researchers must rely on operational definitions. For facial encoding, the people who serve as the stimuli may be asked to convey various states (e.g., emotions) with their face, or to tell about an emotional experience, while being videotaped; the instructed or intended emotion is then used as the correct answer. In the picture-viewing paradigm (Buck, Powers, & Hull, 2017), the researcher surreptitiously records senders (i.e., encoders) while they are watching pictures or videos that vary in emotional content (e.g., scenic, sexual, or unpleasant). Their facial reactions are then watched by new perceivers who guess what the senders were looking at. In this method, the "right answer" is whatever the original stimulus was. Such facial expressions are much more spontaneous and presumably authentic than in the previously described methods because the senders do not know they are being videotaped while watching the stimuli.

For capturing vocal qualities to be used as stimuli in a test, senders may be asked to recite a neutral sentence while varying the emotions they are trying to convey, or they might be asked to describe a past emotional experience, and thereby reexperience the emotion they had felt at the time. If, for example, the request is to "talk about a sad experience you have had," the tone of voice used by a sender could be used by perceivers to guess what emotional state the sender was talking about. If the researcher wants to be sure that verbal cues do not provide the listener with clues as to what emotional message is being conveyed, electronic filtering methods can be applied to make the words unintelligible so that only nonverbal qualities, such as loudness, rhythm, and pitch, remain (see Chapter 11).

The methods described so far involve presenting a set of nonverbal stimuli to perceivers. Such stimuli are often called *thin slices* because they are short excerpts from a longer stream of behavior (Ambady, Bernieri, & Richeson, 2000; Ambady & Rosenthal, 1992; Carney, Colvin, & Hall, 2007; Lippa & Dietz, 2000). The thin slices used in interpersonal accuracy research can range in length from a video of people having a long conversation down to still facial expressions or brief video clips shown for less than 1 second (Matsumoto et al., 2000).

There are many advantages to having the stimuli standardized in a test that can be reused with many different perceivers, enabling direct comparisons between different groups or individuals and allowing for a given perceiver to make judgments of many different people. However, sometimes, a researcher wants to investigate nonverbal communication between individuals who are communicating *with* each other, for example, one spouse with another (Noller, 1980), a subordinate with their boss (Snodgrass, 1992), or one participant with another in the laboratory (Ickes, 2001). Live interaction studies like these are not standardized in the way that a test would be. In a live interaction study, communication accuracy is defined as the correlation or match between Person A's (retrospective) report of what they were thinking or feeling during the interaction and Person B's (also retrospective) report of Person A's thoughts and feelings. In one variation of this method, both parties look at a video of their interaction and report on their own and each other's thoughts and feelings at specific moments (Ickes, 2001, 2003; Ickes, Stinson, Bissonnette, & Garcia, 1990).

The live interaction method presents challenges for several reasons, among them the problem of distinguishing between one person's proclivity to show their thoughts or feelings and the other person's skill in picking up on someone's thoughts or feelings. A person could be an inaccurate perceiver, for example, either because they did not possess much decoding skill or because the other person simply did not send any cues that could enable accurate decoding. However, by showing videotapes of the interactions to a new group of naive judges, it is possible to disentangle these different sources of accuracy (Hall, Rosip, Smith LeBeau, Horgan, & Carter, 2006; Snodgrass, Hecht, & Ploutz-Snyder, 1998).

STANDARDIZED TESTS OF DECODING ABILITY

Researchers have made and validated many different tests of people's ability to decode, or understand, the meanings of nonverbal cues. One of the first and most widely used is the Profile of Nonverbal Sensitivity or PONS test (Rosenthal et al., 1979). The PONS test is a 45-minute video that contains 220 two-second auditory and visual segments portrayed by a white American woman. Five scenes portray a positive-dominant affect or attitude (e.g., "admiring a baby"); five scenes portray positive-submissive behavior (e.g., "expressing gratitude"); five scenes portray negative-dominant behavior (e.g., "criticizing someone for being late"); and five scenes portray negative-submissive behavior (e.g., "asking forgiveness"). Each scene is presented to viewers in 11 different cue channels, representing the single or combined channels of face, body, and content-masked speech (see Chapter 11 for the description of methods used to accomplish this). The test has been administered widely to people of different ages, occupations, and nationalities.

Figure 3-1 shows three still photos taken from the PONS video. Each item has two choices, for example, (a) returning faulty item to a store versus (b) ordering food in a restaurant, or (a) talking about one's divorce versus (b) expressing motherly love. Thus, the PONS test measures the ability to recognize affective or attitudinal states in a situational context.

In contrast, the Diagnostic Analysis of Nonverbal Accuracy (DANVA; Nowicki & Duke, 1994) is based on recognition of pure emotions—happiness, sadness, fear, and anger—not in a situational context. The DANVA has several versions, including tests of facial, vocal, and postural expressions posed by white and black expressors. The facial and postural expressions were generated by asking encoders to pose the different emotions while a photograph was taken, and the vocal cues were generated by asking encoders to say an ambiguous sentence while conveying the four different emotions. The DANVA has been used extensively with children and adults.

One of the most recently developed tests is the Geneva Emotion Recognition Test (GERT; Schlegel, Fontaine, & Scherer, 2019). In this test, actors portray 14 different emotions in video via the combined face, body, and vocal channels. To eliminate verbal clues, the actors used a pseudo language while enacting the different emotions for the camera. The GERT has shown correlations with many other psychological constructs.

In contrast to these tests, in which encoders act out different scenes or emotions, the Interpersonal Perception Task (IPT) emphasizes more spontaneous behavior. Its developers reasoned that in real life, the things we judge about others are often actual events or relationships (Costanzo & Archer, 1989). For example, a man and woman are interacting with two children: Which is their own child? Two women discuss a tennis game they have just played: Who was the winner? A man tells his life story, then he tells it again quite differently: Which story is true? In this video test, one hears the encoders' words but what they say is ambiguous enough not to give away the correct answers. The correct answers on the IPT are authentic; in other words, the scenes are not play-acted or posed. For example, for the item where one has to guess which woman won the tennis game, one of them really did (and that's the correct answer).

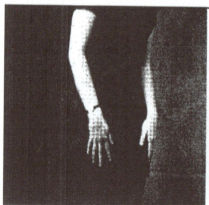

FIGURE 3-1 Still photos from the PONS test.

© Judith A. Hall

PERSONAL FACTORS INFLUENCING THE ACCURACY OF DECODING NONVERBAL CUES

People can be extremely sensitive to nonverbal cues. In Chapter 1, we mentioned that students react to very subtle positive and negative expectancy cues from their teachers. Research shows that first impressions of personality, based on superficial observation and no actual interaction, are quite similar among observers and to targets' own self-descriptions. Thus, people agree on others' sociability or extraversion after the barest exposure to each other, at levels above what would be expected by chance (Albright, Kenny, & Malloy, 1988; Levesque & Kenny, 1993; Marcus & Lehman, 2002).

Similarly, observers' ratings of only a few seconds, or thin slices, of behavior can be surprisingly accurate and predictive of other important variables (Ambady, Bernieri, & Richeson, 2000). The predictive power of thin slices has been demonstrated in a variety of domains, including judgments of teacher effectiveness, the affective style of children and their families, personality traits and psychopathology, rapport during medical examinations, and intelligence (Ambady & Rosenthal, 1993; Carney, Colvin, & Hall, 2007; Fowler, Lilienfeld, & Patrick, 2009; Murphy, Hall, & Colvin, 2003; Oveis, Gruber, Keltner, Stamper, & Boyce, 2009; Roter, Hall, Blanch-Hartigan, Larson, & Frankel, 2011). Regarding teacher effectiveness, people who watch brief silent video clips of teachers' classroom behavior agree remarkably on the teachers' qualities, and their ratings predict performance evaluations by the teachers' own students and principal (Ambady & Rosenthal, 1993). Clips a minute long or shorter produce accuracy above chance levels for a variety of personality traits and intelligence (Carney, Colvin, & Hall, 2007; Murphy, Hall, & Colvin, 2003). In the Carney et al. study, clips of 5 seconds were as good as much longer clips for judging some characteristics (e.g., intelligence).

However, the accuracy with which thin slices are judged varies greatly from study to study and depends both on the method used and the construct being judged. Accuracy may be best when people do not think too much about the judgment process (Ambady, 2010). Accuracy in distinguishing truth from lies is typically not much above the guessing level (Bond & DePaulo, 2006), whereas accuracy in judging basic emotions, and also the status difference between two people, is often very high (Biehl et al., 1997; Schmid Mast & Hall, 2004). Comparisons like this must be made with caution, however, because in developing their tests, investigators have great latitude in determining how easy or difficult the items are (by, for example, varying how much information is made available to perceivers or picking excerpts of a certain difficulty level). In order to detect differences in test-takers' accuracy levels, test developers often strive to make their tests neither too easy nor too difficult.

SELF-ASSESSMENTS AND EXPLICIT KNOWLEDGE OF NONVERBAL CUES

Considering the time required to develop, validate, administer, and score nonverbal tests, you might think it would be cheaper and easier just to ask people to appraise their own skills. Unfortunately, this does not work. People high in ability to judge nonverbal cues are not necessarily those who appraise their own skills highly, although their accuracy in self-evaluation is above the guessing level (Hall, Andrzejewski, & Yopchick, 2009). However, the correlation between people's self-assessments and their scores on actual nonverbal cue judging tests is not nearly high enough for self-assessments to be substituted for tested nonverbal decoding skill. It seems, the cues that people think they use when making nonverbal judgments are often not the ones actually relevant to the judgments they are making, which is one reason accuracy at detecting lies is not very high (Hartwig & Bond, 2011).

Nevertheless, it has been shown that people do have some explicit knowledge of nonverbal communication—that is, knowledge they can articulate on a paper-and-pencil test. Deficits in such knowledge may have important implications for people with subclinical autistic characteristics (Ingersoll, 2011). The Test of Nonverbal Cue Knowledge (TONCK; Rosip & Hall, 2004) and the Geneva Emotion Knowledge test (GEMOK; Schlegel & Scherer, 2017) both measure knowledge of how nonverbal cues are associated behavior, emotion, and other variables. An example from the GEMOK asks, "If somebody uses the word SADNESS to describe an emotional experience, how likely is it that the person opened his/ her eyes widely?" In both tests, the correct answers are based on actual findings in published research. These scores significantly predict accuracy on the PONS, DANVA, and/or GERT nonverbal decoding tests (described earlier), but the correlations are not large enough to permit the TONCK or GEMOK to be used as a substitute for measuring the actual decoding of cues. However, these are good additions to the instruments available for researchers.

GENDER

One of the best-documented correlates of accurate nonverbal perception is *gender*. More often than not, girls and women score higher than boys and men on tests of judging the meanings of nonverbal cues (Hall, Gunnery, & Horgan, 2016; McClure, 2000). Women also show other evidence of better-developed interpersonal skills. They score higher than men on the TONCK, they remember people's appearance and nonverbal cues better than men do (Hall, Murphy, & Schmid Mast, 2006; Horgan, Schmid Mast, Hall, & Carter, 2004), and they are more accurate at picking up social covariations (described earlier; Carter & Hall, 2008). The female advantage in decoding the meanings of nonverbal cues is present from grade school on up. Although the difference is not great—about 2 percentage points between average male and female PONS scores, for example—it is extremely consistent. Females scored higher than males in 80% of 133 different groups given in the PONS test, including a variety of non-U.S. samples (Hall, 1984; Rosenthal et al., 1979). Reviews of research using many other decoding tests have confirmed that this gender difference exists across ages of participants and regardless of whether the encoders are male or female and regardless of which particular test is used. It also holds up, with rare exceptions, from culture to culture (Dickey & Knower, 1941; Izard, 1971; Merten, 2005; Rosenthal et al., 1979).

Although these and other studies indicate a superior ability among females to judge nonverbal cues, most of the research is on judging emotions. Researchers have shown that women do not have an advantage at judging whether another person is lying (Aamodt & Custer, 2006), or when judging status and dominance (Schmid Mast & Hall, 2004). And women's advantage is less consistent when the task is Ickes' empathic accuracy paradigm described earlier, involving the ability to guess another person's thoughts and feelings at particular moments in a conversation (Ickes, Gesn, & Graham, 2000). Tasks that possibly show a weaker female advantage are those in which facial expression plays a less significant role. Indeed, in the empathic accuracy paradigm, the most important cues appear to be verbal rather than facial (Gesn & Ickes, 1999; Hall & Schmid Mast, 2007).

Given how widespread the evidence for females' superiority on nonverbal judgment tasks is, it is no surprise that interpersonal perceptiveness is part of the common stereotype about women (Briton & Hall, 1995). We think it is likely that females' greater skill as interpersonal decoders has been recognized throughout history and contributes to the layperson's notion of "female intuition." Gender differences in nonverbal communication skill are discussed further in Chapter 12.

AGE

Age also has been studied in relation to decoding skill. Provocative research indicates that infants only a few months old have some ability to discriminate among facial and vocal expressions of emotion (Haviland & Lelwica, 1987; Walker-Andrews, 1997; Walker-Andrews & Lennon, 1991). Of course, it is difficult to assess how much infants understand the cues' *meanings*; discrimination per se does not demonstrate this depth of understanding. But research did find that 7-month-olds showed increased attention to faces that matched auditory tones on emotional quality; for example, they looked more at a joyful face than a sad face when the associated vocal tones were ascending, fast oscillating, high, and pulsing (Phillips, Wagner, Fells, & Lynch, 1990). Even more suggestive of emotion understanding is the finding that infants are less likely to trust adults who demonstrate emotions that are incongruent with an event (Crivello & Poulin-Dubois, 2019).

People generally show a gradually increasing decoding skill from kindergarten until ages 20 to 30 (Dimitrovsky, 1964; Harrigan, 1984; Markham & Adams, 1992; Nowicki & Duke, 1994; Rosenthal et al., 1979). More focused investigations have been able to identify the ages when specific skills are gained; for example, children 6 and 7 years old could not tell smiles of enjoyment from those of nonenjoyment, which differ in muscle movements around the eyes, but children 9 and 10 years old could (Gosselin, Perron, Legault, & Campanella, 2002). The great majority of research into developmental trends has been concerned with judging emotions from nonverbal cues. An exception is the study of McLarney-Vesotski, Bernieri, and Rempala (2006), who found improvements across ages 8, 13, and adult for a test of judging personality traits from short video excerpts.

The trend reverses, however, as a person ages. Numerous studies comparing young adults to older adults show a decline in accuracy in judging nonverbal cues among older adults. For example, women averaging 62 years of age scored significantly lower on the multichannel PONS test than women averaging 22 years of age (Lieberman, Rigo, & Campain, 1988), and other researchers have found deficits in adults over age 65 compared to younger adults (college-aged and in their 20s) for face, body, and voice cues examined separately (Isaacowitz et al., 2007; Ruffman, Henry, Livingstone, & Phillips, 2008). Questions currently under study are whether this kind of decline is limited to tests of judging posed emotion expressions and, relatedly, to standardized tests that are context-free (as opposed to the wide array of judgments and contexts that characterize real life). Castro and Isaacowitz (2019) administered an extensive battery of different kinds of interpersonal accuracy tests to young, middle-aged, and older adults and found, as before, an age-specific decline in accuracy on standard posed emotion recognition tests but much more mixed patterns in accuracy for other judgment skills; age-related similarities occurred for judging others' spontaneous expressions of disgust, satisfaction, amusement, interest, and enjoyment.

GENERAL COGNITIVE ABILITY

An important question is whether scores on tests of nonverbal decoding reflect a unique ability related to social intelligence or a general cognitive skill. After all, interpersonal accuracy tests are tests, and, as such, the scores they yield might just reflect general problem-solving or test-taking skills. A large review revealed a small-to-medium positive correlation between general cognitive ability (as measured with IQ and similar tests) and nonverbal judgment accuracy (Schlegel et al., 2019). However, the correlation was small enough to suggest that the two abilities are far from synonymous. We can conclude that a person's skill at judging nonverbal behavior depends to some extent on ordinary cognitive ability but mostly on other factors that are more uniquely connected to social life and social experience.

OTHER PERSONAL CORRELATES

Adults who do well on tests of decoding nonverbal cues have been found to exhibit certain personal and interpersonal characteristics, as reported in much research and published summaries (e.g., Funder & Harris, 1986; Hall, Andrzejewski, & Yopchick, 2009; Hall, Schmid Mast, & West, 2016; Marsh, Kozak, & Ambady, 2007; Pickett, Gardner, & Knowles, 2004; Rosenthal et al., 1979; Schlegel et al., 2019). High-scoring adults are better adjusted, less hostile and manipulating, more interpersonally democratic and encouraging, more tolerant, more helpful to others, more open to experience, more conscientious, more extraverted, more in need of social inclusion, less shy, less anxious, more likely to believe they control what happens to them, more warm, more popular, more likely to be seen by others as interpersonally sensitive, more emotionally intelligent, and better able to judge others' interpersonal sensitivity. In many ways, high-scoring adults appear to have a positive interpersonal orientation to other people. This is interesting because those who are open, positive, agreeable, and invested in interpersonal relationships are also better at judging people's personality traits (Fast, Reimer, & Funder, 2008; Letzring, 2008; Vogt & Colvin, 2003).

The relevance of a positive interpersonal orientation to enhanced interpersonal perception accuracy does not apply to personal life only; it also extends to situations in professional life, such as interactions at the workplace and those between clinicians and patients (Elfenbein, Foo, White, Tan, & Aik, 2007; Hall et al., 2015). Accurate emotion recognition even predicts objective outcomes relevant to workplace success, such as performing objectively better as a salesperson (Byron, Terranova, & Nowicki, 2007) and being a better music teacher (Kurkul, 2007).

Children in preschool and/or elementary school who score higher at decoding face, posture, gesture, or tone of voice have been found to be more popular and more socially competent, less anxious, less emotionally disturbed, less aggressive, and less depressed, and they are higher in internal locus of control (e.g., Baum & Nowicki, 1998; Castro, Cooke, Halberstadt, & Garrett-Peters, 2018; Izard, Fine, Schultz, Mostow, Ackerman, & Youngstrom, 2001; Lancelot & Nowicki, 1997; McClure & Nowicki, 2001; Nowicki, Bliwise, & Joinson, 2019; Nowicki & Carton, 1997; Nowicki & Duke, 1994; Nowicki & Mitchell, 1998).

Children who score higher on nonverbal decoding tests also score higher on academic achievement (Halberstadt & Hall, 1980; Izard et al., 2001; Nowicki & Duke, 1994). Although general cognitive ability may contribute to the ability to understand nonverbal communication, nonverbal skills may also influence academic achievement, possibly through their impact on teacher–student relationships. Halberstadt and Hall (1980) found that children who scored higher on the PONS test were perceived by their teachers as smarter, even when the pupils' actual academic and IQ scores were controlled statistically. Izard and colleagues (2001) found that students' ability to understand facial expressions at age 5 predicted teachers' ratings of these students' academic competence at age 9, controlling for objectively tested cognitive ability. It is possible that nonverbally perceptive youngsters create such a good impression that adults either want to spend more time with them or attribute greater cognitive ability to them, which in turn may create a positive, self-fulfilling prophecy in which these children are taught more and encouraged more, leading to actual gains in their academic achievement. One study has found that decoding skill also seems to have a direct role in the learning process. Bernieri (1991) found that high school students who scored higher on the PONS test learned more from a peer in a brief teaching session than did students who scored lower.

Certain groups tend to have greater nonverbal decoding ability. The top three groups on the PONS test were actors, students studying nonverbal behavior, and students studying visual arts. Buck's (1976) research on the interpretation of facial expressions found that students who were fine arts majors were better decoders than math and science majors. However, clinicians in psychotherapy and medicine appear not to have unusually high abilities in this domain.

Psychologically damaging experiences early in life appear to affect accuracy at decoding nonverbal cues, but a clear consensus does not yet exist. Hodgins and Belch (2000) found that college students who had been exposed to parental violence growing up were worse at judging happy cues than students who had not been, but they did not differ when judging other emotional expressions. Pollak and Sinha (2002) found that abused and maltreated children had a lower threshold for identifying anger in facial expressions. A review of 17 studies of abused children concluded that maltreated children did suffer deficits on emotion recognition tasks (da Silva Ferreira, Crippa, & de Lima Osório, 2014). On the other hand, a large study of children in England found no association between the DANVA emotion recognition test and several kinds of childhood adversity, including caregiver physical or emotional abuse, sexual or physical abuse, maternal psychopathology, and neighborhood disadvantage (Dunn et al., 2018). In fact, the origins of individual differences in ability to judge nonverbal cues are very poorly understood. A database involving measures taken over a 25-year period provides one hint: 5-year-old children who had an easy temperament, parental harmony, and moderate father strictness had higher nonverbal decoding abilities at age 31 (Hodgins & Koestner, 1993). Although this does not demonstrate cause and effect, it does suggest that interpersonal accuracy may develop best in untroubled environments.

People suffering from many kinds of psychopathology score lower than comparison groups on many different tests of nonverbal cue decoding (Cotter et al., 2018). For example, patients with both chronic and acute forms of schizophrenia judge facial and vocal expressions less accurately than unimpaired groups, regardless of whether they are medicated (Edwards, Jackson, & Pattison, 2002; Mandal, Pandey, & Prasad, 1998; Mueser, Penn, Blanchard, & Bellack, 1997). Although groups with various kinds of psychological disturbance often have a generalized decoding deficit, sometimes the deficit is specific; for example, groups with psychopathic personality disorder and other documented antisocial behaviors were selectively worse than control groups when judging fearful facial expressions (Marsh & Blair, 2008), and depressed patients were selectively worse than a control group when decoding sad facial expressions (Surguladze et al., 2004).

People diagnosed with autism have interpersonal communication difficulties. Autism is a disorder largely defined in terms of deficient verbal, and especially nonverbal, communication, and difficulty in relating to other human beings. Deficits in emotion recognition, especially for negative emotions, are often reported (Griffiths & Ashwin, 2016). Even

OXYTOCIN: A JUDGE-GOOD HORMONE?

Oxytocin plays a complicated role in people's social lives. At one time it was considered the "love hormone." However, researchers have expanded their search of its effects to include how people process and respond to social information in general.

People's nonverbal decoding judgments represent one recent avenue of exploration. Oxytocin appears to help individuals with a personality disorder or a history of abuse/neglect correctly judge others' emotion states (Schwaiger, Heinrichs, & Kumsta, 2019; Timmermann et al., 2017). Timmermann and colleagues (2017) noted that people who suffer from antisocial personality disorder show deficits in decoding facial expressions of happiness and fearfulness. However, these deficits disappear when they are given oxytocin intranasally. The authors pointed out that correctly identifying fear in others can inhibit aggression toward them.

Of importance, not all individuals with clinical disorders (e.g., anorexia nervosa, depression) benefit from oxytocin when it comes to interpreting others' emotion states (Leppanen et al., 2017; Rutter, Norton, Brown, & Brown, 2019).

individuals who are classified as high-functioning autistic or having Asperger syndrome show deficits in judging facial, postural, and vocal emotion cues (Baron-Cohen, Wheelwright, Hill, Raste, & Plumb, 2001; Doody & Bull, 2011; Rutherford, Baron-Cohen, & Wheelwright, 2002).

SUBSTANCE ABUSE

Substance abuse can damage the brain, resulting in specific cognitive impairments, including nonverbal decoding skill. Dependence on alcohol, stimulants, and opiates has been linked to a reduced ability to decode facial expressions of emotion (Kornreich et al., 2003; Quednow, 2017). The ability to recognize a change in facial expression from neutral to affective in nature (e.g., sad, angry) is slower among heavy cannabis users (Platt, Kamboj, Morgan, & Curran, 2010). Finally, alcoholic patients score lower than norm groups on the PONS test (Rosenthal et al., 1979). An intriguing experiment using photographs of six emotions found that when nonalcoholic participants were given alcohol, their decoding accuracy was impaired, especially men's ability to identify anger, disgust, and contempt (Borrill, Rosen, & Summerfield, 1987). Perhaps some of the antisocial behavior of drinkers is linked to an impairment in their sensitivity to these cues.

CULTURE

The PONS test, whose encoder is a white American woman, has been administered to people from over 20 nations (Rosenthal et al., 1979). People from countries most similar to the United States in language and culture—modernization, widespread use of communications media, for example—scored highest. This suggests that accuracy is highest when the encoders and decoders share common elements of culture. Elfenbein and Ambady (2002), in a review of many studies, confirmed that people have a slight advantage in accuracy when judging encoders who come from their same culture. This effect could be due in part to motivational factors (e.g., decoders not trying as hard to be accurate when the encoders are culturally dissimilar). However, multiple studies now show that different cultural groups express emotions slightly differently and that these differences are known to decoders from those same cultural groups, giving them an advantage when they decode those expressions (e.g., Dailey et al., 2010; Elfenbein & Ambady, 2003).

TASK FACTORS AFFECTING NONVERBAL DECODING ACCURACY

You may think the particular channels (also called modalities) tested—face, voice, and so on—make a difference in a person's nonverbal receiving accuracy. Generally, judgments of visual channels, especially the face, are more accurate than judgments of the voice, though generalizations like this must be made with caution, because tests of different channels may vary in other methodological ways. Several studies show that emotions and attitudes of liking and disliking are more accurately perceived in the face than in the voice. Although you may be better able to recognize many emotions and attitudes if you get both audio and visual cues, some messages may be more effectively communicated in one mode than in another; for example, vocal cues may be more effective for communicating anxiety and dominance than other communication channels. And studies show that if you are accurate in recognizing facial signals, you will also be accurate in perceiving vocal ones (Zuckerman, Lipets, Koivumaki, & Rosenthal, 1975). Also, accuracy is usually higher if the expressions are posed rather than spontaneous, but if you do well in decoding one of these modalities, you will probably do well in the other (Zuckerman, Hall, DeFrank, & Rosenthal, 1976). It is clear that some emotional and attitudinal states are more difficult to judge than others. At one extreme, it is very difficult to tell if someone is lying, and at the other, it is very easy to identify posed facial expressions showing basic emotions such as disgust or joy.

We might also speculate, as did the PONS researchers, that the amount of time a receiver was exposed to a nonverbal signal would affect their accuracy in identification. The PONS scenes were presented to people with the exposure time varied, for example, 1/24th of a second, 3/24th of a second, and so on up to 2 seconds (Rosenthal et al., 1979). Accuracy did increase as exposure time increased. Yet research on judgments made of exposures varying between 2 seconds and 5 minutes has shown that more information often does not yield higher accuracy, and when it does, the differences are often not dramatic (Ambady, Bernieri, & Richeson, 2000; Carney, Colvin, & Hall, 2007).

People's moods can influence how they perceive others' nonverbal behavior. Positive and negative moods produce a bias to see corresponding emotions in others' faces (Niedenthal, Halberstadt, Margolin, & Innes-Ker, 2000; Schiffenbauer, 1974). A sad mood has been shown to reduce the accuracy of judging others (Ambady & Gray, 2002), which lends support to the argument that sad moods promote a slow and thoughtful information-processing style that can detract from accuracy of nonverbal judgments that would otherwise be made in a more automatic, nonanalytic manner.

CHARACTERISTICS OF ACCURATE NONVERBAL SENDERS

When broadly conceived, a definition of nonverbal sending is even more complex than a definition of nonverbal decoding. In a sense, nonverbal sending is everything of an interpersonal nature that we do without words. Indeed, it is inevitable that nonverbal cues will be perceived and interpreted by others—even if a person's intention is to appear neutral or unexpressive. Attempts to control nonverbal cues by trying not to express them at all are likely to be interpreted as dullness, withdrawal, uneasiness, aloofness, or even deceptiveness (DePaulo, 1992). As it is sometimes said, you cannot *not* communicate nonverbally.

A person's nonverbal sending is a mixture of spontaneous cues and more deliberate or intentional ones. When both spontaneous and posed expressions are obtained from the same people, these two abilities are positively related; that is, if a person's spontaneous facial expression to pleasant stimuli, such as a television comedy scene, and unpleasant stimuli, such as a gory accident scene, were easy to "read," that person would also show skill in performing posed expressions.

In daily life, we deliberately convey a host of impressions of ourselves as nice, smart, youthful, honest, dominant, brave, and so on through nonverbal channels. We also use nonverbal communication intentionally as part of our effort to act socially appropriate, for example, to be respectful to authorities, dignified in a fancy restaurant, or polite in the face of disappointment. Children attain these more deliberate self-presentation skills through a long process that combines social experience with their own development of identity; numerous studies testify to developmental trends in these skills (DePaulo, 1992; Harrigan, 1984; Nowicki & Duke, 1994).

According to DePaulo, success at regulating nonverbal behaviors to promote our public presentation depends on knowledge, skill, practice, experience, confidence, and motivation. The success of nonverbal self-presentation is also limited by the inherent controllability of different nonverbal channels—the face, for example, is believed to be more controllable than voice or body—as well as individual differences among people and the intensity of the reality we might wish to mask. For example, the angrier you are, the harder it will be to act as if everything is fine.

One individual difference that definitely affects self-presentation is spontaneous expressiveness of the sort discussed in relation to the picture-viewing paradigm; for example, a person may not realize how much their face reflects the content of a gruesome or romantic scene viewed on television. Differences in spontaneous expressivity are observable in infancy and remain stable over the course of development. The spontaneously expressive person has many social advantages, as we outline shortly, but may be handicapped whenever self-presentation calls for application of display rules or deception. It is suggested, for example, that a highly expressive person may not make a good poker player (DePaulo, 1992).

Another factor influencing nonverbal self-presentation involves lasting physical and expressive qualities that bestow a particular demeanor on a person. The man with thick, bushy eyebrows may look threatening no matter how gentle he actually is. Research finds that some people's demeanors tend to make them look honest or dishonest or pleasant or unpleasant, no matter what they actually feel or do (Wallbott & Scherer, 1986; Zuckerman, DeFrank, Hall, Larrance, & Rosenthal, 1979). Demeanor can work for or against you, depending on your goals; the socially skilled person may learn to complement demeanor with other expressive cues to enhance self-presentation. For example, a person with a babyish face, which others are likely to perceive as honest-looking (Berry & McArthur, 1986), may develop a repertoire of "innocent" nonverbal cues to enhance the impression of sincerity.

Most research on nonverbal sending accuracy involves emotions. The person who is spontaneously emotionally expressive tends to be female and reports less ability to control their emotions (Tucker & Riggio, 1988). It has been suggested that *not* allowing free expression can take a toll on health and cognitive functioning (Berry & Pennebaker, 1993). People who are less expressive experience a higher level of internal physiological arousal (Buck, 177; Buck, Miller, & Caul, 1974), and when they supress their emotions in experimental studies, it appears to negatively impact their cardiovascular activity, blood pressure, and memory for stimuli presented during the suppression of emotion (Butler et al., 2003; Richards & Gross, 1999).

Accuracy in expressing emotions deliberately increases through childhood, but then it levels off. Borod et al. (2004) compared young, middle-aged, and older adults in their ability to pose several emotions using the face. Clear age effects were observed, with the greatest deficit occurring between the older adult group compared to the other two groups.

The seemingly elusive concept of charisma has been operationally defined as expressiveness, including both spontaneous and more intentional sending. Research with the Affective Communication Test (ACT)—which measures expressiveness through self-reported statements such as "I show that I like someone by hugging or touching that person," "I like being watched by a large group of people," "I don't usually have a neutral facial expression," and "I can easily express emotion over the telephone"—documents that the expressive person is socially influential (Friedman, Prince, Riggio, & DiMatteo, 1980; Friedman & Riggio, 1981; Friedman, Riggio, & Casella, 1988). People who scored as more expressive on the ACT were more likely to have given a lecture, to have been elected to office in a political organization, to influence others' moods, and to be perceived as more likable when meeting new. In a sample of physicians, they were likely to have more patients than their counterparts who scored as less expressive. High scorers were also more likely to have had acting experience, to have had a job in sales, to desire an occupation that uses social skills—such as counselor, minister, or diplomat—and to be extraverted, affiliative, and dominant. Comparable findings have emerged for a longer self-report instrument designed to measure seven dimensions of social skills (Riggio, 1986).

People can have insight into their spontaneous expressiveness, but research often finds a weak relationship between participants' self-reports of posed encoding skill and their ability to act out emotions on purpose (Riggio, Widaman, & Friedman, 1985; Zuckerman & Larrance, 1979). Studies that actually *measure* people's nonverbal sending abilities, rather than asking for self-reports, have also produced a variety of findings. Females demonstrate greater encoding skill than males in both posed and spontaneous facial accuracy (Buck, Miller, & Caul, 1974; Friedman, Riggio, & Segall, 1980; Wagner, Buck, & Winterbotham, 1993; Zaidel & Mehrabian, 1969). Possibly contributing to these effects is that females are more successful than males at mimicking facial expressions shown in photographs and on videotape (Berenbaum & Rotter, 1992). However, evidence is mixed on whether a gender difference applies for vocal encoding of emotions. Also, the gender-related difference in sending ability has not been found with children between 4 and 6 years old for spontaneous facial expressions (Buck, 1975). Buck (1977) actually found preschool boys to be more accurate senders of spontaneous facial cues than preschool girls, but boys' accuracy declined over ages 4 through 6, perhaps due to socialization pressure related to the male gender role.

Just as boys appear to be learning the expression norms for their gender, girls are learning theirs as well. Aside from becoming more facially expressive, girls learn earlier to use nonverbal cues according to "display rules" that dictate what behaviors are socially appropriate. At preschool and elementary school ages, girls showed less negativity than boys after receiving a disappointing gift when in the presence of an adult, although control conditions showed they were no less disappointed than the boys (Cole, 1986; Davis, 1995).

Some personality characteristics also have been associated with accurate senders of nonverbal information. High "self-monitors"—people who are very aware of how they should be acting in various situations and are willing to change their behavior accordingly in order to advance their own self-interests—are better able to send emotional information through facial and vocal channels (Snyder, 1974). People who are more extraverted are higher on behavioral measures of expressiveness, whereas those who are more neurotic are lower on such measures (Riggio & Riggio, 2002). Buck's (1975) personality profile for young children shows many of the same characteristics reviewed earlier for decoders. Children who are effective senders are extraverted, outgoing, active, popular, and somewhat bossy and impulsive. Ineffective senders tend to play alone and are introverted, passive, shy, controlled, and rated as cooperative. Among adults, highly accurate senders are more dominant and exhibitionistic (Friedman, Riggio, & Segall, 1980). Better adult senders also make an impression of greater expressiveness, confidence, and likability, and among males, they use more fluent speech, more fluent body movements, and more smiles (Riggio & Friedman, 1986).

For many years, clinicians and researchers have noticed expression deficits in individuals with schizophrenia. Compared to individuals without the disorder, these people tend to show reduced facial expressivity, are more likely to show negative than positive expressions, show less congruence between verbal and facial messages, and are less accurate in facial and vocal expressions of affect (Mandal, Pandey, & Prasad, 1998). Individuals with *alexithymia*, or difficulty in identifying one's own emotions, also have reduced facial expressiveness when describing positive or negative events from their past (Wagner & Lee, 2008). Finally, socially anxious children may have more problems expressing their anger on their face than do inattentive-hyperactive children (Walker, Nowicki, Jones, & Heimann, 2011).

Noller (1980; Noller & Gallois, 1986) studied the accuracy of husbands' and wives' nonverbal communication to each other. Women were better encoders than men, both in terms of perceivers' ability to judge the women accurately and in terms of the women's correct use of the particular cues associated with a given message (e.g., smiling for a positive message, frowning for a negative message).

PUTTING DECODING AND ENCODING TOGETHER

There are two ways in which decoding and encoding can be considered together. The first way is to ask whether skilled encoders are also skilled decoders. Studies are not very consistent on this question, but a comprehensive review revealed a moderate positive association between encoding and decoding accuracy for intentional displays of emotion (Elfenbein & Eisenkraft, 2010). This makes sense if one that considers both skills rely on (probably) learned understandings of nonverbal cues and their meanings.

The second way we can consider decoding and encoding together is to acknowledge that they occur together in the communication process. Although we have discussed them as separate skills that can be compared, in real interpersonal interaction these skills are used together (Patterson, 2019). A person is required to encode and decode simultaneously—to act out or display feelings, reactions, intentions, and attitudes while at the same time noticing the other's cues, forming impressions, interpreting the meanings of expressions, and evaluating feedback from their own behavior. This "parallel processing" aspect of interpersonal communication puts many demands on the cognitive system, insofar as it is difficult to allocate attention or effort to all of these tasks at the same time. The process is made somewhat easier by the fact that a certain amount of nonverbal processing is so well learned that it is rather automatic, requiring few cognitive resources (i.e., mental attention). The complex sending and receiving of turn-taking cues in conversation is a good example: We know how to do this without much conscious thought. However, when individuals engage in strategic behavior—as in deliberately trying to persuade someone—or when they suffer from social anxiety, considerable expenditure of cognitive resources is required that can negatively affect either the encoding or the decoding process. For instance, socially anxious people tend to be more self-focused, which can distract them from processing another person's cues (Patterson, 1995). Indeed, more socially anxious people do score lower on nonverbal decoding tests than less socially anxious people.

ON BEING AN OBSERVER OF NONVERBAL COMMUNICATION

The observation of Expression is by no means easy.

—Charles Darwin

As you set out to read the remaining chapters of this book, now seems a good time to reflect on how you can best use the knowledge contained there. You will learn quite a lot about the meanings and functions of nonverbal behaviors conveyed in all cue channels. You will learn that nonverbal cues are major indicators of emotion and play a crucial role in making social impressions and influencing others. You have just learned that people differ markedly in their skills in judging and using nonverbal cues. Although certain groups, such as actors and mental patients, fall at the extremes of skill, a great deal of variation from person to person exists even in the typical range of ability.

The research indicates that there may not be strong general skills; instead, there appear to be distinctive skills in different domains. A person may be skilled at judging emotions in the face but not in the voice; another may have the opposite pattern. Sarah may be good at identifying nonverbal deceptions, whereas Jim specializes in recognizing faces, and Martha can tell who stands where in the pecking order simply from hearing their tone of voice. In short, there are many ways to be accurate in nonverbal communication. Because so much of a person's time is spent observing other people, either passively as when observing strangers on a train or bus, or actively as when in direct interaction with others, one is wise to try to develop good observational habits. The following list can be useful to observers of any human transaction. At times some of the following information will contribute to observer bias, but the information may be necessary at some point to interpret the observations fully:

1. Find out about the *participants*—their age, sex, position or status, relationship to each other, previous history, and so on.

2. Find out about the *setting* of the interaction—kind of environment, relationship of the participants to the environment, and expected behavior in that environment.
3. Find out about the *purposes* of the interaction—what are people's stated as well as hidden goals, compatibility of goals, and so on.
4. Find out about the *social behavior*—who does what to or with whom, form of the behavior, its intensity, who initiates it, apparent objective of the behavior, effect on the other interactants, and so on.
5. Find out about the *frequency* and *duration* of such behavior—when it occurs, how long it lasts, whether it recurs, frequency of recurrence, and how typical such behavior is in the situation.

You will also have to decide whether the cues you see are intentional or unintentional. The term *unintentional* may itself have a range of meaning; a behavior may be truly accidental, or it may have significance not recognized by its enactor. Attributions of intention also may vary depending on the nature of the behavior in question. Some people believe that spoken words are generally designed with some goal in mind, but sometimes people say things unintentionally or without much advance planning. Certain environments cause us to focus or attend to the issue of intention more than others. Take the act of being bumped into by another person: At a crowded football stadium, the question of the person's intent may not even be considered, but being bumped into while walking down an uncrowded hallway may be another matter entirely. A full understanding of the nuances of intentionality poses many difficult barriers (Stamp & Knapp, 1990).

THE FALLIBILITY OF HUMAN PERCEPTION

Despite our suggestions concerning how to improve your observational skills, it is important to stress that human behavior and perception are extraordinarily complex. And even though humans are extraordinarily gifted, relative to other life forms, in judging the meaning of behavior, we are not infallible creatures. Even with the best of intentions, it is not unusual for several observers of the same event to "see" several different things, nor is it unusual for one observer to "see" different things in the same event at different times. Consequently, it would be wise of us to take the following into account when considering factors that may contribute to differences in perception.

First, we must recognize that our perceptions are structured by our own cultural conditioning, education, and personal experiences. Adults teach children what they think are critical dimensions of others by what they choose to talk about and make note of. Thus, we form associations that inevitably enter into our observations. For instance, we may be unable to see what we consider to be contradictory traits or behaviors in others; that is, can you conceive of a person who is both quiet and active? Wealthy and accessible? Short and romantic? Another aspect of this internally consistent worldview that may affect our observations concerns preconceptions about what we will see. For example, "My observations will take place in a nursing home. Therefore, the people I will observe will be noncommunicative, sick, and inactive." Social psychological experimentation has produced many demonstrations showing that people see what they expect or wish to see, often without any awareness that they are biasing their observations in this way.

Sometimes, people *project* their own qualities onto the object of attention; they may assume that if they have a certain quality, others must also. Sometimes, such projection stems less from the desire to flatter oneself than from a distorted worldview, as in bullies who see others as hostile and threatening. We sometimes see the reverse of the process as well because people sometimes want to see themselves *unique*: for example, "I am a rational person, but most people aren't." This interaction between a person's needs and desires, or even temporary emotional states, and what they see in others sometimes causes a person to see only what they want to see or causes them to miss what may be obvious to others. This process is known as *selective perception*. Because of these perceptual biases, observers must check their observations against the independent reports of others, or they must check the consistency of their own observations at several different points over an extended period of time.

We must also recognize that perceptions are influenced by which people are observed. You probably do not use the same criteria for observing friends and parents as when observing strangers. You may attribute more positively perceived behaviors to your friend's personality but attribute negatively perceived behaviors to situational constraints. Familiarity can either assist observation or create observational bias, but it does affect perceptions. Furthermore, some phenomena will cause a person to zero in on one particular kind of behavior, observing it very closely but missing simultaneous behaviors occurring elsewhere. It might be that the behavior receiving the scrutiny is bigger, more active, or just more interesting. Or it might be that deviant behavior is monitored more closely than normative or expected behavior. When observing a conversation, it is not possible to attend to everything as it happens. Sometimes one looks for, sees, responds to, and interprets a particular set of cues; at other times, the same cues will go unnoticed or be disregarded. Sometimes, observers fall prey to the natural tendency to follow conversational speaking turns, viewing only the speaker and missing the behavior of the nonspeakers. And of course, some phenomena are so complex, so minute, or so frequent that observer fatigue becomes a major concern.

Even if two people observe the same event and attach similar meanings to it, they may express their observations differently. Others may suspect, then, that the two observers saw two different things, such as the difference in describing a facial expression as happiness, joy, delight, pleasure, or amusement. Or it might be the difference between saying "She struck him" versus "She pushed him," or between describing a girl as "aggressive" and a boy as "exhibitionistic" when they engage in the same behavior. Hence, the language we use to express our perceptions can be an important variable in judging the accuracy of those perceptions.

Finally, we must be aware of the difference between factual, nonevaluative descriptions of behavior and the interpretations given to these descriptions. At the most basic level, we can say that a successful observer is careful not to confuse pure description with inferences or interpretations about the behavior. Failure at the inference stage is aptly illustrated by the familiar story of the scientist who told a frog to jump, and after a few minutes, the frog jumped. The scientist then amputated one of the frog's hind legs, and again told the frog to jump, and told the frog to jump several more times, and eventually the frog made a feeble attempt to jump with one hind leg. Then the scientist cut off the other hind leg and repeatedly ordered the frog to jump. When no jumping occurred, the scientist recorded in his log, "Upon amputation of one of the frog's hind legs, it begins to lose its hearing; upon severing both hind legs, the frog becomes totally deaf." This story illustrates clearly the huge gap that can exist between the factual evidence and the interpretations that are made.

When we are judging the meanings of the highly complex behaviors that make up nonverbal communication, it is quite possible to perceive the behaviors accurately but not know, or be wrong about, what they mean. No dictionary of nonverbal cue meanings exists in which one can simply look up a cue to find its meaning. Thus, a person must constantly be on guard against facile interpretations about meaning. A person must also be cautious about assuming cause-and-effect explanations when, in fact, there could be several different paths of causation between one variable and another.

SUMMARY

This chapter dealt with nonverbal skills and the characteristics of people who have such skills. In the first half of the chapter, we reviewed different definitions of communication skill as well as the major methodologies for measuring sending and receiving skills. We also presented findings on the training of nonverbal skills, using methods such as feedback, observation, and role-playing. The second half of the chapter examined traits and conditions associated with effectiveness in nonverbal sending (encoding) and receiving (decoding). Most research in this area has focused on questions of decoding ability. We reviewed a large number of different correlates of accuracy in encoding and decoding nonverbal cues, among which one of the most consistent is the tendency for females to be more accurate encoders and decoders.

We also discussed how accuracy in decoding may vary with the channel in which the information is presented, what characteristics the encoders have, and how long we heard or saw the behavior. In spite of these possible variations, some evidence suggests that if you are proficient in decoding one channel, you will be proficient in decoding others, and if you are proficient in decoding posed expressions, you will be proficient in decoding spontaneous ones too. We also presented problems associated with simultaneously encoding and decoding nonverbal cues, as routinely happens in conversation. Evidence suggests that being a good decoder implies being a good encoder. It does not necessarily follow that proficiency in one skill, encoding or decoding, always makes a person proficient in the other, however.

Finally, we talked about what being a good observer of nonverbal behavior entails. Knowing the most likely meanings of particular cues and cue combinations is important, but so are other factors relating to attitudes and the context in which observation is taking place.

QUESTIONS FOR DISCUSSION

1. How much insight do you think people have into the cues they use to make judgments about others' states and traits?

2. The ability to decode other people's nonverbal emotional expressions is only one definition of nonverbal judgment accuracy. Think of some other definitions of nonverbal judgment accuracy and discuss why and when they might be useful.

3. Are there any moral or ethical issues related to the decoding and encoding of nonverbal cues?

4. Do you think that too much knowledge or skill in nonverbal communication could be a bad thing? Argue both for and against this hypothesis.

5. Sometimes, it is said that people enact and interpret nonverbal cues automatically, that is, without analytic thought or intention. For different behaviors and/or skills that you can point to, what do you think are the relative contributions of deliberate intention versus automatic processing?

NONVERBAL COMMUNICATION IN ACTION: TRY THIS

You can test yourself on one of the many tests of accuracy in interpreting nonverbal cues. This test, called the Reading the Mind in the Eyes test (Baron-Cohen, Wheelwright, Hill, Raste, & Plumb, 2001), has been used extensively. Women score higher than men, and people on the autism spectrum score lower than non-diagnosed control participants. https://well.blogs.nytimes.com/2013/10/03/well-quiz-the-mind-behind-the-eyes/

PART II

THE COMMUNICATION ENVIRONMENT

The features of the environment within which an interaction takes place can exert a powerful influence on that interaction. Lighting, color schemes, furniture, and architecture, among other features, affect what one says and even how often they say it. Sometimes people deliberately structure these features in order to obtain certain responses from others. Part II explores the way humans affect and are affected by the space within communication environments, as a preface to discussing, in Parts III and IV, the behavior of the people who do the communicating.

CHAPTER 4

THE EFFECTS OF THE ENVIRONMENT ON HUMAN COMMUNICATION

Every interior betrays the nonverbal skills of its inhabitants. The choice of materials, the distribution of space, the kind of objects that command attention or demand to be touched—as compared to those that intimidate or repel—have much to say about the preferred sensory modalities of their owners.

—J. Ruesch and W. Kees

When people communicate with one another, features of the surrounding environment always exert an influence on their interaction. What are these environmental features, and what are their effects?

First, let us look at a familiar communication environment: the classroom. Modern architects experiment with different designs, but many classes still take place in a rectangular room with straight rows of chairs for student seating. A row of windows along one side of the room may determine the direction students face, and consequently determine the front of the room. It is not uncommon for classroom seats to be permanently attached to the floor for ease of maintenance and tidiness. Classrooms typically have some type of partition, often a desk or lectern, that serves as a boundary between the teacher and students. It is not hard for students and teachers to identify problems encountered in environments designed for learning: poor lighting and acoustics; inadequate climate control; external construction noises; inoperative or nonexistent electrical outlets; immovable seats; gloomy, dull, or distracting color schemes; unpleasant odors; and so on. Both students and teachers recognize that such problems impede the purpose for gathering in these rectangular rooms: to increase knowledge through effective student–teacher communication. The influence of the classroom environment on student and teacher behavior remained relatively unexplored until Sommer (1967, 1969, 1974) took a closer look. He focused on the influence of classroom design on student participation.

Sommer selected several different types of classrooms for study. He wanted to compare the amount of student participation in these classrooms and to analyze aspects of participatory behavior in each type. He selected seminar rooms with movable chairs, usually arranged in a horseshoe shape; laboratories—complete with Bunsen burners, bottles, and gas valves—that represented an extreme in straight-row seating; a windowless room; and a room with an entire wall of windows. Among other things, Sommer concluded the following:

1. Students and teachers who dislike their learning environment will try to avoid it or change it.
2. In general, the amount of student participation decreases as the number of students in the class increases. The length of a student's participation is also longer in smaller classes.
3. The content of student participation in large classes is more likely to be devoted to questions of clarification or requests to repeat an idea rather than participation focused on the ideas themselves.
4. Participation was most frequent among those students within range of the instructor's eye gaze. In a seminar room, the students sitting directly across from the instructor participated more. A follow-up study by Adams and Biddle (1970) found a zone of participation in the center of the room (see FIGURE 4-1). This center zone is most likely to occur when the instructor stands in the middle of the room because it is highly dependent on the instructor's visual contact with the students. If the instructor moved to the side and maintained visual contact with the students to their front, the zone of participation would no longer be in the center. But there is more to this story: Koneya (1973) found that when high-, moderate-, and low-participating students were given a chance to select any seat they desired, high participators were most likely to select seats in the central zone of participation.

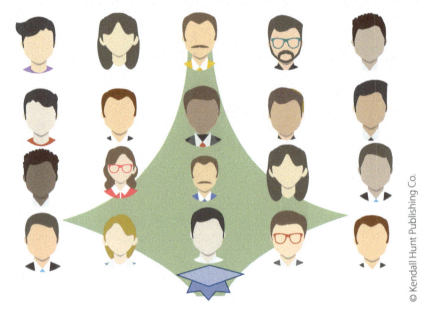

© Kendall Hunt Publishing Co.

FIGURE 4-1 The zone of class participation.

We can conclude from this that student participation can be facilitated by visual contact with the instructor, but students who are likely to participate tend to position themselves in seats that are close to the instructor or within the instructor's likely field of gaze. Also note that an instructor's gaze can be used to inhibit communication as well as facilitate it. When students feel they will be punished—or at least not rewarded—for participating, the zone of participation is inoperative.

5. What happens when you take moderate- and low-participating students and deliberately seat them in the zone of participation? Koneya (1973) found that moderate participators increased their participation, but low participators remained low. This suggests that where students sit can alter their classroom participation, but this is less likely with low participators. Haber (1982) found that ethnic, racial, and religious minorities at five colleges tended to select seating peripheral to the zone of participation—even when they were a majority at a particular college.

From these studies, we can conclude that classroom seating is not random. Certain types of people gravitate toward seats that are close to the instructor and/or within the instructor's expected pattern of gaze. The instructor's gazing patterns create a zone where students are more likely to verbally participate, unless they are students who initially sought seating outside of this zone and were moved within it. Even then, we might find increased participation at some point if a teacher rewards and supports student participation.

Brooks (2011) examined the relationship between classroom design and student learning in a face-to-face setting. Most of the participants in the study were first-year, first-semester students taking Principles of Biological Science with the same instructor. Some of these students were enrolled in a traditional classroom where they sat at tables facing the front of the classroom, which had a whiteboard, projection screen, and teacher's desk. The other students were enrolled in an active learning classroom that had round tables (which have been shown to promote greater collaborative and student-centered learning), laptop technology, an instructor station, and marker boards along the perimeter of the room. With respect to learning outcomes, the difference between actual grades and predicted grades based on college entrance exam scores was greater for those in the active learning classroom than it was for those in the traditional classroom. This meant that the active learning environment benefited students' performance to a greater extent than did the traditional classroom.

More recent work by Shernoff and colleagues (2017) showed that where students sit matters in terms of their grades. They found that college students who sat in the back of a large lecture room were more likely to earn lower grades, possibly because they were less attentive to and less engaged with the class.

The world of education has changed dramatically since the time of Sommer's research. Students take notes (and, of course, check their Facebook pages) on laptops, enroll in online classes, participate with other students in "discussion boards," meet with the instructor during virtual office hours, and so on. For some who are shy in face-to-face settings, an online setting might afford them more opportunities to participate in a class. For those who need to see the instructor in person, an online format might be detrimental to the quality of their education. Either way, teachers need to be aware of their nonverbal immediacy behaviors (use of emoticons, promptness of feedback, audio, etc.) in online classes, as such behaviors lead students to feel more engaged with the class (Dixson, Greenwell, Rogers-Stacy, Weister, & Lauer, 2017).

Even though many classrooms have changed in form (to more technologically rich) or location (cyberspace), educators must still be aware of the setting in which students learn. For example, online classes should be designed to be user-friendly. A virtual classroom should be designed so as not to make one group, such as females, feel less welcome because it is more stereotypically masculine in appearance (Cheryan, Meltzoff, & Kim, 2011). Even what learners sit on in traditional classroom settings may matter. Preschoolers' attention during "circle time" appears to increase when they sit on inflatable cushions as opposed to harder surfaces, such as the floor (Serfert & Metz, 2017).

The preceding discussion of the classroom is an example of a specific context in which spatial relationships, architecture, and objects surrounding the participants influence the amount of interaction and learning that occurs. We will examine other environmental factors that impinge on human communication behavior shortly. As a cautionary note, though, you should remember that the environment is only one element in structuring such behavior. If students, administrators, teachers, office staff, and custodians want to run a school or university like a prison or a dehumanized bureaucracy, changes in the classroom structure will likely have little impact.

Throughout this chapter, we discuss a number of characteristics of environments. Let us initiate our exploration by examining the way people perceive their surroundings, because this can significantly influence the way they feel and the way they choose to communicate.

PERCEPTIONS OF SURROUNDINGS

The number of places for communication with others is limitless: buses, homes, apartments, restaurants, offices, parks, hotels, sports arenas, factories, libraries, movie theaters, museums, and so on. Despite this diversity of places' people probably evaluate these environments along similar dimensions. Once an environment is perceived in a certain way, those perceptions may influence the messages people send. And once these messages have been sent, the environmental perceptions of the other people in that setting may be altered. Thus, people influence and are influenced by their environments.

How do people see environments? We believe the following six dimensions are central to perceptions and consequently to the messages that are sent and received.

PERCEPTIONS OF FORMALITY

One familiar dimension for classifying environments is a formal–informal continuum. Reactions may be based on the objects and people present, the functions performed, or any number of other variables. Individual offices may be more formal than a lounge in the same building; a year-end banquet takes on more formality than a Superbowl-watching party; an evening at home with one other couple may be more informal than an evening with 10 other couples. The greater the formality, the greater the chances that the communication behavior will be less relaxed and more superficial, hesitant, and stylized.

Of importance, what one expects to see along the formal–informal continuum in a particular setting matters. Less formal behavior and dress are expected in informal settings and more formal behavior and dress in formal settings. Trouble can arise when these expectations go unmet. Consider the likely reactions of sunbathers at a beach to a group of men and women sitting on leather chairs and discussing corporate strategy in their business suits. In FIGURE 4-2— dubbed the "flip-flop flap"—expectations were violated, leading to negative reactions on the part of some viewers. The problem was that several members of Northwestern University's championship lacrosse team wore flip-flops when they had their photo taken with then-President Bush at the White House ("NU's Lacrosse Team," 2005). To some people, flip-flops were disrespectful footwear in such a lofty setting.

AP Photo/The White House, David Bohrer

FIGURE 4-2 Northwestern Women's Lacrosse Team at White House.

PERCEPTIONS OF WARMTH

Environments that feel psychologically warm encourage people to linger, relax, and feel comfortable. It may be some combination of the color of the curtains or walls, paneling, carpeting, texture of the furniture, softness of the chairs, soundproofing, and so on. Even the exterior of an environment can affect anticipated feelings of comfort. Students viewed slides of 34 different medical facilities, and the expected quality of care and degree of comfort varied with different types of buildings (Devlin, 2008).

Consumers' perceptions of environmental warmth matter in the business world. Business owners might be interested in knowing that customers experience more psychological warmth in a store that appears visually warm to them (Baek, Choo, Oh, & Yoon, 2017). For other business owners, the level of perceived warmth may matter more. Fast-food chains, for example, try to exhibit enough warmth in their decor to seem inviting but enough coldness to encourage rapid turnover among customers.

Interestingly, environments that make people feel psychologically warm may also make them feel physically warmer. Students were asked to spend 2 hours studying or reading in a room with a neutral decor, similar to that of a classroom. Then they were asked to read or study in a room that resembled a walk-in meat cooler. Nearly all the students felt the second room was cooler, even though the temperature was actually the same in both rooms. Then the meat cooler room was paneled, carpeted, and equipped with subdued lighting and other appointments. Another group of students was asked to read or study in each room. This time, the redesigned meat-cooler room was judged to have a higher temperature than the classroom. Again, actual temperatures were the same (Rohles, 1980).

Lastly, one's own behavior may impact how warm an environment feels. Hu, Li, Jia, and Xie (2016) found a short-term benefit of behaving altruistically: Those who demonstrated altruism felt warmer afterwards in their immediate surroundings than did those who chose not to help another person.

PERCEPTIONS OF PRIVACY

Environmental settings on the ground (e.g., a park) as well as up in the air (e.g., in a plane) impact people's sense of privacy (Ahmadpour, Kuhne, Robert, & Vink, 2016). In general, enclosed environments usually suggest greater privacy, particularly if they accommodate only a few people. If the possibility of other people entering and/or overhearing a conversation is slight, even if it is outdoors, there is a greater feeling of privacy. Personal items such as toiletries, low or focused lighting, high-density situations, partitions, noise, and other environmental factors can affect perceptions of privacy (Buslig, 1999). With greater privacy, people will probably use close speaking distances and more personal messages. In today's world, people's sense of privacy is likely being impacted by the presence of numerous cameras. It seems as if they are everywhere. At your college or university, a camera is likely trained on you when you enter one of its buildings or dorms and when you walk around campus alone or with your friends. Seeing them may give you a sense of security but also the feeling of being watched and monitored too often.

PERCEPTIONS OF FAMILIARITY

When you meet a new person or encounter an unfamiliar environment, your responses typically are cautious, deliberate, and conventional. Unfamiliar environments are laden with rituals and norms you do not yet know, so you will probably go slowly until you can associate this unfamiliar environment with one you know. One interpretation for the stereotyped structure of fast-food restaurants is that they allow people to readily find a familiar and predictable place that will guarantee minimal demands for active contact with strangers. In unfamiliar environments, the most likely initial topic of conversation will be the environment itself: Have you ever been here before? What is it like? Who comes here?

PERCEPTIONS OF CONSTRAINT

Part of one's total reaction to an environment is based on whether, and how easily, one can leave it. Some students feel confined in their own homes during school holiday breaks. But consider the differences between this 2-week constraint and a permanent live-at-home arrangement. The intensity of these perceptions of constraint is closely related to the space available as well as the privacy of this space during the time one is in the environment. Some environments seem to be only temporarily confining, such as an automobile during a long trip. Perceptions of confinement in other environments, such as prisons, spacecraft, or nursing homes, will likely be more enduring. Lengthy at-home confinement during the COVID-19 pandemic lockdowns and quarantines likely has had many ramifications for people's mental health and relationships.

PERCEPTIONS OF DISTANCE

Sometimes responses within a given environment are influenced by how far away other people are. This may reflect actual physical distance—an office on a different floor, a house in another part of the city—or it may reflect psychological distance, with barriers clearly separating people who are fairly close physically. You may be seated close to someone and still not perceive it as a close environment: for example, interlocking chairs facing the same direction in an airport. When the setting forces you into close quarters with strangers, as in elevators or crowded buses, you will probably try to increase distance psychologically to reduce threatening feelings of intimacy. This can be done through less eye contact, more body tenseness and immobility, cold silence, nervous laughter, jokes about the intimacy, and public conversation directed at all present.

The perceptions just described represent only some of the dimensions of communication settings. Generally, more intimate communication is associated with informal, unconstrained, private, familiar, close, and warm environments. In everyday situations, however, these dimensions combine in complex ways. The mixture of intimate and nonintimate factors can be seen in an elevator if it is perceived as close, familiar, and temporarily confining but also public, formal, and cold.

REACTING TO ENVIRONMENTS

Once these perceptions are made, how do they affect a person's reactions? Sometimes the impact of the environment will be slight, but it has the potential to play a significant role in affecting behavior at school. In a study of 98 child-care classes for 3- and 4-year-olds, Maxwell (2007) concluded that perceptions of the physical environment were related to measures of the children's cognitive and social competency, especially for the 3-year-olds.

Mehrabian (1976) argued that people react emotionally to their surroundings. These emotional reactions can be accounted for in terms of (1) how *arousing* the environment is, (2) how *pleasurable* it makes a person feel, and (3) how *dominant* it makes a person feel. *Arousal* refers to how active, stimulated, frenzied, or alert one is. *Pleasure* refers to feelings of joy, satisfaction, and happiness. *Dominance* refers to feelings of being in control, important, and free to act in a variety of ways.

Preferences for particular types of environments might embody all three of these reactions. Evolutionary psychologists have argued that humans should prefer the environment that was most conducive to their survival in the distant past, namely, the savanna (see Orians & Heerwagen, 1992). The savanna, where there is tall grass and scattered trees, would have allowed human ancestors to not only hide from predators but also to scan their surroundings for possible threats and opportunities to acquire needed resources. On the other hand, the rainforest might have been linked to low pleasure because not being able to see predators (snakes!) might have been too arousing due to feelings of having less control (i.e., low dominance) over the surroundings. Falk and Balling (2010) found that even those who reside in a rainforest prefer savannalike environments. Whether there is a "universal preference" among humans for the savanna landscape has been challenged recently, though (Joelson, Ferreira, Silva, & Albuquerque, 2008).

Novel, surprising, and complex environments probably produce higher arousal. People often think of environments in the physical sense, even though, nowadays, new technologies allow individuals to be immersed in virtual ones. These environments can be arousing as well. In fact, one study showed how being immersed in a virtual environment led to increased levels of arousal among viewers of adult content (Simon & Greitemeyer, 2019).

Those people less able to screen out unwanted information from the environment inevitably have to respond to more stimuli and, in turn, become more aroused. Although everyone probably responds as *screeners* and *nonscreeners* on occasion, some people tend to respond habitually as one or the other (Mehrabian, 1977). Nonscreeners are less selective in what they respond to in any environment. They see, hear, smell, and otherwise sense more stimuli. Screeners, in contrast, are selective in what they respond to. They impose a hierarchy of importance on various components in a complex situation. Nonscreeners not only become more aroused than screeners in novel, changing, and sudden situations but also remain aroused longer—even after leaving the arousing environment. That is why nonscreeners are most attracted to environments that are both arousing and pleasurable.

The Highly Sensitive Person Scale (Aron & Aron, 1997) measures hypersensitivity to environmental stimuli (and other types of stimuli), with items such as *Are you easily overwhelmed by strong sensory input? Do you seem to be aware of subtleties in your environment?* and *Are you easily overwhelmed by things like bright lights, strong smells, coarse fabrics, or sirens close by?* It is theorized that persons high on this temperament are especially vulnerable to stress and arousal in reaction to negative environments, with children with the trait being especially at risk for disturbed development in adverse environments. On the other hand, it may be that people high on this trait also respond especially well to highly positive environments. Overall, highly sensitive individuals tend to score low on extraversion and high on neuroticism (Greven et al., 2019).

Introversion–extraversion definitely influences how people respond to arousing environments. Research by Geen (1984) has shown that introverts require less stimulation to reach their desired level of physiological arousal than do extraverts. This means that introverts could become overly aroused in an environment that is comfortable for extraverts. Knowing this, extraverts and introverts may choose some environments over others, avoiding those that will not be arousing enough or too arousing for them. In line with this, Campbell and Hawley (1982) found that introverted students preferred quiet, socially isolated settings when studying, whereas extraverts sought noisier settings where they could socialize with others.

Ambient aroma is an environmental factor that influences how people behave in an environment. Research by Baron (1997) showed that pleasant odors increase willingness to help members of the same gender. The increased helpfulness seems to be due to the pleasant odors making people feel better. It also appears that clean scents increase people's willingness to be charitable (Liljenquist, Zhong, & Galinsky, 2010). A review of experimental studies in the context of retail sales and service found that environments where ambient odors (presumably pleasant ones) were introduced produced reactions of greater pleasure, satisfaction, and behavioral intentions (Roschk, Loureiro, & Breitsohl, 2017). Importantly, these environmental effects are likely to be nonconscious, suggesting that, more often than a person might like, their behavior could be under the influence of the odors wafting through or lingering in the spaces they pass through.

PERCEPTIONS OF TIME

Time is also a part of the communicative environment. At first, it may seem strange to include something as seemingly intangible as time in the same environmental package as chairs, walls, noise, or even weather conditions. However, the human brain may be wired to encode time and place information after an event that is tragic or of momentous importance. Many people can still vividly "see" the details of where they were when they learned of a loved one's death, President Kennedy's assassination, the Challenger space shuttle disaster, or 9/11. When such situational details are burned into your memory, it is called a *flashbulb memory*. In the United States, people treat time as something tangible, a commodity that can be divided up, saved, spent, and made.

Time is important to everyone. It governs when people eat and sleep, it often determines how much they get paid at work, and it sets limits on how much material students can learn in a given class period. Time plays a key role in social interaction as well. It influences perceptions of people: for example, responsible people are on time, boring people talk too long, or good romantic partners make time for joint activities yet give the other person some time to themselves (Leonard, 1978; Werner & Baxter, 1994). A course in time management is a staple for anyone expecting to climb the corporate ladder in U.S. organizations. Time plays such an important role in daily life that people carry the date and time on their wrists or cell phones. Cars have clocks, and GPS tells a person how long it will take to drive from one location to another. People are very much aware of the stress time can create and think of a vacation as a retreat to a place where time matters less. Ironically, vacations are usually thought of as a set period of time.

Time is perceived very differently in other cultures (Hall, 1959). These varying orientations to time are often a central factor in misunderstandings among members of different cultures. Psychology professor Robert Levine gives this account of his teaching experience in Brazil:

> As I left home for my first day of class, I asked someone the time. It was 9:05 a.m., which allowed me time to relax and look around the campus before my 10 o'clock lecture. After what I judged to be half an hour, I glanced at the clock I was passing. It said 10:20! In a panic, I broke for the classroom, followed by gentle calls of "Hola, professor" and "Tudo bem, professor?" from unhurried students, many of whom, I later realized, were my own. I arrived breathless to find an empty room. Frantically, I asked a passerby the time. "Nine forty-five" was the answer. No, that couldn't be. I asked someone else. "Nine fifty-five." Another said, "Exactly 9:43." The clock in a nearby office read 3:15. I had learned my first lesson about Brazilians: Their timepieces are consistently inaccurate. And nobody minds. My class was scheduled from 10 until noon. Many students came late, some very late … none seemed terribly concerned about lateness …. The real surprise came at noon … only a few students left immediately. Others drifted out during the next fifteen minutes, and some continued asking me questions long after that (Levine & Wolff, 1985, p. 30).

Biologically, the human body seems to be programmed so that "internal clocks" regulate physical, emotional, and intellectual functioning as well as the sense of time (Luce, 1971; Meissner & Wittmann, 2011). However, it is possible to experience distortions in the perception of time, some of which are influenced by events, whereas others by personality variables.

Distorted time perception underlies the saying that "a watched pot doesn't boil" and one's impatience in the waiting room at a physician's office. Examples of events that seem to slow time down—that is, the perceived duration is longer than the actual duration—include scary ones (e.g., skydiving for novices) and seeing angry or fearful faces compared to neutral faces (Campbell & Bryant, 2007; Effron, Niedenthal, Gil, & Droit-Volet, 2006; Gil & Droit-Volet, 2011). On the other hand, highly exciting events can make time "fly" (Campbell & Bryant, 2007).

Individual differences in the perception of time have been linked to neurological and psychological differences (Westfall, Jasper, & Zelmanova, 2010; Zimbardo & Boyd, 1999). Zimbardo and Boyd (1999) pointed to individual differences in people's attitudes toward time, which can influence their decisions and judgments. These include the past-negative type (you view your past negatively, and your past still upsets you), the past-positive type (you have a nostalgic view of your past), the present-hedonistic type (you think more about partaking in pleasures of the present than consequences in the future), the present-fatalistic type (you feel stuck in the present and unable to change your future), and the future-focused type (you are focused on accomplishing goals important to your future). These orientations may represent a long-term style or may be subject to change; for example, a present-hedonistic type, who "lives for the moment" at one point in life, might later adopt a future-focused style that involves evaluating today's "moments" in terms of the long-range picture (Gonzalez & Zimbardo, 1985). (Find out your time perspective; see www.thetimeparadox.com/zimbardo-time-perspective-inventory/.)

We devote the remainder of this chapter to the characteristics of environments that form the bases of the perceptions just outlined: perceptions of surroundings and perceptions of time. Each environment has three major components:

1. The natural environment—geography, location, and atmospheric conditions
2. The presence or absence of other people
3. The architectural design and movable objects

THE NATURAL ENVIRONMENT

Some live in densely populated urban areas, some in smaller towns, some in suburban areas on the outskirts of cities and towns, and others in rural areas. Within these broad areas are other environmental features that affect the nature of human interaction and health: for example, apartment complexes, neighborhoods, high-rise buildings, and urban settings with forested areas. The places for living, play, and work are bound to have an impact on behavior. The number of people communicated with can influence one's interaction style, but perhaps more important is the number of different people for whom a person has to adapt their messages. Some environments are very homogeneous and provide inhabitants with fewer experiences and fewer examples of diverse styles, behavior, and values. The pace of life and the time devoted to developing social and personal relationships may also vary as a function of where one lives. In some troubled cities, the social disorder perceived by residents may be a key factor linked to their mental health and substance abuse (O'Brien, Farrell, & Welsh, 2019).

BROKEN WINDOWS. BROKEN RULES?

© Salienko Evgenii/Shutterstock.com

Imagine entering an urban neighborhood with few people around. You pass by numerous buildings that have been vandalized (e.g., broken windows, graffiti on the outside walls, and litter all around). Do these represent clues to the existing norms of conduct operating in that environment? Do you think that the buildings are not monitored and that getting caught for littering or damaging property further is very unlikely?

Wilson and Kelling (1982) and others (Kelling & Coles, 1996) proposed the so-called broken windows theory to account for how the appearance and upkeep of an environment is one signal of the social norms there, the extent to which the setting is monitored, and whether criminal behavior occurs in that area. These, in turn, are relevant to the occurrence and prevention of some criminal activity.

In principle, one way to prevent petty criminal activity is to repair damaged property and not let trash accumulate because this lets would-be vandals know that the area is monitored and that vandalism will be detected and dealt with. On the other hand, the presence of litter, broken windows, and other signs of vandalism might encourage some individuals to engage in similar petty or even serious criminal activity in the neighborhood. Furthermore, additional criminal activity can lead to a further deterioration of the appearance of the area, only making matters worse. For example, law-abiding citizens may decide to flee the area.

The broken windows theory has received some empirical support, but it has also been criticized. Survey research has shown that aspects of the theory have utility in explaining residents' concern about neighborhood safety as well as students' perceptions of social disorder in their school (Pitner, Yu, & Brown, 2012; Plank, Bradshaw, & Young, 2009). Experimental work has revealed that littering, trespassing, and stealing are greater when there are signs that people are violating other rules; littering was greater, for example, when participants saw graffiti on a wall marked with a "no graffiti sign" than when that same wall had no graffiti on it (Keizer, Lindenberg, & Steg, 2008). However, the research of Cialdini, Kallgren, and Reno (1991) suggests that it might be important for us to see another person behave in a way that is consistent with the existing norms in the environment. They found that participants were more likely to litter in a messy garage than a clean garage when they had first seen another person litter in that garage. Stated differently, the litterer brought the norm ("It's OK to litter") to participants' awareness when they were in the messy garage.

As a theory, broken windows has been criticized on a number of fronts. First and foremost, it cannot explain the causes of serious criminal activity. Of course, most of the people who live in economically depressed areas do not turn to a life of violent crime. Moreover, a criminal may be little concerned with the upkeep of a street; a burglar, for instance, may case a luxury home in an exclusive neighborhood and ignore a modest home in a run-down neighborhood because the potential payoffs are greater with the former.

The natural environment also comes with a host of weather-related phenomena. For instance, behavioral scientists have been interested in the effects of barometric pressure: High or rising barometric pressure has been associated with feelings of good health; low or falling barometric pressure is more likely to be linked to feelings of pain or depression, even suicide (El-Mallakh et al., 2017). Optimal student behavior and performance have been observed when the barometer was high or rising and on cool days with little wind and precipitation. Increase in positive air ions also seems to increase people's irritability and tension.

The changing seasons seem to have an impact on behavior and mental health, too. Even in areas of the United States with minimal seasonal variations in temperature, national routines associated with changing seasons are still followed: for example, taking summer vacations and starting school in the fall. Some of the ways in which behavior varies with the seasons include the following:

1. Suicide rates and admissions to public mental hospitals rise dramatically in the spring and peak in the summer.
2. College students tend to break up with their dating partners at the beginnings and endings of semesters.
3. During the summer, people tend to see their friends more often.
4. During the summer, crimes of assault and rape increase.
5. From July to November, people tend to report less happiness but more activity and less boredom.
6. U.S. females born during the fall are more likely to have symptoms related to eating disorders than females born during the other seasons (Javaras, Austin, & Field, 2011), but anorexia nervosa does not appear to be linked to the season of one's birth (Winje, Torgalsboen, & Stedal, 2017).
7. Although seasonal affective disorder (described later in the chapter) can be triggered in spring, the onset is more likely to be during late fall and early winter.

Research related to seasonal effects is growing rapidly. As a consequence, a more nuanced understanding of the relationship between seasonal variations and people's health and behavioral outcomes, including depression, suicide, sleep disorders, and criminal conduct, is being realized by a number of researchers (Chang, Lam, Chen, Sithole, & Chung, 2017; Linning, Andersen, Ghaseminejad, & Brantingham, 2017; Lukmanji, Williams, Bulloch, Bhattari, & Patten, 2019; Moore et al., 2018). The same holds true for the effects of weather; for example, to understand the impact of weather on people's mood, one needs to consider factors such as people's means of travel (public transportation, riding a bike, car, and walking; Ettema, Friman, Olsson, & Garling, 2017).

Seasons come and go gradually along with the weather that typically accompanies them—falling leaves eventually give way to falling snow. However, within seasons, the weather can change suddenly and drastically: For example, a sunny spring day can be followed by violent storm activity that night, with tornadoes touching down and ripping apart neighborhoods. Natural disasters can inflict great psychological damage, sometimes leading to post-traumatic stress disorder (Simpson, Weissbecker, & Sephton, 2011). In a review of studies, Beaglehole and colleagues (2018) confirmed the negative impact of natural disasters on people's mental well-being. Temperature and the way it affects human responses is the climatic factor that has received the most scientific attention—specifically, the extent to which hot temperatures increase aggressive motivation and behavior. Lengthy periods of extreme heat are often associated with discomfort, irritability, reduced work output, and unfavorable evaluations of strangers. In one study, hot temperatures increased aggressive horn-honking for drivers without air-conditioning (Kenrick & MacFarlane, 1986). Vrij, van der Steen, and Koppelaar (1994) studied the reactions of police officers to a simulated burglary in which the temperature varied from comfortably cool to hot. When the temperature was hot, officers reported more aggressive and threatening impressions of the suspect and were more likely to draw their weapon. As Anderson (2001) noted, uncomfortably warm temperatures seem to increase the likelihood that ambiguous social interactions will be viewed as aggressive. A citizen's simple question such as "Is it really necessary that I do that?" may be taken as an aggressive challenge to personal authority that demands some form of retaliation.

An analysis of riots in India over a 22-year period found that most took place during the months when the temperature was between 80 and 90°F (Berke & Wilson, 1951). The *Report of the National Advisory Commission on Civil Disorders* (U.S. Riot Commission, 1968) in the United States said that hot summer nights added to an already explosive situation that eventually resulted in widespread rioting in some cities. An analysis of

102 riots in the United States between 1967 and 1971 concluded that the most likely temperature–riot sequence was one in which the temperature rose to between 81 and 85°F and remained within that range for about 7 days preceding the riot. Rotton and Cohn (2003) conducted two studies, each covering 38 years or more, and found annual temperatures associated with various forms of criminal behavior such as assaults, rapes, robberies, burglaries, and larceny—not murder. Interestingly, aggression may abate when it gets *too* hot: Riots were less likely to occur as temperatures climbed above 90°F (Baron & Ransberger, 1978; Carlsmith & Anderson, 1979).

You might be wondering why heat (up to a point) would lead to more aggression. According to Leonard Berkowitz (1989), the likely culprit is negative feelings. In short, high temperatures can produce negative feelings, and it is these feelings that can trigger anger and hostile thoughts and behaviors toward others. This occurs because such thoughts and behaviors are linked to it in an associated network in memory. This model implies that other environmental stressors that arouse negative feelings in people—excessive noise, traffic jams, pollution, and so on—might also lead to more aggression under the right circumstance.

Obviously, the relationship between temperature, negative affect, and aggression is not simple. Probably a number of factors interact with the temperature to increase the chance of aggression: prior provocation; the presence of aggressive models; and negative affect experienced from sources other than temperature, such as poverty and unemployment, perceived inability to leave the environment, and the nonavailability of resources to relieve any adverse effects of temperature.

Note, however, that sometimes unpleasant environmental factors, such as heat or noise, can increase attraction toward others. In such cases, the aversive stimulus may function as something both people have in common (Kenrick & Johnson, 1979; Schneider, Lesko, & Garrett, 1980). The extent to which heat and other environmental variables increase or decrease attraction to others depends on how these factors intersect with many other factors, such as interactants' personalities and the presence or absence of simultaneously occurring rewarding stimuli.

The effects of the moon and sunspots on human behavior have also been studied scientifically. You might even have heard the phrase "lunar madness." Psychiatrist Arnold Lieber (1978) reasoned that human beings, like the earth, are subject to gravitational forces created by different positions of the moon. (Human beings, like the planet itself, are about 80% water and 20% solids.) Considerable skepticism exists regarding Lieber's theory, however. Reviews of studies that examined the relation of moon positions to psychiatric hospital admissions, suicides, homicides, traffic accidents, and changes in the stock market find no believable relation between moon phases and these behaviors (Campbell & Beets, 1978; Rotton & Kelly, 1985). Recently, Schafer, Varano, Jarvis, and Cancino (2010) did not find a relationship between lunar cycles and reported criminal conduct, and research on the occurrence of stroke and phases of the moon also showed no relation between the two (Rouskanen, Sipila, Rautava, & Kyn, 2018).

Aside from the influence of high temperatures on aggressive tendencies, we do not have a lot of reliable and valid information on how the natural environment affects communication. It seems reasonable to believe that various aspects of the natural environment will have an influence, but the exact nature and degree of this influence are still unknown. One promising avenue is research into the concept of *biophilia*, a proposed need that humans have for a connection with nature and natural beauty. Some research suggests beneficial psychological effects from such exposure (Capaldi et al., 2017; McMahan & Estes, 2015). This line of theorizing also connects to aggression: Wang et al. (2018) demonstrated how exposure to nature helped provoked people regain the self-control they needed in order to refrain from acting aggressively.

Most people seem to believe the weather has less impact on their own behavior than it does on others' behavior, that it has less impact on behavior than it does on emotional states, and that it does not have more impact on negative states than on positive ones (Jorgenson, 1981). Kraut and Johnston (1979) found that people walking on the sidewalk smiled more when the weather was sunny and pleasant than when it was rainy and overcast. This difference was much less significant than the mere effect of being with others, however; people smiled much more when in an interaction than when alone. Thus, compared to more social factors, climate and other environmental variables may have weak influences on some kinds of social behavior.

MINDFULNESS

www.shutterstock.com

How connected do you feel to nature? Some people feel at one with nature, whereas others feel more disconnected from the natural world. What types of people feel a greater connection to nature? Mindfulness is a relatively new term; it refers to experiencing life in the present and being aware and accepting of your thoughts and feelings. Recently, Hanley, Deiringer, and Hanley (2017) found that people who are more mindful by nature feel more connected to nature.

OTHER PEOPLE IN THE ENVIRONMENT

Chapter 5 examines the reactions of people to overpopulated environments. For now, we point out that other people can be perceived as part of the environment and they do have an effect on one's behavior. The other people may be perceived as active or passive participants, depending on the degree to which they are perceived as involved in conversations, either speaking or listening. In many situations, these people are seen as active, especially if they are able to overhear what is being said. In some situations, another person is given the dubious status of *nonperson* and observers behave accordingly. This may occur in high-density situations, but it is also common with just one other person. Taxi drivers, janitors, and children are accorded nonperson status with regularity. The presence of nonpersons, of course, allows the uninhibited flow of interaction because as far as the active participants are concerned, the nonpersons can be ignored as though they are not present. For example, parents sometimes talk to others about personal aspects of their child knowing the child is hearing the conversation.

"Not there" might also apply, in a different sense, to what you see in your day-to-day encounters with others. You physically see a person driving, but they are interacting via text with someone you do not see, and this interaction is distracting the driver to the point that their car is now swerving over to your lane. You might see "smartphone zombies," who are apparently so afraid of missing out on something that they are walking around distracted by their virtual interactions with others (Appel, Krish, Stein, & Weber, 2019). Even your face-to face interactions might be compromised by others who are not present but, nevertheless, intrude on your conversations, which has been termed technoference (see Sbarra, Briskin, & Slatcher, 2019). Indeed, a recent study by Dwyer, Kushler, and Dunn (2018) showed that people were more distracted and derived less enjoyment from face-to-face interactions when smartphones were present versus not.

Other people in the environment are active influencers in big crowds, for example a sporting event or concert. Research shows that the home team was usually the winner in sporting events (Jamieson, 2010). One study found this to be true 53% of the time in professional baseball, 58% in professional football, 60% in college football, 67% in professional basketball, and 64% in professional hockey. Possible reasons are the home team's familiarity with the home field or the visiting team's travel fatigue. However, an important factor contributing to the home team's victories seems to be the spectators, who provide psychological support that improves performance. In contrast, unfriendly home crowds may increase performance errors (Schwartz & Barsky, 1977; Thirer & Rampey, 1979). Some analyses of home team performances before supportive fans have suggested a tendency for the home team to choke in championship games, but this may not be true for baseball or basketball (Schlenker, Phillips, Boniecki, & Schlenker, 1995).

The ways in which groups influence individual performance are too numerous and too large a topic to discuss here. Two examples illustrate the subtlety of some of these effects:

1. In one of social psychology's first experiments, boys wound line on fishing reels faster when others were present performing the same activity, even though there was no competition and no emphasis on speed (Triplett, 1898). Many studies have since found this *social facilitation* effect whereby performance—on simple and well-learned tasks, at least—is enhanced by the mere presence of others.
2. If people feel others are working with them on a joint task, they often slack off without realizing it. This *social loafing* is strongest when people feel their own contributions cannot be tallied or evaluated (Harkins & Szymanski, 1987).

ARCHITECTURAL DESIGN AND MOVABLE OBJECTS

The architectural design of rooms that people enter in everyday life can be very obvious to them, such as how spacious and open they are as well as how much privacy they afford. The effect of these factors likely hinges on a number of situational, social, work, and personal factors. A small room may seem cozy to one person but confining to someone who suffers from claustrophobia. College students who want to socialize with others may be drawn to their school's commons area but seek out a room with a door they can close when they need to study.

The architectural elements of spaciousness, openness, and privacy also can impact behavior in various rooms. Dawson, Hartwig, Brimbal, and Denisenkov (2017) found that, relative to a small room, individuals were more likely to disclose important information in a spacious room. Relative to a closed cafeteria space, students made more trips to the buffet in a cafeteria with an open floor plan where the food was more visible and easier to get to (Rollings & Wells, 2017). Weziak-Bialowolska, Dong, and McNeely (2018) noted that workers at an architectural firm (of all places!) experienced reduced privacy and job satisfaction in an open-plan office environment.

Hall (1966) labeled the architecture and objects in an environment as either *fixed feature* space, referring to space organized by unmoving boundaries such as walls in rooms of houses, or *semifixed feature* space, referring to the arrangement of movable objects, such as tables or chairs. Both can have a strong impact on communication.

BRAINS AND BUILDINGS

At the intersection of neuroscience and architecture exists a new domain of study: neuroarchitecture (see Coburn & Chatterjee, 2017). Two questions from this domain are of potential interest to the field of nonverbal communication. How does the human brain respond to different architectural designs? How can that knowledge be used to design structures that promote healthy interactions among people in various settings (e.g., home or business)? Nonverbal communication researchers have yet to tackle such questions.

© graphicsdunia4you/Shutterstock.com

At one time in U.S. history, banks were deliberately designed to project an image of strength and security. The design frequently featured large marble pillars, an abundance of metal bars and doors, uncovered floors, and bare walls. This style generally projected a cold, impersonal image to visitors, yet oddly enough, it also gave customers some measure of comfort because in such a place their money would likely be safe. Later, bankers perceived a need to change their environment, to create a friendly, warm, homey place where people would enjoy sitting down and discussing their financial needs and problems with someone who was "on their side." Bank interiors began to change. Carpeting was added, wood replaced metal, cushioned chairs were added, potted plants and art were brought in for additional warmth, and coffee was sometimes offered. This is only one example of the recognition that the interior in which interaction occurs can significantly influence the nature of the interaction. Some churches have tried to make their environments more inviting by having greeters, PowerPoint presentations, musicians who sing and play guitars, and the like. Nightclub owners and restaurateurs have long been aware that dim lighting and sound-absorbing surfaces—such as carpets, curtains, and sound-absorbing ceilings—provide greater intimacy and cause patrons to linger longer than they would in an interior with high illumination and no soundproofing.

The earliest studies to focus on the influence of interior decoration on human responses were conducted by Maslow and Mintz (1956) and Mintz (1956). They selected three rooms for study: One was an "ugly" room, designed to give the impression of a janitor's storeroom in disheveled condition; another was a "beautiful" room, complete with attractive decoration that included carpeting and curtains; and another was an "average" room—a professor's office. People sitting in these rooms were asked to rate a series of negative print photographs (to control for color, shading, etc.) of faces. The experimenters tried to keep all factors—time of day, odor, noise, type of seating, and experimenter—constant from room to room so that results could be attributed to the type of room.

People in the beautiful room gave significantly higher ratings on "energy" and "well-being" to the faces than did participants in the ugly room. Experimenters and subjects alike engaged in various escape behaviors to avoid the ugly room, which was variously described as producing monotony, fatigue, headache, discontent, sleep, irritability, and hostility. The beautiful room, however, produced feelings of pleasure, comfort, enjoyment, importance, energy, and a desire to continue the activity. Similar studies found that students do better on tests, rate teachers higher, and solve problems more effectively in beautiful rooms than in ugly ones (Campbell, 1979; Wollin & Montagre, 1981).

Of course, the aesthetics of a room comprise only one source of influence on perceptions. Sometimes it is a powerful force, but sometimes the relationship between the two parties, an understanding of or tolerance for clutter, positive behavior on the part of the other person, and other factors offset any negative effects emanating from an ugly environment.

Sometimes home environments send very definite person- or couple-related messages (see FIGURE 4-3). The designation of places in the home for certain activities and not for others, the symbolism attached to various objects in the home, and ways of decorating the home may tell a lot about the nature of a couple's relationship (Altman, Brown, Staples, & Werner, 1992). Sometimes the way a home is decorated reveals whether the inhabitants decorated their home for themselves, for others, for conformity, or for comfort (Sandalla, 1987). It is easier to judge aspects of other people's personalities when they feel that their home decor expresses their personality (Hâta, 2004).

Lohmann, Arriaga, and Goodfriend (2003) were able to use decorative objects in a home to determine the closeness of the inhabitants' relationship. They asked couples who were either married or living together in a romantic relationship to identify objects in their homes they most wanted visitors to notice and to specify their favorite objects. Each object was also identified as either individually acquired or jointly acquired. Couples completed questionnaires that measured their relationship commitment and closeness. The couples who had greater commitment and closer relationships were also couples who had a higher proportion of jointly acquired objects that they wanted visitors to notice and had more jointly acquired favorite objects.

© bbrown/Shutterstock.com

FIGURE 4-3 Environmental Perception Test: (a) Describe the people who live here. (b) Tell why you would or would not like to meet the people who live here. (c) How much communication takes place here? (d) What topics are most likely discussed? (e) Which dimensions listed on pp. 67–69 influenced your perceptions the most? (f) Compare your answers with others.

PERSONALIZATION

There has been a growing interest in understanding what people think about and learn about others based on how they decorate and maintain their personal spaces. These spaces can be physical in nature, such as a bedroom or office (Horgan, Herzog, & Dyszlewski, 2019), or virtual by design, such as a Facebook page (Gosling, Augustine, Vazire, Holtzman, & Gaddis, 2011).

Personalization is a term used by environmental psychologists to describe how people may leave traces of who they are by how they arrange, decorate, and maintain their personal spaces (Altman, 1975; Harris & Brown, 1996; Harris & Sachau, 2005). For example, the appearance of your bedroom or office may contain traces of your personality, which not only reinforce who you are to yourself but to visitors as well (e.g., a sports fan; a student at a specific university).

Wells and Thelen (2002) outlined six dimensions of personalization. These include items pertaining to your friends/coworkers and loved ones (the picture of your boyfriend on your desk), your interests in various activities and the arts, and your interests in the domains of your intellect (chemistry books) and senses (your nice wineglasses). Of importance, some of these items may be valid indicators of your personality, whereas other items may not actually reflect who you are, even though visitors think they are valid clues to your traits. Regarding the latter, you may display items in your dorm room to "look cool" to those who visit you, even though those items do not represent anything meaningful about you beyond your desire to look cool to others. Or, the rare pile of dirty clothes on the floor may mislead an observer into thinking you are a negligent person when you are not.

Gosling and colleagues were interested in whether personality characteristics could accurately be predicted from a person's office or bedroom (Gosling, 2008; Gosling, Gaddis, & Vazire, 2008; Gosling, Ko, Mannarelli, & Morris, 2002). Observers who entered various offices and bedrooms guessed the extent to which the room reflected the person's extraversion, agreeableness, emotional stability, openness to experience, and conscientiousness. The personality profile of the people who worked in the offices and slept in the bedrooms was obtained from their own responses to personality measures. These environments did have enough signals associated with conscientiousness and openness to enable the observers to effectively judge inhabitants with those characteristics. For example, a variety of reading material was linked to openness to experience, and being neat was linked to conscientiousness. Other research showed that individuals who arranged their desk so as not to impede interaction tended to be more extraverted (McElroy, Morrow, & Wall, 1983; Morrow & McElroy, 1981).

Even when not necessarily accurate in judging other people's personality from the way they construct their environment, people will still make such judgments. In judging characters in a story, perceivers judged those who kept a dirty house to be less agreeable, less conscientious, less intelligent, and less feminine but more open and more neurotic than the clean housekeepers (Harris & Sachau, 2005). Campbell (1979) found that a clean professor's office led perceivers to assume that the professor had other positive qualities, such as being welcoming (Campbell, 1979). Horgan and colleagues (2019) noted that individuals tend to see a researcher who has a very messy office as more careless and cranky as well as less caring than a researcher with a neat, uncluttered, and clean office.

The way people decorate their rooms may also forecast future behavior. In one study, researchers took photographs of 83 first-year students' rooms. When the photographs of the rooms of students who had dropped out of school a year and a half later were analyzed, it was noted that the dropouts had more decorations reflecting high school and home and fewer related to the university community. Dropouts also seemed to have fewer ways to protect their privacy; their favorite way to combat unwanted noise was to override it with more noise of their own (Vinsel, Brown, Altman, & Foss, 1980).

COLOR

Researchers have been investigating how color affects behavior, from how food tastes to how people judge others or a shopping experience (Elliot & Niesta, 2008; Harrar, Piqueras-Fiszman, & Spence, 2011; Roschk et al., 2017). In a recent literature review on studies dealing with the shopping experience, Roschk and colleagues found that warmer colors produce more arousal than cool colors, but cool colors led to more satisfaction than warmer colors.

People believe that colors can affect behavior. In fact, some believe "prisoner mischief" will vary as a function of the colors surrounding prisoners. For example, the walls of the San Diego city jail were at one time reportedly painted pink, baby blue, and peach on the assumption that pastel colors would have a calming effect on the inmates. In Salem,

MESSY RESEARCH

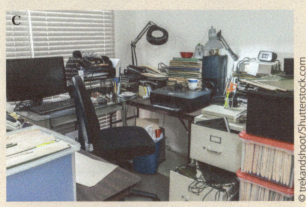

As noted in the book, Gosling and colleagues (2002) found that perceivers saw owners of messy personal spaces as having lower conscientiousness. Horgan and colleagues (2019) wondered if degree of messiness in one's personal space might matter in terms of whether perceivers would view the owner as having one or more negative traits. In three studies, participants entered a researcher's office that was either neat, clean, and uncluttered (office A) or one that was somewhat messy (office B) or very messy (office C) in appearance. They found that perceivers thought the owner of the somewhat messy office was lower in only conscientiousness than the owner of the nonmessy office. However, the owner of the very messy office was seen as not only less conscientious but also less agreeable and more neurotic than the owner of the nonmessy office. This provided evidence that a very messy office led perceivers to form an evaluatively consistent impression (and not a very good one at that!) of the owner. Because people's perceptions matter, these findings have potential real-world implications. If you are an owner of a business that depends on good customer relations, it could prove problematic for you if potential customers thought that one of your employees was careless, uncaring, and cranky because their office was very messy in appearance.

Oregon, the cell bars of Oregon's correctional institution were painted soft greens, blues, and buffs; some cell doors were painted bright yellow, orange, green, and blue. The superintendent of the institution said the color schemes would be continually changed to keep it "an exciting place to work and live in." Initial studies of people exposed to environments painted a particular pink called Baker-Miller found decreasing heart rates, pulse, and respiration. Subsequent studies in adult and juvenile correctional facilities, psychiatric hospitals, and controlled laboratory studies with undergraduate students supported the belief that this pink color aided in suppressing violent and aggressive behaviors (Pelligrini & Schauss, 1980; Schauss, 1985). In 2005, the sheriff of Mason County, Texas, painted the bars and walls of his five-inmate jail pink and issued pink sheets, pink slippers, and pink jumpsuits to his prisoners. He claimed it led to a 70% decrease in repeated offenses (Phinney, 2006).

But not all experiences with pink have been so positive. The county jail in San Jose, California, reportedly painted two holding cells shocking pink in the belief that prisoner hostility would be reduced. Prisoners seemed less hostile for about 15 minutes, but soon the hostility reached a peak; after 3 hours, some prisoners were tearing the paint off the wall. This result is consistent with the research of Smith, Bell, and Fusco (1986) who found pink to be arousing rather than weakening. In fact, any color that is highly saturated and bright is likely to be more arousing and will garner more attention than paler colors (Camgoz, Yener, & Guvenc, 2004; Garber & Hyatt, 2003). When prisoners are allowed to paint their cells with colors they choose, it may have an aggression-reducing effect, but the effect may have more to do with the prisoner's control over the choice of colors than the colors themselves. Nevertheless, the preceding reports show how various institutions have tried, with mixed results, to apply the findings from color research to affect the nature of human interaction in certain environments.

Ball's (1965) summary of the color research prior to 1965 found what others have found since then: that people associate serenity and calm with the colors blue and green, and that red and orange are perceived to be arousing and stimulating. The research of Wexner (1954) and Murray and Deabler (1957) are representative of this tradition. Wexner (see Table 4-1) presented 8 colors and 11 mood-tones to 94 research participants. The results show that a single color is significantly related to some mood-tones; for others, two or more colors may be associated.

It is difficult to interpret this research. First, research participants were asked to judge colors outside of any context, even though the colors in daily life are perceived within a particular context. Separating color from the objects and forms that give it shape, the surrounding colors, and other contextual features may elicit some learned stereotypes about the relationship of mood and color, but each stereotype may or may not be relevant when given a context. Pink may be your favorite color, but you may still dislike pink hair.

Table 4-1 Colors Associated with Moods

Mood-Tone	Color	Number of Times Chosen
Exciting/stimulating	Red	61
Secure/comfortable	Blue	41
Distressed/disturbed/upset	Orange	34
Tender/soothing	Blue	41
Protective/defending	Red	21
	Brown	17
	Blue	15
	Black	15
	Purple	14
Despondent/dejected/unhappy/melancholy	Black	25
	Brown	25
Calm/peaceful/serene	Blue	38
	Green	31
Dignified/stately	Purple	45
Cheerful/jovial/joyful	Yellow	40
Defiant/contrary/hostile	Red	23
	Orange	21
	Black	18
Powerful/strong/masterful	Black	48

Hines (1996) found that residents of four American cities believed red meant danger, warmth, love, strength, and safety, but when these same people were asked to think about red in terms of products, they said red meant Coca-Cola. Because the color red is associated with male dominance and testosterone levels in some nonhuman animals, Hill and Barton (2005) wondered whether the wearing of red would play a role in winning sporting contests. In the 2004 Olympic games, contestants in four combat sports—tae kwon do, boxing, Greco-Roman wrestling, and freestyle wrestling—were randomly assigned red or blue outfits. In all four competitions, the contestants wearing red won significantly more fights. The researchers later compared the performances of five soccer teams that varied the color of their uniforms and found that they won significantly more games when wearing red. The researchers caution, however, that wearing red may only be a favorable factor in winning when the combatants are reasonably matched in skill: wearing red will not overcome a lack of talent. Several studies show that the color of uniforms—red in some sports, black in some others—affects players' behavior or observers' (sometimes referees') judgments, or both (Frank & Gilovich, 1988; Greenlees, Eynon, & Thelwell, 2013; Ilie, Ioan, Zagrean, & Moldovan, 2008; Krenn, 2015; Webster, Urland, & Correll, 2012).

Studies suggest that the color red enhances the attractiveness of members of the other sex. In one experiment, young men saw the same black-and-white photo of a woman in one of two conditions: in either a red background or a white background. Men's ratings of the woman's attractiveness were higher when she was featured in the red as opposed to the white background (Elliot & Niesta, 2008). Similarly, Elliot et al. (2010) found that young women thought a man was more attractive when he was shown on a red background compared to a white one. The authors proposed that for men looking at women, red unconsciously primed the concept of sexiness, whereas for women looking at men, red unconsciously primed the concept of dominance or high status.

There is considerable worry in today's world about the impact of retailers and their products on the planet's health. The idea of "going green" has been tied to the color green. Sundar and Kellaris (2015) have noted that green is one of the colors that people associate with eco-friendliness. The use of the color green on products can be beneficial in terms of enhancing the positive environmental message of those products (Seo & Scammon, 2017). However, the color green might also inflate the perceived ethical practices of retailers (Sundar & Kellaris, 2017).

We cannot make conclusive judgments about the impact of color on human interaction from the research to date, but common sense tells us that colors in the environment will affect people's responses: we simply do not know how or how much. What we do know is that research in this area needs to continue, and that its scope must be broadened to new interaction environments. For instance, because many people visit websites on a daily basis, researchers should examine how color in those websites impacts visitors both within and across various cultures (e.g., Cyr, Head, & Larios, 2010).

SOUND

Types of sounds and their intensity can also affect interpersonal behavior, task performance, and mental and physical health. Most people are aware that music can affect moods and that the selection of music may be designed to match or even change one's mood. Depressing music can add to the intensity of an already gloomy mood; uplifting music can enhance a joyful feeling. Beginning with ideas like this, Honeycutt and Eidenmuller (2001) asked couples to work at resolving a source of conflict in their relationship, while background music was varied. Some couples experienced positive and uplifting music, while others experienced negative or dreary music. Agitating music was linked to arguments in this study, and the intensity of the music affected the intensity of the interaction. In a related study, uplifting or annoying music was played for users of a university gym. Following their workout, they were asked to sign up for a helping task that did not involve much effort or commitment or one that did. People exposed to both types of music signed up for the easy task, but significantly more people who heard the uplifting music signed up to help with the more difficult task (North, Tarrant, & Hargreaves, 2004). Lastly, greater cooperativeness was observed among those making decisions in a group setting when happy music was played in the background (Kniffin, Yan, Wansink, & Schulze, 2017).

Music can also affect consumer behavior. At one British restaurant, diners were exposed to classical, pop, or no music. When dining to the sound of classical music, people spent significantly more money (North, Shilcock, & Hargreaves, 2003). Obviously, different types of music are suitable for different environments, and the music that is most effective for an environment is music that is compatible with perceptions of other environmental features. Scientists at the University of Leicester in England displayed four French and four German wines in a local supermarket. The wines from the two countries were similar in price, sweetness, and dryness. For 2 weeks, a tape deck on a nearby shelf alternated each day with either French accordion music or German beer-hall music. Researchers found that sales were clearly linked to the type of music being played: When French music was played, French wines outsold German wines, and when German music was played, German wines outsold French wines. Only about 7% of those purchasing wines were willing to acknowledge that the music may have influenced their decision (North, Hargreaves, & McKendrick, 1997).

Concern has grown in the general public about the effects of music on young people's behavior. It is important to remember that the music most young adults listen to (pop, rap, rock and roll, soul, country, etc.) contains lyrics. Teasing apart the impact of the music versus the lyrics is thus important. For example, it appears that violent lyrics contribute to aggressive thoughts and behaviors, prosocial lyrics contribute to helping behavior, and romantic lyrics contribute to romance-related behavior (namely, women's initial openness to having phone contact with a male; Anderson, Carnagey, & Eubanks, 2003; Greitemeyer, 2009; Guéguen, Jacob, & Lamy, 2010; Mast & McAndrew, 2011). More important, it seems that it is the lyrics and not the music per se that is responsible for the increase in aggressive thoughts and behavior. Here again, co-occurring verbal cues must be taken into consideration when we evaluate the impact of a nonverbal cue, such as music. We also should not ignore individual differences. Huang and Shih (2011), for instance, found that music negatively affected workers' concentration when the music was either strongly liked or disliked by the worker.

Szalma and Hancock's (2011) review revealed that noise negatively impacts performance, including communication that is both oral and written. However, they noted that the extent to which noise hurts performance depends on a variety of factors, including noise intensity, whether the noise is intermittent or continuous, the type of noise, noise duration, and the type of task being done under noisy conditions. As an illustration of some of these factors, Glass and Singer (1973) asked participants to perform a variety of tasks varying in complexity, while noises were manipulated by the experimenters. Noise levels were varied: Some noise followed a predictable pattern, and some did not. Various noise sources were tested, including typewriters, machinery, and people speaking a foreign language. Although noise alone did not seem to have a substantial effect on performance, deterioration was observed when noise interacted with other factors; for instance, performance decreased when the workload was high and the noise was uncontrollable and unpredictable. Other factors that determine whether noise is a problem or a pleasure include the type of noise—for example, music versus people talking—the volume, the length of time it lasts, and whether the listener is accustomed to it or not. Obviously, some individuals are more influenced by noise than others. Noise-sensitive incoming college students perceived more noise than other students, and these perceptions increased after 7 months into the school year. The noise-sensitive students also received lower grades, felt less secure in their social interactions, and had a greater desire for privacy than did their peers who were less sensitive to noise (Weinstein, 1978). (Noise, as a type of environmental stimulation, ties to our earlier discussion of environmentally sensitive individuals.)

Noise can also have short- and long-term effects on learning, motivation, behavior, and health at school, work, and home. Ryan and Mendel (2010) reported that the noise levels surrounding physical education settings (e.g., gymnasium) are too high for Florida school-aged children (elementary, middle, and high school), which could be detrimental to their learning. And Graziose and colleagues (2019) observed that young children ate fewer fruits and vegetables in noisier than quieter cafeteria settings.

Jahncke, Hygge, Halin, Green, and Dimberg (2011) noted that participants were less motivated and felt more tired when working in an open-plan office space that had high- versus low-noise conditions. The distraction caused by noise may be key to understanding the short-term effects of noise on behavior, including increased alcohol consumption (Stafford, Fernandes, & Agobiani, 2012).

If negative feelings from hot temperatures can lead to aggression under the right circumstances, then noise, which also can produce negative feelings in people, should lead to aggression at times too, as well as other problematic outcomes for people. This is, indeed, the case with respect to aggression (Geen & McCown, 1984). Richburg and Slagley (2019) found that people living in rural areas reported more sleep disturbances and worries about their health from environmental noises stemming from "fracking." Lastly, with respect to hearing acuity, a study in Michigan found that 70% of participants were exposed to typical noise levels that exceeded Environmental Protection Agency guidelines; such exposure levels could negatively impact their hearing over the long term (Flamme et al., 2012). Much concern (and evidence) exists about hearing loss induced by chronic exposure to loud music (Weichbold, Holzer, Newesely, & Stephan, 2012).

It is not all gloom and doom with respect to environmental noise and sounds. Efforts are underway to understand how to reduce the negative impact of noise on people or help them cope better with situational stressors. Pouyesh and colleagues (2018) found that nature sounds helped reduce the anxiety that patients felt while waiting for their coronary angiography procedure. There is the possibility that electric cars may reduce the negative impact of traffic noise on people (Walker, Kennedy, Martin, & Rule, 2016). What about hearing a distracting voice when trying to work? Headphones alone (without music playing in them) may not help short-term memory in this situation unless that voice is also masked by the sounds of nature (Jahncke, Bjorkeholm, Marsh, Odelius, & Sorquist, 2016).

LIGHTING

Lighting also helps structure perceptions of an environment, and these perceptions may influence communication. In a dimly lit or candlelit room, people may talk more softly, sit closer together, and presume that more personal communication will take place (Meer, 1985). When dimly lit university counseling rooms were compared with those that had brighter lighting, students reported feeling more relaxed in the dimly lit rooms. The dimly lit counseling rooms also elicited more self-disclosure from the students and higher ratings of the counselors in those rooms (Miwa & Hanyu, 2006).

When a dimly lit environment is suddenly brightened, it tends to invite less intimate interaction. For example, the flashing of bright lights in nightclubs that previously maintained dim lighting is often a signal that closing time is near, and this allows patrons some time to make the transition from one mood to another. Carr and Dabbs (1974) found that the use of intimate questions in dim lighting with nonintimates caused a significant hesitancy in responding, a significant decrease in eye gaze, and a decrease in the average length of gaze. All of these nonverbal behaviors appear to be efforts to create more psychological distance and decrease the perceived inappropriateness of the intimacy created by the lighting and questions.

The absence of light seems to be a central problem for people who suffer from *seasonal affective disorder*, a form of depression particularly acute in winter months (Rosenthal, 1993). Therapists have successfully treated those who suffer from seasonal affective disorder by exposing them to extremely bright light on a schedule (Lewy et al., 1998; Menculini et al., 2018). Increasingly, researchers are looking at how lighting in indoor and outdoor environments affects behavior and physical and mental health. Relative to bright lighting, dim lighting in a restaurant setting appears to lead diners to select less healthy food (Biswas, Szocs, Chacko, & Wansink, 2017). A number of studies have documented the ill effects of what has been called light pollution, such as the presence of artificial outdoor lights at night. Min and Min (2018), for example, found evidence that outdoor light at night may contribute to mental health problems in people (depressive symptoms and suicidal behaviors). Part of the concern is that artificial lighting might disrupt basic biological processes (endocrine, circadian, and melatonin; Gooley et al., 2011; Russart & Nelson, 2018; Tähkämö, Partonen, & Pesonen, 2019) and lead to poor health outcomes in people (weight and cardiovascular; Obayashi, Saeki, & Kurumatani, 2015; Park, White, Jackson, Weinberg, & Sandler, 2019).

MOVABLE OBJECTS

If we know that the arrangement of certain objects in the environment can help structure communication, it is not surprising that people often try to manipulate objects to elicit specific responses. Politicians and government officials do this routinely when choosing backdrops for their speeches. Manipulating objects in the environment to communicate particular messages also occurs in personal living spaces. In preparation for an intimate evening at home, a person may light candles, play soft, romantic music, fluff the pillows on the couch, and hide the dirty dishes.

Employees often use objects to personalize their offices. These signs of personal identity make them feel more satisfied with their work life and provide visitors with information to initiate a conversation. Because the company also wants to communicate its identity, the amount and kinds of personal objects employees display must also be consistent with the image the company wants to project. Objects in the work environment can also be arranged to reflect certain role relationships, to demarcate boundaries, or to encourage greater affiliation. The interior of an executive suite may clearly indicate the perceived status of the inhabitant, for example, with expensive paintings, a large desk, plush sofas and chairs, and the like (Monk, 1994). Such an atmosphere may be inappropriate for a personal counseling situation, but it can be rearranged to make it more conducive to such a purpose. Of course, sometimes people are able to communicate well in seemingly inappropriate settings by blocking out the messages being sent by the environment, as when lovers intimately say goodbye in relatively cold and public airport terminals.

Desks and their usage seem to be important objects in the conduct of interpersonal communication. Physicians, for example, invite a more engaged conversation with a patient if they are not seated behind their desk. Student–student interaction in classrooms can be constrained by eliminating any possible movement of the student desks or seats (see Figure 4-4). And student–teacher relationships can also be affected by desk placement (Zweigenhaft, 1976). Faculty

FIGURE 4-4 A classroom design with immovable chairs discourages student–student interactions.

members were asked to sketch the furniture arrangement of their offices. These sketches were collected and analyzed with other information obtained from the professors, and a schoolwide teacher evaluation was conducted. It was found that 24 of 33 senior faculty members put their desks between themselves and their students, but only 14 of 30 junior faculty members did so. Furthermore, students rated the "unbarricaded" professors as more willing to "encourage the development of different viewpoints by students," and ready to give "individual attention to students who need it." However, students expect greater formality in student–teacher relationships in some situations, and the basis for an effective working relationship may have been established outside the professor's office, so the barrier may not always be perceived as such.

The arrangement of other furniture items can facilitate or inhibit communication. The location of the television set in a room will likely affect the placement of chairs and, in turn, the patterns of conversation in that room. Even when conversational possibilities have been maximized, not everyone will talk to everyone else. Consider the arrangement of FIGURE 4-5. Without considering other factors, such as the relationship of the interactants or their knowledge of the subject, we would predict exchanges marked by the arrows to be most frequent. The four people seated on the couch, as well as persons F and G, will probably talk to each other less frequently. The four on one end are not likely to communicate very often with the four on the other end.

In some environments, people are not expected to linger, so chairs are deliberately designed without comfort in mind. Hotel owners and airport designers are well aware of the "too comfortable" phenomenon. You may have noticed the slightly uncomfortable nature of the 10 degree forward angle of chairs in some fast-food restaurants. This feature encourages customers to eat and move along quickly to provide seats for others.

STANDING ORDERS

In some work environments, movable objects now include the desks that employees use to do their computer work. These adjustable desks give workers the option to sit down or stand up while they are working. The possible dangers of sitting too long at one's desk (Young et al., 2016) may have given rise to the popularity of these desks. However, standing too long can be problematic for some individuals. What may be more important to workers is being able to move and change the positions of their body throughout the day (see Mula, 2018).

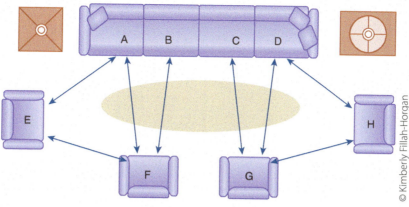

FIGURE 4-5 Seating arrangement and conversation flow.

© Kimberly Fillah-Horgan

The Port Authority Bus Terminal in New York replaced its old wooden seats with folding plastic seats only 8 inches deep that "require so much concentration to balance that sleeping or even sitting for long is impossible." This was done to keep homeless people from sleeping in the terminal (Rimer, 1989).

STRUCTURE AND DESIGN

Much time is spent in buildings. Most people spend the day in a dwelling supposedly designed for effective performance of work; in the evening, they enter another structure supposedly designed for the effective conduct of personal and family life. The architecture of these buildings can go a long way toward determining who meets whom, where, and perhaps for how long.

Signs and structural designs within buildings also communicate where certain activities occur and who is permitted to be in particular spaces. A visit to the bathroom is a part of life, whether you are at work or school, and signs are used to let people know where the facilities are. And the structure of bathrooms—for example, a row of urinals—lets men know that this is the place where women are not allowed. However, where do you go to go when you do not identify as male or female? Gender-inclusive signs can be hung and unisex urinals installed to accommodate everyone who needs a bathroom. The use of gender-inclusive bathrooms may have psychological benefits to other individuals, such as women and minorities, because they may signal a more egalitarian social climate within an organization (Chaney & Sanchez, 2018).

The life of domestic animals is controlled through, among other things, fences, flap doors, litter boxes, or the placement of food and water in particular locations. Although verbal and nonverbal actions help control human situations, manipulation of barriers, openings, and other physical arrangements is also helpful. Meeting places can be appropriately arranged to regulate human traffic and, to a certain extent, the network of communication.

U.S. office buildings often are constructed from a standard plan that reflects a pyramidal organization. A large number of people are under the direction of a few executives at the upper levels. These executives generally have the most space, the most privacy, and the most desirable office locations, usually on the highest floor of the structure. Achieving a height above the masses and occupying a significant amount of space are only two indications of power. Corner offices, large picture windows, and private elevators also are associated with status and power (Monk, 1994). An office next to an important executive may also be a formidable power base. A similar pattern seems to exist in academic settings as well, with the higher-ranking professors normally accorded more space, windows, privacy, and choice of office location (Farrenkopf & Roth, 1980). The offices of top-level executives are often hard to reach, the assumption being that the more complicated the path to get to the executive, the more powerful they must be. FIGURE 4-6 is a hypothetical but not far-fetched example of the long and circuitous route to an executive's office. To get to the office,

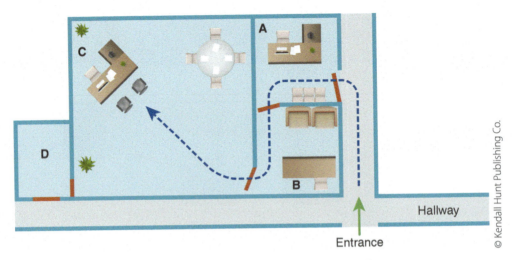

FIGURE 4-6 Getting to the president's office. A, receptionist; B, private assistant; C, president; D, private room with rear exit.

the visitor must be screened by a receptionist and a private assistant and, in either or both places, may be asked to sit and wait. So, although the status and power of an executive may be related to their inaccessibility, assistants and receptionists may value open views that allow them to act as lookouts and defenders against unwanted intrusions. It is common for people on the lowest rungs of the organizational ladder to find themselves in a large, open "pit." These so-called offices—really only desks, sometimes encompassed by a temporary enclosure—have little or no privacy, and complaints are common. Although privacy is minimal, communication opportunities are plentiful.

Some dormitories are built from floor plans that resemble many office buildings and old hotels. It has been speculated that these corridor-type dorms tend to encourage bureaucratic management, which seems to fit the orderly and uniform structure. Rigid rules are easier to enforce in these structures, and interaction among the residents is discouraged. Compared with suite-type dorms, corridor-type dorms are perceived by residents as more crowded, less private, and more conducive to avoiding others (Baum & Valins, 1979). A sense of community and the resulting responsibility for the living space are difficult to achieve. Lounges are sometimes intended to facilitate interaction, but their usefulness has been questioned by architects and behavioral scientists. Lounges, like other design features, must be integrated into the entire architectural plan developed from an analysis of *human needs*—not inserted in places where they fit nicely or look good for parents and visitors.

If you look carefully, you can see many environmental structures that inhibit or prohibit communication. Separating yards with fences creates obvious barriers, even if they are only waist high; locating laundry rooms in dark, isolated areas of apartment buildings discourages their use, particularly at night; and so on.

Other environmental situations seem to facilitate interaction. Homes located in the middle of a block seem to draw more interpersonal exchanges than those located in other positions. Houses with adjacent driveways draw the neighbors together and invite communication. The likelihood of interaction between strangers at a bar varies directly with the distance between them. As a rule, a span of three bar stools is the maximum distance over which patrons will attempt to initiate an encounter. Most bars are not designed for optimal interaction.

Some designs for housing the elderly have taken into consideration the need for social contact, for example by having the doors of the apartments open onto a common entranceway. This greatly increases the probability of social exchange compared to buildings where apartment doors are staggered on either side of a long hallway with no facing doorways. If you want a structure that encourages social interaction, you must have human paths that cross, but if you want people to interact, there must be something that encourages them to linger. Differences in interaction frequency are often related to the distances people must travel between activities. For example, consider this comparison made between two high schools: One was "centralized" with classrooms in one or two buildings and one was "campus style" with classrooms spread among several buildings. The campus design prompted more interactions in the halls, stairs, and lobbies but fewer interactions in the classrooms, as well as fewer interactions between students and teachers before and after class (Myrick & Marx, 1968). It is no secret that the architecture of a school can affect a student's motivation to learn, a teacher's motivation to teach, how much students and teachers talk to each other, and, to a certain extent, what they talk about. Older school designs were often based on how to maintain strict discipline, emphasize status differences between students and teachers, and minimize informal talking.

A more complete analysis of physical proximity and spatial distance appears in Chapter 5, but it is clearly relevant to this discussion on environments as well. Over 60 years ago, Stouffer (1940) made this observation about what social psychologists call the *propinquity effect*, which holds true today:

> Whether one is seeking to explain why persons go to a particular place to get jobs, why they go to trade at a particular store, why they go to a particular neighborhood to commit a crime, or why they marry a particular spouse they choose, the factor of spatial distance is of obvious significance. (p. 845)

Many studies have confirmed Stouffer's remark. Students tend to develop stronger friendships with students who share their classes, dormitories, and apartment buildings, or who sit near them than with others who are geographically distant. Workers tend to develop closer friendships with those who work near them. The effect of proximity seems to be stronger for employees with less status in the organization; managers are likely to choose their friends at the office according to their status rather than their proximity (Schutte & Light, 1978). There is evidence that more contact between members of different social groups will assist in reducing prejudice (Pettigrew & Tropp, 2006). Although close proximity may bring about positive attitude changes between different groups, we must exercise caution in generalizing. If the two groups are extremely polarized, or if they perceive no mutual problems or projects requiring cooperation, proximity may have little effect or may even magnify hostilities.

A number of studies have shown how proximity influences friendships. Classic studies examine actual living arrangements. In a townhouse development, most friendships occurred between people who lived within 100 feet of each other. Next-door neighbors became close friends 46% of the time; neighbors who lived two or three doors away became close friends 24% of the time; and people who lived three or four doors away became friends 13% of the time (Athanasiou & Yoshioka, 1973). Historically, the most famous such study, conducted by Festinger, Schachter, and Back (1950) in a housing development for married students, found similar results, where proximity could be on one's floor, or sharing a common stairwell. Clearly, architects can have a tremendous influence on the social life of residents in apartment buildings.

Making friends takes many forms these days. Physical proximity and architectural design are augmented by the Internet. People start relationships with others through online dating services (e.g., Albright & Simmens, 2014; Rosenfeld & Thomas, 2012; Whitty, 2009). The number of people who get married to someone they met through online dating services is growing. Because of physical distance or lack of opportunity to cross paths with each other, these couples might never have met in the pre-Internet days. Moreover, people can start and maintain friendships with others via their Facebook accounts. In modern classrooms, for example, college students can stay in touch with someone from their hometown while ignoring someone who is sitting nearby. The current design and structure of the setting the student is in, whether it is the dorm, classroom, or student lounge area, may not matter anymore. However, as is the case in traditional settings, the more you interact with someone, even via e-mail, the more you come to like them due to the effects of familiarity on attraction (Reis, Maniaci, Caprariello, Eastwick, & Finkel, 2011). How well frequency of Internet interaction substitutes for frequency of in-person interaction is a question needing an answer.

REGULATING ENVIRONMENTS AND COMMUNICATION

It should be clear by now that communication is often affected by the social and physical environment. And people have some control over structuring these environments; you can paint the walls a different color, substitute candles for electric lights, and so on. But communication environments are influenced by others, too. Earlier in this chapter, we noted how architects affect social interaction, but laws and government regulations also play an important role in creating the environments that affect communicative behavior. It is important to conclude the chapter with this reminder because gaining control over the environment that affects communication may mean becoming a community activist or leader.

Zoning laws, for example, determine whether a part of the environment will be used for industrial, commercial, or residential activity. Zoning laws also determine the population density of an area by defining how many housing units per acre are allowed. When business hours of operation are regulated, it affects when streets are empty, when they are crowded, and what segment of the population occupies the street. Some communities have specific laws governing signs and billboards, where they can be placed, their size, materials, and colors that can be used, and so on. Obviously these and similar regulations governing parking areas, parks, display windows, and vending machines impact social life.

HOSTILE ARCHITECTURE

© JohnGK/Shutterstock.com

Would you want to sleep on this bench? No, because you cannot actually sleep on it. That is the idea behind *hostile architecture*. The goal of hostile architecture is to discourage particular behaviors in public settings, such as sleeping on the benches that people use when waiting for public transportation. Needless to say, such measures target specific groups of people, such as the homeless. These designs might have unintended consequences, though. A very large person might not be able to fit in the middle part of the bench shown here, if two people are already seated on the ends of it.

In addition, there are penal codes that punish loitering, smoking, drinking alcoholic beverages, and other behaviors. Smoking regulations determine where smokers are allowed to congregate. As a consequence, smokers today may have a greater feeling of us (namely, the in-group of smokers) versus them (namely, the out-group of nonsmokers) than did smokers of the past. Moreover, in places that prohibit smoking, including college campuses, smokers may be viewed as and feel deviant for the practice of lighting up. Thus, in an effort to safeguard the well-being of those who occupy it, an environment may be restructured both in a physical way (designated smoking areas) and in a psychological way (e.g., regulations that recast the behavior of smoking).

GREEN WITH ... *FROWNING?*

© AR42/Shutterstock.com

Imagine getting ready to throw out a plastic bottle or piece of paper. A trash can and a recycling bin are nearby. Would the presence of a frowning face on the trash can make you more likely to place your bottle or paper in the recycling bin? Research by Meng and Trudek (2017) suggests that it would. In two studies—a field study with elementary children and a lab study with college students—they found that participants were more likely to recycle when a frowning emoticon was placed on a trash can. This research shows that the presence of a simple, inexpensive, and commonly seen emoticon on trash cans near recycling bins might go a long way in helping individuals "go green."

SUMMARY

The environment in which people communicate frequently contributes to the overall outcome of their encounters. We have seen that both the frequency and the content of messages are influenced by various aspects of the communication setting. We have seen how the environment influences behavior, but we also know that environments can be altered to elicit certain types of responses. As knowledge of environments increases, people may deliberately use them to help obtain desired responses. In many respects, everyone is the product of their environment, and if we want to change behavior, we need to learn to control the environment in which we interact.

Throughout this chapter, we referred to a number of different types of environments: classrooms, dormitories, offices, fast-food restaurants, homes, and bars. We suggested several different ways of looking at environments. Mehrabian (1976), following research in other areas of human perception, commented that all environments could profitably be examined by looking at emotional reactions to them. These emotions can be plotted on three dimensions: arousing–nonarousing, pleasant–unpleasant, and dominant–submissive. We suggested six perceptual bases for examining environments: formal–informal, warm–cold, private–public, familiar–unfamiliar, constraining–free, and distant–close. We also pointed out that people perceive temporal aspects of their environments: when things happen, how long they last, how much time exists between events, and the pattern or rhythm of events.

Each environment seems to have three major characteristics: (1) the presence or absence of nature or natural features, (2) the presence or absence of other people, and (3) the architectural design and movable objects, including lighting, sound, color, and general visual-aesthetic appeal. The quality and quantity of the research in each of these areas vary considerably, but it is clear that any analysis of human behavior must account for the influence of environmental features.

QUESTIONS FOR DISCUSSION

1. Select a familiar environment that effectively encourages or discourages human interaction. Now indicate all the changes you would make so this environment would have the exact opposite effect.

2. Assume the role of a stranger entering your own apartment or your family's home. What messages does the environment communicate?

3. The impact of environmental features on human behavior will vary as a function of context, but what features do you think play a large or small role across different contexts? Explain your choices.

4. How do people communicate time-related messages by their behavior?

NONVERBAL COMMUNICATION IN ACTION: TRY THIS

You know already that people behave differently in different environments, but have you ever really looked closely? Exercise your observational and analytical skills in this activity:

Watch people in different settings—examples would be people in a coffee shop, students in transit between classes, people lining up to go into a concert or bar, or people riding public transportation. Analyze how they are behaving and how the behavior differs between these settings. Pay particular attention to how the environment either limits or facilitates their behavior (e.g., talking or physical contact between strangers).

CHAPTER 5

THE EFFECTS OF TERRITORY AND PERSONAL SPACE ON HUMAN COMMUNICATION

Spatial changes give a tone to a communication, accent it, and at times even override the spoken word.
—E. T. Hall

"If you can read this, you're too close," announces a familiar automobile bumper sticker in an attempt to regulate the amount of space between vehicles for traffic safety. Signs reading "Keep Out," "Private Property," and "Authorized Personnel Only" are also attempts to regulate space among human beings. People do not put up signs in daily conversation, but they use other signals to avoid uncomfortable crowding and other perceived invasions of personal space. The use of space—one's own and others'—can dramatically affect ability to achieve desired communication goals, whether those goals involve romance, diplomacy, or aggression. A fundamental concept in any discussion of human spatial behavior is the notion of territoriality. An understanding of this concept provides a useful perspective for our later examination of conversational space.

THE CONCEPT OF TERRITORIALITY

The term *territoriality* has been used for years in the study of animal and bird behavior. Generally, it means behavior characterized by identification with a geographic area in a way that indicates ownership and often involves defense of this territory against perceived invaders. For humans, territoriality concerns physical items ("my book") and physical space ("my dorm room"), objects or ideas ("my proposed solution") that a person feels psychological ownership of, as well as some combination of the two (plagiarism is stealing another person's thoughts by using their words and claiming them as your own).

There are many kinds of territorial behavior, and frequently such behaviors perform useful functions for a given species. For instance, territorial behaviors may help coordinate activities, regulate density, ensure propagation of the species, hold the group together, provide a sense of well-being, and offer hiding places. Most behavioral scientists agree that territoriality exists in human behavior. It helps regulate social interaction, but it also can be the source of social conflict. Like other animals, the more powerful, dominant humans seem to have control over more territory—as long as the group or societal structure is stable.

Altman (1975) identified three types of territories: (1) primary, (2) secondary, and (3) public. The key distinction is the extent of ownership felt or warranted. *Primary territories* are clearly the exclusive domain of the owner. They are central to the daily functioning of the owner, and they are guarded carefully against intruders. For this reason, the invisible buffer zone surrounding one's body also qualifies as a primary territory. It is not stationary and visible, like other territories, but the degree of ownership is extremely high, access to others is often very limited, and the defense against intrusions can be particularly fierce.

Homes or bedrooms often qualify as primary territory. Goffman's (1971) description of *possessional territories*—which include personal effects such as jackets, and even dependent children—also seems to fit the requirements of primary territory. In this same category, Goffman discusses objects that can be claimed temporarily by people, for example, a magazine, a television set, or eating utensils. These objects, however, seem to be more representative of what Altman calls *secondary territories*, which are not as central to the daily life of the owner, nor are they perceived as clearly exclusive to the owner. The neighborhood bar or those objects like magazines or television sets are examples of secondary territories. More frequent conflicts are apt to develop over these territories because the public–private boundary is blurred. The following exchange is an example of this conflict: "Let me watch my program on TV. I was here first." "It's not your TV. You don't own it."

Public territories are available to almost anyone for temporary ownership. Parks, beaches, streets, seats on public transportation, telephone booths, a place in line, or an unobstructed line of vision to see a particular object of interest are examples. The terms *temporary occupancy* or *ownership* are important. If a cleaning person enters an office to clean while the occupant is in it, it might seem normal and inoffensive because the intrusion is temporary and job related. It would be a different story, however, if the cleaning person settled down to eat their lunch. The chairs in a classroom are theoretically available to anyone in the class for temporary occupancy, but frequent use or a desirable location can result in greater perceived ownership and territorial behavior (Kaya, 2007).

Territorial behavior seems to be a standard part of daily contact with others, and it also is evident when sufficient social contact is denied. In a classic study, Altman and Haythorn (1967) analyzed the territorial behavior of socially isolated and nonisolated pairs of men. For 10 days, two individuals lived in a small room with no outside contact while a matched group received outside contacts. The men in the isolated groups showed a gradual increase in territorial behavior and a general pattern of social withdrawal; they desired more time alone. Their territorial behavior first evidenced itself with fixed objects, areas of the room, and personal objects such as beds. Later they began to claim more mobile and less personal objects. When the two men living together were incompatible with respect to dominance and affiliation, this resulted in greater territorial behavior.

Sports teams often perform better when playing on their home turf. This "home advantage" is no doubt due to multiple factors including fan support, less travel fatigue, and familiarity with the idiosyncrasies of the home field (a famous one being the "Green Monster" wall in left field at the Boston Red Sox's Fenway Park, which is a notorious challenge for visiting teams). An additional theory to account for the home advantage is territoriality on the part of the home team: playing more aggressively to "defend" their home territory from an interloper. This would fit with evolutionary theory, according to Furley (2019), who points out that testosterone concentrations go up before home games compared with away games, which may influence muscle function. Territoriality may also increase risk-taking behavior as well as team members' self-presentation as dominant and confident.

TERRITORIALITY: INVASION AND DEFENSE

A person has to deal with the potential of other people invading their physical territory at many different levels, including their body, personal belongings, personal space, home, neighborhood, work/school environment (Brown & Robinson, 2011), and nation. For example, instructions to police interrogators sometimes suggest sitting close to the suspect without the intervention of a desk that might provide protection or comfort. This theory of interrogation assumes that invasion of the suspect's personal territory, with little opportunity for defense, will give the officer a psychological advantage. Other examples of human territorial invasion and defense include members of adolescent gangs and ethnic/cultural groups who stake out territory in urban areas and defend it against intruders. Preserving national boundaries often underlies international disputes.

Obviously, not all territorial encroachments are the same. Lyman and Scott (1967) identified three types:

1. *Violation* involves the unwarranted use of another's territory. This may be done with the eyes (staring at somebody eating in a public restaurant); with the voice or other sounds (somebody talking loudly nearby on a cell phone or construction noise next to a classroom); or with the body (taking up two seats in public transportation by splaying the legs, often called "manspreading"—a practice now discouraged as seen in public service ads and even local laws in some places).
2. *Invasion* is more all-encompassing and permanent. It is an attempt to take over another's territory. This may be an armed invasion of another country or the act of a wife in a heterosexual couple who has turned her husband's

"man cave" into her home office. When children move away from the parental home for college, work, or military duty, the "ownership" of their bedrooms can be a point of confusion and conflict, as the parent may not consider the child to have the same permanent right to the space as the child does. Ledbetter and Vik (2012) created a scale to measure young adults' feelings of parental invasion. Here is a sample item of each of its three factors: For mediated invasion, "My parents read my text messages without my permission"; for verbal invasion, "My parents ask personal questions that I don't want to answer"; and for spatial invasion, "My parents go through my personal belongings without my permission." College students reported more privacy invasions when their family placed less value on open and frequent conversation and when the family had more conformist (rule-following) attitudes.

3. *Contamination* is defiling of one's perceived territory, not by someone else's current presence but by past presence, including what they left behind. When taking temporary occupancy of a hotel room, for instance, the hotel patron does not want to find the previous "owner's" toilet articles and soiled sheets. Similarly, most people are upset when someone else's dog leaves feces in their yard, or when they find food particles on "their" silverware in restaurants.

Encroachments on perceived territory do not always produce defensive maneuvers. The intensity of our reaction to territorial encroachment varies depending on a number of factors, including the following:

1. Who violated the territory? People may have very different reactions to friends' or acquaintances' violations as opposed to those of strangers. People may be more inclined to share personal things, including space, with people they know (Kaya & Weber, 2003). They may also react differently depending on the gender, status, and age of the violator.

2. What was the reason for the violation of territory? If one feels that the violator "knew better," they might react more strongly than if they felt the other "couldn't help it" or was naive.

3. What type of territory was it? People are likely to perceive a violation of primary territory as far more serious than the violation of a secondary or public territory, although people sometimes attribute more ownership to secondary and public territories than they deserve.

4. How was the violation accomplished? Was it done in a threatening way? If one's body is touched, they may be more aroused and defensive than if someone walks across one's yard. On the other hand, sometimes any intrusion, whether made in a threatening manner or not, will be perceived as a threat (Ruback & Kohli, 2005).

5. How long did the encroachment last? If the violation is perceived as temporary, reactions may be less severe.

6. Does one expect further violations in the future? If so, the initial territorial defense may be more intense.

7. Where did the violation occur? The population density and opportunities for negotiating new territorial boundaries will surely affect the reaction.

The two primary methods for territorial defense are *prevention* and *reaction*. Prevention is a means of staking out territory so others recognize it as claimed and go elsewhere. People may position themselves in such a way so as to keep others away from "their" space (see FIGURE 5-1). A person's mere presence in a place can keep others from entering it. If one stays in a place long enough or often enough, others think it is "owned" it (e.g., a seat in a classroom). Sometimes a person will ask others to assist them in staking out and defending territory: "Would you hold my seat while I go get some popcorn?"

Objects are also used as territorial markers to designate "your" spatial area. In places with relatively low density, markers such as umbrellas, coats, and notebooks are often effective; indeed, sometimes these markers will reserve not only a seat in a public area but also an entire table. Markers that appear more personal may be more effective in preventing violations but are also vulnerable to theft. If the marked territory is highly desirable to many others in the immediate area, markers probably will maintain their effectiveness for shorter periods of time. In public territories, it may be more effective to leave several markers, as these areas are open to nearly everyone. Commuters on trains with a seating arrangement that requires three passengers to sit side by side illustrate how territorial intrusion is sometimes the result of the combined behavior by the protector of the territory and the intruder. Passengers seated on the inside and outside of the three-seat arrangement position their legs, belongings, newspapers, and so on, to convey the idea that sitting in the middle seat in "their" territory is forbidden. At the same time, many commuters who could sit in the

© Terrence Horgan

FIGURE 5-1 Territorial defense.

vacant middle seats with two strangers on each side may decide that taking the middle-seat territory is less desirable than standing or sitting on the floor (McGeehan, 2005).

If the prevention of territorial violations does not work, how do people react? When people come "too" close in face-to-face encounters, it creates physiological arousal, and increased heart rate and galvanic skin responses (Finando, 1973; McBride, King, & James, 1965). (Note that these are generalized arousal responses, not sexual ones.) Men take longer to start urinating, and urinate for a shorter time, when another man is standing at a closer compared to a farther-away urinal (Middlemist, Knowles, & Matter, 1976). These arousal responses are not restricted to approaching humans; Llobera, Spanlang, Ruffini, and Slater (2011) found that people also showed signs of increased physiological arousal the closer they were "approached" by virtual characters.

Once aroused, one needs to label the experienced state as positive (liking, love, or relief) or negative (dislike, embarrassment, stress, or anxiety). If the aroused state is labeled negatively, according to Patterson (1976), the behavior eliciting it will be labeled negatively, and one will take measures to compensate. If someone is aroused by another person's approach and identifies it as undesirable, we could predict behavior designed to restore the proper distance between the interactants: looking away, changing the topic to a less personal one, crossing the arms to form a frontal barrier to the invasion, covering body parts, rubbing the neck to point the elbow sharply toward the invader, and so on.

Russo conducted a 2-year study of invading the territory of female college students seated in a college library (Sommer, 1969). The study compared the responses of those invaded and a similar group that was not invaded. Several different invasion techniques were used: sitting next to these unwitting participants, across from them, and so on. The quickest departure or flight was triggered when the researcher sat next to a participant and moved her chair closer by approximately a foot. Other researchers have suggested that when strangers are involved, males feel more stress from frontal invasions, whereas women react more unfavorably to adjacent invasions (Fisher & Byrne, 1975). After approximately 30 minutes, about 70% of the participants Russo approached at the 1-foot distance moved. From Russo's study, a whole vocabulary of defense was developed. For instance, defensive and offensive displays included the use of position, posture, and gesture. *Position* refers to location in the room; a newcomer to the room will interpret the situation differently if the other person has selected a corner position rather than one in the middle of the room. *Posture* refers to indicators such as whether a person has materials spread out like they owned the space. *Gestures* can be used to indicate receptivity or rejection of communication, for example, hostile glances, turning or leaning away, and blocking with hands or arms. Although verbal defense is not a common first reaction, requests or even profanity can be effectively used. Russo's work is summarized by Sommer (1969):

> There were wide individual differences in the ways victims reacted—there is no single reaction to someone's sitting too close; there are defensive gestures, shifts in posture, and attempts to move away. If these fail or are ignored by the invader, or he shifts position too, the victim eventually takes to flight. [...] There was a dearth of direct verbal responses to the invasions. [...] Only one of the eighty students asked the invader to move over. (pp. 35–36)

It is worth remembering that the norm of politeness may be strong enough to inhibit such direct verbal responses. This demonstrates one important feature of nonverbal communication: It is often off the record and can convey messages subtly without provoking confrontation. The person who glares, shuffles papers, or leans away does not have to acknowledge publicly their irritation. Barash (1973) conducted a study similar to Russo's, but the library invaders' status was manipulated. Students fled more quickly from more formally dressed, "high-status" invaders. Knowles (1973) also experimented with a familiar type of invasion: talking to somebody in a hallway leaving other people to decide whether to walk through the conversants or around them. Only 25% of the people in this study walked through, but when the conversants were replaced with barrels, 75% of the passersby walked through. The fewest intrusions occurred with four-person groups, rather than a pair of people, and "high-status" conversants (i.e., those older and more formally dressed). This study illustrates that, besides not wanting others to violate one's territory, people generally do not want to violate others' territory either, as the mumbled apologies and bowed heads of some of Knowles's invaders testified.

Increasing population density also results in territorial violations. What happens when the population becomes so dense that the usual territorial behavior cannot be exercised?

DENSITY AND CROWDING

During the 1960s, many people were alarmed about the rapidly increasing world population, and books were written that spread alarm at a rapidly rising birth rate and the predicted death of hundreds of millions of people due to overpopulation. The occurrence of urban violence also fueled concern for the effects of population growth. The central question was this: If worldwide population were to increase dramatically, would there be dire consequences? Some highly publicized research with rats seemed to fully support the fear that bad things would happen in highly dense populations (Calhoun, 1962).

Calhoun noted that with plenty of food and no danger from predators, Norway rats in a quarter-acre outdoor pen stabilized their population at about 150. Calhoun's observations, covering 28 months, indicated that spatial relationships are extremely important. He then designed an experiment in which he could maintain a stressful situation through overpopulation while three generations of rats were reared. He labeled this situation a "behavioral sink," an area or receptacle where most of the rats exhibited gross distortions of normal behavior. Some of Calhoun's observations are worth noting:

1. Some rats withdrew from social and sexual intercourse completely; others began to mount anything in sight; and, in general, courtship patterns were disrupted.
2. Nest-building, ordinarily neat, became sloppy or nonexistent.
3. Newborn and young rats were stepped on or eaten by invading hyperactive males.
4. Unable to establish spatial territories, dominant males fought over positions near the eating bins; the hyperactive males violated all territorial rights by running around in packs and disregarding any boundaries except those backed by force.
5. Pregnant rats frequently had miscarriages; disorders of the sex organs were numerous; only a fourth of the 558 newborns in the sink survived to be weaned.
6. Aggressive behavior increased significantly.

Can we generalize from rats to people? Some early studies that found moderate correlations between various socially undesirable outcomes such as crime, delinquency, mental and physical disorders, and high population density seemed to suggest so. Others facetiously contended that the only generalization we could make from Calhoun's work was "Don't crowd rats!" But even this is an overstatement. Judge (2000), who analyzed numerous studies of high density among animal populations, would probably say "Don't crowd rats with aggressive tendencies." In Judge's words,

> The individual characteristics and aggressive tendencies of animals that compose populations can influence aggression more so than increasing population density. Even the results of Calhoun's (1962) influential rat studies were dictated by the unique behavior of a few individuals. The infamous "behavioral sinks" developed when a few dominant adult males established breeding territories in quarter sections of the compartmentalized pens used in the experiments. The remainder of the colony became restricted to single compartments. In colonies in which males did not establish territories or did so in a manner that did not restrict the rest of the colony, no "behavioral sinks" developed (Calhoun, 1962). This outcome of increased density is rarely cited. (p. 144)

More recent studies on rats and different kinds of primates show that animals often do not respond to high density in negative or aggressive ways (Barker, George, Howarth, & Whittaker, 2017; Judge & de Waal, 1993; Judge, Griffaton, & Fincke, 2006; van Wolkenten, Davis, Gong, & de Waal, 2006). Indeed, crowding can even produce a reduction in aggressive behavior. A tension-reduction mechanism has been proposed whereby primates engage in behaviors that offset elevated stress due to close proximity to others, for example grooming other animals or displacement through pacing or self-grooming. In one study, the number of aggressive acts performed by monkeys living in environments of differing densities, from cages to free-ranging activity on an island, was compared (Judge & de Waal, 1997). Aggression was not significantly more prevalent in high-density environments, but coping behavior was. As density increased, the following types of coping behavior also increased: mutual grooming, rapid reconciliation after a fight, and the use of specific facial expressions to indicate the desire to avoid trouble. This tendency to develop ways to cope with high-density life in ways other than aggression is much like the human adaptations reported in the next two sections. Behavioral sinks are not an inevitable result of unchecked population growth.

Stress and aggression among those in high-density situations may also be affected by the amount of space available, the duration of the high-density experience, the ability to enact coping behavior, the extent to which key relationships can be maintained, and other factors. In other words, the widely publicized results of Calhoun's work, which suggested unequivocally harmful consequences of increasing population density, are incorrect. Based on human-density and crowding research conducted thus far, the results are complex and do not lend themselves to a simple "crowding is bad" conclusion.

To understand the effects of population density on human beings, we must first distinguish between the terms *density* and *crowding*. *Density* refers to the number of people per unit of space; *crowding* is a feeling state that may develop in high- or low-density situations. Perceptions of being crowded may be elicited by the following factors:

1. *Environmental factors*, such as reduced space; unwanted noise; the lack of needed resources or the ability to obtain them; and the absence of territorial markers, such as screens and partitions.
2. *Personal factors*, such as personality characteristics reflecting low self-esteem, high dominance, or high need for control; a low desire for social contact; and prior unpleasant experiences with high density.
3. *Social factors*, such as a high frequency of unwanted social contact from many people at close quarters and the inability to change such patterns; inescapable interactions with people from an unfamiliar group; and unpleasant interactions that may be perceived as hostile or competitive. As one example, aggression at night clubs may be due, in part, to interior designs that lead to crowding; specifically, Macintyre and Homel (1997) found that high-risk clubs for aggression had interior designs that resulted in more cross-flow traffic (i.e., people going in two directions) and thus more opportunities for unintended contact (e.g., bumping) between people. In psychiatric hospitals, there is also concern with aggression due to density and crowding (Ulrich, Bogren, Gardiner, & Lundin, 2018). Density per se seems to have no consistent impact on aggression, but design features do, for example not giving persons adequate means to seek privacy or regulate their relationships with others.
4. *Goal-related factors*, such as the inability to accomplish one's tasks.

The central theme characterizing most of the research in this area is that perceptions of crowding tend to increase as a person perceives a decrease in ability to control and influence their physical and social surroundings. Although the factors in the preceding list may contribute to perceptions of crowding, most high-density situations are characterized by some factors that decrease control and some that do not. Given these conditions, what can we say about the effects of high density and human reactions to it?

THE EFFECTS OF HIGH DENSITY ON HUMAN BEINGS

Definitions of density are complex and varied. Correlational studies have used the number of people per city, per census tract, or per dwelling unit; the number of rooms per dwelling unit; the number of buildings per neighborhood; and so on. Experimental studies sometimes put the same-sized group into different-sized rooms; others vary the number of people in the same room. Laboratory studies that vary density to analyze its effects on perceptions of crowding may have relevance only to those situations in which high density is a temporary condition, such as on elevators and buses. Few studies have considered the rate at which high density evolves, or whether participants feel they had any control over the development of a high-density situation. In spite of these variations in measurement, the following conclusions seem warranted.

First, increased density does not automatically increase stress or antisocial behavior in human beings. Sometimes people even seek the pleasures of density (see FIGURE 5-2). Football games and rock concerts are familiar examples. If one takes responsibility for their presence in a highly populated situation, and if they know the condition will terminate in a matter of hours, the chances of negative effects seem to be greatly reduced. The key element here may be the personal sense of control. Nevertheless, negative effects of density do occur. In one study, classroom density decreased girls' academic achievement and negatively affected boys' behavior (Maxwell, 2003). In another study, residential density was positively associated with the likelihood of adolescents being overweight in Nanjing, China (Xu et al., 2010). Other studies have found results—such as aggression, stress, criminal activity, hostility toward others, and a deterioration of mental and physical health—that might fit into a behavioral-sink theory. However, we find other studies in which other environmental factors may offer greater explanatory power or that fail to confirm these highly negative effects altogether. With regard to adolescents, it may be that their proximity to crime contributes more to their substance abuse problems than does the population density of their neighborhoods (Mason & Mennis, 2010). When negative outcomes are not found, the explanation usually lies in the fact that the environmental, personal, social, and goal-related factors mentioned earlier could provide a form of control that was influential in offsetting undesirable influences. Some high-density neighborhoods that are highly cohesive actually have a lower incidence of mental and physical health problems.

Second, sometimes high density is blamed for undesirable effects, either because it is an obvious feature of the situation and has a reputation for causing problems, or because the real causes are things people do not wish to face.

FIGURE 5-2 A high-density beach.

High density can produce a host of problems, but human beings do not stand by passively in situations that demand a long-term commitment to high density; instead, they try various methods to cope with or offset potentially harmful effects. What are some of the methods of coping?

COPING WITH HIGH DENSITY

City dwellers are often exposed to an overload of information, people, things, problems, and so forth. As a result, they engage in behavior designed to reduce this overload, which sometimes causes outsiders to see them as distant and emotionally detached from others. Here are some of the methods for coping in populated cities:

1. Spending less time with each input, for example, having shorter conversations with people
2. Disregarding low-priority inputs, for example, ignoring the intoxicated person on the sidewalk or not talking to people seen on a commuter train every day
3. Shifting the responsibility for some transactions to others, for example, relieving bus drivers of the responsibility for making change
4. Blocking inputs, for example, using attendants to guard apartment buildings

Nigerian students used nine different strategies to cope with high-density conditions in their residence halls (Amole, 2005). Strategies used to clearly define personal territory and studying in less dense locations were two of the most common. Evans and colleagues (2010) showed in both the United States and UK that the link between household crowding, measured as the number of people per room, and children's lack of readiness for school may be due, in part, to a reduction in maternal responsiveness.

Evans, Lepore, and Allen (2000) undertook an international study to test the belief that cultures vary in their tolerance for being crowded. They made the important distinction between perception of crowding and tolerance for it. As they concluded,

> Consistent with proxemic and collectivist theory, we found that Mexican Americans and Vietnamese Americans perceive crowding differently than do Anglo-Americans and African Americans. Members of high-contact, collectivist cultural groups perceive their homes as less crowded. (p. 208)

On the other hand, the authors found that the stereotype that people of Asian or Latin descent can better withstand or tolerate the adverse psychological consequences of crowding was not substantiated. In their research, Anglo-Americans, African Americans, Vietnamese Americans, and Mexican Americans did not differ in psychological distress as a function of residential density.

Now let us shift our attention from spatial relationships in overpopulated conditions to those involved in a two-person conversation.

CONVERSATIONAL DISTANCE

Children are exposed to gradually increasing distances for various communication situations. The first few years of life provide a familiarity with what is known as *intimate distance;* the child then learns appropriate conversational distances for an increasing number of acquaintances and friends; and by about age 7, the child may have incorporated the concept of public distance into their behavioral repertoire. So by about the third grade, children have learned that conversational distance has meaning. As they age, children will gradually reflect adult norms for their culture as they make spatial adjustments for interactants who are known or unknown, tall or short, higher status or lower status, and so on. What are these adult norms? What are comfortable conversational distances? (see FIGURE 5-3).

To answer these questions, first we turn to the astute observations about human spatial behavior made by anthropologist Edward T. Hall (1959, 1966). Hall identified several types of space, but our concern here is with what he called *informal space*. Others have referred to this as *personal space*, but because the space between people is the result of negotiating their personal preferences, it is more appropriately labeled *interpersonal space*. The study of personal space is often called the study of *proxemics* and we will use that term as well. The informal space for each individual expands and contracts under varying circumstances, depending on the type of encounter, the relationship of the communicating persons, their personalities, and many other factors. Hall identified four types of informal space: (1)

intimate, (2) casual–personal, (3) social–consultative, and (4) public. According to Hall, *intimate* distances range from actual physical contact to about 18 inches; *casual–personal* extends from 1.5 to 4 feet; *social–consultative*, for impersonal business, ranges from 4 to 12 feet; and *public* distance covers the area from 12 feet to the limits of visibility or hearing. Hall was quick to note that these distances are based on his observations of a particular sample of adults from business and professional occupations, primarily White middle-class males native to the northeastern United States, and any generalization to other demographic groups in the United States should be made with caution.

Sommer (1961) also sought answers to questions about comfortable conversational distance. He studied people who were brought into a room and told to discuss various impersonal topics. Two sofas were placed in the room at various distances, and participants were observed to see whether they sat opposite or beside each other. It was hypothesized that when they began to sit side by side, it would mean the conversational distance was too far to sit opposite each other on the two couches. From 1 to 3 feet, the participants sat on different couches facing each other. Beyond 3.5 feet, people sat side by side. If we measure distance "nose to nose," this would make the participants 5.5 feet apart when they started to sit side by side, assuming they were not leaning forward or backward. In a follow-up study, Sommer used chairs, which allowed him to vary side-by-side distance as well as the distance across. Here he found that people chose to sit across from each other until the distance across exceeded the side-by-side distance; they then sat side by side.

How generalizable are these findings? A critical look at this study immediately leads us to question what other variables may affect the distance relationship. For instance, this study was conducted with people who knew each other slightly, were discussing impersonal topics, and were in a large lounge. How would other factors affect the distance relationship? For a long time, researchers have theorized that distance is based on the balance of

FIGURE 5-3 Variations in conversational distance and position.

DO YOU WALK THIS WAY?

Walking is another area in which interpersonal distance and spatial arrangement have been investigated. In a naturalistic study, Costa (2010) filmed people as they walked by a designated area in one of two Italian cities. He examined the alignment (i.e., the degree to which people were walking side by side), spatial arrangement (i.e., how people were positioned in relation to one another), and walking speed of people as a function of the size (two to five people) and gender composition of the group (only males, only females, mixed gender). The findings for alignment and spatial arrangement follow:

- Mixed-gender dyads were the most aligned (e.g., when looking at the two people from the side, the horizontal distance between their heads was the shortest). Male–male dyads were the most out of alignment. And female–female dyads were somewhere in between.
- In mixed-gender dyads, males were more likely than females to be the person walking ahead of the other.
- The spatial arrangement found in triads, from the most to the least likely, was as follows: (1) The two side people were walking aligned and ahead of the middle person; (2) all three were out of alignment with the middle person behind one person on one side and ahead of the other person on the other side; (3) the two people on the sides were walking in alignment behind the middle person; and (4) all three people were walking in alignment.

approach and avoidance forces. What are some of these forces? Burgoon (1978) and Burgoon and Jones (1976) said that the distances used in a given conversation are a function of cultural and personal expectations for appropriate distances. When someone violates these expectations, it attracts attention. Sometimes the violation is so immediately aversive that one flees or becomes very defensive. On other occasions, one will mentally process the nature of the violation and the violator to determine a response. The violation of personal space may be judged to be more positive or more negative than the expected behavior, after which one adapts accordingly. When the positive or negative nature of the violation is not clear, one assesses their perceptions of the violator. A positive evaluation of the violator should lead to a positive evaluation of the space violation and vice versa. What are some of these expectations for conversational distance, and how do they develop? What factors lead to certain conversational distances?

Answering these questions is the focus for the remainder of this chapter. Again, however, we must sort through conflicting results due to variations in research methodology and conceptualization of personal space. Logically, we know that conversational distance is the product of both interactants' negotiations. But some research is based on the behavior of a single person; some research does not distinguish between actual physical distance and perceptions of distance; some research measures distance by floor tiles or space between chair legs and totally ignores the ability of the communicators to vary the "psychological distance" by changes in topic, eye gaze, and body angle; and most research does not distinguish between initial distance and changes that take place over the course of a conversation. Because the methods of measuring personal space vary, we even have to be cautious about results that agree with other studies. Sometimes people complete questionnaires about preferred distances; sometimes they are asked to approach nonhuman objects, such as coat racks and life-sized photographs; sometimes people are unknowingly approached at various distances by others; and sometimes they are asked to arrange miniature dolls, photographs, or silhouettes as if they were in various communication situations. With these factors in mind, we selected the following important sources of variation in conversational distance.

GENDER

Many studies have looked at gender differences in interpersonal space using all the methodologies listed earlier (Hall, 1984). In naturalistic interaction, settings in which people are interacting more or less naturally and are not aware of being observed, females predominantly choose to interact with others of either gender more closely than males do, as long as the conversations are neutral or friendly. When the conversations are threatening or alienating, females assume a greater conversational distance (Bell, Kline, & Barnard, 1988).

Another way of understanding gender differences in interpersonal distance is to examine how the *other* person's gender influences the distance between people. The research shows convincingly that people approach females closer

MANSPREADING

©Terrence Horgan

If the second image made you do a double take, then you are aware of the double standard regarding how men and women are permitted to position their legs when they are seated. Relative to women, men are allowed to relax their legs more by spreading them. This practice of manspreading results in men taking up more space than women and even intruding upon the space of others at times.

than they approach males, and this remains true no matter what kind of methodology is used. When the effects for one's own gender and those for the other's gender are combined, they show that female–female pairs interact most closely, male–male pairs interact most distantly, and mixed-gender pairs set intermediate distances. This pattern shows up frequently in research, especially in Anglo-American samples.

Several theories have been put forth to explain these gender differences in conversational distances. One popular notion is rooted in the different amounts of space children experience. It has been noted, for example, that the same stimuli may cause parents to put male infants on the floor or in a playpen but to hug the females or put them in a nearby high chair. Boys are frequently given toys (e.g., cars, trains) or balls (e.g., a football) that seem to encourage activities demanding more space, often away from the confines of the home itself. Girls, in contrast, may receive dolls, dollhouses, and other toys that require less space. Some observational studies have confirmed that young boys at play utilize more space than young girls.

One hypothesis is that women choose a closer interaction distance because people with less status in society are accorded less space and women have internalized this expectation. Focusing instead on socioemotional factors, another hypothesis is that women are more socially oriented than males, so they should prefer distances that connote and promote warmth, trust, and friendship, as closer distances do in neutral or friendly interactions. Eagly (1987), arguing in this vein, invoked the more person-oriented and prosocial roles that women play in society, which produce various kinds of behavior, including interaction distances consistent with such roles. Another contributing factor could simply be height (Hall, 1984; Pazhoohi et al., 2018): because people generally interact with larger interpersonal distances from tall people (and people taller than themselves), the height difference between women and men could account partly for the gender difference in preferred distances. Height is also relevant to the age differences discussed next.

AGE

If distance reflects general comfort with a person, it seems reasonable to predict that people would interact more closely to people in their own general age range. The exceptions, of course, are the very old and very young who, for various reasons, often elicit interaction at closer quarters from adults. Generally, interaction distance seems to expand gradually from about age 6 to early adolescence, when adult norms become established in parallel with the attainment of near-adult height (Aiello & Aiello, 1974). Adults are also more likely to hold older children responsible for understanding adult norms. When 5-year-olds invaded the personal space of people waiting in line to see a movie, they were received positively; but when 10-year-olds were the invaders, they were met with negative responses (Fry & Willis, 1971). Obviously, these reactions are modified by the communicative context, but these studies do suggest that adults expect the norms for conversational distance to be learned before the child is 10.

CULTURAL AND ETHNIC BACKGROUND

Volumes of folklore and isolated personal observations suggest that spatial relationships in other cultures with different needs and norms may produce very different distances for interacting.

Infants reared in different cultures learn different proxemic patterns. A group of Japanese mothers spent more time in close contact with their infants than a comparable group of mothers in the United States. Mother, father, and infant in Japan often sleep in the same room. In the Nyansongo culture of Kenya, infants are always in close proximity to a family member, and the infant sleeps in the mother's arms at night (Caudill & Weinstein, 1972). It is not hard to see how such patterns provide a different sense of distance when compared to the patterns of children who are put into a separate room to sleep several times during the day as well as at night.

Edward T. Hall (1966) used the terms *contact* and *noncontact* to distinguish the behavior of people from different cultural groups. Compared to noncontact cultures, interactants in contact cultures are expected to face one another more directly, interact more closely with one another, touch one another more, look one another in the eye more, and speak in a louder voice. These general predictions have been borne out over years of research, for example by Watson (1970), where the contact cultures were Arabs, Latin Americans, and southern Europeans and the noncontact cultures were Asians, Indians, Pakistanis, northern Europeans, and people living in the United States. Beaulieu (2004) conducted an observational study of people from 11 countries who entered a room for an interview and could position their chair anywhere they wanted vis-à-vis the interviewer. In order from greatest to least distance were people from the United States, UK, and English-speaking Canada; people from China, Japan, and Thailand; those from Austria, France, Netherlands, and French-speaking Canada; and finally those from Brazil and Italy (together called "Latino"). Furthermore, the Latino interviewees uniformly sat directly facing the interviewer while the other groups chose to sit at an angle to the interviewer.

It is important to remember that these broad cultural norms may or may not manifest themselves in any particular conversation within a culture (Remland, Jones, & Brinkman, 1991) and furthermore that broad geographic categories like "Asian" obscure important cultural differences between and within countries in the region. Whether interactants know each other, whether the interaction has positive or negative affect, whether they are talking to a person of their same gender, and a host of other factors may offset these broad cultural tendencies, as is clearly evident from Sorokowska et al.'s (2017) questionnaire study of nearly 9,000 adults in 42 countries. Those authors did not group countries into contact and noncontact, but it is clear from their results that no simple grouping is possible. For example, although respondents from Peru and Argentina preferred the closest distances and Asian countries preferred larger distances than many other countries, there were differences among Asian countries, and some countries in close geographical proximity in Eastern Europe showed dramatically different spatial preferences.

Shuter's (1976, 1977) systematic field observations in contact and noncontact cultures revealed early on that somewhat different proxemic norms may apply for groups within the larger culture. He found, for instance, significant differences within the so-called Latin American cultural group. Costa Ricans interacted more closely than did Panamanians or Colombians. And contrary to predictions, he found no significant differences in interaction distance and touching for women in Milwaukee, Wisconsin, and Venice, Italy. Italian men did not manifest closer interaction positions or face their interaction partners more directly than German men, but they did engage in more touching.

Variations in proxemic patterns in the United States have been the subject of several research projects. For example, the question of whether Black Americans interact at closer distances than White Americans has been studied. Developmental studies show that when entering elementary school, Black children may exhibit closer interaction distances than White children, but by the fifth grade, these differences are minimized; and by age 16, Black Americans tend to maintain greater conversational distances (Aiello & Thompson, 1980; Halberstadt, 1985). Obviously, the racial composition of the schools and the socioeconomic class of the students will also play an important role in determining comfortable interaction distances. Most studies reveal that interactions involving Black and White communicators occur at greater distances than those involving persons of the same race.

Another large cultural group in the United States, Hispanic Americans, has also been observed. These studies generally support the prediction that Hispanic Americans interact at closer distances than do Anglo Americans. Scherer (1974) contended that any differences between Black and White people, and presumably also Hispanic Americans, may be confounded by socioeconomic factors not attributable to ethnic background. This study found that middle-class children maintained greater conversational distance than economically disadvantaged children, but there were no differences between middle-class Blacks and Whites or economically disadvantaged Blacks and Whites. Because proxemic norms are learned, it is reasonable to assume that people who grow up in the same neighborhood—no matter what their skin color or ethnic heritage—will share more expectations for comfortable conversational distance than those raised in different parts of a city, state, or country.

TOPIC OR SUBJECT MATTER

Erickson (1975) wanted to find out if proxemic shifts forward or backward were associated with specific events in a conversation. By coding co-occurring behavior, he determined that proxemic shifts may mark important segments of the encounter, such as beginnings, endings, and topic changes.

In an effort to examine the limits of conversational distance, Sommer tried to use impersonal topics that would presumably not influence the distances chosen. For intimates, personal topics may demand less conversational distance unless other factors, such as an impersonal setting, neutralize such inclinations. Leipold's (1963) work demonstrates how anticipated treatment of the same general topic can influence conversational distance. Students entered a room and were given either a negative comment ("Your grade is poor, and you have not done your best"); praise ("You are doing very well, and Mr. Leipold wants to talk to you further"); or a neutral comment ("Mr. Leipold is interested in your feelings about the introductory course"). Students given the negative comment sat farthest from the experimenter; those who were praised sat closest. Following insults, people may want to assume a greater distance than they normally would with that person, particularly if the person giving the insult is perceived as a higher status person (O'Neal, Brunalt, Carifio, Troutwine, & Epstein, 1980). Using a creative design, Vagnoni, Lewis, Tajadura-Jiménez, and Cardini (2018) showed the same desire to distance oneself when a negative (in this case aggressive) scenario was witnessed. Those researchers recorded actors having a neutral versus aggressive interaction, and then merged the voices with the sound of approaching footsteps to create the auditory impression that the conversants were getting closer. Participants listened to the interactions and indicated when they started to feel uncomfortable. Discomfort started sooner when the conversants were having the angry conversation.

SETTING FOR THE INTERACTION

Obviously, the social setting makes a great deal of difference in how far people stand from others in conversation. A crowded cocktail party demands a different distance than a comfortable evening in the living room with a spouse or significant other. Lighting, temperature, noise, and available space affect interaction distance. Some authors have hypothesized that as room size increases, people tend to sit closer together. Noisy urban street locations outside an office building may prompt people to stand closer to one another than they do when conversing inside the building. And if the setting is perceived as formal or unfamiliar, we would predict greater distances from unknown others and closer distances to known others.

PHYSICAL CHARACTERISTICS

Height seems to make a difference in the distance people select for interacting. Irrespective of gender, shorter individuals seem to invite smaller interpersonal distances than taller individuals (Caplan & Goldman, 1981). When the two communicators are vastly different in height, the distance has to be adjusted so that faces can be seen. Evidence also indicates that obese people are accorded greater interaction distances (Lerner, Venning, & Knapp, 1975).

Studies by Kleck (1969) and Kleck and Strenta (1985) showed that people interacting with stigmatized individuals (a left-leg amputation was simulated with a special wheelchair) choose greater initial speaking distances than with nonstigmatized persons but that this distance decreases as the length of the interaction increases. Similar results have been found for people perceived to have epilepsy and people with facial disfigurations such as scars and port-wine stains. Kleck points out that when people with physical disabilities expect others to behave in a distant manner, they may prepare themselves for such reactions and thereby increase the chances it will happen.

This is a good place to remind the reader that nonverbal behaviors typically do not have fixed meanings, but rather depend on context. For example, standing farther away from someone could reflect very diverse intentions and emotional states, including antagonism, repulsion, uncertainty, anxiety, fear, intimidation, respect, or deference.

ATTITUDINAL AND EMOTIONAL ORIENTATION

Some experiments have been conducted by telling a person that they were going to interact with a person who was either "warm and friendly" or "unfriendly." Not surprisingly, greater distances were chosen when interacting with a person perceived to be unfriendly. Similarly, when told to enter into conversation with another person and to behave in a friendly way, people chose closer distances than when told to "let him/her know you aren't friendly." This friendly/unfriendly relationship to distance seems to manifest itself even with preschool children (King, 1966). In some instances, anger will cause a person to withdraw from others, but if a person seeks retaliation, interpersonal distance may shrink (Meisels & Dosey, 1971).

Variations in emotional states, such as depression, fatigue, excitement, or joy, can sometimes make vast differences in how close or far away people want to be from others. The traumatic experiences of abused children probably explain why they assumed significantly greater conversational distances than their nonabused peers in one study (Vranic, 2003). This was true for males and females and was exacerbated by frontal approaches by males. A study reported by Patterson (1968) indicates that a variety of interpersonal judgments are made about others based on distance. People were told to interview others and secretly rate them on traits of friendliness, aggressiveness, dominance, extraversion, and intelligence. The interviewees were actually confederates who approached the interviewers at different distances and gave standard answers to the questions asked. The mean ratings for all the traits at four different distances were tabulated, revealing that the most distant position yielded significantly lower, less favorable ratings. So barring any contradictory information, people choosing closer distances are often seen as warmer, more likeable, more empathic, and more understanding. When seeking to win another's approval, conversational distance is reduced as opposed to instances when approval is not desired. Females seeking approval maintained a mean distance of 57 inches; those trying to avoid approval averaged 94 inches. When the distance was held constant at 5 feet, approval-seekers compensated by smiling more and engaging in more gestural activity (Rosenfeld, 1965, 1966).

CHARACTERISTICS OF THE INTERPERSONAL RELATIONSHIP

A number of studies also show that conversational distance varies as a function of the relationship with the other person. Strangers begin conversations at a greater distance than acquaintances, and acquaintances are a bit more distant than friends. In a study of 108 married couples, husbands were asked to walk toward their wives and stop when they got to a comfortable conversational distance. The more dissatisfied the husbands were with their marriage, the greater the distance they chose (Crane, Dollahite, Griffin, & Taylor, 1987). Preschoolers seem to be able to use distance as a criterion for determining liking or disliking. Like adults, children seem to maintain greater distances with unknown adults, unfriendly or threatening persons, teachers, and those with a heavyset body type.

Reversing cause and effect, Shin et al. (2019) arranged for a female confederate to sit closer or farther from a male participant and obtained the male's ratings of how much he liked her. Single men but not men already in a relationship liked her more when she was close.

These and other studies suggest that closer relationships are likely to be associated with closer interaction distances. Obviously, there is a point at which we would not expect interactants to get any closer, no matter how close their relationship (at least in public). And even people who are very close will not always interact at close distances due to the ebb and flow of their relationship.

PERSONALITY CHARACTERISTICS

Much has been written about the influence of introversion and extraversion on spatial relationships. The bulk of the evidence seems to indicate that introverts tend to stand farther away than extraverts and to generally prefer greater interpersonal distances. Other studies suggest that anxiety-prone individuals maintain greater distances, while closer distances are seen when people have a high self-concept and affiliative needs or when they are low on authoritarianism or high on interdependence. People with various personality abnormalities can probably be counted on to show greater nonnormative spatial behavior, choosing interactive distances both too far away and too close.

Typically, the origins of individual differences, whether in personality or behavior, are hard to pin down. Most research is simply correlational and furthermore causation is a multistage process wherein one "cause" may be the consequence of a yet earlier "cause," and so forth. Nevertheless, in the case of individual differences in interpersonal distance preferences, Perry, Nichiporuk, and Knight (2016) have proposed a biological factor, possibly not learned, as a source of interpersonal distance preferences. The variable they suggest is called *sensory sensitivity*, defined as a hyperreactivity (the experience of overload) to stimuli such as touch, sound, and light. Perry and colleagues showed that those with such hypersensitivity chose greater interpersonal distances when approaching, or being approached by, another person in the laboratory.

In addition to studying human spatial behavior in high-density situations and in conversation, some researchers have examined such questions in the context of small groups, particularly in regard to seating patterns.

SEATING BEHAVIOR AND SPATIAL ARRANGEMENTS IN SMALL GROUPS

The significance of psychological and cultural factors in seating arrangements is illustrated by the fact that, at the end of the Vietnam War, it took a full 8 months for the negotiators to agree on the shape of the table to be used by the various parties at the Paris Peace Talks of 1968 (McCroskey, Larson, & Knapp, 1971).

Not all seating decisions are as fraught as those were, but people clearly have preferences based on many factors. People will select a place to sit on a long-term basis, such as returning to the same seat again and again in a course they are taking in college or having a general preference for a part of a college classroom. Hemyari et al. (2013), in observing medical students in a large classroom, found that 82% closely maintained their seating position over a semester even though they were free to sit anywhere and the room was not crowded. College students experience greater feelings of comfort, confidence, and being in control when they are able to return to a preferred seat or area (Avni-Babad, 2011). Reasons for these seating choices are hard to determine in naturalistic observation studies, but correlations are documented. Students who sit in front and central sections generally perform better, but the chicken-and-egg nature of this correlation is obvious.

Interest in seating arrangements extends beyond the academic world to real-world settings, including medicine, business, and education (Li & Robertson, 2011; Robson, Kimes, Becker, & Evans, 2011; van den Berg, Segers, & Cillessen, 2012). For example, owners of restaurants probably do not want their patrons to sit at tables that are too close to other tables when they know that these people want to have a romantic night out (Robson et al., 2011). On the other hand, educators might consider having grade-school children who do not get along sit closer to each other in the classroom, as this may promote liking and lead to fewer problems related to victimization (van den Berg et al., 2012).

The specific body of work dealing with seating behavior and spatial arrangements in small groups is known as *small group ecology*. What is clear from this research is that seating behavior is not generally accidental or random. Explanations for why people select a particular seat in relation to the other person or persons vary according to the task at hand, the degree of relationship between the interactants, the personalities of the two parties, and the amount and kind of space available. We summarize some of these in the following sections.

LEADERSHIP AND STATUS

It seems to be a norm, in the United States at least, that leaders are expected to be found at the head or foot of the table. In households, whoever is considered the head of the household is likely to be found sitting at one end of a rectangular dinner table. Elected group leaders generally put themselves in the head positions at rectangular tables, and the other group members try to position themselves so they can see the leader. In mock jury deliberations, a man seated on the end position is more likely to be chosen as the leader. The reaction to women who are positioned at the head of a table of men and women has been less consistently linked to the leadership role (Porter & Geis, 1981), although this phenomenon like many others may change as societal norms and values change. In that research, as long as the group consisted of all women, the one at the head of the table was perceived as the leader. With the continuing growth of women in positions of leadership in business and government, we hope women seated at the end position in groups of men and women to be chosen as the leader, too. The study of Jackson, Engstrom, and Emmers-Sommer (2007) suggests not a lot of progress has been made, however. When shown diagrams of six persons at a table with a man at one end and a woman at the other, participants tended to choose their own gender as the leader, with this same-gender bias being much stronger for men than for women: 94% of the male participants chose the man, while only 64% of the female participants chose the woman, meaning that a substantial minority of women still chose the man.

Howells and Becker (1962) added further support to the idea that a person's position in a group is an important factor in leadership emergence. They reasoned that spatial position determines the flow of communication, which, in turn, determines leadership emergence. Five-person decision-making groups were examined: Three people sat on one side of a rectangular table, and two sat on the other side. Because previous work suggested that communication usually flows across the table rather than around it, the researchers predicted that the side with two people would be able to influence the most people, or at least talk more, and therefore emerge more often as group leaders. This hypothesis was confirmed.

An experiment by Ward (1968) helps unravel how seating position can create leaders. College males were assigned at random to sit in particular seats at a round table. The experimenters arranged it so that more people were seated around one half of the table than the other; only two people sat at the less populated end, and these two seats were considered visually central because their occupants would receive more undivided gaze from people at the other, more densely occupied end. As predicted, occupants of these visually central seats received higher ratings of leadership after discussions had taken place. But were they really leaders or just perceived to be? Other research (Taylor & Fiske, 1975) does indicate that the person on whom attention is centered will appear to be an initiator and a person causally responsible for the course of the conversation. But in Ward's study, evidence indicated that those who were visually central also behaved differently: They talked more. It would be interesting to unravel further the complex routes by which seating position might affect leadership. For example, does the visually central person think, "I'm in a central position; I'd better start acting like a leader"? Or do the attention and subtle cues of the other members of the group trigger leadership behaviors, perhaps without the visually central person even realizing it? Probably both of these processes are at work.

People seem well aware of the different perceptions and communicative potentials associated with different seating positions. When people were asked to select seats to convey different impressions, they chose end positions to convey leadership or dominance; positions with the closest distances to convey interpersonal attraction; and seats that afforded the greatest interpersonal distance, and the least visual accessibility vis-à-vis the end positions, to indicate they did not wish to participate (Reiss & Rosenfeld, 1980).

Russo (1967) found that people rating various seating arrangements on an "equality" dimension stated that one person seated at the head and one on the side indicated more unequal status than if they were seated side by side or both on the ends. In an analysis of talking frequency in small groups, Hare and Bales (1963) noted that people in positions 1, 3, and 5 (see drawing) were frequent talkers. Subsequent studies revealed that these people were likely to be dominant personalities, whereas those who avoided the central or focal positions by choosing seats 2 and 4 were more anxious and actually stated they wanted to stay out of the discussion. Positions 1, 3, and 5 also were considered positions of leadership but leadership of different types, depending on the position. The two end positions, positions 1 and 5, attracted *task-oriented leaders*, whereas the middle positions attracted *socioemotional leaders*, those concerned about group relationships and getting everyone to participate.

TASK

Seating preferences of students and nonstudents engaged in different tasks have been studied (Cook, 1970; Sommer, 1969). In each case, people were asked to imagine sitting at a table with a same-gender friend in each of the following four situations:

1. *Conversation.* Sitting and chatting for a few minutes before class, or before work for nonstudents
2. *Cooperation.* Sitting and studying together for the same exam, or sitting doing a crossword together, or some similar activity for nonstudents
3. *Coaction.* Sitting studying for different exams, or sitting at the same table reading for nonstudents
4. *Competition.* Competing to see who will be the first to solve a series of puzzles

Each person was shown a round table and a rectangular table. Each table had six chairs. The combined results for all the groups surveyed in these two studies are presented in Table 5-1 for rectangular tables and Table 5-2 for circular tables.

There were many similarities among the different groups concerning their order of preference. Conversations before class or work involved primarily corner or "short" opposite seating at rectangular tables and side-by-side seating at round tables. Cooperation seems to elicit a preponderance of side-by-side choices. Coaction—that is, studying for different exams or reading at the same table—necessitated plenty of room between the participants, and the most distant seating positions were generally selected. Most participants wanted to compete in an opposite seating arrangement. However, some students wanted to establish a closer opposite relationship; apparently this would afford them an opportunity to see how the other person was progressing and would also allow them to use various gestures, body movements, and eye contact to upset their opponents. The more distant opposite position would presumably prevent spying.

Table 5-1 Seating Preferences At Rectangular Tables

	X X ▭	X ▭ X	X X ▭	X ▭ X	X ▭ X	X ▭ X
Conversation	45%	36%	12%	1%	4%	2%
Cooperation	23%	13%	42%	8%	10%	4%
Coaction	8%	8%	10%	21%	34%	19%
Competition	6%	22%	7%	40%	19%	6%

Source: From Cook, M. (1970). Experiments in orientation and proxemics. *Human Relations, 23,* 61–76. Copyright © 1970, The Tavistock Institute. Reprinted by permission of Sage Publications.

Table 5-2 Seating Preferences at Round Tables

	X X ◯	X ◯	X ◯ X
Conversation	60%	27%	13%
Cooperation	68%	13%	19%
Coaction	18%	32%	50%
Competition	12%	23%	65%

Source: From Cook, M. (1970). Experiments in orientation and proxemics. *Human Relations, 23,* 61–76. Copyright © 1970, The Tavistock Institute. Reprinted by permission of Sage Publications.

PERSONALITY AND PHYSICAL CHARACTERISTICS

Extraverts are likely to choose to sit opposite of others, either across the table or down the length of it, and disregard positions that would put them at an angle to another person. Extraverts may also choose positions that would put them in close physical proximity to another person. Introverts generally choose positions that would keep them more at a distance, visually and physically, from others. This was found as well in Hemyari et al.'s (2013) study of medical students, where the more introverted students gravitated to the back of the classroom. That study found other personality correlates as well. Students in the front were less agreeable, and got better grades; students low in conscientiousness tended to sit in back and on the aisles; and those higher in openness to experience sat in the back (and had more absences).

Physical similarity is another factor influencing seating choice. Mackinnon, Jordan, and Wilson (2011) observed college students in a computer laboratory, noting whether the students wore glasses or not, and their gender, in relation to where they chose to sit. Students with glasses chose to sit near another with glasses, and students without glasses chose to sit near another without glasses, at a statistically significant rate. Also there was gender homophily: people sat near someone of their own gender. In their second study, on lecture classes, there was again the gender and eyeglasses similarity effect, as well as for race and hair length; and in a third study (a controlled experiment), similarity in physical attractiveness contributed to seating distance to a confederate. Thus, several aspects of physical similarity predict whether someone will want to sit next to another person.

SUMMARY

Perceptions and use of space contribute extensively to various communication outcomes. Some spatial behavior is related to a need to stake out and maintain territory, and territorial behavior can be helpful in regulating social interaction and controlling density; it can also be the source of conflict when territory is disputed or encroached upon without permission. We identified three different types of territories—*primary*, *secondary*, and *public*—and several different levels at which territorial behavior exists: *individual*, *group*, *community*, and *nation*. Although people may vigorously defend their territory, the type of defense depends very much on who the intruder is, why the intrusion is taking place, what type of territory is being intruded upon, what type of intrusion occurs—*violation*, *invasion*, or *contamination*—how long the intrusion takes, and where it occurs. People often try to prevent others from moving into their territory by marking it as "theirs." This can be achieved by physical presence, the presence of a friend or even a stranger who agrees to watch one's territory, or by using markers—fences, coats, and the like. When someone does invade another person's territory, the invadee's physiological arousal increases, and various defensive maneuvers may be used, such as flight, hostile looks, turning or leaning away, blocking advances with objects or hands and arms, and verbal behavior. Just as people do not like others to invade their territory, they are also reluctant to invade the territory of others, often apologizing when it cannot be prevented.

We examined density and crowding in both animal and human interaction. Some animal studies showed undesirable effects from overpopulation. High-density human situations, however, are not always disruptive; sometimes people *want* the company of many people. The best predictor of individually stressful and socially undesirable outcomes seems to be the number of people per room rather than other density measures. When people do feel the stress of a crowded situation, they seek ways to cope with it. We also distinguished between density, or the number of people per unit of space, and crowding, a feeling brought on by environmental, personal, or social factors.

Our examination of spatial behavior in conversations revealed many ways of conceptualizing and measuring this behavior. As a result, some generalizations about conversational space remain tentative. We do know that each person seeks a comfortable conversational distance that varies depending on age, gender, cultural and ethnic background, setting, attitudes, emotions, topics, physical characteristics, personality, and the relationship with the other person.

Finally, we discussed seating arrangements in small groups. Distances and seats chosen do not seem to be accidental. Leaders and dominant personalities tend to choose specific seats, but seating position also can determine a person's role in a group. Seating also varies with the topic at hand, the nature of the relationships among the parties, and certain personality and physical variables.

QUESTIONS FOR DISCUSSION

1. Identify a secondary territory you have experienced in which ownership was disputed. Discuss what happened, why it happened, and how the conflict could have been prevented.

2. What factors are likely to cause a person who comes to the United States from another culture, with different norms for conversational space, to maintain the norms from their culture of origin? What factors are likely to cause an immigrant to manifest conversational space that is more typical of the United States?

3. When is someone's purse likely to be perceived as a primary territory? When can it become a secondary territory?

4. Do you think the findings associated with leadership, dominance, and seating behavior apply to females as well as males? Why or why not?

5. The next time you are walking with two other people, note the spatial arrangement of the group. Does this pattern change when the age, status, or gender composition of the group changes?

6. What happens when somebody invades your territory? For instance, how do you feel when the car behind you is tailgating? When you have to stand in an overpopulated theater lobby or bus? When somebody sits in "*your*" seat? What do you do?

NONVERBAL COMMUNICATION IN ACTION: TRY THIS

Do your own "invasion study": First choose a place in public or on campus that is safe for the following intervention. This might be a library reading room or a campus cafeteria; be sure there is ample choice of seats. Then, seat yourself next to someone or across from them (depending on the arrangement of furniture) at a distance or in a position that you think will be perceived by that person as "too" close given the context. Be sure your seat choice is not so inappropriate that the person will be angered or frightened. Go about your business (reading, eating, etc.) while noticing the behavior of the other person. Do they emit nonverbal or verbal responses? Do they move their possessions to expand "their" space? Do they get up and leave? Take careful notes. If someone gets angry at you, explain the nature of your study to them right away.

PART III

THE COMMUNICATORS

People's nonverbal behavior is typically marked by change, for example, during a conversation when people are constantly expressing themselves and adapting to each other. But some of these nonverbal signals remain relatively unchanged during the course of the interaction. These are the individual features of each communicator: skin color, hairstyle, facial features, height, weight, clothes, and so on. These features affect others' perceptions and how they communicate.

CHAPTER 6

THE EFFECTS OF PHYSICAL CHARACTERISTICS ON HUMAN COMMUNICATION

By a man's finger-nails, by his coat-sleeve, by his boots, by his trouser-knees, by the callosities of his forefinger and thumb, by his expression, by his shirt-cuffs—by each of these things a man's calling is plainly revealed. That all united should fail to enlighten the competent inquirer in any case is almost unconceivable.

—**Sherlock Holmes**

Picture the following stereotyped scene: Mr. and Mrs. America wake and prepare to start the day. The Mrs. takes off her sleep bra and replaces it with a slightly padded uplift bra. While she lets her teeth-whitening strips work their magic, she puts on her tummy-flattening undergarment and begins to "put on her face." This may involve foundation, eyeliner, eye shadow, false eyelashes, mascara, lipstick, and blush. She has removed the hair under her arms and on her legs. She takes a curling iron to her hair. False fingernails, nail polish, and tinted contact lenses precede the deodorant, perfume, and numerous decisions concerning clothes. The Mr. shaves the hair on his face and, if he is an older man, might put a hairpiece on his head and remove his false teeth from a solution used to whiten them. He then gargles with a breath sweetener, selects his aftershave lotion, and begins making his clothing decisions.

This is an extreme hypothetical example, of course. Nevertheless, people do go to great lengths to make themselves attractive. And it is not just an American obsession. Venezuela, a country that has won more international beauty contests than any other country, at one point was spending more than a billion dollars each year on cosmetic products, and some teenage girls get a breast enlargement as a coming-of-age present when they are 15 years old (Pearson, 2006). South Korea boasts the highest rate of cosmetic surgeries in the world, most in the service of beauty standards (*Huff Post*, 2019).

Surgery to enhance physical attractiveness is increasing. Plastic surgeons can reconstruct a nose; change breast size; eliminate bags, wrinkles, or birthmarks; flatten ears; "tuck" thighs or tummies; vacuum fat from the body by liposuction, or insert fat by lipofilling; or even remove the upper layer of skin via a "chemical peel" or microdermabrasion if it appears too blotchy, red, or rough. Over a million Americans have cosmetic surgery each year, including adult women/men and adolescents. Why do people expend so much effort and invest so much money trying to improve their physical attractiveness?

THE BODY: ITS GENERAL ATTRACTIVENESS

People care a great deal about their appearance. If a friend tells you about someone you have not met, you are likely to ask what the person looks like—you want a face to associate with the information you are receiving. Why? Novelists present intricately detailed descriptions of their characters' appearance. Why? Publishers put photos of book authors on book jackets and in book ads. Why? Most newspapers publish photos of newsmakers. Why must readers *see* the person being discussed in an article on airline deregulation, stock fraud, or the manufacture of computer chips? The answer: It is because people think they learn things from appearance. Looks are taken as indicators of a person's background, character, personality, talents, and likely future behavior.

TRANSGENDER CUES?

People who transition from living as one gender to another face a number of challenges. As you will learn in this book, there are a number of appearance and nonverbal cues linked to a person's biological sex as well as to their assigned or chosen gender. One challenge for some transgender individuals concerns whether they look physically like the gender with which they identify. Another challenge is whether they exhibit nonverbal cues linked to their identified gender, including how they walk and sit, express themselves facially, and use their voice.

Only one study could be located that examined efforts related to altering the nonverbal cues of transgender individuals. Hancock and Garabedian (2013) reviewed treatments aimed at helping males transitioning to the female gender produce vocal sounds that better reflect their identified gender, given that pitch and resonance can be markers of their biological sex at birth.

At this point, it is unclear the extent to which people's nonverbal cues change or do not change as they transition from one gender to another. It also is unclear if transgender individuals display nonverbal cues that are unique, that is, different from the cues of cisgender males or females.

Like everyone, transgender individuals have a wide repertoire of behaviors they can choose from, indeed probably more so than cisgender individuals who may have adopted one predominant "male" or "female" repertoire. How a transgender person chooses to deploy elements of their repertoire undoubtedly shows great individual variation. And, of course, because gender is a continuum rather than a dichotomy, there are many individuals who identify as nonbinary, androgynous, and/or pangender, meaning they reject aligning their identities with any particular prototype.

Although it is not uncommon to hear people muse about inner beauty being the only thing that really counts, research suggests that outer beauty, that is, physical attractiveness, plays an influential role in determining responses for a broad range of interpersonal encounters. The evidence from our culture overwhelmingly supports the notion that *initially* people respond much more favorably to those perceived as more physically attractive than to those seen as unattractive. Behavior toward unattractive people seems to be largely negative. However, for attractive people, positive reactions run the gamut from the sound of someone's voice to the broader inferences that are made (Hatfield & Sprecher, 1986; Herman, Zanna, & Higgins, 1986; Hughes, Farley, & Rhodes, 2010). Numerous studies reveal that physically attractive people are perceived to exceed unattractive people on a wide range of socially desirable evaluations that include success, personality, popularity, sociability, sexuality, persuasiveness, and, often, happiness. And, perhaps not surprisingly given such expectations, a recent longitudinal study by Datta Gupta, Etcoff, and Jaeger (2016) found that more attractive people actually enjoy greater psychological well-being.

Judgments linked to a person's attractiveness begin early in life. One study found that children as young as 2 to 3 months looked significantly longer at an attractive face (as judged by adults) than at an unattractive one. This preference for attractive faces among infants occurs regardless of the age (young, old), gender, or race of the face or whether the infant's mother is attractive or unattractive (Gamé, Carchon, & Vital-Durand, 2003; Langlois, Ritter, Roggman, & Vaughn, 1991; Langlois et al., 1987; Slater et al., 1998).

Cultural guidelines for physical attractiveness are well established by age 6 (Cavior & Lombardi, 1973; Dion, Berscheid, & Walster, 1972). It is not surprising, then, to find peer popularity and physical attractiveness highly correlated in elementary and secondary school. The perceptions of attractiveness in a child's world are not limited to their peers. Teachers tend to see attractive children as more intelligent, more socially adept, higher in educational potential, and more positive in their attitudes toward school—even when the unattractive children had similar academic performance. The compensatory power of beauty is such that it might benefit individuals of lower socioeconomic status more than those in higher socioeconomic ranks in terms of their educational attainment (Bauldry, Shanahan, Russo, Roberts, & Damian, 2016).

As children develop, they are exposed to these attitudes and evaluations made by teachers and parents. Teachers interact less, and less positively, with the so-called unattractive elementary schoolchild. In a study of 9- to 14-year-old boys, differences in perceived physical attractiveness were systematically related to social acceptance (Kleck, Richardson, & Ronald, 1974). Although much evidence testifies to the existence of a norm that says "what is beautiful is good," physical attractiveness also may be associated with undesirable traits; for example, vanity, egotism, snobbishness, unsympathetic attitudes toward oppressed people, and a greater likelihood of having marital problems (Dermer & Thiel, 1975). And, in the world of online dating, women with a more attractive picture are seen as less trustworthy by men (McGloin & Denes, 2018). These negative attributions, and the knowledge that beautiful people sometimes experience appearance-related problems, suggest all is not perfect for these people.

Although some would like to believe that "everything is beautiful in its own way," there are many reasons to believe that things are often beautiful in the same way to many people. Within the United States, people are constantly exposed to standards for male and female beauty through the mass media, so it is not surprising to find a great deal of agreement on standards for beauty within American culture. For instance, Lee, Loewenstein, Ariely, Hong, and Young (2008) showed that there tends to be consensus about the attractiveness of photographed members of online picture-rating sites that does not depend on the raters' own level of judged attractiveness. And studies in which perceivers are asked to rate the attractiveness of faces typically find very good agreement among them.

There is also evidence that there may be some inherent standards for physical attractiveness that cut across cultures. Studies involving people from Australia, Austria, China, England, India, Japan, Korea, and Scotland have found significant agreement on facial attractiveness (Etcoff, 1999; Langlois et al., 2000). Dion (2002) points out, however, that agreement is higher when the judges are students from other countries who are studying in the United States and when comparisons are made among different ethnocultural groups within a culture. Agreement is not as high with more geographically isolated groups. Even if there is a universal and biologically based standard for human beauty, cultures or environmental circumstances (e.g., availability of food) may impose certain variations (Anderson, Crawford, Nadeau, & Lindberg, 1992). Nevertheless, participation in global activities like the Miss World contest may affect local standards. Miss World 2001 was Miss Nigeria. In her home country, she was far too skinny to be considered attractive, even though many young Nigerians reportedly favored the new look.

We also should not overlook situational factors that impact how attractive others appear. Van Osch, Blanken, Meijs, and van Wolferen (2015) found that a group of people is judged to be more attractive than what would be expected based on the average of the combined ratings of each member's attractiveness. This presumably occurs because the more attractive members of the group are disproportionately impacting the perceived attractiveness of the entire group. Also, average-looking women may appear more attractive when they are evaluated alongside attractive women. So it appears that women can boost their perceived attractiveness by being seen with more attractive women, and this association does not seem to decrease the attractive women's perceived attractiveness (Geiselman, Haight, & Kimata, 1984).

DATING AND MARRIAGE

Physical attractiveness is probably more important to dating partners than it is to friends or married couples, although perceptions of physical attractiveness still can play an important role in marital relationships. Physical attraction may be most important when dating involves short-term goals and more public, rather than private, activities. Online daters, for example, may be particularly aware of the importance of physical appearance in enticing visitors to read about them on the rest of their profile page. Toma and Hancock (2010) found that individuals who were lower in attractiveness were more likely to enhance their physical appearance by altering their profile picture and misrepresenting descriptions of their physical characteristics on online dating sites. And, perhaps due to greater societal pressures to be attractive, it appears that women are more likely than men to post photos of themselves on dating websites that have been presented in such a way as to increase their physical attractiveness (Hancock & Toma, 2009).

Concern about one's attractiveness is not limited to women on the dating market. In recent years, men have become increasingly invested in their own physical appearance, such as their fitness and muscularity as well as the need for periodic "manscaping." Men, in fact, often think physical appearance is more influential in women's preferences for them than women indicate. One group of women—those who are physically attractive and financially independent—did, however, place a high value on male physical appearance (Pertschuk, Trisdorfer, & Allison, 1994). Apparently, highly attractive women "want it all," or at least think they deserve it, preferring a man who is masculine, sexy, and rich in resources (e.g., money or the potential for wealth), who will be a loving and caring partner, and who shows a desire to establish a home and raise children (Buss & Shackelford, 2008).

Based on the preceding information, one might suspect that actual dating patterns would reflect the preference for a physically attractive partner. This hypothesis was confirmed in a series of "computer dance" studies at the universities of Texas, Illinois, and Minnesota, in which physical attractiveness superseded a host of other variables in determining liking for one's partner and a desire to date in the future (Walster, Aronson, Abrahams, & Rottmann, 1966). Brislin and Lewis (1968) replicated this study with 58 unacquainted men and women and again found a strong correlation between "desire to date again" and physical attractiveness. In addition, this study asked each person whether they would like to date anyone else at the dance. Of the 13 other people named, all had previously, and independently, been rated as very attractive. Last, Luo and Zhang (2009) found that physical attractiveness was the best predictor of men's and women's interest in someone in an actual speed-dating situation.

In light of the many findings that seem to favor the physically attractive, it is worthwhile to note that there are times when the very physically attractive do not enjoy all the benefits. For example, women who had more variable attractiveness ratings—that is, they were not uniformly judged as very attractive or unattractive—were the group most satisfied with their socializing in general with both men and women. They also had as many dates as the most attractive women. Some men did not seek dates with the extremely attractive women because they felt the chances of rejection were high and that the women might perceive their interest as limited to their physical attractiveness (Reis et al., 1982; Reis, Nezlek, & Wheeler, 1980). When less attractive women are in the company of attractive women, this also seems to increase the chances that they will be seen as a good choice for a date.

So it seems that although there is a strong preference for people who are physically attractive, other forces obviously enable those who fall short of the ideal in physical attractiveness to date, marry, and have satisfying relationships. One powerful influence is described by the *matching hypothesis*, which says that each person may be attracted to only the best-looking partners, but reality sets in when actual dates are made. If you select only the best-looking person available, you may face an unwanted rejection, so the tendency is to select a person similar to yourself in physical attractiveness—preferably a little above your self-perceived attractiveness (Hinsz, 1989). Since this hypothesis was presented, other studies have confirmed its validity, including a study that included users of an online dating site (Taylor, Fiore, Mendelsohn, & Cheshire, 2011). So it seems the least good-looking people must settle for each other after all the very good-looking people choose each other (Kalick & Hamilton, 1986). However, if you have high self-esteem, you might seek out highly attractive partners in spite of a considerable gap between your looks and theirs (Berscheid & Walster, 1969). Self-esteem, in this case, may buffer the perception of, and possible reaction to, rejection.

Sometimes, couples' physical attractiveness seems to be mismatched. One study suggests that evaluations of men may change dramatically if they are viewed as married to someone very different in general attractiveness (Bar-Tal & Saxe, 1976). Unattractive men who were seen with attractive women were judged, among other things, as making more money, being more successful in their occupations, and being more intelligent than attractive men with attractive partners. Judges must have reasoned that for an unattractive man to marry an attractive woman, he must have offset this imbalance by succeeding in other areas. Unattractive women seen with attractive men, however, did not receive compensating attributions. This study raises the question of what "other resources" unattractive women are perceived to have to offset deficits in their physical attractiveness.

Even though physical attractiveness may be valued by both men and women, it seems to play a more dominant role in the perceptions of women by men. Buss (1994) found this gender difference reflected in every one of the 37 different cultures he studied. Women may desire physical characteristics, such as strength or facial attractiveness, but often rank characteristics like ambition, social and economic status, dependability, and stability above physical features—particularly for mate selection. (One must keep in mind that this literature assumes heterosexual relations only.)

The relative importance of physical attractiveness for men and women is also likely to vary with age, desired length of relationship, and possibly even budgetary concerns.

- For adolescent boys and girls, the attractiveness, not the social status of a potential partner, is important to their desire to date that person (Ha, Overbeek, & Engels, 2010).
- For short-term or casual sexual relationships, both adult men and women place a high value on physical attractiveness, even though women more than men would also like to have some desirable social and personality characteristics to go along with the physical attractiveness. For long-term relationships, both genders value other characteristics over physical attractiveness, even though adult men still rate it as more important. In one study, male college students said they were interested in different characteristics in a woman depending on whether it was a purely sexual relationship or one expected to be long term. A wide range of features associated with physical attractiveness were chosen for the sexual partner, but such features played a far less important role for long-term partners. Female students wanted virtually the same qualities in a long-term relationship as the men—honesty, fidelity, sensitivity, warmth, personality, kindness, character, tenderness, patience, and gentleness—but unlike the men, they also wanted more than mere physical attractiveness for the sexual relationship (Nevid, 1984).
- Human mating obviously involves more than each gender's stated preferences for members of the other gender. Horgan and colleagues (2015) had women watch a video of a man introducing himself to them after they had been induced to think about him as either a short-term or long-term partner. Women's memory for his appearance (e.g., physical features) and verbal statements was tested afterward. Women in the short-term mating condition had better memory for his appearance than his statements, and better memory for his appearance than did women in the long-term mating condition. Women in the long-term mating condition, on the other hand, had comparable memory for his appearance and statements, and better memory for his statements than women in the short-term mating condition. These findings suggested that women's preference for attractiveness in a short-term partner impacted their memory; they were processing information about his appearance to a greater extent than what he was saying to them. In the long-term condition, however, they were devoting their memory resources equally to what he looked like and what he said, suggesting that they were processing information about his personal and social qualities as much as the quality of his physical attributes.
- Li, Bailey, Kenrick, and Linsenmeier (2002) had men and women design their marriage partner by purchasing spouse attributes with play money under one of two budgetary conditions. When they were given a lot of money to spend, men spent somewhat more on physical attractiveness than did women, whereas women spent somewhat more on social status than did men. Importantly, these gender differences were even greater when each gender had only a little money to spend.

Two physical features of men preferred by women for short-term or casual sexual relationships were features of masculinity in the face—thicker eyebrows, smaller eyes, thinner lips, and a squarer jaw—and a high shoulder-to-waist ratio. Broader shoulders and a smaller waist may be perceived as markers of "good genes" (Braun & Bryan, 2006; Kruger, 2006), and these features may be most attractive during periods when conception is most likely (Little, Penton-Voak, Burt, & Perrett, 2002).

Apparently, the face also reveals a lot about a person's sexual attitudes as well as their suitability as a long-term partner. Boothroyd, Jones, Burt, DeBruine, and Perrett (2008) photographed students and asked them to fill out a questionnaire about their past sexual behavior and their attitudes toward sex. Women were less attracted to men who professed a strong interest in casual sex, but men preferred the faces of women who had a high "sociosexual orientation" (i.e., a greater willingness to have sexual relations with minimal commitment to and from their partner). In another study, men's testosterone levels were measured, and they were asked to fill out a questionnaire dealing with interest in infants. Photos of these men were shown to women who rated their physical attractiveness, their masculinity, the extent to which they perceived them as kind, their potential as a short- or long-term lover, and whether they seemed to like children. Women were skilled at distinguishing the men with high testosterone and those who liked children. Furthermore, they perceived the more masculine faces as attractive for short-term relationships, but were drawn to the faces of the men for long-term relationships who liked children more (Roney, Hanson, Durante, & Maestripieri, 2006).

BEAUTY ON THE JOB

Physical attractiveness may be an advantage in obtaining a job, obtaining a more prestigious job, and being hired at a higher salary (Cash, Gillen, & Burns, 1977; Dipboye, Arvey, & Terpstra, 1977; Hamermesh & Biddle, 1994). Unless the job is deemed inappropriate or irrelevant to the applicant's level of attractiveness, the more attractive applicants are more likely to get the job, assuming all other qualifications are equal. Sometimes, attractiveness provides an edge even when the less attractive competitor is more qualified for the position. Once a position has been obtained, less attractive workers may be discriminated against on performance appraisals, unless they maintain a consistently high level of productivity. And, over time, more attractive individuals may end up earning more money because of greater sponsorship from the organizations they are part of, relative to their less attractive counterparts (Dossinger, Wanberg, Choi, & Leslie, 2019).

The association between one's looks and job earnings is complex, though. Factors that covary with attractiveness, including a person's health, intelligence, and personality traits (e.g., more conscientious and extraverted, and less neurotic), may explain why attractive individuals earn more money than unattractive individuals (Kanazawa & Still, 2018).

Even though both men and women can profit from their physical attractiveness in the workplace, it is not always beneficial for a number of reasons:

- Highly attractive job applicants might be evaluated negatively by same-gender evaluators who feel threatened by them (Agthe, Spörrle, & Maner, 2011).
- Attractive workers might worry that positive evaluations of their work are based on how they look rather than how they actually perform (Major, Carrington, & Carnevale, 1984).
- Even though sexual harassment charges brought by unattractive women may garner less credibility with a jury (Seiter & Dunn, 2000), the attractiveness of both parties involved and the gender of jury members are factors that may work against advantages normally associated with physical attractiveness (Wuensch & Moore, 2004).

PERSUADING OTHERS

Getting others to agree with you or do something for you is often based on the extent to which you can demonstrate your knowledge or expertise as well as your ability to marshal effective supporting arguments (Maddux & Rogers, 1980). But as several research projects show, being physically attractive also may help (Chaiken, 1986), and people may strategically use their attractiveness around those they hope to persuade (Vogel, Kutzner, Fiedler, & Freytag, 2010). Persuasion success is especially likely when the effects of initial impressions are crucial to achieving influence. The association of persuasive effectiveness with physical attractiveness has even been documented in the behavior of 10- and 11-year-old children (Dion & Stein, 1978).

One of the earliest studies of physical attractiveness and persuasion used cosmetics to make one woman look more or less attractive. The experimenter suggested to a group of students that they would complete some questionnaires more quickly if a volunteer would read the questions aloud and indicate what they meant. The volunteer was either the attractive or the unattractive woman. The attractive woman, especially when she stated her desire to influence the audience, was far more effective in modifying the opinions of college students toward issues dealing with higher education (Mills & Aronson, 1965). Other studies also support the influence of physical attractiveness in persuasive situations (Horai, Naccari, & Faloultah, 1974; Widgery, 1974).

The preceding research focused primarily on female communicators, but attractiveness also seems to help male persuaders. Independent assessments of their verbal performance, as well as their ability to obtain signatures on a campus petition, showed attractive men and women outperforming those who were rated as unattractive. In another study, physically attractive men and women were judged to have better sales skills, were treated more cordially, and elicited more willingness from people to contribute to a charitable organization (Reingen & Kernan, 1993).

Is the persuasiveness of attractive communicators due solely to their looks, or do they actually have persuasive skills? An examination of previous tests showed attractive students to have higher grades, higher SAT scores, better self-concepts, and better communication skills (Chaiken, 1979).

SELF-ESTEEM

Is physical attractiveness associated with high self-esteem? One would think so. But the answer seems to be, for the most part, no. Being physically attractive does not guarantee high self-esteem or even happiness (Diener, Wolsic, &

Fujita, 1995; Feingold, 1992; Langlois et al., 2000). In fact, it may be linked to lower self-esteem among children entering adolescence (Mares, de Leeuw, Scholte, & Engels, 2010). Nonetheless, there is some evidence that people use a person's attractiveness as a cue to accurately detect how close others perceive that person's self-esteem (Hirschmuller, Schmukle, Krause, Back, & Egloff, 2018).

This does not mean that efforts to enhance one's appearance have no self-reinforcing effects. Women aged 18 to 60 who used cosmetics to improve their appearance also reported psychological benefits from doing so. Greater attractiveness for those between the ages of 40 and 60 was perceived as most beneficial for masking the aging process and improving one's physical and mental health (Graham & Jouhar, 1982). And training in the use of cosmetics for elderly women has reportedly had a positive effect on their self-image.

ANTISOCIAL BEHAVIOR

What happens when attractive and unattractive people are charged with committing a criminal act? Are judges and juries influenced by a person's looks? As expected, attractive defendants are less likely to be arrested, to be judged guilty, and, if convicted, more likely to receive a shorter sentence in real-life or simulation studies (Beaver, Boccio, Smith, & Ferguson, 2019; Efran, 1974; Kulka & Kessler, 1978; Weiten, 1980).

Obviously, a defendant's attractiveness is rarely assessed in isolation in the courtroom, and other factors interact with attractiveness, including the extent to which the defendant expresses repentance, the degree of commitment jurors have toward impartiality, the extent to which jurors discuss the case, the perceived similarity of jurors and defendant, defendant verbalizations, and the nature of the crime being examined. For some crimes, attractiveness may be a liability for the defendant, as when it is used to commit a crime such as a swindle. Swarmi, Arthey, and Furnham (2017) found no differences in perceptions of guilt between attractive and unattractive individuals when their plagiarism was minor, but attractive individuals were seen as guiltier and more deserving of harsh penalties when their plagiarism was severe.

THE POWER OF PHYSICAL ATTRACTIVENESS: SOME IMPORTANT QUALIFICATIONS

As the preceding sections attest, much research supports the benefits and power of physical attractiveness. No doubt it can be discouraging to the great majority of human beings who are less than gorgeous. Without ignoring the potentially powerful effects of physical attractiveness in some situations, the goal of this section is to review research that shows that physical attractiveness is not always such a dominant factor in constructive interpersonal outcomes.

THE EFFECTS OF INTERACTION

Methodological issues may provide some comfort to those who perceive themselves as less attractive. Although it is not true of all studies of physical attractiveness, most use frontal facial photographs that had been judged prior to the study to fall into the beautiful or ugly category. Hence, in most cases, we are not reporting results from living, moving, talking human beings in a particular environment, nor are we generally dealing with subtle differences in physical attractiveness that lie between the extremes of beautiful and ugly.

We know little about the socially skilled but unattractive person whose communicative beauty is greater than perceptions of their photographic beauty. We do know that talk and nonverbal behavior can significantly affect perceptions; in fact, interaction behavior and facial beauty are the two primary contributors to overall judgments of physical attractiveness (Riggio, Widaman, Tucker, & Salinas, 1991). Berg (2004) found that even a 6-minute get-acquainted conversation could significantly affect perceptions of the physical attractiveness of moderately attractive people—and more positively than negatively. Interaction often elicits information about a person's personality, and that information can significantly change initial perceptions of physical attractiveness not only for physically attractive people but also for neutral and unattractive ones (Lewandowski, Aron, & Gee, 2007). Many romantic partners tell stories about how their initial perception of their partners' physical attractiveness was not particularly high when compared with their ideal, but say that continued positive interaction changed this perception.

THE EFFECTS OF CONTEXT

The perception of appearance may be relative to the context in which it is judged and the motives of the perceiver. Bars have been studied as a unique context for judging physical attractiveness. One research team wanted to find out if the song about how "all the girls get prettier at closing time" had any validity to it. Pennebaker and colleagues (1979) obtained information about the general attractiveness of bar patrons at several different bars at different times leading up to closing time. True to the lyrics of the song, both men and women perceived a significant increase in the attractiveness of others as closing time drew near. Although the gradually dwindling pool of potential partners may have had some effect, especially for those not in a committed relationship already (Madey, Simo, Dillworth, & Kemper, 1996), research also shows that even moderate alcohol consumption tends to increase perceivers' ratings of the physical attractiveness of members of the other gender (Jones, Jones, Thomas, & Piper, 2003).

STEREOTYPES ARE NOT ALWAYS VALID

Even though people often agree on others' physical attractiveness, the self-ratings of the people being judged may be quite different. Thus, people seen as physically attractive (or not) may not perceive themselves that way and, as a result, may manifest very different characteristics than others presume they have. Physically attractive people are typically *perceived* as having a wide range of socially desirable characteristics, and although actual measures do show physically attractive people to be more socially skilled and popular, only a negligible relationship appears to exist between perceptions of a highly attractive person's personality and mental ability and their actual traits (Eagly, Ashmore, Makhijani, & Longo, 1991; Feingold, 1992; cf. Kanazawa & Still, 2018).

ATTRACTIVENESS OVER TIME

Judgments of attractiveness may change over the course of a lifetime. Ratings of facial attractiveness appear to be somewhat stable from about age 16 to age 50, but the overall ratings of attractiveness for both men and women tend to decline in middle and old age, and the decline is more severe for women.

In one study of the effects of time on attractiveness, the high school pictures of 1,300 men and women were rated for attractiveness. The lives of these people were examined 15 years later. Attractive girls in high school had husbands with more education and higher salaries, but their own occupational status and income were not significantly different from those of their less attractive counterparts. The least attractive boys in high school had more prestigious occupations and more education, and they married women with more education than did boys judged as attractive in high school. The authors speculate that the social ostracism of the less attractive men in high school may have turned their attention to educational achievements that paid off later in life (Udry & Eckland, 1984).

Because appearance can be changed, people judged unattractive are not necessarily doomed to a long list of pitfalls or problems. Changes in makeup and hairstyle can increase ratings of general attractiveness as well as ratings of desired personality characteristics (Graham & Jouhar, 1981). Cosmetics have been used to aid the recovery and adjustment of people recuperating from illnesses. Moreover, older individuals can emphasize other positive qualities they have, such as their health and connectedness to others, which they do more often than younger people on online dating profiles (Davis & Fingerman, 2016).

Now that we have examined the global concept of attractiveness, we can ask the following questions. What *specific* aspects of another's appearance do people respond to? Does it make any difference how people perceive their own body and appearance? We focus on the answers to these questions in the remainder of this chapter.

THE BODY: ITS SPECIFIC FEATURES

ATTRACTIVENESS AND THE FACE

Even though the face has long been the specific body feature most commonly examined in studies of physical attractiveness, a basic question remained unanswered: What is facial beauty? Before we report on the research it is essential to note that unquestionably the great majority of faces being judged, as well as the people making those ratings, are White American college students. These results may not pertain when faces and raters belong to different cultural or ethnic groups. Some features, such as smooth skin and youthfulness, make intuitive sense (Rhodes, 2006); others, such as averaged or symmetrical features, not so much. Nevertheless, Langlois and Roggman (1990) found that physically attractive faces approximate the mathematical average of all faces in a particular population. These researchers took pictures of 96 college males and 96 college females. The photos were scanned by a video lens connected to a computer that converted each picture into a matrix of tiny digital units with numerical values. The male and female faces were subsequently divided into three subsets of 32 faces each. From each subset, the computer randomly chose two faces and mathematically averaged their digitized values. It then transformed this information into a composite face of the two individuals. Composite faces then were generated for 4, 8, 16, and 32 members of each set. Ratings by students showed that composite faces were more attractive than virtually any of the individual faces, and the most attractive faces were composites of 16 and 32 faces. There is an important qualification to this effect, though: It depends on the initial attractiveness of the faces used to form the composites (Braun, Gruendl, Marberger, & Scherber, 2001). Specifically, if the faces used are unattractive, the composite remains unattractive, too.

Langlois and her colleagues acknowledge that in some cases people are perceived as attractive by large numbers of people even though their features obviously are not the population average. In fact, the most attractive faces are not likely to be average at all. The most attractive faces tend to emphasize those features associated with physically attractive faces. A woman, for example, would have a higher-than-average forehead, fuller-than-average lips, shorter-than-average jaw, and smaller-than-average chin and nose. Other female facial features often associated with physical attractiveness are clear skin, high cheekbones, lustrous hair, and big eyes. A woman of any age who has small eyes, a relatively large nose, and wide, thin lips will look older, more masculine, and be seen as less attractive.

The prominence of the jaw is linked to attractiveness in a gender-specific way, with greater prominence being seen as more attractive for male than female faces (Mogilski & Welling, 2018). Women's mating goals also need to be taken into consideration. The faces of men with a higher ratio of muscle mass seem to be more appealing to women seeking a short-term sexual relationship with a man (Lei, Holzleitner, & Perrett, 2019). However, a face with a powerful jaw and facial hair, although indicators of male facial attractiveness, may need large eyes and a wide smile to avoid being seen as too masculine.

Another promising approach to identifying facial attractiveness is based on the principle of symmetry (Grammer & Thornhill, 1994; Saxton, DeBruine, Jones, Little, & Roberts, 2011). Photographs of male and female students were precisely measured to determine whether features on one side of the face are equidistant to a midpoint as the same features on the other side of the face. On perfectly symmetrical faces, all the midpoints meet and roughly form a vertical line. Movie actor Denzel Washington has a very symmetrical face, whereas musician Lyle Lovett does not. Some asymmetry is desirable; otherwise, the face may not look real. Horizontal symmetry was also calculated, and the most symmetrical faces were also those chosen as the most attractive. The researchers believe these results are consistent with findings that show symmetry is also a powerful attractant for other animal and insect species. Indeed, it influences how attractive people find animals (dogs) and objects (cars), too (Halberstadt & Rhodes, 2003). It may be that across species, symmetry reflects better health and, thus, better genetic fitness in an evolutionary sense (e.g., Shackelford & Larsen, 1999). Of importance, symmetry, like averageness, is likely to garner high ratings of facial attractiveness, but neither is a guarantee of the most attractive faces (Cunningham, Barbee, & Philhower, 2002).

JUDGMENTS OF THE FACE

Because the face is so central in judgments of attractiveness, it is no surprise that it is the source of stereotyping—often based on glances of 1 second or less. The idea that the shape of a person's face reveals their character was made famous by Johann Kaspar Lavater in the 18th century. Lavater called this pseudoscience "physiognomy" and it was widely accepted across Europe and beyond. Reportedly, Charles Darwin was nearly rejected from his famous trip on the *Beagle* because the captain, a follower of Lavater, did not like the shape of Darwin's nose. Even in the modern era, people's judgments suggest that they believe the human face reveals important information about a person's personality (Hassin & Trope, 2000; Laser & Mathie, 1982). Laser and Mathie, for example, asked an artist to prepare nine charcoal drawings of a male face, varying the thickness of the eyebrows and lips and the shape of the face. People rated these faces with adjectives. The features had marked effects on these ratings: The face with thick eyebrows was seen as less warm, angrier, sterner, less cheerful, and less at ease than those with thin or normal brows; thicker lips connoted warmth and less tension than thinner lips; and narrow faces were seen as more tense and suspicious.

There is evidence that some face-based judgments are accurate, whereas others are not, although in examining this literature, it is often difficult to tell when perceptions are based on facial features or facial expressions. It seems that people might be able to tell whether people are criminals, dominant or submissive, or wealthy, as well as their sexual and sociosexual orientation by simply looking at pictures of their face (Berry & Wero, 1993; Boothroyd, Cross, Gray, Coombes, & Gregson-Curtis, 2011; Boothroyd et al., 2008; Rule & Ambady, 2008a; Tskhay, Clout, & Rule, 2017; Valla, Ceci, & Williams, 2011).

What might account for this accuracy? Perhaps people who are very high or very low in particular personality traits, such as extraversion, might share configural properties of the face that can be reliably detected (Penton-Voak, Pound, Little, & Perrett, 2006). This could occur if facial cues to a person's personality are due to a history of personality-trait-driven expressions and emotional experiences (Adams, Garrido, Albohn, Hess, & Kleck, 2016; Bjornsdottir & Rule, 2017). Maybe people bring out what they expect to see from others due to shared stereotypes about the meaning of their facial features. Last, the appearance of targets also could reflect what they think society expects from them based on their given names (Zwebner, Sellier, Rosenfeld, Goldenberg, & Mayo, 2017).

Of course, face-based judgments are not always accurate. One study showed that people's perceptions of baby-faced individuals as more suggestible and persuadable were not accurate. (Bachmann & Nurmoja, 2006). People think they can accurately judge intelligence and health from physically attractive faces, but they are not very good at it. This false belief seems to be the result of overgeneralizing based on an accuracy in judging intelligence and health in *unattractive* faces (Zebrowitz & Rhodes, 2004). People also may misjudge the meaning of appearance cues on the human face; although makeup can enhance female attractiveness, it is mistakenly seen as a cue to greater unrestrictiveness in their sociosexuality (Batres et al., 2018).

Whether a stereotype reflects actual behavior or not, people often act as if it does. As an example, let us discuss baby-faced people. McArthur and her colleagues examined the facial features associated with age and the kinds of interpretations people make of faces that have more or less youthful features; in particular, they focused on the adult with baby-faced features such as a large forehead, short chin, and big eyes. McArthur and Baron (1983) proposed that people correctly differentiate traits that accompany younger age but then incorrectly ascribe these traits—that is, they overgeneralize them—to people with younger-looking faces, even though they are not necessarily young. Berry and McArthur (1986) found, in support of this, that people rated babyish adult faces as weaker, more submissive, and more intellectually naive than mature-looking faces.

These investigators also simulated a courtroom trial in which a male defendant was charged with an offense that was marked either by negligence or by deliberate deception; the defendant was either baby-faced or mature-faced. Participants acting as jurors more often convicted the baby-faced man for crimes of negligence and the mature-faced man for intentional crimes. This result was predicted based on the earlier finding that adults with babyish features were perceived as more naive and more honest.

So it seems that a number of social outcomes are consistent with the principle that baby-faced people are more likely to acquire influence, jobs, and judicial convictions when the influence strategies, job descriptions, or alleged crimes fit the characteristics they are expected to have (Zebrowitz, 1997).

In sum, there is no doubt that the way a person's face is structured and contoured creates strong impressions on others. Facial endowment may harm or benefit a person, depending on the stereotypes associated with the features. Future research may reveal to what extent actual personality traits and ways of expression will override initial impressions based on facial stereotypes. We suspect such initial impressions are easily overturned by behavioral evidence. As one example, baby-faced soldiers are not expected to be very brave. As a consequence, when mature-faced and baby-faced soldiers exhibit valor, the baby-faced soldier is more likely to be decorated (Collins & Zebrowitz, 1995).

BODY SHAPE

There has been some research attempting to relate personality traits to different body types, sometimes called *somatotypes* (Cortés & Gatti, 1965). Generally, such research is concerned with a person's physical similarity to three extreme varieties of human physique, shown in Figure 6-1, but obviously most people do not fit these extremes. *Endomorphy*, *mesomorphy*, and *ectomorphy*, in their extremes, would describe a corpulent person, a broad-shouldered and athletic person, and a very skinny person, respectively.

Although stereotypes about the personalities of people with different bodies are easy to find, evidence for actual differences in personality is lacking. And, even if relations between body type and personality are found, it cannot be assumed that the body *causes* temperament traits. Any correspondence between temperament traits and body builds may be due to life experiences, environmental factors, self-concept, and a host of other variables, including the stereotypes

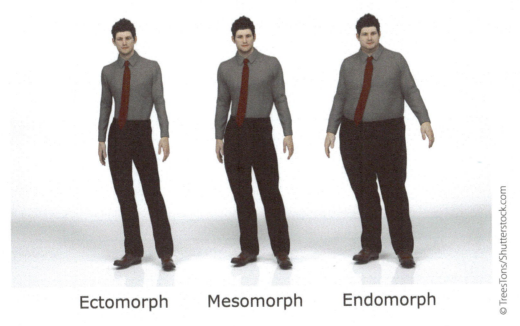

© TreesTons/Shutterstock.com

Ectomorph   Mesomorph   Endomorph

FIGURE 6-1 On the left, the ectomorph (tall, thin, fragile); middle, the mesomorph (muscular, athletic); on the right, the endomorph (soft, round, fat).

themselves. This does not mean that biological factors do not contribute, directly or indirectly, to people's traits. Ellis, Das, and Buker (2008), for instance, have argued that underlying differences in androgen exposure influence not only the development of people's brains—and thus their traits, such as their propensity for criminality—but also the development of their physical features (e.g., how muscular and hairy they are).

Nonetheless, if there are clearly defined and generally accepted physique–temperament stereotypes, we can reason that they will have much to do with the way people are perceived and responded to by others (see Hu, Parde, Hill, Mahmood, & O'Toole, 2018). Wells and Siegel (1961), for example, measured stereotypes by showing 120 adults silhouette drawings of the endomorph, ectomorph, and mesomorph and asking them to rate them on a set of 24 adjectives, such as lazy-energetic, intelligent-unintelligent, and dependent-self-reliant. Their results show the following (Table 6.1):

Clearly, the evidence shows people do associate certain personality and temperament traits with specific body builds. We must recognize these stereotypes as potential stimuli for communication responses.

One question is when people start to prefer particular body types. Male and female infants spend more time looking at a female figure than a male figure (Alexander, Hawkins, Wilcox, & Hirshkowitz, 2016). And, as early as kindergarten, children seem to prefer the more muscular mesomorphs to either the thin or heavyset body types (Johnson & Staffieri, 1971; Lerner & Gellert, 1969; Lerner & Korn, 1972; Lerner & Schroeder, 1971; Staffieri, 1972). Youngsters seem to have a particular aversion to the heavyset physiques. Older children who select descriptive adjectives for these body types tend to see the mesomorph as "all things good," with ectomorphs and endomorphs attracting a host of unfavorable descriptors. Again, we remind readers that most of this research would pertain mainly to White (as well as young, college, Westernized) populations, because of gaps in the research.

Negative reactions to overweight individuals are frequently reported, as well as negative psychological consequences of weight discrimination (Hunger, Dodd, & Smith, 2019; Pearl, 2018). College students with a higher body mass index have been shown in more than one study to receive less support from parents than slimmer students, and in fact heavier young people appear less likely to be in college at all (Incollingo Rodriguez et al., 2019). There is one

TABLE 6.1 Three Physique Categories and Temperament Stereotypes

Ectomorphic	Mesomorphic	Endomorphic
Detached	Dominant	Dependent
Tense	Cheerful	Calm
Anxious	Confident	Relaxed
Reticent	Energetic	Complacent
Self-conscious	Impetuous	Contented
Meticulous	Efficient	Sluggish
Reflective	Enthusiastic	Placid
Precise	Competitive	Leisurely
Thoughtful	Determined	Cooperative
Considerate	Outgoing	Affable
Shy	Argumentative	Tolerant
Awkward	Talkative	Affected
Cool	Active	Warm
Suspicious	Domineering	Forgiving
Introspective	Courageous	Sympathetic
Serious	Enterprising	Softhearted
Cautious	Adventurous	Generous
Tactful	Reckless	Affectionate
Sensitive	Assertive	Kind
Withdrawn	Optimistic	Sociable
Gentle-tempered	Hot-tempered	Soft-tempered

notable exception favoring heavier people: heavyset individuals are less likely than mesomorphic individuals to be misidentified as the perpetrator of a violent or nonviolent crime in line-ups in which the actual perpetrator is not shown (Shaw & Wafler, 2016).

Nevertheless, it is safe to say that being excessively overweight in our culture is often a handicap. Researchers who followed 10,000 people between the ages of 16 and 24 for 7 years found obesity meant you were less likely to marry, more likely to have a lower income, and more likely to receive less schooling (Gortmaker, Must, Perrin, Sobol, & Dietz, 1993). In certain domains, the gender of the overweight person matters; for example, women's weight seems to impact the quality of their intimate relationships more than does men's (Boyes & Latner, 2009).

Although heavier women might represent the ideal in some cultures (Anderson et al., 1992), the cultural ideal for U.S. women has tended toward thinness. This ideal might apply more to White women in this culture, however, as heavy women are judged more harshly in terms of their looks by White female students than by Black female students (Hebl & Heatherton, 1998). Generally, women have tended to be more conscious of their weight than have men. In recent years, there may be growing acceptance of female bodies that are not extremely slender, and this may reflect the fact that the U.S. population is gaining weight, as is much of the rest of the world. Still, however, a content analysis of female portrayals on primetime TV showed that the women are more and more underweight (Mastro & Figueroa-Caballero, 2018). Another trend in recent years has been toward the development of healthy bodies— "eating right," exercising, and developing muscle strength. These fitness-related body standards apply to both men and women and will probably constitute some of the features that make up the next cultural standard for the ideal body shape.

Perceptions of body type attractiveness is gender-specific. Research has shown that women view the mesomorphic male body type as more attractive than either the ectomorphic or endomorphic types (Dixson, Dixson, Bishop, & Parish, 2010). Women say their favorite male physique has a medium-wide upper trunk, a medium-thin lower trunk, and thinner legs—a V-shaped look (Singh, 1993, 1995). The most disliked male physique has a thin upper trunk and a wide lower trunk, or a pear-shaped look. Women who see themselves as traditionally feminine and conservative in their lifestyle seem to favor "muscle men"; more feminist women like thinner, more linear bodies; and big women tend to go for big men. The best clue to a woman's favorite male physique, however, is the type of physique belonging to the man who is "most important to her at that time" (Beck, Ward-Hull, & McLear, 1976; Lavrakas, 1975; Pertschuk et al., 1994; Wiggins & Wiggins, 1969).

The *waist-to-hip ratio* of women plays an important role in men's judgments of women's physical attractiveness (Singh, 1993, 1995; Streeter & McBurney, 2003). A waist-to-hip ratio of 0.70 means the waist is 70% the size of the hips, which is considered the "ideal." By contrast, the ideal ratio for men is between 0.80 and 0.95. Singh says early Greek paintings, ancient Indian sculptures, Miss America winners, and *Playboy* centerfolds all show waist-to-hip ratios very close to 0.70. He surveyed people of many age groups, cultures, and ethnic groups, and their preferences are for the 0.70 waist-to-hip ratio. A study using eye-tracking techniques showed that, although men looked at the breasts of a female target more often and longer than her waist, face, pubic area, and legs, they rated the female target with the 0.70 waist-to-hip ratio as the most attractive irrespective of her breast size (small, medium, large; Dixson, Grimshaw, Linklater, & Dixson, 2011). Electrophysiological evidence has emerged showing that different brain activation occurs in men than in women when both are viewing dressed or undressed women who possess the 0.70 waist-to-hip ratio (Zotto & Pegna, 2017). Moreover, it appears that men have better memory for the appearance and biographical information of women whose waist-to-hip ratio is closer to 0.70 as opposed to farther away from it (e.g., 0.50, 0.90; Fitzgerald, Horgan, & Himes, 2016). This suggests that men may process information about women more deeply the closer she is to having the "ideal" waist-to-hip ratio. It is important to bear in mind that studies that have focused on men's perceptions of a women's waist-to-hip ratio did not factor in how the women walked; this is a problem because a walking woman is more likely to be seen by men in the real world. In addition to the static cue of a woman's waist-to-hip ratio, such dynamic cues also play a role in how attractive women appear (Morrison, Bain, Pattison, & Whyte-Smith, 2018).

Why might men prefer women with a 0.70 waist-to-hip ratio? Women with a lower waist-to-hip ratio seem to be healthier and more fertile than those with a higher waist-to-hip ratio. Other research, however, reveals that in a few cultures, women with a greater waist circumference and a higher waist-to-hip ratio are preferred by men.

Others argue from their research that the preferred waist-to-hip ratio will increase as body size and weight increase, even though small and medium waists and hips are preferred regardless of weight (Forestell, Humphrey, & Stewart, 2004; Tassinary & Hansen, 1998). There is no doubt that the waist-to-hip ratio is one of several features that affect perceptions of female attractiveness by men. Other cues include having a youthful, attractive face and firm breasts (Buss & Schmidt, 2019; Havlicek et al., 2017).

Another feature, which has not received as much research attention, concerns the leg-to-body (LBR) ratio of women (i.e., length of legs relative to height; Frederick, Hadji-Michael, Furnham, & Swami, 2010; Kiire, 2016; Swami, Einon, & Furnham, 2006). Findings have been mixed as to whether longer or more mid-range leg-to-body ratios are seen as most attractive. However, Kiire (2015) used more realistic three-dimensional images of men and women and found that perceivers judged average LBRs to be the most attractive in men and women.

HEIGHT

Height also influences interpersonal responses. People seem to know that height can be important to their social and work lives. Pediatricians report that parents are often concerned that their child is not as tall as expected at a certain age. Children themselves are asked to focus on height when their teachers tell them to line up by height. Adults seem to overestimate their own height, and shorter men do so to a greater extent than taller men (Bogaert & McCreary, 2011; Cameron, Oskamp, & Sparks, 1978).

Height derives its importance from a widespread belief that major deviations from median heights—about 5 feet, 4 inches for women and 5 feet, 9 inches for men—will incur negative judgments from others. Although some may believe it is possible to be too tall, most negative judgments are thought to be associated with shortness. Is there any truth to this? The anecdotal evidence is far more plentiful than the empirical research, and most of the research focuses on men only (Roberts & Herman, 1986). In a study of 956 students in Grades 6 through 12, Sandberg, Bukowski, Fung, and Noll (2004) concluded that being too tall or too short had a minimal impact on peer perceptions of social behavior, friendship, or acceptance. Some psychiatrists echo the belief that sometimes short kids are teased, but that they get over it and do not experience lasting psychological problems. And there seems to be little evidence supporting significant differences in the lives of short children whose parents have authorized giving them human growth hormone to increase their stature. Still, the belief that tallness is favored in the United States persists, so we will examine some dominant perceptions associated with height: *status, attractiveness, marriage, gender*, and *competence*.

HEIGHT AND STATUS. Height has long been a metaphor for power and prestige. Some evidence suggests that height is positively related to authority/status on the job for men but not for women (Gawley, Perks, & Curtis, 2009). The taller of the two U.S. presidential candidates has usually won since 1900, with Jimmy Carter and George W. Bush as notable exceptions. When Carter debated President Ford, his campaign advisers did not want him to be seen standing next to the 6-foot-1-inch president. Consequently, they asked that the debates be conducted from a sitting position. Ford's advisers refused. The compromise involved placing the lecterns far apart. Further testimony to the stigma associated with shorter people and power is that behavior labeled *competitive* for a taller man is labeled a *Napoleonic complex* for a shorter one.

Often, height interacts with other factors, such as general body size, girth, and facial features. In your own experience, you probably can recall some tall individuals who seemed almost frighteningly overpowering, whereas others of the same height did not have this quality. Height can be difficult to disentangle from build and also from behavior, with some individuals seeming more formidable for a variety of interrelated reasons (Lukaszewski, Simmons, Anderson, & Roney, 2016). Nevertheless, taller people are perceived as more intelligent and as better leaders and actually attain higher status in political and organizational settings. Judge and Cable (2004) concluded that taller people have higher self-esteem, are more likely to be in leadership positions, make more money, and get better performance evaluations at work than shorter people. This was more likely to be the case with men, but there was a strong relationship for women as well. It can also go the other way, with people whom one admires or aligns oneself with appearing taller than reality would suggest (Knapen, Blaker, & Pollet, 2017).

HEIGHT AND ATTRACTIVENESS, MARRIAGE, AND SEX. People's height impacts their self-perceptions as well as others' perceptions of them in the area of attractiveness. In a study of couples from Chile, both taller men and women perceived themselves to be more attractive (Buunk, Fernandez, & Muñoz-Ryes, 2019).

In terms of other's perceptions, taller men are frequently perceived as more attractive than shorter men. The ideal male lover is not described as "*short*, dark, and handsome." Male romantic leads in movies are usually either tall or made to look tall by camera angles. Numerous sources attest to the important role of height in perceptions of attractiveness, but obviously people do not make judgments of another's attractiveness based on height alone. Therefore, we can conclude that height is just one feature involved in judgments of attractiveness.

You have probably noticed that shorter people are more likely to be romantically involved with each other, and taller people are similarly paired up. It seems that romantically involved couples do indeed tend to be more similar to each other in height than randomly paired couples (Warren, 1966). Of course, there are exceptions, and they tend to be striking when they occur. Sometimes, they are even a source of amusement, as when the 5-foot-11-inch Nicole Kidman stated that "I can wear heels again" after her marriage was over to the 5-foot-7-inch Tom Cruise. Perhaps not surprisingly then, advertisements for romantic partners often give height as a critical piece of information about themselves (Harrison & Saeed, 1977).

There are benefits and burdens associated with height for men and women in relationships. Pawlowski, Dunbar, and Lipowicz (2000) have found that married men tend to be taller than their unmarried counterparts. And taller adult men

FIGURE 6-2 At 5′10˝ inches tall, larger-than-life action superstar Sylvester Stallone is fairly average in real life in terms of his stature.

report having more frequent sexual intercourse (Eisenberg, Shindel, Smith, Breyer, & Lipshultz, 2010). Short and tall women, on the other hand, appear to be more jealous and competitive toward other women than are women of average height (Buunk, Poliet, Klavina, Figueredo, & Dijkstra, 2009).

BODY IMAGE

So far we have largely discussed how people perceive others. An equally important topic is what people think of themselves. Self-image is the root system from which overt communication behavior grows. In short, what you are—or rather what you think you are—organizes what you say and do. An important part of your self-image is body image, perhaps the first aspect of self-image formed in young children.

Many studies document negative body image concerns, as well as poor psychosocial correlates of negative body image, in both men and women, although the problem is more extreme in women (Mellor, Fuller-Tyszkiewicz, McCabe, & Ricciardelli, 2010; Tiggemann, 2015; Varnes et al., 2013). Being an athlete buffers women somewhat from negative body image, but not entirely. Body image problems cut across different ages and gender minorities, although African and Hispanic women may suffer less in this regard than Western White women. Adult males seem to be most satisfied with their bodies when they are somewhat larger than normal; females are most satisfied when their bodies are smaller than normal and their breasts are larger.

In today's world of social media, posting "selfies" and viewing others' "selfies" are common practices. Mills, Musto, Williams, and Tiggemann (2018) found that young women who posted (vs. those who did not) selfies experienced a temporary drop in their self-confidence and perceived attractiveness as well as an uptick in their anxiousness. However, idealized images of women without make-up does not seem to negatively impact female viewers' body image (Fardouly & Rapee, 2019).

Sex researchers have frequently noted emotional problems in men stemming from a perceived incongruence between their genital size and the supposed masculine ideal perpetuated by our literary and folklore heritage. However, more than 71% of the women in one survey agreed or strongly agreed that "men seem too concerned with the size and shape of their genitals" (Pertschuk et al., 1994). And for women, reduced sexual satisfaction may stem from greater dissatisfaction with the appearance of their genitals (Schick, Calabrese, Rima, & Zucker, 2010).

As people develop, they learn the cultural ideal of what a body should be. This results in varying degrees of satisfaction with the body, particularly during adolescence. Researchers believe that the standards of beauty promulgated in the mass media are oppressive and create an undesirable yearning for often unreasonable goals. Such standards can influence viewers' current level of self-esteem. The self-esteem of neurotic women seems particularly vulnerable to the effects of being exposed to thin models in the media (Roberts & Good, 2010). A national survey of several thousand adults indicated that between 1972 and 1986, both men's and women's dissatisfaction with their bodies rose sharply. Weight was a major factor of dissatisfaction (Cash, Winstead, & Janda, 1986). If the prediction of the U.S. Centers for Disease Control and Prevention holds true, that 42% of Americans will be classified as *obese* by 2030, dissatisfaction with weight may increase if the popular standards do not adapt. On the other hand, new norms may develop that offset the negative impact of being weightier. Already in television ads, one sees many heavy and even obese people; possibly, the advertisers are striving for more inclusiveness and they may also believe viewers will identify positively with people who look more like them and will buy their products more. Or perhaps advertisers are trying to reverse the "thin is beautiful" standards that are impossible for most people to achieve.

People are not always accurate in their perceptions of their own body size and weight. In some cases, constant exposure to ideal body images in the media contributes to misperceptions of one's body shape and size (Bissell & Zhou, 2004; Myers & Biocca, 1992). In addition to misjudgments of one's own body size and weight, people may also misjudge the body type that is most appealing to others. Women seem to think men prefer a thinner woman than men actually report; men seem to think women want a heavier man than women actually report. Men thought that having an attractive face and body build was more important to women than women said it was (Fallon & Rozin, 1985; Pertschuk et al., 1994).

BODY COLOR

People make judgments about temporary color changes on people's bodies. On light-skinned people, for example, a pale color may indicate illness, a rosy flush may indicate embarrassment, and a red neck can appear with anger. But permanent skin colors have been the most potent body stimulus for determining interpersonal responses in our culture. Some Asian Americans use whitening creams and lotions on their faces, arguing that the desire for pale skin is an ancient Asian tradition associated with delicacy and femininity. Younger Asian Americans wonder if this is really an effort to blend into a culture where there is less discrimination against White-skinned individuals, or even a manifestation of prejudice against those with darker skin. There is no need to review the abuses heaped on Black people in America on the basis of skin color alone. These abuses are well documented.

As U.S. demographics change and the number of mixed-racial marriages goes up, the variety of skin colors will continue to increase, and sharp distinctions among people's skin colors will become increasingly difficult to make. Still, there will always be those who want a simple method of classifying their social world, and skin color is easily observed. We can only hope that the number of people who believe skin color to be an accurate gauge for identifying friend and foe will continue to decrease.

The standards for beauty are usually set by the economically dominant group within a society. People in less dominant groups may try to mimic the standards of the dominant group. The standards in the United States have traditionally been those associated with the features of the people whose ancestors immigrated here from Northern and Western Europe. Among other features, they had "White" skin. There is nothing inherently more attractive about "White" skin or the features shared by these Americans who had a Northern or Western European heritage. In fact, pale skin is more likely to have freckles and is more prone to skin cancer and wrinkles than the skin of many Asians and Africans.

Earlier we discussed that averaged faces are perceived as more attractive. Given that children of mixed-racial parents may have a blend of facial features from each race, one wonders if these children will be perceived as more attractive. In support of this, Rhodes et al. (2005) found that White and Japanese participants perceived a mixed-race composite face (i.e., White, Japanese) as more attractive than faces depicting either exaggerated White or Japanese features, and Lewis (2010) found the same when Black, White, and Black–White biracial faces were rated on attractiveness.

BODY SMELL

It is obvious that vision and hearing are the most important sensors for social situations in Western societies, but the sense of smell also may influence responses. The scientific study of the human olfactory system is fairly new, but we know other animals obtain a great deal of information from their sense of smell: the presence of an enemy, territorial markers, finding members of the same species or herd, sexual stimulation, mate selection, and emotional states. Dogs are known for their ability to sense fear, hate, or friendship in human beings and to track them by only the scent from clothing.

Americans do not seem to rely *consciously* on their sense of smell for much interpersonal information, unless perspiration odor, breath, or some other smell is unusually strong or inappropriate to the situation. Perhaps people could enhance their olfactory sensitivity if our language had a better-developed vocabulary for differentiating among odors. If it is true that people tend to neglect their olfactory skills, it seems ironic that they spend so much time and money on artificial scents. Each year American men and women spend millions of dollars on deodorants, soaps, mouthwashes, breath mints, perfumes, aftershave lotions, and other products to add to or cover up natural body scents. Publicly, the so-called natural scent seems to have a low priority in our cultural development.

What is the role of human odors in daily interaction? Reactions may be consciously or unconsciously processed, but the message can be quite meaningful. Odors collect in the mouth and in regions of the body with hair. Several experiments attest to the fact that people are usually able to identify the odors of specific other human beings. These "dirty T-shirt" studies instructed people to wear a cotton T-shirt for periods ranging from 1 day to 1 week and to avoid using any perfumes and deodorants. Seventy-five percent of the people tested were able to sniff out their own T-shirt and those of a male and female stranger. Parents can identify their children's T-shirt, even in infants only 2 hours old, with accuracy rates that sometimes exceed 90%, and children are generally able to identify their siblings (Lord & Kasprzak, 1989; Porter, Cernoch, & Balogh, 1985; Porter, Cernoch, & McLaughlin, 1983; Porter & Moore, 1981; Russell, 1976). Rodriguez-Lujan et al. (2013) suggested that people's hand odor may serve as a biomarker of their identity. By the age of 6 weeks, infants respond to the odor on a breast pad from their mother but not from a stranger. An important qualification is in order with odor-based recognition research: Although people do seem to be able to identify others by smell, the accuracy rate depends a great deal on how many competing stimuli there are. It may be much easier to choose a spouse's T-shirt from 2 than from 20.

Body odor may also be linked to personality traits. Specifically, others' odor-based judgments of a person may align with that person's self-judgments, such as on the trait of dominance, even when wearing fragrant cosmetics (Sorokowska, Sorokowska, & Havlíček, 2016). Others have shown, though, that fragrances can interfere with people's judgments of others' sexually relevant characteristics (Allen, Cobey, Havlíček, & Roberts, 2016). In addition, one's current affective state also may be evident to others via body odors. A literature review by de Groot and Smeets (2017) provided evidence that body odor can reveal alarm states, such as fear, anxiety, and stress, to others.

Smells not only help in identifying people and their characteristics but may also play a role in mating and sexual-related behaviors. Women rate single men's body odor as stronger than that of partnered men's, presumably because single men have higher levels of testosterone in them (Mahmut & Stevenson, 2017). Men appear to be sexually responsive to the odors women produce when they are sexually aroused during their luteal phase (Hoffman, 2019). Moreover, men are more likely to demonstrate the valued social characteristic of cooperation after being exposed to the body odor of ovulating women (Oren & Shamay-Tsoory, 2019). When unmarried women were asked to select a man's T-shirt that had an odor that they would like to smell if they had to smell it all the time, they selected T-shirts from men who were genetically similar, but not too similar, to their fathers (Jacob, McClintock, Zelano, & Ober, 2002). Major histocompatibility complex (MHC) appears to be a factor. MHC is made up of genes that influence tissue rejection in the immune system, and if a child is conceived with a person who is too similar in MHC, the fetus is at a greater risk of rejection. Animals often use smell to detect MHC differences in potential mates, and now we know humans can, too. Women preferred the smell of male T-shirts that were safely different in MHC from their own, even though women taking birth control pills were not nearly as consistent in selecting safely different MHC (Garver-Apgar, Gangestad, Thornhill, Miller, & Olp, 2006; Wedekind & Füri, 1997; Wedekind, Seebeck, Bettens, & Paepke, 1995). With respect to relationship maintenance, Lundström and Jones-Gotman (2009) found that the more women expressed love for their current boyfriend, the less able they were to identify the body odor of a male friend, suggesting that this might be a means of deflecting attention away from other males as potential mates.

Homosexual men seem to react differently to male chemical signals than heterosexual men, and they prefer the odors of gay men. Heterosexual men and women, as well as lesbians, do not prefer the odor from homosexual males (Martins et al., 2005; Savic, Berglund, & Lindström, 2005).

Heterosexual males seem to be affected by different odors given off by females at different times in the ovulation cycle. Eighteen strippers (lap dancers) recorded their tips over the course of 60 days. When they were ovulating, they earned $67 an hour; when they were not ovulating or menstruating, they earned $52 an hour; when they were menstruating, they earned $37 an hour. Strippers who were taking a contraceptive pill did not show a peak in earnings during estrus (Miller, Tybur, & Jordan, 2007).

Odor also seems to play a role in synchronizing female menstrual cycles. It was discovered that friends and college roommates moved from an average of 8.5 days apart in their menstrual cycles to less than 5 days apart during the school year. Another experimenter attempted to explain why by taking odor samples from the underarm of a female colleague, which was called *Essence of Genevieve*. This odor was dabbed on the upper lips of female volunteers three times a week for 4 months. Another group of women were dabbed with alcohol. The alcohol group showed no change, but the group receiving Essence of Genevieve tended to synchronize their cycles with Genevieve's. This group went from an average of 9.3 days apart in their cycles to 3.4, with four women moving to within 1 day of Genevieve's cycle. Subsequent work has examined the role of a man's perspiration odor on women's menstrual cycles. The procedures used in the Essence of Genevieve study were replicated using women whose cycles were longer than normal and shorter than normal. Those whose upper lips were dabbed with the male odor developed cycles closer to normal; the control group did not (Cutler et al., 1986; McClintock, 1971; Russell, 1976; Stern & McClintock, 1998).

In addition to affecting the menstrual cycle, male perspiration also seems to have a positive effect on women's moods in the form of stress reduction and relaxation (Preti, Wysocki, Barnhart, Sondheimer, & Leyden, 2003). In addition, people may be sensitive to competitive signals (and thus potential threat) that are being communicated via male sweat. Larger skin conductance responses were observed from people when they were exposed to the sweat of men who had participated in a competitive sport (and thus had higher levels of testosterone) relative to those in a sports control condition (Adolph, Schlösser, Hawighorst, & Pause, 2010).

The preceding studies are important reminders of the connection between physiological processes and odor. Physicians have long known that people with certain illnesses tend to give off certain odors, but now it seems that certain physiological processes can be modified by odor. It is not surprising that such effects take place in the animal or insect worlds, but until recently we have not thought of human behavior in this way. Today, some people even practice aromatherapy, using odors to alleviate anxiety, headaches, and hypertension, for example.

Another source of odor is flatulent air, generally adding an embarrassing or insulting aura to an interpersonal encounter in our culture (Lippman, 1980). Under certain conditions, however, emission of flatulent air may be used deliberately to draw attention to oneself. The extent to which odors attributed to flatus or unpleasant body odors are evaluated negatively is probably related to the extent of which others believe people are aware of it and whether it is controllable.

BODY HAIR

The length of a person's hair can dramatically affect perceptions and human interaction. In 1902, the U.S. Commissioner of Indian Affairs sent out an order to forcibly, if necessary, cut all male Native Americans' hair so they would look "civilized." Historically, this is only one of many instances in which hair length triggered an undesirable response.

During the 1960s, White men who allowed the hair on their head to grow over their ears and foreheads, and sometimes to their shoulders, found they frequently attracted abuse. Cases of discrimination in housing, school admittance, jobs, and commercial establishments, to mention a few, were numerous.

The media have regularly reported stories involving reactions to, or regulations directed toward, human hair, mostly male hair. Even if standards change and a given practice becomes accepted over time, it is instructive to be reminded the extent to which hair can upset people. Here are some examples:

AUSTIN, TEXAS (1973) Long hair on boys and men is the "sign of a sissy" and should be banned from American athletic fields, according to the lead article in the May issue of the *Texas High School Coaches Association's* magazine. A head football coach at a junior high school in Houston said God made man to dominate woman and, therefore, meant for man to wear short hair. Simpson told his fellow coaches in the article that "a good hair code will get abnormals out of athletics before they become coaches and bring their 'losers' standards into the coaching profession."

NEW JERSEY (1973) The headmaster of a well-known preparatory school, who sported a beard and a mustache, said about 60 seniors would be suspended if they did not cut their hair to meet regulations on hair grooming. One student reported he was told by the headmaster, "I hold your diploma. Either you get a haircut or [you] don't get your diploma."

CONNECTICUT (1975) A woman was fired from her waitressing job because she refused to shave her legs.

SEOUL, SOUTH KOREA (1980) The national police were ordered to refrain from arresting men because of their long hair. During the first 8 months of the year, 14,911 men were arrested on such a charge.

LUBBOCK, TEXAS (1990) A mother in Texas did not see how the rat-tail hairdo her 11-year-old son had been wearing for 3 years was suddenly in violation of the Lubbock Independent School District's dress code. School officials were enforcing a policy that prohibited boys from having longer than shoulder-length hair, ponytails, rat tails, patterns shaved into their hair, and braids. Her son, a Boy Scout and honor student before his withdrawal, was being tutored at home because he refused to conform to the new policy.

WASHINGTON, D.C. (1994) A woman with a moustache alleged that her facial hair was the reason she was fired.

COLUMBIA, SOUTH CAROLINA (1995) Prisoners at a correctional institution stabbed five guards and took three hostages to protest a policy that would require them to cut their hair.

BASTROP, TEXAS (1996) A state appeals court ruled that school officials were out of bounds when they sent a ponytailed 8-year-old boy to the equivalent of solitary confinement. The school district's claims that its hair rule was needed to prevent gangs, teach gender identity, and maintain discipline were sheer nonsense, the Third Court of Appeals said.

HARLINGEN, TEXAS (2004) A 16-year-old student who had several cases of cancer in his family wanted to grow his hair long and donate it to a nonprofit organization that uses donated hair to create custom-fitted hairpieces for children suffering from medical hair loss. School officials said this would violate the policy that forbids boys to grow hair that hangs below their shoulders.

Most negative reactions against long hair are directed at men, consistent with a general societal tendency to enforce appearance norms more stringently for men than for women. For example, it is extremely rare to see men wearing a skirt but women wear pants anytime they want. Women are also allowed to dress in a more revealing and sexualized manner than men are; they have more hairstyle choices; they have much greater license to wear jewelry; and even the color palette of their wardrobe is allowed to have more variety.

Men are increasingly concerned about the appearance of their hair (Ricciardelli, 2011). Some are concerned that naturally occurring baldness will detract from their attractiveness, but just as often, women report that it does not. The motivation for negative responses to "extreme" hairstyles such as Mohawks, shaved heads, and buzz cuts by some members of our culture is an important question but not our major concern here. The fact that hair length and style, in and of itself, elicits feelings of either appreciation or repugnance is the important point (see Figure 6-3).

FIGURE 6-3 How do hair length and style influence your perceptions?

© keko-ka/Shutterstock.com

© Terrence Horgan

FIGURE 6-4 The popularity of beards on men has grown in recent years.

Other body hair also seems to be important in judgments of attractiveness as well. One study that looked at male facial hair from a historical perspective suggested that men sport more facial hair when they want to be more attractive to women during times when marriage is valued and the competition for brides is intense (Barber, 2001). In the present day, beards on men are growing in popularity, even on professional sports teams. One study showed that women preferred bearded over clean-shaven male faces, and that this preference was unrelated to their monthly hormonal cycle (Dixson, Lee, Blake, Jasienska, & Marcinkowska, 2018). However, the type of beard on men seems to matter, with patchy beards being rated as less sexually appealing than fuller ones by women (Dixson & Rantala, 2016).

Other studies suggest that beards do not necessarily enhance men's physical attractiveness to women, but suggest other male characteristics that are valued by women. The degree of beardedness positively influences women's ratings of a man's social status, masculinity, health, and parenting ability (Dixson & Brooks, 2013; Dixson & Vaseo, 2012). Beards may also help men appear more threatening to others, another characteristic suggesting the highly valued trait of dominance in men. Craig, Nelson, and Dixson (2019) observed that facial expressions of anger were more quickly and accurately decoded when they appeared on a bearded man's face.

Similar to food stuck in a man's beard, there are some unsightly social consequences associated with facial hair. Shannon and Stark (2003) have found that beards may not be much of an asset to men in terms of obtaining a management-trainee position. And a beard may actually be a liability in the political sphere, as women and feminists appear less likely to vote for men with facial hair (Herrick, Mendez, & Pryor, 2015).

Although men with a lot of body hair are attractive to some women and repulsive to others, women in California and New Zealand found men to be more and more unattractive as the amount of hair increased on the their chest and abdomen (Dixson et al., 2010). Nonetheless, it appears that preference for male body hair among women might be shaped by experience. For instance, Finnish women showed a preference for male torso hairiness that was correlated with that of their fathers or current romantic partners (Rantala, Pölkki, & Rantala, 2010).

What about the hair on women's bodies? For years, *Playboy* magazine neatly airbrushed or did not display pubic hair on its models. Even magazines depicting figures in nudist colonies were so well known for such alterations of pubic hair that many subsequently advertised their magazines as unretouched. And the practice of shaving or

SPLITTING HAIRS?

The presence versus absence of a beard on the two presidential candidates in the top row is a trivial detail. Nonetheless, it is interesting to note that, from a historical perspective, Charles Evens Hughes was the last bearded major-party candidate to run for president of the United States of America http://www.slate.com/articles/news_and_politics/politics/2012/04/beards_in_politics_there_hasn_t_been_a_bearded_major_party_presidential_nominee_in_almost_100_years_why_.html (*Slate*, Justin Peters, 2012). This political contest occurred over a century ago, in 1916, just in case you are wondering. Also, Hughes lost to the beardless Woodrow Wilson.

Below is the group of candidates who were vying to be the Democratic party nominee for the 2020 presidential race. Obviously, these individuals look quite different from the older white men shown above. Nonetheless, among the male candidates, none of them is sporting facial hair, let alone a beard, and neither does Donald Trump, the former occupant of the White House.

trimming one's pubic hair is common among college-aged women (e.g., bikini or Brazilian wax) and men in the United States and Australia, even though the reasons for doing so may be different for each gender (Smolak & Murnen, 2011).

When nude photographs of the pop singer Madonna appeared in two national magazines, many people commented more about the hair under her arms than about her lack of clothing. Some liked the underarm hair; others did not. Many people in the United States find underarm hair unattractive on women even though this perception is not shared in other countries. It is reported that the Cacobo Indians of the Amazon rain forest carefully trim and groom their head hair but feel that other body hair is unattractive; they methodically eliminate eyebrows by plucking them. The lack of eyebrows on the Mona Lisa is some evidence that at one time it may have been desirable to pluck them for beauty's sake.

The shape of bodies, skin color, smell, and body hair are major factors affecting responses to one's own and others' personal appearance. Still, many other body features, in any given situation, may play an important role; for example, freckles, moles, acne, and so-called beauty marks. We now turn to how people alter their appearance with clothing, decorations, and artifacts such as eyeglasses, jewelry, and piercings.

CLOTHES AND OTHER ARTIFACTS

As early as 1954, Hoult's experiments verified what seems like common sense today—that you can change people's perceptions of someone by changing that person's clothing. We do not have to look far to find evidence to confirm Hoult's finding. The Associated Press once reported that the Lutheran Church believed the attire worn by clergy in the pulpit was responsible for some churchgoers' switching denominations. Many tailors, manufacturers, and sellers of clothes claim to be "wardrobe engineers" who structure their clients' outward appearance to increase their sales, assert their authority, or win more court cases. Career specialists say that a job applicant's attire and grooming are important indicators of their attitude toward the company and that appropriate dress is an asset for career advancement. Clothes are definitely an important factor in first impressions.

School dress codes provide clear testimony that people believe clothes communicate important messages. The Associated Press reported in 1994 that several Houston-area school districts outlawed what they called the *grunge look*. Students were prohibited from wearing baggy pants; untucked shirts; piercings in the lips, nose, and eyebrows; torn or ripped clothing; duster-type coats; or trench coats. Earrings were prohibited for boys, and girls could not wear miniskirts, tank tops, cutoffs, halter tops, strapless garments, or casual pants, dress slacks, or skirts worn on hips. These school administrators, like administrators in other school districts with similar dress and grooming restrictions, wanted to ban clothing that could hide weapons, that might convey gang or drug-related messages, or that seemed sexually provocative, and to encourage clothing that would convey what they believed to be a safe, respectful, and positive learning environment. Sometimes, prohibitions regarding dress can shake a whole society, as happened when the French government, starting in 1989, began banning Muslim headscarves in schools. Conflict between national identity and religious identity as expressed in clothing remains a thorny issue in that country ("Facing History and Ourselves," 2019).

We can draw two important conclusions from the preceding examples: (1) right or wrong, many people believe clothes communicate important messages; (2) clothing communicates most effectively when it is adapted to the wearer's role and the attendant surroundings. This second conclusion relates to the earlier testimony about how to dress for job interviews and make positive first impressions. It is also supported by research in which well-dressed participants and participants who were dressed sloppily asked strangers for money to make a phone call. When well dressed, those requesting aid received more cooperation in a clean, neatly appointed airport, where most of the people were also well dressed; when participants were poorly dressed, the greatest cooperation was obtained from strangers in a bus station, where the people and surroundings more closely resembled the participant's state of poor dress (Hensley, 1981). The need to change clothes to fit situational demands even manifests itself in how users alter the appearance of their avatars depending on whether the virtual situation for them is a video game or a "job-themed social network" (Triberti, Durosini, Aschieri, Villani, & Riva, 2017).

Sometimes, a person is very much aware of what attire fits the situation. Most people know, for example, that the business outfits of working women on television programs would not be appropriate for women who do not work "on camera" (White, 1995). Other situations are not so clear, as Victoria Clarke, then assistant secretary of defense for public affairs, found out in 2003. She was criticized for wearing bright colors while answering questions about the war in Iraq. Some, mainly men, argued that pink is not an appropriate color in time of war (Givhan, 2003).

Examine the clothing types shown in Figure 6-5. What are your first impressions?

The following is a list of 20 characteristics that may be associated with one or more of these clothing types. Check the spaces you think apply to specific clothing types, and compare your impressions with those of your friends, family, and associates.

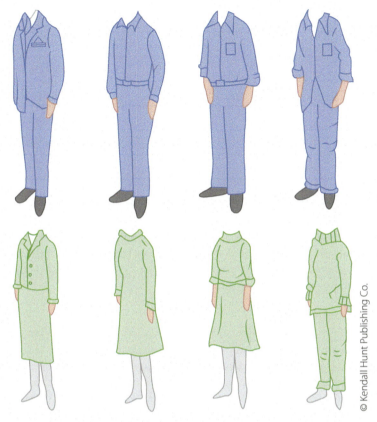

© Kendall Hunt Publishing Co.

FIGURE 6-5 Four clothing styles.

Males				Females				
1	2	3	4	1	2	3	4	
___	___	___	___	___	___	___	___	1. Has smoked marijuana
___	___	___	___	___	___	___	___	2. Is shy, doesn't talk much
___	___	___	___	___	___	___	___	3. Is a fraternity or sorority member
___	___	___	___	___	___	___	___	4. Is a Democrat
___	___	___	___	___	___	___	___	5. Is involved in athletics
___	___	___	___	___	___	___	___	6. Is married
___	___	___	___	___	___	___	___	7. Is generous
___	___	___	___	___	___	___	___	8. Drives a sports car
___	___	___	___	___	___	___	___	9. Is a Republican
___	___	___	___	___	___	___	___	10. Is vocationally oriented
___	___	___	___	___	___	___	___	11. Is active politically
___	___	___	___	___	___	___	___	12. Is dependable

___	___	___	___	___	___	___	___	13. Listens most to classical music
___	___	___	___	___	___	___	___	14. Lives with parents
___	___	___	___	___	___	___	___	15. Has long hair
___	___	___	___	___	___	___	___	16. Has many friends
___	___	___	___	___	___	___	___	17. Is intelligent
___	___	___	___	___	___	___	___	18. Is religious
___	___	___	___	___	___	___	___	19. Is open-minded
___	___	___	___	___	___	___	___	20. Is older

Did you find any similarities in your responses and those of your peers? Were there any major differences between your responses and the responses of people with distinctly different backgrounds? Later in this chapter, we focus on what specific messages and impressions clothes communicate, but first let us consider the fundamental question: Is clothing, in and of itself, an important factor in communicating?

FUNCTIONS OF CLOTHING

To understand the relationship between clothes and communication, we must be familiar with the various functions clothes can fulfill: decoration, physical and psychological protection, comfort, sexual attraction, self-assertion, self-denial, concealment, group identification, persuasion, attitude, ideology, mood reflection or creation, authority, and status or role display (Barnard, 2001). Clothing can be used to conceal the body, but that function may mean different things depending on the person. For instance, with age, older women (over 62) may become increasingly drawn to clothing that is comfortable, convenient, and not too revealing of their body (Lövgren, 2016). For younger women (aged 18–52), though, the use of clothing for camouflage purposes may be linked to their greater dissatisfaction with their body (Tiggemann & Lacey, 2009).

Other functions are related to norm adherence and gender-role expectations and opportunities. Because some widely accepted cultural rules and social norms apply for combining certain colors and styles of dress, clothes can function to inform the observer of a person's knowledge or awareness of such rules (see "The Lowdown on Fashion Trends"). For instance, the costumes children wear on Halloween may reveal their adoption of gender-role expectations, with older children wearing more gender-typed costumes than younger children (Dinella, 2017).

Learning about fashion is something that women spend a lot of time on, especially during adolescence through young adulthood, due to societal expectations. This activity may thus function as a common, acceptable form of recreation for them (Bloch, 1993). It is interesting to note that this behavior is even observed in virtual settings. Guadagno, Muscanell, Okdie, Burk, and Ward (2011) found that women were more likely than men to buy clothes/objects for their avatars. However, on the downside, Internet games that focus on appearance seem to make young girls feel more dissatisfied with their body (Slater, Halliwell, Jarman, & Gaskin, 2017).

Clothing that functions as a means of persuasion has been the subject of numerous studies. An old but classic study tested the ability of people dressed in "high-status" clothing to get unsuspecting bystanders to violate a traffic light. Lefkowitz, Blake, and Mouton (1955) found pedestrians much more likely to violate a traffic light at an intersection if another person violated it ahead of them, especially if that other person's attire represented a person with social status. Other studies have found that a variety of requests—to make change, accept leaflets, give detailed street directions, return money left in a phone booth, and so on—are more easily accomplished if the requester is dressed to fit the situation or is dressed in what would be considered high-status clothing (Fortenberry, MacLean, Morris, & O'Connell, 1978; Levine, Bluni, & Hochman, 1998). Bickman (1974a, 1974b), for example, had four men stop 153 adults on the streets of Brooklyn and make various requests. The men's clothing varied and included civilian clothing, comprising a sport jacket and tie; a milkman's White uniform; and a guard's uniform, with a badge and insignia but no gun. The men asked pedestrians to pick up a bag, to put a dime in a parking meter for someone else, or to stand on the opposite side of a bus-stop sign. In each case, when dressed in the guard uniform, the men received greater compliance. In fact, 83% of those who were asked to put a dime in the parking meter obeyed, even after the person in the guard uniform had left the scene. Uniforms do help people identify the wearer's probable areas of expertise, and this knowledge can be persuasive—but obviously overgeneralized. In public service announcements, the same woman dressed as a nurse or as a businesswoman asked for contributions to fight leukemia. The nurse was judged to be more knowledgeable and received more pledged contributions (Lawrence & Watson, 1991). Uniformed police officers want their uniform to be persuasive, but it is sometimes difficult because of the different goals associated with their job. It was debated whether the same uniform can communicate approachability and friendliness as well as authoritativeness in enforcing the law (Young, 1999). Officers in the NYPD Community Affairs division wear baseball caps with NYPD logo and windbreakers instead of the standard police uniform to minimize their threat to the citizens whose problems they try to solve. Lawyers have long known that their clients' manner of dress can have a persuasive impact on the judgments made by a judge or jury. Some defendants have even been encouraged to put on a ring that simulates a wedding ring to offset any prejudice against single people.

THE LOWDOWN ON FASHION TRENDS

What nonverbal message is a woman wearing jeans so low they show her butt crack communicating? As a college student in the United States in the later 20th century, she was likely signaling her awareness and acceptance of fashion norms concerning how she can identify herself as female through style of dress. Interestingly, what was acceptable then was not earlier in the century. It used to be referred to as *plumber's butt*, a decidedly pejorative label. This illustrates how nonverbal messages linked to fashion may be subject to shifting conformity pressures. Wearing pants that low is no longer as fashionable. Women who continue to do so might be communicating a different nonverbal message to others, such as "I'm old-fashioned."

Take a look at these other fashion trends. Do they reflect shifting conformity pressures for men and women? Will they be fashionable 10 years from now?

© Terrence Horgan

© Alones/Shutterstock.com

FIGURE 6-6 Dress and conformity?

CLOTHING AS INFORMATION ABOUT THE PERSON

To make a list of the things invariably communicated by clothes would be impossible; such a list would vary with the demands of each particular situation, ethnic group, time of day and era, region of the country, and, for women, even the phase of their monthly ovulatory cycle. Women, for example, may choose sexier clothes to wear when they are close to ovulating (Durante, Griskevicius, Hill, Perilloux, & Li, 2011). Making the task even harder is the fact that any given item of clothing can be worn in such a way as to convey multiple meanings, as any kind of nonverbal behavior can. Wearing a tie may convey sophistication and status, but the way it is knotted or worn—tight or loose, thrown over the shoulder—can send other messages.

Some of the personal attributes communicated by dress include gender, sexual orientation, age, nationality, relation to a companion (e.g., matching sweaters), socioeconomic status, identification with a specific group, occupational or official status, mood, personality, attitudes, interests, and values. Clothes also set expectations for the behavior of the wearer. When the target of observation is an acquaintance, that knowledge will guide our interpretations of clothing. One might, for example, see radical clothing changes as representing temporary moods rather than lasting personality changes. Obviously, the accuracy of such judgments varies considerably; age, gender, and socioeconomic status are typically signaled with greater accuracy than more abstract qualities such as attitudes, values, and personality. T-shirts with slogans may be needed to communicate attitudes that might otherwise be more difficult to assess. In the Vietnam War era, many such shirts said "Make Love, Not War," while in 2018-2019 one of the bestselling said, "The Future is Female."

DRESS AND SEXUAL ORIENTATION

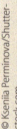

A woman's dress and grooming style can signal her sexual orientation. Krakauer and Rose (2002) noted that lesbians may deliberately dress themselves in a less "feminine" way after coming out, possibly as a way of signaling their sexual orientation to other lesbians. For example, they may wear more masculine- or androgynous-looking clothes and less to no makeup at all. This does not apply to all lesbians, though; the appearance of "lipstick lesbians" and "femmes" is more prototypically "feminine."

© Kseniia Perminova/Shutter-stock.com

EFFECTS OF CLOTHING ON THE WEARER

What about the effect of clothing on the self-image of the wearer? In an earlier generation, a woman was said to buy herself a new hat when she felt down in the dumps. Although a modern woman (or man) might not take recourse to a new hat, surely many have improved their mood with a clothing purchase. A new outfit may promote feelings of gaiety and happiness; people may feel less efficient in shoes that hurt; and self-consciousness may result from wearing the "wrong" outfit, a common feeling for adolescents trying to grapple with their developing self-image. Some graduate teaching assistants dress "up" when teaching to distinguish themselves from their students, who frequently are almost the same age. Such attire may send its messages back to the wearer, giving them added confidence or assurance in dealing with their students (Gorham, Cohen, & Morris, 1999; Roach, 1997). The identity claim that is conveyed by choice of clothing no doubt helps to reinforce that identity because not only do others see and respond to the clothing (and the claim it suggests), the wearer also sees and responds to it.

Even clothes that are arbitrarily assigned to be worn can influence the wearer. Participants who were told to come to the lab in either White or Black clothes scored differently on an implicit self-concept measure (implicit meaning the task would not elicit deliberate responding): Wearing White produced a temporarily more moral self-concept compared to wearing Black (Uebayashi, Tado'oka, Ishii, & Murata, 2016). Consistent with this, the wearing of Black athletic uniforms appears to increase the aggression of those who wear them (Frank & Gilovich, 1988). Finally, when nurses had to wear "patient clothing" they experienced comfort but also stigmatization and depersonalization (Edvardsson, 2009).

The issue of wearing uniforms to school has gained a great deal of notoriety in recent years. One of the prominent arguments for adopting school uniforms is that the style of dress changes how wearers feel about themselves and, in turn, changes behavior. One large-scale study of 10th-grade students did not find any direct effects of uniforms on substance use, behavioral problems, or attendance but did find a negative effect on achievement (Brunsma & Rockquemore, 1998). For some students, uniforms provide a needed form of structure and control, and they are a symbol of school unity, but it is not realistic to expect uniforms to eliminate most of the problematic behaviors manifested by troubled teens. School uniforms by themselves—without the support of students, teachers, school administrators, and parents—are not likely to accomplish much.

CLOTHING AND PERSONALITY

People do use how others are dressed to make assumptions about them, rightly or wrongly. Stereotypes about people based on their clothing are easy to find, and some have been documented. Koukounas and Itsou (2018) observed that both men and women perceived greater "sexual intent" in a woman wearing more versus less sexually provocative clothing (exposed legs and cleavage vs. pants, long-sleeved shirt) while interacting with a man. Gillath, Bahns, Ge, and Crandall (2012) documented personality stereotypes associated with the appearance of college students' shoes. Observers saw the shoes and guessed the personalities of their owners. Shoes in better repair were thought to be worn by more conscientious people, more colorful shoes by people open to experience, brand-revealing shoes by extraverted people, and high-top shoes by people low in agreeableness (among other associations).

Can observers *accurately* perceive traits from the way people dress? It appears that a person's style of dress can provide diagnostic clues to their traits, which can be used accurately by observers in guessing those traits (Back, Schmukle, & Egloff, 2010; Borkenau & Liebler, 1993a; Vazire, Naumann, Rentfrow, & Gosling, 2009). For example, the clothes that a person chooses to wear may provide a clue to their narcissism (Han et al., 2016; Vazire, Naumann, Rentfrow, & Gosling, 2008). Stylish clothes and haircuts can contribute to accurate judgment of extraversion (Borkenau & Liebler, 1993b). Fancy clothes can also contribute to the initial positivity that people feel toward those whose personality traits can be problematic in the long run, such as is the case with narcissists (Back et al., 2010). In the shoe-judging study, accuracy was significantly above guessing for agreeableness (the agreeable targets really did wear fewer high-top shoes, for example), but accuracy was not above the guessing level for the other Big Five traits. Lack of accuracy was due to two factors: Shoes did not actually reveal much about personality, and sometimes observers used incorrect cues in guessing personality. Extraversion, for example, was not actually associated with wearing shoes that showed the brand.

ARTIFACTS AND BODY DECORATIONS

People adorn themselves with badges, tattoos, masks, earrings, personal aids and devices (glasses, watches), accessories (hats), and jewelry, among other things. We must take these artifacts and decorations into consideration in any discussion of clothing because they are also potential communicative stimuli. A ring worn on a particular finger, a fraternity or sorority pin worn in a particular configuration, and a single earring worn in a particular ear all may communicate something about the nature of a person's relationships and self-image.

People around the world choose to decorate and alter their bodies in a vast variety of ways, sometimes temporarily with body paint, sometimes permanently with tattoos (see Figures 6-7 and 6-8), scarring, or mutilation (in the case of binding infants' feet or heads, the bone structure is actually reshaped). In our society, parents circumcise many male children, and the piercing of various body parts with rings has become increasingly popular with young adults. Tattoos used to be tied to a person's occupation or criminal background. Today, tattoos are common among college students and young adults in general. There are some correlates, however, in terms of personality and demographics (Sagoe, Pallesen, & Andreassen, 2017; Swami et al., 2016). Yet, other research has shown that consumers do not seem to respond differently to a tattooed versus nontattooed server's mistake in a restaurant setting (Ozanne, Tews, & Mattila, 2019).

People sometimes react strongly to a particular artifact or decoration. These reactions may be positive, negative, or a mixture of the two. Women perceive tattooed men as healthier and more masculine, dominant, and aggressive (compared to non-tattooed men), and as worse partners and parents (Galbarczyk & Ziomkiewicz, 2017). Wohlrab, Fink, Kappeler, and Brewer (2009) observed that tattooed avatars were viewed as more adventure-seeking, less inhibited, and having more previous sexual partners than their nontattooed counterparts. The presence of tattoos might

© Tinxi/Shutterstock.com

FIGURE 6-7 A woman body-painting a man.

© Terrence Horgan

FIGURE 6-8 People around the world use tattoos to decorate their bodies.

hurt a person's perceived hireability in jobs in which workers have to face customers (Timming, Nickson, Re, & Perrett, 2017). Lipstick on women may be positively viewed due to its positive association with greater femininity and attractiveness (Stephen & McKeegan, 2010). Yet, as noted earlier, it is mistakenly seen as a cue to greater female unrestrictiveness in their sociosexuality (Batres et al., 2018).

Of course, we do not know for certain how people will respond to even the most common of personal artifacts. Consider the following question: Do people who wear eyeglasses seem more intelligent to us? Surprisingly, given the frequent depictions of smart but nerdy bespectacled people on TV, the answer to this question is not clear (Harris, Harris, & Bochner, 1982; Lundberg & Sheehan, 1994; McKelvie, 1997). Some early research found that wearing glasses created the impression of intelligence, temporarily at least, but this effect was not consistent. Perhaps because glasses are now a fashion item as well as an ocular necessity, stereotypes about their wearers have become more complex. And of course the type of glasses would influence stereotypes and impressions greatly.

SUMMARY

Appearance and dress are part of the total nonverbal stimuli that influence interpersonal responses, and under some conditions, they are the primary determinants of such responses. Physical attractiveness may be influential in determining whether a person is sought out, and it may have a bearing on whether a person is able to persuade or manipulate others. It is often an important factor in the selection of dates and marriage partners, and it may determine whether a defendant is deemed guilty or innocent. Physical attractiveness may be a major factor contributing to how others judge personality, sexuality, popularity, success, and often happiness. Fortunately for some, and unfortunately for others, such judgments begin early in life. Most children are not conventionally beautiful. There are indications that teachers not only make attractiveness judgments about young children but also treat the unattractive ones with fewer and less positive communications. A sizable proportion of the American public still thinks of the ideal man or woman in terms of physical attractiveness.

In spite of the overwhelming evidence that physical attractiveness is a highly desirable quality in interpersonal situations, other factors temper these general findings. For instance, all positive findings for attractiveness are based on probabilities, not certainty. Many less attractive people are not evaluated unfavorably. For example, judgments can be tempered by who people are seen with, the environment in which they are judged, other communicative behavior they engage in, or the time of life at which they are evaluated. In addition, many attractiveness studies have used photographs rather than live, interacting human beings, and we know that the dynamics of interaction influence perceptions.

In addition to the importance of general physical attractiveness in influencing the responses of others, we have some information on stereotyped responses to specific features: general body build, facial appearance, skin color, odor, hair, and clothes. These specific features may have a profound influence on a person's self-image and hence on patterns of communication with others.

The way people clothe their bodies may also communicate important messages in work and social life, and it is one of the first things people perceive about a person. Age, gender, and socioeconomic status are more easily judged from clothing than attitudes or beliefs, unless a clear attitudinal message is sent (as with a slogan T-shirt). Wearing attire that others perceive as similar to theirs, appropriate to the situation, or representative of an expert or authority figure gives a persuasive element to clothing. We also know that clothing and the other ways of body decoration—jewelry, colors, tattoos, and so on—affect how people feel about themselves, which in turn affects the communication process.

QUESTIONS FOR DISCUSSION

1. Can verbal behavior affect the way people perceive one's physical attractiveness? What verbal behavior might cause people to perceive a person as less physically attractive? What verbal behavior might make a person appear more physically attractive? Do the answers to these questions vary with context? If so, give examples.

2. Do you know of romantic couples in which one member is significantly less attractive than the other? Why do you think they are attracted to each other, despite this difference in their attractiveness?

3. Does the impression of physical attractiveness emerge differently in photos versus videos with no sound? List and discuss some of the reasons why there might or might not be differences.

4. People have been refused employment or fired from their jobs because of perceived problems with their height, weight, odor, clothing, hair, or general attractiveness. Under what conditions, if any, do you think such characteristics are legitimate reasons for not hiring a person or for firing an employee?

NONVERBAL COMMUNICATION IN ACTION: TRY THIS

Go to a public place where you can conveniently watch the people. For each of 10 people, first form your "first impression" of the person from their appearance and clothing—your first impression includes their personality, background, occupation, attitudes, or demographic group. Then, revisit your first impression by analyzing in detail what features of their appearance and clothing produced your impression. Does the careful analysis change any part of your impression?

THE COMMUNICATOR'S BEHAVIOR

Most nonverbal behavior involves change or movement. Different gestures, postures, and body movements occur during an encounter, possibly with *self* or *other* touching. The face, eyes, and voice are displayed in myriad patterns. Part IV examines these behaviors individually, but in everyday conversation, these signals work in concert with one another to communicate messages. The ways nonverbal signals work together is the subject of Part V.

CHAPTER 7

THE EFFECTS OF GESTURE, POSTURE, AND MOVEMENT ON HUMAN COMMUNICATION

We respond to gestures with an extreme alertness and, one might say, in accordance with an elaborate and secret code that is written nowhere, known by none, and understood by all.

—**Edward Sapir**

Sapir's view, quoted here, aptly characterized the prevailing view of gestures during the first part of the 20th century. If he were alive today, his assessment would no doubt be somewhat different. Spoken language and gestures are commonly acknowledged as building blocks of human interaction, both in informal conversation and in more formal public discourse. But unlike language, gestures received relatively little scholarly attention until the last part of the 20th century. Kendon (1981a) identified only six scholarly books on gesture published between 1900 and 1979 in the English language. Now, however, gestures are carefully scrutinized by scholars from around the world, and the academic journal *Gesture*, specifically devoted to gesture research, was launched in 2001. As a result, knowledge of how people use and respond to gestures has greatly increased.

Even though hand and arm gestures are the primary focus of this chapter, the concept of gesture can also include other body parts, and we broaden the concept in the chapter to include the way people walk and their posture. (See Box **Posture Like Jagger**) These behavior modalities have several psychological and interpersonal functions—they can express emotional states, send messages, be interpreted by others, help regulate interpersonal interaction, and even provide feedback to one's brain and nervous system that can shape emotional or cognitive states. Gesture also has an intimate relation to linguistic communication (the words we use) and even to the learning process. As this list suggests, our interest is in the communicative functions of gesture, not in all kinds of gestures in the literal sense. For example, the movements of grooming, smoking, eating, drawing, or hammering a nail are *instrumental*, that is, required by the task at hand. We do not include these in our discussion, unless they have an additional communicative meaning.

POSTURE LIKE JAGGER

© Bruce Alan Bennett/Shutterstock.com

The musical group *Maroon 5* wrote a popular song that referenced the iconic front man Mick Jagger of the legendary rock-n-roll group *The Rolling Stones*. It was called "Moves Like Jagger," in celebration of a man's ability to excite a young woman with his dance moves.

Another song called "Posture Like Jagger" would be a good one for elderly folks. People tend to experience postural decay, whereby they start to hunch or stoop over as they get older. This represents a possible postural cue to a person's advanced age.

What is remarkable about Mick Jagger, who is well into his seventies now, is that there do not appear to be any noticeable signs of postural decay in him, whether he is standing, prancing, skipping, or running on stage during concerts. His genes, active lifestyle, and rigorous fitness routine likely contribute to his upright posture in old age.

EMOTION IN RELATION TO GESTURE AND MOVEMENT

A number of emotions can be judged at above-chance levels just from viewing photos or videos of body movements. Researchers have studied what body movements or posture cues differentiate one emotion from another. Dael, Mortillaro, and Scherer (2012) demonstrated that clusters of movement patterns could reliably distinguish among 12 different emotions. Hot anger, amusement, and elated joy had particularly distinct movement patterns, but the overall level at which the emotion could be predicted from movement patterns (55%) was far in excess of the level expected by chance (8%).

Several studies have shown that emotions such as sadness, anger, and happiness can be accurately identified by a person's gait (Janssen et al., 2008; Montepare, Goldstein, & Clausen, 1987; Montepare & Zebrowitz, 1993; Montepare & Zebrowitz-McArthur, 1988). Arm swing, stride length, heavy-footedness, and walking speed play a central role in these perceptions. Hadjikhani and de Gelder (2003) found that perceptions of fear communicated solely by a person's body, with the expressor's facial features blurred, activated the same areas of a perceiver's brain that are activated when responding to facial expressions of emotion. And Gilbert, Martin, and Coulson (2011) demonstrated that people can identify an angry body posture more quickly than a happy body posture located in a neutral crowd. This finding pertaining to postural cues is in line with other research showing that people have an attentional bias for threatening nonverbal cues, such as angry faces and insulting gestures (Flaisch, Hacker, Renner, & Schupp, 2011; Hansen & Hansen, 1988).

In the emotional disorders seen in psychiatry, body cues can help with diagnosis and with tracking outcomes. Fiquer et al. (2018) found that patients with major depression, compared to healthy controls, showed more shrugging, holding the head down, and "adaptive" hand gestures (which usually take the form of self-touching).

The terms *embodiment* and *embodied cognition* were coined to reflect the phenomenon of one's body informing one's emotions and thoughts, through various pathways including neurological. This phenomenon has been mostly studied with regard to internal feedback from facial expressions (see Chapter 9), but experimental research shows that the body can do the same. Stepper and Strack (1993) found that achieving success on a task produces more feelings of pride when the person sits upright rather than slumped. And Nair, Sagar, Sollers, Consedine, and Broadbent (2015) found that, when under stress in a laboratory task, participants who were positioned in an upright posture reported higher self-esteem, better mood, and lower fear, and used fewer negative emotion words, compared to participants who were placed in a slumped posture.

CULTURE: UNIVERSALITY OR CULTURAL SPECIFICITY?

At one point, it was thought that different cultures develop their own unique codes of gestural communication. This is actually far from true, although there are some ways in which cultures differ in how they use gesture, in terms of both meaning and usage. As we have said elsewhere in this book, with nonverbal behavior all-or-nothing statements rarely hold up. With regard to culture in particular, different cultures (countries, regions, etc.) might use cues in different frequencies or in different contexts, but the core meaning of those cues might be shared across cultures. An example would be kissing: One sees wide variation in the form, frequency, and settings for kissing as well as in who is encouraged or prohibited from kissing whom. Nevertheless, in all likelihood, the kiss has a universal meaning as a sign of affection or friendly intent.

As an example of gestural universality, some head gestures seem to transcend culture and language. Arabic, Bulgarian, Korean, and African-American speakers all used lateral head movements to accompany expressions of inclusivity, changed their head position for each item on a list, oriented their head toward a specific location when referring to absent or abstract entities, and used head nods to elicit active listening nods from their listeners (McClave, 2000; McClave, Kim, Tamer, & Mileff, 2007).

Differences in gestures across cultures can develop for various reasons, including differences in cognition, ecological/social requirements, geographical coincidence, and linguistic differences (Kita, 2009; Morris, Collett, Marsh, & O'Shaughnessy, 1979). Although not all cultures in the world have been compared, comparative data does exist as well as many within-culture studies. To give one example of how a common functional purpose can coexist with specific cultural variations, Kita (2009) described how in Naples, Italy, there are four distinctly different kinds of pointing used in different contexts (index-finger pointing with the palm vertical, index-finger pointing with the palm down, open hand pointing with the palm vertical, and thumb pointing). Similarly, an Australian Aboriginal group was documented to have even more pointing gestures, each with a contrastive function: index-finger pointing, open-hand pointing with the palm down, open-hand pointing with the palm vertical, "horn-hand" pointing (with the thumb, the index finger and the pinkie extended), lip pointing (a pointing by protruded lips), and eye pointing.

Many types of gestures are commonly employed in everyday interaction, and these gestures have been categorized in many ways (Kendon, 2004; McNeill, 2000; Morris, 1977, 1994). We will use a classification system based on the extent to which a gesture is dependent on speech for its meaning. This is a useful distinction, and we can learn a lot about gestures by classifying them as either *speech independent* or *speech dependent.* At the same time, it is important to recognize the difficulties in neatly categorizing a behavior which, on the surface, may seem relatively uncomplicated. Take, for example, the head shake (Kendon, 2002). Many cultures use the head shake as a speech-independent gesture meaning "no." But while a "no" meaning can be communicated without speech, sometimes people will say "no" during the shake. The meaning of the shake has a greater dependence on the accompanying speech when it is used to signal disapproval or doubt, which may occur while saying "Well, I guess I could talk to her ...." In addition, the head shake also accompanies statements to underscore intensity or impossibility, as in "You just wouldn't believe how big his muscles were." Furthermore, the tone of voice influences meaning (loud or soft, questioning or assertive, etc.) as well as situational factors. The head shake, like the pointing gestures just discussed and, in fact, all the gestures discussed in this chapter, can be used and interpreted in different ways, depending on the way it is enacted and the context in which it occurs. With this in mind, let us examine those gestures that are less dependent on speech for their meaning. The theme of culture will come up again in this section.

SPEECH-INDEPENDENT GESTURES

Speech-independent gestures are most often called *emblems* (Ekman, 1976, 1977) but sometimes *autonomous gestures* (Kendon, 1984, 1989a, 1989b). They are nonverbal acts usually performed by the hands, but not always, that have a direct verbal translation that one could state in a word or two or a phrase. In having distinct and fairly invariant meanings—within cultures or subcultural groups—they stand out from most other nonverbal behaviors, which are more fluid and more context-dependent for their meanings. With emblems there is high agreement among members of a culture or subculture on their verbal translation. These gestures are the least dependent on speech for their meaning and most commonly occur as a single gesture. The "ring gesture" in Figure 7-1 is an example of a speech-independent gesture found in several cultures.

Children are able to decode some of these speech-independent gestures by the time they are 2 years old, and this ability increases dramatically by age 5 (Konishi, Karsten, & Vallotton, 2018; Kumin & Lazar, 1974; Michael & Willis, 1968, 1969). When the gestures were deliberately modeled by caretakers, toddlers as young as 1 year old understood hand-arm movements to represent many acts, emotions, and needs, such as "all done," "eat," and "cold" (Acredolo & Goodwyn, 1996; Konishi et al., 2018). In a different study, 4-year-olds accurately decoded the emblems for "yes," "no," "come here," "quiet," "good-bye," "two," "I won't listen," "blowing a kiss," "I'm going to sleep," and "I won't do it" but not the hand gesture for "crazy." Generally, children at this age understand and decode accurately more speech-independent gestures than they actually use in their own interactions and younger toddlers use gestures more than words to make their needs and emotions known.

Emotional self-regulation—that is, controlling or changing one's emotions when in distress—develops in stages through infancy, starting with reactive behaviors requiring little planning, such as head turning to an aversive stimulus, and moving to more deliberate strategies such as self-distraction (engaging with a toy) and strategies involving gestures, such as the child resisting temptation by shaking their head in a "no-no" gesture. Konishi et al. (2018) systematically observed toddlers' use of gestures to regulate their distress in a daycare center. Here is one example:

> As Clara (20 months) watches her mother leave, she begins to whimper ... Clara's caregiver says "It's hard to say goodbye to mom today, it's hard." [...] Clara begins to sob while saying "No, no, no" ... The caregiver says "You don't want to play?" Clara signs "Book" by opening and closing her hands ... Her caregiver responds, "You would like to look at the book with pictures of your family?" Clara replies "Uh huh" and nods her head. (p. 739)

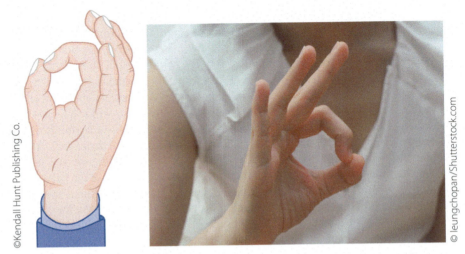

©Kendall Hunt Publishing Co.

© leungchopan/Shutterstock.com

FIGURE 7-1 The ring gesture signifies "A-OK" or "good" in the United States as a speech-independent gesture. It may stand for "zero" or "worthless" in other cultural contexts.

This event, like others reported by the researchers, showed that the toddler deliberately self-regulated via communicating in the gesture modality.

Adults' awareness of their own speech-independent gestures is about the same as that of word choice. In other words, it is a behavior people are usually very conscious of enacting. An exaggerated nose wrinkle may say "I'm disgusted!" or "Phew! It stinks!" To say "I don't know," "I'm helpless," or "I'm uncertain," you might turn both palms up, shrug the shoulders, or do both simultaneously. (The context and other nonverbal cues would determine which of these doubt-related messages you intended—another demonstration that even emblems do not have 100% consistent meanings.)

Facial emblems may look in some respects like spontaneous emotional expressions; for example, the nose-wrinkle emblem for disgust might also be a reflexive emotional reaction, done without deliberate intent. Bavelas and Chovil (2018) demonstrated that, rather than being spontaneous readouts of emotion, facial expressions are often more like emblems, in that they are *referring to* an emotional reaction (which may not be felt in the moment) or *commenting on* something or someone, in the past or present. Researchers believe facial emblems differ from spontaneous facial expressions of emotion in two ways: They are more stylized; and they are enacted for either a longer or shorter duration than the emotional expression. When people talk about their experiences, they may portray certain feelings emblematically by selecting and emphasizing a single feature of a multifeatured facial expression of emotion. An example might be mechanically dropping the jaw or dramatically raising the eyebrows to indicate surprise.

In some cultures, speech-independent gestures are strung together to form a sequential message, but this is unusual in the United States. But it could happen if you are on the phone when a visitor enters your office and you need to convey "Wait a minute," "come in," "I'm on the phone," "sit down," and "don't say anything." Sometimes an entire system of speech-independent gestures develops, such as with underwater divers, umpires, and television directors. Even though these gestures form a system of signals related to performing a specific task, such systems can grow beyond the boundaries of those tasks. In the sawmills of British Columbia, for example, the noise level made spoken communication very difficult. A system of task-related gestures developed that eventually came to include messages not associated with the tasks of the sawmill (Meissner & Philpott, 1975). Gesture systems not limited to a specific task are known as *sign languages.* Sign language is commonly thought of as a form of communication for the hearing impaired, but sign languages also develop in other contexts. Examples include religious orders in which vows of silence are taken as well as social situations in which some are forbidden to speak to others, such as has been reported historically for Armenian wives in the presence of their husbands (Kendon, 1983). (Even though full-scale sign languages such as American Sign Language use the hands [also the face] as the modalities of communication, we do not discuss sign languages as "nonverbal communication" in this book.)

Speech-independent gestures may be used when verbal channels are blocked or fail, but they also are used during verbal interaction. A person may be telling the story of another person's strange behavior and may conclude by making a gesture that communicates "he's crazy." In this case, the circular gesture at the side of the head is a substitute for the statement. Listeners may also use speech-independent gestures to comment on or qualify what the speaker is saying. "Yes" and "no" gestures are common listener responses during another's speech.

DECODING DECISIONS

© CREATISTA/Shutterstock.com

How would you interpret this gesture? As discussed already, there is generally high agreement about the verbal meaning of speech-independent gestures in a culture. Nevertheless, even within a culture, there may be uncertainty regarding the meaning of such gestures. Contextual, regional, and ethnic background factors may alter the emotional valence or verbal translation of them. In the picture, the "L" shape near the forehead means "loser" in the United States. You probably know that someone might do that in jest if the goal is to playfully tease another person about not succeeding at something they should have. It also might be a display of derision about another person's lack of success or low station in life.

As reported in the news in 2006, the late Supreme Court Justice Antonin Scalia cupped a hand under his chin and flicked his fingers out in response to a question about his critics. For the Italian Scalia, this was meant to signal that these critics were not worthy of his consideration. For others who were present, though, Scalia was signaling that he would say "f**k off" to them. If you had to rule on this one, what decoding decision would you have made?

Thus, even though speech-independent gestures can communicate messages without attendant speech, their meanings are still influenced by context. Giving someone "the finger" can be humorous or insulting, depending on who performs it, who the target is, and what other behaviors accompany it. Facial expressions and eye movements accompanying speech-independent gestures are likely to expand the range of possible meanings associated with a hand gesture. Some of these emblematic gestures are specifically adapted to particular subgroups within a given culture. In the United States, for example, the finger-wag gesture indicating "no-no" is used primarily when adults are addressing children or pretending another adult is a child; the "shame on you" gesture seems limited to usage by children (see Figure 7-2).

Sherzer's (1974) detailed work on the pointed-lip gesture used by the San Blas Cuna of Panama and the thumbs-up gesture used by urban Brazilians further illustrates how gestures may have a general meaning that is modified by context. For example, the thumbs-up gesture has a general meaning of "good" or "positive" (see Figure 7-3). Context, however, expands the range of its meanings. It can be used to indicate understanding the point of what someone said or did; to acknowledge a favor granted; to greet someone; to indicate knowledge of the next move in an interactional sequence and who is going to perform it; to request permission to carry out an action, as when a customer signals a waiter about the availability of a table; and as a sexual insult.

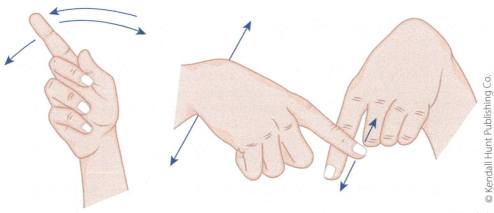

© Kendall Hunt Publishing Co.

FIGURE 7-2 Finger emblems used in the United States for "no-no-no" (left) and "shame on you" (right).

© Christopher Halloran/Shutterstock.com

FIGURE 7-3 The thumbs-up gesture by 2008 presidential candidate John McCain.

Sometimes the context does not affect the meaning so much as the slight changes in the way the gesture is performed. When the forefinger is extended vertically, with the other fingers curled, and is held motionless and facing another person, the meaning is "wait a minute." When the hand turns sideways and the finger repeatedly moves up and down, the meaning shifts to one of emphasis or reprimand. When the same finger is put perpendicularly in front of the lips, it means "be quiet." When placed on the chin, it can mean "I wonder …" and when placed on the temple the meaning can be "I'm thinking." As stated earlier, when it points toward the temple and circles in the air, it means "crazy!" These are North American meanings; elsewhere there are others. When that finger pulls down one lower eyelid in France, it means "I don't believe you," and when it is twisted gently into the cheek, it means "Mmm, tastes good" in Italy. In all of these cases, chances are other behaviors will co-occur via the eyes, mouth, or head movements that help convey the message.

There are published lists of emblematic gestures for cultures around the world (Armstrong & Wagner, 2003; Axtell, 1991; Barakat, 1973; Creider, 1977; Johnson, Ekman, & Friesen, 1975; Morris et al., 1979; Poggi, 2002; Saitz & Cervenka, 1972; Sparhawk, 1978; Trupin, 1976; Wylie, 1977). Kendon's (1981b) analysis of over 800 emblematic gestures contained in some of these lists revealed three broad categories of meaning that accounted for 80% of the speech-independent gestures observed in the United States, Colombia, France, southern Italy, and Kenya and 66% of those found in Iran. These categories were (1) interpersonal control, (2) announcement of one's current state or condition, and (3) an evaluative response to the actions or appearance of another. Ekman's studies of five cultures indicate that each has emblematic gestures for greeting and departing, replying, directing locomotion (all forms of interpersonal control), insulting or evaluating another's actions or appearance, referring to a person's physical and affective state, or announcing a person's current condition or state. As yet, no speech-independent gestures have been found that are made the same and have the same meaning in every culture studied. Future research may identify some, however. The most likely candidates are gestures having to do with affirmation and negation; stopping; not knowing; and sleeping, eating, and drinking (i.e., functions all human beings share).

Far more common are examples of gestures of similar form that differ in meaning from culture to culture. From 1877 through 1878, Bulgaria and Russia combined forces to fight Turkey. The alliance discovered a real problem in that the Russian way of saying "no" was to shake the head from side to side, but a very similar Bulgarian gesture, a head sway or wobble, meant "yes" (Jacobson, 1972). The ring gesture, with the thumb and forefinger touching to make a circle (see Figure 7-1), indicates "you're worth zero" in France and Belgium; "money" in Japan; "asshole" in parts of southern Italy; and in Greece and Turkey, it is an insulting or vulgar sexual invitation. Of course, to many U.S. residents, it means "A-OK." Things certainly would not be "A-OK" if the ring gesture was used in cultures that attach other meanings to it.

The thumb signals the number "1" for Germans, whereas it does not for French or English Canadians (Pika, Nicoladis, & Marentette, 2009). The thumbs-up gesture pictured in Figure 7-3 is usually decoded as positive, meaning "good" or "OK" in the United States, but in the Middle East, it is an obscene gesture. The thumb inserted between the index and middle fingers—the "fig" gesture—is an invitation to have sex in Germany, Holland, and Denmark but is a wish for good luck or protection in Portugal and Brazil (see Figure 7-4). During World War II, Winston Churchill made the "V for victory" gesture world famous, and it continues to mean "victory" in some cultures. But if the palm is facing toward the performer, it is a sexual insult in Great Britain—a meaning former Prime Minister Margaret Thatcher learned the hard way, when she essentially said "screw you" to a crowd of people, thinking she was giving a sign of victory. In the United States, the British meaning of sexual insult is not associated with the "V" sign facing inward; it simply means the number "2." Nor is there any distinction the other way—with the palm facing outward—between the "V" for victory and the "V" for peace, the latter being a meaning that gained popularity during the anti-Vietnam War protests of the 1960s (see Figure 7-5).

© Kendall Hunt Publishing Co.

FIGURE 7-4 The "fig" gesture.

(a)

(b)

© Vernon Merritt III/Contributor/The LIFE Picture Collection/Getty Images

(c)

FIGURE 7-5 (a) "V" gesture used as an insult in Britain and (b) Richard Nixon makes the "V for victory" gesture at the 1968 Republican Convention in Miami. (c) People at an anti-Vietnam War demonstration in Washington, DC, using the "V" gesture to signify "peace."

© Icon Sportswire/Contributor/Getty Images

(a)   (b)   (c)

FIGURE 7-6 (a) The double horn gesture in Naples means "cuckolded." (b) University of Texas football mascot gives the school's "Hook 'em Horns" gesture. The "I love you" gesture (c) is similar to the hook 'em gesture (a and b) except that the thumb is extended in the former (c).

The vertical horn sign pictured in Figure 7-6 (a) is normally decoded "cuckold" in Portugal, Spain, Italy, and places in Central and South America ("cuckold" meaning a man whose wife has cheated on him). Students from cultures in which this gesture indicates "your wife has been unfaithful to you, and you are either too stupid to know it or not man enough to satisfy her" would, indeed, be surprised if they were to attend the University of Texas. Here, and throughout Texas, the horn sign is used to show identification with the university and represents school spirit. It is modeled after longhorn cattle and literally represents the University of Texas Longhorns. Consider the reaction of people who associate the sign with "cuckold" viewing a University of Texas football game with 85,000 fans making the sign vigorously, repeatedly, and in unison!

Many readers will recognize the "Vulcan Salute" made famous by Mr. Spock in the television series Star Trek (Figure 7-7). Most will know that "Live long and prosper" is its meaning. The actor who played Mr. Spock, Leonard Nimoy, reported that he was inspired to use this gesture by remembering rabbis in his childhood synagogue who used it, with both hands, as a blessing.

Many emblems have no equivalent in other cultures. In France, for example, one can signal drunkenness by making a fist around the nose and twisting. Many messages have different gestural forms from culture to culture. Cultural and historical factors can contribute to differences in gestures for suicide. In ancient Japan, for example, Samurai warriors sometimes performed hari-kari (see bottom image in Figure 7-8).

One of the problems in comparing studies of speech-independent gestures across cultures is the lack of a uniform method for identifying them. Johnson, Ekman, and Friesen's (1975) study of American emblematic gestures offered a systematic procedure that other researchers may want to use. The authors asked members of a particular group or culture to produce emblems associated with a list of verbal statements and phrases. They reported that after about 10 or 15 informants had been tested, a great majority of the emblems had been identified. To qualify as a "verified" emblem, at least 70% of the encoders must have performed the action in a similar way. The emblems similarly encoded were then presented to a group of decoders, who were asked to identify the meaning of the gestures and the extent to which they reflect natural usage in everyday conversation. A different method was used by Morris et al. (1979) in their survey of people in 25 places in Europe, Great Britain, and North Africa. They showed pictures depicting 20 different hand emblems to people in public places and asked them whether each one was used locally and, if so, what it meant. Morris and colleagues were able to draw maps showing the clustering of usages across locations and were able to relate these patterns to geographical and historical factors.

FIGURE 7-7 Actor Leonard Nimoy making his famous "Live long and prosper" gesture.

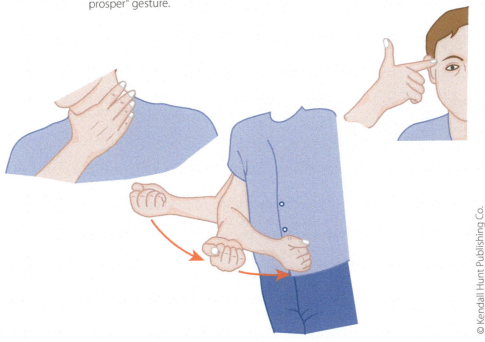

FIGURE 7-8 Historical and cultural variations in suicide gestures: the South Fore, Papua New Guinea (top left);
Japan (bottom); the United States (top right).

SPEECH-RELATED GESTURES

Speech-related gestures, sometimes called *illustrators* or *cospeech gestures*, are directly tied to or accompany speech. The meanings and functions of these gestures are revealed as we examine how they relate to the associated verbal messages. Attempts to classify the various types of speech-related gestures have used different terminology (Efron, 1941, 1972; Ekman, 1977; Kendon, 1989a, 1989b; McNeill, 1992, 2000; Streeck & Knapp, 1992), but four common types have emerged:

1. Gestures related to the speaker's referent, concrete or abstract
2. Gestures indicating the speaker's relationship to the referent
3. Gestures that act as visual punctuation for the speaker's discourse
4. Gestures that assist in the regulation and organization of the spoken dialogue between two interactants

REFERENT-RELATED GESTURES

As a person talks, they use gestures to characterize the content of their speech. At first glance, these movements may seem random and you may have commented that someone was "waving their hands around" while they talked. Actually, the common observation that someone "talks with their hands" may be, quite literally, closer to the truth. Hand movements that occur while one is speaking are, perhaps surprisingly, not random. Sometimes these movements depict fairly concrete referents, whereas other times, vague and abstract ideas. Research shows that hand gestures and speech are closely connected in the brain and, indeed, have been referred to as a common system (McNeill, 1985).

Sometimes the gestures reflect what is being said, sometimes they add to what is being said, and sometimes they even help the speaker figure out their choice of words. Although these same functions likely hold true for singers, such as rappers, this is a domain of study where little research has been done (see Box **It's Not a Wrap**). In the following, we will describe speech-related gestures and their purposes. Note that it takes many words to describe gestures that, if seen in context, would take but a moment to be fully (if nonconsciously) processed and understood; this underscores the fact that, in practice, these gestures both carry meaning and facilitate speech and interaction.

IT'S NOT A WRAP

© Christian Bertrand/Shutterstock.com

Many readers have no doubt noticed the finger, hand, and arm gestures used by modern rap and hip-hop artists when they are performing on stage. These gestures can be tied to the content of their songs as well as the properties of their music. However, a program of research does not currently exist in the world of nonverbal communication that is devoted to understanding the precise properties and functions of such gestures.

Pointing movements, formally called "deictic movements," can help indicate a specific person, place, or thing being discussed. In toddlers, pointing may involve the whole hand or only the index finger depending on what the child is attempting to communicate (Cochet & Vauclair, 2010). The referent may be in the immediate conversational environment or may be more distant, as is the case when a person says, "Want to go to that restaurant down Broadway?" while pointing their finger in the direction of the referred-to place. Gestures that draw the referent's shape or movement, and gestures that depict spatial relationships, can be used to help a listener visualize features associated with concrete referents. When you say, "I had to bend the branch way back" or "she was eating her food like an animal" while illustrating how these events occurred, the gesture bears a close relationship to the concrete semantic content of your speech. Referent-related gestures that depict an action (as in acting out the act of hammering a nail) or outline the referent by drawing a picture in space are called iconic gestures. However, if one makes an hourglass figure to signify a shapely woman, it may function as an emblem (speech-independent), depending on the context. The test for determining whether such a picture may be speech independent is if 70% of the members of the usage community respond with "shapely woman" when shown the gesture portrayal without any speech context.

More abstract referents are involved when one sketches the path or direction of an idea in the air, when one makes a series of circular movements with the hand or arm to suggest one means more than the specific words used, and when one uses expansion and contraction gestures such as those of an accordion player to indicate the breadth of the subject being discussed. Sometimes people represent abstract content via gestural metaphors. For example, cup-shaped gestures in the following sample of discourse (McNeill, 1985) represent containers of what could be supposed. When they spread apart, they seem to convey the idea that anything is possible, and their sudden disappearance suggests that what might have been did not happen:

"Even though one might [*both hands form cups and spread wide apart*] have supposed [*cups vanish abruptly*] ...."

Thus far the focus has been on the speech-related referents of gestures. However, people also gesture when trying to solve a problem in silence. These cothought gestures reflect internal thought processes and are not necessarily intended to communicate information to others. Chu and Kita (2011) found that when participants were experiencing difficulties in solving a spatial-visualization problem, such as a mental rotation task, their cothought gestures increased, and that these gestures eventually helped them to solve more problems.

GESTURES INDICATING A SPEAKER'S RELATIONSHIP TO THE REFERENT

These gestures comment on the speaker's orientation to the referent rather than characterizing the nature of the thing being talked about. The positioning of the palms can show quite different orientations toward one's own message (see Figure 7-9).

For example, palms facing up show more uncertainty ("I think" or "I'm not sure"), palms down show certainty ("clearly" or "absolutely"), palms out and facing the listener show assertion ("Let me say this" or "Calm down"), and palms facing the speaker allude to embracing a concept ("I've got this great idea …"). Palm positions can have other speech-related associations, such as a speaker's palms-up gesture when pleading, begging, or even anticipating closeness in greetings.

Oscillating hand movements suggest that a speaker is unsure or could go either way. Charles de Gaulle, former president of France, was noted for his grasping gesture, which many felt signified his desire to control the subject under discussion (see Figure 7-10).

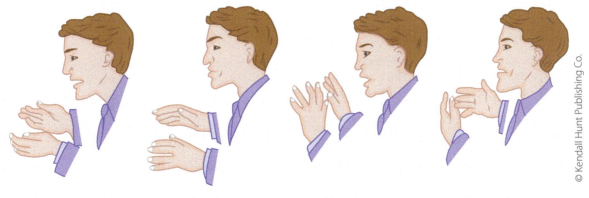

© Kendall Hunt Publishing Co.

FIGURE 7-9 Palm gestures.

© Francis CHAVEROU/Contributor/Gamma-Rapho/Getty Images

FIGURE 7-10 Former French President Charles de Gaulle's characteristic gesture, perceived by many as "grasping for control of an idea."

PUNCTUATION GESTURES

Punctuation gestures accent, emphasize, and organize important segments of the discourse. Such a segment may be a single word or a larger utterance unit, such as a summary or a new theme. When these gestures are used to emphasize a particular word or phrase, they often coincide with the primary voice stress. Punctuation gestures can also organize the stream of speech into units. When we speak of a series of things, we may communicate discreteness by rhythmic chopping hand gestures, for example, "We must consider A (gesture), B (gesture), and C (gesture)." A single chopping gesture after C could indicate that C will be considered separately, or it could mean that A, B, and C will be considered as a group. A slight downward movement of the head may accompany the hand gestures. Pounding the hand or fist in the air or on another object also acts as a device for adding emphasis and visually underlining a particular point being made (see Figure 7-11).

Punctuation can, of course, be accomplished with body movements other than the hands. The "eye flash" (not the "eyebrow flash" discussed in Chapter 2) is one such display (Bull & Connelly, 1985; Walker & Trimboli, 1983). The momentary widening of a speaker's eyelids, without involving the eyebrows, has been found to occur most often in conjunction with spoken adjectives and is used for emphasis.

INTERACTIVE GESTURES

Thus far, the gesture categories discussed have focused on the content of the speaker's monologue. *Interactive gestures* acknowledge the other interactant relative to the speaker and help regulate and organize the dialogue itself. Because they are directed at the ongoing involvement and shared roles of the interactants, these gestures occur only in the presence of others.

Bavelas (1994) and colleagues (Bavelas, Chovil, Coates, & Roe, 1995; Bavelas, Chovil, Lawrie, & Wade, 1992) identified four different types of interactive gestures and the functions they serve.

1. The speaker and the person spoken to are in the process of exchanging information, so it is natural that this relationship be acknowledged with several types of gestures that acknowledge the delivery of information. These are called *delivery gestures*. These gestures may refer to the delivery of new information as in the gestures accompanying "Here's my point" in Figure 7-12. They may also accompany information that the speaker thinks the addressee already knows with the meaning, "As you know ..." Other forms of delivery gestures are also interpreted by the addressee as asides (e.g., "Oh, and by the way ...) or an indication that the speaker is asking the addressee to extrapolate additional information not given as in "or whatever."

2. Several types of speaker gestures refer to a previous comment made by the addressee. These are called *citing gestures* with one type illustrated in Figure 7-12 when the speaker says, "As you said earlier ...." Citing gestures also acknowledge an addressee's response to a speaker and essentially mean "I see that you understood me."

FIGURE 7-11 Punctuation gestures.

© Kendall Hunt Publishing Co.

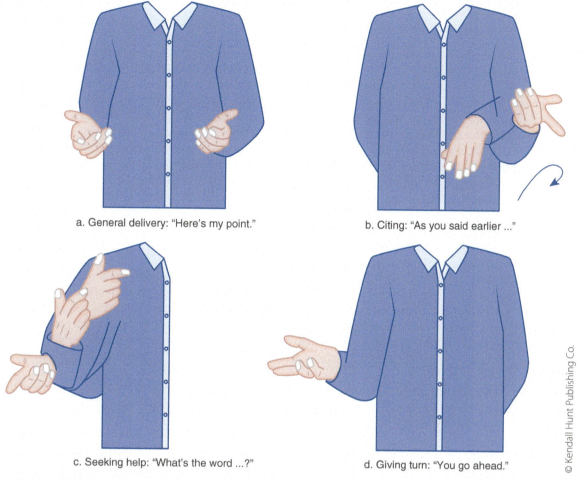

a. General delivery: "Here's my point."

b. Citing: "As you said earlier ..."

c. Seeking help: "What's the word ...?"

d. Giving turn: "You go ahead."

FIGURE 7-12 Interactive gestures.

© Kendall Hunt Publishing Co.

3. Some interactive gestures are designed to seek a specific response and are appropriately called *seeking gestures*. For example, in Figure 7-12 (c) the speaker's gesture is seeking help in identifying a word or phrase they want to use. The "thinking face" is a facial gesture that may also elicit participation from one or more addressees in a speaker's word or idea search. Sometimes, however, the speaker is seeking agreement from the addressee rather than help and the gesture means, "Do you agree?" Gestures that query the addressee's understanding are the verbal equivalent of "ya know?" at the end of a unit of talk. While seeking gestures invite responses from an audience, the Goodwins point out that self-touching contributes to a state of conversational disengagement or the opposite of inclusion (Goodwin, 1986; Goodwin & Goodwin, 1986).

4. *Turn gestures*, as noted in more detail in Chapter 12, occur during the exchange of speaking turns. This may signal "you go ahead and talk" as illustrated in Figure 7-12, but turn gestures may also accompany the taking of a turn or an awkward transition when no one is assuming the turn at talk.

Although the preceding fourfold classification of speech-related gestures is useful, there can still be individual and cultural differences. Efron's (1941, 1972) classic cross-cultural comparison illustrates this. He found that as southern Italians talked, they made extensive use of gestures that had a close resemblance to their referent (e.g., pictorial), whereas Eastern European Jews made very little use of such gestures. It seems reasonable that different cultures value different kinds of information, and gestures vary accordingly. Even the number of gestures in all categories may vary from culture to culture.

GESTURE FREQUENCY

The frequency of gesturing can be influenced by several factors.

1. We would expect to find more gestures in face-to-face communication and when the speaker expects the recipient will see the message (Alibali & Don, 2001; Bavelas, Kenwood, Johnson, & Phillips, 2002; Cohen, 1977; Cohen & Harrison, 1973). People do, of course, use some gestures when listeners cannot see them, for example, when talking on the phone (see Figure 7-13). These may occur because one feels that the other person is still present, but the gesturing can also help retrieve a particular word from our mental lexicon (Hadar, 1989; Pine, Gurney, & Fletcher, 2010). Continued communication without visible contact, however, may reduce the number of gestures used.

2. Gestures are also likely to increase when a speaker is enthusiastic and involved in the topic being discussed.

3. We would expect speakers concerned about their listeners' comprehension to use more gestures, too—especially in difficult or complex communicative situations, as when the listener is perceived as not paying attention, the listener is not comprehending, or the speaker cannot find the right words to express an idea (Bavelas, Coates, & Johnson, 2002; Goldin-Meadow, 2003; Holler & Beattie, 2003). Even though exposure to gestures that accompany speech may often facilitate more accurate decoding on the part of the listener, there are some occasions when the contribution is negligible (Krauss, Dushay, Chen, & Rauscher, 1995).

4. Speakers trying to dominate conversations would be expected to use more speech-related gestures.

5. Speech content also plays a role in the number of gestures used. When answering questions about manual activities—such as "Explain how to change a car or bicycle tire," or "Explain how to wrap a box for a present"—we would expect more gestures than when answering questions about visual or abstract images (Feyereisen & Havard, 1999).

6. A communicator's cognitive abilities can affect gesture production. In one study, the rate of gesturing by speakers with a combination of low phonemic fluency and high spatial skill was especially high (Hostetter & Alibali, 2007).

7. Cultural background is related to gesture frequency. Americans, for instance, gesture more than the Chinese when telling stories (So, 2010).

8. When people share information that has been learned verbally and visually, they use more representational gestures compared to when they learn this information only verbally (Hostetter & Skirving, 2011). Thus, having a mental image of the to-be-shared information may facilitate gesturing.

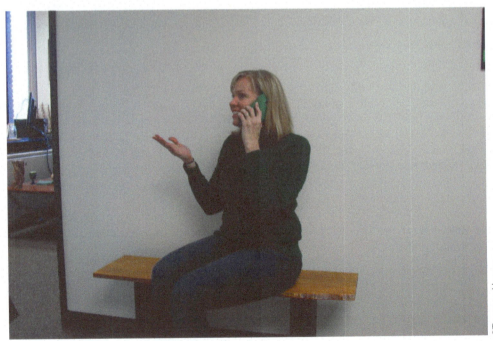

©Terrence Horgan

FIGURE 7-13 Gesture made while speaking on a cell phone.

As noted, speech and gesture are intimately linked, and it would be hard for anyone to abstain completely from gesturing while speaking. Even if it were possible, it would be ill advised because gestures play an important role in communication and cognition. As long ago as 1931, a Soviet researcher asked participants to talk while inhibiting all gestures of the head, hands, face, and body. It is reported that no one was able to carry out the instructions completely, and "the speech … lost its intonation, stress and expressiveness; even the very selection of words needed for the expression of content became labored; there was a jerkiness to the speech, and a reduction of the number of words used" (Dobrogaev, 1931). The impact on fluency of not being able to gesture has been noted often in other research (e.g., Rimé, 1982). Without gestures, speakers also would have to increase the number of phrases and words used to describe spatial relations and would probably pause more often (Graham & Heywood, 1976). Gestures help speakers retrieve words from their mental lexicon (Hadar, 1989; Krauss, Chen, & Chawla, 1996; Krauss & Hadar, 1999; Morrel-Samuels & Krauss, 1992). Support for the word-retrieval function of gestures has been found using children, adults, and those with a language disability (Hanlon, Brown, & Gerstman, 1990; Pine, Bird, & Kirk, 2007; Rauscher, Krauss, & Chen, 1996). This important role of gestures in speech production is often underemphasized, but it is clear that gestures facilitate both the invention of messages and their organization and delivery.

Lastly, adults and children enjoy certain cognitive and memory benefits from gesturing; for example, gesturing can help children learn a new concept, recall information they have previously learned, and verbally report more details of a story they are not familiar with (Cameron & Xu, 2011; Cook, Mitchell, & Goldin-Meadow, 2008; Cook, Yip, & Goldin-Meadow, 2010; Goldin-Meadow, 2018; Ping & Goldin-Meadow, 2010). Listeners are also likely to experience a serious loss from not seeing gestures because gestures, like speech, are listener adapted (Beattie & Shovelton, 2006; de Ruiter, 2007). For example, when a speaker talks to others who have experienced the event the speaker is talking about, the speaker's gestures are smaller and less precise than when the same event is communicated to people who have not experienced the event (Gerwing & Bavelas, 2004). Since gestures are listener adapted, it is no surprise that they often facilitate comprehension and help listeners access linguistic cues in their memory (Berger & Popelka, 1971; Church, Garber, & Rogalski, 2007; Rogers, 1978; Woodall & Folger, 1981). Gestures out of synchrony with the vocal/verbal stream are distracting and interfere with listener comprehension (Woodall & Burgoon, 1981).

THE COORDINATION OF GESTURE, POSTURE, AND SPEECH

Earlier we said that speech-related gestures are tied to, or accompany, speech. That they are connected to speech is easily understood, but the exact nature of that connection is more difficult to understand. Most scholars agree that body movements and gestures are not randomly produced during the stream of speech but are inextricably linked as parts of the same system. The disagreements among scholars in this area focus on how to define coordination, or synchrony, of speech and movement. Must two things happen at exactly the same time to be in sync? Must they happen for the same length of time? If speech and gesture are closely coordinated, does the same part of the brain control both systems? Is there a synchrony of speech and movement between two speakers, as well as within the behavior of a single speaker? This section focuses on the research on these issues. The first part addresses the coordination of a single speaker's speech and movement, and the second examines the coordination of two speakers' behavior.

SELF-SYNCHRONY

In the early 1960s, William S. Condon began a microscopic analysis of the coordination between movement and speech. By examining individual frames of a 16-mm film, he was able to match body movements with a speech transcript. This allowed him to observe speech–body orientation accurate to 1/24th of a second. Condon and Ogston (1966) and Condon (1976) showed that speech and movement are rhythmically coordinated even at the most microscopic levels, for example, in syllables and even smaller segments. Just as speech units can be grouped together to form larger units, so can movement units. A sweep of the arm or a turn of the head may occur over an entire phrase of several words, but we may see movements of the face and fingers coordinated with smaller units of speech. Using digital video annotation, Loehr (2007) examined the rhythmic relationship between the hands, head, and voice of four speakers during spontaneous interaction. He, too, found a complex process of self-synchrony. Stressed syllables often aligned with gestural strokes and even eye blinks.

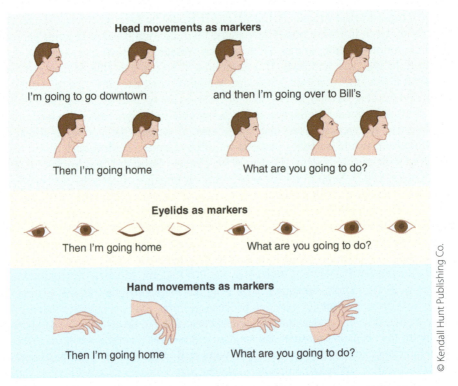

FIGURE 7-14 Some postural-kinesic markers of syntactic sentences in the United States.

The smallest idea unit in spoken language is called the *phonemic clause.* This group of words, averaging about five in length, has only one primary stress—indicated by changes in pitch, rhythm, or loudness—and is terminated by a juncture. This unit commonly has shown systematic relationships to body movements. Slight jerks of the head or hand often accompany the primary stress points in the speech of American English speakers. Gestures also seem to peak at the most salient part of the idea unit. At the junctures or boundaries, we also find movements of the head or hands that indicate completion or initiation.

Birdwhistell's (1966) analysis of nonverbal activity that accompanies verbal behavior led him to identify what he calls *kinesic markers.* Markers seem to operate at several different levels. For instance, we might see an eye blink at the beginning and end of some words, or a tiny head sweep may be seen during the expression of a compound word that would hyphenated in written form. Figure 7-14 shows head, hand, and eyelid markers occurring at the end of statements and questions. Similarly, after making a point, speakers may turn the head to one side or tilt, flex, or extend the neck, signaling the transition to another point.

Another level of markers is characterized by gross shifts in postural behavior. One such marker is the shift from leaning back when listening to leaning forward when speaking. The observation that postural shifts mark new stages of interaction or topic shifts, particularly at the beginning or ending of speech segments, has been made by several researchers (Bull & Brown, 1977; Erickson, 1975; Scheflen, 1973). Kendon's (1972, 1980, 1987, 1988, 2004) detailed analyses of speech and body movement confirmed the notion of self-synchrony. He also supported the idea of a hierarchy of body movements that acts in conjunction with speech behavior. Kendon found that the wrist and fingers tended to change positions most often, followed by the forearm, then the upper arm. Elements of the face generally changed more often than the head, and trunk and lower limb movements were rare. The larger units of body movement were related to the larger units of speech, and the smaller body units were related to the smaller units of speech.

Kendon also observed when movements occur in one's speech stream. Some movements accompany speech, but many precede speech units. The time between the speech-preparatory body movement and the onset of speech is apparently related to the size of the impending speech unit, with earlier and more extensive behavior involving more body parts, for larger speech units. A change in body posture, for instance, may precede a long utterance and may be held for the duration of the utterance. Hierarchically structured body movements convey information about verbal structure and communicative involvement. The positions of the head, limbs, and body sometimes forecast information to a listener, such as the length of utterance and change in argument strategy or viewpoint. The act of forecasting upcoming components of speech through gesture is a crucial function in social interaction. Speakers often shift their gaze to their hands during the production of iconic gestures, thereby calling them to the attention of the listener. Speaker gaze returns to the listener as the speech unit projected by the gesture is completed. In this process, gaze acts as a gesture pointer (Streeck, 1993; Streeck & Knapp, 1992).

The preceding research leads us to conclude that speech and gesture are coordinated within the individual. But why? It is most likely because they are two components used in the expression of a single unit of content. Both systems are being guided by the same overall purpose, and both systems seem to be under the governance of the same parts of the brain (Cicone, Wapner, Foldi, Zurif, & Gardner, 1979; Gentilucci & Dalla Volta, 2008; Kimura, 1976). As Kendon (2000) said, "[A]lthough each expresses somewhat different dimensions of the meaning, speech and gesture are co-expressive of a single inclusive ideational complex" (p. 61). It should therefore not surprise us that gestures and speech both break down in aphasia (McNeill, 1992).

Developmentally, gesture and speech also appear to grow up together and follow similar developmental trajectories (Göksun, Hirsh-Pasek, & Golinkoff, 2010; Graham & Kilbreath, 2007). Because these gestures occur throughout the life span, they can offer clues to the development or deterioration of a person's cognitive and linguistic skills (Goldin-Meadow & Iverson, 2010). Children use more gestures as they develop, just as they use more words (McNeill, 1992). Children eventually learn how to combine words and gestures. Because gesture–speech combinations (pointing at food and saying "eat") occur earlier than speech–speech combinations ("eat food") in children, they can serve as a developmental marker of sorts (Bates & Dick, 2002). Boys tend to produce gesture–speech combinations later than girls, and thus also produce speech–speech combinations later than girls do (Ozcaliskan & Goldin-Meadow, 2010).

In addition to being coordinated with speech, body movements are coordinated with other body movements. In their study mentioned earlier, Dael et al. (2012) analyzed 49 body movements used by actors while expressing 12 emotions on video, using standardized vocal utterances. Certain body movements clustered together, for example, one co-occurring cluster included finger movements, movements of shoulder and elbow, and arm movements that were lateral, back, up, down, and forward. A different cluster included beats, emblems, and illustrators.

INTERACTION SYNCHRONY

The preceding section revealed a speech–body movement coordination within the actions of a single speaker. This section provides information about speech–body movement coordination or the coordination of body movements between two speakers—a kind of social rhythm or interaction synchrony (Bernieri & Rosenthal, 1991). Sometimes the term *mimicry* is used, with mimicry sometimes referring to the frequency or occurrence of specific behaviors (e.g., leaning) or expressions (e.g., smiling), whereas synchrony sometimes refers to more holistic coordination of movement over time. These terms are not always clearly distinguished by authors, however. Interactional synchrony has been studied in several ways.

Without always being very aware of it, human beings commonly tend to mimic the mannerisms, facial expressions, postures, and other behaviors of the people they interact with. This has been called the "chameleon effect" (Chartrand & Bargh, 1999)—not because people, like chameleons, change colors to match their environment but because people change their postures, gestures, and mannerisms to match those of their interaction partners. Interestingly, some individuals are more chameleon-like than others, such as those who tend to see their "self" as more connected to other people (Van Baaren, Horgan, Chartrand, & Dijkmans, 2004).

Mimicry usually occurs completely outside of conscious awareness, even though one might use matching behavior intentionally when trying to communicate affiliation. Also, situational factors can affect mimicry; van der Schalk and colleagues (2011) showed that people are more likely to mimic the facial displays of members of their ingroup than those of outgroup members. However, mimicking the behavior of outgroup members, such as people from a different racial group, may be one way of reducing prejudice toward them (Inzlicht, Gutsell, & Legault, 2011).

Matching the behavior of a fellow interactant may occur in several different ways. Sometimes a speaker's behavior is followed in kind by the listener when the listener becomes the speaker (Cappella, 1981). Here the matched behavior occurs not simultaneously but in sequence. Chapter 11 reports research that shows how people tend to match a partner's utterance duration, loudness, precision of articulation, latency of response, silence duration, and speech rate. Of importance, when people mimic gestures they might better understand their meaning (Alibali & Hostetter, 2010). In some instances, though, the speaker's behavior elicits an offsetting or compensatory behavior from the other person, as we mention in several chapters of this book. For example, if a speaker is leaning toward a listener and the listener perceives the interaction distance to be too close, the listener will likely lean away or increase the interaction distance in other ways. Although this is definitely a reaction, one would not call it mimicry.

Other researchers have been interested in occasions when both interaction partners exhibit the same behavior at the same time. Postural congruence is one of those frequently matched behaviors. It may involve crossing the legs and/or arms, leaning, head propping, or any number of other positions. Notice the variety of postural congruence in Figures 7-15 to 7-18. When the listener's behavior is a mirror image of the speaker's, this form of matching is called *mirroring*.

Postural congruence has been observed to occur during periods of more positive speech, is rated by observers as an indicator of rapport and cooperation, and has been implicated in creating rapport (Charney, 1966; LaFrance, 1979, 1985; LaFrance & Broadbent, 1976; Trout & Rosenfeld, 1980). Body synchrony between clients and psychotherapists was shown to occur to a higher degree than in a control comparison group, consisting of "pseudo" dyads created by pairing the videos of clients and therapists from different interactions. More synchrony in the real dyads was also associated positively with several aspects of relationship quality and outcome (Ramseyer & Tschacher, 2011).

Nonconscious mimicry occurs more often with people who enter an interaction with a stronger desire to affiliate or establish rapport (Lakin & Chartrand, 2003; Yabar, Johnston, Miles, & Peace, 2006), and interpersonal synchrony is stronger among those with a prosocial (vs. proself) orientation (Lumsden, Miles, Richardson, Smith, & Macrae, 2011). When one person deliberately mimics or moves in synchrony with the other person, positive outcomes ensue (assuming there is not suspicion; Chartrand & Bargh, 1999; Vicaria & Dickens, 2016). Thus, mimicry seems to occur more often when the person is other-oriented; for example, when wanting to be liked by others, feeling concerned about others, seeking a closer relationship with others, showing dependence on others, and seeing one's "self" as more connected to other people. However, mimicry can also occur due to greater conversational involvement rather than positive emotion or affiliative motives.

© Terrence Horgan

FIGURE 7-15 Postural congruence.

FIGURE 7-16 Examples of postural congruence through head propping and leaning and matching hand positions.

FIGURE 7-17 Two women show evidence of bent-knee congruence and arm mirroring (touching the wall) while interacting with the woman in the center of their group.

A related phenomenon is *motor mimicry*. A common example of motor mimicry is when a person you are near drops a heavy weight on their foot. As the injured party reacts in pain, your wincing facial expression might mean you are having a burst of sympathy, or are even vicariously feeling what they feel. Bavelas and colleagues do not deny such an inner experience, but their research also shows that motor mimicry can often be a *communicative* phenomenon. In

© stockfour/Shutterstock.com

FIGURE 7-18 A daughter and her father exchange similar facial expressions. Also notice how they are holding their colored pencils.

their research, wincing in reaction to another's injury depended strongly on the visual accessibility of the injured party and the possibility of making eye contact with that person. More motor mimicry was seen as the probability of eye contact went up. Furthermore, the pattern and timing of the wincer's reaction was determined by the probability of eye contact with the victim (Bavelas, Black, Chovil, Lemery, & Mullett, 1988; Bavelas, Black, Lemery, & Mullett, 1986). In a related study, Kimbara (2008) found that visual accessibility to another interactant during a joint description of previously viewed video clips also led to a greater similarity in the shape of their hand gestures than the same task without visual access to their partner.

This tendency to match and mimic others' behavior posturally, facially, vocally, and so forth sometimes leads to *emotional contagion*, that is "catching" the other person's emotion. Two of the essential conditions for this process include strongly felt emotions and communicators who are skilled encoders and decoders (Hatfield, Cacioppo, & Rapson, 1994). Some people are more susceptible to emotional contagion than others, so that more susceptible people might feel better around a happy friend, and more miserable around a sad one. As evidence of this, Magen and Konasewich (2011) noted that women's positive emotion was more likely to suffer than men's after interacting with a troubled friend, thus showing a potential downside to a strong susceptibility to another person's negative emotion state. Currently in the professions of medicine and psychotherapy, there is much concern with "burnout," or feelings of emotional depletion and loss of sensitivity to others' distress; the burnout phenomenon may be exacerbated in individuals who are especially responsive to others' emotions.

Interaction synchrony may also be a precursor of language learning. Condon and Sander (1974) found babies 12 hours old whose head, hand, elbow, hip, and leg movements tended to correspond to the rhythms of human speech. When the babies were exposed to disconnected speech or to plain tapping sounds, however, the rhythmic pattern was not observed. Bernieri, Reznick, and Rosenthal (1988) found that mothers significantly synchronized their movements with those of their 14-month-old babies.

As the reader can tell, interpersonal coordination does not have to involve the same body parts; in other words, one kind of behavior may coordinate in a systematic way to a different kind of behavior. The category of behavior called "listener responses" or "back channel responses" fits this description. These are behaviors such as head nods, some eyebrow raises, some facial movements, and minimal utterances such as "yeah," "uh-huh," and "mm-hmm" that signal attention, comprehension, and encouragement to the speaker. These responses appear at specific junctures in the speech of a partner, specifically at the ends of rhythmical units of the other person's utterance, that is, at pauses within phonemic clauses but mainly at junctures between these clauses.

Dittmann (1972) noticed that adults sometimes believe children are not listening to them and badger them with questions like "Did you hear me?" Dittmann reasoned that this common adult perception of children may be associated with the absence of listener responses. In his study, children in grades 1, 3, and 5 barely used these listener responses except under "the strongest social pull" by the other interactant. Subsequent studies indicated the major deficiencies were in "mm-hmm" and head-nod responses. By 8th grade, a dramatic increase in these listener responses was found. By early adolescence, peers begin to lengthen their response duration, providing more opportunity for such listener responses.

Much evidence shows that human interactants do exhibit a speech–body movement interaction synchrony as well as body–body movement synchrony. It is also clear that this synchrony may take place on very microscopic levels. Still, there are questions: Are there social contexts that intensify the degree of synchrony? How much synchrony is desirable? At least one study suggests that *moderately* rhythmic social interactions are evaluated most positively (Warner, Malloy, Schneider, Knoth, & Wilder, 1987). Is it possible to predict which behaviors will synchronize with which other behaviors at certain times? And, finally, what is the best method of measuring behavioral coordination (Gatewood & Rosenwein, 1981; McDowall, 1978a, 1978b; Rosenfeld, 1981)?

SUMMARY

Gestures aid communication in many ways: They replace speech when people cannot or do not want to talk and help regulate the back-and-forth flow of interaction. They establish and maintain attention, add emphasis to speech, and assist in making speech content memorable. Although people do gesture when interaction partners are not visible, such as over the telephone, gestures are more frequent when both interactants are visible to each other. More gestures occur when the speaker is knowledgeable about the topic being discussed, highly motivated to have listeners understand the message, trying to dominate a conversation, excited and enthusiastic about the topic being discussed, and speaking about manual activities. Gestures also play a role in word retrieval and speech production. So the absence of gestures may negatively affect the speaker's message as well as a listener's comprehension.

Two major types of gestures were discussed: *speech independent* and *speech related*. Speech-independent gestures are operationally defined as gestures that show high local consensus about their meaning and usage, and which would be understood even without accompanying words or knowing about the social context. People are normally keenly aware of using this type of gesture. Culture affects the number, frequency, and meanings associated with speech-independent gestures. Although no universal gestures of this type have been found—that is, none has the same meaning and form in every culture studied—the functions they serve are very likely universal. These include conveying affirmation, negation, "stop," and "I don't know" and gestures that indicate sleeping, eating, drinking, and insult. Most speech-independent gestures are culture specific to some extent; that is, they are not found in the same form in other cultures. Many gestures have basically the same form but different meanings from culture to culture, and these different meanings can produce cross-cultural misunderstandings.

The other major category of gestures is *speech-related gestures*. Some of these gestures characterize the content of speech, and some show the speaker's relationship to the referent by indicating whether the speaker is certain or uncertain, embracing an idea or distancing herself or himself from it, and the like. Some speech-related gestures are used to accent or emphasize speech units. Interactive gestures, unlike the other speech-related gestures, focus on the dialogue rather than the speaker's monologue. Interactive gestures focus on the ongoing involvement of the interactants and their shared roles.

The last part of this chapter examined coordination within a person or between people in the relation of gesture, movement, and speech. Interaction synchrony can manifest itself through matching behavior—similar behavior occurring at the same time (postural congruence or motor mimicry) or similar behavior occurring in sequence (one speaker raises their voice, followed by the next speaker raising their voice). Interaction synchrony can also manifest itself in the moment-to-moment coordination of changes in the direction and timing of behavior.

QUESTIONS FOR DISCUSSION

1. Spend some time during the day interacting without using hand gestures. What problems did you encounter, if any? How did other people react? What does your experience tell you about the relationship of gestures to speech?

2. Some researchers have found matching behavior to be associated with rapport between the interactants. Can you think of a situation in which rapport would not involve matching behavior? Can you think of a situation in which matching occurred but there was not much rapport?

3. Select a speech-independent gesture. Discuss the meaning of this gesture when accompanied by different facial expressions and speech.

NONVERBAL COMMUNICATION IN ACTION: TRY THIS

On the Internet (e.g., YouTube), find a clip at least 20 seconds long of people engaged in conversation. First, watch them without sound and see if you can describe and classify their hand gestures, and make a guess at how the gestures are related to what they might be conveying through their speech (this will require repeated viewings). Then, watch them again with the sound turned on and see if your silent-viewing analysis still makes sense. Again, repeated viewings will be required.

CHAPTER 8

THE EFFECTS OF TOUCH ON HUMAN COMMUNICATION

We often talk about the way we talk, and we frequently try to see the way we see, but for some reason we have rarely touched on the way we touch.

—**Desmond Morris**

The scene is a university library, but it could just as easily be the local supermarket, bank, or restaurant. What happens takes about half a second and is not noticed by most of those experiencing it. Remarkably, however, this event influences their experience in the library. What could be so mysterious and so powerful?

The answer begins with three researchers at Purdue University (Fisher, Rytting, & Heslin, 1976), who wanted to investigate systematically the effects of a brief, seemingly accidental touch in a nonintimate context. They had male and female clerks return library cards to some students by placing their hand directly over the student's palm, making very brief and apparently incidental physical contact; other students were not touched. Outside the library, a researcher approached the students and asked questions about their feelings toward the library clerk and the library in general. Students who were touched, especially the females, evaluated the clerk and the library significantly more favorably than those who were not touched. This was true for students who were aware of being touched and those who were not.

Awareness of the power of a seemingly insignificant touch may be one reason why politicians are so eager to "press the flesh" or give the "glad hand" (shake hands in a warm but insincere way, in political slang). However, like many nonverbal behaviors, touch is often ambiguous in its meaning, and recipients of touch may have widely different reactions depending on their own sensitivities and the intentions they attribute to the toucher. Also, societal expectations change. One example, spotlighted in the #MeToo movement, is growing intolerance for one person touching another in a perceived sexualized manner, or even at all, without consent. A casual attitude about touching others has now come to haunt some politicians—former Senator Al Franken, former President Donald Trump, and President Joe Biden are some examples—as well as many others in Hollywood and in workplaces and campuses around the world. Whether casual touching is perceived to be sexual, friendly, manipulative, or merely accidental is an intensely fraught question and underscores not only the evolution of social norms but also the complex psychological functions of nonverbal behavior.

Touch serves many functions and conveys many messages (Hertenstein, 2011). Its presence (or absence) is a crucial aspect of most face-to-face relationships. People may not consciously notice the presence or absence of touching, unless a norm or expectation is violated or a specific wish is fulfilled; nevertheless, at a less conscious level, people monitor each other's touch (or lack of it) constantly. The act of touching is like any other message: It may elicit positive, neutral, or negative reactions, depending on the configuration of the touch, the people involved, and the circumstances. Happiness may be lying in another person's arms. You may feel indifferent to a handshake done out of convention. You can be provoked into anger from touching that seems inappropriate, and you may reciprocate with a not-so-subtle form of touching (e.g., push, slap, or punch). Some people respond positively to being touched and need a lot of it, while others seem to evaluate almost all touching negatively. Variability in the need for and reaction to touch may be related to differences in temperament as well as childhood experiences. In the next section, we discuss the importance of touching throughout the life span.

TOUCHING AND HUMAN DEVELOPMENT

Tactile communication is probably the most basic and primitive form of communication. Touch develops before other senses in utero, where the fetus responds to vibrations of the mother's pulsating heartbeat, which impinge on the child's entire body and are magnified by the amniotic fluid. Touch is the most developed sense at birth, especially via the mouth and hands. Newborns can discriminate different textures with both their mouth and hands, and they are also sensitive to pain. Interventions such as massage and giving the infant the opportunity to suck during a painful experience can serve as pain relievers via distraction or because the additional tactile stimulation competes neurologically with the pain signal (Field & Hernandez-Reif, 2008). Infants of depressed mothers have been shown to benefit in utero from the massage therapy that their mothers had received (Field, Diego, Hernandez-Reif, Deeds, & Figueiredo, 2009).

Research shows that touch is critical to normal physiological growth in newborns. The animal literature shows that social touch in infancy, often in the form of grooming, promotes social bonding and social adequacy during development. Maternal licking of rat pups stimulates production of growth hormone, and massage with pressure stimulates weight gain in preterm infants and continues to be associated with mental and motor development a year later (Field, 2019). Parent–infant bonding may also be fostered by tactile contact during a critical period in the first hours after birth, but the research on this is mixed (Hertenstein, Verkamp, Kerestes, & Holmes, 2006). There is no question, however, that early bonding is related to adequate and appropriate "contact comfort" between babies and caretakers; research showing that mothers with depressive symptoms engage in less, and less engaging, touching of their infants during stressful tasks points to a potentially important risk factor for these infants' development (Mantis, Mercuri, Stack, & Field, 2019). A self-perpetuating cycle may exist whereby less childhood touching by parents predicts future depression (Takeuchi et al., 2010), which in turn creates disturbed touch patterns with those individuals' own children.

The importance of touch early in life to children's development and interactions with others has been clearly documented (Bales et al., 2018; Cascio, Moore, & McGlone, 2019; Feldman, 2011; Moszkowski, Stack, & Chiarella, 2009; Stack & Jean, 2011). A particularly extreme illustration came in the 1990s after the fall of Romania's Communist regime, when horrendous conditions in underfunded Romanian orphanages shocked the world. Over 100,000 orphan children spent part or most of their early childhood in extreme deprivation, which included no human physical contact much of the time. The lasting cognitive and neurological deficits of these children have been extensively documented (Nelson, Zeanah, & Fox, 2019).

WHEN IS A BABY LIKE A KANGAROO?

As everyone knows, a baby kangaroo lives for its earliest time out of the womb in the mother's pouch—touching her skin, soaking up her warmth, and accompanying her day and night. What if a human baby had that experience? What if the baby was born undeveloped, just like a baby kangaroo? That describes the human preterm infant.

The method known as "Kangaroo Care" was first developed in Bogota, Colombia, for the care of preterm infants as an alternative to putting the infants into an incubator for extended periods. In Kangaroo Care, the infant spends extended periods lying naked on the mother's chest, enjoying her warmth, body rhythms, and opportunities for intimate psychological contact. This method has been extensively studied, with comparisons to routine incubator care.

The evidence is clear: Babies and families both benefit from this approach. Physiological indicators in the postnatal period as well as many outcomes measured as far as ten years after birth reveal benefits. For the babies, these include a better stress response, better sleep, less emotional negativity, and enhanced cognitive development; for the mothers, lower blood pressure (which could help reduce anxiety and depression in preterm mothers); and for parent–infant relations, more interpersonal sensitivity, less behavioral intrusiveness, and more dyadic reciprocity. The fact that the kangaroo experience even influences how fathers interact with the infants suggests multiple pathways to these desirable outcomes.

Rarely does a no-cost, easy-to-do intervention have such dramatic psychological and physiological rewards.

Even among physically healthy infants, touch in the form of massage has benefits to infants that should be of interest to parents, including positive effects on their patterns of sleep (Underdown, Barlow, & Stewart-Brown, 2010). It seems that, in general, positive early tactile experiences are crucial to infants' later physical, mental, and emotional adjustment. Youngsters who have little physical contact during infancy may be slower to learn to walk and talk, and some instances of difficulties and lag in reading and speech are also associated with early deprivation of tactile communication. Physical violence in adults may also be related to deprivation of touch during infancy. Although most research focuses on an infant's needs and desires for physical contact, there are individual differences, as we discuss later: some infants and children invite more touch than others. Aversion to being touched has, in fact, been observed in children who later develop a diagnosis on the autism spectrum (Mammen et al., 2015); the complex interplay of infants' temperament and behavior with parental responses could in this situation, as in many others, produce a magnifying effect over time.

Ashley Montagu (1971) cited many animal and human studies to support the notion that tactile satisfaction during infancy and childhood is of fundamental importance to subsequent healthy behavioral development. He maintained that it is not possible to handle a child too much, as "there is every reason to believe that, just as the salamander's brain and nervous system develops more fully in response to peripheral stimulation, so does the brain and nervous system of the human being" (p. 188). Harlow's (1958) famous "surrogate mother" experiments on monkeys offer supporting evidence from the animal world for the importance of touch for infants in stressful situations. Harlow constructed a monkey mother-figure out of wire that could provide milk and protection; then he constructed another one out of soft rubber and toweling that did not provide milk. Because infant monkeys consistently chose the cloth mother, Harlow concluded that contact comfort was a more important part of the mother–child relationship for monkeys than was sustenance per se.

Maternal touch also has been shown to reduce the impact of stressful situations on human infants (Feldman, Singer, & Zagoory, 2010). (We write "maternal" to reflect the research, with no implication that the same would not hold for paternal touch.) Researchers are investigating the type and pace of touch as well as the simple fact of touch. In particular, "C tactile" touch is transmitted by unmyelinated slow-conducting nerve receptors called C tactile or CT afferents, which are sensitive to gentle movements on the skin and which are associated with a pleasure experience in numerous studies, not only on infants (Field, 2019). Van Puyvelde, Gorissen, Pattyn, and McGlone (2019) found that infants' physiology responded more favorably to mothers' stroking compared to static touch, and furthermore that mothers intuitively stroked their infants at a rate optimal for the CT nerves to fire, which is to say gently, with low force touch, and a medium stroking velocity rate.

Infants gain knowledge of themselves and the world around them through tactile explorations with their mouths and hands. Their mental representations depend on the integration of input from touching and seeing objects in their surroundings. During early childhood, words accompany touch until the child associates the two; then words may replace touch entirely. A parent may gently stroke or pat an infant for consolation. As the child grows older, the parent may stroke and pat the child while murmuring encouraging words. Eventually, instead of being touched, the child might simply hear a call from another room, "It's all right, I'm here." As words replace touch, an intimate closeness may still be present because of the earlier associations.

Gender differences show up early, likely owing to conscious or nonconscious parental socialization practices. After 6 months of age, girls are not only allowed but encouraged to spend more time touching and staying near their parents than boys. Indeed, girls' tendency to stay nearer to the mother is one of several well-established behavioral gender differences in children over 3 years of age, along with play grooming (girls more), rough-and-tumble play (boys more), and play fighting (boys more). All of these behaviors imply touching, or the opportunity to touch, other people. The pattern suggests that searching for an overall gender difference may not be helpful, because the gender difference varies with the behavior. The pattern suggests early manifestation of the distinction that is well-documented in teens and adults between "communal" and "agentic" behaviors (Trapnell & Paulhus, 2012). Girls' pattern suggests more composed and harmonious touch encounters, while boys' pattern suggests more active and aggressive (although playful) touch encounters. These patterns fit with general positive touching tendencies related to gender. In a study of parents engaging in a playful versus more conversational task with their 4- to 6-year-olds, fathers touched the child more than mothers did in the playful task (Aznar & Tenenbaum, 2016).

Within the family, nonaggressive touch frequency is positively associated with positive affect; in other words, more touch may be a marker for good family adjustment as well as a predictor of future emotional health (Takeuchi et al., 2010). Harrison-Speake and Willis (1995) gathered adults' views on the appropriateness of different kinds of parental touch with children of different ages. Clear norms were evident: Touch was seen as increasingly inappropriate as children grew from toddlers to young teenagers, especially for fathers and for boys. This same decrease in parent–child touch was seen in Aznar and Tenenbaum's (2016) observational study of 4- and 6-year-olds. Several observations of touching behavior have been made in the context of the developing child's school experiences. In one study, preschool boys tended to touch their male teachers more than their female teachers; preschool girls touched teachers of both genders about equally. The teachers themselves usually touched children of their own gender more (Perdue & Connor, 1978). However, in general, teachers may be using nurturing (or any) forms of touch less these days because of concerns about how their touch will be viewed by others (Fletcher, 2013; Owen & Gillentine, 2011).

Willis and colleagues (Willis & Hoffman, 1975; Willis & Reeves, 1976) observed children in elementary school and junior high school. From kindergarten through sixth grade, the amount of touching steadily declined but still surpassed most reports of adult touching. This same trend occurred in junior high, with about half as much touching as in the primary grades. The most touching occurred between same-gender dyads. African-American children, especially African-American females, tended to exhibit more touching behavior. Although touching in the primary grades is more often initiated with the hands, junior high students showed much more shoulder-to-shoulder and elbow-to-elbow touching. Junior high females began to show more aggressive touching, and junior high boys were touched in more places, primarily because of the play fighting so common at that age. During adolescence, tactile experiences with members of the same gender, and then the opposite gender, become increasingly important.

The use of touch to communicate emotional and relational messages to the elderly may be crucial, particularly as the reliance on verbal and cognitive messages wanes. Sehlstedt et al. (2016) found that gentle touch (specifically, C-tactile stroking) produced lower ratings of intensity as participants aged (across the range of 13 to 82 years) yet the relation of age to perceived pleasantness was positive. Thus, even though sensitivity decreased with age, the psychologically rewarding aspects of touch increased with age.

Although older Americans seem to be given a greater license to touch others, it is not clear how much others touch them. No doubt the infirmities of age require more touching, but it may make a big difference whether this increased touching is merely functional and professional or whether it expresses affection and is actually appreciated. Observations of touching among residents in four homes for the elderly revealed that females tended to initiate more touching than did males. And, as in childhood, same-gender touch was more likely than touch between members of the opposite gender (Rinck, Willis, & Dean, 1980).

WHO TOUCHES WHOM, WHERE, WHEN, AND HOW MUCH?

The amount and kind of contact experienced in adulthood varies considerably with the age, personality, gender, situation, culture, and relationship of the parties involved. We explore these factors briefly here.

IN TOUCH WITH THE BIG O

Physical intimacy serves many emotional, psychological, and physiological needs. Regarding the latter, two people can choose to engage in sexual behavior with each other in order to experience pleasure, which may culminate in an orgasm for both of them. The words "may culminate" apply more to heterosexual women than heterosexual men. An orgasm gap exists, with men being more likely than women to climax during sex (Frederick, St. John, Garcia, & Lloyd, 2018).

Factors linked to the orgasm gap include the anatomical features of women and sexual/gender scripts. Due to its location, the clitoris may not receive a lot of direct stimulation during sexual activity that focuses only or mostly on penile–vaginal intercourse, which might be why women have more difficulties orgasming this way than men do. In terms of scripts, if heterosexual couples believe that sex culminates in sexual intercourse, then women may be at a disadvantage relative to men for the anatomical reason noted earlier.

Closing the orgasm gap requires more varied touching and better communication. Orgasm success for women seems to depend on having a number of their erogenous zones touched, especially the clitoral region of their body. For women in same-gender relationships, more manual and oral stimulation of the clitoris may explain why they are more likely to orgasm than women in heterosexual relationships (Frederick et al., 2018).

Given that physical intimacy serves many emotional, psychological, and physical needs, it makes sense that sex is better and orgasm frequency greater for women when these needs are being meant, such as in longer-term relationships (not "hookups") marked by satisfaction and better sexual communication (Armstrong et al., 2012; Frederick et al., 2018; Kontula & Miettinen, 2016). When women are more satisfied in their intimate relationships, they tend to have more frequent and consistent orgasms (Klapilova, Brody, Krejcova, Husarova, & Binter, 2015; Young, Denny, Luquis, & Young, 1998). In terms of sexual communication, women in established relationships might be more willing to tell their partners how they need to be touched in order to get an orgasm. Perhaps not surprisingly then, women in established relationships with men are more likely to receive manual and oral stimulation of their clitoris (Armstrong et al., 2012).

There are reports of married couples who have so little to say to each other, or who find it so difficult to establish closeness through verbal contact, that physical contact during sexual encounters becomes a primary mode of establishing closeness. Of course, communication problems may be so bad for some couples that they neither talk to nor touch each other all that much. Many factors in the development of American society have led to a common expectation that touching is conducted only in extremely personal and intimate relationships, which leads to the belief that all touching is somehow sensuous in nature. This is far from true, as this chapter amply illustrates. Actually, long-term intimates probably touch each other less, and less intimately, than those who are either working to establish a romantic relationship or working to restore one that is losing intimacy (Emmers & Dindia, 1995; Guerrero & Andersen, 1991; McDaniel & Andersen, 1998). For intimates in long-established romantic relationships, the quality of touch has likely replaced the quantity needed to initially establish the relationship as an intimate one. In married relations also, people are more likely to reciprocate touch than in dating relationships (Guerrero & Andersen, 1994).

For some individuals, the contact occurring in a crowded commuter train or theater lobby is very uncomfortable, especially opposite-gender contacts for some women and same-gender contacts for some men. Explanations for such feelings are numerous. Some children grow up learning not to touch a multitude of animate (and inanimate) objects. They are told not to touch their own body and later not to touch the body of their dating partner. Care is taken such that children do not see their parents touch each other intimately. Touching is associated with admonitions of "not nice" or "bad" and is punished accordingly. Because of such experiences, some people become nontouchers in any situation.

Self-report scales to measure people's frequency and acceptability of interpersonal touching have been developed since the 1980s (e.g., Andersen, Andersen, & Lustig, 1987; Deethardt & Hines, 1983). Recent additions are the Touch Experiences and Attitudes Questionnaire (TEAQ; Trotter, McGlone, Reniers, & Deakin, 2018) and the Comfort with Interpersonal Touch scale (CIT; Webb & Peck, 2015).

Self-reports of one's attitudes about touch have been shown to have validity. One ubiquitous finding is that females report more comfort with touch than males. For the TEAQ, which covers positive touch (such as hugs, kisses, skin–skin, and hair–skin contact, with subscales for childhood touch, friends and family touch, current intimate touch, attitude to self-care, attitude to intimate touch, and attitude to unfamiliar touch), a strong correlate of touch aversion proved to be report of childhood psychological trauma including abuse; also, more positive touch attitudes were related to current social support (Trotter et al., 2018). The CIT (Webb & Peck, 2015), with separate subscales for initiating versus receiving touch, produced a wealth of validational findings: People more comfortable with touch were more extraverted, less likely to be chronic electronic gamers (i.e., socially reclusive), more likely to participate in roller derby (a sport high in physical contact), and more liking of massage as well as ballroom dancing, getting a haircut, having a garment personally fitted by a tailor, and being in more crowded shopping environments—all experiences involving physical contact, or the likelihood of it, with others. Touch-avoiders stand farther from others, respond negatively to touch in a live interaction, and touch their relationship partners less in public (Andersen, 2005). Other studies show that nontouchers, when compared with touchers, report more anxiety and depression in their lives, less satisfaction with their bodies, and more suspicion of others. This body of research shows that there are real differences between people in their tolerance for touching and that these differences can be seen in their personal and social experiences.

Certain situations have a facilitating or inhibiting effect on touching behavior. Several studies have demonstrated that in public places, where most observational research is done, touching can be quite infrequent. As an example, Hall and Veccia (1990) observed 4,500 pairs of people in public places and found that only 15% were already touching or engaged in touch during the observation period. Similarly, Remland, Jones, and Brinkman (1991) observed dyads in public places in several European locations and found that people touched in only 9% of the interactions observed.

Henley (1977) gathered people's opinions on touch patterns and concluded that people think that the likelihood of touch is increased in the following situations, which imply underlying themes of power, intimacy, and emotion:

1. Giving information or advice rather than asking for it
2. Giving an order rather than responding to one
3. Asking a favor rather than agreeing to do one
4. Trying to persuade rather than being persuaded
5. Participating in a deep, rather than casual, conversation
6. Interacting at a party rather than at work
7. Communicating excitement rather than receiving it from another
8. Receiving messages of worry from another rather than sending such messages

Greetings and departures at airport terminals are communicative situations that reflect a higher incidence of touching than would normally be expected. In one study, 60% of the people observed in greetings touched; another study reported that 83% of the participants touched (Greenbaum & Rosenfeld, 1980; Heslin & Boss, 1980). Heslin and Boss found that extended embraces and greater intimacy of touch were more likely to occur during departures than greetings. The stronger the emotion, as reflected in facial expressions, and the closer the perceived relationship, the greater the chances of increased touching. Actual relationship closeness, such as in romantic relationships as opposed to friendships, has, in fact, been shown to predict the amount of interpersonal touching in public (Afifi & Johnson, 1999; Guerrero, 1997).

Another situation likely to show a higher incidence of touch than normally found in public settings involves team sports. In one study, the touching behavior of bowlers during league play was observed and found to be far more frequent than observations during normal social interaction (Smith, Willis, & Gier, 1980). Similarly, Kneidinger, Maple, and Tross (2001) counted touches made on the field during college baseball and softball games and found a high touching rate, averaging more than 20 touches per inning. The excitement and camaraderie of the team experience may lower inhibitions and create a "safe" environment for showing team solidarity.

Anthropologists and travelers, as well as researchers, have noted that touch patterns differ according to culture and nationality. Some cultures seem very tactile, and others are more "hands off" (DiBiase & Gunnoe, 2004; McDaniel & Andersen, 1998). Cultures can differ in overall quantity of touch, the contextual rules that determine when and how people touch, and in the meanings expressed by touch. Research has not progressed far in mapping out these sources of variation. A strong likelihood is that most touches have common meanings in different cultures, but the norms for who can touch whom, and when, follow local customs. Thus, the amount of touch might differ while the meanings remain much the same. Most of our knowledge about the psychology of touch and other nonverbal behaviors is based on the study of White Americans.

Gender and relationships influence touching patterns. In a classic study, Jourard (1966) asked college students what parts of the body they thought are touched most often, using a questionnaire. Students indicated which of 24 body parts they had seen or touched on others, or that others had seen or touched on them, within the previous 12 months. The other people were specified as mother, father, same-gender friend, and opposite-gender friend. Among other findings, Jourard's study found that females were perceived as considerably more accessible to touch by all of the people specified than males were. Opposite-gender friends and mothers were reported as doing the most touching. Many fathers were recalled as touching not much more than the hands of the participants. The likelihood of opposite-gender touching of course depends greatly on the relationship between the parties, and this kind of touch is more likely when intimacy and familiarity are high (Stier & Hall, 1984).

Jourard's data were gathered over 50 years ago. A replication of this study more than a decade later revealed about the same results—with one exception (Rosenfeld, Kartus, & Ray, 1976). Both males and females were perceived as even more accessible to opposite-gender friends than they were in the preceding decade, with increased touching reported for body parts normally considered more intimate, such as chest, stomach, hips, and thighs. Of course, when people are asked to recall where they have been touched and how often, there is always the possibility that these recollections will not be accurate. Jones (1991) found that the number of body parts actually contacted was consistently fewer than those anticipated or recalled by students filling out a questionnaire.

We pursue the topic of gender differences in touch further in Chapter 12. Suffice it to say here that the observation of gender differences in nonverbal behavior raises many interesting questions about determinants. Henley (1977) proposed the hypothesis that gender differences in touch, as well as several other nonverbal behaviors, are closely tied to gender differences in dominance and power, with the general hypothesis being that differences between men and women parallel differences between powerful and weak people in society at large. The evidence supporting Henley's hypothesis is mixed and is undermined by the very inconsistent evidence of systematic differences in nonverbal behavior, including touching, according to the dominance–power dimension (Hall, 2011b; Hall, Coats, & Smith LeBeau, 2005; see Chapter 12). For instance, gender differences have been found among men and women in supervisory roles, with women reporting nonsexually touching their subordinates more than their male counterparts (Fuller et al., 2011). If power differences solely accounted for gender differences in touching behavior, one might expect male and female supervisors to report similar levels of positive touching behavior on the job.

DIFFERENT TYPES OF TOUCHING BEHAVIOR

Argyle (1975) listed the following kinds of bodily contact as most common in Western culture:

Type of Touch	Bodily Areas Typically Involved
Patting	Head, back
Slapping	Face, hand, buttocks
Punching	Face, chest
Pinching	Cheek
Stroking	Hair, face, upper body, knee, genitals
Shaking	Hands, shoulders
Kissing	Mouth, cheek, breasts, hand, foot, genitals
Licking	Face, genitals
Holding	Hand, arm, knee, genitals
Guiding	Hand, arm
Embracing	Shoulder, body
Linking	Arms
Laying on	Hands
Kicking	Legs, buttocks
Grooming	Hair, face
Tickling	Almost anywhere

(We made the following alterations to the original list: (1) changed *bottom* to *buttocks*; (2) added *genitals* to four categories; and (3) added *shoulders* to the shaking category.)

Morris (1977) reported on field observations that led to the naming of 457 types of body contact, falling into 14 major types of public body contact occurring between two people. Some of these forms of touch can be seen in Figure 8-1. Sometimes the specific nature of a relationship can be deduced by observing the way touching is enacted. Morris's major categories of nonaggressive touching include the following:

1. **The handshake.** The strength of the tie or desired tie between the participants can often be observed by watching the nonshaking hand.

2. **The body-guide.** Here, touching is a substitute for pointing. The person guiding the other's body is frequently the person in charge during that encounter.
3. **The pat.** Morris says that when adults pat other adults, it is often a condescending gesture or a sexual one. The well-known exception is the congratulatory pat, which can be on the buttocks following a successful performance in team sports.
4. **The arm-link.** This may be used for support when one person is infirm, but it is also frequently used to indicate a close relationship. The person in charge, says Morris, is less likely to be the person grasping the other's arm.
5. **The shoulder embrace.** This half-embrace is used in male–female romantic relationships as well as to signify buddies in male–male relationships.
6. **The full embrace or hug.** This gesture frequently occurs during moments of intense emotion, sporting events, romance, greetings, and farewells. It is also used ritualistically to show a relationship closer than a handshake would indicate.
7. **The hand-in-hand.** When adults hold hands with children, it is designed for support, to keep children close, or to protect them. As adults, handholding suggests an equality within the relationship, because both parties are performing the same act. It is often thought of in opposite-gender relationships, but same-gender handholding is not uncommon, even between males (e.g., children, high-contact cultures).
8. **The waist embrace.** According to Morris, the waist embrace is frequently substituted for the full embrace when the participants wish to signal more intimacy than handholding or a shoulder embrace yet still remain mobile.
9. **The kiss.** The location, pressure, duration, and openness of a kiss help signal the closeness or desired closeness between two people at a particular moment.
10. **The hand-to-head.** Given the highly vulnerable nature of the head area, letting someone touch the head shows a trusting, often intimate, relationship.
11. **The head-to-head.** Two people touching heads render them incapable of regarding other ongoing activities in a normal manner, so this is usually thought of as an agreement by both parties to shut out the rest of the world— a condition especially common to young lovers.
12. **The caress.** This signal is associated with romantic feelings for a partner, although like any signal, it can be used by nonintimates who are trying to deceive others about the depth of their relationship.
13. **The body support.** Parents often support children by carrying, lifting, or letting them sit in their laps. Such support may be sought among adults in playful situations, or when one person feels physically helpless.
14. **The mock attack.** Aggressive-looking behaviors are sometimes performed in a nonaggressive manner: for example, arm-punches, hair-rufflings, pushes, pinches, and ear-nibbles. Such gestures are sometimes allowed or even encouraged with friends to signal a high degree of behavioral understanding. And sometimes these mock-attack touches are substitutes for more loving touches that may be too embarrassing, such as in the case of some fathers wishing to show love for their sons.

Another method of categorizing the various types of touching was undertaken by Heslin and Alper (1983). This taxonomy is based on the functions of the messages communicated and ranges from less personal to more personal types of touch. Accidental touches and aggressive touches seem to be a part of the intimacy continuum but are not presented in this list.

1. **Functional/professional**. The communicative intent of this impersonal, often cold and businesslike, form of touching is to accomplish some task or to perform some service. The other person is considered an object or nonperson to keep any intimate or sexual messages from interfering with the task at hand. Examples of such situations may include a golf pro with a student, a tailor with a customer, or a physician with a patient. A functional/professional relationship may, unfortunately, offer convenient cover for touching that is far from professional, as what made national news in 2016 when Larry Nassar, a former national team doctor for *USA Gymnastics*, was found to have engaged in years of sexual abuse under the pretense of providing medical treatment to young athletes, hundreds of whom eventually filed lawsuits against him. Nassar was sentenced to 60 years in prison, but sadly many such cases go unreported because of reticence on the victims' part or ambiguity (in the victims' minds) about the true nature of the touch.

FIGURE 8-1 Some common forms of touch.

PROFESSIONAL TOUCH?

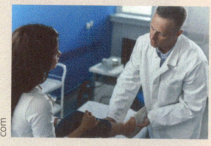 

The professionals shown here are not sexually harassing their clients. However, the risk of inappropriate touching by professionals in these occupations (medicine and yoga) is real for two reasons. One, professionals in these occupations need to touch their clients. Two, it may not always be clear to clients that they have been touched inappropriately. Although clients may feel uncomfortable with how they are being touched, they may assume the professionals are just doing their jobs.

2. **Social/polite**. This type of touching affirms the other person's identity as a member of the same species, operating by essentially the same rules of conduct as functional or professional touch. Although the other is treated as a person, there is still very little perceived involvement between the interactants. The handshake is the best example of this type of touching. Although the handshake is only about 150 years old, it was preceded by a handclasp, which goes back at least as far as ancient Rome.

3. **Friendship/warmth**. This kind of touching behavior begins to recognize more of the other person's uniqueness and expresses a liking for that person. However, this type of touch may engender uneasiness, because it can be misunderstood as intimate or sexual touching. Private situations may exacerbate this problem, so it probably will take place in public if the toucher anticipates the possibility of misinterpretation.

4. **Love/intimacy**. When one lays a hand on the cheek of another person, or fully embraces that person, one is probably expressing an emotional attachment or attraction through touch. The various kinds of touching at this point are probably the least stereotyped and the most adapted to the specific other person.

5. **Sexual arousal**. Although sexual arousal is sometimes an integral part of love and intimacy, it also may have characteristics distinct from that category. Here we are primarily looking at touch as an experience of physical attraction only. The other person is, in common parlance, a sex object.

Morris (1971) proposed that heterosexual couples in Western culture normally go through a sequence of steps, similar to courtship patterns in other animal species, on the road to sexual intimacy. Aside from the first three, notice that each of the following steps involves some kind of touching: eye to body, eye to eye, voice to voice, hand to hand, arm to shoulder, arm to waist, mouth to mouth, hand to head, hand to body, mouth to chest, hand to genitals, and genitals to genitals or mouth to genitals. Whether this sequence is the same for men and women, and whether it is similar in same-gender and opposite-gender interactions, is not well understood.

It is a challenge to study touching behavior at all. Because people do not touch much in public, at least in Western societies, observers must wait long periods, and observe a great many people, to see many touches. Furthermore, the private settings in which touch occurs more often tend to be ones to which researchers do not have access. Therefore, naturalistic observation is more difficult and time-consuming than for other kinds of nonverbal behavior. For this reason, touch researchers use self-report methodology relatively more. To demonstrate effects of touch, other challenges arise. Often, to create experimental control, experimenters will train helpers (confederates) to deliberately engage in the behavior, or not, as in the library study mentioned at the chapter's beginning. Experiments are an important way of studying the impact of specific behaviors. Lewis, Derlega, Shankar, Cochard, and Finkel (1997) offered a valuable caution about the use of confederates who are expected to control their behavior precisely. Despite training, confederates may have difficulty controlling one behavior, such as touch, without simultaneously changing other behaviors, such as smiling and gazing. This issue also occurs in naturalistic studies, where one wonders if a given outcome is due to the touch per se or to other behaviors that co-occurred. It is sometimes hard therefore to know which behavioral cue was crucial in influencing the recipient of the cues. A critical reader is wise to consider possible confounding effects of unintended cues when evaluating research.

THE MEANINGS AND IMPACT OF INTERPERSONAL TOUCH

Data gathered by Jones and Yarbrough (1985) indicate a wide range of meanings associated with touch. In their study, 39 male and female university students recorded the details of each touch experience over a 3-day period. Over 1,500 acts of social touching were analyzed. The following discussion incorporates their findings, along with others.

TOUCH AND POSITIVE AFFECT

Positive touching may involve support, reassurance, appreciation, affection, and sexual attraction, or, if the touch is sustained, it may send a message of inclusion (i.e., "We're together"). The enhanced positive affect that can be produced by even fleeting touches may generalize to the entire local environment, as found in the library study described earlier and in the consumer studies of Hornik (1991, 1992) in which shoppers touched by student greeters evaluated the store more favorably. A light, comforting pat by a female has been shown to even increase the financial risk-taking behaviors of others, presumably because they feel more secure (Levav & Argo, 2010).

Some kinds of touching behavior from nurses would fit into the category of positive touching, if it is perceived as comforting and relaxing to the patient. Back rubs and massages may also express positive feelings from a friend but may be perceived as task related when performed by a professional massage therapist. Yet, even then, the effect may be to increase positive affect. Psychotherapists, too, recognize the importance of performing touch in such a way that it communicates positive regard but not too much intimacy. If touch is perceived as an indication of interpersonal warmth, it may bring forth other related behaviors, including increased verbal output from patients and improved patient attitudes toward nurses (Aguilera, 1967; Pattison, 1973).

TOUCH AND NEGATIVE AFFECT

The students in Jones and Yarbrough's study did not report many touches in this category, but people clearly perceive some touches as an expression of negative attitudes and emotions. An expression of anger or frustration may be conveyed by hitting, slapping, pinching, or tightly squeezing another's arm so the person cannot escape. Generally, negative touch is much more likely among young children than adults.

Depending on the situation and other factors, any touch can be perceived negatively, as we alluded to earlier when discussing unwanted touches by politicians. Even the most well-meaning touch can have a negative impact. As alluded to earlier and discussed in more detail later, casual and innocuous touches can promote good mood and compliance. However, context and perceived intentions would qualify all interpretations, and the previous such studies focused on intentional touches. Martin (2012) showed that, in a store setting, being *accidentally* brushed on the shoulder blade by a confederate customer (as opposed to having the customer simply pass by closely) resulted in more negative brand evaluations and less time spent shopping among both men and women, with significant effects for both male and female touchers. Mechanisms for this negative effect could be several, from feeling the space is not safe to projecting one's negative reaction onto the products being examined.

Similarly, Camps, Tuteleers, Stouten, and Nelissen (2013) demonstrated that the same pat on the shoulder by another student (who was actually a confederate delivering the pats or not) could make the participant either more or less generous depending on whether their joint task was cooperative or competitive. This study gives clear evidence of how touch can take its meaning from the context and not from its intrinsic properties.

TOUCH AND DISCRETE EMOTIONS

Touch can do more than convey generalized positive and negative affect; it can convey discrete emotions, and may even be the preferred channel for communicating certain feelings, such as love and sympathy (App, McIntosh, Reed, & Hertenstein, 2011). Hertenstein, Keltner, App, Bulleit, and Jaskolka (2006) videotaped participants (touchers) while they tried to convey different emotions just by touching the hand and forearm of another person (recipients). Viewers who watched the video were able to identify, at levels better than guessing, the emotions of anger, fear, happiness, disgust, love, sympathy, and disgust. Analysis of the videos provided insight into how these emotions were conveyed. For example, sympathy was expressed with stroking and patting, anger with hitting and squeezing, and disgust with a pushing motion. There were also differences in intensity and duration.

Touch can be experienced both by seeing it and by receiving it. Hertenstein, Keltner, et al. (2006) also asked the original recipients of the touch to guess what emotion was the toucher was trying to convey. They could not see the touches, because the touching was done while their arm was sticking through a curtain—they could only *feel* the touches. Anger, fear, disgust, sympathy, love, and gratitude could be identified at better than guessing levels, but some other emotions could not be accurately identified by those receiving them, such as embarrassment, envy, pride, happiness, and surprise. In a follow-up study by Thompson and Hampton (2011), however, romantic couples but not strangers were able to communicate pride and envy to each other via touch. This finding suggests that the relationship between two people may be important to either the encoding or the decoding of emotions that are more self-focused in nature among touchers.

To extend the paradigm in a more naturalistic direction, Hertenstein, Holmes, McCullough, and Keltner (2009) allowed participants to touch another participant on any part of the body they wished, not just the arm as in Hertenstein et al.'s (2006) study. Recipients, who could not see the toucher, guessed whether the toucher was trying to convey anger, disgust, fear, happiness, sadness, sympathy, love, or gratitude. All eight emotions were identified at a greater than chance level, with anger being the highest and sadness and disgust being the lowest. Distinctive types, durations, and intensities of touch were observed for the different emotions. For example, anger was conveyed by shaking and pushing with strong intensity and relatively short duration, while sympathy was conveyed by patting, hugging, and rubbing with light intensity and relatively long duration.

People can also identify discrete emotions on another person's face by *feeling* that person's face with their hands, as a blind person might do—another connection between touch and emotion. Even normally sighted individuals with no special experience in doing this decoded six emotions at levels well above guessing, with the highest accuracy for happiness, sadness, and surprise (Lederman et al., 2007).

TOUCH AND PLAY

Sometimes touching is perceived as an attempt to reduce the seriousness of a message—whether it is affection or aggression. When one person goes through the motions of landing a knockout punch on the other person, then stops the forward movement of the fist just as it makes contact with the other person's skin, the message is "I'm not fighting, I'm playing." An accompanying smile or laugh may further reinforce this message.

The ultimate in playful touch is tickling, a phenomenon first addressed by psychologists nearly a century ago and discussed even by Charles Darwin. One question is why people cannot tickle themselves, and whether the "other" who does the tickling must be human or could as easily be a mechanical device. According to Harris and Christenfeld (1999), a machine can tickle as well as a person provided there is an element of unpredictability to it. Harris and Alvarado (2005) analyzed facial movements during tickling, discovering that the face showed signs of both happiness and pain.

TOUCH AND INFLUENCE

Touch is associated with influence when its goal is to persuade the other to do something. Jones and Yarbrough called these *compliance touches*, which may include a variety of behaviors from fulfilling social obligations to actual helping behavior, as evidenced by the following studies:

- Restaurant servers who touched diners got bigger tips (Crusco & Wetzel, 1984). Relative to nontouched customers, those who were touched briefly by their server drank more alcohol compared to their partners (Kaufman & Mahoney, 1999).
- Customers in stores who were touched by a greeter spent more time shopping and bought more (Hornik, 1991, 1992).
- Psychologists who touched students on the shoulder when requesting help obtained greater compliance (Patterson, Powell, & Lenihan, 1986).
- People who were touched after agreeing to fill out a survey answered a significantly larger number of items than people who agreed but were not touched (Nannberg & Hansen, 1994).

The psychological mechanism accounting for these findings is likely to be positive affect and the personal bonding that may be implied (nonconsciously) by even a fleeting and seemingly insignificant touch between strangers. These findings suggest that one could try to use touch manipulatively. Such efforts would of course backfire if the touch recipients did not like the touch, if they perceived a manipulative intent, or if the implied personal bonding was too threatening. Regarding the latter, men in Poland were found to be less likely to agree to a request from a man who had touched them, presumably due to homophobic attitudes (Dolinski, 2010). Note that touches in these studies were likely perceived as intentional; a negative effect of accidental touches was described in an earlier section.

Because an innocuous touch can create positive affect, Seger, Smith, Percy, and Conrey (2014) speculated that it might even promote positive associations toward a different racial group. In three experiments with either African American or Asian confederates and participants who were not members of those respective groups, the confederate either touched the participant lightly during study administration or not. Afterward, a measure of implicit racial associations on the negative-positive dimension was administered. In all three studies, implicit associations became more positive toward that racial group after having been touched, and the effect was not due to memory for the touch. Thus, touch can affect nonconsciously held outgroup attitudes.

Aside from using touch to achieve discrete goals, such as bigger tips or a favor, people may also use touch for more general impression-management purposes; an example would be to convey the impression of strength, dominance, or self-confidence. Barack Obama, when he was president, could often be seen gripping another person's upper arm with one hand while shaking hands with the other. He may have done this to convey an aura of being in control, though he could also intend to convey warmth and friendliness. Whatever the motive, the recipient might interpret it as either a welcome expression of solidarity or an offensive act of interpersonal control.

TOUCH AND INTERACTION MANAGEMENT

A conversation can be structured or controlled in many ways. These *management touches* may guide someone without interrupting verbal conversation; get someone's attention by touching or tugging at that person's arm, or tapping them on the shoulder; or fulfill some ritualistic function, such as touching a baby's head at a baptism.

Greetings also can serve as vehicles for management touches, as the participants choose to use gestures that signal to the self, the other, and any observer what kind of relationship exists and what kind of interaction can be expected. Greetings between heterosexual men may be especially fraught, at least in U.S. society, given common anxiety about being perceived as homosexual (Bowman & Compton, 2014). Ironically, in societies with strict laws and norms against homosexuality, public expressions of intimacy in male heterosexual dyads may be less fraught because no actual homosexuals would dare display male–male intimacy in public. The Saudi Crown Prince in Figure 8-2 used his touch to manage the ensuing interaction, probably much to President Bush's surprise.

FIGURE 8-2 Crown Prince Abdullah of Saudi Arabia holds hands with President George W. Bush at Bush's ranch in Crawford, Texas, April 25, 2005.

TOUCH AS PHYSIOLOGICAL STIMULUS

Obviously, touch is preeminently important at all stages of sexual interaction. Touch is also a strong but complex stimulus in more mundane interactions and, crucially, in appropriate neurological and social development (Bales et al., 2018). Touch can be physiologically arousing or soothing, depending on many contextual factors. When people are in experiments in which they are forewarned that they will be touched in a professional, innocuous manner, researchers find predictable heart rate decreases (Drescher, Gantt, & Whitehead, 1980), which is said to demonstrate that touch is intrinsically calming and relates to the evolutionary importance of mother–infant bonding. However, when touch is unexpected and/or unexplained, the heart rate goes up; for example, when females were touched unexpectedly on the wrist for 10 seconds by a male experimenter, a significant increase in heart rate was found, and, moreover, all participants showed increases in blood pressure in this condition compared to a no-touch condition and a condition in which touch was expected, such as taking a pulse (Nilsen & Vrana, 1998). Such research underscores that the physiological impact of touch depends on social–contextual factors and on the interpretations given to the touch.

TOUCH AND INTERPERSONAL RESPONSIVENESS

Sometimes the meanings attributed to touch concern the level of involvement, responsiveness, or activity of the communicator (Afifi & Johnson, 1999). Sometimes touch simply means that the intensity of the interaction, or the interactants' level of involvement in the conversation, is high. Interpersonal responsiveness may be perceived as positive affect when it is mutually felt, or when one person feels they contributed to the other's behavior. Probably more than any other nonverbal behavior, acts of touch that are perceived as deliberate are extremely salient in interaction; they are almost certain to be noticed and are likely to produce strong reactions, either positive or negative.

In emotionally upsetting situations, or in situations of pain or fear, a person often desires social support yet verbal messages such as "Can I have a little support please?" or "Tell me this will be OK" can be hard to deliver, out of pride, inhibition, or concerns about rejection. And sometimes the verbal response ("Don't worry, you'll do fine") is not convincing. Here interpersonal touch serves a crucial support function. Robinson, Hoplock, and Cameron (2015) observed the behavior of dating couples when they were reunited after one member of the couple had undergone a stressful laboratory task. The more distressed the first person was, the more they were observed to reach out for physical contact to their partner, and the more contact they received the more comforted they felt. Interestingly, it did not seem that the second person's touch was motivated by their sensitivity to the first person's distress; instead, the authors concluded that the power of the reciprocity norm produced touch in response to the first person's initiative, producing good effects even though an explicit appeal and explicit recognition of need were both lacking.

TOUCH AS TASK RELATED

There are times when we need to help someone get out of a car, or our hands touch as the result of passing something back and forth. These touches, associated with the performance of a task, are similar to what Heslin called *functional/professional* touch. As people get older, they may for instance need assistance walking. Fortunately, even a light touch, something that might be done by aides in a nursing home, has been shown to reduce postural sway in the elderly (Johannsen, Guzman-Garcia, & Wing, 2009). Of course, as with any other message, the two communicators may not share a similar meaning for the touch. What seems routine or functional to one person may seem intrusive or too personal to another. Trappings and rituals help prioritize the functional purpose of the touch: The paper gown worn by a patient during a medical exam may serve no real function other than signaling the impersonality of the exam.

Often, people have to endure functional touch, even from strangers—as in airport screening situations or with a new dental hygienist. Here, the burden of maintaining a desired level of intimacy (in this case, a desired lack of intimacy) can fall upon both parties. Unlike the reciprocity example we just described, here the individuals are likely to engage in *compensation*, which is behaving in a way that offsets the intimacy implications of the situation. Schroeder, Fishbach, Schein, and Gray (2017) demonstrated in several experiments how the experience of functional intimacy makes a person engage in psychologically distancing behaviors. For example, when the pulse was taken on the neck rather than on the wrist, recipients recommended "improvements to the procedure" that included making the pulse-taker wear plastic gloves and a lab coat, and stand farther away. (The pulse-taker had stood the same distance from the participant, regardless of the neck or wrist condition.)

TOUCH AS HEALING

A miraculous cure is one that cannot be explained by recognized medical or physiological therapy. Throughout recorded history, wondrous healings of the sick and infirm by religious workers, royalty, and other charismatic persons have had interpersonal touch as a major ingredient. Jesus was said to heal by touch, and he was often described as being surrounded by crowds hoping for his touch. The French and English kings were widely believed to be able to accomplish healing by the laying on of hands. In later centuries, healing touch became the province of ministers and of others who attributed the healing touch to the power of God. The healing power of touch in the so-called miraculous cases has not been studied in a controlled way that could establish its effectiveness or the mechanisms by which it may work. Although it may be difficult to rule out the power of God or some unknown physical forces, certainly one can point to psychological factors in miraculous healing such as the patient's intense hope for a cure, having trust in the healer, and being embedded in a social group with a shared belief system about the power of healing touch. Placebo effects, or the phenomenon whereby the body responds to beliefs about treatments even when they have no active ingredients, are well established in medicine.

The medical and nursing professions are interested in touch as a form of therapy (Borelli & Heidt, 1981; Kerr, Wasserman, & Moore, 2007; Krieger, 1987). Some touch therapies involving what researchers call *light touch* have been shown to reduce pain (Kerr et al., 2007). Massage, long known for its relaxing and pleasurable properties, has positive effects on outcomes such as brain activity, attentiveness and alertness, pain relief, anxiety and depression, stress hormones, sleep, appetite, pulmonary function in asthmatic children, immune function, weight gain in preterm infants, and other clinical indicators of health (Field, 1998, 2001, 2010; Field, Diego, & Hernandez-Reif, 2007). It has been suggested that specific neurologic (electroencephalogram) and parasympathetic nervous system activity (e.g., the pressure stimulates the vagal nerve, which lowers physiological arousal and stress hormones) may be the mechanisms underlying massage's favorable impact on people's well-being (Field, 2010). Even a single massage-therapy session has beneficial effects on anxiety, blood pressure, and heart rate (Moyer, Rounds, & Hannum, 2004).

Other therapies involving touch are more controversial. Reiki, in particular, is a popular modality wherein the practitioner supposedly transfers energy to the patient by holding their hands on or near to the patient's body. Some studies show beneficial effects, but the scientific community is skeptical as there is no established scientific principle to point to, and the studies were designed poorly (Lee, Pittler, & Ernst, 2008).

Whether owning pets is, in general, associated with positive health outcomes is not a settled empirical matter (Herzog, 2011; McNicholas et al., 2005; Wells, 2011). Nevertheless, the beneficial effects of touch may partially underlie whatever positive physiological and psychological effects pets have on us, because our relationships with pets typically entail high levels of touching (Allen, 2003). Animal-assisted therapy has been employed to help treat physical, cognitive, and emotional disturbances, often with beneficial effect (e.g., Virués-Ortega, Pastor-Barriuso, Castellote, Población, & de Pedro-Cuesta, 2012). The specific mechanisms involved in these therapeutic effects have not been untangled—for example, how much is due to the physical contact versus companionship, play opportunities, and increased human connection from the therapists.

Mental health professionals and physicians debate whether touch should be incorporated into the therapeutic process (Hetherington, 1998; Smith, Clance, & Imes, 1998; Young, 2007). Risk of sexual involvement, or simply risk that clients will take offense, is weighed against the potential value of human physical contact during stressful moments. Certainly therapists, and medical doctors as well, need to be highly sensitive to the responses that clients may have to being touched.

Outside the clinical situation per se, research shows that affectionate touch provides beneficial emotional, psychological, physiological, and health effects not just in infancy, as we have already discussed, but throughout life (Jakubiak & Feeney, 2017).

TOUCH AS SYMBOLISM

Perhaps because touch outside of intimate relationships is so infrequent, it is highly salient when it occurs. Touch can be so fraught with meaning that the act of touch itself comes to represent the significance of the relationship or occasion.

Sometimes, the symbolism of a touch is experienced at a very personal level through one's own experience of touch. Everyone has seen photographs of fans reaching out to touch a famous rock star or professional athlete. Figures 8-3 and 8-4 show the eagerness of people to touch public figures. Even in everyday situations, people often find value in

FIGURE 8-3 Crowd members reaching for Meghan Markle, Duchess of Sussex

touching someone who is important to them. They might say proudly after such an encounter, "I shook his hand!" The vicarious symbolic power of touch is sometimes evident even when the touch is one step removed from the actual person, as when one can touch or possess a remnant or other souvenir of the important person. Even an autograph fits this description because the important person has touched the pen and paper. Certainly, throughout the history of Christianity, it has been very meaningful to claim to own a piece of a saint's body or clothing.

One study of touch patterns in a state legislature noted that though the governor was touched by many, he was not seen to touch anyone during the observation period (Goldstein & Jeffords, 1981). The daughter of the Buddhist Panchen Lama, a holy man second in importance to the Dalai Lama, recollected a trip to Tibet when she was 7 years old: "They told me that there were people lining the road for fifty miles. Thousands and thousands of people, all wanting to touch me" (Hilton, 2004). On another trip, at age 17, she told of being exhausted by the crowds surrounding her. But, she said, "I can't complain, because it makes them so happy to see me and to touch me." But she had to ask her bodyguards to stop them from lifting up her skirt to get to her legs.

Touching in some situations, such as in Figure 8-4, gives touchers the feeling of acquiring something important: Something has rubbed off on them. It does not always seem to matter whether the significant other person is the toucher or the recipient of the touch. What is rubbed off can vary, too. Sometimes it is vicarious power: One can feel more important among peers after touching a famous person. Other times, what is gained is less definable though no less important: We might say that one feels one has acquired some piece of the other's essence through touch. Whatever the valuable quality possessed by the other, people feel they have gained a bit of it through even a very minor touch. This somewhat magical way of thinking has its reverse side, too, when we feel contaminated by touching or being touched by undesirable people. It is surely no coincidence that members of the lowest caste in traditional Hindu society in India were called *untouchables*.

CONTEXTUAL FACTORS IN THE MEANING OF INTERPERSONAL TOUCH

The meanings of touch depend on many environmental, personal, and contextual variables, as previous sections have made clear. Indeed, it is likely that much of the time, the meaning of touch derives from such qualifying variables and not from the nature of the touch per se. Often, touch intensifies ongoing emotional experiences rather than conveying specific meanings or messages. The relationship between the interactants provides an important context for interpreting the meaning of touch. A touch on the arm, which might be interpreted as a social/polite or merely friendly gesture, may

© PAUL J. RICHARDS/Staff/AFP/Getty Images

FIGURE 8-4 The audience is eager to touch President Obama after one of his speeches.

acquire sexual overtones depending on setting, acquaintanceship, and the recipient's expectations. An embrace may take on different intimacy connotations if two men embrace on the sports field versus in a bar (Kneidinger et al., 2001).

Interpretations of touch are also related to other contextual variables such as duration, the specific form of the touch, other verbal and nonverbal cues, and other contextual features, singly and in combination; for example, a touch might seem more intimate if it is accompanied by prolonged gaze, the touch is held an instant longer than necessary, the environment is private, and so forth. Certain parts of the body connote greater intimacy than other parts, but intimacy is also linked to the manner of touch. For instance, a touch and release on any part of the body is likely to be perceived as less intimate than a touch and hold.

Men and women may also attribute different meanings to similar types of touch. In a hospital study by Whitcher and Fisher (1979), female nurses touched patients during an explanation of procedures prior to surgery. Females reacted positively, showing lower anxiety, more positive preoperative behavior, and more favorable postoperative physiological responses. But men who were touched in the same way reacted less positively. A similar result was obtained by Lewis and colleagues (1995), who obtained ratings of photographic representations of nurses touching or not touching patients at the bedside. Men who looked at the photos rated both male and female nurses as more supportive if they did not touch the patient, whereas women viewers thought the nurses were more supportive if they did.

Heslin, Nguyen, and Nguyen (1983) found that men and women responded differently in a questionnaire study regarding people from whom touching would be considered the greatest invasion of privacy. Women indicated that touch from a stranger would be the greatest invasion of privacy, whereas men felt that touch from a same-sex person would be the greatest invasion of privacy. Men reported themselves to be as comfortable with touch from women strangers as they were with touch from women partners. Both men and women agreed that the most pleasant type of touch was stroking in sexual areas by an opposite-sex partner. But the second most pleasant type of touch reported by women was for a male friend to stroke their nonsexual areas, whereas the second most pleasant type of touch reported by men was for a female stranger to stroke their sexual areas.

Marital status influences how men and women interpret different kinds of touches. Over 300 individuals who were in an intimate relationship, either married or not, reported on what it meant to them when their significant other touched them on various parts of the body (Hanzal, Segrin, & Dorros, 2008). Confirming results found by Nguyen, Heslin, and Nguyen (1976), unmarried men found more pleasantness and warmth or love in being touched than unmarried women did, but this pattern was reversed among those who were married—in this group, the women found greater reward in being touched. Moreover, this result was not due to the difference in age between the unmarried and married groups.

TOUCH CAN BE A POWERFUL NONCONSCIOUS FORCE DURING INTERACTIONS

As studies cited earlier indicate, being touched can influence perceptions, moods, and behaviors even when it is fleeting, subtle, and possibly even unnoticed. But just as the influence of touch can be nonconscious on the part of the person being touched, so too can it be nonconscious on the part of the *toucher*. A prime example can be found in the phenomenon called *facilitated communication*, a technique developed for improving the communication of individuals with autism, severe intellectual disabilities, and physical diseases that impair motor abilities and communication, such as cerebral palsy. Facilitated communication was hailed on several continents as a breakthrough in the ability of speech-impaired individuals to communicate, and it became widely practiced and taught in the 1980s and 1990s (Jacobson, Mulick, & Schwartz, 1995; Spitz, 1997), and remains popular even in this century.

How does facilitated communication work? The technique is based on close tactile contact between the facilitator and the communicator (i.e., patient or person who otherwise has impaired ability to communicate), as well as a close psychological relationship in which trust is established. The facilitator holds and steadies the communicator's hands while the communicator types words or sentences on a keyboard. Using this method, many communication-impaired clients typed out highly revealing, often eloquent accounts of their feelings and thoughts. To many observers, it seemed that at last individuals with impairments could overcome their isolation and break out of their terrible enforced silence. Or so it seemed.

Unfortunately, facilitated communication proved not to reveal the impaired communicators' thoughts but rather the thoughts of the facilitators themselves. Research has unveiled facilitated communication as a pseudoscience, although usually practiced by sincere believers. Studies showed that the communicators were able to answer questions only when their facilitators knew the question and its answer, and furthermore communicators' responses often seemed much too verbally advanced for their intellectual level. In fact, communicators could even type out answers to questions when they were not looking at the keyboard (Kezuka, 1997; Spitz, 1997)!

Proceeding against a wave of protest by those who believed in the system, researchers persisted in conducting controlled experiments that ultimately revealed that typically the facilitated communication effects were due to the facilitator nonconsciously guiding the communicator's hand to type out what was already in the facilitator's mind. Research showed that when facilitators were fed incorrect information about the communicator's background, and then had to ask the communicator about those same facts, the answers given reflected the misinformation, not the true answers (Burgess et al., 1998). Kezuka (1997), using mechanical methods of determining physical force exerted by facilitators, demonstrated that facilitators did, indeed, use tiny muscle movements of their hand, and sometimes facial and other cues, to influence the position of the communicator's hand. Thus, the facilitators were the real communicators.

What makes facilitated communication fascinating and important for behavioral science is the fact that, in all likelihood, the great majority of facilitators were not frauds or charlatans but sincere believers (Spitz, 1997). Needless to say, the exposure of the true nature of facilitated communication was a great disappointment to those who believed in it. However, the actual—that is, nonconscious—mechanism of its effect is no less astonishing than the original claims. How could the facilitators be expressing their own thoughts without being aware of it?

Actually, this is not the first phenomenon involving nonconscious movement that has been documented. In the 19th century, great interest was paid to pendulums purported to swing in response to mysterious forces. Forked sticks called *dowsing rods* are said to suddenly point downward when the person using them walks over a place where there is underground water (Vogt & Hyman, 2000). And furniture has suddenly moved or turned, supposedly under the influence of spirits (Spitz, 1997). In all of these cases, there were no supernatural forces at work, only strong expectancies that produced motor responses that were out of awareness. According to Wegner, Fuller, and Sparrow (2003), all of these phenomena reflect "authorship confusion," whereby the true source of the action is attributed to a wrong person or object.

SELF-TOUCHING

People also communicate nonverbally through self-touching that includes nail chewing, skin picking, twirling the hair, hand wringing, lip biting, holding, stroking, and self-grooming activities. It is not clear what psychological functions are served by these actions, though researchers generally agree that they are more an out-of-awareness expression of personal needs than reflective of intentional communication (i.e., more "signs" than "signals"). However, intentional communication sometimes involves self-touching, as when a sexual invitation includes self-stroking or self-preening. Various kinds of self-touching, or self-touching used in different circumstances, may serve different functions. Figure 8-5 shows two kinds of self-touching. Morris (1971) listed various kinds of self-touching:

© Terrence Horgan

© Terrence Horgan

FIGURE 8-5 Self-touching.

1. **Shielding actions**. These behaviors usually involve reducing input or output: for example, covering the mouth or ears with the hands.
2. **Cleaning actions**. Sometimes the hands are brought up to the head to scratch, rub, pick, or wipe—for literal cleaning. But sometimes similar self-touching is used for attending to one's appearance: for example, hair grooming, clothes straightening, and other types of preening. People in the process of building an intimate relationship did more preening than those whose intimate relationship had been established for some time (Daly, Hogg, Sacks, Smith, & Zimring, 1983).
3. **Self-intimacies**. Self-intimacies, according to Morris, are comforting actions that generally represent nonconsciously reproduced acts of being touched by someone else. Examples include holding one's own hands and hugging one's own legs. Thus, self-touching can be a substitute for comfort that might otherwise be provided by others.

Some self-touching behaviors, including Morris's self-intimacies, have been called *adaptors* or *self-manipulators* (Ekman & Friesen, 1972). As the term implies, they are self-soothing behaviors in response to certain situations. There is consensus that adaptors are generally associated with negative feelings but also mental concentration (which may be associated with stress). Self-adaptors include rubbing, scratching, or kneading (as with the hands).

Research on psychiatric patients has found that self-adaptors increase as a person's psychological discomfort, anxiety, or depression gets worse (Ekman & Friesen, 1972; Freedman, 1972; Freedman, Blass, Rifkin, & Quitkin, 1973; Freedman & Hoffman, 1967; Waxer, 1977). If, however, the anxiety level is too high, a person may freeze, engaging in little movement. Ekman and Friesen (1972) also discovered picking and scratching self-adaptors to be related to a person's hostility and suspiciousness. Theoretically, this picking and scratching is a manifestation of aggression against oneself or aggression felt for another person that is directed inward. Other hypotheses about self-adaptors include the possibility that rubbing is used to give self-assurance; that covering the eyes is associated with shame or guilt; that self-grooming shows insecurity about one's self-presentation and that self-touching is an outlet for nervous energy. On the other hand, many people have self-adaptor habits (such as picking on one's cuticles) that probably do not reflect any deep psychological mechanism.

A number of studies have, indeed, indicated that self-touching is associated with situational anxiety or stress. This is the case in baboons and rats as well as in people (Castles, Whitens, & Aureli, 1999; Nephew & Bridges, 2011). Ekman and Friesen (1974a) asked people to watch one of two films, one highly stressful and the other quite pleasant. Viewers were then instructed to describe the film as pleasant to an interviewer. Thus, those watching the stressful film had to deceive, which in itself can be considered stressful. Participants in the unpleasant film group engaged in more self-touch than those simply describing the pleasant film as pleasant. Also, in a study of physician–patient communication, patients were more likely to touch their bodies when talking about anxiety-producing hidden agendas than when talking about the primary complaint (Shreve, Harrigan, Kues, & Kagas, 1988).

Interracial interaction is another context in which stress can produce self-touching. Olson and Fazio (2007) measured self-manipulations—such as scratching the head, playing with the hair, or kneading the hands—by White participants when interacting with Black and White confederates. The participants' general racial attitudes were measured as well as their attitudes about the particular Black confederate they interacted with. When these two kinds of attitudes were discordant—such as when their general attitude was negative, but their attitude toward the particular Black confederate was positive—participants engaged in significantly higher levels of self-touching. This study well illustrates the complexity of interpreting the meaning of nonverbal communication by reminding us that nonverbal behavior in interracial situations can reflect uncertainty or internal conflict rather than general negative attitudes.

Another source of body-focused movements is cognitive, or information-processing, demand. When engaged in a monologue, people touched themselves more than when simply sitting still. Heaven and McBrayer (2000) showed that people touched themselves more when answering questions about a passage they had heard than when simply listening to it. When asked to read the names of colors that were printed in contradictory colors, such as the word *red* printed in blue, people touched themselves more than if they were given color-consistent color names to read (Kenner, 1993). These results suggest that mental concentration and stress can lead to more self-touching.

Though not much direct evidence exists for how aware people are of their self-touching, it is generally assumed that, compared to some other nonverbal behaviors, self-touching is low in awareness. Hall, Murphy, and Schmid Mast (2007) found that, indeed, when asked how much of several nonverbal behaviors they engaged in during a videotaped interaction, people were least accurate in remembering how much they had engaged in self-touching, though they did remember their self-touching at levels better than chance.

Object-adaptors involve the manipulation of objects for no obvious functional purpose. These movements often involve touching objects in a repetitive or fidgety way, such as when a stressed person manipulates a pencil or paper clip over and over, or an anxious child rubs the tag or other part of their favorite stuffed toy. Object-adaptor behaviors also may be derived from the performance of some instrumental task, such as writing with a pencil or smoking. Some people engage in these mannerisms more than others. Although people are typically not very aware of performing self-adaptor behaviors, they are probably more aware of object-adaptors. These movements are often learned later in life, and fewer social taboos seem to be associated with them. As with self-adaptors, object-adaptors are likely to be associated with anxiety, stress, or cognitive load.

Because there are social constraints on displaying some self-adaptors, they are more often seen when a person is alone. At any rate, in public we would not expect to see the full act. As an example, alone you might pick your nose without inhibition, but when around other people, you may just touch your nose or rub it casually.

Individual and group differences in self-touching have been found. In a study of children from four countries, those from England and Australia engaged in significantly less self-touching during experimental tasks than did Italian children and French-speaking children in Belgium. Possibly, touching of other people may parallel these self-touching differences across these cultures. Also in those samples, significant individual variation was revealed, meaning that some children were consistently more likely to touch themselves during a variety of experimental tasks (Kenner, 1993). Another group difference relates to gender: Women touch themselves in interpersonal interaction more than men do (Hall, 1984). It is not clear to what extent this may reflect greater social anxiety or arousal on the part of females, a heightened self-consciousness about appearance, or the simple fact that women's clothes and hair more often demand readjustment.

SUMMARY

Humans' first information about themselves, others, and the environment probably comes from touching. The act of touching or being touched can have a powerful impact on responses to a situation, even if that touch was unintentional. In some cases, touching is the most effective method for communicating; in others, it can elicit negative or hostile reactions. The meanings we attach to touching behavior vary according to what body part is touched, how long the touch lasts, the strength of the touch, the method of the touch, and the frequency of the touch. Touch also means different things in different environments—institutions, airports, and so on—and varies with communicators' age, gender, culture, personality, and relationship. Indications are that children in the U.S. touch more than adults do, with a decreasing amount of touch from kindergarten through junior high school. Investigators agree that early experiences with touch are crucial for later adjustment.

The common types of interpersonal touching and self-touching may communicate a variety of messages that include influence, positive affect, negative affect, play, interpersonal responsiveness, interaction management, and task requirements. Touch can have powerful symbolism, and its possible healing and therapeutic power has received much attention throughout history and in modern research laboratories. Touching can also intensify whatever emotional experience is occurring. Touch can be a powerful source of behavioral influence, and both the toucher and the recipient of touch may be unaware of its occurrence and effects.

QUESTIONS FOR DISCUSSION

1. Think of a person you know personally who does not like touching or being touched. What analysis can you offer for this person's characteristic? How much do you think it reflects personal history and personality versus social and cultural norms?

2. What do you think about the ethics of using touch to achieve compliance or a favor from someone? Is it different from using persuasive language or using other forms of nonverbal communication, such as smiling or generally "being nice"?

3. Most studies find that touch is a rather infrequent event. Do you think this is correct? Discuss exceptions to this generalization. Why do you think touch might seem to be not very common?

4. Sometimes people are eager to touch others because they gain something of psychological value by doing so, yet people often feel violated by being touched. Discuss these different perspectives on the phenomenon of touch.

5. It has been suggested that sometimes a person's friendly intentioned touch is misperceived as being a sexual invitation. Have you ever had such an experience? Do you think this is a true phenomenon?

NONVERBAL COMMUNICATION IN ACTION: TRY THIS

For a day, pay close attention to your own and others' use of self-touching. Try to analyze the circumstances under which people engage in this behavior. Note what brings it on, what situations it occurs in, and what kind of people do it more or do it less. What kind of psychological function do you think self-touching serves?

CHAPTER 9

THE EFFECTS OF THE FACE ON HUMAN COMMUNICATION

Your face, my thane, is a book where men may read strange matters.

—Shakespeare, Macbeth, Act I

The face is rich in communicative potential. It is a primary site for communication of emotional states, it reflects interpersonal attitudes, it provides nonverbal feedback on the comments of others, and some scholars say it is the primary source of communicative information next to human speech. For these reasons, and because of the face's visibility, people pay a great deal of attention to the messages conveyed by faces of others and weigh them heavily when making important interpersonal judgments, whether those judgments are justified or not. In innumerable situations, people want to see another person's face, even when it's not particularly relevant to any actions or personally relevant consequences. Imagine looking at the engagement or wedding pages of a newspaper without seeing couples' faces! Or imagine not being able to tell one person's face from another person's face (see Box **Face Blindness**). Fascination with the face begins when an infant takes special interest in the huge face peering over the crib and tending to their needs. Most of the research on facial expressions and various components of the face has focused on the display and interpretation of emotional signals. Although this is the major focus of this chapter, we also emphasize that the face may be the basis for judging another person's personality, and it can—and does—provide information on much more than our emotional state.

FACE BLINDNESS

Imagine not recognizing a coworker or family member because you have difficulties discriminating one face from another. This is what some individuals suffering from prosopagnosia or face blindness have to deal with in everyday life. This condition forces them to use other cues from close others, such as their body size and voice, in order to identify them. Needless to say, afflicted individuals report having problems during social interactions, including anxiety about not recognizing others. These worries can negatively impact their social and work lives; they might, for example, avoid social or work gatherings because, in such situations, recognizing others is important (Yardley, McDermott, Pisarski, Duchaine, & Nakayama, 2008). However, very little research has been devoted to examining the social, occupational, and life outcomes linked to this condition.

Dr. Julie Broadbent: One Face of Prosopagnosia

I've always had problems recognizing people. I have difficulty following the plot in a movie or TV show because I can't distinguish between the characters. As a professor, I often mistake one student for another, even at the end of the semester. I can't picture the face of my sister or my husband when I close my eyes. I am nervous and careful in social situations. Why? Because I'm never sure who I am talking to! I have to wait for the conversation to begin for hints as to who they are.

I always assumed my difficulties were due to inattention, a bad memory, or being too vain to wear my glasses as a young teenager. But those factors don't explain my problem. Despite being a neuroscientist, I wasn't aware a neurological condition called prosopagnosia—more commonly known as face blindness—existed until I came across a brief description of it in the textbook I was using for my biopsychology class. That's when the light bulb lit up! That's when everything started to make sense! It was a huge relief to know the cause of many embarrassing moments in my life.

Some people have a severe form of prosopagnosia. Neurologist Oliver Sacks, for example, could not recognize his own face in a mirror. Others, like myself, are moderately affected by the condition. (Like many, however, I have never been officially tested for prosopagnosia.) I have no problem recognizing colleagues I work with every day. However, I may not recognize others I am not so familiar with, especially if I see them in an unexpected context, such as an airport. In these situations, I tend to smile tentatively at anyone who looks my way, just in case I know them.

At the other end of the continuum, you have superrecognizers. Superrecognizers can see someone's face once and, on encountering them again, will recognize that they have seen them before. My husband, who annoyingly turns out to be a superrecognizer, has been teasing me for 35 years about my inexplicable inability to recognize people. He still teases me even though he is now aware that this disorder is often associated with changes in the fusiform gyrus (due to abnormal development, trauma, or disease) on the ventral surface of the right temporal lobe in the human brain.

Now that I am aware of prosopagnosia, it's a relief to be able to tell my students on the first day of class that I am moderately affected by this disorder and forewarn them of the inevitable embarrassing moments that will occur during the semester. When those moments occur, my students now just shrug and say, "It's just Dr. Broadbent!"

THE FACE AND PERSONALITY JUDGMENTS

The human face and its features come in many sizes and shapes. As reviewed in Chapter 6, people have long believed that certain personality or character traits can be judged from the shape or features of a person's face. For example, high foreheads are believed to reveal intelligence, thin lips conscientiousness, and thick lips sexiness (Secord, Dukes, & Bevan, 1959). *Facial primacy*, or the tendency to give more weight to the face than to other communication channels, may stem in part from these facial stereotypes.

But facial primacy probably stems even more from the *dynamic* nature of the face—its ability to make practically an infinite number of expressions. Many different muscles are used routinely in making facial expressions (Rinn, 1984). The look of a person's face is due in part to the genetic blueprint that endows it with certain physical features, in part to transient moods that stimulate the muscles to move in distinctive ways, and in part to the lingering imprint of chronically held expressions that seem to set in and become virtually permanent over the years.

People make personality attributions based on facial expressions. For example, a person who smiles warmly upon introduction is immediately perceived to be nice. Likewise, a sour-faced old man might be assumed to be mean and selfish. Little research exists on the validity of such stereotypes. It is certainly possible that the person with the warm smile is a cutthroat manipulator and the mean-looking man is a tenderhearted grandpa. Research does show that facial expressions influence impressions of personality. In Knutson's (1996) study, this was based on static images, while the 2011 study of Hall, Gunnery, and Andrzejewski used videos of target people assigned to watch emotion-inducing film clips. New participants then watched the videos of the targets' facial expressions and guessed the target people's personalities. When the film clips were geared to arouse disgust, fear, or sadness, the target people were rated as more neurotic, and when the film clips were happiness-inducing the target people were rated as more extraverted, open to experience, and agreeable. These ratings were not related to the target people's actual personalities but were solely influenced by the expressions they were showing while watching the films.

Some facial expression stereotypes have validity. Riggio and Riggio (2002) reviewed published studies relating participants' actual extraversion and neuroticism (according to personality inventories they filled out) to their facial expressiveness as measured in laboratory situations. More neurotic people were less expressive, and more extraverted people were more expressive.

Another study lending support to the validity of facial expression stereotypes was done by Harker and Keltner (2001). The more women's faces showed positive emotional expression in their college yearbook pictures, the more observers of the pictures thought the women would be rewarding to interact with. And, indeed, the women who had more positive expressions had more affiliative personalities and reported experiencing more positive affect, not only at age 21 but also decades later, and they were more likely to be married by age 27 than women who had less positive yearbook photos.

Many more studies have documented whether people's appearance and expression are thought to be, and actually are, related to their personalities. In general, viewers agree with each other in assigning personality, and often their judgments are correct, at least in the sense of being more accurate than just guessing. In terms of facial expressions in particular, Kaurin, Heil, Wessa, Egloff, and Hirschmüller (2018) found, for example, that in "selfie" photos, people with arrogant expressions were judged as more narcissistic and they actually were more narcissistic. The same match between the perceived and actual trait held for conscientiousness (mouth more closed) and agreeableness (more smiling). Naumann, Vazire, Rentfrow, and Gosling (2009) found that smiling had this same match between perceived and actual agreeableness, and extraversion did as well. Results like these led Walker and Vetter (2016) to take the next step and develop a database of facial expressions of real people that were altered slightly so that they would produce systematically different personality impressions. (See Figure 9-1)

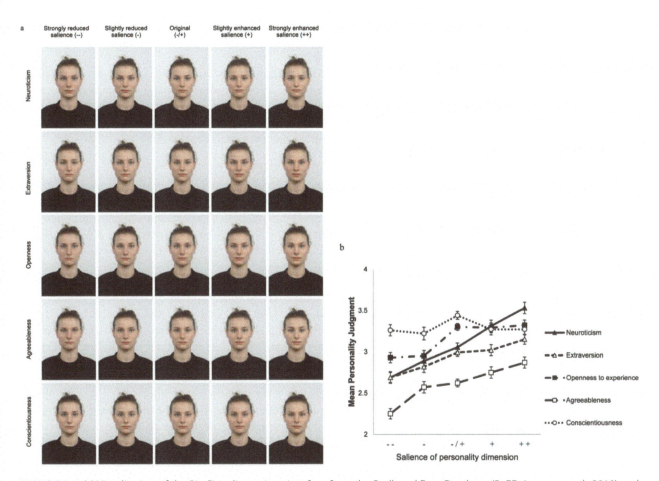

FIGURE 9-1 (a) Visualization of the Big Five dimensions in a face from the Radboud Face Database (RaFD; Langner et al., 2010) and (b) Linear Trend Analyses for the Big Five dimensions. Error bars represent standard errors of the means.

THE FACE AND INTERACTION MANAGEMENT

The face is also used to facilitate and inhibit responses in daily interaction. Parts of the face are used to:

1. Open and close channels of communication
2. Complement or qualify verbal and/or nonverbal responses
3. Replace speech

Behaviors can, of course, serve several functions simultaneously. For example, a yawn may replace the spoken message "I'm bored" and also may serve to shut down other channels of communication, such as eye contact.

CHANNEL CONTROL

When people want a speaking turn, they sometimes open the mouth in readiness to talk, which is often accompanied by an inspiration of breath. Others notice such signals and decide whether to ignore or respect them. As noted in Chapter 2, the eyebrow flash found in greeting rituals, which is frequently accompanied by a smile, is another facial cue that signals a desire to interact. Interestingly, smiles also are found in situations in which there is a desire to close the channels of communication—for example, a smile of appeasement as a person backs away from someone threatening physical harm. Smiling can be used to flirt with others—an invitation that not only opens the channels of communication but also suggests the type of interaction desired.

Although smiles often show emotion or attitudes, they actually have many complex functions. Brunner (1979) showed that smiles serve as "listener responses" or "back channels" in conversation in that they signal attentiveness and involvement just as head nods, "uh-huh," and "yeah" do. These smiles do not indicate joy or happiness in the sender but are meant to facilitate and encourage the other person's speech. These cues achieve channel control by keeping channels open and also serve a reinforcing function.

COMPLEMENTING OR QUALIFYING OTHER BEHAVIOR

In normal conversational give and take, there are instances when one wishes to underline, magnify, minimize, or contradict messages. The speaker or listener may give these signals. A sad verbal message may acquire added emphasis with eyebrow movements that normally accompany the expression of sadness. A smile may temper a message that could otherwise be interpreted as negative. The hand emblem for "A-OK" may be accompanied by a wink, leaving little doubt that approval is being communicated. Thus, facial cues can combine with other cues to avoid confusion and magnify or qualify messages.

REPLACING SPOKEN MESSAGES

Ekman and Friesen (1975) identified what they call *facial emblems*. Like hand emblems, these displays have a fairly consistent verbal translation. Facial emblems are different from spontaneous emotional expressions in that the sender is trying to talk *about* an emotion, or *represent* it. These facial emblems can occur in contexts not likely to trigger the actual emotion; they are usually held for a longer or shorter time than the actual expression and are usually performed by using only part of the face. When you drop your jaw and hold your mouth open without displaying other features of the surprise expression, you may be saying that the other person's comment is surprising or that you were dumbfounded by what was said. Widened eyes without other features of the surprise and fear expressions may serve the same purpose as a verbal "Wow!" If you want to comment nonverbally on your disgust for a situation, a nose wrinkle or raising one side of your upper lip should get your message across. Sometimes one or both eyebrows communicate "I'm puzzled" or "I doubt that." Other facial messages with common verbal translations that are not associated with expressions of emotion include the "You know what I mean" wink and sticking your tongue out to convey insult or disapproval (Smith, Chase, & Lieblich, 1974).

Facial movements play an important role in managing conversation (Bavelas & Chovil, 1997; Chovil, 1991/1992). According to Chovil, the most frequent function is *syntactic display*. Syntactic facial displays act as markers, functioning as visible punctuation for words and clauses; they are directed toward the organizational structure of the conversation to mark beginnings, endings, restarts, continuations, and emphasis. Raising and lowering the eyebrows is a central activity in syntactic displays. Facial actions made by a speaker that are directly connected with the content of what is being said are called *semantic displays*. These displays may be redundant with the verbal behavior or they may involve additional commentary on the spoken words, such as personal reactions to what is being said. The face also provides *listener responses*, those little cues that indicate attentiveness (among other things) while someone else is speaking.

Smiles have many types; Brannigan and Humphries (1972) identified nine smiles, representing various types and degrees of intensity, many of which seem to occur in distinctly separate situations. Ekman and Friesen (1978), using an anatomically based coding system we will describe shortly, found over 100 distinctly different human smiles. A function-based typology was developed by Niedenthal and colleagues, who documented that distinctly different kinds of smiles are used for different purposes: to reinforce desired behavior, to invite and maintain social bonds, and to dominate other people (Martin, Rychlowska, Wood, & Niedenthal, 2017; Niedenthal, Mermillod, Maringer, & Hess, 2010). Most extensively, researchers have distinguished between smiles that are more and less likely to be indicative of true positive affect, as discussed later in this chapter.

THE FACE AND EXPRESSIONS OF EMOTION

The intellectual roots of our modern interest in facial expression stem from the mid-19th century. Charles Darwin's *The Expression of the Emotions in Man and Animals* (1872), although not as famous as his other writings on natural selection, was a major work of theory and empirical observation that largely focused on the face (Ekman & Oster, 1982). To Darwin, the study of emotional expression was closely tied to his case for evolution, for he held that the capacity to communicate through nonverbal signals had evolved just as the brain and skeleton had. The face becomes increasingly mobile as one moves up the phylogenetic ladder. In many animals, the face is a fixed mask with little to no capacity for mobility, but in primates we see a great variety of expressions (Redican, 1982). Because it would support his theory of evolution, Darwin considered it extremely important to document similarities in the nature of emotional expression across species and across human cultures. Several strands of contemporary facial research can be traced to Darwin's insights, including conducting judgment studies to find out what meanings observers ascribe to different expressions, undertaking cross-cultural studies, studying the movements of particular facial muscles, and testing the hypothesis that making facial expressions can intensify the expressor's experience of emotion. We review each of these topics here.

DISPLAY RULES AND FACIAL EMOTION EXPRESSION

Consider the following situations:

1. A student who feels sure they got a "C" on a paper is told by the instructor that the paper got an "A." The student's internal reaction is total surprise, followed by glee. However, facially there is only mild surprise and verbally the student only mumbles a quick thank-you.
2. A poker player draws a fourth ace in a game with no wild cards. The other players don't see any response.
3. Courtney receives a nice holiday present, but it is nothing spectacular. Courtney's facial expression and comments, however, lead the gift-giver to believe Courtney thought it was a spectacular gift.
4. Sarah, a fledgling executive, and Dan are married. Dan is forced to attend Sarah's boss's party and is told explicitly that his behavior will have a profound impact on Sarah's future with the company. Dan is nervous and also annoyed. But, according to those who describe the party later, he was the very picture of charm.

These four examples illustrate *display rules* that dictate how emotions should be displayed to other people (Ekman & Friesen, 1969b). The student illustrated a *deintensified affect*—strong surprise was made to look like mild surprise. The poker player was trying to *neutralize feelings* to make it appear there was no emotion at all. The person reacting to the holiday present tried to make mild happiness appear to be strong happiness—an *overintensification* of the affect. The husband of the fledgling executive was trying to *mask feelings* of tension or annoyance with happiness and confidence. These display rules are learned but are not always used at a conscious level of awareness. They are learned, culturally prescribed norms for when and how much emotion to display. People also develop personal display rules based on their needs or perhaps the demands of their occupation (e.g., as a politician or salesperson). Through experience, people learn that some affect displays are appropriate in some places but not others, for some status and role positions but not others, or primarily for one gender.

The existence of display rules helps explain why some anthropologists have believed that emotions are expressed in sharply different ways from culture to culture. Although the same potential for showing a particular facial expression of emotion (e.g., anger) may exist in all humans, cultural upbringing influences when and how it is shown (Matsumoto, Yoo, & Chung, 2010). Another example concerns grief. In one society, people may weep and moan at a funeral, whereas in another they may celebrate with feast and dance. However, the underlying emotion, grief, is likely experienced and expressed similarly in private. The difference is that in public, the cultural norms—display rules—regulate behavior. In the first society, the rule says "Show how sad you are," but in the second, it says "Affirm social bonds" or "Show hope for the future."

The topic of deception is taken up in a later chapter, but let us say here that the face, along with other nonverbal cues, can certainly be used to deceive others about feelings and thoughts. Deception may be driven by situational factors, such as when a customer does not want a salesperson to know how much they really want a costly product (Puccinelli, Motyka, & Grewal, 2010). The line between deception and display rules can be fuzzy, but in general it can be said that display rules, because they are shared, reflect a collective understanding of socially appropriate behavior, whereas deception is generally considered to be done to convey a message that does not have a shared understanding. Therefore, basing nonverbal behavior on display rules tends to be looked on with approval, as an indication of social astuteness or maturity, whereas deception is generally disapproved of.

People can also have their own idiosyncratic "rules" for expression. Ekman and Friesen (1975) developed a classification system for various styles of facial expressions. The styles are heavily based on personal display rules and represent extremes. A style may be displayed in a less extreme fashion in some situations or at certain times in the person's life, but some people manifest a given style with consistency. These styles include the following:

1. **The withholder**. The face inhibits expressions of actual feeling states. There is little facial movement.
2. **The revealer**. This style is the opposite of the withholder. The face of the person who lets it all hang out leaves little doubt how the person feels—continually.
3. **The unwitting expressor**. This pattern usually pertains to a limited number of expressions that a person thought were masked in a given situation. Thus, this person might ask, incredulously, "How did you know I was angry?"
4. **The blanked expressor**. In this style, the person is convinced an emotion is being portrayed, but others see only a blank face.
5. **The substitute expressor**. Here, the facial expression shows an emotion or sends a message other than the one the person thinks is being displayed. A person might go around with a furrowed brow, for example, to convey what a deep thinker they are, but a viewer might think the person is always conveying disapproval or bad mood.
6. **The frozen-affect expressor**. This style manifests at least part of an emotional display at all times. Some people are born with a facial configuration that in a relaxed, neutral state shows the down-turned mouth associated with sadness; others habitually experience an emotion so much that traces of the emotional display are permanently etched into the face, an idea that Darwin proposed. Research shows that supposedly "neutral" faces do convey hints of different emotions, due to physiognomy or muscular habits. When viewers attribute emotional experience to such faces, it is called the emotion overgeneralization effect (Franklin & Zebrowitz, 2013).

The preceding discussion of display rules and styles of emotional facial expression demonstrates that people have considerable control over their facial expressions, and this control is manifested in a variety of ways. Although facial messages can send messages that are not felt, sometimes the lie is imperfect because the enacted expression occurs at the wrong time; because it occurs too often or for too long, as when an insincere smile is displayed too long; or because various facial muscles are used inappropriately. These factors may help separate genuine emotions from pseudoexpressions of emotion on the face.

People undeniably are aware of the communicative potential of the face and tend to monitor it carefully by inhibiting or exhibiting its movements. With the constant feedback one receives about their own facial expressions, a person can become rather proficient at controlling them.

The way emotions are experienced can be quite complex. Sometimes one moves rapidly from one emotion to another. Sometimes one is not sure what emotion they are feeling, or might feel many emotions at once. Simultaneously felt emotions may even be contradictory, as when one is both attracted and repulsed by a grisly accident scene. When there is more than one emotion, a person might try to control one while dealing with the other. These are only some of the many ways people experience emotions (Ellis, 1991).

FIGURE 9-2 Facial blends.

Because emotional experience is complex, understanding emotion through facial expression is correspondingly difficult. People do not always portray pure or single emotional states, in which all the parts of the face show a single emotion. Instead, the face conveys multiple emotions. These are called *affect blends* and may appear on the face in numerous ways. For example, one emotion is suggested by one facial area, and another is suggested by another area, as when brows are raised as in surprise and lips are pressed as in anger. Or two different emotions are shown in one part of the face, as when one brow is raised as in surprise, and the other is lowered as in anger. Such displays may merely confuse a viewer, or they may convey a new meaning that is different from either of the elements. The brows just described might, for example, convey skepticism.

Figure 9-2 shows two examples of facial blends. One photograph shows a blend of happiness, evidenced by a smiling movement in the mouth area, and also surprise, evidenced by the raised eyebrows and forehead, wide eyes, and a slight dropping of the jaw. Such an expression could occur if you thought you were going to get an "F" on an exam, but you received an "A" instead. In the other photograph, the eyebrow, forehead, and eye area show anger while the mouth shows sadness. This combination might occur if your instructor told you that your grade on an exam you considered unfair was an "F." You feel sad about the low grade and angry at the instructor.

A final note about the complexity of faces concerns *micromomentary* facial expressions, or simply *micro* expressions. While studying nonverbal communication between therapist and patient, Haggard and Isaacs (1966) ran films at slow motion and noticed that the expression on the patient's face would sometimes change dramatically—from a smile to a grimace to a smile, for example—within a few frames of the film. Further analysis revealed that when they ran the films at 4 frames per second, instead of the normal 24 frames per second, 2.5 times as many changes of expression could be discerned. The existence of these very brief expressions can explain why a photograph of someone during an emotional experience might seem to convey an emotion quite different from the predominant one. Research on micro expressions has yielded evidence that skill at detecting them can be trained and that it is a skill worth having (Hurley, Anker, Frank, Matsumoto, & Hwang, 2014).

One hypothesis about the causes of micro expressions is that they reveal actual emotional states that are condensed in time because of repressive processes. For example, one patient, saying nice things about a friend, had a seemingly pleasant facial expression; however, slow-motion film showed a wave of anger cross her face. Although agreeing that micro expressions may show conflict, repression, or efforts to conceal an emotion, Ekman, Friesen, and Ellsworth (1982) actually found them to be "very rare events" based on extensive analysis of facial movements. However, this does not mean they do not have an impact, possibly a subliminal one, when they occur.

THE FACIAL EMOTION CONTROVERSY

One tradition, originating with Darwin and associated today with the work of Paul Ekman and Carroll Izard, emphasizes the close connection between facial displays of emotion and concurrently felt emotions with a corresponding emphasis on emotion-expressive display linkages as being biologically grounded. This approach has fueled ambitious programs of cross-cultural research on the recognition of facial expression. A simplistic version of such a theoretical position would hold that, at least for certain basic emotions, experiencing a given emotion always produces a certain expression, which could be a single muscle movement or a complex pattern of movements, and conversely that this expression always signifies the occurrence of its associated emotion. According to such a view, facial expressions are always a *readout*—an honest, unpremeditated, uncontrolled indication—of internal emotional states.

A bit of reflection on everyday experience should make the reader skeptical of such a view, however, and it is unlikely that any theorist holds such an extreme position. As we discussed in the previous section, people can feign emotions by willfully putting on different expressions. They also are sensitive to situations in which it would be inappropriate to show certain expressions; for example, a winner who shows too much happiness could be seen as gloating. A rising tide of research now shows that a purely spontaneous nonverbal "readout" of emotional states may be a rarer event than some think (Bonanno & Keltner, 2004; Russell, Bachorowski, & Fernández-Dols, 2003). The term *loosely coupled* is used to describe emotion and expression systems that coincide only occasionally or under certain circumstances.

Many studies support this argument that expressions are not a perfect window into emotional experience. Researchers have sought to create or observe situations in which the experience of an emotion can be confirmed, so that they can see what expressions are produced. People bowling with friends have been observed in the United States and Spain. After a good roll, and at other moments when they reported feeling happy, bowlers smiled much more when turning to face their friends than when facing the pins, suggesting that the smile was more a message of happiness to their friends than a spontaneous sign of their emotional state. Similarly, soccer fans watching a match on television smiled much more during happy moments when facing their friends than during happy moments when they were not interacting with them directly. During their noninteractive happy moments, they showed expressions indicative of several different emotions not shown in the interactive happy moments (Fernández-Dols & Ruiz-Belda, 1997; Kraut & Johnston, 1979; Ruiz-Belda, Fernández-Dols, Carrera, & Barchard, 2003). Thus, a person can be very happy yet not show it in a prototypically "happy" facial expression.

Further evidence that facial expression and experienced emotion are only loosely coupled, and that the nature of the social situation is a strong determinant of what is displayed on the face, is that facial *motor mimicry*—displaying what another person is feeling, such as wincing when a friend stubs his toe—decreases when no one is there to see the facial display (Bavelas, Black, Lemery, & Mullett, 1986; Chovil, 1991). Furthermore, college students watching emotionally provoking slides were more facially expressive when they watched with a friend than a stranger (Wagner & Smith, 1991), and college students recounting positive and negative experiences showed facial expressions that inconsistently matched their reported affect (Lee & Wagner, 2002). At the Olympic Games, gold medal winners were filmed at three moments: while standing behind the podium away from public view, while standing on the podium interacting with authorities and the public, and while standing on the podium facing the flagpoles and listening to their national anthem (Fernández-Dols & Ruiz-Belda, 1995). While their feelings of happiness probably did not vary across these three closely spaced periods, the winners smiled the most during the public-interactive period, suggesting again that a facial expression may have more to do with the social circumstances than to the emotion being experienced.

Audience effects such as these may even occur when a person is alone and behaving spontaneously, for even then a person may respond to fantasies or memories of social interaction. In support of this notion, Fridlund (1991) found that college students watching a pleasant film smiled more when watching with a friend than when watching alone. But students who watched the film in a different room from their friend and were aware that the friend was watching the same film also smiled more than students who watched the film alone. Thus, even the *imagined* presence or experience of others may serve to stimulate or facilitate facial displays.

Another way of testing whether expressions match inner feelings is to compare people's expressions to what they say about their emotional states. When viewers were asked about their emotions during neutral or scary film excerpts, almost no matching occurred (Fernández-Dols & Ruiz-Belda, 1997)—only 2 of 35 viewers who reported a basic emotion showed the expression that theoretically should have been produced by that emotion, and 3 showed expressions that suggested entirely different emotions from those reported.

Fridlund's (1994, 1997) *behavioral ecology theory* of facial expression asserts that facial expressions are virtually never simply emotional and are, instead, always enacted for social purposes. In Fridlund's view, spontaneous expression of emotion would not have been a selected trait during evolution because always showing one's feelings would not serve the expressor's interest, and it could possibly even serve the interests of rivals by depriving the expressor of the ability to deceive. Fridlund's argument that facial expressions are meant to *communicate* rather than to simply *reveal* is consistent with many examples of functional expressive behavior in the animal kingdom, as well as with everyday observation of human interaction.

However, most researchers would not accept the extreme position that facial expressions are almost always messages and are hardly ever purely spontaneous readouts of one's emotional experience. There are certainly many instances when a face shows feelings without the person being aware of it—sometimes feelings that they would very much have wanted to conceal. The fact that audience presence effects can sometimes work in reverse, with people showing *more* facial expressions when alone than with others present, suggests that people do, indeed, produce spontaneous emotional expressions (Buck, 1984, 1991; Wagner & Lee, 1999). Facial expressions are not only for social communication purposes.

MEASURING THE FACE

ANATOMICAL DESCRIPTION For many years, descriptions of facial movements tended to be impressionistic or idiosyncratic (Ekman, 1982; Rinn, 1984). This changed dramatically with the work of Carroll Izard (1979) and of Paul Ekman and Wallace Friesen (1978), who independently developed precise systems for describing facial action based on muscle movements. Izard's work focused on infant expressions. Ekman and Friesen's Facial Action Coding System (FACS) has been applied more generally. Although it is a system comprehensive enough to describe nearly any combination of muscle movements, it requires many hours of training and practice and is extremely time-consuming to apply.

Ekman and Friesen developed the FACS by painstakingly learning how to move all their facial muscles and by studying anatomy texts. They studied the faces of other people who had learned how to control specific muscles and considered what movements an observer could reliably distinguish. These movements are called *action units*. Sometimes an action unit involves more than one muscle, if those muscles always work in tandem or if an observer cannot see the difference. Altogether, the FACS can identify over 40 distinct action units in the face. For illustration, Figure 9-3 presents the action units identified by Ekman (1979) for the brow and forehead. Altogether, seven different muscles can influence this region of the face.

The FACS allows emotion researchers to describe objectively what movements have occurred on the face, and further work with this system allows a face to be categorized as showing a given prototypical emotion based on extensive data relating those movements to other criteria, mainly observers' judgments of facial expressions. Through years of collecting such judgments, Ekman and his colleagues developed a catalogue of prototypical movements associated with seven different judged emotions. For example, Ekman and Friesen (1978) determined that in the brow/forehead

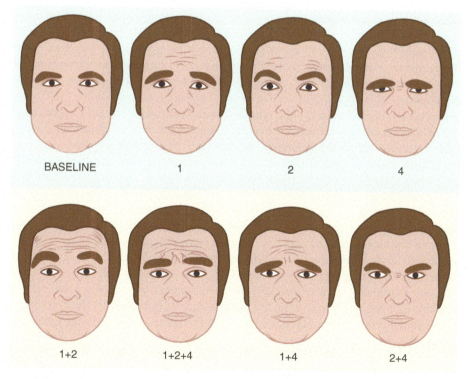

FIGURE 9-3 Action units for the brow/forehead.
Source: From p. Ekman, "About Brows: Emotional and Conversational Signals" in von Cranach, et al., eds. *Human Ethology*, p. 174.

region (shown in Figure 9-3), action units 1 or 1 + 4 occur in sadness, along with associated movements across the rest of the face. In surprise, we see 1 + 2; in fear, 1 + 2 + 4; in anger, 4; and so forth.

Recall that we discussed the role of the face in interaction management. Ekman explains how the brow/forehead area contributes to these conversational signals as well

- Accent a word, 1 + 2 (Actor Woody Allen uses 1 + 4 for this, according to Ekman)
- Underline a phrase, 1 + 2 or 4
- Punctuate, like a "visual comma," 1 + 2 or 4
- Question mark, 1 + 2 or 4
- Word search, 4
- Listener response (back channel), 1 + 2
- Indicate lack of understanding, 4

Although the FACS method is laborious to apply, the results can be very interesting and lessons derived from it can be possibly quite useful in daily life. For example, facial muscle movements can reveal implicit attitudes, perception of different tastes (e.g., sour or sweet), as well as the occurrence of sexual excitement, pain, and even different pain sources, such as pain from immersion of the hand in cold water versus electric shock (Fernández-Dols, Carrera, & Crivelli, 2011; LeResche, 1982; Lynch, 2010; Patrick, Craig, & Prkachin, 1986; Wendin, Allesen-Holm, & Bredie, 2011). The facial signs of pain, measured in both infants and adults, include the following: a tightening of the muscles surrounding the eyes, which narrows the eyes and raises the cheeks; the corrugator and other forehead muscles lower the eyebrows and wrinkle the bridge of the nose; and the levator muscles raise the upper lip and may produce wrinkles at the side of the nose (Prkachin & Craig, 1995). The faces of terminal cancer patients differ according to the stage of disease progression. In the early stages, signs of fear are more prominent ("whole eye tension combined with tension … in the lower eyelid"), but these give way to signs of sadness (in the brow/forehead region) in the late stage (Antonoff & Spilka, 1984–1985).

Some of the most subtle and fascinating work studying facial muscle movements concerns different kinds of smiles, referred to as *Duchenne smiles* and *non-Duchenne smiles* after the 19th-century neurologist who first described them. The muscle called the *zygomaticus major,* which stretches out the lips when we smile, is the common denominator. Ekman has shown that the frequency, duration, and intensity of action by the zygomaticus major differentiated among facial displays made by people watching different kinds of films, and it also correlated with how much happiness people said they felt while viewing them (Ekman, Friesen, & Ancoli, 1980). However, other muscles besides the zygomaticus major are crucial to understanding what the smile really means. Darwin proposed that in a "felt" or genuinely happy (Duchenne) smile, the *orbicularis oculi* muscle—the muscle that makes crow's-feet at the corner of your eyes, called the "cheek raiser" in FACS terminology—is involved, but that it is not involved in an emotionally phony or mechanical (non-Duchenne) smile. Figure 9-4 shows the difference between "felt" and "unfelt" smiles.

To document the different kinds of smiles, Ekman and colleagues asked student nurses to watch either a pleasant or a stressful film, while those shown the stressful film were asked to act as though the film were pleasant. The smiles of those who saw the pleasant film showed more felt (Duchenne) smiles with no muscular activity associated with negative emotion. Those trying to look pleasant while watching the stressful film showed more "masking" or non-Duchenne smiles, involving the zygomaticus major but not the orbicularis oculi, and they also showed more movements of the 10 or so muscles associated with fear, disgust, contempt, sadness, or anger.

In another comparison of smiles, Matsumoto and Willingham (2006) analyzed the expressions of athletes in the 2004 Olympic judo competition. Compared to silver medal winners, both gold and bronze medal winners showed many more Duchenne (felt enjoyment) smiles, especially the open-mouthed variety, when receiving their medals and when on the podium. Although you might have expected silver medalists to be happier than bronze medalists, apparently coming in second felt like a defeat, whereas coming in third felt like a victory over the many other athletes who did not win any medal at all.

The distinction between enjoyment smiles and more purely social smiles has been supported in numerous studies, even among infants as young as 10 months of age (Ekman, Davidson, & Friesen, 1990; Ekman & Friesen, 1982; Fox & Davidson, 1988). Numerous studies show that Duchenne and non-Duchenne smiles produce different impressions on observers. The review by Gunnery and Ruben (2016) found that Duchenne smiles were seen by viewers as more

© Asier Romero/Shutterstock.com

© eurobanks/Shutterstock.com

FIGURE 9-4 The woman and man are displaying so-called "unfelt" and "felt" smiles, respectively. Interestingly, even though the "felt" smile has been considered a "genuine" smile (i.e., the person is actually happy), many people are able to produce such a smile deliberately.

authentic, genuine, real, attractive, and trustworthy than non-Duchenne smiles. The distinction between enjoyment and social smiles, although very important, is still a probabilistic one. This means that in any particular instance, there may be uncertainty about the smile's true meaning. Although it may be unlikely that a smile involving only the mouth is a true expression of pleasure or happiness, it is possible for a smile involving the eye muscles to be produced by someone who has good control over the facial muscles. The fact that an enjoyment smile can be posed, as in Figure 9-4, underscores this point. Research shows that a sizable minority of people can deliberately produce a Duchenne smile (e.g., Gunnery, Hall, & Ruben, 2013; Krumhuber & Manstead, 2009).

AUTOMATED FACIAL MEASUREMENT Because anatomical description of the face, such as that used in the FACS, is so time-consuming to learn and employ, there is strong interest in developing computer programs that can describe facial movements and even "recognize" emotions. This is a major challenge because of the many possible muscle movements and the existence of great differences between individual faces in shape and musculature. The challenge is especially great for stimuli that are not standardized in terms of head position and other movement parameters. Early systems were not very practical, because they required attaching small dots to the face to serve as landmarks for the computerized analysis (Kaiser & Wehrle, 1992). Automated systems that can analyze movement under more natural circumstances and in real time are currently being developed and have very promising validity as tested against trained human coders for recognizing discrete emotions (Cohn & Ekman, 2005). Software has also been developed (e.g., FACSGen 2.0) that enables researchers to reliably create various facial expressions on humanlike avatars (Krumhuber, Tamarit, Roesch, & Scherer, 2012).

Another approach that eliminates human judgment is based on automatic measurement of facial movements that may be too slight to be seen with the naked eye. Electrodes attached to the face measure electromyographic (EMG) responses, that is, electrical activity indicative of incipient or very slight muscle movements. This method can identify (for example) movement of the zygomaticus muscle, which expands the mouth, under happy conditions, and movement of the corrugator muscle between the brows, which responds under sad, angry, and fearful conditions (Matsumoto, Keltner, Shiota, O'Sullivan, & Frank, 2008). Studies that use EMG recordings have shown that facial muscles respond in predictable ways to simply seeing others' emotional expressions (Blairy, Herrera, & Hess, 1999; Dimberg, 1982; Lundqvist, 1995). Thus, the face responds with corrugator activity to seeing angry expressions and with zygomatic activity to seeing happy expressions. The face also responds in mimicking fashion to facial expressions of sadness and disgust. Nonemotion states (e.g., confusion) as well as attitudes (e.g., positive affect in response to images of slim people) are also detectable using EMG responses (Durso, Geldbach, & Corballis, 2012).

SIMPLE OBSERVATION Although much is to be gained from the FACS's fine-grained anatomical analysis and EMG technology, researchers most often employ less highly trained human observers for their facial measurement and judgment tasks. Observers are frequently asked to count the frequency of facial expressions, rate their intensity, or time their duration, either with or without a period of training (Kring & Sloan, 2007). As long as adequate interobserver agreement is obtained, these approaches can have high validity and many studies rely on human observers (who sometimes use assistance from computer software that allows, for example, time stamping for understanding temporal aspects of the behavior and for coordinating one person's movements with another's). Extensive training of observers is not always even necessary; Sato and Yoshikawa (2007) studied unconscious mimicry of facial expressions by unobtrusively videotaping participants while they watched videos of faces that were showing either angry or happy expressions. Untrained observers were just as good as trained FACS coders at distinguishing which kind of video the participants had watched.

Because coding (counting, rating, or timing) nonverbal behavior on the face or other parts of the body can be very time-consuming, researchers often decide to code only a portion of their recorded behavior—for example, coding smiling for 1 minute of a 15-minute conversation. Excerpts like this have been dubbed "thin slices" (Ambady & Rosenthal, 1992). For behaviors that show reasonable consistency in their production, this method has been shown to be trustworthy, meaning that not much valuable information is lost in using thin slices instead of entire recordings (Murphy, 2005; Murphy et al., 2019).

MEASURING EMOTION RECOGNITION

Emotions can be identified at levels much higher than chance from posed facial expressions, as Ekman and colleagues (1987) have shown, and also from spontaneously expressed facial displays (Tcherkassof, Bollon, Dubois, Pansu, & Adam, 2007), though accuracy is lower for spontaneous expressions than for posed ones. But before going further, measurement issues must be discussed (and there is much more on emotion recognition in Chapter 3, where the emphasis is on people's skill in judging others' states and traits).

THE RESPONSE FORMAT Examine the three faces shown in Figure 9-5, then consider the following methods of measuring your accuracy.

1. In the space provided, write in the emotion being expressed in each of the faces you observed.

   A._____   B._____   C._____

2. From the choices given, select the one emotion that best describes Face A, Face B, and Face C.

Face A	**Face B**	**Face C**
Rage	Happiness	Sadness
Anger	Joy	Despair
Wrath	Delight	Solemnity
Indignation	Amusement	Despondency
Resentment	Pleasure	Melancholy

3. From the following list, select the term that best describes Face A, Face B, and Face C: happiness, sadness, surprise, fear, anger.

This exercise illustrates one of the many problems involved in testing the accuracy of judgments about facial expressions or other nonverbal cues. In this case, judgment accuracy would depend a great deal on which set of instructions the judge received. The first, involving a free response from the judge (synonymous terms are perceiver or decoder), will produce a wide range of responses, and researchers will be faced with the problem of deciding whether the judge's label corresponds with the "correct" label for the emotion. The labels used by the researcher and those used by the judges may be different, but both may respond the same way to the actual emotion in real life or may be thinking of the same emotion. To illustrate, some individuals may label an angry face with the word *disgusted*, which, for them, means the person is thoroughly fed up and annoyed, whereas for others that word means the person finds something, such as a food item or an image, to be sickening.

In the second testing condition, the discrimination task is too difficult because the emotions listed in each category are too much alike. We can predict low accuracy for judges given these instructions because different perceivers will make slightly different construals. In contrast, the last set of instructions is the opposite of the second set—the discrimination task may be too easy. Because the emotion categories are discrete and rather different from each other, we can predict high accuracy for the third condition.

Accuracy is also influenced by biases in judgment patterns. Consider a facial judgment task with equal numbers of sad, happy, and angry faces. If a judge guesses "happy" all the time, to state the extreme case, they would score as very accurate on happy faces, and we might conclude that such a judge is an excellent judge of happiness. But obviously the judge has no *differential* accuracy, because she or he gave only one answer to all the items. For the same reason, the low accuracy obtained by such a judge on the other emotions is less an index of actual inaccuracy than of a rating bias. Another factor determining the accuracy level is how many choice options the judge has: with four emotion choices, the guessing level would be 25%; with three, 33%; and so on. Therefore, any given level of accuracy cannot be evaluated in absolute terms but rather must be appraised in terms of how much higher or lower it is than the guessing level.

Yet other factors influence the levels of accuracy that will be obtained by a researcher. The duration of exposure to the facial expressions will likely have an impact, though accuracy can be obtained with surprisingly short exposures (see Ambady, Bernieri, & Richeson, 2000; Matsumoto et al., 2000). Also, sometimes researchers deliberately choose facial stimuli that are easier or harder to judge, and, finally, some judgments are simply harder than others. It is much

© Terrence Horgan

FIGURE 9-5 How should these facial expressions be read?

harder to tell whether a person on video is lying or telling the truth than to tell whether they have a happy, sad, or angry facial expression. Thus, when we ask how accurate people are in such judgments, we must consider many factors (Hall, Andrzejewski, Murphy, Schmid Mast, & Feinstein, 2008).

CREATING THE FACIAL STIMULUS Researchers use various methods to elicit the emotional expressions that observers are asked to identify. Some researchers tell actors (or regular people) to behave as if they were in different emotion-arousing situations; others give a list of emotions and tell the actor to portray them via posing; and others gather examples of facial expressions of people in real situations that were not posed or acted. One early study (Dunlap, 1927) used some ethically unacceptable methods: A camera was set up in a laboratory, ready to catch the expressor's face at the proper moment. To elicit an expression of pain, the experimenter bent the person's finger backward forcibly; to produce a startled look, the experimenter fired a pistol behind them at an unexpected moment; apprehension was elicited by saying the pistol would be fired again, close to the expressor's ear, on the count of three—at the count of two, the photo was taken. Amusement was captured when the experimenter told some jokes; disgust resulted when the expressor had to smell a test tube containing tissues of a dead rat; and finally—unbelievably—to elicit an expression of grief, the expressor was hypnotized and was told several family members had been killed in a car wreck. "Unfortunately," says the experimenter, "the camera could not catch intense grief because the subject bowed his head and cried."

Presenting people with a controlled stimulus and then observing their reactions, although carried to an unethical extreme in Dunlap's study, still underlies some research on spontaneous expressions. Expressors are shown stimuli (pictures or videos) that differ in their content while a video camera unobtrusively records their facial reactions. Judges later observe the expressors' faces and try to guess what the stimulus was or how the expressor felt about it (Buck, 1979; North, Todorov, & Osherson, 2012). This method can capture completely unpremeditated expressions. However, because expressors are not in a truly communicative situation, their behavior may be no more generalizable to real social interaction than are expressors' attempts to pose various emotions on the command of the experimenter. Another method, asking participants to reexperience an emotional event and then talk about it, has been used sometimes as a more natural alternative that blends some elements of deliberate and spontaneous communication (Hall et al., 2011).

CONTEXT OR NOT? Though researchers often present faces of strangers out of context, many contextual factors can influence perception of the expressions. The context can be visual, as when perceivers are shown the situation, including people who may be in it. Or the context can be narrative, as when observers are told a background story and then shown a facial expression of a person supposedly in the story. Also, the context can consist of other cues of the target person to which the perceiver is exposed.

Although a number of investigators have pursued the question of whether context or expression dominates perceptions, and how they work together, the issue is far from resolved and replete with methodological issues (Fernández-Dols & Carroll, 1997; Matsumoto & Hwang, 2010). In perhaps the most extensive investigation, Cowen and Keltner (2019) obtained 1,500 naturalistic photographs of expressions and asked judges to rate them on 28 different emotion terms (examples are confusion, contemplation, anger, awe, elation, embarrassment, and relief). Judges showed agreement among each other, producing strong evidence that the 28 terms had unique connections to different expressions, although the emotion categories and their expressions were "bridged by smooth gradients that correspond to continuous variations in meaning" (p. 2). To investigate the impact of context, the authors removed any background information or hand/body movements, leaving only the facial expressions, and obtained a new set of judgments. The presence of context made little difference to the overall conclusions, except for triumph, pride, and love, where perceivers' interpretations were influenced by context.

Context effects are sometimes very evident, however. Other people's expressions influenced perceptions in Cline's (1956) classic study, where perceivers saw pictures of two people in apparent interaction and rated the emotional state of one of them. The expression on one face influenced interpretation of the other face. When the smiling face was paired with a glum face, the smiling face was seen as that of a vicious, gloating, taunting bully. When the smiling face was paired with a frowning face, the smiling face seemed peaceful, friendly, and happy.

The nature of other people's expressions can have different impact depending on the judge's cultural background. Masuda et al. (2008) showed that the interpretation of a facial emotion display varied between U.S. and Japanese perceivers, as a function of other people's expressions in the immediate social context. Japanese perceivers were more influenced by the expressions of the other people in the picture. Kuwabara and Son (2011) also found a culture–context effect in children: Japanese children's judgments concerning the proper emotional expression of a face were more sensitive to changes in the accompanying context than was the case with their counterparts from the United States.

Although the question is often asked in terms of which matters more, expression or context (see the review by Fernández-Dols & Carroll, 1997), this either–or approach is too simplistic. Often, a judgment depends not on which source of information wins out in observers' judgments but rather on whether the two sources of information can be meaningfully integrated. Sometimes this is done by reinterpreting the information from one source, for example, by deciding that a "sad" story context might actually produce angry feelings, too. Other times, a true integration is made, as when a facial expression of "fear" plus a context of "anger" produces the overall interpretation of "pain" (Carroll & Russell, 1996).

Some writers argue that facial expressions are more inherently ambiguous than generally assumed, even for so-called basic emotions. A person may be consciously aware of using contextual information at times, whereas at other times this influence may be automatic in that it occurs outside of conscious awareness and control (Aviezer, Bentin, Dudarev, & Hassin, 2011; Hassin, Aviezer, & Bentin, 2013). Furthermore, the prevailing paradigm within which research participants are shown facial expressions without any context has been criticized as not representing what happens in real life. The relevance of contextual information in the processing of expressions has been particularly highlighted by Isaacowitz and colleagues (e.g., Kunzmann & Isaacowitz, 2017).

EMOTIONS INFERRED FROM THE FACE

Many factors influence how emotions are inferred from the face, but the compelling fact remains that they *can* be inferred and often with extremely high levels of accuracy. Some emotions are more likely to be confused, but six basic emotions—happiness, anger, sadness, disgust, surprise, and fear (and contempt, possibly)—are judged with very high accuracy among observers in many studies. However, a photograph of a "basic" emotion is one that tends to be prototypical and exaggerated, and thus quite easy to identify. In one large database, the ordering of accuracy from highest to lowest followed the list just given, but the emotions differed in how accuracy was influenced by how long the expression was shown (Calvo & Lundqvist, 2008). Happiness was equally easy to judge across exposures ranging from 25 to 500 milliseconds—that is, up to a half a second—but all of the other emotions showed increases in accuracy as the exposures got longer.

Figures 9-6 to 9-11 show the standard six "basic" emotions with a description of their characteristic facial actions, each of which can also be described in terms of which action units are involved. These expressions are recognized at high levels not only in the United States but also around the globe (see Chapters 2 and 3; Ekman, Sorenson, &

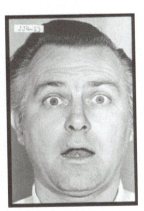
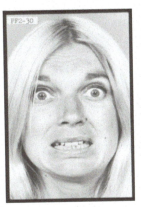
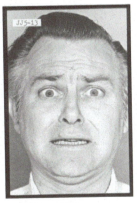

© Paul Ekman, PhD

© Paul Ekman, PhD

FIGURE 9-6 *Surprise:* The brows are raised so that they are curved and high. The skin below the brow is stretched, and horizontal wrinkles go across the forehead. The eyelids are opened: The upper lid is raised, and the lower lid is drawn down; the white of the eye—the sclera—shows above the iris and often below as well. The jaw drops open so that the lips and teeth are parted, but there is no tension or stretching of the mouth.

FIGURE 9-7 *Fear:* The brows are raised and drawn together. The wrinkles in the forehead are in the center, not across the entire forehead. The upper eyelid is raised, exposing the sclera, and the lower eyelid is tensed and drawn up. The mouth is open, and the lips are either tensed slightly and drawn back or stretched and drawn back.

FIGURE 9-8 *Disgust:* The upper lip is raised. The lower lip is also raised and pushed up to the upper lip, or is lowered and slightly protruding. The nose is wrinkled, and the cheeks are raised. Lines show below the lower lid, and the lid is pushed up but not tense. The brow is lowered, lowering the upper lid.

© Paul Ekman, PhD

FIGURE 9-9 *Anger:* The brows are lowered and drawn together, and vertical lines appear between them. The lower lids are tensed and may or may not be raised. The upper lids are tensed and may or may not be lowered by the action of the brow. The eyes have a hard stare and may have a bulging appearance. The lips are in either of two basic positions: pressed firmly together, with the corners straight or down, or open and tensed in a squarish shape, as if shouting. The nostrils may be dilated, but this is not essential to the anger facial expression and may also occur in sadness. There is ambiguity unless anger is registered in all three facial areas.

© Paul Ekman, PhD

FIGURE 9-10 *Happiness:* The corners of the lips are drawn back and up. The mouth may or may not be parted, with teeth exposed or not. A wrinkle, the nasolabial fold, runs down from the nose to the outer edge beyond the lip corners. The cheeks are raised. The lower eyelids show wrinkles below them and may be raised but not tense. Crow's-feet wrinkles go outward from the outer corners of the eyes (covered by hair in these photographs).

© Paul Ekman, PhD

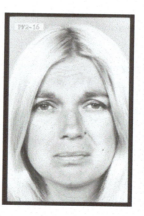

FIGURE 9-11 *Sadness:* The inner corners of the eyebrows are drawn up. The skin below the eyebrows is triangulated, with the inner corner up. The upper eyelid inner corners are raised. The corners of the lips are down, or the lips are trembling.

© Paul Ekman, PhD

Friesen, 1969; Izard, 1971). Biehl and colleagues (1997) demonstrated that seven emotions shown on the faces of both Japanese and White individuals were judged with high levels of agreement by viewers in Hungary, Japan, Poland, and Sumatra, and by Whites and recently immigrated Vietnamese in the United States.

One could argue that in today's world of global media exposure and cross-cultural contact, such a result is not at all surprising. Ekman and his colleagues set about to find out how remote tribal people in New Guinea, who had not been exposed to Western facial expression norms, would respond. Even in New Guinea, photos of U.S. citizens' faces showing these six basic emotions were judged correctly for the most part. Moreover, some New Guineans were photographed while showing how they would react in different situations, such as "you feel sad because your child died," and U.S. respondents later guessed with great accuracy which scenario was being communicated (Ekman & Friesen, 1971).

Most cross-cultural research has dealt with depictions of the face showing very pure configurations for the major emotions. However, as noted earlier, facial expressions can be complex blends, with different muscles simultaneously showing elements of different emotions. Also, expressions can be weakly displayed or partial. The question of whether cross-cultural universality also applies to secondary, more subtle expressions led Ekman and a team of colleagues to introduce a new methodology into the cross-cultural research. These researchers obtained ratings of faces on a variety of emotions from subjects in 10 places around the world, including Estonia, Sumatra, Scotland, Japan, Italy, and Hong Kong. There was dramatic agreement across cultures not only on the primary emotion being shown by the faces but also on the secondary emotion (Ekman et al., 1987).

Although accurate recognition of certain emotions is generally well above chance everywhere it has been tested, variability still exists between individuals and from place to place. Sometimes there is an *in-group advantage*, such that accuracy is higher when the perceivers share the target persons' culture or background (Elfenbein & Ambady, 2002, 2003). This boost in accuracy can result from motivational factors (e.g., trying harder, attending better to the faces of people you perceive as being like yourself). Young and Hugenberg (2010) observed that accuracy was higher when perceivers were judging facial expressions from people who they thought had the same personality type as themselves, as opposed to people who they thought had a different personality type.

But the in-group advantage can result because different cultures actually express emotions slightly differently, for which the term *emotion dialects* has been used (Elfenbein, 2013). Early evidence of this could be seen in the research of Russell (1994), who found that facial expressions, mainly of Westerners' faces, were more accurately recognized by other Western groups than by non-Western groups. Since then, a number of studies have confirmed this phenomenon.

A compelling demonstration of the role of emotion dialects is Elfenbein and Ambady's (2003) study using photographs of mainland Chinese people in China and Caucasian Americans expressing different emotions through the face. The groups whose accuracy was tested were mainland Chinese people in China, mainland Chinese people in the United States, Chinese Americans—that is, U.S. citizens of Chinese extraction—and non-Asian U.S. citizens. The accuracy of these four groups conformed exactly to the authors' "dialect" predictions: The more the group was familiar with mainland Chinese expressions, the better they were on Chinese compared to Caucasian expressions, and the more the group was familiar with American expressions, the better they were on Caucasian compared to Chinese expressions. In addition, an analysis of how long the Chinese-American families had been in the United States showed that the longer the families had been in the country, the better they were at judging Caucasian compared to Chinese faces. These data lend strong support to the emotion dialects concept.

Although researchers do not agree on how many basic emotions there are, most research describing facial movements associated with emotion has concentrated on the six shown in Figures 9-6 to 9-11. Recently, attention has turned to other expressions, including shame, embarrassment, compassion, contempt, and pride. Whether these represent basic emotions signaled by universally recognizable facial displays is debatable. Widen, Christy, Hewett, and Russell (2011), for example, found that agreement on the emotions being communicated by facial displays of shame, embarrassment, compassion, and contempt dropped when participants had to freely choose an emotion label for each of the faces. Nonetheless, these and other expressions are believed to be signaled by specific cues:

1. *Contempt* is thought to be signaled by a slight tightening and raising of the corner of the lip on one side (Ekman et al., 1987).
2. *Threat* is conveyed by several facial signals, such as V-shaped brows, wide eyes, open mouth, and down-turned mouth.
3. Facial signs for *anxiety* have been shown to include increased blinking and more facial movements associated with fear, such as a horizontal mouth stretch and more facial movements overall (Harrigan & O'Connell, 1996).

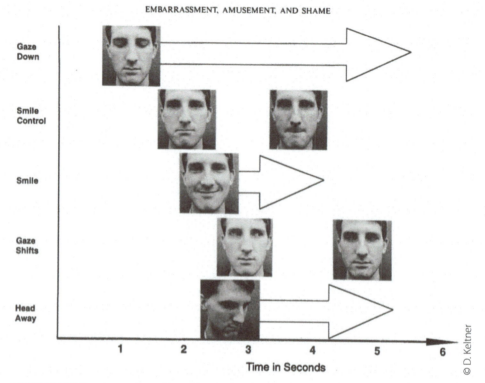

EMBARRASSMENT, AMUSEMENT, AND SHAME

Gaze Down

Smile Control

Smile

Gaze Shifts

Head Away

Time in Seconds

© D. Keltner

FIGURE 9-12 Representation of a prototypical embarrassment response. The mean duration of each action is equal to the interval beginning with the leftmost edge of the photograph and ending with the end of the arrow.

Copyright © 1995 by American Psychological Association. Reproduced with permission. From "Signs of appeasement: Evidence for the distinct displays of embarrassment, amusement, and shame," Keltner, Dacher; Journal of Personality and Social Psychology, 68(3), 441–454. 1995.

4. *Pride* in its prototypical form includes a small smile in conjunction with other cues: head tilted back slightly, expanded posture, and hands on the hips (Tracy & Robins, 2004, 2007).

5. *Embarrassment* has been shown to be signaled by looking down, shifting the eyes, turning the head away, touching the face, and engaging in "controlled smiles," which are smiles a person tries to counter with other facial movements (Keltner, 1995). Keltner has also studied the temporal ordering and relative duration of the components of facial embarrassment (Figure 9-12).

PHYSIOLOGY AND THE FACE

INTERNALIZERS AND EXTERNALIZERS

You must have friends with faces that remain as still as a rock, no matter how much excitement swirls around them. You also have friends with faces that seem as sensitive as a butterfly's wings to every shift of the emotional winds. What you may not know is that these differences, aside from being quite real and enduring, also are associated with differences in physiological functioning. *Internalizers*, those who show little facial expression, experience high physiological reactivity on measures such as heart rate and electrodermal responding; *externalizers*, the expressive ones, show the opposite pattern (Buck, Savin, Miller, & Caul, 1972; Lanzetta & Kleck, 1970; Notarius & Levenson, 1979). Most theorizing about this relationship has pointed to learned factors; for example, the notion that society encourages people to suppress their overt emotional reactions, and that individuals who do so must experience their emotions or arousal in some other way, perhaps through internal activation of the nervous system. The metaphor of discharge can be applied: The emotion is released, either externally or internally (Notarius & Levenson, 1979). Research on newborns finds a similar negative relationship between expressiveness and physiological response, suggesting that inherited temperamental factors may be at work, too (Field, 1982).

FACIAL FEEDBACK

Adding to the complexity and fascination regarding the relation between the face and physiology is the *facial feedback hypothesis* put forth by Darwin, who believed that if an emotion is freely expressed, it will be intensified. The facial feedback hypothesis states that expressions on the face can intensify emotional experience via direct connections between facial muscles and emotion centers in the brain, even without any conscious awareness of what the face is showing.

EMBODIED COGNITION

© Anatomy Image/ Shutterstock.com

The mind and body used to be thought of as two separate entities. Later, it was understood that the human brain is responsible for what is called the "mind," and that the mind controls the body. You can make the decision to smile, for example, when you want to let another person know that you like them.

However, can the body influence the mind? Yes, according to those who subscribe to the notion of embodied cognition (Lakoff & Johnson, 1999). For example, one key to recognizing others' emotion states may be the ability to experience emotion states yourself (Wearne, Osborne-Crowley, Rosenberg, Dethier, & McDonald, 2019). Another example is how motor processes, such as those involved in smiling, can influence your thoughts about emotion states. Consider a situation in which you see a Duchenne smile on another person's face. If you happen to mimic that expression (which often happens involuntarily), you are activating motor processes in your face that are linked to your cognitive-based experience and understanding of happiness. This, in turn, might help you recognize happiness in the other person. These ideas are currently being explored by those who are interested in applying the notion of embodied cognition to the study of nonverbal behavior (Niedenthal et al., 2010).

The evidence for this perspective on emotion recognition is mixed. Facial mimicry does provide information that aids the process of judging the meaning of a smile (Maringer, Krumhuber, Fischer, & Niedenthal, 2011). But what if your ability to mimic another's facial expression was impaired (e.g., from Botox injections, which can paralyze muscles used in some facial expressions)? Would emotion recognition be impaired as well? Research shows that people are slower at reading emotion-evoking sentences when they cannot facially express the emotion that the sentences were designed to arouse (Havas, Glenberg, Gutowski, Lucarelli, & Davidson, 2010). However, other research shows that feedback from facial expressions is not necessary for the experience of emotion states or for the recognition of others' emotion states (Bogart & Matsumoto, 2010; Davis, Senghas, Brandt, & Ochsner, 2010). It could be that facial mimicry is helpful—but not always required—in identifying emotion states. When you cannot or do not mimic the other person's facial expression, you may still be accurate by calling upon your beliefs about how a person should be feeling in a particular situation, or by drawing on your knowledge of which facial movements are associated with particular emotions   .

Is the facial feedback hypothesis valid? The idea that one's emotions can be regulated via their own facial behavior—that authentic emotional experience can result from inauthentic outward expressions—has important ramifications for child rearing, psychotherapy, and many other domains (Izard, 1990). The facial feedback hypothesis has been debated at length, in part because early studies had methodological problems (Matsumoto, 1987). Such early experiments asked participants to pose their faces in various ways and then measured their emotional state through self-report (Laird, 1974; Tourangeau & Ellsworth, 1979). The flaw in such a study is that expressors may realize their posed expression is meant to look like fear or happiness (or whatever the target emotion is). If this happens, it is no surprise that they obediently report feeling those emotions.

Fortunately, studies exist that do not share this problem. In a particularly well-designed study, a group of investigators disguised the purpose of the facial posing by telling participants they were helping develop ways for persons with disabilities to hold a writing implement; it could be held sideways between the teeth, which naturally expands the lips, or it could be held by the lips, pointing forward which contracts them. Unknown to the participants, these two manipulations differ in whether the smiling muscles around the mouth are activated. Those holding the pen between their teeth, which activated the smiling muscles, rated cartoons as funnier than the other participants did (Strack, Martin, & Stepper, 1988). This effect is generally robust (Marsh, Rhoads, & Ryan, 2018). Thus, the position of the facial muscles can, indeed, "feed back" to influence the expressor's emotion state. Subsequent research using this same pencil-in-the-teeth paradigm showed that inducing expressors to activate their eye-corner muscles as well as their mouth-widening muscles, which produce Duchenne smiles, resulted in higher levels of enjoyment when viewing positive video clips than occurred when expressors made non-Duchenne smiles (Soussignan, 2002). This makes sense when you consider that the Duchenne smile is said to reflect more genuine positive emotion than the non-Duchenne smile. In another feedback experiment, participants' faces were immobilized (using tape impeding forehead movements and a mouth guard impeding mouth movements) during a risk-taking task that normally produced facial expressions of anxious anticipation. Those with an immobilized face engaged in riskier behavior in the laboratory task (Carpenter & Niedenthal, 2019).

Strack and Neumann (2000) extended the facial feedback phenomenon beyond emotional responses. Under the guise of studying how working on a computer produces tension, participants were asked to furrow their brows or not while doing a computer judgment task. On the task, participants made ratings of how famous various celebrities and noncelebrities were. Those who maintained the furrowed brow rated the individuals as less famous than those in the control group, presumably because the furrowed brow unconsciously put them in a skeptical frame of mind.

A sufficient number of studies now exist that one can have confidence that facial feedback is a real phenomenon. However, not much is known about the exact mechanisms that produce psychological changes, such as emotions, following facial movement. Although well-designed studies can rule out a cognitive explanation—that is, that people simply report the feelings they know their movements suggest—the nature of the physiological mechanism is still an open question. Although most investigators assume feedback occurs through the nervous system, a novel theory called the *vascular theory of emotional efference* holds that certain facial movements and breathing patterns change the temperature of the blood flowing into the brain, which then influences affective state, suggesting that perhaps cooler blood produces more positive affect (McIntosh, Zajonc, Vig, & Emerick, 1997; Zajonc, 1985).

Thus, it appears that expressions, whether deliberately put on or spontaneously mimicked in response to others' expressions, can produce corresponding emotions or can intensify or deintensify experiences already in progress. The process of *emotional contagion* (Hatfield, Cacioppo, & Rapson, 1994) may contribute to the ability to understand others' emotional states. Indeed, when Surakka and Hietanen (1998) showed the "felt" and "unfelt" smiles to viewers, they found that EMG recordings of both eye and cheek muscles were stronger for those who saw the felt smiles and that more pleasure was subsequently experienced by those who saw those smiles.

Though mimicry of others' facial expressions can occur entirely without awareness, it is not immune to social influences. In a good demonstration of this, facial EMG responses—specifically, the zygomaticus major responding to a happy facial expression and the corrugator responding to a sad facial expression—occurred only when the participants had acquired positive associations to the target person by being told she had traits such as niceness and likability. When the target person had negative traits, such as being "deceitful" and "aggressive," participants' faces showed no mimicking activity (Likowski, Mühlberger, Seibt, Pauli, & Weyers, 2008).

Researchers studying the face and physiology also have discovered that posed and spontaneous facial expressions are controlled by different pathways within the brain. This has been demonstrated by certain forms of brain injury that result in a person losing the ability to produce facial expressions deliberately but not losing the capacity to laugh, cry, frown, and so on when genuinely experiencing an emotion; the reverse form of disability also exists (Rinn, 1984). When brain damage occurs, facial expressiveness is especially impaired when the damage is to the right hemisphere of the brain, which is considered the more nonverbal hemisphere (Buck & Duffy, 1980). Researchers have found that the left side of a person's face tends to be more expressive (Borod, Koff, Yecker, Santschi, & Schmidt, 1998; Nicholls, Wolfgang, Clode, & Lindell, 2002; Skinner & Mullen, 1991) because the left half of the face is controlled by the right hemisphere. However, consistent with the notion of separate neural pathways, this asymmetry is present only for posed expressions; spontaneous, more genuine ones tend to be symmetrical (Ekman, Hager, & Friesen, 1981; Skinner & Mullen, 1991). Perhaps now you will think differently about your friend with the crooked smile.

Thus far we have mostly examined the face in terms of what its movements mean. Researchers also have asked questions about the impact of facial expressions in the real world. In the next section, we focus on several such settings.

FACIAL EXPRESSIONS IN REAL-WORLD APPLICATIONS

HEALTH AND CLINICAL SETTINGS

An important application of knowledge of facial expressions occurs in the context of health and the helping professions. One such application is the face in relation to the existence and severity of mental disorders. For example, when distressed, toddlers with autism show less expressivity in their face than do those children without the disorder (Esposito, Venuti, & Bornstein, 2011). Extensive work has been conducted on the interaction between mothers who have depression and their infants (Field, 2002; Lundy, Field, & Pickens, 1996). Depressed mothers seem less able to identify happy expressions in infants, which means they may be less responsive to such cues (Arteche et al., 2011). Infants of depressed mothers have less expressive faces than other infants, do not orient as well visually to adults, and show more facial negativity. In Field's (2002) study, the depressed mothers displayed the same kinds of behaviors that were then seen in their infants, such as more negative facial expressions and less looking around, as well as less vocalization and less tactile stimulation.

Ekman, Matsumoto, and Friesen (1997) noted that more contempt and more "unfelt" happy expressions at the time of psychiatric hospital admission were related to less improvement at discharge, and that different diagnostic groups showed different facial emotion patterns: People with major depression showed more sadness and disgust; people in a manic condition showed more "felt" and "unfelt" happiness and less anger, disgust, and sadness; and people with schizophrenia showed fear and low levels of all the other coded emotions.

In an even more precise and revealing investigation of depressive individuals' expressions, Reed, Sayette, and Cohn (2007) asked how such individuals would handle a situation in which a positive stimulus—in this case, a video clip of a well-known comedian—could not be avoided. Would they be unmoved by the stimulus or would they respond with happy feelings and expressions, the same as individuals with no depressive tendencies? The answer was some of both. The video affected all participants equally in terms of self-rated happiness and number of elicited smiles. However, participants with current depression symptoms and a depression history were five times more likely to try to control their smiles with additional muscle movements than other participants. It was as though these individuals were fighting off the urge to smile.

The face is also relevant to physical health. Could restraining the outward expression of emotion be damaging to health (Mauss & Gross, 2004)? A "repressed" style of expression was related to indications of coronary artery disease and even to the actual occurrence of a heart attack (Friedman & Booth-Kewley, 1987; Friedman, Hall, & Harris, 1985). Malatesta, Jonas, and Izard (1987) found that women who showed less expression on their face when talking about an angry experience had more arthritis symptoms, and women who showed less facial expression during a sad account had more skin problems. Further evidence for a relation of emotional expression/suppression to health comes from research on *alexithymia*, a term used to describe people who have a pronounced inability to describe their own emotions. These patients are deficient in facial expressiveness and also seem to suffer from a disproportionate number of psychosomatic ailments (Buck, 1993). What is cause and what is effect in such research remains an open question.

The patient's face is not the only face that is important in a clinical situation. Physicians' and therapists' facial expressions have an impact on patients. Ambady, Koo, Rosenthal, and Winograd (2002) found that the facial expressions of physical therapists predicted changes in elderly patients' physical and psychological functioning over the course of treatment. Specifically, facial "distancing" or not smiling and not looking at the patient was associated with decreases in functioning, whereas facial expressiveness—that is, smiling, nodding, and frowning—was associated with increases in functioning. Ruben, Blanch-Hartigan, and Hall (2017) studied the impact of a physician (who was an actor) displaying more or less supportive nonverbal cues, which included facial expressions, to a participant who was (really) undergoing a painful procedure. High nonverbal support produced greater pain tolerance in the participants and a reduction in the amount of pain they expressed via their faces.

SALES AND SERVICE

Interactions between service providers and customers provide yet another forum in which facial expressions can have impact. In an experiment in which role-playing "customers" watched videos of hotel clerks interacting with someone who was checking in, the clerk who displayed a smile that appeared authentic received higher customer satisfaction ratings than the clerk whose smile appeared inauthentic—but only when the clerk was performing their tasks competently. When the clerk made errors, the kind of smile had no impact (Grandey, Fisk, Mattila, Jansen, & Sideman, 2005). Thus, the context was an important qualifier of whether the smile mattered. Kulczynski, Ilicic, and

Baxter (2016) found that a smiling endorser in an ad fostered positive feelings in viewers, which, in turn, promoted more brand favorability and purchase intentions. But like the preceding study, there were qualifications: The endorser needed to be familiar and relevant to the product in order for the smile to have this effect.

GROUPS AND LEADERSHIP

Evaluative affect displays are subtle ways that audiences can enhance or devalue speakers. Butler and Geis (1990) investigated male and female leaders in groups. Each group had a male or female leader who had, unknown to the group members, been trained to offer identical suggestions and arguments. However, the group members, who were the subjects of study, displayed more pleased responses (smiling and nodding) and fewer displeased responses (furrowed brow, mouth tightening, head shaking) when listening to the male leader than when listening to the female leader. Group members were apparently unaware of their gender-biased behavior or denied it, for they later revealed no gender bias in written evaluations of the leaders. Koch (2005) replicated these results both in the lab and in real organizational groups. The potential importance of this finding in real groups is obvious: Subtle signals of devaluation sent by audience members could undermine a female leader's performance and could even create negativity in other audience members who were not initially biased against her.

MEDIA

Facial expressions are related to gender stereotyping, ridicule, as well as discrimination against men and women in the media and small groups. Leppard, Ogletree, and Wallen (1993) noted that, in medical advertisements, men were more often shown with serious/neutral facial expression, whereas women were more often shown with pleasant expressions. Sometimes the natural expressions of others are ridiculed in the media (see Box **Resting Bitch Face**).

Another connection between the face and gender discrimination involves the "face-ism" or *facial prominence* phenomenon. In magazine and newspaper pictures, proportionately more of the picture is devoted to men's faces, whereas pictures of women show more of the body. Archer, Iritani, Kimes, and Barrios (1983) found this pattern in publications from 11 different cultures and in artwork over 6 centuries, as well as in people's amateur drawings. Both Archer and later researchers (Zuckerman, 1986) have made the case that face-ism is a form of devaluing women. Matthews (2007) found higher facial prominence in magazine photographs of individuals who had intellectually oriented as opposed to physically oriented occupations, especially if the person in the photograph was a man. Consistent with the view that depicting less of the face devalues the person in the picture, Zuckerman and Kieffer (1994) demonstrated that face-ism favoring White over Black people also exists in magazines and art.

EVERYDAY LIFE

The smile is a profoundly influential social cue that has been studied in many contexts. People reciprocate smiles quite predictably (Hinsz & Tomhave, 1991; Jorgenson, 1978). You can imagine how, after returning someone's smile, facial feedback or attributional processes could produce real changes in your emotional state or your attitude toward the smiler (e.g., "I just smiled at Jim. I must really like him!"). Smiles are positive reinforcers that can change behavior just as other, more traditional reinforcers can. For example, receiving a smile from one stranger can make you more helpful toward a different stranger (Solomon et al., 1981), and receiving a smile from your waitperson can lead you to leave a larger tip (Tidd & Lockard, 1978).

Angry faces are a potent stimulus, too. Hansen and Hansen (1988) compared people's ability to pick out an angry face in a crowd of happy faces to their ability to pick out a happy face in a crowd of angry faces. As they predicted, picking out the angry face was faster and more error free than picking out the happy face. It is possible that our survival as a species has some relation to sensitivity to possible threat, whether physical or social, signaled by others' angry facial expressions.

The influence exerted on us by others' facial expressions is not limited to those faces that are consciously seen and noted. Nonconscious, subliminal perception effects have been uncovered as well. Murphy and Zajonc (1993) showed people a happy or an angry face for only 4 ms, an interval much too short to allow for conscious perception of the faces, followed by unfamiliar stimuli—in this case, written Chinese characters. When the experimenters asked the participants how much they liked each Chinese character, they found that characters preceded by a happy face were liked more than those preceded by an angry face. Dimberg, Thunberg, and Elmehed (2000) found that subliminally exposing people to happy or angry facial expressions produced corresponding facial movements according to EMG measurements. In this case, both the stimulus (the faces seen) and the response (the small facial movements picked up by EMG recording) occurred nonconsciously.

RESTING BITCH FACE

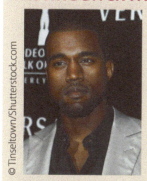

© Tinseltown/Shutterstock.com

© Denis Makarenko/Shutterstock.com

A new phrase has emerged in popular culture, the so-called resting bitch face (RBF). It refers to a look of mild anger, annoyance, contempt, or discontent in the face of a woman or man who is (apparently) not otherwise feeling any of those emotion states. The RBFs of celebrities Kanye West and Kristen Stewart are often featured in the media.

Judgments of people sometimes hinge on interpretations of their facial features and expressions. As can be inferred from the term "bitch" in RBF, the label is decidedly critical of the men and women showing that expression.

Questions remain about whether the RBF is a true facial expression and, if it is, how individuals who display it might be received by the people they interact with in day-to-day life. To date, the research community has not tackled these questions. This neglect should not be countenanced given the potential social implications of the RBF to people's lives, and how the term may be misused in the domain of popular culture.

SUMMARY

The face is a multimessage system. It can communicate information regarding personality, interest, and responsiveness during interaction, emotional states, and how people want to present themselves to others. Although we know that people associate certain personality characteristics with certain expressions and facial features, we do not fully know how accurate these impressions are. We know the face is used as a conversational regulator that opens and closes communication channels, complements and qualifies other behaviors, and replaces spoken messages.

Facial expressions are very complex entities to deal with. Of all the areas of the body, the face seems to elicit the best external and internal feedback, which makes it easy for people to follow a variety of facial display rules. Not all facial displays represent single emotions; some are blends of several emotions. Sometimes people show aspects of an emotional display when they are not actually feeling emotional, as with facial emblems that represent commentary on emotions. At other times the emotion or current feeling is not very predictably shown on the face. The question of how often the face spontaneously reveals emotional experiences in daily life is hotly contested.

Accuracy in judging the face tends to be high, at least when prototypic expressions are presented. Furthermore, certain basic emotions have been found to be accurately judged in cultures around the world: anger, fear, disgust, sadness, happiness, surprise, and contempt. To understand what the face actually does during the expression of emotion, anatomically based coding systems, such as the FACS, have been developed. The FACS can identify which muscles are prototypically involved in different kinds of expressions.

A psychophysiological approach has added much to our understanding of facial behavior. People with more expressive faces have less activity in their autonomic nervous systems than do less expressive people; this is interesting partly because of its health implications. Under certain circumstances, facial movements can influence the emotions felt by the expressor; thus, the face may not only read out emotions but also actually produce them. Studies of minute facial movements show that people nonconsciously mimic the facial expressions of others, even those expressions too quick to be consciously perceived. And researchers are finding out more about which activities of the brain and nervous system are associated with different emotions. We concluded with a sampling of studies showing that facial expressions can have a strong impact on the people in our social environment.

QUESTIONS FOR DISCUSSION

1. Facial expressions can show emotions, but they also are used for conversation management. Give examples of each, and state which function you consider the most important.
2. Consider men's and women's nonverbal behavior. Does the concept of display rules help you explain any differences?
3. The distinction between a feigned or posed facial display and an authentic or spontaneous one may be hard to make. Discuss the issue of intentionality in facial expressions. Is it important to be able to make such a distinction? Do you think you can make such a distinction yourself, and if so, how do you think you do it?
4. The chapter gives examples of how the face is a potent influence on others. Think of some other examples of this, and discuss whether the face is more or less influential than other nonverbal channels in terms of its social impact.
5. Can you think of any occasions when you might have experienced intensification, or even the creation, of an emotion as a result of facial feedback?
6. Some people are more aware of the expressions that occur on their faces than other people. Discuss this phenomenon. What kind of people do you think are more self-observant than others? What impact do you think this kind of self-accuracy has?

NONVERBAL COMMUNICATION IN ACTION: TRY THIS

Go to an art museum, or go online, and find portraits of people done in different centuries. Analyze each face carefully, writing down what you see in the overall expression and attitude it conveys, as well as the specific details of eyes, brows, and mouth positions and any muscle movements you detect. Are there any differences in expressions according to when the portrait was done, or according to other variables you can identify (such as gender, social class, or ethnicity)?

CHAPTER 10

THE EFFECTS OF EYE BEHAVIOR ON HUMAN COMMUNICATION

He speaketh not; and yet there lies a conversation in his eyes.
—**Henry Wadsworth Longfellow**

Throughout history, people have been preoccupied with the eyes and their effects on behavior. You have probably heard these phrases:

"It was an icy stare."

"He's got shifty eyes."

"Did you see the gleam in his eye?"

"We're seeing eye to eye now."

"His eyes shot daggers across the room."

"She could kill with a glance."

These phrases do not just describe eye movements; they convey what people think those eye movements *mean*. It is common for people to attribute a wide range of emotions, intentions, or traits to the appearance and movements of the eyes: Downward glances are associated with modesty; wide eyes with frankness, wonder, naiveté, or terror; a constant stare with coldness or accusation; and eyes rolled upward with intention to disparage someone's behavior.

In addition, our society has a number of eye-related norms. As examples, you should not look at strangers for a long time, and do not look at particular body parts on other people (e.g., their legs, chest) for too long, except under special circumstances (e.g., flirting, foreplay, etc.).

Fascination with eyes has led to the exploration of almost every conceivable feature of the eyes and the areas surrounding them. This includes eye size, color, position, eyebrows, and wrinkles around the eyes. Eye rings are found mainly in other animals, but some speculate that human eyebrows are residual "rings," to be raised during surprise or fear and lowered for focus during threat and anger; certainly eyebrows can convey many messages (recall the eyebrow action units described in Chapter 9). Eye "patches" are the colored eyelids sometimes seen in primates, but these are not a part of the natural human communicative repertoire, although some people use eyeliner and eye shadow to achieve a similar effect. Another nonhuman feature that has received scholarly attention is "eyespots," eye-shaped images located on various parts of some animals' bodies. These can be seen on peacock feathers, butterflies, and certain fish and are considered an evolved way that a relatively helpless creature can distract or scare away enemies.

Researchers have examined the degree to which eyes open or close as a reflection of various emotional states. Some feel that excessive blinking may be associated with various stages of anxiety—as if attempting to cut off reality. Psychiatrists report that some patients blink up to 100 times per minute; normal blinking, needed to lubricate and protect the eyeball, occurs about 6 to 10 times per minute in adults. Some evidence shows that when a person is attentive to objects in the environment, or deep in concentrated thought, the blinking rate decreases. Ophthalmologists warn patients that staring for a long time at a computer screen greatly reduces the blink rate and can lead to dry eyes and other problems.

Some eye-related behaviors can occur without much conscious awareness, such as the crinkles around the eyes when a person is feeling genuine enjoyment, but others are used very deliberately. An example of the latter is the "eye flash," in which the eyelids are briefly opened without the accompanying involvement of the eyebrows, for less than a second, used to emphasize particular words, usually adjectives (Walker & Trimboli, 1983). The *eyebrow* flash is yet another but quite different gesture, discussed in depth in Chapter 2.

Further diversity in the significance of the eyes comes from research on eye color. Blue eyes are a genetically based marker for inhibition and shyness, and people perceive greater dominance in men with brown eyes than blue eyes (Kleisner, Kočnar, Rubešová, & Flegr, 2010; Rosenberg & Kagan, 1987).

Of the many eye-related topics of inquiry, this chapter focuses on two: The first is known by terms such as *eye contact*, *mutual glances*, *visual interaction*, *gazing*, or *line of regard*. The second concerns pupil dilation and constriction under various social conditions.

GAZE AND MUTUAL GAZE

We begin by looking at the terminology we will be using: *gaze* and *mutual gaze* (Argyle & Cook, 1976; Kleinke, 1986; Rutter, 1984). *Gaze* refers to an individual looking at another person; *mutual gaze* refers to a situation in which two interactants are looking at each other, usually in the region of the face (see Figure 10-1). Eye contact—that is, looking specifically in each other's eyes—does not seem to be reliably distinguished by receivers or observers from gazing at the area surrounding the eyes (von Cranach & Ellgring, 1973). In fact, much of what is considered "looking someone in the eye" is a series of rapid, repeated scans of several parts of the face. Indeed, if someone did look fixedly without moving the eyes, the impression would be one of vacant staring. Gaze and mutual gaze can be reliably assessed by observers. At a distance of 3 meters, face-directed gazing can be distinguished, and shifting the direction of the gaze by 1 centimeter can reliably be detected from a distance of 1 meter.

People do not look at another person the entire time they are talking, nor do they avert gaze 100% of the time. What are considered normal gazing patterns? Obviously, the answer varies according to the background and personalities of the participants, the topic, the other person's gazing patterns, objects of mutual interest in the environment, and so on. The speaker's fluency also affects gazing patterns. During fluent speech, speakers tend to look at listeners much more than during hesitant speech. We will discuss some of these factors in more detail later in this chapter. Keeping such qualifications in mind, we can get a general idea of normal gazing patterns from research on focused interaction between two people (e.g., Argyle & Ingham, 1972). Generally, people gaze about half the time; there are notable individual differences in the amount of other-directed gaze; and people gaze more while listening than while talking.

Whatever one's preferred overall amount of gazing during conversation is, it tends to be a very consistently manifested style. This has been documented in research where a video of a person in conversation is "sliced" up into much shorter excerpts, for example 30 seconds or one minute in duration. Then gazing is measured, in duration, within each of these slices. Researchers find that the amount of gazing is very predictable from one slice to another, meaning that if they tend to gaze a lot (or a little) in any given slice, they will predictably gaze a similar amount in other slices (Murphy et al., 2015).

© Monkey Business Images/Shutterstock.com

FIGURE 10-1 Mutual gaze.

FUNCTIONS OF GAZING

Kendon (1967) identified four functions of gazing: (1) *regulatory*—responses may be demanded or suppressed by looking; (2) *monitoring*—people may look at their partner to indicate the conclusions of thought units and to check their partner's attentiveness and reactions; (3) *cognitive*—people tend to look away when having difficulty processing information or deciding what to say; and (4) *expressive*—the degree and nature of involvement or emotional arousal may be revealed through looking.

Our discussion follows a similar pattern, as gazing has been shown to serve several important functions:

1. Regulating the flow of communication
2. Monitoring feedback
3. Reflecting cognitive activity
4. Expressing emotions
5. Communicating the nature of the interpersonal relationship

These functions do not operate independently, nor are there fully unique eye behaviors associated with each of these functions. In addition, visual behavior not only sends information but is also one of the primary methods for collecting it. Looking at the other person as you finish an utterance may not only tell the other that it is their turn to speak but is also an occasion for you to see how they are reacting to what you have said.

REGULATING THE FLOW OF COMMUNICATION

Visual contact occurs when a person wants to signal that the communication channel is open. In some instances, eye gaze establishes a virtual *obligation* to interact. When you seek visual contact with your server at a restaurant, you are essentially indicating that the communication channel is open and that you want to say something to them. You may recall instances when an instructor asked the class a question, and you were sure you did not know the answer. Establishing eye contact with the instructor was the last thing you wanted to do. Police use this knowledge to identify drivers who may be engaged in illegal activity because they consider drivers who avoid eye contact to be suspicious. People routinely use gaze avoidance to prevent unwanted social interactions. As long as one can avoid eye gaze in a seemingly natural way, it is much easier to avoid interaction.

When passing unknown others in a public place, people typically acknowledge them with a brief glance, but this initial glance is followed by the avoidance of gaze unless further contact is desired, or unless the other person signals a desire for further contact by gazing back or by smiling. However, the time it takes us to look away from another person might vary as a function of a number of factors, such as the person's attractiveness and emotional state. Belopolsky, Devue, and Theeuwes (2011) found in a laboratory study that it took participants longer to visually disengage from an angry face than a face with a neutral or happy expression. One wonders whether this would hold true in real-life settings where directing any extra gaze at an angry person might pose a risk, while gazing at a happy person would likely be pleasant and less dangerous.

A length of gaze that exceeds an acknowledgment glance is likely to signal a desire to initiate a conversation (Cary, 1978), and violation of this *civil inattention* norm—a term coined by Goffman (1963)—can produce negative feelings in the recipients (Zuckerman, Miserandino, & Bernieri, 1983). When you want to disavow social contact, your eye gaze will likely diminish. Thus, there would be more mutual gazing in greeting sequences and greatly diminished gazing when people are wanting to bring an encounter to an end.

Within a conversation, gazing at the other can command a nonverbal, as well as verbal, response. Because speakers gaze less than listeners, it is the speaker's gazing that determines moments of mutual looking. During these moments, it is highly likely that the listener will respond with a *listener response*, also called a *backchannel response*, that signifies attention (Bavelas, Coates, & Johnson, 2002). These responses can include smiles and other facial expressions, sounds such as "mm-hmm," and head nods. Thus, the speaker's behavior is an important determinant of the timing of these responses. However, gazing is not the only determinant: Listener responses also occur when people do not see each other, as when talking on the phone. In these situations, people are likely to increase their level of verbal back channel responses, such as "uh-huh," as a means of communicating their attention to the speaker (Boyle, Anderson, & Newlands, 1994).

In addition to opening and closing the channel of communication and commanding responses from the other, eye behavior also regulates the flow of communication by providing turn-taking signals. As we have said, speakers generally look less often than listeners. But speakers do seem to glance during grammatical breaks, at the end of a thought unit or idea, and at the end of the utterance. Although glances at these junctures can signal the other person to assume the speaking role, these glances are also used to obtain feedback, to see how one is being received, and to see if one can continue talking. This feedback function is addressed in the next section. The speaker–listener pattern is often choreographed as follows: As the speaker comes to the end of an utterance or thought unit, eye gaze toward the listener will continue as the listener assumes the speaking role; the listener will maintain gaze until the speaking role is assumed, at which point they will look away.

Research on naturally emerging and appointed leaders in three-person male groups has found that the leader controlled the flow of conversation using this cue pattern: The leader showed an increased tendency to engage in prolonged gaze at someone when he was done with a speaking turn, as if inviting, or possibly instructing, that person to take the floor. This "prolonged gaze" pattern (Kalma, 1992) has also been seen in three-person conversations in maternity hospitals, where the nurse "selected" the mother over the father most of the time to answer questions about new parenthood, by using this same gaze-control method (Tiitinen & Ruusuvuori, 2012).

A speaker's gaze at the completion of an utterance may help signal the yielding of a speaking turn, but listener-directed gazes do not always accompany the smooth exchange of speaking turns (Beattie, 1978; Rutter, Stephenson, & White, 1978). For instance, even though the speaker glances at the listener when yielding a speaking turn, the listener delays a response or fails to respond. Further, when a speaker begins an anticipated lengthy response, they are likely to delay gazing at the other beyond what would normally be expected. This pattern of adult gazing and looking away during speech seems to have its roots in early childhood development. Observations of the gazing patterns of 3- to 4-month-old infants and their parents revealed temporal similarities between their looking-at and looking-away sequence and the vocalizing and pausing sequences in adult conversations (Jaffe, Stern, & Peery, 1973).

Finally, people can use gaze to signal the presence of socially meaningful information in the interaction environment to another person, such as a friend. If you notice the sudden appearance of a stranger, a quick glance at the stranger can cue your friend to look that way. Your use of gaze here should help your friend (or whomever you are talking with) to more quickly notice looked-at information in the environment. This phenomenon, called the *gaze-cuing effect*, has, in fact, received extensive research. The gaze-cuing effect has been observed not only in humans but in a number of species, and is not limited to the assessment of environmental threats (Brauer, Call, & Tomasello, 2005; Frischen, Bayliss, & Tipper, 2007).

The gaze-cuing effect can be influenced by characteristics of the gazer and perceiver, as well as contextual factors including the number of people involved. When an observer saw that one individual was looking at the target but two others were not (33% looking), the gaze-cuing effect was triggered in the observer, but it took three individuals looking at the target when there were five potential lookers (60% looking) to produce the same effect (Capozzi, Bayliss, & Ristic, 2018). In addition, females show quicker cue-gazing responses than do males, and more dominant-looking female faces seem to elicit greater cue-gazing effects (Alwall, Johansson, & Hansen, 2010; Jones, Main, Little, & DeBruine, 2011). Seeing two people look at—but not away from—each other before they both look in one direction leads to the gaze-cuing effect (Böckler, Knoblich, & Sebanz, 2011). Lastly, whether person A looks where person B has looked may depend on the match between B's facial expression and what A is searching for in the environment. Kuhn and Tipples (2011) found that participants who were looking for a threatening target were more likely to follow the gaze of a fearful face than a happy one.

MONITORING FEEDBACK

When people seek feedback concerning the reactions of others, they gaze at the other person. If the other person is looking back, it is usually interpreted as a sign of attention to what is being said. Listener facial expressions and gazing suggest not only attention but also whether the listener is interested in what is being said.

Being seen is a profound form of social acknowledgment, and its lack—the experience of having others "look right through you"—undermines a person's very existence as a social being, as many people in subordinate roles or stigmatized social categories can testify. The averted gaze of another can lead to feelings of being ostracized (Wirth, Sacco, Hugenberg, & Williams, 2010). A child on a playground who demands to be watched by their parent while doing feats on the jungle gym is not simply asking for added safety or security. Far more importantly, the parent's gaze *infuses meaning* into the child's actions. Without a witness, the actions may feel pointless or even unreal.

On the other hand, under some circumstances being seen—especially in the sense of being *watched*—can feel like a violation of privacy and can be very uncomfortable, especially when one cannot look back at the person watching. One type of being watched is called *objectifying gaze*, usually discussed within the context of men engaging in this kind of gazing at women, although objectifying gaze can be found in other contexts as well. Many women experience being "ogled" or "leered at," often to their great displeasure. Laboratory research shows that when women are looked at in a sexualized way, their cognitive performance decreases and body shame increases. Bareket, Shnabel, Abeles, Gervais, and Yuval-Greenberg (2018) used eye-tracking technology (a way of precisely measuring where the eyes are directed when looking at various stimuli) to document a connection between men's holding objectifying attitudes toward women and what parts of a woman's body they look at. Items on the objectification scale included "If a woman is attractive, she doesn't need to have anything interesting to say" and "Commenting on women's physical features is only natural." While making general ratings of a diverse set of photographs of women (not in sexy clothes or poses), men who held more objectifying attitudes spent more time looking at the women's sexualized body parts (chest, waist, and hips), compared to their face, than men with less objectifying attitudes.

Putting such toxic gaze patterns aside, effective monitoring of others via gaze may have useful practical consequences. In studies of physician–patient interaction, physicians who engaged in more patient-directed gaze recognized their patients' degree of psychosocial distress better and obtained more psychosocial information from them (Bensing, Kerssens, & van der Pasch, 1995; van Dulmen, Verhaak, & Bilo, 1997). Monitoring others' reactions during group discussions is crucial to planning responsive statements and maintaining group harmony and morale. Crosby, Monin, and Richardson (2008) showed that when a White member of a group made an offensive statement about Black people, visual attention was shifted to the Black member of the group, but only when listeners thought he could hear the offensive remark. Presumably, group members wanted to know how the affected person reacted before deciding how to respond themselves. Effective monitoring of group members via gaze has been shown to be higher in women than men: During group interaction, women spread their gaze more evenly around a group than men do (Koch, Baehne, Kruse, Zimmermann, & Zumbach, 2008).

REFLECTING COGNITIVE ACTIVITY

The use of gaze and attention to others' gaze are related to higher-order cognitive processes in children and adults alike. For example, toddlers' theory-of-mind skills were the strongest predictor of their tendency to gaze longer at the face of a person (as opposed to other objects around her) who became sad after having her ball taken away from her (Poulin-Dubois et al., 2018). Adult may use the gaze of a speaker to process what they are saying (Jachmann, Drenhaus, Staudte, & Crocker, 2019).

At other times, whether as a listener or speaker, people may avoid gazing at others, such as when trying to process difficult or complex ideas. In each case, looking away serves to reduce the cognitive demands placed on the person. This averted gaze, which may include closing the eyes, reflects a shift in attention from external to internal matters, as well as an effort to exclude or interrupt external stimulation, such as that inherent in the processing of face-to-face social cues (Markson & Paterson, 2009). People avoid gaze more on reflective questions than factual ones and on more difficult questions—more difficult in factual content or in terms of the length of the temporal search required, as in "Name a professor you currently have" versus "Name a professor you had two semesters ago" (Glenberg, Schroeder, & Robertson, 1998). Furthermore, when participants were required to answer factual questions, either with their eyes closed or while looking directly at the experimenter, performance was better in the eyes-closed condition, thus demonstrating the functional utility of excluding external stimulation while engaging in difficult cognitive activity. Gaze aversion also benefits children on difficult cognitive tasks, largely by helping them manage the cognitive demands (Doherty-Sneddon & Phelps, 2005; Glenberg et al., 1998).

When thinking about others' questions, gaze aversion appears to be a cognitive load-reducing strategy used by typically developing individuals as well as those with autism and Williams syndrome (Doherty-Sneddon et al., 2013). The use of gaze aversion while answering challenging questions appears to be something that can be taught to very young children, resulting in superior performance (Phelps, Doherty-Sneddon, & Warnock, 2006).

EXPRESSING EMOTIONS

A glance at the eye area can provide a good deal of information about the emotion being expressed. In fact, greater attention to the eyes might account for why some (women) are better than others (men) at reading emotion states on the face (Hall, Hutton, & Morgan, 2010). If there are tears near the eyes of a person, an observer would likely conclude that the person is emotionally moved, although without other cues, the observer may not know whether the tears reflect grief, physical pain, frustration, joy, anger, some complex blend of emotions, or feigned grief, as in "crocodile tears" (tears that are not real expressions of grief). And, as we indicate later, cues such as downcast or averted eyes are often associated with feelings of sadness, shame, or embarrassment.

The extensive studies of Paul Ekman and Wallace Friesen have provided valuable insights into facial configurations for six common, basic emotions shown in the photographs here. The descriptions shown pertain to the brow and eye area, and the eye photographs are from Ekman and Friesen's collection. As the photographs illustrate, it may be difficult to judge what emotion is being expressed without being able to see the brows. Similarly, some expressions may be ambiguous unless the entire face can be seen. In everyday life, of course, there are mainly dynamic as opposed to static facial expressions involving the eyes and mouth as well as facial blends in which the eyes tell one story, and other parts of the face tell another.

SURPRISE Brows are raised so that they are curved and high. Skin below the brow is stretched. Eyelids are opened; the upper lid is raised, and the lower lid is drawn down; and the white of the eye shows above the iris, and often below as well.

© Paul Ekman, Ph.D.

FEAR Brows are raised and drawn together. The upper eyelid is raised, exposing the white of the eye, called the *sclera*, and the lower eyelid is tensed and drawn up.

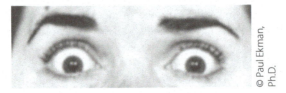

© Paul Ekman, Ph.D.

DISGUST is shown primarily in the lower face and in the lower eyelids. Lines show below the lower lid, and the lid is pushed up but not tense. The brow is lowered, lowering the upper lid.

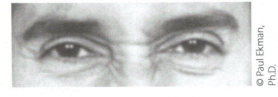

© Paul Ekman, Ph.D.

ANGER The brows are lowered and drawn together, and vertical lines appear between them. The lower lid is tensed and may or may not be raised. The upper lid is tensed and may or may not be lowered by the action of the brow. The eyes have a hard stare and may have a bulging appearance.

HAPPINESS is shown primarily in the lower face and lower eyelids. The lower eyelid shows wrinkles below it and may be raised but is not tense. Crow's feet wrinkles go outward from the outer corners of the eyes.

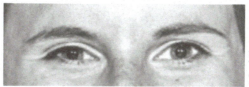

SADNESS The inner corners of the eyebrows are drawn up. The skin below the eyebrow is triangulated, with the inner corner up. The upper-eyelid inner corner is raised.

The eye-tracking study of Eisenbarth and Alpers (2011) showed that participants looked initially or relatively longer at different parts of the face when decoding specific emotions; for instance, initial fixations to the eyes were more common with sad than happy, angry, or fearful expressions, and longer fixations to the mouth were seen with happy expressions. The authors interpreted this as evidence that people look at those areas of the face that are most diagnostic for the given emotion. But do the eyes, for example, display emotion better or worse than other parts of the face? Ekman, Friesen, and Tomkins (1971) demonstrated that the eyes were better than the brows, forehead, or lower face for the accurate perception of fear but were less accurate for anger and disgust. Baron-Cohen, Wheelwright, and Jolliffe (1997) tested university students' accuracy at identifying 16 emotional states, posed by an actress, by evaluating each area separately: the eye area, including brows, the mouth area, and the whole face. The authors included "basic" emotions such as angry, afraid, and happy, and "nonbasic" states such as admiring, flirtatious, arrogant, and thoughtful. The eye region was not quite as accurately judged as the whole face for the basic emotions but was indistinguishable for the nonbasic states (see Figure 10-2). Can you identify the emotions posed by the person in this study? (Answers are at the end of the chapter.) Both the eyes and the whole face were judged much more accurately than the mouth. Consistent with the research by Ekman et al. (1971), accuracy for the mouth region, although not superior to the eye region, was similar to that of the eye region for distinguishing disgust and anger and much lower than the eye region for distinguishing fear.

Most research on recognizing facial expressions of emotion presents faces with direct forward gaze. However, it has been shown that the direction in which the eyes are gazing has an influence on judgments of emotion in the face (Adams & Kleck, 2003, 2005). In one of the studies, a face shown with the eyes gazing directly forward made viewers more likely to see approach-orientation emotions, such as anger and joy, in the face, but the same face with an averted gaze made them more likely to see avoidance-orientation emotions, such as fear and sadness. In another study,

a

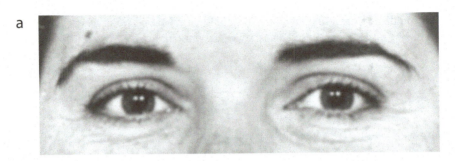

b

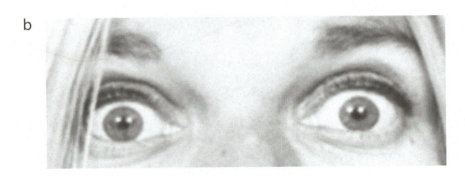

c

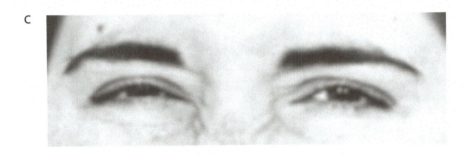

d

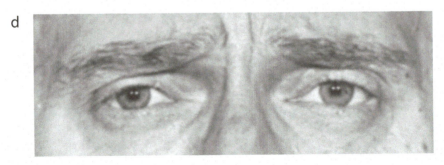

FIGURE 10-2 Can you judge the emotions in these eyes? (a) happy or surprised, (b) angry or afraid, (c) sad or disgusted, (d) distressed or sad. (See answers at the end of the chapter.)

Source: From Baron-Cohen, S., Wheelwright, s., Jolliffe A. T. (1997, September 1). Is there a "Language of the Eyes"? Evidence from normal adults, and adults with autism or Asperger syndrome. *Visual Cognition, 4*(3), 311–331(21), reprinted by permission of the publisher (Taylor & Francis Group, www.informaworld.com).

identical facial blends of fear and anger were presented to viewers with direct versus averted gaze; more anger was attributed to the face that had direct gaze, and more fear was attributed to the face that had averted gaze. Thus, when the expression was ambiguous, gaze direction influenced emotional perception.

COMMUNICATING THE NATURE OF THE INTERPERSONAL RELATIONSHIP

The direct gaze of a live person is important to the initial stages of processing their facial information, which obviously is relevant to the possibility of some sort of relationship (Pönkänen, Alhoniemi, Leppänen, & Hietanen, 2011). Even the direct gaze of a "person" in a painting can trigger interpersonally relevant reactions in those who are viewing it (see Box **Looking into Your Mind**).

LOOKING INTO YOUR MIND

© Adam Eastland Art + Architecture / Alamy Stock Photo

It appears that the visual system is designed to process eyes that are looking directly at you more quickly and accurately than eyes looking away from you, even when those eyes are drawn as opposed to real (von Grünau & Anston, 1995). You have no doubt experienced the feeling of being followed by the eyes of a "person" in a famous painting, such as the one shown in the picture here (Titian's *Venus of Urbino*). Based on the research of Kesner and colleagues (2018), your brain is likely reacting as if you were being looked at by a "watchful intelligent being." Her direct gaze triggers this reaction in you. You may experience other conscious and nonconscious reactions, including the feeling that she is more trustworthy (Kaisler & Leder, 2016) as well as a generalized sense of greater interpersonal closeness (Cui, Zhu, Lu, & Zhu, 2019).

In terms of cognitive processing and benefits, her direct gaze is probably making you spend more time looking at her eyes and mouth than would be the case if she were looking away from you (Kesner et al., 2018). The straight gaze of others may also help you process other information about their face better, such as their gender (Framorando, George, Kerzel, & Burra, 2016).

Gazing and mutual gazing are often indicative of the nature of the relationship between two interactants. For instance, relationships characterized by different status or dominance levels may be reflected in the eye patterns; one example was given earlier—the way the leader in a group seems to pick the next speaker via gaze direction. The gaze of observers also might reflect a sensitivity to status differences among people. Foulsham, Cheng, Tracy, Henrich, and Kingstone (2010) found that participants watching a video of a decision-making group looked more at the high-status than low-status individuals in the group.

Another indicator of status or dominance is the *visual dominance ratio*—the percentage of time spent looking at another while speaking to them divided by the percentage of time spent looking at the other person while that person is speaking. People with higher status or dominance gaze relatively more while speaking and relatively less while listening, compared to people with lower status or dominance. This has been observed in laboratory dyadic settings as well as in real-world workplace settings involving groups of people (Koch, Baehne, Kruse, Zimmermann, & Zumbach, 2010). Although subtle patterns such as these distinguish people with higher and lower dominance, a simple measure of overall gazing does not, according to numerous studies (as reviewed by Hall, Coats, & Smith LeBeau, 2005). On the other hand, stereotypes about gazing and dominance indicate a belief in such an association. When asked to imagine how much gazing people of high or low dominance would display, in terms of either personality or rank in a workplace, participants thought the higher dominant person would gaze more (Carney, Hall, & Smith LeBeau, 2005). And across many studies, when shown video excerpts of people gazing different amounts, viewers attributed higher dominance to those who gazed more (Hall et al., 2005).

On the flip side of visual dominance is the notion of "visual egalitarianism" (Koch et al., 2010). Here, equality among members of a group might be revealed in gaze patterns that suggest all members of the group are being looked at to relatively the same extent. Koch and colleagues found that visual egalitarianism was greater in groups headed by a female team leader than a male team leader.

Several studies testify that people gaze more at people and things perceived as rewarding. Efran and Broughton (1966) found that males gazed more at other males with whom they had engaged in a friendly conversation preceding an experiment and with those who nodded and smiled during the person's presentation. Exline and Eldridge (1967) found that the same verbal communication was decoded as being more favorable when associated with more gaze than when presented with less gaze. Exline and Winters (1965) reported that people avoided the eyes of an interviewer and disliked him after he had commented unfavorably on their performance. Self-relevance influences responses to gaze, too. Faces are considered more likable if the eyes are shown shifting toward the viewer than if the eyes are shown shifting away (Mason, Tatkow, & Macrae, 2005).

Mehrabian (1972b) asked a group of people to imagine they liked a person and to engage this person in conversation. Even in this role-playing situation, increased gazing was associated with increased liking. Mutual liking, revealed in the form of participants' rating of rapport, was similarly related to gazing when interactants debated a controversial topic (Bernieri, Gillis, Davis, & Grahe, 1996). Interestingly, when engaging in a more cooperative discussion, eye contact was not related to rapport judgments.

What you are gazing at and how long you are gazing at someone are often considered in the context of human courtship. When people are described as potential mates for you (as opposed to potential friends), you may spend more time looking at the head and chest regions of their bodies and more time gazing at them if you are single (Gillath, Bahns, & Burghart, 2017). And, of course, whom you are attracted to can affect whom and what you gaze at; for example, men and "sexually fluid" women gaze at the breasts of nude women, and women gaze at the hips and groin regions of nude men (Widman, Bennetti, & Anglemyer, 2019). Your relationship status and environmental factors, such as the availability of resources, may also influence whom you prefer and how long you gaze at a person's face (Lyons, Marcinkowska, Moisey, & Harrison, 2016).

The maintenance of mutual gaze longer than otherwise expected is a primary way of signaling desire for heightened intimacy. In movies, one can almost always predict when a first kiss is coming because the characters share an unusually long mutual gaze. An increased amount of gaze can both signal a wish for more involvement and be an indication that heightened involvement has occurred. In one study, for example, single men (but not single women) showed more gazing toward an attractive than unattractive opposite-sex interaction partner (Van Straaten, Holland, Finkenauer, Hollenstein, & Engles, 2010). Several sources confirm an increase in gazing between two people who are seeking to develop a more intimate relationship. Rubin's (1970) analysis of engaged couples indicated more mutual gaze, and Kleinke, Bustos, Meeker, and Staneski (1973) found that longer glances or reciprocated glances were perceived as an indicator of a longer relationship. It may be that the amount of gazing increases as relationships become more intimate, but it may also be true that after maintaining an intimate relationship for years, gazing returns to levels below those observed during more intense stages of the relationship's development.

Argyle and Dean (1965) proposed an intimacy equilibrium model to help explain why and how much people gaze in an interpersonal interaction. This model suggests that intimacy is a function of the amount of eye gazing, physical proximity, intimacy of topic, and amount of smiling. Thus, gaze is part of a network of other behaviors that have important relations to one another in a total system reflective of the overall psychological intimacy in a given interaction. Clearly, other variables might be inserted into the equation, for example, body orientation, the form of address used, tone of voice, other facial expressions, and forward lean. The central idea behind this proposal is that as one component of the model is changed, one or more of the other components also will change in the opposite direction, as a form of compensation to keep the overall intimacy or stimulation at a constant, desired level. For example, if one person looks too much, the other may look less, move farther away, smile less, talk less about intimate matters, and so on to reestablish the initial desired level of intimacy. In addition, when one person is forced to increase the implied intimacy of a behavior—for example, by standing close to another in a crowded elevator—the other will compensate by gazing less, talking about impersonal topics, and so forth.

Cross-cultural research shows that in societies that emphasize a greater amount of physical contact between mothers and infants, mutual gaze between them is lower than in societies where the norms prescribe more physical autonomy and distance. Here again is evidence of a compensatory mechanism, whereby the crucial psychological connection between mothers and infants is maintained in different but equivalent ways. The same trade-off between physical contact and mutual gaze has also been observed in chimpanzee mother–infant interactions (Bard et al., 2005).

Although this compensatory model has received extensive support, there are many occasions when, rather than counter or offset the other's behavior, people will *reciprocate* it; for example, gazing will elicit gazing, and smiling will elicit smiling. This can be seen in personal interactions as well as between strangers; glancing at a passing stranger is likely to produce a glance in return (Patterson et al., 2007; Patterson, Webb, & Schwartz, 2002).

Several scholars have proposed alternatives to the intimacy equilibrium model (Cappella & Greene, 1982; Patterson, 1976) in an attempt to accommodate both compensation and reciprocation. These theories argue that the tendency to exchange the same behavior (i.e., to reciprocate) or to offset the other's behavior (i.e., to compensate) is a result of the type and amount of arousal that is felt and desired. A general rule suggests that one tends to reciprocate or match another's nonverbal behavior when the other's behavior is perceived as congruent with one's own expectations and preferences, or when one wants to initiate an upward or downward spiral in intimacy. When the partner's behavior is not congruent with one's expectations and preferences, there will likely be compensatory or offsetting behavior (see also Chapter 12).

When the relationship between the two communicators is characterized by negative attitudes, we might see a decrease in gazing and mutual gazing but not always. This is because gaze, like touch, can sometimes serve more to intensify or highlight whatever feeling or intention is present at the moment than to communicate a specific message. In addition, gaze does not occur in isolation from other cues—a threatening stare and a loving look may both be long, but the rest of the face is likely to be doing quite different things.

To illustrate one of the preceding points, satisfied married couples in one study tended to look at each other *less* than couples who were dissatisfied with their relationship, with this being particularly true when negative messages were exchanged (Noller, 1980). Increased gazing served to emphasize the confrontational nature of the relationship while simultaneously providing a way to monitor the other's reactions during critical moments. This is a good example of how the immediate context can never be ignored when interpreting the meaning of nonverbal behavior.

A hostile or aggressive orientation may also trigger the use of staring to produce anxiety in others. A gaze of longer than 10 seconds is likely to induce irritation, if not outright discomfort, in many situations. In one study, drivers sped away more quickly from an intersection when stared at by a pedestrian (Ellsworth, Carlsmith, & Henson, 1972). Several studies confirm that mutual gaze is physiologically arousing. Hostility toward another can be expressed by visually and verbally ignoring the other person, especially when the other person knows one is deliberately doing so. But insult can also be conveyed by looking at that person too much, that is, by not providing the public anonymity that they expect. Sometimes, you can elicit aggressive behavior from others just because you happen to look too long at their behavior. Threats and aggressive action can be elicited in zoo monkeys by human beings who stare at them too long.

Thus, if we are looking for a unifying thread to link gazing patterns motivated by positive and negative feelings toward the other, it would seem to be this: People tend to look at those with whom they are interpersonally involved. Gazing motivated by hostility or affection *both* suggest an interest and involvement in the interpersonal relationship. Contextual information, and other verbal and nonverbal cues, are needed to decide whether to interpret extended gazing positively or negatively. One such contextual cue may be the type of smiling associated with the gaze; Canadas and Schmid Mast (2017) found that people showed a preference for objects/people that were looked at by faces displaying a more genuine-looking smile (with crow's feet around the eyes).

CONDITIONS INFLUENCING GAZING PATTERNS

DISTANCE

As suggested by intimacy equilibrium theory, gazing and mutual gazing often increase as the physical distance between two people grows. In this case, gazing psychologically reduces the distance between communicators and allows for better monitoring. On the other hand, there may be less visual contact when the two parties feel too close in terms of physical distance, especially if they are not well acquainted. Reducing one's gaze in this situation, then, increases the psychological distance. Several studies by Aiello (1972, 1977) found that extending the conversational distances to as much as 10 feet produced a steady increase in gazing for men, but for women, being more than 6 feet from their interactant brought a sharp decline in their gazing. It is probable that because women prefer closer interaction distances (see Chapter 5), they may find it difficult to define interactions at relatively great distances as normal and friendly, and they may react by ceasing their attempts to maintain involvement.

GROUP AND PHYSICAL CHARACTERISTICS

Who we are viewing is likely to impact our gazing behavior. Consider a group of people who appear mostly happy, mostly angry (the other expressions are neutral in each case), or happy or angry. Interestingly, people appear to gaze longer at the happy faces than the angry faces, and they are better able to tell when the crowd is mostly happy versus mostly angry (Bucher & Voss, 2019).

One might think that when interacting with a person who is disabled or stigmatized in some way, gaze would be less frequent. The evidence for this is mixed, though, and may hinge on the nature of the disability or situational demands present during the interaction. Bowers, Crawcour, Saltuklaroglu, and Kalinowski (2010) noted that college-aged participants were more likely to look away from a speaker's eyes when he was stuttering as opposed to speaking fluently. Kleck (1968), on the other hand, found that the amount of gazing between nondisabled and disabled interactants did not differ significantly from interactions between those considered nondisabled. Possible explanations are that in such situations, the nondisabled person is seeking information that might suggest the proper mode of behavior, or the disabled person is a novel stimulus that arouses curiosity. These factors would counteract any tendency to avoid looking. A subsequent study, however, found that when a strong possibility arose that a nondisabled person would have to engage a disabled person in conversation, gaze avoidance increased. When conversation was not expected, people without disabilities tended to stare more at people with disabilities than those without (Thompson, 1982).

PERSONAL CHARACTERISTICS AND PERSONALITY

There are definitely stereotypes about gaze and personality. Kleck and Nuessle (1968) showed observers a film of people looking at their partners either 15% or 80% of the time, and the observers were asked to select characteristics that typified the interactants. Those who looked at their partner only 15% of the time were labeled as cold, pessimistic, cautious, defensive, immature, evasive, submissive, indifferent, and sensitive; those who looked 80% of the time were seen as friendly, self-confident, natural, mature, and sincere. Napieralski, Brooks, and Droney (1995) presented viewers with 1-minute videotaped interactions in which the target person gazed for 5, 30, or 50 seconds at an interviewer. The less a person gazed, the more state and trait anxiety were attributed to that person by viewers.

During actual interactions, of course, gaze patterns are influenced by situational factors and the mood, state of mind, and intentions of the gazer. As one example, lonelier people gaze more at the faces of people they do not know during face-to-face interactions (Lodder, Scholte, Goossens, Engels, & Verhagen, 2016). Nevertheless, some patterns have emerged in the relations between gazing patterns and personality traits. Dependent individuals seem to use eye behavior not only to communicate more positive attitudes but also to elicit such attitudes when they are not forthcoming from others (Exline & Messick, 1967). Dependent males directed more gaze toward a listener who provided them with few, as opposed to many, social reinforcers, whereas dominant males decreased their eye gaze with listeners who reinforced less.

Kalma (1993) distinguished between two personality styles relating to dominance: *sociable dominance* and *aggressive dominance*. The sociably dominant person agrees strongly with statements such as "I have no problem talking in front of a group" and "No doubt I'll make a good leader." The aggressively dominant person agrees strongly with statements such as "I quickly feel aggressive with people" and "I find it important to get my way." In an experimental setting, Kalma observed people who varied on these dominance styles and found that the sociably dominant person engaged in more mutual gaze, whereas the aggressively dominant person engaged in more looking around; that is, they showed lack of interest in others.

A particular kind of social dominance is sexual harassment. Male college students' proclivity to sexually harass women was measured using a questionnaire that asked how likely they would be to exploit a woman under varying hypothetical circumstances, such as rewarding her for sexual favors. Videotapes that were surreptitiously made of the same men interacting at a later time with a subordinate female revealed that, among other behaviors, the men more likely to harass engaged in more direct eye contact with the woman (Murphy, Driscoll, & Kelly, 1999).

Self-esteem and self-confidence are associated with gazing patterns. A study of attributions found that interviewees were rated by observers as having increasingly lower self-esteem as their gazing decreased (Droney & Brooks, 1993). Variations in gazing at another person during positive and negative feedback may be related to self-esteem. When receiving favorable feedback on their performance, people with high self-esteem tended to gaze more, and negative feedback reduced their gazing behavior. But the pattern was reversed for those with low self-esteem. These people gazed more during feedback that criticized their performance than during feedback that complimented it (Greene & Frandsen, 1979).

Intelligence is also a trait people display during social interactions. Evidence shows that people who score higher on standard tests of cognitive ability, such as an IQ test, engage in more interpersonal gaze and responsiveness, and that perceivers who watch these people on videotape can use these cues to accurately judge their intelligence levels (Murphy, Hall, & Colvin, 2003).

Other personality traits—as measured by the self-report of the gazers—have been associated with more gazing. Such traits include extraversion, agreeableness, and openness (Berry & Hansen, 2000; Mobbs, 1968), although some studies do not find correlations between gaze and personality (Dabbs, Evans, Hopper, & Purvis, 1980; Gifford, 1994; Harrison, Binetti, Coutrot, Johnston, & Mareschal, 2018). For example, Gifford (1994) failed to find associations between interpersonal gazing and trait measures of ambitiousness, gregariousness, warmth, unassumingness, laziness, aloofness, coldness, and arrogance.

Shyness is related to gazing behavior, but this correlation can depend on whether the shy person is of a sociable or unsociable type. In a laboratory experiment, Cheek and Buss (1981) classified college students on both a shyness scale and a sociability scale and then observed them in a get-acquainted session. Although shy individuals engaged in less gazing overall, and in more self-touching and less talking, this effect was mainly present if the person was both shy (e.g., "I am socially somewhat awkward"; "I feel inhibited in social situations") *and* sociable (e.g., "I like to be with people"; "I prefer working with others rather than alone"). Thus, the behavioral deficits associated with shyness appear mainly in shy people who crave social interaction; shy people who would just as soon be left alone had gaze patterns much like people who were not shy.

Social anxiety, another related concept, is also associated with less gazing. In one study, women who were high in social anxiety avoided eye contact with male avatars that were staring at them from a distance in a virtual reality experimental setup (Wieser, Pauli, Grosseibl, Molzow, & Mühlberger, 2010). In another study, in which socially anxious people were asked to present a viewpoint to two confederates, the socially anxious ones were especially likely to reduce gaze toward a confederate with opposing views compared to one with agreeing views (Farabee, Holcom, Ramsey, & Cole, 1993). In an experiment in which participants had choices of which face to look at on a computer screen, Mansell, Clark, Ehlers, and Chen (1999) found that socially anxious people whose anxiety was heightened by being told they would be giving a public talk avoided faces that showed emotional expressions, preferring to give their visual attention to neutral-expression faces. Under such circumstances, the socially anxious person may have an especially strong need to avoid the arousal engendered by emotional faces, which, in turn, may be related to a history of finding emotionally charged social interactions to be aversive. Highly anxious individuals also avert their eyes sooner from an extended facial display of anger compared to less anxious individuals (Rohner, 2002). Of importance, not all studies have found greater gaze avoidance among socially anxious individuals (Wieser & Pauli, 2009). When negative facial expressions are very intense, more trait-anxious individuals actually look at them more (Mogg, Garner, &Bradley, 2007).

As we mentioned earlier, *gaze cuing* refers to the automatic tendency to look in the direction of someone else's gaze. This effect is especially pronounced when the target person's face looks fearful. When viewers saw a fearful face with eyes averted, as though the target person was looking at something frightening in the environment, their own gaze shifted in that direction more than was the case when the averted eyes were shown on a happy face (Putnam, Hermans, & van Honk, 2006). Furthermore, this effect is especially notable for viewers who are high on trait anxiety: Highly anxious individuals are especially quick to use gaze direction as a cue when the gazer has a fearful facial expression, suggesting that anxiety makes a person especially visually attuned and responsive to evidence of threat in their environment (Fox, Mathews, Calder, & Yiend, 2007; Mathews, Fox, Yiend, & Calder, 2003; Putnam et al., 2006).

Finally, there are gender differences related to gaze avoidance and the use of gaze. Larsen and Shackelford (1996) found that gaze-avoidant females (but not males) were viewed negatively in terms of their social characteristics (e.g., disagreeable, unattractive). As shown in many studies, females look at others during interaction more than males do, and such differences have been observed in infancy and early childhood as well as in adulthood (Hall, 1984; Leeb & Rejskind, 2004). In addition, women are gazed at more than men are by others in an interaction. (Gender differences are discussed further in Chapter 12.)

PSYCHOPATHOLOGY

A number of research studies find special gazing patterns, usually less gaze, in some psychopathological conditions. While giving a speech, individuals diagnosed with a clinical anxiety disorder are more likely than those without the disorder to avoid looking at audience members' emotional gestures (Chen, Clarke, MacLeod, Hickie, & Guastella, 2016). Individuals with bipolar manic disorder showed more gaze avoidance than controls in a virtual reality–based social interaction (Kim et al., 2009). Depressed patients are characterized by nonspecific gaze patterns and looking-down behaviors that revert to more normal patterns with clinical improvement (Schelde & Hertz, 1994). Mothers with depressive symptoms spend less time gazing at their infants, and their infants respond by averting gaze more than control infants (Field, 1995). Nonetheless, infants of depressed mothers react in a similar fashion to the still-face paradigm (i.e., the mom looks at her child but does not respond facially to them) in terms of their gazing behavior (it is reduced; Graham, Blissett, Antoniou, Zeegers, & McCleery, 2018). Finally, paranoid schizophrenic patients show a deficit in judging the gaze direction of others, which is consistent with everyday conceptions of paranoia: Paranoid individuals are more likely than comparison subjects to perceive another as looking at them, when the person is actually looking away (Rosse, Kendrick, Wyatt, Isaac, & Deutsch, 1994).

The term *autism spectrum disorder* (ASD) is used to represent the nature of autistic symptoms ranging from severe (childhood disintegrative disorder) to mild (Asperger's syndrome), with *classic autism* being somewhere in between the two extremes. Of importance, deficits in either attention to or the processing of social information, such as eye and facial cues, may be present in each case but not necessarily to the same extent.

Clinicians and researchers cite gaze aversion, among other social interaction deficits, as a characteristic of their autistic patients (Adrien et al., 1993; Hutt & Ounsted, 1966; Walters, Barrett, & Feinstein, 1990). Autistic individuals also may have more difficulties detecting the direction of another's gaze (Senju, Yaguchi, Tojo, & Hasegawa, 2003), monitoring a speaker's gaze direction, and directing someone else's gaze via the pointing gesture (Baron-Cohen et al., 1997).

Baron-Cohen, Wheelwright, Hill, Raste, and Plumb (2001) reported that individuals with autism or Asperger's syndrome were less accurate overall than normally functioning participants in judging emotions from the eye region of the face. And Baron-Cohen et al. (1997) also found that the patients were especially impaired for nonbasic—that is, more complex—expressions, and when the eye region alone was being judged as opposed to the full face. (See Figure 10-2 for some of the eye expressions used in this study.) Gaze measurement confirmed that individuals with autism fail to use information from the eye region when making emotion judgments (Spezio, Adolphs, Hurley, & Piven, 2007), a deficit that directly impacts their ability to distinguish genuine from posed smiles, for which attention to the eye region is necessary (Boraston, Corden, Miles, Skuse, & Blakemore, 2008).

One theory to account for these deficits holds that individuals with autism find direct gaze to be overwhelmingly arousing, and they avoid it for that reason. This may also contribute to their poorer face-recognition abilities, because our attention to the eye region of others is important to our subsequent ability to recognize their faces (Royer et al., 2018; Tanaka & Sung, 2016). Indeed, Kliemann, Dziobek, Hatri, Steimke, and Heekeren (2010) found that children diagnosed with ASD were more likely than control children to move their eyes away from the eyes of facial stimuli. Using an experimental method that varied the direction of a poser's gaze (looking at or away from the camera), while zooming the image in larger to suggest an approaching person, Kylliäinen and Hietanen (2006) found that autistic children's skin conductance (a measure of physiological arousal) was greater in the direct gaze compared to averted gaze condition, but for control children, there was no difference.

There may be a breakdown in the autistic person's ability to synchronize an interaction by reciprocating another person's direct gaze. Chen and Yoon (2011) observed that individuals who reported more autism-associated traits did not show a greater tendency to look at eyes staring at them versus away from them, whereas those with fewer traits did.

Needless to say, social problems are likely to ensue as a consequence of autistic kids' deficits in using other people's facial cues, including more loneliness, poorer social skills, and more social problems than is the case with their typically developing peers (e.g., Deckers, Muris, & Roelofs, 2017). Efforts are underway to improve the socioemotional skills of children who suffer from ASD, such as using computer programs designed to help them attend to and use facial cues (Chen, Lee, & Lin, 2016; Hopkins et al., 2011). FaceSay is a computer program that allows these children to practice attending to eye gaze and recognizing faces and emotions with avatar assistants, with some positive results being reported (Hopkins et al., 2011).

FACESAY™

© nasharaga/Shutterstock.com

Children who suffer from autism have interpersonal difficulties related to understanding other people's emotion states. Understanding others' emotion states depends, in part, on attending to their facial cues. Children with autism show deficits in following the eye gaze of others and appear not to use information in the eye region of people's faces adequately when making emotion judgments.

Symbionica, LLC created FaceSay, which is an interactive computer game designed to help children with autism develop skill in recognizing facial expressions of emotion. These children play games that have them follow the eye gaze of an avatar, focus on the eye region of an avatar, and decide whether faces are showing the same expression.

To illustrate, in one game, a child views the head and face of a female avatar that is encircled by various objects, including a sun, leaf, and eye mask (a mask that goes over the eye region with holes in it for the eyes). She says, "These do look fun" as she scans the objects around her head. She then says, "Can you please click on the one I'm looking at?" while she is looking at the eye mask, which is to her right. During a pause in speaking, she looks forward at the child and then right back to the eye mask.

The child needs to click on the object that the avatar was looking at. If they select the right one—in this case, the eye mask—the avatar says, "Thank you, that's just what I wanted." During this time, the eye mask appears on the avatar's face, which is looking at the child again, and the child earns a point for the correct answer.

This game helps children with ASD focus on the eyes and gaze pattern of the avatar. Getting comfortable doing so, as well as gaining experience using social information from the eyes, are social skills that can help these children interact more successfully with their peers at school.

Another promising, and likely related, new avenue of insight involves the role of the neuropeptide oxytocin in the ability of humans, both those with and without psychopathology, to develop social attachments and to be sensitive and responsive socially. Especially relevant to the present chapter is the study of Guastella, Mitchell, and Dadds (2007), who found that experimental administration of oxytocin to male college students via nasal inhalation caused them to give added attention to the eye region of faces shown to them in photographs. The authors suggested that oxytocin administration might have therapeutic benefits for groups such as those with schizophrenia and autism, who have chronic difficulties in social communication. This possibility found empirical support in a study by Andari and colleagues (2010), who noted that individuals with autism spent more time gazing at the eyes of pictured faces after they had inhaled oxytocin. Future therapies will likely involve a combination of interventions and will need to be tailored to meet the specific deficits associated with the various ASDs.

TOPICS AND TASKS

Common sense suggests that the topic being discussed and the task at hand affect the amount of gazing. We would expect, for instance, more gazing when the topic is happy rather than sad or interesting as opposed to not. For example, one study found that typically developing children as well as children diagnosed with high-functioning autism exhibited more looking at an adult face when talking about a topic of interest to them (Nadig, Lee, Singh, Bosshart, & Ozonoff, 2010). We would expect interactants who have not developed an intimate relationship with each other to gaze less when discussing intimate topics, assuming other factors, such as the need for affiliation or inclusion, are controlled. People also may gaze differently during competitive tasks and cooperative tasks. In one study, cooperators used longer gazes and mutual gazes to signal trust, liking, and honesty. Gazes also were used to aid coordination. Competitors, however, seemed to use frequent, short gazes to assess their partner's intentions while not giving away their own (Foddy, 1978).

Discussing topics that cause embarrassment, humiliation, shame, or guilt might be expected to engender less gazing at the other person. Looking away during such situations may be an effort to insulate oneself against threats, arguments, information, or even affection from the other party. When subjects were caused to fail at an anagram task and were publicly criticized for their work, not only did they report feeling embarrassed, but the amount of gaze from them slipped from 30% to 18% (Modigliani, 1971). When people want to hide some aspect of their inner feelings, they may try to avoid visual contact—for example, in situations where they are trying to deceive a partner. The extent to which this occurs may vary with age and personality characteristics. Young children, for example, may be more likely than adults to break eye contact when lying than when telling the truth (McCarthy & Lee, 2009). Exline, Thibaut, Hickey, and Gumpert (1970) designed a fascinating, although possibly ethically unsound, experiment. A paid confederate induced research participants to cheat on an experimental task. Later, the experimenter interviewed the participants with the supposed purpose of understanding and evaluating their problem-solving methods. With some participants, the experimenter grew increasingly suspicious during the interview and finally accused the participant of cheating and demanded an explanation. Participants included both those who scored high and low on tests of Machiavellianism, a characteristic of a person who uses cunning and shrewdness to achieve a goal without much regard for how unscrupulous the means might be. Figure 10-3 shows that high Machiavellian participants used gazing to present the appearance of innocence after being accused of cheating; low Machiavellian participants, in contrast, continued to look away.

In the study by Bensing and colleagues mentioned earlier, physicians' average levels of gaze at patients were much greater when the patients were talking about social and emotional topics than when talking about more physiological problems, and levels were also high when the physicians were verbally conveying empathy or psychosocial interest. Patients were also more satisfied with their visits when the physicians gazed more.

Persuasion is another common communicative task. We know that gazing can add emphasis to a particular point, and along the same lines, Mehrabian and Williams (1969) found that a person trying to be persuasive gazes more overall. And research shows that listeners judge speakers who gaze more as more persuasive, informed, truthful, sincere, and credible, and even pictured faces appear more trustworthy when the eyes are showing a direct versus an averted gaze (Wyland & Forgas, 2010).

The application of such findings in a simulated courtroom situation found that witnesses who testified while looking slightly downward, rather than directly at their questioner, were judged less credible—and the defendant for

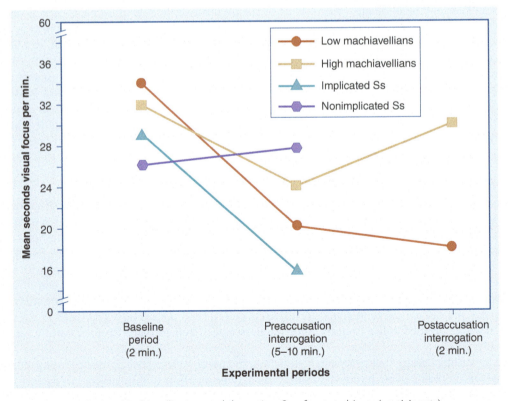

FIGURE 10-3 Gazing, Machiavellianism, and deception. Ss refers to subjects (participants)

whom they were testifying was more likely to be judged guilty (Hemsley & Doob, 1978). In another important study, actors reenacted the actual verbal answers given by surgery students during medical school oral examinations, using a nonverbal style marked either by direct gaze and a moderate speech rate or by indirect gaze and a slower speech rate. Surgery faculty from 46 medical institutions who judged the competency of these reenacted oral examinations gave significantly higher scores to the actor who used direct gaze and a moderate rate of speech, even though the answers were the same as in the other condition (Rowland-Morin, Burchard, Garb, & Coe, 1991). It is clear from these studies that in real-life situations, the presence or absence of gaze can have a profound impact, yet the impact can be highly unfair or damaging. You would not want to be the honest witness, the sincere speaker, or the competent medical student who had the misfortune to gaze less than expected.

CULTURAL AND RACIAL BACKGROUND AND RACIAL ATTITUDES

Eye behavior also varies according to the environment in which social norms are learned. Sometimes gazing patterns show differences between "contact" cultures, such as Arab cultures, and "noncontact" cultures, such as northern European cultures (see Chapters 5, 8, and 13). Sometimes cultural rules dictate whom you should or should not look at. One report says that in Kenya, conversations between some men and their mothers-in-law are conducted by each party turning their back to the other.

We may find different racial patterns within our own culture. White people are found to gaze significantly more at their partners than Black people do, and this difference may be especially pronounced with authority figures—a tendency that could create cross-racial misunderstanding. The gaze patterns of Blacks and Whites during cross-racial interactions may be changing, but the research on this is not consistent (Fehr & Exline, 1987; Halberstadt, 1985). Interestingly, when a face is gazing at you as opposed to away from you, you are likely to have better memory for it when it is of the same race rather than a different race than your own (Adams, Pauker, & Weisbuch, 2010). In addition, how a fearful face is processed may vary as a function of the gaze and racial match of the person being viewed. For instance, Adams and colleagues had Japanese and U.S. White participants view fearful Japanese versus U.S. White faces; greater responsiveness (namely, neural activity) was observed when the faces were of the same race as the viewer and looking away, whereas direct gaze from opposite-race faces elicited greater neural reactions. Such findings underscore the variety of factors that may influence and be affected by gaze in each encounter.

Of course, one's cultural inclinations may be suppressed, neutralized, or emphasized by other forces attendant to the situation. And, although cultural experiences may alter gazing patterns and the total amount of gaze, perceived extremes in gaze may elicit similar meanings in different cultures. For instance, too much gazing may signal anger, threat, or disrespect; too little may signal dishonesty, inattention, or shyness.

Because people often enact nonverbal behavior without conscious awareness, psychologists have suggested that nonverbal cues may sometimes be subtle indicators of social attitudes, especially those that may be denied or not consciously acknowledged, such as negative feelings toward members of minority groups (Crosby, Bromley, & Saxe, 1980; Word, Zanna, & Cooper, 1974). Dovidio, Kawakami, Johnson, Johnson, and Howard (1997) predicted that the amount of gaze directed by interviewees toward Black versus White interviewers would be related to the interviewees' implicit racial attitudes. As predicted, interviewees who had displayed more implicit racial bias gazed less at the Black than the White interviewer and also blinked more, suggesting greater negative arousal and tension. However, these nonverbal cues were not related to explicit, and more reactive, paper-and-pencil reports of prejudice by the interviewees.

PUPIL DILATION AND CONSTRICTION

Researchers currently utilize video-based eye-tracking tools that measure where people are looking, how long they are looking at something, and how their pupils respond to what they are looking at and doing, cognitively speaking (Wang, 2011). Of interest here is how people's pupils, which, as you know, can dilate and constrict, might signal their interest level, attitudes, memory, decision-making processes, as well as various disorders. We will first review the groundbreaking but somewhat controversial early work in this area before turning to current research trends.

You might think that the pupils of the eyes respond only to the presence of bright light (by constricting) and the absence of light (by dilating). In the early 1960s, however, Eckhard Hess and colleagues ushered in a new way of thinking about pupil dilation and constriction by suggesting that these were possible indicators of interest. In an early experiment, Hess and Polt (1960) presented five pictures to male and female participants. Males' pupils dilated more than females' pupils in response to pictures of female nudes; and females' pupils dilated more than males' to pictures of a partially clothed "muscle man," a woman with a baby, and a baby alone. Thus, it seemed pupil dilation and interest in the stimulus were related. In a follow-up study, Hess, Seltzer, and Shlien (1965) found that the pupils of homosexual males dilated more when viewing pictures of males than did the pupils of heterosexual males, whose pupils dilated in response to female pictures.

This research suggests that pupil size may reflect psychological processes, not just ambient light levels. The pupils seem to register a person's *interest* in the stimulus. Indeed, this is true, but the research on sexual interest is somewhat mixed. Of course, what is sexually interesting or arousing depends on the sexual orientation of the person. Rieger and Savin-Williams (2012) demonstrated that individuals' pupils do, in fact, dilate to erotic videos depicting the type of people they are attracted to in life. For example, bisexual men, who are attracted to both men and women, showed pupil dilation to videos depicting men or women. Interestingly, however, heterosexual females showed this same pattern as well. Lesbians, on the other hand, responded more like heterosexual men in that they both showed more pupil dilation to women than men (e.g., Rieger, Savin-Williams, Chivers, & Bailey, 2016). Finally, Snowden, McKinnon, Fitoussi, and Gray (2019) found that both heterosexual men and women showed more pupil dilation to images of nude *males* than females. These conflicting findings point to the need for additional research on this topic.

Other research suggested that pupil changes could reflect attitudes, not just interest. Barlow (1969) selected participants who actively supported either liberal or conservative candidates. He photographed the pupil of their right eye while they watched slides of political figures and found what seemed to be a perfect correlation between pupillary response and political attitudes: Dilation occurred for photographs of liked candidates and constriction occurred for photographs of disliked candidates.

Several of Hess's studies suggested that pupil response might be a *bidirectional* index of attitudes, such that pupils dilate for positive attitudes and constrict for negative ones. His oft-cited finding in support of this theory was the constriction of the pupils of subjects who viewed pictures of concentration camp victims, dead soldiers, and a murdered gangster. In Hess's (1975a) words, "The changes in emotions and mental activity revealed by changes in pupil size are clearly associated with changes in attitude." Hess continued to advocate this position, although he acknowledged the need for more research on the pupil's reaction to negative stimuli (Hess, 1975b; Hess & Petrovich, 1987).

Woodmansee (1970) tried to improve on Hess's methodology and measuring instruments and found no support for pupil dilation and constriction as an index of attitudes toward African Americans. Hays and Plax (1971) found that their subjects' pupils dilated when they received supportive statements, such as "I am very much interested in your speech," but constriction did not follow nonsupportive statements, such as "I disagree completely with the development of your speech." Some research has found pupil dilation in response to both positive *and* negative feedback (Janisse & Peavler, 1974; Partala & Surakka, 2003). Other research has found dilation to be associated with arousal, attentiveness, interest, and perceptual orientation as opposed to a reliable index of a person's attitudes. Thus, the intriguing hypothesis that pupil size can be a bidirectional indicator of attitudes appears not to be viable.

Pupil-size research is difficult to do in part because many stimuli can cause variations in pupil size. Tightening muscles anywhere on the body, anticipation of a loud noise, drugs, eyelid closure, and mental effort all alter pupil size. People also have varying absolute pupil sizes. Children, for instance, have larger absolute pupil sizes than adults. Future research needs to untangle the relative contributions of attitudinal processes and these nonattitudinal factors to instances of pupil dialation in people.

The relations between pupil size and cognitive ability and cognitive processes (e.g., deception, interpreting others' intentions) have been explored as well (Kim, Lee, Kim, & Lee, 2019; Quesque, Behrens, & Kret, 2019; Tsukahara, Harrison, & Engle, 2016). Although controversial, a person's baseline pupil size has been shown to be positively related to their fluid intelligence (Tsukahara et al., 2016). In terms of recognition memory, people's pupils dilate more when they are viewing items that they have seen before (versus unfamiliar items), and also pupil dilation might reflect the strength of a person's memory for an item (Otero, Weekes, & Hutton, 2011). It appears that this old-versus-new effect is not something one can consciously control. Heaver and Hutton (2011) found that participants' pupils dilated more to old items than new items even when they were instructed to "feign amnesia" or report "all items as new." This suggests that measures of pupil dilation might be a means of determining whether a person is pretending to have forgotten things that they really have not or whether they are possibly not consciously aware of something recognizable to them at a nonconscious level.

"I RECOGNIZE THAT MELODY"

© Knapp, Hall, & Horgan

Weiss, Trehub, Schellenberg, and Habashi (2016) have shown that people's pupils dilate more to melodies they have heard before compared to ones they have not. Pupil dilation may thus index recognition memory for melodies.

Eye pupils also might signal when one has reached a decision or how one is processing information about others (Einhäuser, Koch, & Carter, 2010; Goldinger, He, & Papesh, 2009). Goldinger and colleagues had White and Asian participants study faces from each other's race as well as their own. They noted that participants made longer but fewer visual fixations, attended to a different set of facial features, and had more dilated pupils when looking at faces from the other race. These findings point to possible differences in effort needed to initially process faces from another race.

Pupil-dilation research has been directed at understanding social phobias (Cheval et al., 2016) as well as developmental (Martineau et al., 2011), clinical (Steidtmann, Ingram, & Siegle, 2010), and personality disorders (Burley, Gray, & Snowden, 2019). Cheval and colleagues (2016) suggested that, relative to men low in homophobia, those high in homophobia may be less interested in sexual stimuli in general, given that their pupils do not increase as much when exposed to such material. With respect to clinical disorders, there is some evidence that the pupils of those who suffer from autism or depression react differently to various stimuli relative to control participants without those the disorders. Martineau and colleagues (2011) noted that the average pupil size of children with ASD was smaller than that of control children while viewing slides of neutral faces, avatar faces, and objects, and Steidtmann et al. found that people with a history of depression showed greater overall pupil dilation to negatively toned words than did their nondepressed counterparts. Such findings point to the possible diagnostic value of eye-tracking methodologies as well as to how pupillary responses might offer clues to neurologically linked information-processing differences among those with and without various social phobias or clinical conditions.

Another approach to studying pupil size is to investigate its impact on a viewer. Hess (1975a) cited a study that showed photographs, like those in Figure 10-4, where a woman's pupils were retouched to appear large in one photo and smaller in the other. Although male subjects did not tend to pick either picture as consistently more friendly or attractive, they tended to associate positive attributes with the woman who had larger pupils and negative attributes with the one with smaller pupils. Hensley (1990) attempted to replicate Hess's work and obtained the responses of over 500 students to the photographs of models with constricted and dilated pupils used by Hess. The students evaluated the photos on 22 characteristics, including attractiveness, social skills, persuasiveness, friendliness, and outgoingness. No statistically significant differences were found between responses to photos of models with constricted pupils and those with dilated pupils on any of the 22 characteristics, raising doubts about Hess's claim.

However, several studies have shown that observers are sensitive to pupils of different sizes, and the impact is especially pronounced in the context of a sad facial expression. In a study that varied three levels of pupil size, observers saw more intensity and more negativity when a sad face had smaller pupils (Harrison, Wilson, & Critchley, 2007). Seeing smaller pupils might also make people want to help more (Küster, 2018).

One study suggested that pupil dilation may be influential when working with others or when selecting interaction partners or even dates. Kret and De Dreu (2019) found that participants tended to trust game partners more when those partners had dilating versus constricting pupils. In Stass and Willis's (1967) study, participants had to choose which of two confederates seemed the most trustworthy, pleasant, and easy to talk to on an intimate basis. The confederates varied (on purpose) in their gazing and pupil dilation, which was achieved through use of a drug. Gazing was an

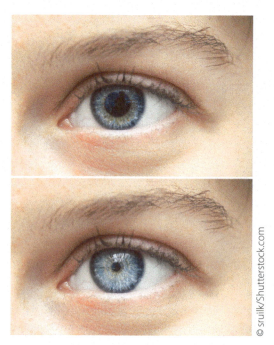

FIGURE 10-4 Stimulus photographs with pupils small and large.

overwhelming factor in which confederate the participants chose, but pupil dilation also was a factor. Thus, for both women and men, pupil dilation seemed to be an influential attraction device. Perhaps this would be no revelation to those women who, in the Middle Ages, put drops of the drug belladonna into their eyes to enlarge their pupils, or to those expert romancers who suggest a dimly lighted meeting place.

SUMMARY

Although researchers have examined the size, color, and position of the eyes, eye rings, eyebrows, and eyespots in humans and other animals, our major concern in this chapter was with people's gaze and mutual gaze. We said that gazing served many interpersonal functions:

1. Regulating the flow of communication, both to open the channels of communication and to assist in the turn-taking process.
2. Monitoring feedback.
3. Expressing emotion.
4. Communicating the nature of the interpersonal relationship, for example, to show variations due to status, liking, and disliking.

We also outlined a number of factors that influence the amount and duration of gaze in human relationships; for example, distance, physical characteristics, personal and personality characteristics, topics and tasks, and cultural background. From this review, we would predict *more* gazing in the following situations:

- You are discussing easy, impersonal topics.
- You are interested in your partner's reactions and are interpersonally involved.
- You like or love your partner.
- You are from a culture that emphasizes visual contact in interaction.
- You are an extravert and not shy.

- You have high affiliative or inclusion needs.
- You are dependent on your partner, and the partner has been unresponsive.
- You are listening rather than talking.
- You are female.
- You do not have a mental disorder such as depression, autism, or schizophrenia.
- You are not embarrassed, ashamed, sorrowful, sad, or trying to hide something.

The preceding list is not exhaustive. Indeed, some of the findings depend on certain important qualifications. For example, you may have less gaze and less mutual gaze when you are physically close—unless you happen to love your partner and want to get as close physically and psychologically as you can. This list is not intended to replace the qualified principles that appear in the chapter.

The last part of this chapter dealt with pupil dilation and constriction. We reviewed the findings of Eckhard Hess and others who have pursued his ideas. At this time, pupil dilation has been associated with arousal, attentiveness, mental effort, interest, and perceptual orientation. Aside from Hess's own work, however, mixed support has been found for the idea that pupils reflect attitudinal states. Dilation occurs under conditions that seem to represent positive attitudes, but not much support exists for the belief that constriction of pupils is associated with negative attitudes.

QUESTIONS FOR DISCUSSION

1. How do you use gaze in your everyday life? When are you more likely to gaze at someone for a long period of time? When are you more likely to gaze for a very short period of time?

2. Try to recall a time when you had a conversation with someone with a physical disability, someone on crutches or in a wheelchair, for example. Did your gazing patterns change when interacting with this person as opposed to interacting with an able-bodied person? How did your gazing patterns change?

3. As an experiment, try looking continuously at the eye region of a person you are conversing with. Is this difficult? Did the person react to this in any way—for example, by reducing gaze, moving back, or commenting?

4. People of higher status are sometimes said to gaze more and for longer periods than people of lower status. What do you think of this? Think of examples that would and would not be supportive of this theory.

5. Go to a bus or elevator that is crowded and observe how you, as well as the other people, use gaze in such a circumstance. How much, when, where, and at whom do people gaze?

NONVERBAL COMMUNICATION IN ACTION: TRY THIS

Watch yourself in a mirror, and try to convey the following emotions using only your eyes and eyebrows: fear, anger, disgust, surprise, happiness, and sadness. How do your eye positions and movements change? Now, take selfies of yourself making those expressions with your whole face BUT cover up the lower part of your face with a piece of paper so that only your eyes show. Then, show those photos to a friend and see if they can guess, just from seeing your eyes, which emotion you were showing.

Answers to Figure 10-2: (a) happy, (b) afraid, (c) disgusted, (d) distressed

CHAPTER 11

THE EFFECTS OF VOCAL CUES THAT ACCOMPANY SPOKEN WORDS

I understand a fury in your words
But not the words.

—Shakespeare, Othello, Act IV

Ideally, this chapter would not be in written form. Instead, it would be a recording you could listen to. A recording would give you a greater appreciation of the vocal nuances that are the subject of this chapter or, as the cliché goes, *how* something is said rather than *what* is said. But the dichotomy set up by this cliché is misleading because *how* something is said is frequently *what* is said.

Some vocal cues are deliberately produced to communicate various meanings. Robert J. McCloskey, spokesperson for the State Department during the Nixon administration, reportedly exemplified such behavior:

> McCloskey has three distinct ways of saying, "I would not speculate": spoken without accent, it means the department doesn't know for sure; emphasis on the "I" means "I wouldn't, but you may—and with some assurance"; accent on "speculate" indicates that the questioner's premise is probably wrong. (*Newsweek*, 1970, p. 106 [see "Next Army Chief," 2003])

Most people do the same kind of thing when emphasizing a particular part of a message. *Prosody* is the word used to describe all the variations in the voice that help to convey words' meanings. Notice how different vocal emphases influence the interpretation of the following message:

1. *He's* giving this money to Herbie. (*He* is the one giving the money, nobody else.)
2. He's *giving* this money to Herbie. (He is *giving*, not lending, the money.)
3. He's giving *this* money to Herbie. (The money being exchanged is not from another fund or source; it is *this* money.)
4. He's giving this *money* to Herbie. (*Money* is the unit of exchange, not flowers or beads.)
5. He's giving this money to *Herbie*. (The recipient is *Herbie*, not Eric or Bill or Rod.)

Vocal pitch indicates the end of a declarative sentence (by lowering it) or a question (by raising it). Sometimes, tone is consciously manipulated to contradict the verbal message, as in sarcasm. For instance, you can say, "I'm having a wonderful time" so it means "I'm having a terrible time." If you are perceived as being sarcastic, the vocal cues probably superseded the verbal message.

THE RELATIVE IMPORTANCE OF CHANNELS

The assumption that vocal cues will predominate in forming attitudes based on contradictory vocal and verbal content prompted Mehrabian and colleagues to conduct research on the topic. In one study, listeners heard single words that had previously been rated as positive, neutral, or negative spoken in positive or negative vocal tones (Mehrabian & Wiener, 1967). This experiment led to the following conclusion:

> The variability of inferences about communicator attitude on the basis of information available in content and tone combined is mainly contributed by variations in tone alone. For example, when the attitude

communicated in content contradicted the attitude communicated by negative tone, the total message was judged as communicating negative attitude. (p. 109)

A similar study, pitting vocal cues against facial and verbal cues, found facial cues to be more influential (Mehrabian & Ferris, 1967). From these studies, Mehrabian devised the following formula, which illustrates the differential impact or weighting of verbal, vocal, and facial cues:

Perceived attitude of communicator = 0.07 *(verbal)* + 0.38 *(vocal)* + 0.55 *(facial)*

Obviously, the formula is limited by the design of Mehrabian's experiments. For instance, we do not know how the formula might change if some of the variables were manipulated more vigorously, or if more or different people did the judging. We do not know whether the formula would apply to verbal materials longer than one word. And we do not know whether these respondents were reacting to the inconsistency itself as a source of attitudinal information (see Lapakko, 1997, for a critique). The fact that respondents resolved inconsistencies by relying on nonverbal cues does not mean evaluative information is conveyed by nonverbal cues alone, or even mainly, in more realistic communication. In realistic settings, we would expect that the message(s) conveyed by vocal cues would align with that being communicated by facial cues and words more often than not.

The relative importance of vocal cues is likely to vary according to a number of factors, such as the nature of the message, age of the decoder, the nature of the decoding task, as well as various combinations of these three. Friedman (1979a, 1979b) found that for some kinds of messages, words mattered more than the facial expressions. Others have suggested that bodily action cues, such as facial expressions, posture, and hand gestures, send a stronger message of frustration during arguments than does the combination of verbal and nonverbal cues of frustration (e.g., pitch; Yu, 2011). Still others have shown that, although words alone, prosody alone, and the two combined can help people make decisions about whether a face is happy, sad, or grimacing, one method is not necessarily better than the others (Pell, Jaywant, Monetta, & Kotz, 2011).

The preference to base interpretations on words versus vocal cues changes with age: Young children rely much more on verbal content, older children show a mixed pattern, and adults rely much more on nonverbal tonal qualities (Bugental, Kaswan, & Love, 1970; Morton & Trehub, 2001). However, even within a particular age, some emotional messages might be recognized better than others in the vocal channel. For instance, preschoolers appear to recognize sadness in the voice alone better than the emotions of happiness, fear, and anger.

The nature of the decoding task also needs to be taken into consideration. Paulmann and Pell (2011) had participants make emotion judgments when only one cue was available (face shown on a computer, voice heard over headphones, or text on a computer screen), two cues (face and prosodic cues or prosodic cues with words) were available, or all three were available. In terms of identifying emotion states, having access to more emotionally congruent cues was more helpful than just having one. This research also showed that if only one cue was available, the visual cues from the face or text tended to be more informative than the prosodic cues. In another study, Paulmann, Titone, and Pell (2012) had participants select facial expressions that matched their task instructions ("click on the happy face"). They found that participants looked longer at facial expressions that matched their task instructions irrespective of whether the available prosodic cues matched or did not match the emotion on the face that they were told to identify. This suggests that semantic information may exert a more powerful influence than prosodic cues on such tasks.

When viewers were asked to guess the thoughts and feelings of people shown on videotape engaged in natural conversation, their accuracy was based far more on the words that were spoken than on the nonverbal cues of the speakers (Gesn & Ickes, 1999; Hall & Schmid Mast, 2007). Nonverbal cues did contribute to accuracy, though, especially when the viewers were asked to focus on the target person's feelings.

Sometimes, the emotion state of other people changes during an interaction. Chen, Clarke, MacLeod, Hickie, and Guastella (2016) found that changes in others' emotion states were more easily and accurately detected when both their facial and vocal cues were available to decoders opposed to either cue alone.

Nowadays, with text messaging and email, people rely a great deal on communication via words alone, and it is reasonable to ask what might be missed in such a medium. Kruger, Epley, Parker, and Ng (2005) found that when affective messages were conveyed through email, they were much less accurately decoded than when the same messages were conveyed in voice-to-voice and face-to-face conditions. Furthermore, adding facial cues did not improve accuracy beyond the voice-only condition. In this instance, vocal cues were crucial to fully conveying attitudinal intent.

Above and beyond issues of accuracy, prosodic cues in face-to-face interactions offer a means of emotional support that emails and text messages cannot provide. Seltzer, Prososki, Ziegler, and Pollak (2012) found that girls who did text messaging with their mothers after undergoing a stressful experience had cortisol levels—which is one marker of current stress level—similar to children who did not interact with a parent at all, whereas those who had either interacted with their mothers on the phone or in person (thus having access to prosodic cues from their mothers' voice) showed increases in oxytocin, which is thought to be linked to the experience of positive relationships with others. In short, vocal cues were important in helping these girls cope with the stress, whereas text messages were not. Because of this, it is likely that highly valued video-chat technologies, such as FaceTime, where individuals can hear and see each other over their cell phones, will become increasingly important to families, friends, and lovers.

The relative importance of the voice may hinge on the nature of the message being communicated and judgment task. Studies comparing impressions made by the voice to those made by the face have found the voice especially suited to conveying degrees of dominance or potency. Vocal clues to dominance include speed, tendency to interrupt, and loudness; the most obvious clue to pleasantness in the face is a smile. The face has a greater impact on judgments of pleasantness or positivity (Zuckerman, Amidon, Biship, & Pomerantz, 1982; Zuckerman & Driver, 1989).

In terms of tasks, if one wants to understand others' emotions, then paying attention to their voice might be especially important (Kraus, 2017). Paying attention to a person's voice might also be important to understanding the empathy that they are experiencing toward another person (Karthikeyan & Ramachandra, 2017).

Thus, even though the impact of the voice relative to other channels of communication may vary according to many factors, there is no doubt that vocal cues exert a great deal of influence on listener perceptions. Often these responses are based on stereotypes associated with various vocal qualities. Not surprisingly, the existence of such stereotypes means that some vocal qualities are preferred over others. Zuckerman and Driver (1989) documented that listeners generally agree on whether a voice is attractive, and also that people whose voices are considered more attractive are believed to have personality traits such as dominance, competence, industriousness, sensitivity, and warmth. Other stereotypes relating to the voice will be described later in this chapter.

THE INGREDIENTS AND METHODS OF STUDYING PARALANGUAGE

The physical mechanisms for producing nonverbal vocal qualities and sounds, also called *paralanguage*, are extremely complex (Juslin & Scherer, 2005). Figure 11-1 illustrates the many muscles and other structures involved in producing vocal sounds; these include the throat, nasal cavities, tongue, lips, mouth, and jaw. In this chapter, however, we focus on the impact of paralanguage rather than the mechanisms by which it is produced. Many techniques and methods have been developed for studying the role of vocal nonverbal cues in the communication process (Scherer, 2003). We provide just a short introduction here.

In one approach to studying nonverbal vocal communication, listeners are asked for their impressions or inferences about a voice sample, for example, how anxious or competent the voice sounds. Using this method, a researcher may gain insight into the social meanings of vocal cues because listeners' impressions are based on their store of experience, knowledge, and beliefs. However, a researcher learns little about what specific vocal cues created a given impression because listeners are interpreting the vocal cues as a totality to reach a final impression. Listeners may know an angry voice when they hear one, but may not be able to pinpoint the acoustic properties that made it sound angry. (Whether their impressions are correct is a separate issue from the question of how the impressions are formed.)

In contrast, sometimes researchers want, and need, to measure specific vocal characteristics, also called *acoustic properties*, and for this they use automated devices or trained coders. Voice researchers use automated measurement by computers much more than do researchers who study nonvocal modalities of communication, in part because the technology exists for doing so. Commonly measured acoustic properties include the following: *speech rate*, or words per unit of time; *fundamental frequency* (F_0), which is the vibration rate of the vocal folds in the throat and the main contributor, along with the harmonics and resonances thus produced, to the perception of pitch; and *intensity*, which

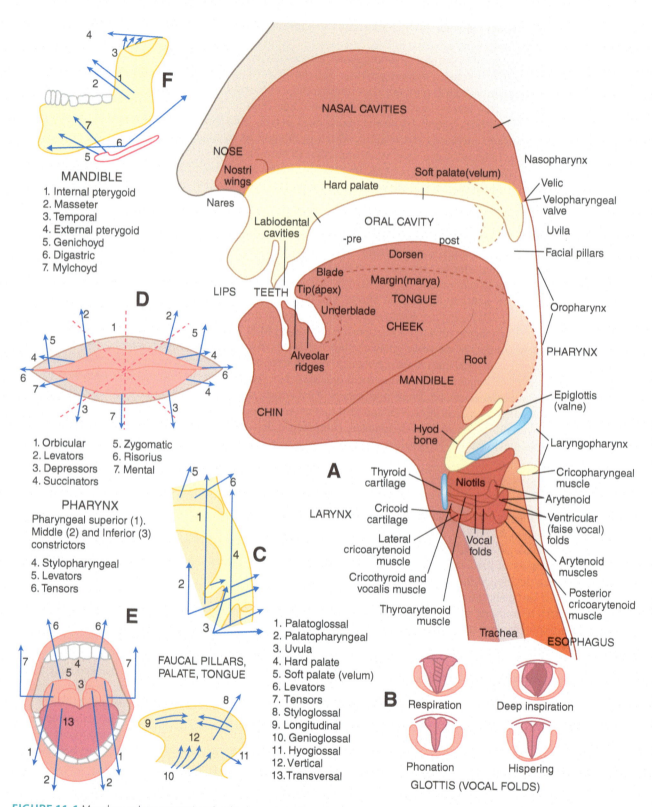

FIGURE 11-1 Muscles and structures involved in speech and paralanguage.
Source: From Poyatos, F. (1993). *Paralanguage: A linguistic approach to interactive speech and sound* (p. 49). Amsterdam, NL: Benjamins. With kind permission by John Benjamins Publishing Company, Amsterdam/Philadelphia. www.benjamins.com.

is the energy value for a speech sound, perceived as loudness. Each of these can be measured as an average value over an utterance or over some other unit of time, or they can be described more dynamically in terms of range, variation, and contour (Scherer, 1986).

It is also possible to assess vocal nonverbal behavior at a level *between* these impressionistic and purely descriptive extremes. A listener might be asked to characterize a voice as whiny, breathy, or abrupt but not to go to the next level of inference by attributing a trait or mood. For instance, from the three adjectives just named, a listener might infer that the speaker is weak, sexy, or rude, respectively. You can see that the last three descriptions are further removed from the actual vocal cues and more inferential than the first three. Perceptions at this midway point are a crucial link in understanding the relationship between acoustic features of voices and their social impact (Scherer, 1982).

The fact that the voice has acoustic features perceived and interpreted by listeners according to their knowledge, stereotypes, and other cognitions is part of what is called the *lens* model of nonverbal judgment (Scherer, 2003), which we have described elsewhere in this book. According to this model, a full understanding of vocal and other nonverbal phenomena must acknowledge a series of interlocking steps: A person's state or trait (A) is reflected in acoustic behavior (B), which is perceived by a listener (C), who forms an impression or attribution (D), which may then be the basis for behavioral reaction or change in the listener (E). Studies hardly ever include all of these elements. One study might document how a speaker's emotional state is reflected in acoustic changes (A–B), whereas another might relate acoustic properties of the voice to listeners' impressions of personality (B–D).

Researchers are also interested in the development of skill in using acoustic cues as well as in disturbances to this ability. To this end, experiments are conducted with infants and children to understand if or when they can use prosodic cues in the processing of language (Berman, Chambers, & Graham, 2010; Sakkalou & Gattis, 2012). Also, children and adults who suffer from specific disorders, such as Williams syndrome (where there are deficits in the production and comprehension of prosody), are compared to typically developing children in an effort to isolate the neurologic mechanisms that might contribute to their underlying problem in processing emotional cues from language (Pinheiro et al., 2011).

All approaches for measuring vocal behavior have strengths and weaknesses. The choice depends on the questions being asked in the particular study. Hall, Roter, and Rand (1981), for example, were interested in the impact of physicians' and patients' communication of emotion during medical visits. Accordingly, they asked listeners to rate the emotions conveyed in content-masked audiotapes of doctors and patients talking during medical office visits. (Content masking obscures the verbal information while retaining nonverbal vocal properties, as explained later in this chapter.) They found that if the physician sounded angry, anxious, or content, the patient did also, and vice versa; in other words, there was a reciprocation of expressed feelings. In that study, gathering judges' impressions made more sense than measuring acoustic properties, such as fundamental frequency or loudness, because the interest was in social impact, not the specific cues. But another researcher might focus on uncovering the relationship *between* the descriptive and impressionistic levels, that is, finding out what increased fundamental frequency, intensity, and so on mean in terms of listeners' perceptions.

The voice is capable of a great variety of sounds (Poyatos, 1993; Trager, 1958). The components most closely tied to speech include the three already mentioned—frequency, intensity, and speed—as well as vocal lip control, ranging from sharp to smooth transitions; articulation control, either forceful or relaxed; rhythm control, varying from smooth to jerky; and resonance, describing voice ranges from resonant to "thin." Other nonverbal vocal behaviors are less tied to speech and may even substitute for speech. These include laughing, crying, whispering, snoring, yelling, moaning, yawning, whining, sighing, and belching, along with the common "uh," "um," "mmm," "uh-huh," and other such sounds, some of which merge with our definitions of linguistic behavior. Also included as paralanguage are *non-sounds*, such as pauses between words or phrases within one person's speech and pauses when a new speaker begins, also called a *switching pause* or *speech latency*. Some related phenomena, which Mahl and Schulze (1964) placed under the broad heading of *extralinguistic phenomena*, are also relevant to any discussion of communication and vocal behavior. These include dialect or accent, nonfluencies, duration of utterance, and interaction rates.

Now that we have reviewed the ingredients of paralanguage, we can ask the next logical question: What reactions do vocal cues elicit, and how are they important to communication?

THE SOUNDS OF ILLNESS

You undoubtedly have heard the hoarse or whisper-like speaking voice of a friend and realized that they had laryngitis, a physical condition in which swollen vocal cords affect the sound of the voice. Clinicians, such as psychologists and psychiatrists, also listen to the speech of others, but generally for the purpose of identifying possible clues to disturbances of the mind. They rely on the *Diagnostic and Statistical Manual of Mental Disorders* to diagnose various psychological disorders. The *DSM* lists the features associated with each mental disorder, and speech is sometimes one of many different features mentioned. The following are examples of speech cues that are linked to various disorders in the *DSM* and research:

© Ohyperblaster/Shutterstock.com

Autism (in children): Greater pitch variability and range in the voice (Bonnch, 2010).

Attention-deficit/hyperactivity: Talking excessively, loud voice.

Schizophrenia: Disorganized speech, flat voice, poor vocal emotion expression.

Manic episode: Pressured speech.

Depression: Slow speech, long pauses.

Major depression with catatonic features: Echolalia (the person repeats words or phrases that others have just spoken).

Histrionic personality disorder: Speech is excessively impressionistic and lacking in detail.

Schizotypal personality disorder: Less pitch variability in the voice (Dickey et al., 2012).

© Rido/Shutterstock.com

VOCAL CUES AND SPEAKER RECOGNITION

You may have had this experience: You pick up the phone and say, "Hello." The voice on the other end says, "Hi, how ya doin'?" At this point you realize two things: (1) The greeting suggests an informality found among people who are supposed to know each other, and (2) you don't know who it is! So you try to extend the conversation without admitting your ignorance, hoping some verbal cue will be given, or that you eventually will recognize the caller's voice. As a result, you say something like, "Fine. What have you been up to?" Speaker recognition is important not only to all of us in everyday life but also to law enforcement officials and governments. Joseph Stalin assigned teams of imprisoned scientists and engineers to develop speaker-recognition technology so Stalin's police could easily identify "enemies of the state" (Hollien, 1990).

A complex acoustical signal is produced each time you speak. It is not exactly the same each time you speak, even if it is the same word, nor is the acoustic signal you produce exactly the same as the one produced by other speakers. The probability that greater differences will exist between the voices of two different speakers than the voice of a single speaker at two different times has led to considerable interest in the process of identifying speakers by their voices alone. There are three primary methods for identifying speakers from the voice:

1. Listening
2. Visual comparison of spectrograms (voiceprints)
3. Recognition by computers that compare the acoustic patterns of a standard spoken message to stored versions of the same message previously spoken by the same speaker

Although machines are credited with many accomplishments in today's society, ordinary human listening compares favorably with the other two techniques for accuracy in most speaker-recognition tasks. Under certain circumstances, human beings can recognize speakers with a high degree of accuracy. In one study, a single sentence was enough to identify 8 to 10 work colleagues at more than 97% accuracy (Van Lancker, Kreiman, & Emmorey, 1985). In another study, 83% accuracy for 29 familiar speakers was achieved (Ladefoged & Ladefoged, 1980). Computer-based methods of speaker recognition appear to be developing, however (Kelly et al., 2019; Tiwari, Hashmi, Keskar, & Shivaprakash, 2019).

It appears that listeners use numerous acoustic cues to identify a speaker, but it is not clear which ones reliably distinguish one speaker from another, as some cues, such as speaking rate, are important to the recognition of some voices but not others (Creel & Bregman, 2011; Van Lancker, Kreiman, & Wickens, 1985). Moreover, even when listeners accurately identify a speaker from their voice, they are probably not able to explain the perceptual bases for their decision.

Law enforcement and judicial agencies have a special concern for identifying speakers objectively from their vocal characteristics. At the famous trial of Bruno Hauptmann, the kidnapper of Charles and Anne Morrow Lindbergh's baby, Charles Lindbergh claimed he recognized Hauptmann's voice as the voice of the kidnapper, even though it had been about 3 years since he had heard it. Skeptical about the accuracy of this identification, McGehee (1937) conducted research that found accuracy tends to drop sharply after 3 weeks, and after 5 months it dips to about 13%. Subsequent research has also found reductions in accuracy over time, but often not as dramatic as those McGehee found. Accuracy of identification by listeners also falls notably as the speech samples are made shorter, when various distortions or distractions occur—such as more speakers, disguised voices, whispering, and dialects (Vestman, Gowda, Sahidullah, Alku, & Kinnunen, 2018) and when the target voice is paired with another that sounds similar to it (Hollien, 1990; Kerstholt, Jansen, van Amelsvoort, & Broeders, 2006). And, of course, accuracy varies with how many times one has heard the voice in question.

One effort to find a more objective method of speaker identification involves the *spectrogram*, also called a *voiceprint*, which is a visual picture of a person's speech. A spectrogram is a plot of vocal energy in different frequency bands as a function of time. Although some have made strong claims for the accuracy and reliability of spectrographic analysis, it seems to be quite fallible (Bolt et al., 1973). Errors in human judgment occur as interpretations of the visual data are made. Two similar spectrograms of two different people uttering a single word make it sufficiently clear that relying on spectrograms as evidence at trials is hazardous (Hollien, 1990). Spectrograms are not like fingerprints. True, no two voices are exactly alike, but depending on the voice sample obtained and the equipment used, two different voices may appear very similar. In contrast, fingerprints, unlike voices, show little variability from one measurement to the next, unless, of course, smudges or smears have occurred. One study asked speakers to produce the same sentence using their normal voice and a number of "disguises"—speaking like an old person, using a hypernasal voice, a hoarse voice, a slow rate of speech, and a disguise of the speaker's own choosing. These voice samples were then submitted to spectrographic analysis by experts who were paid $50 if they achieved the highest accuracy of identification. Normal voices were matched with about 57% accuracy, but all the disguises significantly interfered with identification. The least accuracy was achieved when speakers chose their own type of disguise (Reich, Moll, & Curtis, 1976). Hollien (1990) concluded that spectrographic recognition is a still unvalidated methodology.

The neuroscience of person recognition is a promising avenue of research exploration. New technologies allow researchers to identify areas of the human brain linked to recognizing people based on their vocal qualities (Anzellotti & Caramazzam, 2017; Roswandomitz, Kappes, Ohrig, & von Kriegstein, 2018) and understand how the human brain processes familiar versus unfamiliar voices differently (Maguinness, Roswandowitze, & von Kriegstein, 2018).

VOCAL CUES AND PERSONALITY

One cultural syndrome that aptly illustrates people's association of vocal cues with certain personality characteristics concerns the low, deep voice associated with men and masculinity. Salespeople, radio and television announcers, lawyers, and many others try to emulate low vocal tones, which they perceive as being more sophisticated, appealing, sexy, or masculine than higher-pitched voices.

Numerous research efforts have tried to determine whether certain personality traits are actually expressed in the voice and whether listeners are sensitive to these cues. It is common to find the following:

1. High agreement among judges of the voices regarding the presence of certain personality characteristics
2. Inconsistent agreement between the judges' personality perceptions and the speaker's actual score on personality tests
3. A very high correspondence between the judges' perceptions and actual criterion measures for some voices and some personality traits

We can make several points about these findings. First, the criterion measures—personality tests—are also frequently imperfect measures, meaning there might be a higher correspondence than the data seem to indicate. Furthermore, research has often ignored differences among listeners with respect to personality, culture, and developmental traits, which may profoundly impact the listener's accuracy in perceiving personality traits based on vocal cues. Research also suggests that a given personality trait may not be expressed similarly in the voices of people from different cultures.

The finding that listeners cannot always detect personality from vocal cues does not mean the voice does not contain any cues to personality. There are several lines of positive evidence on this issue. Extraversion/introversion is the trait dimension best-documented in vocal cues of American speakers. Cues associated with a speaker's actual, not just perceived, extraversion, when compared to introversion, are more fluency—that is, shorter pauses when the speaking turn switches from one speaker to another, shorter silent pauses within a person's speech, and fewer hesitations—faster rate, louder speech, more dynamic contrast, higher pitch (up to a point), and more variable pitch. In addition, extraverted people have been shown to talk more, in both number of words and total speaking time (Lippa, 1998; Siegman, 1987).

Imagine you are listening to only the voice of other people. Based on their vocal qualities alone, could you possibly determine who has had a history of infidelity? The research conducted by Hughes and Harrison (2017) suggests that the answer to this question is *yes*.

© Andrey_Popov/
Shutterstock.com

Lippa (1998) also inquired about several dimensions of masculinity and femininity relative to vocal qualities, defining the masculinity–femininity dimensions in terms of the participants' gender-typical preferences for occupations, hobbies, and other activities. Among men, those who were more masculine by this definition had poorer enunciation and less expressive, lower-pitched, slower, and louder voices; among women, there was a correlation only for voice pitch—more masculine women had lower-pitched voices. Listeners' perceptions partially matched these associations, with higher ratings of masculinity being given to targets whose voices were less expressive and lower pitched.

The trait of dominance also has been documented to have an associated speech style, and some of its elements overlap with those found for extraversion. Individuals who speak louder are perceived as more dominant (Harrigan, Gramata, Luck, & Margolis, 1989; Tusing & Dillard, 2000), and indeed more dominant individuals do tend to have voices that are louder than those of less dominant individuals (Hall, Coats, & Smith LeBeau, 2005; Siegman, 1987; Weaver & Anderson, 1973). With respect to men, a lower-pitched voice has been linked to greater bodily masculinity/strength in them and possibly to the ability to intimidate other males more (Hughes, Dispenza, & Gallup, 2004; Puts et al., 2016; Sell et al., 2010). Compared to women with higher voices, women with lower voices are perceived as more dominant by men and women alike (Borkowska & Pawlowski, 2011). Because the stereotype and the actual behavior associated with dominance coincide, it is not surprising that Berry (1991a) found that listeners were accurate in judging the personality trait of assertiveness in voices recorded while expressors recited the alphabet.

How personality is actually expressed in speech may be complex, but there is no dearth of evidence that people believe speech contains clues to personality. Addington (1968) conducted one of the most complete studies in this area. Male and female speakers simulated nine vocal characteristics, and judges responded to the voices by rating them on 40 personality characteristics. Judges were most reliable, meaning they agreed most with each other, in ratings of masculine–feminine, young–old, enthusiastic–apathetic, energetic–lazy, and attractive–ugly personality dimensions in vocal characteristics. Addington concluded that the male personality generally was perceived in terms of physical and emotional power, whereas the female personality was apparently perceived in terms of social faculties. Table 11-1 summarizes his results.

Addington posed some interesting questions for researchers studying vocal cues and personality. To what extent are these stereotyped impressions of personality maintained in the face of conflicting personality information? And what is the relationship between a given personality impression and vocal cues? For example, Addington's research indicated that increased pitch variety led to more positive personality impressions, but is it not possible that, at some point, increasing pitch variety could become so exaggerated as to evoke negative perceptions? Zuckerman's research on vocal attractiveness suggests this may be so, because extremes of pitch, pitch range, shrillness, and squeakiness produced more negative impressions. Attractive voices were more moderate on such acoustic qualities.

Another question is the accuracy of some stereotypes. Consider the following. Do gay males show vocal characteristics that are more similar to heterosexual females than heterosexual males? In stereotype, gay men possess female-like qualities, including the pitch of their voice. In fact, male actors use a higher voice pitch when portraying a gay character (Cartei & Reby, 2012). However, a study of actual pitch characteristics of gay men as well as heterosexual men and women revealed that, although gay men do use a higher pitch than heterosexual men, it is significantly lower than that of the typical heterosexual female (Baeck, Corthals, & Van Borsel, 2011). Thus, there is no evidence that gay men's voice pitch usually matches that of heterosexual females.

Yet there is some evidence that, relative to their heterosexual counterparts, lesbians tend to have a lower pitch and show less pitch variation (Van Borsel, Vandaele, & Corthail, 2013). Moreover, people's sexual orientation may be linked to some differences in their vowel production; as one example, gay males tend to use an expanded vowel space (Pierrehumbert et al., 2004). Degree of nasality in the voice, however, does not appear to be related to people's sexual orientation (Vanpoucke, Cosyns, Bottens, & Borsel, 2018).

People with more attractive voices are, in general, rated as having better personalities than people with less attractive voices, and are perceived as less neurotic, more extraverted, and more open, warm, agreeable, powerful, honest, and conscientious (Berry, 1992; Zuckerman, Hodgins, & Miyake, 1990; Zuckerman & Miyake, 1993). Moreover, people assume that attractive and unattractive voices belong to attractive and unattractive faces, respectively (Hughes & Miller, 2016).

There is some evidence that the quality of a person's voice is linked to their genetic fitness. Hill and colleagues (2017) found that people with less attractive voices showed indications of lower genetic fitness in their faces, namely, greater fluctuating asymmetry. Moreover, within each gender, those with more stereotypically desirable physiques—that is, men with higher shoulder-to-waist ratios and women with lower waist-to-hip ratios—tend to have more attractive voices (Hughes et al., 2004). Perhaps not surprisingly then, people with more attractive voices, as judged by independent listeners, are sexually active earlier and have more partners than those with less attractive voices.

Zuckerman's research, as well as that of others (Bloom, Moore-Schoenmakers, & Masataka, 1999; Bloom, Zajac, & Titus, 1999; Riding, Lonsdale, & Brown, 2006), also uncovered the particular speech qualities that produced higher ratings of vocal attractiveness. Voices rated "more attractive" were more resonant, less monotonous, less nasal (even in infants) and for adult male voices, lower in pitch.

Personality stereotypes also exist about people with babyish voices. Both adults and young children with more babyish voices are perceived as more warm and honest but less powerful and competent than people with more mature-sounding voices. It seems the general qualities attributed to children are attributed to people with younger-sounding voices no matter what their actual age (Berry, 1992; Berry, Hansen, Landry-Pester, & Meier, 1994). This might explain why, although a higher pitch in the female voice is perceived as attractive, too high of a pitch is not, as this could be a vocal cue of sexual immaturity (Borkowska & Pawlowski, 2011).

Table 11-1 Simulated Vocal Cues and Personality Stereotypes

Simulated Vocal Cue	Speakers	Stereotyped Perceptions
Breathiness	Males	Younger, more artistic
	Females	More feminine, prettier, more petite, effervescent, high-strung, shallower
Thinness	Males	Did not alter the listener's image of the speaker; no significant correlations
	Females	Increased social, physical, emotional, and mental immaturity; increased sense of humor and sensitivity
Flatness	Males	More masculine, more sluggish, colder, more withdrawn
	Females	More masculine, more sluggish, colder, more withdrawn
Nasality	Males	A wide array of socially undesirable characteristics
	Females	A wide array of socially undesirable characteristics
Tenseness	Males	Older, more unyielding, cantankerous
	Females	Younger; more emotional, feminine, high-strung; less intelligent
Throatiness	Males	Older, more realistic, mature, sophisticated, well adjusted
	Females	Less intelligent; more masculine; lazier; more boorish, unemotional, ugly, sickly, careless, inartistic, naive, humble, neurotic, quiet, uninteresting, apathetic
Increased rate	Males	More animated and extraverted
	Females	More animated and extraverted
Increased pitch	Males	More dynamic, feminine, esthetically inclined
Variety	Females	More dynamic and extraverted

VOCAL CUES AND GROUP PERCEPTIONS

A related line of study involves associating various characteristics with voices representative of groups of people. The study of dialects and accents is illustrative. In George Bernard Shaw's play *Pygmalion*, and its musical adaptation *My Fair Lady*, Eliza Doolittle spent considerable time and effort trying to correct her dialect so she could rise in social standing. Professor Higgins says, "Look at her—a pris'ner of the gutters; Condemned by ev'ry syllable she utters" (*My Fair Lady*, Act I, Scene 1). Eliza's training, according to one study, was appropriate. It suggests that if we expect a speaker to reflect a nonstandard or "lower-class" dialect, and the speaker actually presents themselves in accordance with standard or "upper-class" models, the evaluation will be very positive. The reverse also was true: Speakers who were expected to speak "up" but who spoke "down" instead were evaluated negatively (Aboud, Clement, & Taylor, 1974).

Aspects of speech may change due to nonconscious or conscious process. For example, Smith-Genthôs and colleagues (2015) found that people nonconsciously mimic a speaker's tone of voice. However, there may be times when people deliberately adjust their speech to match those of the class of people they aspire to in life (LaBov, 1966) or to fulfill perceived role expectations (Cartei & Reby, 2012). Regarding the latter, as noted earlier, male actors may adopt a higher-pitched voice when depicting gay characters mainly because of the stereotype that gay males have a higher pitch (Cartei & Reby, 2012). Sometimes, though, there may be a fine line between adapting to an audience and violating expectations based on our own background. For example, if an audience thinks you are faking something or concealing who you "really are," they could judge you harshly.

Although there are some exceptions, ordinarily dialects other than the one spoken by the listener receive less favorable evaluations than those considered standard for the listener's group. Generally, these negative responses occur because the listener associates the speaker's dialect with an ethnic or regional stereotype and then evaluates the voice in accordance with the stereotype. Nonnative accents can obviously be a liability in the workplace (Russo, Islam, & Koyuncu, 2017).

Beyond stereotypes, do aspects of a person's voice reveal the region of a country they are actually from? The answer is clearly yes; virtually anyone raised in the United States can distinguish a southern accent from a northern accent. Subtler regional distinctions could be harder to detect, of course. Aubanel and Nguyen (2010) showed that people's accents provided a clue to which region of France (e.g., southern and northern France) they came from.

A related question is whether regional varieties of speech differ in prestige value. U.S. listeners in Maine, Louisiana, New York City, Arkansas, and Michigan rated 12 voice samples of American dialects and one foreign accent (Wilke & Snyder, 1941). The most unfavorably regarded was the foreign accent and so-called New Yorkese. Such speakers may seek help with their accents when they are looking to land jobs that have audiences expecting to hear Standard American English (e.g., TV news anchors).

Several investigators have pursued the question of exactly how we judge the speech and dialects of others. By far, the most extensive work in this direction was done by Mulac (1976). Mulac's experiments used regional and foreign dialects, broadcasters, various speech pathologies, prose and spontaneous speech, and different modes of presentation such as written format, audiotape, videotape, and sound film. This work shows that people tend to respond to samples of speech along three primary dimensions:

1. *Sociointellectual status*, that is, high or low social status, blue or white collar, rich or poor, and literate or illiterate
2. *Aesthetic quality*, that is, pleasing or displeasing, nice or awful, sweet or sour, beautiful or ugly
3. *Dynamism*, that is, aggressive or unaggressive, active or passive, strong or weak, loud or soft

These results confirm the findings of studies in many other areas of perception, some of which are discussed elsewhere in this book, that show that the world and the things and people in it are perceived according to the fundamental dimensions of power, evaluation, and activity.

VOCAL CUES AND JUDGMENTS OF SOCIODEMOGRAPHIC AND DEVELOPMENTAL CHARACTERISTICS

The study of vocal cues relating to the sociodemographic characteristics of a speaker might focus on the judgment process itself or the accuracy of the judgments. In terms of the judgment process, researchers have examined how people recognize cues to a person's dialect from spoken words as well as the phonological markers of regional difference in accent (Aubanel & Nguyen, 2010; Scharinger, Monahan, & Idsardi, 2011).

In terms of judgment accuracy, Pear (1931) did pioneering work on vocal cues and judgments of personal characteristics. Using nine speakers and over 4,000 listeners, he found a speaker's age could be estimated fairly accurately, the speaker's gender with remarkable accuracy, birthplace with little accuracy, and occasionally vocation with surprising accuracy. The actor and clergy were consistently identified from among the nine professionals represented. Since that time, others have been interested in judgments of such characteristics as body type, height, weight, age, occupation, status or social class, race, gender, education, accents, and dialect region.

There are three characteristics that are judged accurately and with some consistency from vocal cues, namely, gender, age, and social class or status. These will be discussed in detail next. This is followed by a discussion of how speakers' vocal cues might change in response to the characteristics of the people they are speaking to in everyday life.

GENDER

Listeners who heard six recorded vowels of 20 speakers were able to identify the sex of the speaker 96% of the time when the tape was not altered in any way. Accuracy decreased to 91% for a filtered tape and to 75% for a whispered voice sample (Lass, Hughes, Bowyer, Waters, & Broune, 1976). These authors argued that the fundamental frequency is a more important acoustic cue in speaker gender identification than the resonance characteristics of the voices. More recently, Pernet and Belin (2012) noted that timbre and pitch are the major markers of gender; most notably, men tend to have a lower pitch than women. Women's voices also are more variable or expressive but less resonant than men's.

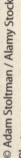

Monica Seles and Jimmy Connors were not grunts in the world of tennis. These two heavy-hitters were famous not only for their play but also their loud grunting on the tennis court. Research by Raine, Pisanski, and Reby (2017) found that the fundamental frequency of grunts serves as a cue to the gender of the grunter.

In terms of pitch, many social, cultural, and biological factors can, of course, qualify differences between men and women, differences within each gender, and variations expected from individual women. For instance, males and females interacting with each other may manifest different vocal cues than when they present monologues or interact with a member of the same gender (Markel, Prebor, & Brandt, 1972). Pitch differences between women from various cultures reflect the adoption of cultural or gender rules. Many travelers and scholars have noted the high pitch of Japanese women's voices and speculated on the reasons. Greater societal pressure for women to be "feminine" in Japan than is the case in the Netherlands may explain, for example, why the pitch of the former group tends to be higher than that of the latter group (Van Bezooijen, 1995). Adult women experience hormonal changes with their menstrual cycle. Such changes affect their vocal pitch. Some research suggests that women's pitch gets higher prior to ovulation, a change that men find attractive, whereas other research shows that this change is not likely detectable by men in everyday life (Bryant & Haselton, 2008; Fisher et al., 2011). Thus, women's pitch may not be a useful cue in detecting the time of their peak fertility.

At the borderline between verbal and nonverbal behavior falls an area of study concerned with speech styles, or *speech registers*. A speech register refers to a total way of communicating through speech, which can include both nonverbal and verbal forms, and it is believed to vary systematically with social characteristics of the speakers, for example, how socially powerful a person is (Erickson, Lind, Johnson, & O'Barr, 1978). This research is pertinent to our discussion of speaker gender because it has been suggested that certain verbal forms associated with power differentiate the speech styles of men versus women (Lakoff, 1975). Examples of less powerful speech stereotypically associated with females include *tag questions* ("It's a nice day, *isn't it?*"), *hedges and qualifiers* ("sort of," "maybe"), *disclaimers* ("I don't know, *but*"), and *intensifiers* ("The puppy was *so* cute"). Leaper and Robnett (2011), in a review of the research, concluded that women did speak somewhat more tentatively than men, but this was not due to women taking a submissive role in conversation. Rather, they concluded that using more tentative speech is an aspect of women's greater interpersonal sensitivity (see Chapter 3).

Interruptions, another interactional strategy that can reflect dominance, also have been hypothesized to differentiate men from women in the direction we might expect based on stereotype. People certainly do have well-developed stereotypes about how men and women speak, but the evidence supporting the hypothesis of gender differences in language use and interruptions is extremely mixed (Aries, 1987; Dindia, 1987; Hirschman, 1994; Irish & Hall, 1995; Kramer, 1978; Marche & Peterson, 1993; Mulac, Lundell, & Bradac, 1986; Nohara, 1992; Turner, Dindia, & Pearson, 1995). The fact that interruptions can signify enthusiastic, active participation in a conversation, rather than efforts to attain or express dominance, is probably one reason why studies are mixed as to which gender interrupts more.

Because interruptions can mean very different things, discussing them without drawing functional distinctions can be very misleading. For example, in a study of married and cohabiting couples by Daigen and Holmes (2000), the total number of interruptions in the couples' conversations, as measured in a laboratory interaction, was not related to marital satisfaction. But interruptions that conveyed disagreement and disparagement of the other's message did predict lower satisfaction, both at the time and 2 years later—especially when the latter kind of interruption was directed from the man to the woman. Further evidence that the impact of interruptions might differ between men and women comes from Farley's (2008) study showing that, in general, speakers who interrupted often were less liked by listeners than speakers who did not interrupt, but that this effect was especially pronounced when the interrupter was a woman.

Upspeak/Uptalk is another example of how men's and women's vocal qualities can be impacted by situational factors. Upspeak/Uptalk is when a speaker uses a rising pitch and uncertain tone at the end of a declarative sentence, which are often assumed to reflect less confidence or lower dominance. Linneman (2012) noted that men used Uptalk less and women used it more when each was having success on a TV show. Is it possible that, due to gender roles or constraints, women use Upspeak more as a way of downplaying their success?

AGE

As we mentioned, studies show age to be fairly accurately assessed from vocal cues. In one study, age was judged quite accurately from the voice, and not much less so than when judgments were made from a full-length photograph of the speaker (Krauss, Freyberg, & Morsella, 2002). Several studies have investigated males' voice pitch during infancy, childhood, adolescence, early adulthood, and middle and advanced age. There is a general lowering of pitch level from infancy through middle age, with some studies finding a subsequent reversal, such that men's pitch level rises slightly with advancing age.

With advancing age, speech slows down, and disfluencies and perturbations in fundamental frequency increase (Hummert, Mazloff, & Henry, 1999). Indeed, research by Gordon, Andersen, Perez, and Finnegan (2019) showed that older people speak more slowly and that their speech rate was one of the cues that listeners used to accurately judge their age. Changes in pitch flexibility, tremor, speech rate, loudness, vocal quality, articulatory control, and the like may also give clues to a speaker's age. But it is likely that listeners rely on a host of these cues as opposed to only one when judging a voice to be that of an old person (Harnsberger, Brown, Shrivastav, & Rothman, 2010).

SOCIAL CLASS OR STATUS/DOMINANCE

Several studies show listeners to be amazingly accurate in judging social class or status on the basis of voice alone (Brown & Lambert, 1976; Harms, 1961). Harms used a standard system to determine social class for nine speakers. Each speaker recorded a 40- to 60-second conversation in which he responded to questions and statements such as "How are you?" and "Ask for the time." Results showed that listeners were able to identify the speakers' status, with many of them stating that they had made their decision after only 10 to 15 seconds of listening to the recording. And Brown and Lambert noted that listeners could accurately detect differences in the vocal qualities of blue- versus white-collar French Canadian workers.

Status, of course, can be an enduring characteristic of a person, something they project in everyday life, or one that is temporary, as when a person is called upon to occupy a higher-status or more powerful role in a group or dyadic setting. Changes in a person's pitch and loudness appear to reflect a person's desired, actual, or assigned status in group/dyadic settings. Chen and colleagues (2016) observed that individuals who initially used a deepening pitch in a group setting were more likely to end up as higher-ranking members of the group. Leongómez and colleagues (2017) found less pitch variability in a dyadic setting from individuals who were higher in self-perceived dominance. Finally, Ko and colleagues (2014) noted specific pitch and loudness cues from those assigned more power or status. Specifically, relative to their less powerful counterparts, these individuals tended to use a higher and less variable pitch, and they were more variable in their loudness. A literature review by Hall, Coats, and Smith LeBeau (2005) found that, overall, people higher (versus lower) in status or personality dominance spoke more loudly, but there was an interesting reversal in a study of social class, where white-collar participants spoke less loudly than blue-collar participants.

CHARACTERISTICS OF RECIPIENTS

So far we have been discussing ways in which a speaker's personal characteristics are reflected in their nonverbal speech style. But it would be very surprising if a person's speech style did not also reflect characteristics of the *other* person in an interaction. After all, reactions to different kinds of people may produce many emotions and thoughts that may, in turn, be reflected in vocal expression. Also, people are aware of how they *ought* to talk to different kinds of people.

A well-studied example of such a "target effect" is baby talk, also called *Motherese or infant-directed speech*. When adults speak to babies, listeners will likely hear the following: changes in their timbre, pitch (it gets higher), and speech rate (it gets slower); they become more repetitive and rhythmic in speech; and they start using shorter and simpler sentences, more extreme vowels, and exaggerated emotional tones (Grieser & Kuhl, 1988; Kuhl et al., 1997; Piazza et al., 2017; Saint-Georges et al., 2013; Snow & Ferguson, 1977; Trainor, Austin, & Desjardins, 2000).

It appears that this type of speech of adults to infants occurs around the world, with some variability of course, and that even young children talk this way to babies. This suggests that infant-directed speech may be an evolved solution to an adaptive problem (e.g., Broesch & Bryant, 2017; Narayan & McDermott, 2016; Sulpizio et al., 2017).

In terms of evolved solutions to adaptive problems, infant and parents need to bond, and parents need to communicate and teach their language to their children. The fact that infants prefer baby talk to normal adult speech suggests that it serves a variety of attachment- and information-related functions, including getting an infant's attention, promoting language development, clarifying the speaker's message, and creating an emotional bond. These propositions have been supported by research showing that Motherese is part of an attachment vocalization repertoire that humans are especially sensitive to (Chan & Thompson, 2011); notably, infants show greater event-related potentials (ERPs) to familiar and unfamiliar words when they are spoken in infant-directed speech compared to adult-directed speech (Zangl & Mills, 2007). As further evidence of this, Gordon, Zagoory-Sharon, Leckman, and Feldman (2010) found that the amount of Motherese displayed was linked to oxytocin, a hormone thought to promote mother–infant bonding. Finally, Trainor and colleagues (2000) noted that baby talk contains more free emotional expression than typical adult-directed speech, but that it is very similar in terms of acoustic characteristics to adult-directed speech that emphasizes the communication of emotion.

Certain groups of people who have childlike qualities attributed to them—or who are perceived (often erroneously) as cognitively impaired, such as the elderly or the deaf—are also spoken to in a way that resembles baby talk. Zebrowitz, Brownlow, and Olson (1992) found that the facial characteristics of children influenced how much baby talk they received from adults; those with more babyish faces received more baby talk than same-age children who had more mature-looking faces.

Psychologists are especially interested in this kind of "secondary" baby talk because of the possibility that it contributes to the stigmatizing of groups perceived as dependent or incompetent (Caporael, 1981). Elderspeak is when speakers talk to the elderly in a manner similar to how they would talk to infants. As examples, they may use shorter sentences, a higher pitch, and a slower rate of speech (Kemper, 1994). Needless to say, if you are an elderly person, you may perceive this type of talk as patronizing. And you may be less receptive to treatment, especially if it is used by those who are supposed to be trying to help you (Ryan et al., 1995; Williams et al., 2011).

Men and women use others' vocal qualities, such as pitch, to assess the attractiveness of members of the same and other gender as well as to communicate their attractiveness to members of the other gender. Regarding the former, both men's and women's feelings of jealousy were shown to be greater when they had imagined a member of the other sex with a more attractive vocal pitch flirting with their romantic partner (O'Connor & Feinberg, 2012). Regarding the latter, women were observed to use a higher-pitched voice, which males find attractive, when leaving a voicemail for a man they found to be attractive (Fraccaro et al., 2011). Women, on the other hand, tend to find lower-pitched voices in men more attractive (Simmons, Peters, & Rhodes, 2011). However, men appear to adopt a sing-song pitch around attractive women; they are presumably trying to strike a balance between signaling their masculinity with a lower pitch, but not too much of it (i.e., masculinity) because that could be perceived by women as threatening (e.g., Leongómez et al., 2014).

VOCAL CUES AND EMOTION

Humans appear to be designed to detect emotional information from sound, whether that sound comes from a person speaking, singing, or playing an instrument (Juslin & Laukka, 2003; Sachs, Habibi, Damasio, & Kaplan, 2018; Scherer, Trznadel, Fantini, & Sundberg, 2017). In this section, we will examine what is known about emotional expression in the human voice. Such cues are widespread among many animal species for communication about territory, relationship, identity, alarm, physical states, and emotion (Kitchen, Cheney, & Seyfarth, 2003; Marier, Evans, & Hauser, 1992). In fact, Darwin viewed the voice as a primary channel for emotional signals in both humans and animals.

One persistent question is whether people can identify emotions in the voice. The answer is definitely "yes," whether the person is speaking or singing (e.g., Juslin & Laukka, 2003; Scherer et al., 2017). There is substantial accuracy even when speakers and listeners are not from the same culture, and listeners in different cultures tend to make the same errors and confusions when judging emotions in the voice, though there appears to be some advantage in judging voices from one's own culture (Juslin & Laukka, 2003; Scherer, 2003; Scherer, Banse, & Wallbott, 2001). Pittam and Scherer (1993) concluded that the recognition of emotion from the voice is four to five times what would be expected if listeners were simply guessing, and Juslin and Laukka (2003) concluded that across five different emotions, accuracy of judgment averaged 90% when calculated against a guessing rate of 50%. Of course, accuracy depends on how clear and potent the vocal expressions are; subtle emotional expressions would probably not achieve such high levels of recognition accuracy.

Other questions are more closely related to contextual variables. Jaywant and Pell (2012) observed that participants made fewer errors in judging facial expressions when they had first heard vocal cues expressing the same emotion state as the face. Sauter, Eisner, Ekman, and Scott (2010) had participants from distinct cultural groups (English-European and the Himba from Namibia) listen to a story in their native language that was designed to arouse a specific emotion state, such as sadness. Next, participants listened to two vocalizations of emotions. These emotional vocalizations were produced by members from their own cultural group as well as from members of the other cultural group. More important, one of two emotional vocalizations matched and the other did not match the emotional content of the story. Results showed that members of both cultures were able to match emotion states in vocal cues (anger, fear, disgust, amusement, sadness, surprise) to the emotional content of the story and that they were able to do this using vocal cues from members of their own cultural group as well as those from members of the other cultural group.

Concerned that most emotion-judgment tasks present several negative emotions—such as anger, sadness, and fear—but typically only one positive emotion, namely happiness, Sauter and Scott (2007) presented five different positive emotions for judgment through the vocal channel. Listeners in both Great Britain and Sweden showed significant accuracy in distinguishing between amusement, contentment, sensual pleasure, achievement/triumph, and relief. With respect to cross-cultural comparisons, though, Sauter et al. (2010) found that English participants recognized the nonbasic positive emotions of achievement/triumph, relief, and sensual pleasure in the vocalizations of Himba speakers, but that Himba participants did not recognize these emotions in the vocalizations of English speakers.

Neumann and Strack (2000) further demonstrated that hearing voices expressing different emotions elicits the corresponding emotional feelings, as reflected both in the listener's own voice tone and in self-ratings of their mood. These, like other findings on "emotional contagion" (see Chapter 9), show that emotions can be conveyed and shared outside of conscious awareness (Chartrand & Bargh, 1999).

The notion that a listener might respond with the same kind of emotion as expressed in the speaker's voice suggests a parallel situation: listening to music. Music can create potent emotional effects, and indeed experimenters often use music to induce emotion states in participants. Some researchers have studied the accuracy of identifying emotions in music using methods very similar to those used to study the communication of emotion in the voice. For example, a performer might be asked to play a passage on the piano so as to convey anger or happiness. Accuracy on the part of listeners can then be measured. Juslin and Laukka (2003) found, in reviewing these studies, that accuracy for judging emotions in music is very similar to accuracy in judging emotions in the voice, and furthermore that many of the same acoustic qualities account for the effects. For example, tempo and intensity increase in anger and happiness in both modalities, and variability in intensity is increased for anger and fear but is decreased for sadness and tenderness in both modalities. As more specific evidence of this, it appears that the "minor third" is important both in music and in the pitch of the human voice for communicating the emotion state of sadness (Curtis & Bharucha, 2010).

You may have wondered how it is possible to separate the nonverbal voice qualities from the words being spoken in studies of vocal communication. Several methods have been used to accomplish this essential goal, and accuracy may vary somewhat depending on the method used (Juslin & Scherer, 2005). Some studies use "meaningless content," usually having the speaker say numbers or letters while trying to convey various emotional states. As early as 1964, studies of this type were conducted (Davitz, 1964). Speakers in Davitz's studies were instructed to express 10 different feelings while reciting parts of the alphabet. These expressions were recorded and played to listeners, who were asked to identify the emotion being expressed from a list of 10 emotions. Generally, emotions or feelings were communicated far beyond chance expectation. It is difficult to tell, of course, whether the communicators were using the same tonal or vocal cues they would use in real-life emotional reactions.

Studies have also controlled verbal cues by using "constant content," in which a speaker reads a standard passage while attempting to simulate different emotional states. The underlying assumption is that the passage selected is neutral in emotional tone. Another approach is for the listener to try to ignore content and focus attention on the pauses, breathing rate, and other characteristics that suggest the speaker's emotional state. This method is frequently used in psychotherapy to identify signs of anxiety.

Some studies have used electronic filtering to eliminate verbal content (Rogers, Scherer, & Rosenthal, 1971). A low-pass filter will hold back the higher frequencies of speech on which word recognition depends. The finished product sounds much like someone talking on the other side of a wall. One problem with the electronic filtering technique is that some of the nonverbal vocal cues are eliminated in the filtering process, creating an artificial stimulus. Although some aspects of vocal quality may be lost in the filtering process, a listener can still adequately perceive pitch, rate, and loudness in order to judge emotional content. An advantage of the filtering method is that naturally occurring speech can be used, in contrast to the previous methods, which require the speaker to recite a standard text.

Filtered speech is the most popular method of making words unintelligible and has produced some very intriguing results, some of which we summarize here. In a study of doctors, Milmoe, Rosenthal, Blane, Chafetz, and Wolf (1967) found that when more anger was perceived in the filtered voices of doctors talking about their alcoholic patients, the less successful they were in getting those patients into therapy. Later research verified that the tone of voice used when talking *about* patients carries over into the way doctors talk *to* patients (Rosenthal, Vanicelli, & Blanck, 1984). Another study of physicians found that those who provided more medical information to their patients—and were more competent, according to technical standards for conducting a proper interview, diagnosing correctly, and so on—were those with the lowest ratings of boredom in short, filtered clips of their voices (Hall, Roter, & Katz, 1987). In another recent study of this type, primary care physicians' voices were recorded during medical visits. Independent listeners' ratings of their filtered speech revealed that physicians whose patients were more satisfied had voices that were warm and supportive (Haskard, Williams, DiMatteo, Heritage, & Rosenthal, 2008).

Although, on average, accuracy for judging emotions from the voice is very high, studies do vary in how accurately emotions are judged from voice cues. One reason for this involves the differing methods by which such observations may be made, for example, how long the voice samples are, which content-masking technique is used, or how dissimilar the response alternatives are. Another reason is that speakers and listeners vary widely in how accurately they can express and recognize different emotions (see Chapter 3). For example, in the Davitz and Davitz (1959) study, one speaker's expressions were identified correctly only 23% of the time, whereas another speaker communicated accurately over 50% of the time. In that study, like many others, accuracy was defined in terms of how well listeners could identify the emotion the speaker was asked to express. Listeners' accuracy in recognizing the intended emotion varied widely, just as the speakers' sending accuracy did.

Thus, depending on the skills that individuals bring to a communication situation, they may or may not succeed in sending and receiving vocal emotion cues well. Accuracy in judging emotions from the voice develops with age and appears to be correlated with similar psychological characteristics as is skill in judging other nonverbal cues (Baum & Nowicki, 1998). For example, children appear to learn vocal expressions of emotion later than expressions of the face or body (Nelson & Russell, 2011). Deficits in more than one domain have been noted for various disorders. For example, persons with autism and Asperger syndrome score lower than comparison groups on judging both vocal and facial emotion cues (Rutherford, Baron-Cohen, & Wheelwright, 2002), and the same is true for people with anorexia nervosa (Kucharska-Pietura, Nilolaou, Masiak, & Treasure, 2004).

Another qualification to any statement about the voice's overall ability to communicate emotions is that some emotions are easier to communicate than others. For example, one study found that vocal anger was identified 63% of the time, whereas vocal pride was identified correctly only 20% of the time. Another study found that joy and hate were easily recognized in the voice, but shame and love were the most difficult to recognize. In general, anger, joy, and sadness are easier to recognize in the voice than fear and disgust (Banse & Scherer, 1996; Pittam & Scherer, 1993).

In a review of studies on accuracy of judging anxiety, Harrigan, Wilson, and Rosenthal (2004) found that accuracy for judging *state anxiety*—that is, anxiety being experienced at a given moment—was higher when judgments were based on the voice alone than when they were based on video cues alone. However, for *trait anxiety*, which is a personality tendency to be anxious, this was reversed—in fact, listeners could not judge trait anxiety from the voice at all. Perhaps trait anxiety is not manifest unless immediate circumstances are creating physiological arousal.

In addition to demonstrating that emotions can be conveyed through the voice, researchers have learned a great deal about *how* the voice conveys emotion. Although efforts are under way to specify the acoustic features associated with nonverbal vocalizations of specific emotion states (Sauter, Eisner, Calder, & Scott, 2010), there currently is no precise "dictionary" of emotion cues for the voice, any more than there is for any nonverbal channel. You cannot identify key acoustic features and then look them up in a book somewhere to understand exactly how the speaker is feeling.

Many factors enter into the total picture of emotional expression: contextual cues, the words being spoken, other nonverbal behaviors, individual differences in the people, and the fact that there is undoubtedly more than one way to express a given emotion. Other factors include whether the expression is spontaneous versus posed (Juslin, Laukka, & Bänziger, 2018) as well as the age of the expressor (Morningstar, Ly, Feldman, & Dirks, 2018). Regarding the latter, it may be easier for listeners to detect an emotion in adults' voices than children's because of adults' better use of pitch when expressing various basic emotions (Morningstar, Dirks, & Huang, 2017). And, as with the face, there also is a range of specific emotion states within a particular valence that need to be taken into consideration. For example, the positive emotion of interest is associated with distinct vocal cues, but the positive emotion of pride is not (see Sauter, 2017). With these qualifications in mind, we now summarize key vocal cues associated with emotion.

Dasgupta (2017) examined the vocal qualities of pitch, sound pressure level, timbre, and length of pauses between words and found that faster talking in a shrill and louder voice was associated with an agitated emotional state. State anxiety is often associated with disfluencies or speech disruptions (Cook, 1965; Mahl, 1956; Siegman, 1987). "Non-Ah" speech disruptions are sentence changes (starting a sentence one way and changing its form part way through), sentence incompletions (starting a sentence and abandoning it to make a different point), stutters, repetitions, omissions (of words or parts of words), tongue slips, and intruding incoherent sounds. In contrast, a final kind of speech disruption, called "Ah" errors or filled pauses, is not associated with anxiety or stress but seems rather to have other meanings (see the section "Hesitations, Pauses, Silence, and Speech").

Personality dimensions related to anxiety have also been studied in relation to the production of speech disturbances. Harrigan, Suarez, and Hartman (1994) obtained anxiety ratings of verbatim transcripts of the speech of individuals who varied in state and trait anxiety as well as in repression, which is the need to deny negative thoughts, impulses, or behaviors. Repressors' speech was judged to be the most anxious, more so than even the speech of people who were highly trait-anxious but not repressive. The authors attributed these effects to differences in the frequency of speech disturbances among the groups. Although repressors do not view themselves as high on trait anxiety, their vocal behavior says otherwise. Perhaps anxious people are more aware of their anxiety and can take steps to conceal or control it, whereas repressive people are not aware of it, increasing the chances that anxiety cues will "leak out" through their voice.

In an experiment on therapeutic treatment for social anxiety, those patients who responded favorably to the intervention showed changes in key vocal variables when asked to give a speech in front of a group—specifically in showing a lower vocal pitch and greater continuity of speech, measured as having a smaller percentage of their speaking time spent in silence (Laukka et al., 2008). In general, stress from any source makes the voice rise in pitch. In one of the earliest demonstrations, Williams and Stevens (1972) analyzed recordings of the radio announcer who described, live on the air, the horrifying explosion and burning of the hydrogen-filled zeppelin *Hindenburg* at Lakehurst,

Table 11-2 Acoustic Concomitants of Emotional Dimensions

Amplitude Variation	Moderate	Pleasantness, activity, happiness
Pitch variation	Moderate	Anger, boredom, disgust, fear
Pitch contour	Down	Pleasantness, boredom, sadness
	Up	Potency, anger, fear, surprise
Pitch level	Low	Pleasantness, boredom, sadness
Tempo	Slow	Boredom, disgust, sadness
	Fast	Pleasantness, activity, potency, anger, fear
Duration (shape)	Round	Potency, boredom, disgust, fear, sadness
Filtration (lack of overtones)	Low	Sadness, pleasantness, boredom, happiness
	Moderate	Potency, activity
Tonality	Atonal	Disgust
	Tonal-minor	Anger
Rhythm	Not rhythmic	Boredom
	Rhythmic	Activity, fear, surprise

New Jersey, in 1937. Comparison of his voice before and immediately after the disaster showed the fundamental frequency rose, with much less fluctuation in frequency.

Scherer's work has encompassed a broad range of emotions. In a 1974 study, he used artificial sounds, rather than spontaneous speech, to approach the question of which vocal features are associated with which emotions. Listeners rated synthesized tones on 10-point scales of pleasantness, potency, activity, and evaluation and indicated whether the stimuli could or could not be an expression of interest, sadness, fear, happiness, disgust, anger, surprise, elation, or boredom. Generally speaking, tempo and pitch variation influence a wide range of judgments about emotional expressions. Table 11-2 summarizes the results of several of Scherer's studies.

Scherer (1986) expanded his examination to include 12 different emotions— such as irritation/cold anger, grief/desperation, elation/joy—and 18 different acoustic variables, including average fundamental frequency, variability in loudness, and speech rate. In comparing theoretical predictions to actual research, Scherer found some impressive consistencies but also considerable variation, partly due to great differences in how the studies were conducted and the number of studies conducted. Joy/elation is well studied and is associated with higher-average frequency, or *pitch*; greater frequency range; greater frequency variability; higher-average intensity, or *loudness*; and faster rate. Consistent with the results for joy/elation, the perception of how much affection is perceived in a speaker is positively predicted by how high-pitched and expressively variable the voice is (Floyd & Ray, 2003). Anger is conveyed by higher frequency and intensity, with a greater frequency range and faster speech rate for "hot" anger. Fear is shown by higher frequency, especially high-frequency energy, and faster speech rate. Sadness—at least the quiet, resigned sort—involves lower-average frequency and intensity, has downward-directed contours, and is slower (Pittam & Scherer, 1993; Scherer, Banse, Wallbott, & Goldbeck, 1991).

VOCAL CUES, COMPREHENSION, AND PERSUASION

In addition to its role in personality and emotional judgments, the voice also plays a part in retention and attitude change, which has been primarily studied in public speaking. For many years, introductory public speaking textbooks have stressed the importance of delivery in the rhetorical situation. Delivery of the speech, rather than speech content, was perhaps the first area of rhetoric to receive quantitative examination by speech researchers. Almost every study that isolated delivery as a variable showed that delivery did matter. It had positive effects on the amount of information remembered, the amount of attitude change elicited from the audience, and the amount of credibility audience members attributed to the speaker.

Typical prescriptions for use of the voice in delivering a public speech include the following:

1. Use variety in volume, rate, pitch, and articulation. The probability of desirable outcomes is less when we use a constant rate, volume, pitch, and articulation. Being consistently over-precise may be as ineffective as being overly sloppy in articulation.
2. Base decisions concerning loud–soft, fast–slow, precise–sloppy, or high–low variations on what is appropriate for a given audience in a given situation.
3. Avoid excessive disfluencies.

Regarding the third prescription, Engstrom (1994) found that participants' ratings of an announcer's competence dropped as the number of speech errors or disfluent speech made by the announcer increased.

VOCAL CUES, COMPREHENSION, AND RETENTION

Several studies tend to support the prescriptions for vocal variety in increasing audience comprehension and retention. Woolbert's (1920) study, perhaps the earliest study of this type, found that large variations of rate, force, pitch, and quality produced high audience retention when compared with a no-variation condition. Glasgow (1952), using prose and poetry, established two conditions for study: "good intonation" and "mono-pitch." Multiple-choice tests, following exposure to these differing vocal samples, showed that mono-pitch decreased comprehension by more than 10% for both prose and poetry. Other research suggests that moderately poor vocal quality and pitch patterns, disfluencies, mispronunciation, and even stuttering do not interfere significantly with comprehension, although listeners generally find these conditions unpleasant (Kibler & Barker, 1972; Klinger, 1959; Utzinger, 1952). All of these studies indicate that listeners are rather adaptable. It probably takes constant and extreme vocal unpleasantries to affect comprehension, and even then the listener may adapt. Poor vocal qualities probably contribute more to a listener's perception of the speaker's personality or mood than to a decrease in comprehension. Poor vocal qualities (along with other nonverbal cues from speakers) might also impact how much listeners think they have learned from speakers (see Box **Fluent and Disfluent Instructors**).

© Terrence Horgan

FLUENT AND DISFLUENT INSTRUCTORS

As you well know, some instructors seem like more effective lecturers than others. The effective or "fluent" ones display appropriate gestures, move around the classroom, and use their voice and pauses well. The ineffective or "disfluent" ones, on the other hand, use fewer gestures, do not move around a lot, have limited eye contact with the class, and use a monotone pitch and awkward pauses. How do these different instructor types impact your perceived and actual learning? Toftness et al. (2008) investigated these very questions. As expected, participants thought that they had learned more from the fluent instructors. Yet there were no differences in participants' actual memory for the material covered by the fluent and disfluent instructors. One implication of this is that measures of students' actual learning may need to be taken into consideration when assessing instructors' effectiveness, especially in situations where students feel that they have not learned a lot in a particular class because the instructor's use of their voice and other nonverbal cues is not very good.

Children are required to understand what adults are referring to when they speak about an object, such as a bunny. Do children use vocal cues to do this? Berman, Chambers, and Graham's (2010) research suggests that 4-year-olds do. They conducted an experiment in which children heard an adult say a sentence, such as "Look at the bunny," in either a neutral, happy, or sad voice. More important, there were three objects the children could look at: a distractor item, such as a horse; a clean, intact bunny; or dirty, ragged, broken bunny. Results showed that 4-year-olds (but not 3-year-olds) visually fixated most often to the "broken" bunny when they heard the sad voice, and most often to the "intact" bunny when they heard the happy voice. These findings suggest that 4-year-old children were using vocal cues to determine which object the speaker might be referring to in the sentence "Look at the bunny." It also appears that children as young as 15 months are aware when a person's action does not match her preceding vocal cue (Hoicka & Wang, 2011).

The study of speaking rate by itself yields additional evidence of listener flexibility and the lack of impact on comprehension of seemingly poor voice-related phenomena. The normal speaking rate is between 125 and 190 words per minute. Some researchers believe comprehension begins to decrease once the rate exceeds 200 words per minute, but other experts in speeded speech place the level of significant decline in comprehension at between 250 and 275 words per minute. King and Behnke (1989) point out that time-compressed speech adversely affects comprehensive listening—that is, understanding a message and remembering it for the future—but does not adversely affect short-term listening (40 seconds or less) or interpretive listening (reading between the lines) until very high levels of compression are reached, around 60%. Obviously, individual ability to process information at rapid rates differs widely. The inescapable conclusion from studies of speech rate, however, is that people can comprehend information at much more rapid rates than they ordinarily are exposed to. In an experiment in which individual listeners were allowed to vary the rates of presentation at will, the average choice was 1.5 times normal speed (Orr, 1968).

VOCAL CUES AND PERSUASION

Before we examine the role of the voice in persuasion, it is important to stress that speakers can communicate intentional, motivational, and attitudinal information to others with their voice alone. As examples, there are vocal cues that distinguish between a speakers' passion and indifference (Truesdale & Pell, 2018), sincerity and insincerity (Fish, Rothermich, & Pell, 2017), and confidence and doubt (Guyer, Fabrigar, & Vaughan-Johnston, 2019; Jiang & Pell, 2017). Moreover, those listening to speakers can quickly key into specific vocal cues. For instance, Zougkou et al. (2017) have examined the ERPs of listeners and found that listeners were able to distinguish between motivational (e.g., controlling tone) and non-motivational speech within 200 ms. Others are exploring how we use the vocal tones of speakers to understand their intentions (Hellbernd & Sammler, 2018).

At the global level, the vocal cues noted above are likely to impact how persuasive a speaker is perceived to be. However, here, we are concerned with the specific contributions that vocal cues make toward changing people's attitudes.

Mehrabian and Williams (1969) conducted an early series of studies on the nonverbal correlates of intended and perceived persuasiveness. The following vocal cues were associated with both "increasing intent to persuade and decoded as enhancing the persuasiveness of a communication": more speech volume, higher speech rate, and less halting speech. This early study has been followed by many studies on the relation of vocal cues to attitude change. The vocal cues listed shortly are associated with greater perceived persuasiveness, credibility, competence, or actual attitude change (Burgoon, Birk, & Pfau, 1990; Leigh & Summers, 2002). However, an upper limit to the effective range on each of these variables is likely, so that extremes would produce less, not more, credibility or persuasion. Also, how these cues impact attitudes may depend on the degree to which listeners are cognitively "elaborating" on the speakers' message (e.g., see Guyer et al., 2019).

- Fluent, nonhesitant speech
- Shorter response latencies, the pauses when speakers switch turns
- More pitch variation
- Louder voice
- Faster speech, as measured by words per minute or length of pauses

Of all these cues, faster speech has received the most attention in its relation to the persuasion process (Miller, Maruyama, Beaber, & Valone, 1976; Street, Brady, & Lee, 1984). Why is fast speech persuasive? Possibly, faster speakers seem more credible because listeners assume they really know what they are talking about and truly believe it themselves. But when listening to a faster-speaking persuader, listeners may also be kept so busy processing the message that they have little chance to develop counterarguments in their heads. Or listeners may be simply distracted by noticing the faster speech, and this interferes with ability to focus on the message and develop counterarguments (Woodall & Burgoon, 1983). It is also important to note that faster speech does not *always* produce more persuasion. Smith and Shaffer (1991) found that faster speech increased persuasion when the message was counterattitudinal—that is, when it favored a position that opposed the listener's preexisting attitude—but it decreased persuasion when the message was consistent with the listener's preexisting attitude.

At this point you may legitimately ask, "So what?" So what if you know the voice's potential for eliciting various responses related to comprehension, attitude change, and speaker credibility? Obviously in real-life situations, visual and verbal cues, prior publicity and experiences with the speaker, and a multitude of other factors can reduce the importance of vocal cues. In short, specific nonverbal cues do not operate in isolation in human interaction, as they do in the experiments reported here.

For the most part, we do not know what their role is in context—that is, in combination with other cues and in settings outside the laboratory. DeGroot and Motowidlo's (1999) study takes us a step in that direction. These investigators asked managers in companies to let themselves be interviewed as though they were applying for their job. The managers' vocal cues were then related to their actual supervisors' performance ratings of them and also to naive observers' impressions of the taped interviews. A vocal composite that consisted of faster speech rate, more pitch variability, fewer pauses, lower pitch, and less amplitude variability was a significant predictor of both the performance ratings and the favorability of listeners' reactions, which led the authors to believe that people who speak with this desirable set of vocal characteristics will be better able to perform well on the job. Burgoon and colleagues (1990) also examined a wide range of different cues, including vocal cues and those relating to face and body, in a study of credibility and persuasiveness. Controlling for other nonverbal behaviors, vocal fluency remained the strongest predictor of judged competence, which is a dimension of credibility, and it was one of the two strongest predictors of judged persuasiveness. Complementing these studies of specific vocal cues, Ambady, Krabbenhoft, and Hogan (2006) used global ratings of electronically filtered speech to predict ratings of sales effectiveness, as made by upper management, in a sample of sales managers. Even though the sales managers' voice clips totaled only 1 minute each, ratings of qualities such as emotion, empathy, cooperation, and enthusiasm as perceived in the voice were strongly correlated with their superiors' positive evaluations of them.

VOCAL CUES AND TURN-TAKING IN CONVERSATIONS

Thus far, we have discussed the role of vocal cues in communicating interpersonal attitudes, emotions, and information about the speaker. Vocal cues also play an important role in managing the interaction and are part of a system of cues that helps people structure their interactions—that is, who speaks when, to whom, and for how long.

Rules for turn-taking, or "floor apportionment," may have as much to do with how a conversation is perceived as does the actual verbal content of the interaction (Duncan, 1973; Wiemann & Knapp, 1975). You can probably recall instances where turn-taking rules played a significant role in your responses, for example, when a long-winded speaker would not let you get a word in edgewise; when a passive interactant refused to "take the conversational ball" you offered; when you were confronted with an "interrupter"; or those awkward moments when you and the other person started talking simultaneously.

Altogether, people do a remarkable job of negotiating turn-taking through nonverbal, including vocal, cues. Only rarely is there need to explicitly verbalize this information—for example, "Okay, Lillian, I'm finished talking. Now it's your turn to talk." Use of these signals is mostly nonconscious but conforms to definite rules of usage nonetheless. These have been described extensively by Duncan and Fiske (1977) in their analyses of two-person conversations held in a laboratory setting. Certain cues were almost invariably present when smooth turn-taking took place, five of which were vocal, either verbal or nonverbal. None of these cues seems to be more important than the others; rather, it seems that a smooth switch is best predicted by the sheer number of these cues. In other words, redundancy—sending several equivalent-meaning cues simultaneously—promotes smooth regulation of conversation. These cues included the speaker's pitch or a drawl at the end of a unit of speech, the grammatical completion of a unit of speech, and the use of certain routine verbal phrases. The next sections elaborate on these and other turn-regulating behaviors identified in research (Cappella, 1985; Rosenfeld, 1987).

TURN-YIELDING

To yield a turn means to signal you are finished and that the other person can start talking. Sometimes, we do this by asking a question, causing the pitch to rise at the end of our comment. Another unwritten rule most of us follow is that questions require, or often demand, answers. We also can drop our pitch, sometimes with a drawl on the last syllable, when finishing a declarative statement that concludes our intended turn. If the cues are not sufficient for the other person to start talking, we may have to add a trailer on the end. The trailer may be silence or may take the form of a filled pause, for example, "ya know," "so, ah," or "or something." The filled pauses reiterate the fact that you are yielding, and they fill a silence that might otherwise indicate the other's insensitivity to your signals or your own inability to make them clear.

TURN-REQUESTING

We can also use vocal cues to show others that we want to say something. Although an audible inspiration of breath alone may not be a sufficient cue, it does help signal turn-requesting. The mere act of interrupting or simultaneous talking may signal an impatience to get the speaking turn. Sometimes, you can inject vocalizations during normal pausing of the other speaker. These "stutter starts" may be the beginning of a sentence ("I … I … I …") or merely vocal buffers ("Ah … Er … Ah …"). Another method for requesting a turn is to assist the other person in finishing quickly. This can be done by increasing the rapidity of our responses, much like the increased rapidity of the head nods when we are anxious to leave a situation in which another person has the floor. Normally, backchannel cues, such as "Uh-huh," "Yeah," and "Mmm-hmm," are used to encourage the other to continue speaking and to signal attentiveness. However, when these cues are used rapidly, the message can be "Get finished so I can talk."

TURN-MAINTAINING

Sometimes, we want to keep the floor. It may be to show our status or to avoid unpleasant feedback, or perhaps it reflects some exaggerated sense of the importance of our own words and ideas. Common vocal cues in these instances may include the following:

1. Increasing volume and rate when turn-requesting cues are sensed
2. Increasing the frequency of filled pauses
3. Decreasing the frequency and duration of silent pauses

Although Lalljee and Cook's (1969) research does not support the use of pauses for control, Rochester (1973) cites several studies that support the following conclusions:

1. More filled pauses and fewer silent pauses are found in dialogue than monologue.
2. More filled pauses and fewer silent pauses are not found when people want to break off speaking.
3. More filled pauses and fewer silent pauses are more likely when the speaker lacks visual means of controlling the conversation, as on the telephone.

TURN-DENYING

In some instances, we may want the other person to keep talking—to deny the turn when offered. The back-channel cues we noted earlier may keep the other person talking by giving reinforcement for what is being said. The rate with which these cues are delivered, however, is probably slower than when we are requesting a turn. And, of course, simply remaining silent may dramatically communicate a turn denial. Silence and pauses are the subjects of our next section.

We wish to reiterate that conversational regulation is a delicate matter involving a complex coordination of verbal behavior, vocal behavior, gaze, and body movement. Research finds that even if we would predict a turn-switch based on words and voice, a switch is very unlikely if the speaker looks away from the listener during the likely switching point or engages in a hand gesture that is maintained or not returned to a resting state.

HESITATIONS, PAUSES, SILENCE, AND SPEECH

Spontaneous speech is actually highly fragmented and discontinuous. Goldman-Eisler (1968) said that even when speech is at its most fluent, two-thirds of spoken language comes in chunks of less than six words, which strongly suggests that the concept of fluency in spontaneous speech is an illusion. Pauses range in length from milliseconds to minutes. Pauses are subject to considerable variation based on individual differences, the kind of verbal task, the amount of spontaneity, and the pressures of the particular social situation.

LOCATION OR PLACEMENT OF PAUSES

Pauses and hesitations are not randomly distributed throughout the speech stream (Goldman-Eisler, 1968; Merlo & Barbosa, 2010). Goldman-Eisler (1968, p. 13) outlined places where pauses do occur—at both grammatical and non-grammatical junctures.

Grammatical

1. "Natural" punctuation points, for example, the end of a sentence.
2. Immediately preceding a conjunction whether (a) coordinating, such as *and*, *but*, *neither*, *therefore*; or (b) subordinating, such as *if*, *when*, *while*, *as*, *because*.
3. Before relative and interrogative pronouns, for example, *who*, *which*, *what*, *why*, *whose*.
4. When a question is direct or implied: "I don't know whether I will."
5. Before all adverbial clauses of time (when), manner (how), and place (where).
6. When complete parenthetical references are made: "You can tell that the house— the one on the corner—is falling into disrepair."

Nongrammatical

1. Where a gap occurs in the middle or at the end of a phrase: "In each of … the cells of the body …."
2. Where a gap occurs between words and phrases repeated: (a) "The question of the … of the economy" and (b) "This attitude is narrower than that … that of many South Africans."
3. Where a gap occurs in the middle of a verbal compound: "We have … taken issue with them and they are … resolved to oppose us."
4. Where the structure of a sentence is disrupted by a reconsideration or a false start: "I think the problem of France is the … what we have to remember about France is …."

Analysis of spontaneous speech shows that only 55% of the pauses fall into the grammatical category, whereas oral readers of prepared texts are extremely consistent in pausing at clause and sentence junctures.

TYPES OF PAUSES

The two major types of pauses are the unfilled, silent pause and the filled pause. A *filled pause* is filled with some type of phonation such as "um" or "uh." A variety of sources associate filled pauses with a range of generally undesirable characteristics. Some people associate filled pauses and repetitions with emotional arousal; some feel that filled pauses may reduce anxiety but jam cognitive processes. Goldman-Eisler (1961) found, in four studies, that unfilled pausing time was associated with "superior (more concise) stylistic and less probable linguistic formulations," whereas higher rates of filled pauses were linked to "inferior stylistic achievement (long-winded statement) of greater predictability." Livant (1963) found the time required to solve addition problems was significantly greater when the participant filled his pauses than when he was silent. Several experimenters reached similar conclusions: When speakers fill pauses, they also impair their performance. Thus, in a heated discussion, you may maintain control of the conversation by filling the pauses, but you may also decrease the quality of your contribution. However, too many filled *or* unfilled pauses may receive negative evaluations from listeners (Christenfeld, 1995). Lalljee (1971) found that too many unfilled pauses by the speaker caused listeners to perceive the speaker as anxious, angry, or contemptuous; too many filled pauses evoked perceptions of the speaker as anxious or bored. Although these studies suggest that filled pauses are generally to be avoided, research also finds that in university lecturers, their use is correlated with more complex thought processes and use of a larger vocabulary (Schachter, Christenfeld, Ravina, & Bilous, 1991; Schachter, Rauscher, Christenfeld, & Crone, 1994).

Filled pauses show up, interestingly, much more in the speech of men than that of women (Hall, 1984). We might think of men as more assertive in general, but Siegman (1987) observed that more filled pauses are usually associated with "cautious and hesitant speech" (p. 398). Perhaps men are more socially uncomfortable than women are. It may be, however, that filled pauses are serving another function altogether—keeping the speaker's turn from being taken over by the other person, which may be of more concern for men.

REASONS WHY PAUSES OCCUR

During the course of spontaneous speech, one is confronted with situations that require decisions as to what to say and what lexical or structural form to put it in. One school of thought relates hesitancy in speech to the uncertainty of predicting the cognitive and lexical activity while speaking. The speaker may be reflecting on decisions about the immediate message or may even be projecting into the past or future—that is, "I don't think she understood what I said earlier" or "If she says no, what do I say then?" Thus, these hesitation pauses would happen due to competing processes taking place in the brain. Goldman-Eisler indeed found that the duration of pause while interpreting cartoons was twice as long as while describing them. It also was observed that with each succeeding trial (i.e., with increasing reductions in spontaneity) there was a decline in pausing. More recent research continues to support the theory that longer speech latencies and a relatively large number of pauses are sometimes due to the complexity of the message being formulated (Greene & Ravizza, 1995).

It has been argued that speakers use fillers, such as "uh" and "um," to signal that the listener should expect either a minor or major delay in speaking (Clark & Fox Tree, 2002). However, recent work by O'Connell and Kowal (2005) has called this into question, finding that such fillers were not usually followed by silent pauses.

Another possible explanation for some pausing behavior involves what is described as "disruption behavior." Instead of representing time for planning, the pause may indicate a disruption due to an emotional state that may have developed from negative feedback or time pressures. These disruptions may take many forms: fears about the subject matter under discussion, desire to impress the listener with verbal or intellectual skills, pressure to perform other tasks simultaneously, or pressure to produce verbal output immediately.

Pauses may also be used to help children learn about turn-taking in conversations. Bergeson, Miller, and McCune (2006) observed that mothers used longer pauses when talking with older as opposed to younger infants, thus giving them extra time to respond.

INFLUENCE AND COORDINATION WITHIN THE DYAD

Thus far, we have considered hesitations and pauses primarily from the speaker's standpoint. Now we consider the interaction process and the effect of one person's interpersonal timing on another. For many years, Chapple (1949, 1953; Chapple & Sayles, 1961) explored the rhythms of dialogue, that is, the degree of synchrony found in the give-and-take of conversations. This involved noting who talks, when, and for how long. He developed a standardized interview in which the interviewer alternates "normal" attentive responding with silences and, later, interruptions. As you might suspect, there are many reactions. Some people respond to a nonresponse, or silence, by speeding up; others match the nonresponse; and most try some combination of the two.

Matarazzo's studies of interviewing behavior found most latencies of response were between 1 and 2 seconds, with the mean of about 1.7 seconds (Matarazzo, Wiens, & Saslow, 1965). Matarazzo also demonstrated response matching, showing how the interviewer could also control the length of utterance by increasing the length of his own utterances. As the interviewer extended the length of his responses, a corresponding increase in the length of responses from the interviewee resulted. In the same manner, there must be times when pauses beget pauses. The interviewer also can control response duration by head-nodding or saying "Mmm-hmm" during the interviewee's response. This demonstrates that these back-channel responses do indeed encourage a speaker to continue speaking.

SILENCE

Most of the hesitations and pauses we have discussed are relatively short. Sometimes, silences may be extended. They may be imposed by the nature of the environment, for example, in churches, libraries, museums, courtrooms, or hospitals; they may be imposed for the duration of a given event, as at a burial or when someone is singing or signing the national anthem; or they may be self-imposed, such as remaining quiet in the woods to hear other sounds, or enjoying with a lover the mutual closeness that silence may bring. Silence can mean virtually anything, and it is charged with those words that have just been exchanged; words that have been exchanged in the past; words that have not or will not be said but are fantasized; and words that may actually be said in the future. For these reasons, it would be absurd to provide a list of meanings for silence. The meaning of silence, like the meaning of words, can be deduced only after careful analysis of the communicators, subject matter, time, place, culture, and so on.

Some of the many interpersonal functions served by silence include the following:

- Punctuation or accenting, drawing attention to certain words or ideas
- Evaluating, providing judgments of another's behavior, showing favor or disfavor, agreement or disagreement, or attacking (e.g., not responding to a comment, greeting, or letter)
- Revelation, making something known, or hiding something
- Expression of emotions: the silence of disgust, sadness, fear, anger, or love
- Mental activity, showing thoughtfulness and reflection or ignorance (Bruneau, 1973; Jaworski, 1993; Jensen, 1973)

There are social and emotional consequences associated with silence. Silence in response to a question like "I'm lost. Do you live around here?" is likely to be viewed as inappropriate (e.g., Brown & Levinson, 1987). Koudenburg, Postmes, and Gordijn (2011) conducted an experiment in which participants imagined being a person whose statement was followed by silence (or not) from others in a videotaped group interaction. They found that silence triggered greater feelings of being distressed, afraid, and hurt as well as feelings of rejection in participants. It seems that people are sensitive to cues of possible social exclusion, one of which appears to be silence from others.

SUMMARY

This chapter should leave you with the overall impression that vocal cues frequently play a major role in determining responses in human communication situations. You should be quick, however, to challenge the cliché that vocal cues only concern how something is said—frequently they are *what* is said. What is said might be an attitude ("I like you" or "I'm superior to you"); it might be an emotion; it might be the coordination and management of the conversation; or it might be the presentation of some aspect of your personality, background, or physical features.

You should also recognize the important role vocal stereotypes play in determining responses. Whether judges are trying to estimate your occupation, sociability, race, degree of introversion, body type, or any of various other qualities about you, they will be very apt to respond to well-learned stereotypes. These stereotypes may not accurately describe you, but they will be influential in the interaction between you and others. Although research has demonstrated considerable interjudge agreement, so far it is difficult to identify many personality traits that seem to be judged with consistent accuracy. Although it is not uncommon for a person speaking a dialect other than one's own to be perceived negatively, speakers who try to correct for speech differences, and severely violate expectations for their speech, may also be perceived negatively.

Accurate judgments—that is, beyond chance levels—of age, sex, and status from vocal cues alone tend to be fairly consistently reported in the literature. Furthermore, people are often able to identify specific speakers from voice alone.

Although studies of judgments of emotions from vocal cues have used different methods, different emotions, listeners with differing sensitivity, and speakers with differing abilities for portraying emotions, the results reveal that people can make quite accurate judgments of emotions and feelings from nonverbal vocal messages. Some indications are that moderately poor vocal behaviors do not interfere with a listener's comprehension of a message and that, if there is variety in volume, pitch, and rate, chances are increased of achieving audience comprehension in public speeches. Unchanging, constant vocal behavior, particularly at the extremes, may be less advantageous in achieving audience comprehension.

Research also suggests that the voice may be important in some aspects of persuasion. More fluency, higher rate, more volume, and less halting speech seem related to intent to persuade and perceived persuasiveness. We know that the credibility of the speaker plays an important role in persuasion in some situations. Some decisions concerning credibility—such as dimensions of trustworthiness, dynamism, likableness, and competency—are made from word-free samples of the voice alone.

Vocal cues also help us manage the give-and-take of speaking turns. In turn-yielding, turn-requesting, turn-maintaining, and turn-denying, we use vocal cues to make our intentions clear.

We also discussed the important role of hesitations or pauses in spontaneous speech. Such pauses, ordinarily between 1 and 2 seconds long, may be greatly influenced by the other interactant, the topic being discussed, and the nature of the social situation. Pauses may be the overt manifestation of time used to make decisions about what to say and how to say it, or they may represent disruptions in the speech process.

Taken together, these findings show that vocal cues alone can give much information about a speaker, and our total reaction to another individual is at least somewhat colored by our reactions to these vocal cues. Our perceptions of verbal cues combine with other verbal and nonverbal stimuli to help frame the nature and flow of our interactions with others.

QUESTIONS FOR DISCUSSION

1. Consider stereotypes you have about the voice—for example, about high or low voices, fast or slow voices, voices with different accents, and so on. Discuss what truth you think there is to the stereotypes, based on as many real examples as you can think of.

2. Analyze the phenomenon of sarcasm in terms of the voice as well as the other cues that might be associated with it. Act out a variety of different comments in a sarcastic manner, and specify the cues you use. Are verbal and non-verbal usages different in teasing (or joking) compared to being sarcastic?

3. Review the different methods for making voices free of verbal content by applying content-masking techniques. Why does the chapter argue that doing this does not free the voice of content?

4. Theorists argue that some nonverbal channels are easier than others to self-monitor and control. Compare the vocal channel to the face and body channels. How would you rank these three channels in terms of how easy they are to monitor and control? What is the basis for your rankings?

NONVERBAL COMMUNICATION IN ACTION: TRY THIS

Spend some time paying special attention to how you use a person's vocal cues to identify their characteristics, such as social class, education, sexual orientation, or personality. A good way to do this would be to sit in a public place and listen to people speaking whom you are not looking at. Or you could listen to the television without looking at it. Analyze the cues you use. Do you have any sense of whether your judgments are correct?

PART V

COMMUNICATING IMPORTANT MESSAGES

Our book concludes with a discussion of how the various nonverbal signals discussed thus far combine as communicators pursue critical and familiar outcomes. Chapter 12 focuses on how nonverbal signals help us effectively communicate and interpret intimacy, power, involvement, identity, and deception in daily interaction. Chapter 13 examines nonverbal messages in advertising, politics, education, culture, health care, and technology. Together, these two chapters show the importance of understanding nonverbal behavior in effectively managing life's most important tasks.

CHAPTER 12

USING NONVERBAL BEHAVIOR IN DAILY INTERACTION

Nothing in nature is isolated; nothing is without connection to the whole.

—Goethe

Try to imagine yourself telling a high school student how to be a successful college student. Your approach probably would break the process into its component parts: social life, or dating and partying; intellectual life, which might include studying, taking notes, and relating to professors; organizational life, that is, what campus and social groups to join; financial life, or how to get by with little money; and so on. As informative as your explanations and advice in these separate areas may be, you know they are not enough. You also need to point out how these parts go together to create complex situations; for example, a person you desire has agreed to go out with you, but the date will cost a lot of money, and it will occur the night before a big test.

In the same way, this book is designed to make you more knowledgeable about human interaction and about nonverbal behavior in particular. The preceding chapters focused on individual parts of the total system: eyes, face, gestures, physical appearance, voice, and so forth. In this chapter, we show how these component parts combine to achieve the various communicative outcomes that people strive for in daily life.

To fully understand any process, one continually must look at the isolated parts that make up the system and at how they combine to achieve the system's purpose. Throughout this book, we have made occasional references to multisignal effects—for example, the role of verbal behavior in judgments of physical attractiveness and the close interrelationship of gestures with verbal behavior. Edward T. Hall, who coined the term *proxemics* to identify the study of distance and space, believed one has to consider 19 different behavioral signals to fully understand proximity in human transactions—and proximity is just one of the many nonverbal modalities that combine to produce total impressions and messages. In this chapter, we look at how nonverbal signals contribute to communicating intimacy, communicating status and power, managing the interaction, communicating identity, and deceiving others.

COMMUNICATING INTIMACY

Humans desire intimate relationships with others. Most people want to have acquaintances, friends, a lover, and to be part of a family. The "need to belong" and be connected to close others is very strong, indeed (Baumeister & Leary, 1995). How people establish close or intimate relationships with others is beyond the scope of this chapter. However, how they express their desire for, or felt intimacy toward, another person is not, for this involves the use of verbal and nonverbal cues (e.g., Guerrero & Jones, 2006; Guerrero & Wiedmaier, 2013; Hall & Xing, 2015; Moore, 2010; Patterson, 1983; Prager, 2000). Some of the same cues, such as self-disclosure and touching, are used by people to establish or maintain close or intimate relationships with others, as these cues signal positive involvement, closeness, and affectionate communication between individuals (Guerrero & Wiedmaier, 2013). Moreover, within the context of human courtship, some cues like touching are used even more by people at many different points in the process, from flirting to the beginning stages of romantic relationships (Andersen, Guerrero, & Jones, 2006; Baxter & Bullis, 1986; Burgoon, 1991; Docan-Morgan, Manusov, & Harvey, 2013; Guerrero & Wiedmaier, 2013; Jesser, 1978; Marston, Hecht, Manke, McDaniel, & Reeder, 1998; Tolhuizen, 1989; Willis & Briggs, 1992).

Scholars have studied nonverbal signals associated with intimacy from four different perspectives, and we will discuss each of them: the display behaviors associated with romantic courtship, courtship behaviors displayed in nonromantic situations, nonverbal behaviors that signal closeness with strangers and acquaintances, and nonverbal behaviors that signal closeness in more well-established intimate relationships.

COURTSHIP BEHAVIOR

We know that some men and women can exude messages such as "I'm available" or "I want you" without saying a word. And it appears that others have the ability to detect these cues in them, especially those given off by men. Place, Todd, Penke, and Asendorpf (2009) found that observers of speed-dating videos were able to detect men's romantic interest in women better than women's romantic interest in men. Perhaps women's cues are subtler than men's.

There are popular books available for those who seek to improve their ability to attract the romantic attention of others via nonverbal signals (Strauss, 2005). These signals include a thrust of the hips, touch gestures, extra-long eye contact, carefully looking at the other's body, showing excitement and desire in fleeting facial expressions, and gaining close proximity. When subtle enough, these moves will allow both parties to deny that either had committed themselves to a courtship ritual.

Academic research focusing on heterosexual flirtation in singles bars, hotel cocktail lounges, online- and speed-dating sites, bars in restaurants, and labs provides some observational data on the role of nonverbal signals in the courtship process (Back, Schmukle, & Egloff, 2010; Brak-Lamy, 2015; Grammer, Kruck, Juette, & Fink, 2000; Grammer, Kruck, & Magnusson, 1998; Hall & Xing, 2015; McCormick & Jones, 1989; Moore, 2010; Perper & Weis, 1987).

Two points should be kept in mind about flirting, though. First, when people flirt with each other, one should not assume that they want to pursue a romantic relationship with each other. Studies have shown that people's actual sexual interest in or desire to date another person is difficult to determine based on their flirtatious behaviors (Back et al., 2011; Grammer et al., 2000; Houser, Marcos, Horan, & Furler, 2008). Second, flirting does not often lead to a romantic relationship (Back et al., 2011; Brak-Lamy, 2015). One must therefore be careful about reading too much into what individuals do nonverbally (and what those nonverbal cues might mean) when they flirt with others.

With those cautionary points in mind, we can sketch out some differences between men and women in terms of how they flirt with each other nonverbally. Although it appears that there is considerable ambiguity about people's intentions early on during courtship (Guerrero & Wiedmaier, 2013), greater uncertainty or cautiousness is seen from women than men. When flirting, men tend to use more assertive cues and women more indirect ones (Clark, Shaver, & Abrahams, 1999; de Weerth & Kalma, 1995). As examples, men are more likely to touch women nonsexually and sexually than vice versa (Ballard, Green, & Granger, 2003; Brak-Lamy, 2015; McCormick & Jones, 1989; Moore, 2010). Women, on the other hand, are more likely use bodily presentation when they are flirting, a subtler cue compared to touching (de Weerth, 1995; Grammer, 1990). The subtle nature of women's nonverbal cues might explain why it is more difficult to gauge women's interest in men than men's interest in women early in the courtship process (Grammer et al., 1999; Place, Todd, & Asendorpf, 2009).

Nevertheless, it is interesting to note that, despite women's greater cautiousness during courtship, they are more likely than men to start or stop that process (Birdwhistell, 1970; de Weerth, 1995; Grammer et al., 1998; McCormick & Jones, 1989; Moore, 2010). According to Moore (2010), women are often the "selectors" because they display nonverbal cues that indicate their readiness to be approached by a specific man. Women use a number cues to do so—gazing at him, self-grooming, and showing a pleasant facial expression (McCormick & Jones, 1989; Moore, 1985, 2010; Whitty, 2004). Additional research has shown that women use gazing and smiling behaviors to successfully attract men (McQuillen, McQuillen, & Garza, 2014; Walsh & Hewitt, 1985). In terms of women's eye gaze, there are three types: a room-encompassing glance; a short, darting glance at a specific man; and a fixed gaze of at least 3 seconds at a specific man (see Figure 12-1). Lastly, given that men tend to value women's appearance more than vice versa, women may also try to enhance their appearance or sexual appeal around men (Brak-Lamy, 2015; Feingold, 1992).

There is some evidence to suggest that women value intelligence and status or dominance in men (Feingold, 1992; Prokosch et al., 2009). Given this, are there male behaviors that increase a man's chances of being selected by a woman? Men have greater success when they display cues related to greater dominance, such as taking up more space, showing an open-body position, and touching other men more (Grammer, 1990; Renninger, Wade, & Grammer, 2004).

Does courtship proceed according to a defined sequence of steps? Several theorists and studies suggest that it does (Birdwhistell, 1970; Eibl-Eibesfeldt, 1971; Givens, 1978a; Morris, 1971; Nielsen, 1962; Perper, 1985).

FIGURE 12-1 A woman flirting with a man.

Nielsen (1962), citing Birdwhistell, described a "courtship dance" of the American adolescent. Later, Givens (1978b) and Perper (1985) described the courtship process in terms of phases. First comes the *approach* phase, in which the two people come into the same general area. The second phase involves *acknowledging* the other's attention and turning toward the other as an invitation to begin talking. Nonverbal behavior during the *interaction* phase involves an increasing amount of fleeting, nonintimate touching and a gradually increasing intensity in gaze. The *sexual arousal* phase consists of more intimate touching, kissing, and other affectionate behaviors, and the *resolution* phase is characterized by intercourse. Obviously, either person can short-circuit the process or skip a step in the sequence at any point.

Even within one point of the courtship sequence, say flirtation, a sequence of events seems to unfold. For heterosexual individuals, this includes noticing others, deciding whether to approach them, talking to them, evaluating them, touching them, and synchronizing their behavior with them (e.g., Cunningham & Barbee, 2008). Flirting is not the same for everyone, though; Hall and Xing (2015), for example, have documented individual differences in flirting style.

When courtship is successful, sexual activity is likely to occur at some point. Whereas women use nonverbal cues to start the courtship process, men apparently are more involved in those steps leading to intercourse (Moore, 2010). However, the nonverbal cues that men use successfully to start a sexual relationship with women are not fully understood. Once in a committed relationship, young men are more likely to initiate sexual activity than young women, and men do so more with their nonverbal behavior than with their verbal behavior (Vannier & O'Sullivan, 2011).

There are several limitations to the research on the courtship process that need to be addressed:

1. Little is understood about the nonverbal courtship signals or behaviors of individuals interested in members of their own gender. As would be expected, touching, smiling, and eye contact are used to signal sexual attraction among lesbians (Rose & Zand, 2002). However, it is not clear how nonverbal cues are used to successfully negotiate the various stages of courtship, from relationship initiation to later sexual activity among people in same-gender relationships.

2. In the 21st century, people are turning more and more to alternative forms of courtship, such as online dating services (Albright & Simmens, 2014; Rosenfeld & Thomas, 2012; Whitty, 2009). Men and women seeking romance must signal their interest in another person and respond to the romantic overtures of others over cyberspace where the use of cues is often limited to profile images, emoticons (e.g., "smileys"), and written background information. However, with more advanced technologies, such as FaceTime, people can now hear and see each other in real time. Nonetheless, two people may be actively courting each other before they have had a chance to gaze, smile, or touch each other in the real world. It is not known if some of the traditional steps in the

COURTING EQUALITY

 © serdjophoto/Shutterstock.com

 © oneinchpunch/Shutterstock.com

Same-gender couples continue to struggle for recognition and acceptance. They have even been left out by researchers in nonverbal communication. Very little is known about how the courtship process unfolds for individuals romantically interested in members of their own gender. For example, how do women flirt with other women nonverbally? In heterosexual couples, gender norms can simplify the "who initiates" question, whereas in same-gender couples there is not a simple social rule to follow. What factors determine initiation in same-gender couples? These questions deserve attention from the research community.

real-world courtship process are altered because of prior online involvement. For example, would the nonverbal signals of interest be stronger or weaker for online daters actually meeting each other for the first time relative to individuals meeting for the first time without having had any prior online contact?

3. Another limitation concerns the lack of attention to the fluctuating nature of some nonverbal courtship cues. Research has shown that women's scent may change during ovulation, leading to potential changes in men's courtship-related behavior. In such studies, men are exposed to samples of women's body odor on low- versus high-fertility days (i.e., the women are currently ovulating). Results show that men rate the high-fertility odors as more attractive and also experience an uptick in their testosterone levels, both of which could motivate greater courtship intentions on their part (Gildersleeve, Haselton, Larson, & Pillsworth, 2011; Miller & Maner, 2010). One intriguing possibility is that, when women are most fertile, their odor cues might increase men's willingness to pursue them when they are also showing other signs that they desire interpersonal contact from men. This fluctuating courtship cue might be beneficial to the extent that it increases women's chances of reproducing. In line with this, Haselton, Mortezaie, Pillsworth, Bleske-Rechek, and Frederick (2007) found that women in relationships appear to dress more attractively when they are ovulating. Finally, men also may shift their courtship behavior, such as their use of language, to appear more attractive when they are around an ovulating woman (Coyle & Kaschak, 2012).

4. As noted already, it is important to bear in mind that flirting is often not successful; that is, the people involved do not go on to date or have a romantic relationship with each other (Back et al., 2011; Brak-Lamy, 2015). Thus, it is crucial to study the nonverbal cues that are used successfully by men and women to signal their desire to change their relationship from nonromantic to romantic. Docan-Morgan et al. (2013) noted that touch was one of the cues used to signal that change.

QUASI-COURTSHIP BEHAVIOR

Scheflen (1965) identified behaviors he called *quasi-courtship* behaviors, meaning they could be used during courtship, but they could also be used to communicate affiliative interest of a nonromantic type. Such behaviors may also be designed to invite affirmations of one's sexual appeal or attractiveness. Depending on the context, then, a particular cluster of behaviors could be considered friendly, flirting, or seductive. This opens up the possibility that the same set of cues could be interpreted differently or incorrectly by perceivers. It is not uncommon, for example, for men to perceive more sexual intent in the friendly behavior of women than women see in the friendly behavior of men (Abbey & Melby, 1986; Egland, Spitzberg, & Zormeier, 1996; Koeppel, Montagne-Miller, O'Hair, & Cody, 1993; Simpson, Gangestad, & Nations, 1996).

NONVERBAL SEXUAL CONSENT?

The ambiguity of nonverbal cues helps a person test the waters with another person when it comes to engaging in sexual activity. You might be interested but unsure, not ready to commit to sexual activity, or worried that your overtures will be rebuffed. Nonverbal behaviors provide, in this domain as in many others, an opportunity to send messages "off the record" and have deniability about what the behaviors meant if those messages are not welcomed or if one wants to make the other person responsible for what happens next.

The advantages of ambiguity are matched by its disadvantages, however. The other person may interpret your cues in a way you did not intend and take actions you do not want. Therefore, although it is obvious that clearly communicating one's consent is necessary, many people do not do so. Consent cues may be verbal or nonverbal, implicit or explicit, and within nonverbal cues there are active versus passive indications of consent (Willis, Blunt-Vinti, & Jozkowski, 2019). Any cue that is implicit opens the door to misunderstanding.

Willis et al. asked nearly 600 demographically diverse women from across the United States to report how they gave consent in their most recent partnered sexual activity, with items such as (1) using explicit verbal cues such as saying, *I want to have sex*, (2) using implicit verbal cues (like hints) such as asking the partner to get a condom, (3) using explicit nonverbal cues such as just starting to do the behavior (e.g., moving the partner's hands toward her genitals or starting to have sex), (4) using implicit nonverbal cues such as making eye contact or touching the partner's arm, back, or legs, and (5) using passive nonverbal behaviors such as letting it happen without resisting or stopping it.

Women's answers revealed how potentially dangerous this situation is for some women. Those who reported passively doing nothing and not resisting (a full 48%) were significantly *unlikely* to use explicit verbal consent and were significantly *likely* to use implicit nonverbal consent, which is ambiguous. Therefore, by their own admission many women's styles of giving consent are open to misunderstanding. We must note that in this study, the large majority of women were in committed sexual relationships. Whether the results would be the same for women in dating relationships is unknown. However, sexual coercion in long- and short-term relationships is common enough for us to worry based on this research.

Quasi-courtship behavior has some elements of courting, or relating to another for romantic purposes, but these behaviors are qualified by some other co-occurring behavior that says, "This is not courtship even though you see some similarities to that behavior." In some cases, quasi-courtship behaviors are used to build rapport; at other times, they are a form of play. The overall message is one of affiliation. Scheflen (1965) made films of numerous therapeutic encounters, business meetings, and conferences. Content analysis of these films led him to conclude that consistent and patterned quasi-courtship behaviors were exhibited in these settings. He then developed a set of classifications for such behaviors:

- *Courtship readiness* defines a category of behaviors characterized by constant manifestations of high muscle tone, reduced eye bagginess and jowl sag, a lessening of slouch and shoulder hunching, and decreasing belly sag.
- *Preening behavior* is exemplified by things such as stroking the hair; putting on makeup; glancing in the mirror; rearranging clothes in an attention-grabbing fashion, such as leaving buttons open, and adjusting suit coats; tugging at socks; and readjusting tie knots.
- *Positional cues* are reflected in seating or standing arrangements that suggest, "We're not open to interaction with anyone else." Arms, legs, and torsos are arranged to inhibit others from entering conversations.
- *Actions of appeal or invitation* include flirtatious glances, gaze holding, rolling of the pelvis, crossing the legs to expose a thigh, exhibiting the wrists or palms, protruding the breasts, and others.

Others have discussed Scheflen's positional cues in terms of who is excluded and who is included. The positioning of torsos in Figure 12-2 suggests, "We're not open to others" (in *a*) and "I'm with you—not her" (in *b*).

FIGURE 12-2 Positional cues.

LIKING BEHAVIOR OR IMMEDIACY

In the late 1960s and early 1970s, Mehrabian (1972b) conducted a number of experimental studies on what he called *immediacy*, that is, behaviors that indicate greater closeness or liking. This cluster of signals distinguishes a positive evaluation of an interaction partner from a negative one:

- More forward lean
- Closer proximity
- More eye gaze
- More openness of arms and body
- More direct body orientation
- More touching
- More postural relaxation
- More positive facial and vocal expressions

A lower frequency of these behaviors, particularly when they are expected, or the manifestation of opposite behaviors were associated with less intimacy or even disliking. While confirming the behaviors Mehrabian linked to immediacy, Ray and Floyd (2006) also found one form of positive vocal expression, vocal variety, but it is primarily limited to female behavior. Mimicking another's behavior may be another way of infusing a greater sense of affiliation in an interaction, although this would not necessarily be a conscious strategy on the part of the mimicker (Vicaria & Dickens, 2016). Smiling is another behavior often considered in the "immediacy" cluster.

Some combinations of Mehrabian's immediacy behaviors also have been found when people are trying to communicate support (Trees, 2000) and politeness (Trees & Manusov, 1998). And as we note in Chapter 13, a teacher's immediacy behaviors with their students have been linked to positive student attitudes, both toward the instructor and the course, as well as some measures of student learning (Rodriguez, Plax, & Kearney, 1996).

BEING CLOSE IN CLOSE RELATIONSHIPS

The work by Mehrabian and others provides a useful perspective for understanding how positive and negative evaluations of interaction partners are associated with clusters of nonverbal signals. In theory, the greater the number of signals activated, the more powerful the message. Immediacy cues are signals to look for in our culture during initial interactions with people one does not know very well. They do not, however, tell much about how friends or lovers communicate intimacy. It is difficult to judge accurately how emotionally close spouses are to each other by observing how much time they spend leaning toward each other with a direct body orientation, how much they gaze at each other in close proximity, and so on (Andersen et al., 2006; Guerrero & Floyd, 2006; Manusov, Floyd, & Kerssen Griep, 1997). Because much of the stereotypical immediacy behavior has presumably happened early on in these relationships, it needs to be displayed only on certain occasions once the relationship has become an intimate one. There are times in established relationships when it is imperative to communicate closeness with utmost clarity, especially when the relationship has been threatened. At such times, we are likely to see again the cluster of immediacy signals by the partner or partners who wish to offset any threat to their current level of intimacy. Partners in an established close relationship also use these stereotyped signals of intimacy when they want to communicate the closeness of their intimate relationship to outsiders, who may not understand the subtle and sometimes idiosyncratic ways intimates communicate their intimacy to each other. But most everyone understands close proximity, gazing into each other's eyes, touching, and all the other signals associated with the stereotyped immediacy cluster.

Time is an important limitation of much of the work on nonverbal behavior associated with intimacy, affiliation, or liking. Mehrabian's cluster of immediacy signals is primarily limited to one-time encounters. Ongoing relationships express different levels of intimacy over time, often indicating liking and disliking in quick succession. Clore, Wiggins, and Itkin (1975a, 1975b) realized that the sequencing of immediacy behaviors may have an important influence. They first collected a large number of verbal statements describing nonverbal liking and disliking; these behaviors were limited to a female's actions toward a male. The large number of behavioral descriptions was narrowed by asking people to rate the extent to which the behavior accurately conveyed liking or disliking. Table 12-1 lists the behaviors in order, rated highest and lowest. An actress then portrayed the narrowed list of these behaviors in an interaction with a male, and the interaction was videotaped. To no one's surprise, viewers of the video felt that warm behaviors would elicit greater liking from the male addressee. The interesting aspect of the studies is what happened when viewers were exposed to a combined video in which the actress's behavior was initially warm but then turned cold, or when her behavior was initially cold but then turned warm. The reactions to these videotapes were compared with responses to videotapes showing totally warm or totally cold portrayals by the actress. Viewers thought the man on the videotape would be more attracted to the woman who was cold at first and warm later than he would be to the woman who was warm for the entire interaction. Further, people felt the woman whose behavior turned from warm to cold was less attractive to the man than the woman who was cold during the entire interaction. Why? It might have to do with the extent to which the judges felt the male had responsibility for the female's change in behavior.

As we alluded to earlier, intimates in established romantic relationships may exhibit quantitatively less nonverbal behavior typically associated with affection and intimacy than they did in forming the relationship. To establish these relationships usually means a high frequency of hugs, kisses, handholding, and so forth; to maintain the relationship, though, it is often the quality of the act, not the frequency, that is important. Perceived sincerity, magnitude of the expression, and perfect timing are examples of qualitative factors. A hand held out to a significant other at just the right moment after a fight may be the equivalent of 10 handholdings at an earlier point in the relationship. The frequency of nonverbal acts of intimacy becomes important in established relationships when it is necessary to offset a threat to the relationship.

Table 12-1 Behaviors Rated as Warm and Cold

Warm Behaviors	Cold Behaviors
Looks into his eyes	Gives a cold stare
Touches his hand	Sneers
Moves toward him	Gives a fake yawn
Smiles frequently	Frowns
Works her eyes from his head to his toes	Moves away from him
Has a happy face	Looks at the ceiling
Smiles with mouth open	Picks her teeth
Grins	Shakes her head negatively
Sits directly facing him	Cleans her fingernails
Nods head affirmatively	Looks away
Puckers her lips	Pouts
Licks her lips	Chain smokes
Raises her eyebrows	Cracks her fingers

(Continued)

Table 12-1 (*Continued*)

Has eyes wide open	Looks around the room
Uses expressive hand gestures while speaking	Picks her hands
Gives fast glances	Plays with her hair's split ends
Stretches	Smells her hair

Source: Adapted from Clore, G. L., Wiggins, N. H., & Itkin, S. (1975), Judging attraction from nonverbal behavior: The gain phenomenon. *Journal of Consulting and Clinical Psychology*, 43, 491–497.

As close or intimate relationships develop, the nonverbal behavior is likely to change. To communicate a wider range of emotional states, more facial and vocal blends may occur. Sharply defined territories become more permeable. Conventionally performed nonverbal acts gradually give way to performances unique to friends or a couple. The increasing familiarity with auditory, visual, and olfactory signals creates a condition for greater accuracy and efficiency in communicating; close female friends, for example, are better able to interpret each other's as opposed to a stranger's low-intensity facial expressions of negative emotions (Zhang & Parmley, 2011). More than acquaintances, intimates rely on a variety of nonverbal signals to communicate the same message. Long-term intimates are also subject to acquiring one another's facial, postural, and gestural styles, making them look more alike over time (Zajonc, Adelmann, Murphy, & Niedenthal, 1987). Intimacy brings with it exposure to more personal nonverbal acts and more talk about them. We would also expect more overt evaluations—that is, approval or disapproval of nonverbal behavior—among intimates than among acquaintances (Knapp, 1983).

In the next section, we discuss how closeness or intimacy is created by the contributions of both parties. Matching, or reciprocity, may involve the *same kind* of behavior, or it may involve behaviors that are not the same but equivalent in their meaning or value. Furthermore, the extent to which one behavior is equivalent to another behavior in terms of its intimacy connotations is negotiated by the relationship partners. Thus, almost any behavior can communicate intimacy if the interaction partners agree that it does, with such shared but possibly idiosyncratic definitions more likely among those with a longer history of interacting with each other.

MUTUAL INFLUENCE

Whatever nonverbal behavior is used to communicate liking or disliking is inevitably the result of what both interactants do. This perspective prompted Argyle and Dean to propose *equilibrium theory* in 1965, which in various forms remains a mainstay of our understanding of relational dynamics. Their theory holds that interactants seek an intimacy level comfortable for both of them. Eye gaze, proximity, smiling, and topic intimacy, according to this theory, signal the degree of intimacy wanted by each interactant, which must then be negotiated in order to achieve harmony and avoid conflict. Some of this negotiation could of course occur verbally, as when "Can I kiss you?" or "Is it okay if I sit next to you?" is met with encouraging or discouraging words. But, there is a great deal of nonverbal negotiation as well.

In the Argyle and Dean theory, if the nonverbal behavior signals an increase or decrease in intimacy, the other interactant compensates by engaging in behaviors necessary to achieve equilibrium. For example, if a mere acquaintance looked at you too much, stood too close, and talked to you about intimate topics, equilibrium theory would predict that you would increase distance, look away, and try to change the topic to something less intimate in order to reestablish your comfort level. Although some attempts to test this theory found support for the predicted compensatory reactions, others found the opposite pattern—*reciprocating* changes in intimacy rather than offsetting them. This finding led to Patterson's (1976) *arousal-labeling model* of interpersonal intimacy, which maintained that gaze, touch, and proximity with another person create arousal. This arousal state is then labeled either positively or negatively. If it is negative—for example, dislike, embarrassment, or anxiety—the reaction will be to compensate or offset the behavior. If the arousal state is considered positive, as in liking, relief, or love, the reaction will be matching behavior or reciprocity.

Although this expanded theory explained why people sometimes compensate for, and sometimes reciprocate, the behavior of another person, it requires time-consuming cognitive labeling of behavior. In many encounters, these changes are too quick to involve this kind of mental processing. This consideration prompted Cappella and Greene (1982) to posit a *discrepancy arousal theory*. This model proposes that people have expectations about other people's expressive behavior. Increases and decreases in involvement by one person that violate the other person's expectations will lead to arousal or cognitive activation. Moderate arousal results from moderate discrepancies from what had been expected; these are pleasurable, and reciprocity ensues. Large discrepancies from what had been expected are highly arousing, leading to negative affective responses and compensation. Little or no discrepancy from expectations is not arousing, so we would not expect to see any compensatory or reciprocal adjustments made.

Burgoon (1978) and colleagues proposed a model specifically focused on one element of immediacy: proximity. Since then, this proximity model of *expectancy violation* has also been used to study and predict involvement in general (Burgoon & Hale, 1988; LePoire & Burgoon, 1994). This model is an important contribution toward our understanding of reciprocal and compensatory reactions, because it relies on both arousal and cognitive responses, and it explicates the important role of how rewarding the communicator is perceived to be.

Burgoon's expectancy-violations model posits that people have expectations for appropriate proximity in conversations, based on culture, personal experiences, and knowledge of specific interactants. When expectations for proxemic immediacy are met, arousal is not likely to play an important role. When violations occur, too far or too close, arousal is heightened, which directs attention to the nature of the interpersonal relationship. Interpretations then are made that guide a person's response. Interpretations vary, according to Burgoon's work, based on the perceptions of whether the violator is rewarding. If the person is rewarding—that is, high in credibility or status, or offers positive feedback—the violation of expectations will be perceived more positively than for nonrewarding interactants.

In an elaboration of the expectancy-violations model, Burgoon, Stern, and Dillman (1995) proposed *interaction adaptation theory*. This theory assumes that each interactant enters into a conversation with requirements, expectations, and desires. Requirements are what one deems absolutely necessary, like being close enough to hear someone. Expectations are what one anticipates happening based on the norms, the people involved, and the situation. Desires are personal goals and preferences for the interaction. This combination of what is believed to be needed, anticipated, and preferred is called an *interaction position*, and it is used as the standard against which the interaction partner's behavior is judged. When the interaction partner's behavior is closely aligned with one's interaction position, this theory predicts reciprocity of behavior. Reciprocity is also expected when the partner engages in major deviations that are more positive than one's interaction position would dictate. However, major deviations by the interaction partner that are more negative than one's interaction position are likely to make a person respond with compensatory behavior.

What should we make of these theories that try to predict when people reciprocate a partner's behavior and when they engage in compensatory behavior? Obviously, a simple bottom-line statement cannot take into account the many subtleties and variations associated with every human transaction, but as a general rule of thumb, one should remember the following: With strangers and acquaintances, people tend to reciprocate or match their nonverbal behavior when it is perceived as generally *congruent* with expectations and involvement preferences for a specific person in a given situation. People tend to compensate or offset the nonverbal behavior of strangers and acquaintances when it is perceived as a *major violation* of expectations and preferences for that person in that situation.

Most research examines one-shot behavior–response sequences to predict reciprocity or compensation. However, in real life an interpersonal interaction is likely to continue on, making for further behaviors and responses. For example, if the desired levels of intimacy of the interactants are discrepant, one could see repeated acts of compensation leading ultimately to one person exiting the scene or taking strong action to confront the other person either about their behavior ("Don't keep touching me!") or about the discrepant intimacy expectations that underlay the behavior patterns. Another kind of cycle can result when behavior is reciprocated: The repeated reciprocation of immediacy behaviors such as smiling or touching may lead to levels of implied intimacy that one or both parties find excessive, in which case compensation may occur. Thus, adjustments are a continuing process.

COMMUNICATING DOMINANCE AND STATUS

Tired of feeling weak and unimportant? Want to unlock the secrets of those who have gained authority and power? Want to know how to dominate friends, enemies, and business associates, with a few simple tips? Sorry, but we cannot tell you how to do that, even though we can understand the motivation behind the questions. People are likely to feel less satisfied with an interaction when they have less power than the other person (Dunbar & Abra, 2010). We can summarize the research on dominance and nonverbal behavior for you, but there are no pat answers. The desire for a simple how-to manual is great in this area, yet the research is too complex to allow it.

Even the basic concepts are complicated. The terms *status*, *dominance*, and *power* are often used interchangeably, but many authors have noted their ambiguities and have offered many definitions (Burgoon & Dunbar, 2006; Edinger & Patterson, 1983; Ellyson & Dovidio, 1985). Others have developed models in which some of these concepts, such as status and dominance, are facets of another overarching interpersonal dimension, such as power (Schmid Mast, 2010). The concepts are certainly related but not perfectly: A figurehead leader has status without power, whereas a low-status member of an organization may wield considerable influence by virtue of personal contacts, shrewd insight, and social interaction skill. Indeed, the term *political skill* has been used to describe such skills (Ferris et al., 2005; Wang & Hall, 2019).

A person's status, which may be detected in their nonverbal behavior (Kraus & Keltner, 2009; Shariff & Tracy, 2009), often connotes a socially valued quality that people carry with them into different situations and interactions, whereas power and dominance are more likely to be situationally defined. But dominance can also be seen as a personality trait expressed in nonverbal cues (Bente, Leuschner, Al Issa, & Blascovich, 2010), in addition to a situationally defined state in people. The tendency to be subordinate also has been viewed as a stable trait linked to nonverbal behaviors associated with a lack of confidence and submissiveness in men (Sturman, 2011), although situational factors—such as being around physically imposing males—might prompt submissive behaviors in men who are customarily dominant around others in day-to-day life. Some researchers would say that any kind of aggressive act is dominant, but for others a behavior is dominant only if it is followed by clear evidence of submission from another individual.

In research, many operational definitions have been used to represent these various concepts, which collectively have been labeled the *vertical dimension of social relations* (Hall, Coats, & Smith LeBeau, 2005). The following are some illustrations of different ways that verticality may be considered: attire, occupation, education, military rank, socioeconomic status, hierarchical position, initiation of contacts, children's attempts to gain precedence in play, giving orders, boasts, not submitting to others, controlling others' behaviors, attacks, control of resources, expertise, experience, and autonomy. All of these may have nonverbal communication aspects.

Another issue is whether nonverbal behaviors used to try to attain higher verticality may be different from those used by someone who has already achieved this goal (Argyle, 1988; Heslin & Patterson, 1982). Thus, acquiring and expressing dominance may not involve the same cues. Recognition of this possibility may help sort out contradictory results. For example, research finds that more gazing is perceived as dominant, and people with more dominant personalities, people who initiate speech more in groups, and people who attain higher status in groups are also less likely to be the first to break a mutual gaze in face-to-face interaction (Dovidio & Ellyson, 1985; Kleinke, 1986; Lamb, 1981; Rosa & Mazur, 1979; Snyder & Sutker, 1977; Thayer, 1969). Many authors have noted that gaze can carry connotations of threat and coercion, and it is often assumed that higher levels of gazing are a hallmark of a dominant, powerful, or high-status individual.

We might think everything adds up—higher status people gaze more—until we also read that people with dependent personalities tend to gaze more, and that people made to feel dependent gaze longer at an experimenter (Kleinke, 1986; Mehrabian, 1972b; Nevill, 1974; Thayer, 1969). Henley (1977) proposed that the reason why women gaze at others more than men do is because low-power people feel the need to monitor others by gazing at them. But, people higher on the vertical dimension do not predictably gaze less at others (Hall et al., 2005). These apparent contradictions may be reconciled if we consider that a person of high status or dominance may feel either secure or defensive, and a person of lower status or dominance may be struggling to gain status or may be signaling to more powerful others that they are no threat to that powerful other. Nonverbal behaviors such as gaze that people use in these different psychological states could differ radically. For example, the person who feels out of control but is striving to gain control might engage in high levels of gaze, whereas the person who accepts a low-status role might avert their eyes so as not to appear threatening. Gaze, touch, and most other nonverbal behaviors take their meanings in a complex way from the situation, from a person's motives, and from other co-occurring nonverbal behaviors.

Another important issue is the difference between the *impression* made by a particular nonverbal behavior and the *actual behavior* of people having different degrees of dominance, power, or status. Here are two examples of why this perceived-versus-actual distinction matters: A nonsmiling face is sometimes perceived as dominant (Keating, 1985), and seeing someone touch another raises the viewer's perception of the toucher's dominance (Major & Heslin, 1982). But these findings do not necessarily mean that dominant or high-status people *actually* smile less and touch more. The evidence is mixed for both, with no overall trends either way (Hall et al., 2005; Hall & Friedman, 1999; Johnson, 1994).

In general, people have well-developed beliefs about how nonverbal behavior is related to verticality. Carney, Hall, and Smith LeBeau (2005) asked college students to imagine interactions among people with differing degrees of dominance, including those with either more or less dominant personalities and those with either more or less status in the workplace. The more dominant person was believed to engage in more "invasive" behaviors, glare and gaze more, interrupt more, stand at a close distance, touch the other more, touch themselves less, show emotions successfully, stand more erect, and pay less attention to the other person, among many other perceived dominance behaviors.

Another way to examine people's beliefs is to show them nonverbal behavior—on videotape, for example—and ask them to rate how dominant or powerful the individuals seem to them. Many studies have done this, as reviewed by Hall et al. (2005). In general, the behaviors that predict higher ratings of verticality concur with those identified more explicitly in the Carney study.

However, for studies that correlated a person's actual degree of verticality with their nonverbal behavior, many fewer relations were found on average (Hall et al., 2005). High actual dominance was associated with more facial expressiveness, more bodily openness, smaller interpersonal distances, better posed expression skill, less vocal variability, louder voices, more interruptions, fewer backchannel responses, fewer filled pauses, and a more relaxed-sounding voice. At the same time, many other behaviors that are generally believed to be related to verticality were not observed. Furthermore, studies vary greatly in how nonverbal behavior is related to actual verticality, sometimes showing diametrically opposite effects.

Such opposite-seeming results could stem from the fact that high and low verticality can have many different emotions and motives associated with it. Considering this, it may not make much sense to seek nonverbal cues that are consistently correlated with a person's verticality. For example, a person low in a workplace's hierarchy who is feeling hostile to management might smile a very different amount from a similarly low-ranking person who is feeling the need to please their supervisor. To make an analogy, knowing how high a person is on a ladder does not tell you how they feel about it. Some might be terrified at being high and some might be delighted; some might find it depressing to be low and some might find it to be a great relief. Because one's feelings cannot necessarily be predicted from one's structural position, it follows that knowing a person's social verticality does not determine their emotions and motives, and therefore their nonverbal behavior. One boss might be kind and nurturant while another is stern and punitive.

In addition, as the readers of this book know by now, the nonverbal behaviors themselves can have ambiguous meanings, and therefore it is risky to label a particular behavior as being intrinsically, or always, dominant or nondominant. For instance, although interrupting others in conversation can be a dominant behavior (Henley, 1977; Kollock, Blumstein, & Schwartz, 1985; Leffler, Gillespie, & Conaty, 1982; Robinson & Reis, 1989), one should not take this interpretation for granted. Interruption is sometimes indicative of a highly involved and participatory conversation and is not necessarily a sign of a power struggle in progress (Dindia, 1987; Kennedy & Camden, 1983).

In contrast to the often-cited ambiguity of nonverbal cues, there is one behavior that has consistently been associated with dominance: the *visual dominance ratio* (Ellyson, Dovidio, & Fehr, 1981; Exline, Ellyson, & Long, 1975). Experiments that defined status, power, and dominance in different ways found that among White college students, the higher status person gazed roughly the same percentage of the time while listening and speaking, whereas the lower status person gazed relatively more while listening. When college students interacted in a laboratory, and one was made to be the expert or was accorded higher status, that individual, regardless of gender, engaged in the visually dominant pattern of gazing relatively more while speaking than while listening. Although subtle, the visual dominance ratio does not go unnoticed. When observers were asked to judge the relative power or potency of individuals displaying different patterns of gazing, they gave higher ratings to individuals engaging in relatively more looking while speaking than to those engaging in relatively more looking while listening.

How much a person talks when in a group is also a very consistent and rather strong indicator of status or dominance, both in terms of observers' perceptions and in terms of actual status or dominance (Schmid Mast, 2002). However, even here there are exceptions. In an interview situation, the interviewee (lower power) is likely to talk more than the interviewer (higher power). And in groups, a person with well-established status or power can often afford to sit back and say very little, knowing that others will attend fully whenever they choose to speak.

Murphy, Driscoll, and Kelly (1999) connected nonverbal dominance to the likelihood that college males would engage in sexual harassment. These authors found that males who scored higher on a scale that had previously been shown to predict sexual harassment engaged in several behaviors that people believe to be related to dominance: more open body postures, more direct eye contact, and less direct body orientation. However, nonverbal behaviors that might be construed as sexual—smiling, head tilting, and flirtatious glances—were not predicted by the scale, leading the authors to conclude that sexual harassment is more dominance related than sexuality related.

In sum, the relation of nonverbal communication to dominance and other power-related qualities is complex and does not lend itself to simple, formulaic approaches. Perhaps this is fortunate, because it would be troubling if it were truly easy to dominate others through nonverbal behavior.

MANAGING THE INTERACTION

Most of the time, you do not engage in much conscious thinking about how to greet people, request a speaking turn, show your conversational partner you believe what they are saying, or say good-bye. Yet you are very skilled in achieving these goals. These barely noticed behaviors structure the interaction—they regulate the processes of coming together, the back-and-forth nature of speaking and listening, and departure. When such acts are the subject of conscious reflection, you can appreciate the importance of the messages involved. However, because these processes are fairly automatic and nonconscious in nature, trying to think too much about them might disrupt the smooth and normal feeling that you typically get while interacting with others.

GREETING BEHAVIOR

Greetings perform a regulatory function by signaling the beginning of an interaction. Greetings also do much more: They convey information about the relationship, reduce uncertainties, signal ways to better know the other, and structure the ensuing dialogue. Some greeting behavior follows certain conventions, like the handshake, but greetings take many forms. In the 1930s, greetings in Germany did not take on any compulsory forms until the "Hitler Salute" was imposed upon the German people by the Nazi regime. This gesture was designed to signal one thing above all else—the greeter's willingness to follow the Nazi party's rules. It was the expected greeting in everyday administrative, commercial, political, and social situations, and it was taught to children at an early age (see Figure 12-3). The salute was a salute to Hitler, so it played no role in establishing a connection between the interacting parties. Allert (2008) argues convincingly that it wounded the sociability and connectedness among Germans of that era.

FIGURE 12-3 Germans performing the Nazi salute.

Without the imposition of any particular convention like the Hitler salute, verbal and nonverbal behavior during greetings may signal status differences, such as those between a subordinate and supervisor; degree of intimacy, as between acquaintances versus between lovers; or a current feeling or attitude, such as aversion or interest. An emotionally charged greeting may reflect our desired involvement with the other person, or it may reflect a long absence of contact. Goffman (1971) proposed an "attenuation rule," which states that the expansiveness of a greeting with a particular person will gradually subside with continual contact with that person, for example, a coworker at an office. Kendon and Ferber (1973) found that the following six stages characterized greetings initiated from a distance.

1. **Sighting, orientation, and initiation of the approach**. A greeting, like any other transaction, requires participation by both interactants. Sometimes, both will agree that acknowledgment is enough. After mutual recognition, an immediate and sustained withdrawal of attention occurs. Goffman (1963) called this common action *civil inattention*. When the greeting continues, we move to stage 2.

2. **The distant salutation**. This is the "official ratification" that a greeting sequence has been initiated and who the participants are. A wave, smile, or call may be used for recognition. Two types of head movements were noted at this point: One, the head toss, is a fairly rapid back-and-forward tilting motion. In the other, the person tended to lower the head, hold it for a while, and then slowly raise it.

3. **The head dip**. Researchers have noted this movement in other contexts as a marker for transitions between activities or shifts in psychological orientation. Interestingly, this movement was not observed by Kendon and Ferber if the greeter did not continue to approach their partner.

4. **Approach**. As the greeting parties continued to move toward each other, several behaviors were observed. Gazing behavior probably helped signal that the participants were cleared for talking. A break in this gaze was seen just prior to the close salutation stage, however. Grooming behavior and one or both arms moving in front of the body were also observed at this point.

5. **Final approach**. Participants at this stage are less than 10 feet from each other. Mutual gazing, smiling, and a positioning of the head not seen in the sequence thus far are now seen. The palms of the hands may also be turned toward the other person.

6. **Close salutation**. As the participants negotiate a standing position, they produce the more stereotyped, ritualistic verbalizations so characteristic of the greeting ceremony: "Hey, Steve! How ya doin'?" and so on. If the situation calls for body contact—handshakes, embraces, and the like—these will occur at this time. Even though the handshake is common in the United States, this kind of greeting behavior is not shared in some other cultures and used much more in others.

The specific nature of greetings varies according to the relationship of the communicators, the setting, and the attendant verbal behavior. Our major concern here is with the nonverbal behavior. The greetings observed by Krivonos and Knapp (1975) were frequently initiated by a vertical or sideways motion of the head accompanied by eye gaze. Smiles, regardless of the degree of acquaintanceship, were also common. Perhaps the smile serves the function of setting a positive, friendly initial mood. Eye gaze signals that the communication channels are open and that an obligation to communicate exists. Other eye-related greeting behaviors included winks and the eyebrow flash (discussed in Chapter 2). The hands are often active in the greeting process with salutes, waves, handshakes (Schiffrin, 1974), handslaps, and various emblematic gestures such as the peace sign, the raised fist, or the thumbs-up gesture. Hands used in greetings have traditionally been open, but in recent years, the "fist bump" has been used by some in the United States. When fists lightly touch each other in greeting, the greeters are signaling friendliness by showing that a potentially threatening gesture is being used in a nonthreatening way. Hands also may be engaged in grooming, such as running fingers through the hair. Touching may take the form of embraces, kisses, or hitting on the hands or arm. The mouth may smile or assume an oval shape, suggesting a possible readiness for talk.

TURN-TAKING BEHAVIOR

Conversations begin and are eventually terminated. Between these two points, people exchange speaking and listening roles, that is, they take turns. Without much awareness of what they are doing, people use body movements, vocalizations, and some verbal behavior to accomplish this turn taking with surprising efficiency. The act of smoothly exchanging speaking and listening turns is an extension of our discussion of interaction synchrony in Chapter 7. And, because a number of the turn-taking cues are visual, it is understandable that it might be harder to synchronize exchanges during telephone conversations.

The turn-taking process is not just an interesting curiosity of human behavior. Important judgments about others are based on how the turns are allocated and how smoothly exchanges are accomplished. Effective turn taking may elicit the perception that you and your partner really hit it off, or that your partner is a very competent communicator; ineffective turn taking may prompt evaluations of "rude" (too many interruptions), "dominating" (not enough turn yielding), or "frustrating" (the inability to discern turn-taking cues).

The turn-taking behaviors we are about to outline have generally been derived from analyses of White, middle- and upper-class adult interactants. Some of these behaviors may not apply to other groups. African Americans, for example, seem to gaze less than Whites do during interactions (Halberstadt, 1985). Other groups may develop speaking patterns with more unfilled pauses, which may communicate turn yielding to those unfamiliar with the group norm. Children who are learning turn-taking rules engage in behaviors rarely seen in adults, such as tugging at their parent's clothing and hand raising to request a speaking turn.

Speakers and listeners negotiate behaviors associated with turn taking, but speakers typically take responsibility for signaling *turn yielding* and *turn maintaining* while listeners typically take responsibility for *turn requesting* and *turn denying*. The behaviors associated with these acts are derived from careful analyses of both audio and visual elements enacted at junctures where interactants exchange or maintain the speaking turn (Duncan, 1975; Duncan & Fiske, 1977; Wiemann & Knapp, 1975; Wilson, Wiemann, & Zimmerman, 1984). Any individual behavior associated with speaker or listener intentions will contribute toward a smooth turn exchange, but the greater the number of signals, the greater the chances for a smooth exchange.

Note, however, that familiarity with the rules of interaction is also an important part of effective turn taking. For example, before any specific turn-taking behaviors are observed, most people enter conversations knowing that speaking roles will generally alternate, and that when one person finishes speaking, the other is generally obligated to take the conversational "ball." Cultures with different conversational rules and specialized systems of communication, such as sign language, require somewhat different turn-exchange processes, although congenitally blind and adventitiously blind communicators also display a range of vocal and bodily behaviors associated with conversational turn taking (Magnusson, 2006).

TURN YIELDING To yield in conversation literally means you are giving up your turn and you expect the other person to start talking. The termination of one's utterance can be communicated with gestures that rise or fall with the speaker's pitch level. Questions are clearly an indication that a speaker is yielding their turn and expects the partner to respond. If it is a rhetorical question the speaker plans to answer, the speaker will probably emit turn-maintaining cues, but a listener who is eager to get into the conversation may attempt to answer even a rhetorical question. Vocally, a person also can indicate the end of an utterance by a decreased loudness, a slowed tempo, a drawl on the last syllable, or a trailer such as "you know," "or something," or "but, uh." Naturally, an extended, unfilled pause (the speaker simply stops talking) is also used to signal turn yielding. More often than not, however, the silence becomes awkward, and the speaker adds a trailer onto the utterance. Body movements that have been accompanying the speech may also be terminated; for example, illustrative gestures come to rest, and body tenseness becomes relaxed. Gazing at the other person will also help signal the end of an utterance. If the listener does not perceive these yielding cues, and gives no turn-denying cues, the speaker may try to convey more explicit cues, such as touching the other, raising and holding the eyebrows in expectation, or saying something like "Well?"

TURN MAINTAINING What happens when the speaker does not want to yield a speaking turn? Voice loudness probably will increase as turn-requesting signals are perceived in the listener. Gestures probably will not come to rest at the end of the verbal utterances, creating a gestural equivalent to the filled pause. Filled pauses probably will increase while the frequency and duration of silent pauses decrease. This minimizes the opportunities for the other person to start speaking without interrupting or to start speaking simultaneously. Sometimes, there is a light touching of the other person by the speaker, which seems to say, "Hold on a little bit longer. I want to make a few more points and then you can talk." This touching is sometimes accompanied by a patting motion, as if to soothe the impatient listener. In some respects, this touch has the effect of the speaker putting their hand over the mouth of the would-be speaker—an act not allowed in interpersonal etiquette in our society.

TURN REQUESTING A person who does not have the floor but wants to talk may exhibit several behaviors. An upraised index finger seems to symbolize an instrument for creating a conversational hole in the speaker's stream of words, but it also approximates a familiar, formal turn-requesting signal learned in school—a raised hand. Sometimes, this upraised index finger is accompanied by an audible inspiration of breath and a straightening and tightening of posture, signaling the imminence of speech. In some cases, certain self-adaptors classified as preening behavior also may signal preparation for a new role. In addition, simply talking over the other person will signal a request for a speaking turn, but to make sure that request is granted, you have to speak louder than your partner, begin gesturing, and look away as if the turn were now yours. When the speaker and listener are well synchronized, the listener will anticipate the speaker's juncture for yielding and will prepare accordingly by getting the rhythm before the other person has stopped talking, much like a musician tapping their foot preceding a solo performance. If the requestor's rhythm does not fit the speaker's rhythm, stutter starts may occur—for example, "I … I … I was …." Sometimes, the turn-requesting mechanism consists of efforts to speed up the speaker, realizing that the sooner one speaker has their say, the sooner the requestor will get theirs. This same behavior was noted when people were anxious to terminate a conversation (Knapp, Hart, Friedrich, & Shulman, 1975). The most common method for encouraging a speaker to finish quickly is the use of rapid head nods, often accompanied by verbalizations of pseudo agreement such as "yeah" and "mmm-hmm."

TURN DENYING Sometimes, a person receives turn-yielding cues from the speaker but does not want to talk. At such times, one might maintain a relaxed listening pose, maintain silence, or avoid eye contact with the speaker. Or one might exhibit behavior that shows continuing involvement in the content of the speaker's words. This might take the form of smiling, nodding, or shaking the head; completing a sentence started by the speaker; briefly restating what the speaker just said; requesting clarification of the speaker's remarks; or showing approval by appropriately placed "mm-hmm's," "yeah's," or other noises such as the "tsk, tsk" sound that suggests "You shouldn't have said that."

Many of the actions listeners perform are called *backchannel* or *listener responses* (Duncan, 1974; Rosenfeld, 1987; Rosenfeld & Hancks, 1980). Listener responses are either nonverbal or minimally verbal and are not attempts to take the floor. They help regulate the flow of information and signal the listener's orientation to the speaker's messages. Listener responses can affect the type and amount of information given by the speaker, the length of the speaker's turn, and the clarity of the speaker's content. At key points while talking, a speaker will look into the face of the listener and this is likely to produce a backchannel response such as a nod or an "mm-hmm" from the listener (Bavelas, Coates, & Johnson, 2002). The primary nonverbal signals are head nods, but postural changes, smiles, frowns, eyebrow flashes, and laughter (Vettin & Todt, 2004) also occur. Common verbal and vocal backchannel signals include saying "yeah," "mmm-hmm," repeating the speaker's words, asking a clarifying question, or completing a sentence for the speaker. These listener responses signal attentive listening, approval, and encouragement for the speaker to continue on.

LEAVE-TAKING BEHAVIOR

Having managed our way through the conversation thus far, it is now time to terminate it. Leave taking seems to serve three valuable functions in daily interaction (Knapp et al., 1975). The primary regulatory function is signaling the end of the interaction. Again, specific nonverbal manifestations of this function vary with the relationship between the communicators, preceding dialogue, anticipated time of separation, body position—that is, whether the communicators are standing or sitting—and other factors. Decreasing eye gaze and positioning one's body toward the nearest exit were the two most frequent nonverbal behaviors observed in this study, and these seem to adequately signal impending absence. Leave-taking rituals may also summarize the substance of the discourse. This is usually accomplished verbally, but a good-night kiss may sufficiently capture the evening's pleasantries to qualify as a summarizer. Finally, departures tend to signal supportiveness, which can offset any negativity that might arise from encounter-termination signals, while simultaneously setting a positive mood for the next encounter—that is, it sends the message, "Our conversation has ended, but our relationship has not." Nonverbal supportiveness may be found in a smile, a handshake, touch, head nodding, and leaning forward. Because signaling supportiveness seems so important, people often use the more direct verbal signals, for example, "Thanks for your time. I'm glad we got a chance to talk."

Head nodding and leaning forward, of course, serve several simultaneous functions. Rapid head nodding toward the end of a conversation reinforces what the speaker is saying, but it is a rather empty reinforcement, because it can also signal a desire to terminate the conversation. And although it is true that people accompany their feelings of liking by sometimes leaning toward another person, it is also necessary to lean forward to stand up in order to exit. So, like words, movements have multiple meanings and serve several functions.

Other nonverbal leave-taking behaviors include looking at a watch; placing the hands on the thighs for leverage in getting up, which also signals to the other person that a "catapult" is imminent; gathering possessions together in an orderly fashion; and accenting the departure ritual with nonvocal sounds, such as slapping the thighs when rising, stomping the floor with the feet when rising, or tapping a desk or wall with the knuckles or palm. Finally, researchers noticed that nearly all the nonverbal variables studied tended to increase in frequency during the last minute of interaction, with a peak during the 15 seconds just prior to standing. This increasing activity in at least 10 body areas just prior to the termination of an interaction may suggest why people are so frustrated when partings "fail," that is, when the partner calls us back with "Oh, just one more thing ...." It means one has to go through the entire process of leave taking all over again.

COMMUNICATING IDENTITY

The evening news shows a group of people entering a building. The narrator explains that a fugitive sought in several states has been apprehended by the FBI. But do you need to be told? Even without the narrative, you can tell a great deal about the people and what is going on. The dress, bearing, and demeanor of some of these people have "Federal agent" written all over them. For example, they do not smile—indeed, they look completely humorless, erect, and controlling. How about behavior of the suspected criminal? That person's posture is likely to be slumped, head bowed, the face wearing a dismal expression, with eyes averted from the camera.

The point of this mental exercise is that appearance and behavior reveal significant information about people's identities—who they are, or in many cases, who they would like to be. Identity includes social attributes, personalities, and those attitudes and roles people regard as self-defining. Thus, being a police officer is a role likely to be deeply connected to a person's self-definition, and portraying that identity appropriately is likely to be important to the person who identifies with that role. Being an arrested suspect is a more fleeting role but could be integral to the self-concept in the case of a career criminal. Sometimes, it is hard to tell when behavior reflects transient emotions and roles or a more enduring and deeply felt identity.

People have a great need to convey their identities. The communication of identity is, in part, self-validating: A person's adoption of cues to identity can, in effect, confirm that identity to the self, because one can see the self through others' eyes. The sociologist Charles Horton Cooley, back in 1902, coined the term *looking glass self* to capture the idea that gradually, through seeing how others perceive the self, one becomes more and more that person (Cooley, 1902). Of course, people have motives for actively displaying their identity to signal belonging, desired belonging, or non-belonging to various social groups.

Clues to another's identity also help people decide how to act toward that person. But direct, concrete evidence of others' identities is sometimes hard to come by, so people rely on cues and gestures (Argyle, 1988). Such cues enable perceivers to be surprisingly accurate at judging important components of other people's identities. In the case of social class, for example, a person's way of dressing tells a great deal, as do other accoutrements such as pens, briefcases, hairstyles, makeup, and jewelry, in addition to various kinds of nonverbal behavior. Relative status among university personnel was well judged from photographs of two people interacting, for example (Schmid Mast & Hall, 2004), and social class (defined as personal income) was judged well from photographs of people on web-based dating sites (Bjornsdottir & Rule, 2017). Several other identity groups have been shown to be judged more accurately than chance from photos or short excerpts of video (Tskhay & Rule, 2013). In those authors' review of the literature, Mormon, Jewish, gay, and politically conservative (versus liberal) people could all be identified at levels above guessing. Some insights into how such identity judgments are successfully made are available. For example, Tskhay and Rule (2015) found that the positivity versus negativity of facial expressions was a significant cue in identifying both sexual orientation and political orientation.

PERSONAL IDENTITY

The concept of identity can be construed at both the personal and social levels. Personal identity consists of a unique configuration of characteristics—personality, attitudes, tastes, values, and features—that the individual perceives as personally defining. Nonverbal styles of expression can also be so distinctive that they become an aspect of identity. Davis and Dulicai (1992) provided an analysis of Adolf Hitler's movements and gestural mannerisms during public appearances. Some of Hitler's movements included finger wagging (the "scolding Dutch uncle"), forward stabs, pounding, slicing, crushing fists, and snapping punches, all of which are performed with extreme control and inward stress. Davis and Dulicai summarize the uniqueness of Hitler's movement style as follows:

> Hitler's movement is very difficult to imitate. In seminars with people who are sophisticated about movement analysis and performance such as dancers and dance therapists, most cannot even approximate the ways in which he controls the action … and sustains such a violent intensity throughout a series of batons (pointing gestures). Those who come close want to stop. It is tortured, painful, relentless, and unyielding motion. To move this way is to be at war with one's body and it is notable that, for all of the aggression that Hitler's oratory displays, it is this war with himself that stands out. (p. 161)

Personality is one of the ways to define personal identity, and personality is fairly consistent across situations and time. Aspects of personality are often documented to be associated with various appearance-related cues or behavioral cues. An important question is how beliefs about behavior–trait associations differ from the actual associations. People may have beliefs that are not substantiated when observational research is done. A useful way of conceptualizing this question is the lens model. As shown in Figure 12-4, the lens model encompasses the relation of both perceived and actual behavior to a criterion, such as the actual personality trait, as well as the relation between the perceived and actual trait—that is, the degree to which observers can judge which targets have the trait in question.

Table 12-2 illustrates this model using Gifford's (1994) study of 60 undergraduates videotaped in conversation. Over 20 nonverbal behaviors were measured by independent observers and then related to both the participants' self-descriptions of personality and the impressions of personality made by observers who watched the tapes with the sound turned off. Table 12-2 shows that for the trait "ambitious-dominant," there were associations between nonverbal behaviors and the personality ratings made by observers. However, actual ambition-dominance—that is, the self-ratings by those who appeared on the tapes—related to fewer behaviors, only two of which appeared on the list of behaviors correlated with observers' ratings. This suggests that observers had a correct "theory" about these two cues but held misconceptions for all the others shown on the other side of the table; in other words, they thought that the more ambitious-dominant people displayed these cues, but they were wrong. The observers did, however, extract enough information to form a significantly accurate overall impression of the targets' ambition-dominance; possibly, they based their impression on additional cues that were not measured, along with the two they used correctly. Many lens-model studies relating nonverbal cues to perceived and actual personality traits have been done (e.g., Back & Nestler, 2016; Borkenau & Liebler, 1995; Murphy, Hall, & Colvin, 2003).

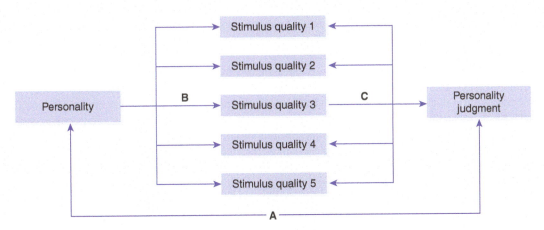

FIGURE 12-4 A diagram of a judgment lens model of social perception.

Table 12-2 Perceived and Actual Correlates of Ambition-Dominance

Correlated with Perceived Trait Only	Correlated with Both Perceived Trait and Actual Trait	Correlated with Actual Trait Only
Head, trunk, and legs more directly facing another	More gestures	More leg lean
Head more tilted back	Legs more extended	Less object manipulation
Arms less wrapped		
More self-touching		
More headshaking		

Source: Adapted from Gifford, R. (1994). A lens-mapping framework for understanding the encoding and decoding of interpersonal dispositions in nonverbal behavior. *Journal of Personality and Social Psychology, 66*, 401.

SOCIAL IDENTITY

Race and gender are among the most salient aspects of social identity, so it is not surprising that research has turned up nonverbal communication differences associated with these categories. It is, of course, an oversimplification to think of these categories as though everyone in them behaves the same. Stereotypic thinking promotes many judgment errors and undesirable behaviors due both to erroneous beliefs and overgeneralization. Overgeneralization can be across individuals (thinking they are all alike) and across contexts (not acknowledging how behavior varies with roles, locations, and relationships). Obviously, people may express their gender identities differently at home than at the office—let us hope they do. Similarly, a racial minority student may have a different behavior style when with friends of the same social group than in a classroom filled with students from the majority group. Also remember that distinctions such as male or female and Black or White may be confounded with other distinctions, such as social class and status. Furthermore, each individual has numerous social identities: A person might identify as a woman *and* a Latina *and* a member of the middle class. Furthermore, each category of social identity is often complex; certainly both race and gender can be defined in various ways and are not binary. Many people cannot easily describe the complexity of their racial, ethnic, and gender identities. Thus, it can be unclear what identity factors explain a given nonverbal behavior.

In mixed-racial interactions, each person may deliberatively or unwittingly communicate their racial identity to the other. A person's choice of clothes or hairstyle may signal their identification with a particular racial group, whereas their interpersonal distance to another may be done out of force of habit. People may use such cues to categorize others into a specific racial group. Their nonverbal reactions to such categorizations may betray their attitude or unease toward members of that racial group (Word, Zanna, & Cooper, 1974). Toosi, Babbitt, Ambady, and Sommers (2012) examined over 40 years of research on same- and mixed-racial (generally Black and White) interactions and found that individuals tended to show more friendly nonverbal behavior toward each other when they were interacting with a member of their own (versus a different) racial group. The more negative-looking behaviors in cross-race interactions often have ambiguous meaning because, although they can reflect hostile feeling, they can also reflect uncertainty and anxiety (Olson & Fazio, 2007). Fortunately, attitudes toward other racial groups can improve via greater interracial contact; thus, signs of nonverbal unease or negativity have and hopefully will continue to decrease over time.

Gender differences in nonverbal behavior have been studied for many years. Essentially, all of this literature is based on the assumption that gender is binary and that the individuals being studied are cisgender (and, moreover, heterosexual). Research on nonverbal behavior in relation to gender minorities and sexual orientation is scarce. Therefore, the research summarized in the following paragraphs do not reflect the differences that might appear in a broader representation of individuals.

Gender roles are collections of attitudes, behaviors, and traits deemed desirable for each gender. In many societies, these roles and their associated expectations are evolving but they have not disappeared. The male gender role, in stereotype, is exemplified by autonomy, assertiveness, dominance, and task orientation; for women, gentleness, empathy, and interpersonal orientation are stereotypical (Cross & Madson, 1997). To a great extent, nonverbal differences correspond to these role prescriptions. People generally want to show the world what gender they identify with, and also that they behave as men or women are expected to behave. Compared to women, men:

- Have less skill in sending and receiving nonverbal, especially emotional, cues.
- Are less likely to notice or to be influenced by people's appearance and nonverbal behavior.
- Have less expressive faces and use fewer expressive gestures.
- Smile and laugh less.
- Look at others less.
- Keep greater distances from others.

The nature of gender differences in interpersonal touching has sparked much debate. When it comes to same-gender touch, the evidence is rather clear that heterosexual men are particularly averse to touching other men, except in certain prescribed settings such as team sports, both as part of the game and as expressions of team spirit. Both self-reported and observational data indicate that same-gender touching is avoided by men, at least in the United States, but is quite welcome by women. One hypothesis for men's avoidance is homophobic attitudes and the fear that touching will be seen as homosexual. This might explain why they are less likely to comply with the request of a man who has touched them (Dolinski, 2010). Moreover, research by Roese, Olson, Borenstein, Martin, and Shores (1992) found that among men, those with the least stated liking for same-gender touching had the highest scores on a homophobia scale with items such as "Homosexuality is a sin and just plain wrong" and "Homosexual behavior disgusts me." In a second study, both male and female college students who were observed to engage in less same-gender touching in a cafeteria had stronger homophobic attitudes when surveyed by researchers.

Studies on opposite-gender touching have been more widely debated, but there is some concurrence that when the individuals are young adults, or the touch is with the hand, or the arm is put around the other person, males do take the touching initiative. However, the woman is more likely to touch the man than vice versa when the couple is in their 40s or older, when the touch is either brief or involves linking arms or handholding (Hall & Veccia, 1990), and when the couple is married rather than dating (Guerrero & Andersen, 1994; Willis & Briggs, 1992).

Although exhaustive research over the life span has not been conducted, there is reason to believe that nonverbal gender differences are especially pronounced in adolescence and the college years, when gender roles are especially salient. For example, the gender difference in smiling is not evident in young children (Dodd, Russell, & Jenkins, 1999; Hall, 1984); it peaks in adolescence and decreases after that, though never completely (LaFrance, Hecht, & Levy Paluck, 2003). Most nonverbal gender differences have been investigated among college students observed in a laboratory situation, but evidence abounds from more naturalistic settings as well. For example, male physicians interacting with patients engage in less smiling, nodding, and backchanneling (saying "mmm-hmm") than female physicians do (Hall, Irish, Roter, Ehrlich, & Miller, 1994).

The nonverbal behaviors that women engage in more than men suggest more openness, sensitivity, and involvement. In some circumstances, these traits may work to women's disadvantage (Henley, 1977). Their smiling may make them appear weak, "too nice," or even insincere; their higher levels of gazing may connote dependency; and their nonverbal style may not be distant or threatening enough to win automatic respect in the professional world. However, if this is the case, we would argue that the problem is with the stereotypic beliefs rather than with the behavior per se. It is only because of cultural blinders that men's behavior is seen as the norm and women's behavior is seen as "different" or in need of correction. Because most evidence suggests that the kinds of nonverbal skills and behavior shown more by women are an asset in daily life, one could make the case that men's nonverbal behavior style and skills are a handicap in social relations.

Women's greater emotional expressivity is consistent with the stereotype that women are more emotional than men. However, several studies have found that self-reports of the intensity of emotional experience do not differ when assessed concurrently with the experience (Kring & Gordon, 1998), while studies that ask about emotional intensity in general or retrospectively find a consistent gender difference in self-reported emotional intensity (Diener, Sandvik, & Larsen, 1985). The latter difference may be biased by the influence of gender stereotypes on self-ratings; alternatively, women may do more subsequent thinking and processing of emotional experiences, which amplifies their intensity with the passage of time. At any rate, although it is clear that women are more emotionally expressive than men, it is not clear that they are also more emotional in terms of their inner experience.

As with race and other group differences, male and female nonverbal differences are not large in absolute terms, and one should not overestimate the size of these differences. Though some of them are large relative to other psychological differences between the men and women, they are still of modest magnitude, and even the largest nonverbal gender difference shows more similarity than difference between males and females. Stated differently, a great deal of overlap exists in the male and female repertoires. Nevertheless, there is a striking correspondence between people's beliefs about these differences and the actual magnitude of such differences (Briton & Hall, 1995; Hall & Carter, 1999), which strongly suggests that people can see these differences in daily life. Of course, societal beliefs can also translate into self-fulfilling prophecies, such that men and women come to have the behavioral repertoire that others expect them to have (Zanna & Pack, 1975).

The gender differences are also not invariant. In fact, they vary considerably as a function of setting and context, including the nature of the situation, the affective tone of an interaction, other nonverbal behaviors, and the characteristics of the other person involved (Aiello, 1977; Hall & Halberstadt, 1986; LaFrance et al., 2003; Putnam & McCallister, 1980). As examples of this variation, the gender difference in gazing is much more evident when people are within conversational distance of one another than when they are standing farther apart. The tendency for women to smile more than men is greatest when they know they are being observed, when they are interacting with others, when they are not very familiar with the other people in the interaction, when the circumstances make them feel more anxious, and when they are White. Finally, people act in the most gender-stereotypic ways when with others of their own gender; in opposite-gender encounters, males and females often accommodate to the other's norms. So, for example, gazing is highest between females, lowest between males, and intermediate in male–female interaction (Hall, 1984). The fact that nonverbal gender differences vary with these contextual factors demonstrates that we still have a great deal to learn about the origins of male and female behavior.

Explanations for nonverbal gender differences focus both on gender expectations and on status/dominance differences. For example, the well-established finding that women score higher on tests of judging the meanings of nonverbal cues has been theorized to stem from women's subordinate status, which leads them to constantly monitor and win the approval of others (Henley, 1977). In fact, little is known about why females are better at decoding nonverbal cues (Hall, 1984; Henley, 1977; Noller, 1986). It is clear, however, that the socialization of females in our society (and in many others) emphasizes expertise in various aspects of social interaction, including knowing the general social rules governing interpersonal relations, the general display and decoding rules appropriate to various situations, and the more specific rules governing the use of nonverbal cues in particular. It is society's expectation not only that females will be attuned to social interactions but also that they will be responsible for how social interactions proceed. These pressures and expectations could easily produce the nonverbal differences documented in research.

DECEIVING OTHERS

One of the most common communicative outcomes people seek is to persuade or influence others, and this is sometimes accomplished through deception. The present section focuses on lying and lie detection, as these have been researched for many years. Four major questions drive the research in this area:

1. What behaviors distinguish liars from truth tellers?
2. What cognitive and emotional processes are at work during acts of lying?
3. How accurate are people at detecting lies?
4. What conditions enhance ability to detect lies?

Identifying behaviors exhibited by liars has, until recently, focused predominantly on nonverbal signals. It was incorrectly assumed that liars could manipulate their words easily but had less control over their nonverbal behavior, which would therefore betray them. Ekman and Friesen (1969a) believed that clues to deception would be found in the areas of the feet and legs first, the hands next, and the face last. Because the face is more likely to be controlled by the liar, Ekman and Friesen argued that facial clues would be more difficult to detect. Ekman and Friesen (1975), however, indicated several ways the face reveals deception, such as micromomentary expressions and the timing and location of the expression. For example, smiles made when people were trying to cover up negative feelings included traces of muscular actions associated with disgust, fear, contempt, or sadness (Ekman, Friesen, & O'Sullivan, 1988). Moreover, attempts to suppress particular facial movements, such as eyebrow movements and smiles, are not entirely successful by those who are lying (Hurley & Frank, 2011).

Attempts to develop a list of behaviors that distinguish liars from truth tellers have always faced the problem that there are many types of lies—prepared or not, short answer or extended narrative, interrogated or not—and many motivations for lying, such as to protect oneself or someone else, to get out of an obligation or promise, or to avoid conflict. For the lies that occur most in our daily interaction, people report they are not serious, are largely unplanned, and do not make them fearful of being caught (DePaulo, Kashy, Kirkendol, Wyer, & Epstein, 1996). In addition, no behavior that occurs while lying is completely unique to lying (Ekman, 1992; Zuckerman, DePaulo, & Rosenthal, 1981). Still, attempts have been made to examine the behavioral indicators of lying regardless of how lying was operationalized. A review of 120 studies performed by DePaulo and colleagues (2003) identified the following profile for liars when compared with truth tellers:

- *Liars are less forthcoming.* As a result, they are likely to manifest shorter responses and less elaboration; they appear to be holding back, speak at a slower rate, and have longer response latencies.
- *Liars tell stories that seem less plausible and with fewer details.* Thus, stories by liars are likely to have more discrepancies and to be less engaging—that is, they contain more word or phrase repetitions. They tend to be less direct; use fewer self-references; are more uncertain and less fluent with more hesitations, errors, and pauses; and tend to be presented in a less active manner with fewer gestures.
- *Liars make fewer spontaneous corrections while telling their stories and are less likely to admit they cannot remember something.*
- *Liars make a more negative impression.* Overall, they seem less cooperative, make more negative statements, and use more words denoting anger and fear. They are also more likely to use offensive language, to complain more and smile less, and they seem more defensive.
- *Liars are more tense.* Their voices are likely to have a higher pitch, their pupils are more likely to be dilated for a longer period of time, and they are more likely to exhibit fidgeting.

In another literature review, Hartwig and Bond (2011) applied the lens model to the detection of deceit and found that people are perceived to be lying when they sound uncertain, indifferent, or ambivalent, and they provide implausible, illogical accounts, and few details. Importantly, they suggest that deceit is not betrayed in a single behavioral cue but rather seems to be tied to the global impressions people form when they are around liars. Hartwig and Bond's analyses led to the conclusion that diagnostic clues to lying do exist but are not highly consistent, and furthermore that perceivers hold some wrong ideas about what cues matter. Together, these factors may explain why, in general, accuracy at detecting lies is low although still better than simply guessing. However, since accuracy judgments usually combine the accuracy for judging truthful and deceptive speakers, and since truthful speakers are usually judged with a much higher degree of accuracy (in part because perceivers operate with a "truth bias"—that is, a tendency to generally think the target people are telling the truth whether they are or not), the actual ability to detect liars may be even lower.

One behavior many people expect of liars is a sharp decrease in eye gaze or the presence of "shifty eyes." Although this behavior may occur with some liars in some situations, it has become so stereotypically associated with lying in this culture that liars often consciously seek to control it. Research shows that shifty eyes are not a good guide to identifying liars.

Although it is difficult to find behaviors that always characterize liars, it is easier to identify behaviors associated with key underlying cognitive and emotional processes that occur during lies (Knapp, Cody, & Reardon, 1987). The two most commonly studied processes are *arousal* and *cognitive difficulty.* Nonpathological liars who know they are telling a high-stakes lie, and who know there will be important consequences if they are caught, are likely to experience one or both of these states. Nonverbally, arousal is indicated by pupil dilation, blinking, speech errors, and higher pitch. Verbally, we might see excessive responses—for example, "Why do you always have to question me?!"—in response to a seemingly natural, nonthreatening question. Curt replies, or extremes in language usage, are also seen. Warren, Schertler, and Bull (2009) suggest that people may not be able to conceal emotionally arousing information from others as well as nonemotionally arousing information. Liars commonly experience cognitive difficulty as well. This may be manifested in speech hesitations, shorter responses, pupil dilation, speech errors, incongruent verbal and nonverbal behavior, and a lack of specific references.

Two other processes typical of the high-stakes lie involve *attempted control* and the *display of an affective state*. Less spontaneous, or what seems to be rehearsed behavior, would indicate attempted control. In 1991, military prisoners of war who were forced to make anti-U.S. statements on Iraqi television were reportedly told as part of their training that if captured they should speak and behave in a wooden and mechanical manner to indicate they were lying. Indirect responses to direct questions also may signal an attempt to control one's behavior. The expected affective state is one of anxiety commonly reflected in fidgeting, stammering, and the like. But other emotional states are also relevant to deception. Anger is very common and is reflected in liars' tendencies to be negative and disaffiliative in their responses. Some liars feel enough guilt that looking away for long periods or covering their eyes with their hands is not uncommon. "Duping delight," the pleasure one may experience in deceiving another, occurs sometimes as well and may be reflected in a smile at the wrong time or a sneer of contempt.

Enhancing the ability to detect deceit is not a simple matter of developing a guidebook of nonverbal cues for lie detection. You must think about the person who is doing the lying, the nature of the lie, how high the stakes are for the liar, the characteristics of the person who is being lied to, and the information available to or used by the person trying to detect deceit. In the remainder of this section, we discuss several of these issues.

Some people are better liars than others (Bond & DePaulo, 2008; Vrij, Granhag, & Porter, 2010). If an individual has a long history of lying, they might be well practiced in executing a lie even under the most trying circumstances, such as an interrogation. Or some people might "naturally" be more successful with their lies; paradoxically, this could sometimes be people who lie the least, because no one is expecting them to lie.

Although there have been claims and some evidence that particular kinds of people are better lie detectors than others, the current consensus among researchers is that, in general, there is not much meaningful variation among individuals (Bond & DePaulo, 2008; Law et al., 2018). Aamodt and Custer's (2006) literature review found that age, experience, education, and gender were all unrelated to lie detection accuracy, and that "professional lie catchers" such as police officers, detectives, judges, and psychologists were no more accurate than members of the general population. However, people who focus on vocal cues as their source of information about deception may fare better than those who concentrate on the face (Anderson, DePaulo, Ansfield, Tickle, & Green, 1999; Zuckerman, Spiegel, DePaulo, & Rosenthal, 1982), and people who have received feedback during training and practice may get somewhat better at detecting deception (deTurck, 1991; deTurck, Feeley, & Roman, 1997).

Analyzing both verbal and nonverbal signals may be more likely to reveal a liar than observing either alone (Vrij, Edward, Roberts, & Bull, 2000). And it may be that perceivers need a sufficient amount of time seeing these cues in order to make more accurate judgments (Masip, Garrido, & Herrero, 2009).

Recently, attention has shifted to thinking about ways of making nonverbal cues to deception more apparent to observers. This direction makes sense for two reasons: Cues to deception are not that strong in the first place and lying appears to be more cognitively demanding (for most people) than telling the truth (Hartwig & Bond, 2011; Vrij, Granhag, Mann, & Leal, 2011). Thus, additional cognitive demands could deplete the already more taxed cognitive resources of liars, leading them to have less control over possible diagnostic cues to their deception. As evidence of this, Vrij, Mann, Leal, and Fisher (2010) found that more cues to deception were available in liars when they were instructed to maintain eye contact with the person they were lying to (an additional cognitive demand), and that this enabled observers to better identify them as liars.

Although some may bemoan the fact that the detection rate is not higher, others believe it would be undesirable if everyone were highly accurate at detecting each other's lies. The ability to withhold information and mislead, it is argued, is just as crucial to the well-being of society as disclosure, openness, and honesty (Knapp, 2008). This point was taken to comic extreme in the movie *The Invention of Lying*. The main character, played by Ricky Gervais, lives in a world in which people never lie and thus do not withhold their thoughts and feelings, no matter how rude or crude they may be. Once the main character discovers how to lie, he is able to dupe others because they assume everything he says must be true. Although never realizing that others can lie would be detrimental, always being suspicious of others would not be much better.

Are machines any better than human beings at detecting lies? Polygraphs, which measure physiological indicators such as heart rate and blood pressure, are sometimes reported to detect liars with more accuracy than human observers. But because they too often label truth-tellers as liars, they are barred as courtroom evidence in most states (Robinson, 1996; Vrij, 2000) and continue to be challenged by scientists (Iacono & Ben-Shakhar, 2019). Other automated approaches include functional magnetic resonance imaging to identify brain activity that would distinguish liars from truth tellers (Kozel et al., 2009; Monteleone et al., 2009), but this method also faces theoretical, procedural, ethical, and accuracy problems (Vendemia, Schillaci, Buzan, Green, & Meek, 2009; Vrij, 2008).

What about people in close relationships? Should they not be more accurate at detecting lies? Because trust is a fundamental reason couples have close relationships, either party is likely to get away with lying quite easily at first. But once suspicion is aroused, those who know a person's behavior well are likely to be the best detectors (Comadena, 1982; McCornack & Parks, 1986). However, often people in close relationships choose not to engage in the sort of monitoring necessary to detect deception (Smith, Ickes, Hall, & Hodges, 2014). They may not want to confront the lie, or they may be afraid of destroying intimacy if they show distrust by their close monitoring (Knapp, 2006).

POLICING YOUR FEELINGS AROUND COPS

© FrameStockFootages/Shutterstock.com

Sooner or later, every driver gets pulled over by a police officer. A sudden surge of anxiety generally accompanies the experience of flashing lights and sirens that direct you to pull over and bring your vehicle to a stop. You might know that your *lead foot* is responsible for your predicament. If you are an African-American motorist, your fear might be that, in the eyes of the officer, you are "guilty" of Driving While Black. However, you might be genuinely puzzled as to what you did or did not do that drew the attention of the officer.

Next, after you get your license and registration out, you roll down your window and sit there and wait.

You wonder what is going on. Your anxiety level does not ease up.

Soon the police officer gets out, approaches your vehicle with an expressionless face, and then says firmly, "License and registration." You hand over each with a *shaky* hand. The officer then says, "Do you know why I pulled you over?" "No," you reply in a *shaky* voice.

The thought, "The cop must think I'm lying or up to no good because I'm so nervous," might run through your mind. You try controlling your anxiety, but it does not work. You still feel anxious.

For their own protection, police officers are trained to use their nonverbal behavior to communicate that they are in control and in charge of a situation. These nonverbal cues of dominance as well as the police uniform—a symbol of authority—can be anxiety provoking to you.

Police officers are also trained to read *your* nonverbal behavior. Ironically, seeing some anxiety from you might be comforting to them because it suggests that getting pulled over is not a common experience for you. Thus, you do not need to keep your anxiety in check.

Police officers will, of course, use your anxiety level as a possible clue to trouble if it seems disproportionate to the situation. This could happen if your anxiety level does not drop when the officer tells you that you are just getting a warning because one of your taillights is out. However, even that nonverbal cue would not be used in isolation. Other cues—nonverbal and verbal—would be assessed to see if further questioning of you is warranted.

SUMMARY

Every day a person needs to accomplish goals that require the effective management and reading of nonverbal signals. This chapter identified what we know about five of those goals.

We began by discussing the various ways we manifest our liking or disliking for others. Even though certain non-verbal signals have been associated with courtship and romantic flirtation, we also know that similar behaviors occur when people are trying to communicate friendliness, interest, and playfulness. These quasi-courtship behaviors can lead to misunderstandings, and they remind us how important context is for interpreting nonverbal signals. The cluster of nonverbal behavior comprising immediacy or liking behavior can be usefully applied to a variety of situations in which one wants to signal positive responses to strangers and acquaintances. Immediacy occurs in established close relationships, too, but mainly when it is important to be clear about one's feelings, when the relationship is threatened, or when a couple wants to communicate their closeness to outsiders. Otherwise, people in close relationships employ a more unique and varied nonverbal repertoire. We concluded this section by noting the ways people adjust the intimacy level through reciprocal or compensatory behavior.

Nonverbal behavior is also highlighted in acts of dominance and efforts to show status. Like intimacy, sometimes people will manifest different nonverbal behavior when seeking dominance/status than after they have achieved it. But, again, context and individual differences are important. An aspiring executive may engage in more eye gaze while seeking the top position in the company, but another executive, equally motivated, may engage in far less eye gaze with their superiors as a sign of respect. There are a number of behaviors that have been associated with dominance and status. Higher status people tend to manifest a higher visual dominance ratio, the tendency to look relatively more while speaking than listening.

Nonverbal signals are also crucial in initiating, managing, and terminating everyday conversations. Smooth turn exchanges are negotiated when speakers signal turn-yielding cues and listeners signal turn-requesting cues. There are times, however, when listeners do not want to assume the speaking turn, and speakers do not want to give it up. These, too, are highly dependent on the manifestation of certain nonverbal signals.

People tell others and themselves who they are by communicating their identity through nonverbal signals. Identity may be personal, such as with individual personality, or it may be social, as in identifying with one's race or gender group. Research has found important differences in the nonverbal behavior of men and women, for example, but often these differences are not large.

Even though most people would not like to think of themselves as deceivers, research indicates people often use deception to manage their social sphere. There is no behavior that is always associated with lying, but research shows that liars tend to be less forthcoming, provide fewer details, give off a negative impression, exhibit more tenseness, and make fewer spontaneous corrections in their speech. Arousal and cognitive difficulty often trigger the observed behaviors seen in high-stakes lying. Last, most people are not very accurate lie detectors in laboratory studies, although on average they do better than just guessing.

QUESTIONS FOR DISCUSSION

1. Research tells us that men typically smile, laugh, and gaze at their conversational partners less than women do. Speculate on why this is and the extent to which it is functional or dysfunctional behavior.

2. What does it mean to collaborate in a lie? Are collaborators and liars subject to similar ethical standards?

3. Identify situations in which controlling behavior is likely to be reciprocated, and when it is likely to elicit compensatory behavior.

4. Try to imagine a social world in which lies could be detected accurately 99% of the time. Describe it.

5. Describe how you nonverbally communicate your romantic involvement with someone when you are in public together. How would the presence of a potential rival influence this, especially if the rival began flirting with your significant other?

NONVERBAL COMMUNICATION IN ACTION: TRY THIS

Ask an acquaintance to participate in this lie-detection activity with you.

Instruct the person to make up a list of 10 questions that you will ask them. The questions can be about anything, but they should be questions you do not already know the answer to. Some examples might be, "What did your bedroom growing up look like?" or "Describe a movie you really liked," or "What kind of relationship do you have with your mother?" Then, instruct the other person to LIE on half the questions and TELL THE TRUTH on the other half but not to tell you when they are lying or telling the truth. (Tell them to mix up the order of lie and truth.) After asking each question and hearing the answer, your job is to guess whether they have been lying or telling the truth, and to analyze what behaviors of theirs you used to reach your decision. Calculate your accuracy, and ask your acquaintance about their experience while lying.

CHAPTER 13

NONVERBAL MESSAGES IN SPECIAL CONTEXTS

The context is the frame of reference for interpreting an action.

—S. W. Littlejohn

If asked what the word "fast" means, you are likely to pause, because you know the word has different meanings in different contexts. If the subject is running, *fast* is associated with speed. Fast is a word used to describe going without food during certain religious observations. Nonverbal behavior has the same multimeaning potential because it can be interpreted differently in different contexts. People who are sad look down at the floor, but so do people who are submissive or shy. Knowing which meaning to attribute to a behavior requires knowledge of the context. A smile displayed by a powerful and energetic person to a submissive and passive person may be seen as sinister, but the very same smile from the same person directed at another powerful and energetic person may be viewed as a happy smile. If any given facial expression can be interpreted in multiple ways—as delight, contentment, pleasure, approval, interest, or sexual invitation—then we need to understand how contextual features help pinpoint the most likely meaning.

What is *context*? Those features of a social encounter that provide key markers for the meaning of any given behavior are usually identified as the context. Philippot, Feldman, and Coats (1999, p. 13) said that "nonverbal behavior can be fully understood only when considered within its social context." You may feel like you understand the meaning of a particular nonverbal behavior because you are aware of certain aspects of context: (1) some personal or background characteristics of the people involved—their relationship, their age, their group membership, their gender; (2) some environmental features—the number of people involved, the accompanying lighting or noise, the time of day, the furniture configuration, the format (face-to-face, social media, virtual); (3) the expectations and norms for the situation—learning, therapy, fun; or (4) various message features—the topic, the emphasis given to the behavior, what other verbal and nonverbal behavior preceded and followed the behavior in question, and so on. These features of context give meaning to nonverbal messages. In this chapter, we discuss nonverbal messages in the context of advertising, politics, education, culture, therapy, and technology.

ADVERTISING AND MEDIA

No one in modern society needs to be told that they are surrounded by advertising. Nevertheless, people routinely underestimate the broad scope of its influence. Television, magazines, and other forms of media do far more than bombard consumers with direct appeals to buy products. To buy a product, you have to lay down your money, but the media exert a powerful influence on people's psychology even when nothing is bought. By immersing the public in images, concepts, and associations, the media and the advertisers shape the values, attitudes, stereotypes, associations, assumptions, and expectations by which people live.

Advertising does far more than tell potential consumers to buy products. It speaks to issues that concern, and sometimes preoccupy, people. One glaring example of this is the practice of tracking your Internet searches. By tracking your searches, specific ads may appear as pop-ups the next time you browse the web, presumably because advertisers assume that, based on your search history, you may be more inclined to purchase their products. A man searching for rugged work shirts from company X may find ads from company X and other companies selling rugged work shirts popping up the next time he goes online to only read the day's news.

Advertising penetrates into areas of intense personal concern for nearly everyone, such as the following:

• What does success mean?
• How does one define beauty?
• How should I behave in order to be socially acceptable?
• How do people belonging to different groups behave, and what do they value?
• On what should I base my self-esteem?
• What kind of a person do I want to be?

Advertising provides, in both blatant and subtle ways, "answers" to these questions. Furthermore, advertising does far more than just supply answers to these questions: It legitimizes the underlying premises that success, beauty, and social acceptance are the keys to happiness and that stereotypes have validity. And it does this without a person putting a penny on the counter—indeed, often without a person even noticing.

Many commentators have railed at the subtle influence and the homogenizing power of the concepts and assumptions that are planted in people's minds by advertising. But individuals who are exposed to advertising, which is everyone, are likely to deny advertising's influence when it comes to themselves. We (and here we include ourselves, the authors, along with you, the readers) are like the "fish who don't know they are wet"—because, if these images are all we know, then that is the only reality we know. People also routinely deny social influences on themselves that they can readily see influencing others. This "I'm immune to what influences other people" fallacy is common. People appear to have a built-in bias against recognizing what influences them. Social psychologists have documented this in countless studies (Nisbett & Wilson, 1977; Wegner, 2002). The sheer fact that researchers can routinely conduct psychological experiments in which situational factors are manipulated to influence behavior without the participants' awareness suggests that people's insight into the sources of their behavior is frighteningly weak (Bargh & Chartrand, 1999).

On those occasions when one is on guard for attempted influence, one is most likely to attend to what is being *said*. Is this person telling me the truth? Are advertisers misrepresenting the product or the issues? But the kinds of influence that are most likely to go unnoticed and remain out of awareness are—you guessed it—*nonverbal* in nature. In advertising, nonverbal information accounts for an overwhelming amount of the total message, especially if one includes the information provided by settings, backgrounds, props, possessions, clothes, hair, makeup, music, and physical and group characteristics of the people shown, in addition to their nonverbal behavior, such as facial expression, tone of voice, and body movements. The nonconscious impact rests more on the nature and juxtaposition of these images and sounds than on what is actually said. The verbal messages contained in advertisements are often silly, irrelevant, meaningless, or not likely to promote distinctive associations to the product. Yet the message can be powerful indeed because the viewer is gripped by the images.

That the influences are mainly nonverbal means that people are less guarded against their influence and less critical of their content. They may think it's merely entertainment, when actually they are being manipulated. Sometimes, viewers think they are ignoring the visual (nonverbal) aspects of the ad, but unfortunately people are *most* vulnerable to such influences when distracted or when not closely attending to, or even resisting, the advertiser's persuasion attempts (Petty, Cacioppo, & Schumann, 1983). When people feel a personal involvement in an issue, they attend closely to the quality of the arguments and are better able to ignore irrelevant information. However, when they are not very involved—which is the state people are in when exposed to most advertising—they are prey to nonconscious influence by irrelevant information, such as how sexy the model is, how charming the puppy in the ad is, how happy the people in the ad appear to be, or how wise and honest-looking the spokesperson is. Thus, people are most vulnerable when in precisely those circumstances under which they experience most advertising. Furthermore, laboratory research shows that even nonverbal cues that are impossible to notice consciously—that is, those presented subliminally—can serve as "primes" that influence subsequent behavior, such as behavior toward certain racial groups (Chen & Bargh, 1997). The images, associations, and stereotypes represented in advertising penetrate our minds through constant repetition and their fleeting and seemingly peripheral nature. But peripheral they are not—they *are* the message.

One area of intense study has been the representation of gender in advertisements. Goffman (1979) listed several ways in which the nonverbal portrayal of women suggests demeaned status relative to men: the relative size of men versus women; how objects or people are touched or grasped; which gender appears to be in charge of the activity; the presence of ritualized subordination gestures, such as averting the eyes; "unserious" clowning or childlike poses; and the occurrence of "licensed withdrawal," when women separate themselves from the ongoing activity. Lest one think Goffman's analysis is outdated, there are current content analyses showing the same themes.

Of course, there are many ways in which the genders are shown stereotypically (Bartsch, Burnett, Diller, & Rankin-Williams, 2000; Ganahl, Prinsen, & Netzley, 2003; Kang, 1997). Gender stereotyping is seen in TV ads from Asian, American, and European countries (Matthes, Prielier, & Adam, 2016) as well as in ads for video games, where female characters are more likely to be submissive and sexualized (Behm-Morawitz, 2017). Analysis of 10 years of Super Bowl ads found good representation of women and minority individuals, but rarely as the primary character, and women were seen predominantly in the home, in emotional roles, and in ads with sexual overtones (Taylor, Mafael, Raithel, Anthony, & Stewart, 2019). Furnham and Lay (2019) analyzed over 50 studies of television advertising done since 2000. Here is their summary:

> The studies revealed that women are usually depicted as young, attractive, and dependent. They promote domestic, personal, and medical products and feature predominately as homemakers. Further, females are usually portrayed more visually. On the other hand, ads usually show men who are middle-aged and are depicted as professionals. Moreover, they are used for voice-overs more than women. Males tend to appear in advertisements promoting cars and automotive accessories, as well as technology. Overall, these themes have been stable over time, channels, products, and countries. (p. 120)

One area of concern is how male and female bodies are depicted in the media, both in terms of its form and function. With respect to form, magazines and television tend to show relatively more of men's faces and relatively more of women's bodies (Archer, Iritani, Kimes, & Barrios, 1983; Copeland, 1989; Dodd, Harcar, Foerch, & Anderson, 1989). Furthermore, photos showing more of the face are seen as more intelligent and dominant (Schwarz & Kurz, 1989; Zuckerman, 1986). In addition, the bodies of actors and actresses in television programs have changed over the years, with more muscular men and thinner women being seen by viewing audiences. Such depictions may communicate erroneous expectations about the typical male and female body type. More disturbing still, the nonverbal behavior of TV characters toward people with particular body types may even help shape people's cultural views concerning body ideals. Weisbuch and Ambady (2009) showed that thin women were the recipients of more positive nonverbal behavior than heavier women by TV characters and that this "nonverbal bias" can result in women holding and thinking that others hold slim body type ideals for females.

Specific nonverbal cues are enacted differently by males and females, too. In advertising aimed at children, boys were found to be dominant, aggressive, effective, victorious, and likely to manipulate objects, whereas girls acted shy, giggled, covered their faces, averted their eyes, lowered or tilted their heads, and touched objects gently (Browne, 1998). In advertising showing adult characters, women smiled more and stood in a more canted position, with weight unevenly distributed (Halberstadt & Saitta, 1987). Because such gender-stereotypical portrayals feel very normal and expected, it is difficult to grasp how profound the assumptions are on which they are based. Only if boys acted "like girls" and vice versa would the viewer suddenly see the stereotyping in action. One might counter that the portrayals of men and women are simply reflecting the way men and women behave in real life. Although to some extent this is true, many of the nonverbal expressions and mannerisms shown in advertising are strong exaggerations of real-life gender differences, or they show behaviors that ordinary men and women do not actually engage in.

Advertising manipulates not only how people think about products but also how people feel emotionally, how they think about social groups, and how they think about themselves. There are positive and negative aspects to this. On the positive side, advertisers sometimes feature individuals who do not conform to rigid societal norms, such as a stay-at-home dad who strives to clean his kids' clothes properly, a woman who is in the boss role in a work setting, a heavyset woman who promotes a beauty product, and a mixed-racial or same-sex couple who show intimacy toward each other. Such ads can help break negative stereotypes about people and expose viewers to a changing world of gender roles, body types, and intimate relationships. Television advertisers sometimes appeal to changing consumer attitudes, as with "femvertising" (female empowerment advertising) that challenges physical and social role stereotypes (Åkestam, Rosengren, & Dahlen, 2017).

WHAT IS IN AN IMAGE?

What is in an image? A young woman scrolls through her social media feed and sees an advertised tutorial to make your lips look bigger and a clothing advertisement with a young thin woman in tight pants that accentuate her buttocks. The young woman finds an interesting post—a music video that repeatedly zooms in on a female music artist's glistening cleavage. Each of these focuses on women's appearance or bodies, and particular parts of their bodies, in a sexualized way. When women are depicted in sexualized ways, when they appear to be for the pleasure or use of someone else, or when women's bodies are portrayed in parts—as when a camera focuses on their legs, hips, or breasts, for example—these women are often not seen as whole persons but as things or as *objects*.

© Diego Cervo/Shutterstock.com

Objectification theory (Frederickson & Roberts, 1997) places images like these among many other objectifying cultural experiences. The camera perspective in these images, like the one shown above, share similarities with the ways that women are sometimes gazed at by heterosexual men. The young woman who steps away from social media might also walk into interpersonal experiences in which someone is looking her up-and-down, someone is making comments about her appearance, or someone is sexually harassing her. Experiences like these form a pattern of regarding women as objects, as less than human, or as some*thing* for the visual consumption or use by others.

Objectifying cultural contexts induce women to internalize this critical male gaze, to focus their attention on their appearance, survey their bodies in evaluative ways, and sometimes modify their bodies in an effort to be viewed more favorably (Roberts, Calogero, & Gervais, 2018). This internalization of the critical observer's view is called *self-objectification*. Many predicted consequences of self-objectification have been found, including appearance anxiety, body shame, and depressive and eating disorder symptoms in women. Self-objectification has also been found to impair some cognitive functioning in women, including reduced attention and math performance, and it may even lead them to speak less. And when they do speak, they may seem less persuasive to listeners who have been primed to think of others in objectifying ways (Horgan, Herzog, Grey, Latreille, & Lindemulder, 2017). In all these ways, objectification is not just an experience with media; it is theorized to be one socializing influence that teaches us what it means to be a woman (Roberts et al., 2018).

© Milles Studio/Shutterstock.com

© Diego Cervo/Shutterstock.com

Images of models can be harmful to the health of viewers' minds and bodies. As discussed in the textbox dealing with the objectification of women, images of thin female models in advertisements can cause mental and physical problems for women. For example, female viewers who are healthy could hurt their physical health and development if they decide to lose weight in order to look like very thin models. Moreover, at the societal level, thin female models do not represent the majority of women in the United States, given that 67% of US women are considered to be either overweight or obese. In an effort to be more inclusive, plus-sized models are increasingly being depicted in advertisements. The presence of more plus-sized models in ads should help women who are naturally heavyset be more accepting of their bodies. However, there is a concern that such images could normalize heaviness and promote unhealthy behaviors related to food consumption (Lin & McFerran, 2016). This could prove problematic for women (and men, of course) whose lifestyle habits (as opposed to their genes) have contributed to their current weight problems. This is potentially a serious public health matter, given that the United States is currently in the grip of an obesity epidemic.

More negative nonverbal behaviors directed at Black versus White characters on TV may be one way in which racial biases are transmitted to viewers (Weisbuch, Pauker, & Ambady, 2009). Images of beautiful people who seem very successful and happy simultaneously invite us to identify with them—"If I drink this beer, I can become just like them"—*and* to think we are sadly inadequate by contrast: "My boyfriend isn't as cute as the guy in the ad, my sex life doesn't seem as exciting, I don't have such a nice car, and my thighs will never look that good." The subtle message that the viewer is inadequate is a large part of advertising's lethal power. Even the current fad for television ads to be rapid-video montages, with many images that change so quickly you hardly know what you saw, is more than just a way to get the viewer's attention. It is a way to make viewers feel slow, dull, and excluded from the exciting, fast-paced life of the people on the screen.

Advertisers use both research and common sense in planning their strategies. No doubt a great deal of advertising research is done in-house and is never published in journals. But there is no shortage of published advertising research, some of it very early indeed. An article from 1923 asked the reasonable question, "How much smiling should an actor show for different kinds of products?" (Burtt & Clark, 1923). Research participants were shown faces with different degrees of smiling and were asked to name products that would sell best with each kind of smile. They thought that clothing would be sold best by a relatively unsmiling face, whereas toilet articles, amusements, and food would sell better if the actors smiled more.

Of course, asking people what kind of advertising messages they think would work best is not the best way to evaluate effectiveness. An advertiser would want to know about actual consumers' responses and about their purchasing choices. Current advertising researchers are especially interested in indirect methods of understanding viewers' emotional responses, and they learn about these responses by measuring brain activity, recording tiny electric impulses in the facial muscles associated with different emotions, and cataloguing which facial muscles move visibly (Hazlett & Hazlett, 1999; Raskin, 2003; Young, 2002). In Chapter 10, we also described early interest in using changes in pupil size as an indicator of viewers' product preferences.

The fields of selling and marketing do not concern themselves only with advertising; consumers also have face-to-face interactions with salespeople. It should come as no surprise to know that salespeople are coached in their nonverbal behavior, for example, to remember to smile at the customer. Researchers evaluate not only the impact of such coaching (Peterson, 2005) but also the relationship between ability to decode nonverbal cues and effectiveness at being a salesperson (Byron, Terranova, & Nowicki, 2007). Salespeople who scored higher on a standard test of decoding emotional expressions in the face were more successful in selling both building supplies and autos.

Should you be worried about advertising's power to exploit and manipulate you with nonverbal cues and images? Yes! But considering that you can hardly take up residence on a desert island (assuming there would be no advertising there), the best you can hope for is to arm yourself against these effects by developing your knowledge of nonverbal communication and the use of psychological tactics (Cialdini, 2007).

POLITICAL MESSAGES

Politicians have long recognized the important role of nonverbal cues, whether those cues come from the people they govern (see Box **Pussy Hat**) or themselves. Regarding the latter, President Lyndon Johnson is said to have been very sensitive to what nonverbal cues can communicate. He reportedly cautioned his staff not to stand in front of the windows and look across the street at the White House the day after President John F. Kennedy's assassination for fear it would appear as if they were looking for power. In journalist Bob Woodward's (2004) book about how and why President George W. Bush and his staff initiated a preemptive attack on Iraq, he notes how members of Bush's cabinet paid close attention to Bush's body language. In the following excerpt involving General Tommy Franks, one can see that Bush, too, felt nonverbal signals played a critical role in understanding a person's reaction:

"I'm trying to figure out what intelligent questions to ask a commander who has just impressed me in Afghanistan. I'm looking for the logic. I'm watching his body language very carefully," Bush recalled. He emphasized the body language, the eyes, the demeanor. It was more important than some of the substance. It was also why he wanted Franks there in Crawford and not as another face on a wall of screens. (p. 66)

PUSSY HAT

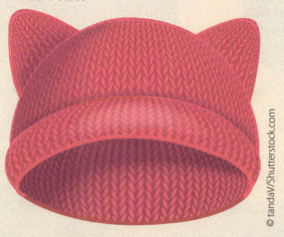

Presidential candidate Donald Trump was overheard saying that, because he was a star, he could do anything he wanted to women. His misogynistic comment that he could "grab 'em by the pussy" set off a firestorm of criticism. One group, the *Pussyhat Project*, utilized the image shown here as a means of symbolizing collective grief over Trump's eventual election to the presidency. This symbol or nonverbal cue unified people (especially women, understandably) and energized them to protest in large national marches, while changing the narrative about women's vaginas from being passive to men's advances to being under the control of women. Controversy followed, as it usually does, because of concerns that the movement might have unwittingly communicated sexist ideas that one part of the female anatomy was tantamount to the whole of women as well as a message of rejection to those women who do not have vaginas or pink vaginas. Nonetheless, this moment exemplified the power of symbols to people, even when they are short-lived. This symbol may, of course, be used in future marches to protest other issues of concern to women, such as LGBTQ+ rights.

© tandaV/Shutterstock.com

According to a 2014 Nielsen report, the average adult American watches over 35 hours of TV a week. Thus, we have to be concerned about the nonverbal messages of politicians, reporters, and everyday citizens shown on TV as well as in new forms of communication, such as social media. Television can highlight nonverbal signals that can influence voters, and political candidates know that the image they project on TV will affect voter choices (see Box **Political Gestures**). Emotion displays from citizens about social issues can increase viewers' motivation to get involved politically (Bas & Grabe, 2016). Last, the political impact of nonverbal communication in the domain of social media is likely great, but this is an area where more research is needed (Dumitrescu, 2016).

POLITICAL GESTURES

© Maverick Pictures/ Shutterstock.com

© David Garcia/ Shutterstock.com

© BestStockFoto/ Shutterstock.com

In early 2020, Joe Biden, Elizabeth Warren, and Bernie Sanders were all vying to be the Democratic nominee for president of the United States. Biden was the "moderate" candidate, whereas Sanders the more radical, angry one. Warren held "progressive" views like Sanders, but projected a more upbeat and less grumpy image than Sanders. Candidates' gestures reflect their personalities and momentary circumstances, along with the advice of their coaches and advisors. In these photos, is Biden trying to show how even-keeled and not extreme he can be? Is Warren broadcasting her high energy and high hopes? Is Sanders showing how relentlessly he would berate all the politicians he considered wrong-minded?

© Justin Sullivan

FIGURE 13-1 President Obama in a debate with Mitt Romney.

Some argue that political candidates in the United States have become so preoccupied with the image they project that their concern for arguments supporting their policies has diminished. If this is true, it is because politicians are well aware that image has the potential to trump their positions on issues (Ailes, 1988; Budesheim & DePaola, 1994). Sometimes, politicians have had to be reminded of this, though. Then-president Obama learned quickly that criticisms are sure to follow when nonverbal mistakes are made; he made the mistake of appearing less engaged than his challenger, Mitt Romney, during their first televised debate (see Figure 13-1). More to this point of how "style obscures substance," Gong and Bucy (2016) showed how inappropriate facial expressions by leaders led to negative evaluations of them by viewers.

Physically unappealing candidates and candidates whose behavior does not signal energy, confidence, likeability, and a connection to voters are not likely to play well on television. Candidates whose nonverbal demeanor signals a positive relationship message on TV—facial expressions that communicate sincerity, body positions that suggest immediacy, and vocal tones that are perceived as caring—are more likely to garner voter support. Television requires what Jamieson (1988) called "a new eloquence—a softer, warmer style of communication." This in no way minimizes the necessity of a candidate also displaying nonverbal signals that would help to communicate assertiveness and energy. How have U.S. presidential candidates fared in the image competition?

During the first of the 1960 television debates between presidential candidates Richard Nixon and John Kennedy, analysts often discussed Nixon's loss in terms of how he presented himself on television, that is, his "five o'clock shadow" showing through the stage makeup, lighting conditions that accentuated a tired face, a suit that blended into the background, and so on. Nixon has been quoted as saying he spent too much time studying and not enough time on his physical appearance (Bryski & Frye, 1979–1980; Tiemens, 1978). A movement analysis by Davis (1995, p. 213) indicated Nixon's appearance was only one of his nonverbal drawbacks.

> Nixon sits with a tense, narrow posture, whereas Kennedy sits with legs crossed, hands resting easily, his weight centered. In the medium camera shots, Nixon can be seen gripping the lectern tightly and not gesticulating for long periods of time, although his head movements are clear and emphatic. And Nixon displays a disastrous pattern of hyperblinking—not just abnormally frequent (more than one per second), but at times with such rapid flutters that his eyes momentarily close. By comparison Kennedy clearly wins despite his rather ordinary and constricted showing.

It was widely reported and believed that radio listeners judged the debate a tie, whereas television viewers felt Kennedy was the winner. Even though the accuracy of this conclusion has been questioned, the belief that it was true may have been largely responsible for subsequent concern about the influence of nonverbal signals in political campaigns and debates (Kraus, 1996; Vancil & Pendell, 1987).

FIGURE 13-2 Bush using a backdrop to create an image.
Ron Edmonds/AP Images

Since 1968, the strategies used to create favorable images of political candidates have become more widespread and more sophisticated. The visuals on candidates' websites are specifically designed to develop the candidate's image in areas that are believed to help the candidate win votes—family photos or videos that imply the candidate is a person with "family values," or images of the candidate dressed casually and speaking to people who work in restaurants and factories to show the candidate's connection to voters (Verser & Wicks, 2006). The communication environment at the candidate's speeches and television appearances is carefully constructed. At a 2004 campaign speech in Indianapolis, White House aides asked people in the crowd behind President George W. Bush to take off their ties so they would look more like the people who would benefit from his tax cut.

Backdrops with pictures and slogans accompanied most of Bush's speeches and became a part of any photo of him, the speaker. For some who saw the photo in the newspaper the next day, the composite message of Bush and the backdrop summed up the speech completely (see Figure 13-2). When President Bush selected the site of a small shipping company to deliver a speech on how his economic plan would favor small business, his aides put up American flags and a backdrop saying "Strengthening the Economy." Boxes near the podium stamped "Made in China" were covered, and a backdrop of boxes labeled "Made in USA" was added.

Analysts of the 1976 Carter–Ford presidential debates argued that Gerald Ford's loss was attributable to less eye gaze with the camera, grimmer facial expressions, and less favorable camera angles (Tiemens, 1978). Subsequently, Jimmy Carter's loss to Ronald Reagan in the 1980 debate was attributed to Carter's visible tension and his inability to "coordinate his nonverbal behavior with his verbal message" (Ritter & Henry, 1990).

Effective leaders are often seen as people who confidently take stock of a situation, perform smoothly, and put those around them at ease. Many saw Presidents Reagan's and Clinton's nonverbal behavior this way. In 1984, Reagan's expressiveness and physical attractiveness were evident, whereas his opponent, Walter Mondale, was perceived as low in expressiveness and attractiveness (Patterson, Churchill, Burger, & Powell, 1992). President Clinton's communication style was a double-edged sword for him. On the one hand, he seemed able to empathize with an audience; on the other hand, his facile verbal and nonverbal style led some to question his trustworthiness, which was evident in the label "Slick Willie."

Expressions of fear and uncertainty may be the biggest turnoff for voters. These include looking down, hesitating, making rapid, jerky movements, or seeming to freeze, as Dan Quayle did when Lloyd Bentsen told him in the 1988 vice-presidential debate, "You're no Jack Kennedy." When Donald Trump was a presidential candidate, his success in the primaries (and subsequent general election) might have been due to his grandiose communication style, which is the opposite of one characterized by fear and uncertainty (e.g., Ahmadian, Azarshahi, & Paulhus, 2017).

FIGURE 13-3 President Bush checks his watch during a debate.

FIGURE 13-4 Trump and Clinton debate.

There have been other notable turnoffs during presidential debates. During a debate with Bill Clinton and Ross Perot, President George H. W. Bush glanced at his watch, which, for many, signaled rightly or wrongly his noninvolvement and impatience with the audience or issues at hand (see Figure 13-3). Finally, in 2000, Al Gore was criticized for excessive sighing as well as for invading the personal space of presidential candidate George W. Bush.

The 2016 presidential race was marked by unconventionality, at least in terms of the contenders. It was the first time a woman (Hillary Clinton) squared off with a man (Donald Trump). The Republican candidate, Trump, had never held an official governmental position, whereas the Democratic candidate, Clinton, had been elected to the U.S. Senate and appointed to President Obama's cabinet as Secretary of State. The average of national polls showed that viewers thought that

Clinton had won all three of their debates. Yet the pull of conventionality was evident. Trump was elected president. And an analysis of their communication patterns showed that Trump's was more "masculine," whereas Clinton's was more "feminine" (Grebelsky-Lichtman & Katz, 2019; see Figure 13-4). Furthermore, as evidence that viewers continue to interpret nonverbal gestures through a gendered lens, research by Everitt, Best, and Gaudet (2016) found that only men's perceived leadership improves when male and female politicians are shown using assertive, expressive, or choppy hand movements.

The fact that the faces of presidential candidates are so prominent in their campaign literature and television ads makes this feature especially important in determining voter perceptions. In one study, individuals whose faces seemed more threatening were less likely to win an election (Mattes et al., 2010). In another study, people looked at facial photos of the candidates vying for congressional offices from 2000 to 2004 and made a decision about which one appeared more competent, based only on the face. Notably, these viewers had no prior knowledge of the candidates or their parties. The candidates rated as more competent in the U.S. Senate races won 71.6% of the time, and the candidates rated as more competent in the races for the U.S. House of Representatives won 68.8% of the time. A follow-up study found similar results when the viewers were allowed only one second or less to view the faces (Olivola & Todorov, 2010; Todorov, Mandisodza, Goren, & Hall, 2005). Thus, people with competent-appearing faces seem to be more electable. Going beyond perceptions of competence, one question is whether people's facial cues can actually predict their success in life, which would represent a real-world indicator of their actual competence (see Box **The Face and Mouth of Success**).

THE FACE AND MOUTH OF SUCCESS

© ArtMari/Shutterstock.com

In a remarkable study, the faces of chief executive officers of the 25 highest and 25 lowest performing U.S. companies were rated on their leadership ability and their power-related traits of dominance, maturity, and competence. When any effects due to age, affect, or attractiveness were removed, the highest ratings on leadership and power-related traits were significantly related to their company's profits (Rule & Ambady, 2008b). In an extension of this research, Re and Rule (2016) looked at a specific feature of the face—namely, mouth width—and its relation to success. They found that the widths of CEOs' mouths were positively related to their perceived and actual leadership success. In their words, "The big man has a big mouth."

Are there facial cues that could lead to higher ratings of competence for individuals vying for political office? Riggio and Riggio (2010) argue that facial cues of dominance coupled with approachability are key. Verhulst, Lodge, and Lavine (2010), on the other hand, argue that more familiarity with the face and greater facial attractiveness can lead individuals to think a person is more competent. Greater facial maturity and attractiveness are other possibilities (Olivola & Todorov, 2010). For example, when one of the candidates has a more "mature" face, and his rival is more baby-faced, judgments of competence will tend to favor the more mature face (Poutvaara, Jordahl, & Berggren, 2009; Zebrowitz, 1997). Keating, Randall, and Kendrick (1999) digitized the faces of Presidents Clinton, Reagan, and Kennedy and made them look more or less mature by altering the size of the eyes and lips. A less mature-faced Clinton, with bigger eyes and lips, was perceived as more honest and attractive, even by those who did not support him in the 1996 election. Clinton's power ratings were not affected by his youthful look, but Reagan and Kennedy were seen as less powerful when their faces were made to look less mature.

If you plan to get involved in politics one day, you might begin to worry about your electability, especially if you have questions about the appearance of your face. However, rest assured, people who are highly involved in selecting a candidate are probably not influenced as much by the facial cues of candidates (Riggio & Riggio, 2010). Moreover, even though a facial quality such as babyfaceness is linked to lower ratings of perceived political competence, this does not mean that a babyfaced candidate is doomed to failure (Poutvaara et al., 2009). Viewers can use other cues, such as the body movements of politicians (e.g., body posture), to judge qualities related to leadership, such as their perceived level of dominance (Koppensteiner, Stephan, & Jäschke, 2016). More important, some of these other cues may be reliable indicators of a politician's future success (see Box **Signs of Future Success?**)

SIGNS OF FUTURE SUCCESS?

Does a U.S. Senator provide clues to their future success as a committee chair? Leanne ten Brinke and colleagues (2016) explored this question by analyzing the verbal and nonverbal behaviors of senators delivering speeches from the Senate floor. They were interested in behavioral displays linked to the presence of virtues and vices in the senators. For example, the use of a sympathetic facial expression and tone of voice would be linked to the virtue of humanity, whereby the person exhibits the traits of love, kindness, and social intelligence. On the other hand, the lack of an emotional expression and use of a smile in response to failure or others' pain would be linked to the vice of psychopathology, which may give off the impression that that person lacks empathy and shows more impulsivity and aggressiveness. The authors found that nonverbally "virtuous" senators were more influential when they assumed greater power as a committee chair, whereas those with nonverbal "vices" (as described above) did not become better able to enlist the help of others on collaborative bill-related efforts.

Fortunately, the image advisors are not yet in control of all the variables, including the public's increasing knowledge of how political images can be molded. A carefully controlled appearance and scripted verbal behavior can readily be offset, or put in perspective, when candidates engage in spontaneous speech and interactive dialogue about substantive issues.

TEACHER–STUDENT MESSAGES

Whether it takes place in the classroom itself or not, the process of teaching and learning is a gold mine for discovering the richness and importance of nonverbal behavior (Andersen & Andersen, 1982; Babad, 1992; Philippot, Feldman, & McGee, 1992; Woolfolk & Brooks, 1983). The following are only a few reminders of the ways in which nonverbal cues play a crucial role in this context:

1. Nonverbal cues between teachers and students signal a close or distant relationship.
2. Students avoid eye gaze with teachers to avoid participation.
3. Students' body postures and facial expressions display their interest in and attention to what the teacher is saying.
4. Students' and teachers' dress, hair length, and adornment affect classroom interaction and learning.
5. Disciplinary enactments by teachers may include negative facial expressions, threatening gestures, or critical vocal tones.
6. Teachers announce they have plenty of time for student conferences but fidget and glance at their watch when students come to see them.
7. Teachers may try to assess student comprehension and learning by visually scanning students' facial expressions.
8. Classroom design—wall colors, space between seats, size and placement of windows—affects student participation and learning.

Subtle nonverbal influences in the classroom can sometimes have dramatic results, as Rosenthal and Jacobson (1968) found. Intelligence quotient (IQ) tests were given to elementary school pupils prior to their entering for the fall term. Randomly—that is, not according to scores—some students were labeled as high scorers on an "intellectual blooming test," indicating they would show unusual intellectual development in the following year. Teachers were given this information. These students showed a sharp rise on IQ tests given at the end of the year, which experimenters attributed to teacher expectations and to the way these students were treated. Rosenthal and Jacobson had this to say:

> To summarize our speculations, we may say that by what she said, by how and when she said it, by her facial expressions, postures, and perhaps by her touch, the teacher may have communicated to the children of the experimental group that she expected improved intellectual performance. Such communications together with possible changes in teaching techniques may have helped the child learn by changing his self-concept, his expectations of his own behavior, and his motivation, as well as his cognitive style and skills. (p. 180)

In an effort to identify the cues associated with teacher expectancies, Chaikin, Sigler, and Derlega (1974) asked people to tutor a 12-year-old boy. The boy was described as either bright to one group and dull to another group, and a third group was given no information about the boy's intelligence. A 5-minute videotape of the tutoring was analyzed for behaviors indicating liking and approval. Tutors of the so-called bright boy smiled more, had more direct eye contact, leaned forward more, and nodded more than either of the other two groups. In general, then, people who expect others to do well, as compared to those who expect poor performance, seem to:

1. Create a warm socioemotional climate
2. Provide more differentiated performance feedback
3. Give more difficult material and more material
4. Give more opportunities for the performer to respond (Blanck, 1993; Harris & Rosenthal, 1985; Rosenthal, 1985)

A related line of research has examined teachers who are perceived as more and less "immediate" in their style of teaching (McCroskey & Richmond, 1992). We explained in Chapter 12 that immediacy behaviors signal liking, warmth, and positive affect, and sometimes immediacy is shown when teachers move around the classroom and gain proximity to their students. Sometimes, it involves teachers smiling more, showing facial expressions of interest when students are speaking, maintaining eye gaze with students, using a friendly vocal tone, or other behaviors that students associate with liking and warmth. Research by Smythe and Hess (2005) found that student perceptions of their teacher's immediacy behavior is not always an accurate reflection of how their teacher actually behaves, but numerous studies show that when college students do associate nonverbal immediacy with a teacher, they are more likely to like the teacher and the course. There is also more teacher–student interaction in these classes, and students report that they would like to take another course from that instructor. Students feel they learn more from teachers who exhibit immediacy behavior, which obviously is an important outcome. Motivational benefits of teacher immediacy include students' desire to persist in college (Wheeless, Witt, Maresh, Bryand, & Schrodt, 2011) as well as students' level of engagement in their online classes (Dixson, Greenwell, Rogers-Stacy, Weister, & Lauer, 2017).

In terms of actual or perceived learning outcomes, the data available at present do not provide consistent and conclusive evidence that students actually feel more competent or learn more from teachers who exhibit more immediacy (Allen, Witt, & Wheeless, 2006; Goodboy, Weber, & Bolkan, 2009; Harris & Rosenthal, 2005; Houser & Frymier, 2009; Witt, Wheeless, & Allen, 2004). At this point, it seems reasonable to assume that perceived teacher immediacy will improve some types of student learning but not others. Nor does it seem unreasonable to assume that certain types of students will profit more or less from perceived teacher immediacy.

Even though plenty of evidence supports the conclusion that *perceived* teacher immediacy behavior has a positive impact on some important student perceptions, the exact nature of that behavior, and the way it is displayed throughout the length of the class, are not well known. For example, does a teacher have to exhibit immediacy behavior throughout every class period to be perceived as "immediate," or is the optimal style a mix of immediate and less immediate behavior? When does immediacy behavior signal that the course is "easy" or that the teacher is a "pushover"? Can a teacher be stern, strict, and businesslike and also communicate positive affect to their students? Woolfolk (1978) and others have found that even negative nonverbal behavior can elicit quality student performance sometimes, but it is unlikely to be an effective teaching style if used for the duration of the class. And even though we know the types of behavior associated with teacher immediacy, it is still not clear how such behaviors should be enacted for them to be perceived as immediate in nature.

Ambady and Rosenthal (1993) added to this literature in two important ways. First they showed that a teacher's nonverbal style when interacting with students (as analyzed via video) predicted both students' end-of-semester evaluations (for college students) *and* principals' overall evaluations of teachers' performance, personality, and appearance (for high school teachers). Qualities such as appearing nonverbally confident, warm, and enthusiastic were among those that accounted for these effects. Furthermore, this was found even when the video clips were silent and were only seconds long. Possibly, who is going to be a "good" teacher is broadcast from the very beginning of students' exposure to them.

In today's world of education, in which more and more students are taking online classes, how the teacher–student relationship can be developed in that format represents a new avenue of investigation. In the old-fashioned face-to-face setting, students are likely to learn more about their teachers than they do in an online format (unless, of course, the class is done in a virtual classroom format). In the former setting, there is more two-way verbal and nonverbal communication between the teacher and student, a situation that allows students to learn about their teachers (we are sure you remember some of your teachers' stories better than what they were lecturing about that day!). In the online format, students may watch only recorded lectures from their teachers. One way teachers can compensate for this and thus foster greater teacher–student satisfaction is to use self-disclosure in their online classes (Song, Kim, & Luo, 2016). Moreover, the language that teachers use to give ego-threatening feedback to online students still matters and should not be ignored by them, for example, by relying solely on emojis to soften the blow of their comments to students (Clark-Gordon, Bowman, Watts, Banks, & Knight, 2018).

Sometimes, teachers treat some students better or worse than others because of race, gender, and other factors, including past interactions with the student. Do students perceive these teacher biases even when the teachers believe they are suppressing them? Not always, but certainly much more than teachers believe. Students are often keenly aware of subtle nonverbal signals that convey messages teachers believe they are effectively masking. For example, a study by Brey and Shutts (2018) found that children believed that students who had received positive nonverbal messages from a teacher (e.g., smiling, nodding, touching) were "smarter," "nicer," and "stronger" than students who had only gotten neutral expressions from that teacher. Such teacher cues may be used by children in the formation of their academic stereotypes about particular groups of children (see Brey & Pauker, 2019). Thus, as a first step, teachers should admit their biases to themselves and recognize that their biases are likely to be perceived by others (Babad, 1992).

Thus far, we have been focusing on teacher behavior, but the classroom is a two-way street in which teachers and students mutually influence one another. As we have observed, teacher immediacy behavior elicits a number of positive outcomes from students. But students who exhibit immediacy can also elicit positive outcomes from teachers (Baringer & McCroskey, 2000). We have much to learn about the nonverbal communication of warmth and closeness in learning environments, and this knowledge will be increasingly important as student exchange programs and distance education continue to increase (Guerrero & Miller, 1998; Mottet, 2000; Park, Lee, Yun, & Kim, 2009).

CULTURAL MESSAGES

When we state that people expect behavior to match the local rules and norms, we are talking about culture. Everyone exists within several cultures—family, religious group, social class, age group, school, workplace, gender, and society. So some cultural teaching is a part of all communication behavior. Culture in this section focuses on large groups of people, possibly millions, who vary in age, sex, gender, and social class but share a set of nonverbal behaviors that help to define them as a culture.

Any behavior identified as characteristic of a large group of people, however, does not mean that every person or every conversation in that culture will always exhibit that behavior. For example, a culture described as one in which people touch each other often may also have some members whose conversations do not involve much touching, and some conversations may be devoid of touching even though the interactants normally do a lot of touching. When touching is identified as a characteristic of a culture, it simply means that this group of people generally tends to touch each other more when compared with other groups of people.

Scholars believe cultures differ on a variety of dimensions (Gudykunst & Ting-Toomey, 1988), but two dimensions in particular are useful for examining variations in nonverbal behavior: (1) high-contact versus low-contact cultures, and (2) cultures that value individualism versus cultures that value collectivism.

HIGH-CONTACT VERSUS LOW-CONTACT CULTURES

Cultural differences in touch have been well documented (Andersen, 2011). For example, people in so-called high-contact cultures establish close interaction distances and touch each other frequently (Hall, 1966). They enjoy the olfactory and tactile stimulation that comes with this kind of interpersonal involvement. Central and South America, Southern Europe, and the Middle East are often classified as high-contact regions; Asia and northern Europe are viewed as low-contact.

The United States has traditionally been labeled a low-contact culture. Informal observations by Jourard (1966) would seem to support this designation. He measured the frequency of contact between couples in cafés in various cities and reported the following contacts per hour: San Juan, Puerto Rico, 180; Paris, 110; Gainesville, Florida, 2;

London, 0. Cultural habits do change. Prior to the COVID-19 pandemic of 2020, people in the United States may have been touching each other more than at any other time in their history. (see "Touchy Topic," 2000; Willis & Rawdon, 1994). In the early 1970s, Barnlund (1975) conducted a comparative study of Japanese and U.S. touching patterns using self-reports from 120 college students in each culture. In almost every category, the amount of physical contact reported in the United States was twice that reported by the Japanese. A much more recent observational study on a U.S. campus of romantically involved cross-sex couples found that Asian couples were far less likely to walk with arms around one another than were Latino couples (Regan, Jerry, Narvaez, & Johnson, 1999). Similarly, McDaniel and Andersen (1998), in a study of cross-sex touch among travelers in a U.S. airport, found that travelers from the United States touched notably more body regions than did Northeast Asians, who touched less than any group observed, including Southeast Asians, Caribbean and Latin Americans, and Northern Europeans. Although this study measures extent of touch, not frequency of touch, it does suggest—as do the other studies reviewed here—that whereas Asia, especially Northeast Asia, may indeed have low contact as its norm, the United States seems to have norms that are further in the "contact" direction. As the U.S. population grows ever more ethnically diverse, any broad label would probably be an oversimplification.

Classifying cultures as either high-contact or low-contact inevitably covers up differences. For example, Central and South America are both classified as "high contact," but Shuter's (1976) systematic observation of people interacting in natural settings suggests that public touching and holding decrease as one moves south from Costa Rica to Panama to Colombia. And as we noted earlier, when we label a culture as high-contact or low-contact, we should not forget that there are likely to be important variations within a culture. Halberstadt (1985), for example, reviewed race differences and nonverbal behavior and found that Black Americans tend to establish larger interpersonal distances for conversation than White Americans do, but they also engage in *more* touch. As we reflect on high- and low-contact cultures, we need to emphasize the difference between *frequency* and *meaning*. Two cultures may display different frequencies of touch, especially in public, but it is a separate question as to whether the meanings attached to those touches are different as well. Communicating intimacy through touch could be similar in both cultures even though one culture allows more public touching than the other.

INDIVIDUALISM VERSUS COLLECTIVISM

Cultures have also been distinguished from one another by the extent to which they manifest individualism or collectivism (Hofstede, 2001; Triandis, 1994). Individualistic cultures emphasize things like personal rights, responsibilities, achievements, as well as privacy, self-expression, individual initiative, and identity based on personal attributes. Regions said to typically manifest behavior aligned with this orientation include the United States, Australia, Great Britain, Canada, the Netherlands, New Zealand, Germany, Belgium, and Denmark. Nonverbal signals that support individualism may include such things as environments designed for privacy; eye gaze and vocal signals that exude confidence, strength, and dynamism; and distinctive clothing. Dion (2002) argued that stereotyping based on facial attractiveness will also be more prevalent among members of individualistic cultures, because facial attractiveness is another way to highlight distinctiveness.

Cultures with a collective orientation tend to emphasize things that show the value they put on their group membership. Of special concern would be things like interests shared with group members, collaborating for the good of the group, maintaining harmony within the group to ensure it functions well, and maintaining traditions that emphasize group values and successes. Global regions typically associated with collectivism include Venezuela, Japan, Pakistan, Peru, Taiwan, Thailand, Brazil, Kenya, and Hong Kong. Among other things, we would expect nonverbal signals in collective cultures to exhibit familiar routines, rituals, and ways of behaving that are widely known and practiced in the culture; a high frequency of deference behavior, such as bowing and gaze avoidance; politeness routines that include the suppression of emotional displays that might offend the group; and behavior designed to avoid calling attention to the actions of an individual when it could be detrimental to the group.

SIMILARITIES ACROSS CULTURES

The fact that cultures exhibit different nonverbal behaviors gets a lot of attention. It should, because these differences can lead to problematic encounters. But it is also important to understand that similarities exist across cultures as well.

Some of these similarities occur because people in one or more cultures adopt a behavior exhibited in another culture. Today, information flows freely across cultures, so it is not difficult to imagine how a gesture or style of adorning the body could become a multicultural phenomenon. Information about behavior in other cultures is regularly exchanged via travelers, magazines, movies, the Internet, and other ways.

Similarities in nonverbal behavior also occur across cultures for another reason: They may be part of an inherited neurological program that members of the human species acquire. These include, but are not limited to, the following:

- The eyebrow raising or eyebrow flash has been observed in greeting behavior in cultures around the world (Eibl-Eibesfeldt, 1972).
- Some of people's emotion states can be recognized from their facial, bodily, or vocal cues by people from various cultural backgrounds (Cordaro, Keltner, Tshering, Wangchuk, & Flynn, 2016; Ekman, 2003; Ekman, Sorenson, & Friesen, 1969; Parkinson, Walker, Memmi, & Wheatley, 2017). This is especially likely when the emotion states are prototypical (e.g., not subtle, not blended).
- Researchers have found considerable cross-cultural agreement regarding which faces are perceived as attractive or unattractive, with speculation that this agreement occurs because it is linked to our species' survival (Cunningham, Barbee, & Philhower, 2002; Dion, 2002; Etcoff, 1999; Rhodes, Harwood, Yoshikawa, Nishitani, & McLean, 2002).
- Mothers from individualistic and collectivistic cultures show similarities in terms of the touching, rocking, and vocalizing they do in response to their infant's expressions of pain, which could represent another adaptation that was vital to the survival of our species (Vinall, Riddell, & Greenberg, 2011).

These underlying similarities among humans are not always readily visible because cultural teachings may direct members to mask or minimize them. For example, the *asiallinen* "matter of fact" nonverbal style in Finland demands expressive restraint in facial displays. People from more expressive cultures may view this as a nonexpression, but Finns see it as a valued expression showing emotional control. In fact, some Finnish leaders have lost credibility with their constituents by publicly showing a lack of emotional control through facial expressions that were too reflective of their feelings (Wilkins, 2005).

Also, as reviewed in Chapter 3, there are cultural differences in the ways emotions are expressed. Even though in a general sense there is wide cross-cultural recognition of such expressions, people from within a given culture have an advantage that has been linked to their familiarity with culturally specific "dialects" of emotion expression.

CLINICAL SETTINGS

Anyone who has ever visited a physician or a psychotherapist knows that the nonverbal cues exchanged in such a visit are important to the outcome of the visit. In this section, we suggest four areas in which nonverbal communication is important in dealing with distress and illness, whether physical or mental:

1. *Understanding the disorder*. How do clinical professionals define different conditions, such as depression?
2. *Diagnosis*. Does the clinician reach correct conclusions about the client's problems, states, and progress?
3. *Therapy*. Is the clinician able to help the client solve their problems and maintain good physical and psychological functioning?
4. *Relationship*. Do the clinician and client develop a positive and trusting interpersonal relationship?

Nonverbal cues play an important part for each of these goals (Blanch-Hartigan, Ruben, & Hall, 2020; Gorawara-Bhat, Cook, & Sachs, 2007; Robinson, 2006; Schmid Mast, 2007). In terms of understanding a disorder, studying nonverbal behavior and skill can help researchers develop theories about the nature of the disorder. In fact, nonverbal behavior might be part of the definition. For example, the definition of depression includes the expression of sadness, and the definition of schizophrenia includes the display of inappropriate nonverbal behavior. Similarly, autism is defined in part by the idea that such patients lack the ability to infer what's going on in someone else's head; therefore, a deficit in the ability to judge emotional expressions would be a definitional element of the disorder. As summarized in previous chapters, and by Perez and Riggio (2003), many groups with psychological disorders—including depression, schizophrenia, alcoholism (Philippot, Kornreich, & Blairy, 2003), and autism (McGee & Morrier, 2003)—score lower on accuracy in judging the meanings of nonverbal cues than do control groups. At present, it is not clear to what extent the nonverbal decoding deficit so evident in impaired groups is tied uniquely to the nature of their disorders or instead reflects other factors, such as a general deficit in cognitive ability, lowered motivation to focus on experimental tasks, or the effect of medications. Studies need to include appropriate control tasks, along with the nonverbal sensitivity tests, to resolve this question.

Nonverbal cues are also important in the process of diagnosis by practicing clinicians. The process of clinical care, either by medical doctors or psychotherapists, involves expert knowledge and cognitive skills acquired through training. Nevertheless, most of what clinical care consists of is interpersonal interaction. Basically, clinicians and clients talk to each other, and it is through the medium of face-to-face communication that therapeutic action occurs. Naturally, nonverbal behavior is a crucial component of this process.

The clinician routinely studies the patient for nonverbal signs that will shed light on problems and progress. In a psychotherapy visit, the therapist's ability to read signs of emotion—especially those that signal issues not brought up verbally, those that are upsetting to clients or are denied by them—is central. In medical visits, the physician must be attuned to emotional and psychosocial issues that might be causing, or be caused by, a medical condition. For instance, a patient might start experiencing depression in the aftermath of a heart attack. Research shows that physicians are not as skilled in reading nonverbal cues as one might wish, which includes emotion cues in general and cues that should be diagnostic of specific disorders (Ruben & Blanch-Hartigan, 2016).

Many studies have investigated the display of different nonverbal cues in relation to different psychological disorders. For example, researchers have shown that the stereotype of the depressed person as downcast and slow in response has validity. The following have been documented in individuals with depression: decreased general movement; decreased expressiveness; decreased speech, gestures, eye contact, and smiling; halting speech; and a deficit in the ability to express emotions (Bouhuys, 2003; Ekman & Friesen, 1974b; Ellgring, 1986; Perez & Riggio, 2003; Waxer, 1976). Fiquer and colleagues (2018) coded the nonverbal behavior of individuals presenting with major depression and found that, relative to controls, they displayed some negative cues more frequently (e.g., shrugs, frowns) and some positive cues less frequently (smiles, eye contact).

Some forms of schizophrenia are marked by a voice that is flat and monotone, and an increase in very subtle muscle activation in the corrugator muscle of the face—the muscle associated with distressed-looking eyebrows—is observed compared to control participants, even when viewing positive stimuli (Kring & Earnst, 2003). Other nonverbal characteristics of schizophrenia include lack of facial expression, inappropriate affect displays, increased self-touching, and less interpersonal gazing. Some nonverbal behaviors are distinctively associated with autism and related conditions such as Asperger syndrome, most notably gaze avoidance but also less smiling and gesturing (McGee & Morrier, 2003).

Another illustration of the diagnostic use of nonverbal cues is in the detection of pain. Obviously, efforts to alleviate pain may not be started if the cues to pain are missed, which would be a real problem for the person who cannot verbally report being in pain. One study showed that family members did not seem to be aware of the nonverbal pain cues of loved ones with dementia (Eritz & Hadjistavropoulos, 2011). Research finds that medical professionals often under-treat pain, perhaps because they have not correctly decoded the relevant pain expressions.

Researchers have documented the configuration of facial cues indicative of different kinds of pain in both infants and adults (Patrick, Craig, & Prkachin, 1986; Prkachin, 1992). Some common indicators include lowering the brows, narrowing the eye openings, raising the cheeks, raising the upper lip, and wrinkling the nose. Analysis of cues may reveal information not forthcoming from self-reports provided by patients. For example, chronic and acute sufferers of temporomandibular joint disorder, which causes painful jaw movement, reported the same amounts of pain, but the chronic group showed more facial indications of pain both when alone and when experiencing painful procedures (LeResche, Dworkin, Wilson, & Ehrlich, 1992). Nonverbal cues can also reveal differences in the behavior of people actually experiencing pain versus those just pretending (Prkachin, 1992).

During medical education, there is a widespread trend to increase training and awareness of communication factors in medical care. Nevertheless, physicians typically receive only a limited amount of training in communicating with patients, including recognizing patients' states and conditions through an enhanced awareness of nonverbal cues. Clearly, physicians can use this kind of knowledge. It is very important that physicians not only notice cues but that they also draw appropriate interpretations from them. Nonverbal cues can also be tied to diagnostic judgments by considering them as an unobtrusive source of information on the patient's progress. Ellgring and Scherer (1996), Ostwald (1961), and others have found that vocal qualities, smiling, movement, and other nonverbal behaviors can change following psychotherapy.

Thus far, we have discussed ways clinicians make use of the client's cues. The client also studies the clinician for signs of understanding, interest, approval, rejection, and reassurance. The clinician's nonverbal behavior may facilitate a good relationship, a high level of trust, and a good exchange of information—what are together called the "therapeutic alliance"—or it may make the client feel disregarded and misunderstood. Hall, Horgan, Stein, and Roter (2002) found that both patients and physicians were able to judge with significant, though not great, accuracy how much they are liked by each other, certainly an impression that could have far-reaching consequences. In that study, patients whose doctors liked them less were less satisfied and more likely to consider changing doctors over the following year. Greater satisfaction and attributions of empathy are associated with doctors who gaze, lean forward, nod, gesture, establish closer interpersonal distances, and have warm and enthusiastic voice qualities. Physicians who are better able to decode the meanings of nonverbal cues have patients who are more satisfied and more likely to keep their appointments (DiMatteo, Hays, & Prince, 1986; DiMatteo, Taranta, Friedman, & Prince, 1980). Those researchers also found that physicians who were more accurate at expressing nonverbal emotion cues in a posed task had more satisfied and compliant patients. So far, it is not known exactly how these nonverbally skilled physicians put their skills into action in the medical encounter, but we can imagine that they might be good at showing empathy, creating a warm atmosphere, or picking up on the patient's unmentioned issues. Indeed, Hall et al. (2014) found that among female medical students, those who scored higher on a test of judging patients' cues were less hurried, more respectful, and more interactive when in a clinical situation.

Medical educators now stress the importance of developing a good relationship with patients. Because what is a good relationship varies from patient to patient, physicians need to be able to adapt their communication style to the type of communication their patients need or prefer (e.g., Carrard, Schmid Mast, & Cousin, 2016). It is a fallacy to think that physicians enact only well-learned roles in a one-size-fits-all way or that physicians are cognitive machines that crank out professional behavior without having feelings or showing emotions. In fact, physicians' positive feelings toward their patients may minimize the negative ones of their patients. For instance, patients may not only better tolerate their pain but also more effectively communicate it around a physician who is showing supportive nonverbal behaviors (leaning forward, eye contact, nodding, smiling, warm voice) toward them (Ruben, Blanch-Hartigan, & Hall, 2017; Ruben & Hall, 2016). For physicians, the worry that if they show empathy they will be seen as warm but less competent by their patients is not supported by the research of Kraft-Todd and colleagues (2017).

Those who supervise physicians and psychologists should be mindful that these professionals, like others in society, might respond differently to patients/clients as a function of the latter's cultural or racial background. For example, clinicians' expressions of empathy toward clients from different cultural groups may not be the same, and these differences can impact the quality of care that clients receive (Lorie, Reinero, Phillips, Zhang, & Reiss, 2017). Elliott, Alexander, Mescher, Mohan, and Barnato (2016) found that physicians responded differently to White and Black elderly patients, not with respect to what they said but how they acted toward them nonverbally. The Black patients who were presenting as needing end-of-life care received fewer "positive, rapport-building nonverbal cues" than did their White counterparts. Disparities in how physicians treat Black patients in terms of communication is now a significant area of research (Johnson, Roter, Powe, & Cooper, 2013).

We also can look for cues that the therapeutic fit or alliance is lacking; these cues could possibly forecast the likelihood of the patient or client terminating treatment early. The extent to which nonverbal synchrony exists between a therapist and patient has been related to patient outcomes (e.g., improvements, dropping out of therapy; Paulick et al., 2018; Schoenherr et al., 2019). Schoenherr and colleagues found less nonverbal synchrony early on between therapists and clients who had social anxiety in situations in which the clients had left therapy before their treatment was completed.

Clinicians and clients of all sorts develop relationships; they may be of a unique and highly structured kind, but they are relationships nonetheless. Therefore, all that we know about the role of nonverbal behavior in attraction, attitudes, impressions, rapport, emotions, and persuasion is relevant to this special context.

A MORE SENSITIVE MCAT?

© Monkey Business Images/Shutterstock.com

When you visit your physician, you are comforted by the knowledge that they understand biology, chemistry, biochemistry, and physics well, especially in relation to the development and health of your body. As you might already know, the Medical College Admission Test (MCAT) assesses this sort of scientific intelligence. What you may not be sure about is your physician's social, psychological, and cultural knowledge of people. There is no test for that, right?

That used to be the case, but not anymore.

If you are interested in becoming a physician, you will need to prepare for a new section of the MCAT (started in 2015), one dealing with the social, psychological, and cultural aspects of human behavior. In this changing and increasingly diverse world, physicians need to be sensitive to how factors such as patients' cultural and social backgrounds might influence patients' health.

Nonverbal cues not only provide clues to a patient's state of health, they are also helpful in determining their likely social and cultural backgrounds. However, a physician's ability to decode patients' nonverbal messages and encode important nonverbal information to patients (e.g., disapproval for medication noncompliance), in a manner that is both effective and sensitive to their patients' background (e.g., age, socioeconomic status, education, race, ethnicity, culture), likely depends on years and years of hands-on training. Years and years of practice do not guarantee the development of this skill, though. Fortunately, some medical educators are developing a curriculum for managing the fears of children and parents in pediatric visits, teaching skillful attention to the child's nonverbal cues and a response repertoire grounded in nonverbal communication and sensitivity to the child's development level (Krauss & Krauss, 2019).

Regrettably, although tests are available that measure a physician's social intelligence or nonverbal communication skills, they are not part of the selection and training of physicians. But there is one test that YOU can apply: You can always choose to leave a physician who does not respond appropriately to you.

TECHNOLOGY AND NONVERBAL MESSAGES

Virtually all the research reported in this book has been designed to enhance your understanding of nonverbal behavior in face-to-face interaction. But an increasing amount of communication is being analyzed and mediated by new technologies. Regarding the former, programs or systems are being developed to help code human hand movements, gestures, and self-touching (Lausberg & Sloetjes, 2016) as well as the verbal and nonverbal cues that occur during job interviews (Naim, Tanveer, Gildea, & Hoque, 2018). With respect to mediated communication, there are two issues emanating from this trend that are especially pertinent to the study of nonverbal communication. First, does technology eliminate the role of nonverbal signals in face-to-face interaction? Second, do changes in the manifestation of nonverbal behavior mediated by technology result in less effective communication?

Before we answer these two questions, which will be the focus of the remainder of this section, let's review recent findings dealing with how technology has interfaced with nonverbal communication in various domains. Positive and negative outcomes are associated with these interfaces.

On the positive side:

- Wearable devices are being used to help deaf individuals "hear" music or visually impaired people recognize facial expression of emotion via tactile sensations on their bodies (Burmer et al., 2018; Design Boom, October 4, 2019).
- Children's ability to learn from robot tutors is being investigated. A study by Kory Westlund et al. (2017) found that preschool children learned new animal names equally well from a human or robot tutor who had used gaze and body orientation to the to-be-recalled animal. Social robots may help children with autism learn gestures that communicate emotions or needs to others (So et al., 2018; see Box **Robots**).
- The presence of emojis (e.g., graphical faces with emotional expressions) in social media messages appears to help readers understand those messages more easily and find them more believable than when those messages have

incongruent or no emojis at all (Daniel & Camp, 2018). One concern, however, is whether people interpret emoji expressions the same from one platform to another (Fugate et al., 2019).

On the negative side:

- When individuals are on their smartphones, their tendency to display affiliative behaviors, such as smiling toward others, declines (Kushlev, Hunter, Prouix, Pressman, & Dunn, 2019). Although they may be connected to an online world, they are more disconnected from the social world around them.
- There is concern that the emotional security that some patients need in psychotherapy is not getting met during Internet-based interactions with their therapists, due to the "loss" of nonverbal cues that are usually present during face-to-face, patient–therapist interactions (Roesler, 2017).

ROBOTS

© Steve Schapiro/Contributor/Corbis Premium Historical/Getty Images

© Steve Schapiro

© CBS Photo Archive

The iconic *Mr. Spock* (pictured on the top left) from the TV series, *Star Trek*, was a half human—half Vulcan character who acted in robotic ways. In today's parlance, his upgrade *Data* (center) of the TV series *Star Trek: The Next Generation* was an actual robot (to be more precise, an android, for those readers who are also *Trekkies*). The intellectual and physical strengths of both characters were offset by their emotional weaknesses. Sure, they were smarter and stronger than their human counterparts. But they looked different from, and were not able to connect emotionally with, humans. And humans were not able to connect emotionally to them very easily.

Mr. Spock and *Data* (center photo) epitomize the challenges facing engineers in the field of robotics. How do you design robots to look humanlike? More important, can humans relate to or learn from them, and what factors influence that process (e.g., social eye gaze, immediacy; Admoni & Scassellati, 2016; Kennedy, Baxter, & Belpaeme, 2017)? In order to relate to robots, do people see humanlike qualities in them, such as facial expressions of "emotion"?

Two robots, *Sophia* (right photo) and *Charles* are going where no robots have gone before. Sophia not only looks more humanlike than previous robots, she can express human emotions such as joy, grief, and frustration on her face (*CNN*, November 2, 2018). Charles can "read" a person's facial expression and then copy it (*Interesting Engineering*, March 28, 2018).

If human-looking robots "read" and then mimic our facial expressions, their ability to connect with us emotionally should increase, at least from our perspective. This might be important to future human–robot "relationships," as nonverbal mimicry fosters a bond between interactants (Lakin, Jefferis, Cheng, & Chartrand, 2003).

Of course, the future success of human–robot interactions will also depend on humans being able to read robots' programmed emotion messages, which can now occur along a number of nonverbal channels. McColl and Nejat (2013) documented some success that life-sized robot *Brian 2.0* had in successfully communicating sadness, joy, and anger to human observers via its body movements and posture.

Computer scientists have become aware of what they call the "uncanny valley" in their development of human-appearing robots and avatars. Note that Mr. Spock and Data are, actually, real humans (actors)—in other words entirely real—whereas the robot shown on page 307 does not look very human. This is deliberate. The uncanny valley phenomenon describes viewers' feelings, which can be eeriness or even revulsion, if a robot or an avatar looks *almost* human but not quite. Perhaps the imperfect human replica suggests human deformity, disease, or simply deviance which viewers find repellant. According to research, if the robot or replica becomes indistinguishable from a real human, viewers' comfort increases.

The answer to the first question—does technology eliminate the role of nonverbal signals in face-to-face interaction?—depends on what kind of communication technology we are talking about and how it is used. Computer-mediated communication may be mainly verbal, as in texting and email; it may have verbal text with an anthropomorphic icon or photograph ("pic"); it may provide ongoing visual images of interactants through videoconferencing or webcams on personal computers; and, in the case of immersive collaborative virtual environments (CVEs), it might involve the interaction of two- or three-dimensional animated representations of the interactants in the form of "avatars" who embody each interactant's desired behavior—including frowns, winks, and smiles.

Text messaging via cell phones may reduce the role of nonverbal behavior, but cell phones also have the ability to instantly complement a written message with vocal cues or a photograph. Even those forms of communication that are mainly verbal, such as text messaging and email, are not completely devoid of extraverbal signals. For example, people associate meanings with the length of time it takes a person to reply, when during the day the message is sent (Walther & Tidwell, 1995), the depth or detail of the reply, and the number of spelling errors—perhaps a sign of how much care went into composing the message, or perhaps the sender's competence. Certainly the media have drawn constant attention to the misspellings and other verbal flubs in President Trump's tweets (theatlantic.com, 2019). The meanings associated with these and other features of the communication will no doubt vary with the nature of the interactants' relationship, their online interaction history, how important or pressing the issue is, and the like (see Döring & Pöschl, 2009). For example, if your male friend is using *Tinder*, you understand what is going on with him if he swipes left after viewing a female's profile picture.

Will communication effectiveness suffer when people communicate in ways that eliminate or severely reduce their opportunity to see, touch, and exercise control over the interaction context? (This is certainly a question being asked all over the world as we write this during the COVID-19 pandemic.) During the early stages of the technology boom, many theorists and practitioners believed that the effectiveness of human communication mediated by technology would suffer. They argued that technology could not effectively restore what would be lost by the lack of human co-presence (Walther, 2006). However, one could argue that the success of Facebook, where people can let their "friends" know what they are doing, post "pics" and videos of themselves and others, respond with a "like" to another's wall post, view others' photo albums, and play games with like-minded friends, suggests that such computer-mediated technologies may be filling a void in the lives of many who lack sufficient interpersonal contact with meaningful others in the real world, and may enhance social engagement even for people who have no deficiencies in that domain. Also, online interactions may be helpful in some conflict-resolution situations because the interactants are not physically around each other (e.g., Shin, Liu, Jang, & Bente, 2017). Tension and hostility might increase more when individuals are physically close to each other while arguing.

Human beings and the ever-increasing number of new communication technologies relate to each other in complex and diverse ways. People can, of course, use face-to-face communication when they need to use more nonverbal messages in an interaction (Riordan & Kreuz, 2010). However, some messages can be effectively communicated through various technological instruments without all the nonverbal signals that might accompany the same message in face-to-face interaction. When messages are short, uncomplicated, and can be easily understood without complementary and redundant information from other channels, almost any type of mediated communication, including text and email messages, can be successful. However, email messages have been found to be less effective in accurately communicating sarcasm, humor, and certain emotions when compared to vocal and face-to-face communication. Adding to the problem is the discovery that the people who sent the email messages greatly overestimated the accurate reading of their messages. Kruger, Epley, Parker, and Ng (2005), who base their conclusions on five studies, point out that it is apparently hard for the senders of email to appreciate the interpretive perspective of the receiver.

What is lost, however, is ongoing feedback and relationship information that could be used to adapt message content. Herbert and Vorauer (2003) found that evaluative feedback was more positive and more accurate in face-to-face interaction than over email. Some believe that the absence of ongoing feedback and relationship information in less personal forms of communication, like email, facilitates less sensitive, self-focused, critical, and deceptive messages (Kiesler, Siegel, & McGuire, 1984). It is not clear, however, whether less personal communication channels are also less civil. Bullying occurs in the classroom and on the playground as well as in cyberspace via email, instant messaging, blogs, and so on (i.e., cyberbullying). But is less civil behavior more widespread in email messages or face-to-face interactions in general? Is less civil behavior more likely in email messages but only under certain circumstances? Is less civil communication behavior more likely related to individual style than it is to the nature of the media used to communicate? We are still seeking the answers to these questions.

Interactive video often allows interactants to accomplish their communicative goals, but remote interaction via video does not seem to generate the same interpersonal impressions as face-to-face interaction does. Storck and Sproull (1995) found less positive feelings among interactants who used interactive video when compared to those who interacted face to face. And in an Australian study dealing with genetic counseling via videoconferencing, practitioners reported difficulties in detecting client nonverbal cues and with rapport building, even though they were satisfied with the delivery format overall (Zilliacus et al., 2010).

Sometimes, the introduction of nonverbal cues to computer-mediated communication can be problematic. Apparently college students already know this. In a study of 1,000 college students, Rumbough (2001) found that 37% used the Internet to meet new people, but only 11% posted a picture of themselves. Without a picture, students did not have to deal with visual cues that might act as a distraction or source of a stereotype—for example, weight, race, or physical attractiveness—that might hinder message credibility and relationship development. These media users want the introduction of any potentially problematic visual cues to be considered in conjunction with a history of positive interactions. However, when photos were introduced to partners who had been working and interacting online on several tasks, it resulted in lower ratings of affection and social attraction for their partners, but it had the opposite effect for unacquainted partners who did not have a history of interaction (Walther, Slovacek, & Tidwell, 2001). Even the introduction of dynamic nonverbal signals in videoconferencing does not guarantee more effective communication, unless the images produced fit the viewers' needs. When videoconferencing focuses on the interactants' faces, it may facilitate communication for more personal messages, but not when an object, such as a new product, is the focus of the discussion, or when the goal of the videoconference is to teach a skill, such as bike repair (Brittan, 1992; Gergle, Kraut, & Fussell, 2004; Kraut, Fussell, & Siegel, 2003).

The effectiveness of technology-mediated messages is also dependent on individual needs and preferences. Some people are more comfortable in contexts with more nonverbal cues, and some are comfortable with fewer. Certain groups of individuals may share a preference—for example, online dating services typically report that males are far more likely to use a photo of the potential date as the basis of a dating decision than are females. Given the adaptable nature of people, it is safe to assume they will not simply be slaves to technology. Before the computer was invented, people typing or handwriting to each other used capital letters, underlining, quotation marks, and parenthetical phrases like "just kidding" to offset the lack of vocal and visual cues. Computers are equipped with even more options to make a sender's message clearer and reduce uncertainties on the part of the receiver, for example, bold lettering. Emoticons such as :) for happy or for something intended as humorous, and :(for sad are commonly used to add information to an email that might otherwise be communicated by facial or vocal expressions. In addition to textual adaptations, the email message itself can be flagged as a priority, or it may be accompanied by a request for an acknowledgment of receipt. Coping also occurs when a communicator uses more than one type of technology to communicate a message, especially important and urgent ones: a text message or email, for example, that is followed by a cell phone call. In short, people who are striving to communicate effectively will learn how to use one or more mediated forms of communication to suit their needs and offset any deficits created by missing nonverbal cues. The ability to effectively decode nonverbal cues sent in the form of computer-generated visuals will also characterize effective communicators in the digital age. Virtually anyone with a computer and some program like Photoshop has the ability to alter visual images. Given the high credibility accorded to visual images in this culture, these altered images can be very persuasive, and they are easily circulated to a broad audience. Just as skilled observers of nonverbal behavior in face-to-face encounters learn what cues to attend to for effective decoding, skilled observers of online photos and videos will need to learn what features raise suspicion about an image's authenticity as well as how they can verify or put those suspicions to rest (Knapp, 2008; Lester, 2006; Messaris, 1994; Mitchell, 1992).

Technology users are not the only ones who are interested in the role of nonverbal signals and effective communication; the makers of new technologies are also looking for ways to make their instruments better reflect face-to-face interaction. The future is likely to offer a greater sophistication in the area of touching (Bailenson & Yee, 2007), smell, and three-dimensional images. The production of avatars with realistic-looking human hair, skin, and smooth movement coordination that reflect cultural, regional, and ethnic differences are yet to be developed. But it seems likely that they will—challenging the study of nonverbal communication in ways we never envisioned.

SUMMARY

Understanding the meaning of nonverbal behavior requires an understanding of context. This chapter examined various forms of nonverbal behavior in several familiar contexts: advertising, politics, education, culture, clinical interactions, and communication technology.

Nonverbal messages embedded in advertising can be extremely influential. A wide variety of nonverbal signals, including music, hairstyle, clothing, possessions, and responsiveness, are used to influence the viewer or hearer. When the target of the ads is distracted during the processing of the ad's information, and multiple exposures to the ad occur, the impact can be even more powerful. These nonverbal signals not only help sell products but can also influence the expectations, perceptions, and attitudes of the people exposed to them as they relate to actual daily social interaction.

It often seems as if political candidates are obsessed with creating the "right" image, and more often than not, displaying the "right" nonverbal signals is a compelling part of that image. Images of a candidate can be honed by carefully structuring the environment—the music, backdrop, others present—within which they are viewed. Managing how the candidate looks with the help of makeup and the appropriate clothes and hairstyles is also important, as is structuring behavior, such as having a candidate "act more assertive." On several occasions, the outcome of televised presidential debates has been attributed to nonverbal signals: calm demeanor versus tension, confidence versus uncertainty, warmth versus coldness, shortness versus height, listening with interest versus smirking, and so on.

The learning process in elementary, secondary, and college classrooms is also influenced by nonverbal messages. Students whose nonverbal signals communicate liking and warmth get positive outcomes from their teachers, and students also believe they learn more from teachers who exhibit such behaviors. Some research, however, indicates that some negative nonverbal behavior by a teacher can have positive outcomes for learning in the short run.

Some nonverbal behavior is common to human beings throughout the world, but many of the behaviors we exhibit are taught to us by our culture. We explored two dimensions along which cultures vary in order to highlight cultural differences in nonverbal behavior. These dimensions focused on close versus distant behavior and behavior focused on highlighting the individual versus highlighting the group. Although these broad cultural characterizations are a useful place to start, it is important to remember that variations also exist within cultures.

The clinical situation is another context in which nonverbal messages are crucial. Therapists and physicians rely on nonverbal signals to help them understand and diagnose depression, schizophrenia, autism, pain, and other mental and physical disorders. Equally important are nonverbal signals that occur as part of the communication between therapist and patient during therapy. Both patient and therapist are especially attuned to cues that may signal emotions being felt. In a similar manner, physicians can learn to read nonverbal signals emanating from their patients, which can be valuable signs of an illness, fear, or how the patient feels about the physician. In the same way, patients can use nonverbal signals to assess how their physician feels about their illness and their relationship.

To varying degrees, nonverbal signals also play an important role in messages mediated by technology. Just as in face-to-face interaction, nonverbal signals accompanying technology may complement, repeat, substitute, accent, regulate, and conflict with verbal behavior. In some cases, however, the number and type of nonverbal signals are quite limited. Despite this, messages can be effectively communicated even though the lack of co-presence often takes its toll on how the participants feel about each other. Sometimes, the introduction of nonverbal cues in computer-mediated communication facilitates effectiveness; sometimes it hinders it. As technology-mediated communication increases, human beings will make adaptations with the signals available to them while seeking to approximate face-to-face interaction as much as possible. At the same time, the makers of new technology will increasingly incorporate alternatives for conveying nonverbal information that more closely approximates face-to-face interaction.

QUESTIONS FOR DISCUSSION

1. Discuss how the nonverbal behavior of a patient and physician can mutually influence each other. Next time you visit a counselor or physician, try to carefully observe that person's nonverbal behavior. Is it as effective and positive as it could be?

2. You are a consultant to a vibrant, physically appealing presidential candidate who is not a deep thinker and so is unable to make good arguments to promote their platform. What would you do to get this person elected? Now reverse the situation: You are advising a person who is a deep thinker who is able to make good arguments, but this person is not dynamic and is physically unappealing. What do you do to get this person elected?

3. Suppose you were hired to advise incoming college freshmen on what nonverbal behavior they should enact to impress their teachers. What advice would you give?

4. Different cultures exhibit different nonverbal behavior, and sometimes these differences cause communication problems when people from those different cultures interact. But it is also true that sometimes these differences occur and yet there are no problems. Under what conditions do you think problems would or would not occur?

5. Select a short scene from your own life in which you were interacting with another person. Then assume you and that person were communicating that same scene via a technology of your choice (e.g., computers, cell phones). Identify the difficulties and advantages the technology has for communicating the information in that scene.

NONVERBAL COMMUNICATION IN ACTION: TRY THIS

Take careful notes on the use of nonverbal communication in television advertisements for an hour or two (for this exercise, keep the sound off). Be as systematic as you can, documenting, for example, how ads differ according to the channel or network, how men and women are portrayed, how different cultural minority groups are portrayed, and what gimmicks or devices are used to capture your attention or change your mood. Did you notice things you had not noticed before?

REFERENCES

Aamodt, M. G., & Custer, H. (2006). Who can best catch a liar? A meta-analysis of individual differences in detecting deception. *Forensic Examiner, 15*, 6–11.

Abbey, A., & Melby, C. (1986). The effect of nonverbal cues on gender differences in perceptions of sexual intent. *Sex Roles, 15*, 283–298.

Aboud, F. E., Clement, R., & Taylor, D. M. (1974). Evaluational reactions to discrepancies between social class and language. *Sociometry, 37*, 239–250.

Acredolo, L. P., & Goodwyn, S. (1996). *Baby signs*. Chicago, IL: Contemporary.

Adams, R. B., Jr., & Kleck, R. E. (2003). Perceived gaze direction and the processing of facial displays of emotion. *Psychological Science, 14*, 644–647.

Adams, R. B., Jr., & Kleck, R. E. (2005). Effects of direct and averted gaze on the perception of facially communicated emotion. *Emotion, 5*, 3–11.

Adams, R. B., Jr., Pauker, K., & Weisbuch, M. (2010). Looking the other way: The role of gaze direction in the cross-race memory effect. *Journal of Experimental Social Psychology, 46*, 478–481.

Adams, R. S., & Biddle, B. (1970). *Realities of teaching: Explorations with video tape*. New York, NY: Holt, Rinehart & Winston.

Addington, D. W. (1968). The relationship of selected vocal characteristics to personality perception. *Speech Monographs, 35*, 492–503.

Adolph, D., Schlösser, S., Hawighorst, M., & Pause, B. M. (2010). Chemosensory signals of competition increase the skin conductance response in humans. *Physiology and Behavior, 101*, 666–671.

Adrien, J. L., Lenoir, P., Martineau, J., Perrot, A., Hameury, L., Larmande, C., & Sauvage, D. (1993). Blind ratings of early symptoms of autism based upon family home movies. *Journal of the American Academy of Child and Adolescent Psychiatry, 32*, 617–626.

Afifi, W. A., & Johnson, M. L. (1999). The use and interpretation of tie signs in a public setting: Relationship and sex differences. *Journal of Social and Personal Relationships, 16*, 9–38.

Agthe, M., Spörrle, M., & Maner, J. K. (2011). Does being attractive always help? Positive and negative effects of attractiveness on social decision making. *Personality and Social Psychology Bulletin, 37*, 1042–1054.

Aguilera, D. C. (1967). Relationships between physical contact and verbal interaction between nurses and patients. *Journal of Psychiatric Nursing, 5*, 5–21.

Ahmadian, S., Azarshahi, S., & Paulhus, D. L. (2017). Explaining Donald Trump via communication style: Grandiosity, informality, and dynamism. *Personality and Individual Differences, 107*, 49–53.

Aiello, J. R. (1972). A test of equilibrium theory: Visual interaction in relation to orientation, distance and sex of interaction. *Psychonomic Science, 27*, 335–336.

Aiello, J. R. (1977). Visual interaction at extended distances. *Personality and Social Psychology Bulletin, 3*, 83–86.

Aiello, J. R., & Aiello, T. C. (1974). The development of personal space: Proxemic behavior of children 6 through 16. *Human Ecology, 2*, 177–189.

Aiello, J. R., & Thompson, D. E. (1980). Personal space, crowding, and spatial behavior in a cultural context. In I. Altman, A. Rapoport, & J. F. Wohlwill (Eds.), *Human behavior and environment* (Vol. 4). New York, NY: Plenum.

Ailes, R. (1988). *You are the message*. New York, NY: Doubleday.

Åkestam, N., Rosengren, S., & Dahlen, M. (2017). Advertising "like a girl": Toward a better understanding of "femvertising" and its effects. *Psychology & Marketing, 34,* 795–806.

Albright, L., Kenny, D. A., & Malloy, T. E. (1988). Consensus in personality judgments at zero acquaintance. *Journal of Personality and Social Psychology, 55,* 387–395.

Alexander, G. M., Hawkins, L. B., Wilcox, T., & Hirshkowitz, A. (2016). Infants prefer female body phenotypes: Infant girls prefer they have an hourglass shape. *Frontiers in Psychology, 7.*

Alibali, M. W., & Don, L. S. (2001). Children's gestures are meant to be seen. *Gesture, 1,* 113–127.

Alibali, M. W., & Hostetter, A. B. (2010). Mimicry and simulation in gesture comprehension. *Behavioral and Brain Sciences, 33,* 433–434.

Allen, C., Cobey, K. D., Havlíček, J., & Roberts, S. C. (2016). The impact of artificial fragrances on the assessment of mate quality cues in body odor. *Evolution and Human Behavior, 37,* 481–489.

Allen, K. (2003). Are pets a healthy pleasure? The influence of pets on blood pressure. *Current Directions in Psychological Science, 12,* 236–239.

Allen, M., Witt, P. L., & Wheeless, L. R. (2006). The role of teacher immediacy as a motivational factor in student learning: Using meta-analysis to test a causal model. *Communication Education, 55,* 21–31.

Allert, T. (2008). *The Hitler salute: On the meaning of a gesture* (J. Chase, Trans.). New York, NY: Metropolitan Books/Henry Holt.

Altman, I. (1975). *The environment and social behavior.* Monterey, CA: Brooks/Cole.

Altman, I., Brown, B. B., Staples, B., & Werner, C. M. (1992). A transactional approach to close relationships: Courtship, weddings, and placemaking. In B. Walsh, K. Craik, & R. Price (Eds.), *Person–environment psychology: Contemporary models and perspectives* (pp. 193–241). Hillsdale, NJ: Lawrence Erlbaum.

Altman, I., & Haythorn, W. W. (1967). The ecology of isolated groups. *Behavioral Science, 12,* 169–182.

Altmann, S. A. (1968). Primates. In T. A. Sebeok (Ed.), *Animal communication* (pp. 466–522). Bloomington: Indiana University Press.

Alwall, N., Johansson, D., & Hansen, S. (2010). The gender difference in gaze-cueing: Associations with empathizing and systemizing. *Personality and Individual Differences, 49,* 729–732.

Ambady, N., Bernieri, F., & Richeson, J. A. (2000). Toward a histology of social behavior: Judgmental accuracy from thin slices of the behavioral stream. In M. Zanna (Ed.), *Advances in experimental social psychology* (Vol. 32, pp. 201–271). San Diego, CA: Academic Press.

Ambady, N., & Gray, H. M. (2002). On being sad and mistaken: Mood effects on the accuracy of thin-slice judgments. *Journal of Personality and Social Psychology, 83,* 947–961.

Ambady, N., Hallahan, M., & Conner, B. (1999). Accuracy of judgments of sexual orientation from thin slices of behavior. *Journal of Personality and Social Psychology, 77,* 538–547.

Ambady, N., Koo, J., Rosenthal, R., & Winograd, C. H. (2002). Physical therapists' nonverbal communication predicts geriatric patients' health outcomes. *Psychology and Aging, 17,* 443–452.

Ambady, N., Krabbenhoft, M. A., & Hogan, D. (2006). The 30-sec sale: Using thin-slice judgments to evaluate sales effectiveness. *Journal of Consumer Psychology, 16,* 4–13.

Ambady, N., & Rosenthal, R. (1992). Thin slices of expressive behavior as predictors of interpersonal consequences: A meta-analysis. *Psychological Bulletin, 111,* 256–274.

Ambady, N., & Rosenthal, R. (1993). Half a minute: Predicting teacher evaluations from thin slices of nonverbal behavior and physical attractiveness. *Journal of Personality and Social Psychology, 64,* 431–441.

Ambady, N., & Skowronski, J. J. (Eds.). (2008). *First impressions.* New York, NY: Guilford.

Amole, D. (2005). Coping strategies for living in student residential facilities in Nigeria. *Environment and Behavior, 37,* 201–219.

Andari, E., Duhmel, J., Zalla, T., Herbrecht, E., Leboyer, M., & Sirigua, A. (2010). Promoting social behavior with oxytocin in high-functioning autism spectrum disorders. *Proceedings of the National Academy of Sciences of the United States of America, 107,* 4389–4394.

Andersen, J. F., Andersen, P. A., & Lustig, M. W. (1987). Opposite-sex touch avoidance: A national replication and extension. *Journal of Nonverbal Behavior, 11,* 89–109.

Andersen, P. A. (2005). The Touch Avoidance Measure. In V. Manusov (Ed.), *The sourcebook of nonverbal measures* (pp. 57–65). Mahwah, NJ: Lawrence Erlbaum.

Andersen, P. A. (2011). Tactile traditions: Cultural differences and similarities in haptic communication. In M. J. Hertenstein & S. J. Weiss (Eds.), *The handbook of touch: Neuroscience, behavioral, and health perspectives* (pp. 351–371). New York, NY: Springer.

Andersen, P. A., & Andersen, J. (1982). Nonverbal immediacy in instruction. In L. L. Barker (Ed.), *Communication in the classroom*. Englewood Cliffs, NJ: Prentice Hall.

Andersen, P. A., Guerrero, L. K., & Jones, S. M. (2006). Nonverbal behavior in intimate interactions and intimate relationships. In V. Manusov & M. L. Patterson (Eds.), *The SAGE handbook of nonverbal communication* (pp. 259–277). Thousand Oaks, CA: SAGE.

Anderson, C. A. (2001). Heat and violence. *Current Directions in Psychological Science, 10*, 33–38.

Anderson, C. A., Carnagey, N. L., & Eubanks, J. (2003). Exposure to violent media: The effects of songs with violent lyrics on aggressive thoughts and feelings. *Journal of Personality and Social Psychology, 84*, 960–971.

Anderson, J. L., Crawford, C. B., Nadeau, J., & Lindberg, T. (1992). Was the Duchess of Windsor right? A cross-cultural review of the socioecology of ideals of female body shape. *Ethology and Sociobiology, 13*, 197–227.

Anokhin, A. P., Golosheykin, S., & Health, A. C. (2010). Heritability of individual differences in cortical processing of facial affect. *Behavior Genetics, 40*, 178–185.

Antonoff, S. R., & Spilka, B. (1984–1985). Patterning of facial expressions among terminal cancer patients. *Omega, 15*, 101–108.

Aoki, H. (2021). Some function of speaker head nods. In J. Streeck, C. Goodwin, & C. LeBaron (Eds.), *Embodied interaction. Language and body in the material world* (pp. 93–105). Cambridge, UK: Cambridge University Press.

Aoyama, S., Toshima, T., Saito, Y., Konishi, N., Motoshige, K., Ishikawa, N., & Kobayashi, M. (2010). Maternal breast milk odour induces frontal lobe activation in neonates: A NIRS study. *Early Human Development, 86*, 541–545.

App, B., McIntosh, D. N., Reed, C. L., & Hertenstein, M. J. (2011). Nonverbal channel use in communication of emotion: How may depend on why. *Emotion, 11*, 603–617.

Archer, D., Akert, R., & Costanzo, M. (1993). The accurate perception of nonverbal behavior: Questions of theory and research design. In P. D. Blanck (Ed.), *Interpersonal expectations: Theory, research, and applications.* Cambridge, UK: Cambridge University Press.

Archer, D., Iritani, B., Kimes, D. D., & Barrios, M. (1983). Face-ism: Five studies of sex differences in facial prominence. *Journal of Personality and Social Psychology, 45*, 725–735.

Argyle, M. (1975). *Bodily communication*. New York, NY: International Universities Press.

Argyle, M. (1988). *Bodily communication* (2nd ed.). London, UK: Methuen.

Argyle, M., & Cook, M. (1976). *Gaze and mutual gaze*. New York, NY: Cambridge University Press.

Argyle, M., & Dean, J. (1965). Eye contact, distance and affiliation. *Sociometry, 28*, 289–304.

Argyle, M., & Ingham, R. (1972). Gaze, mutual gaze and proximity. *Semiotica, 6*, 32–49.

Argyle, M., Trower, P., & Bryant, B. (1974). Explorations in the treatment of personality disorders and neuroses by social skills training. *British Journal of Medical Psychology, 47*, 63–72.

Aries, E. (1987). Gender and communication. In P. Shaver & C. Hendrick (Eds.), *Review of personality and social psychology* (Vol. 7, pp. 149–176). Newbury Park, CA: SAGE.

Armstrong, N., & Wagner, M. (2003). *Field guide to gestures*. Philadelphia, PA: Quirk Books.

Aron, E. N., & Aron, A. (1997). Sensory-processing sensitivity and its relation to introversion and emotionality. *Journal of Personality and Social Psychology, 73*, 345–368.

Arteche, A., Joorman, J., Harvey, A., Craske, M., Gotlib, I. H., Lehtonen, A., . . . Stein, A. (2011). The effects of postnatal maternal depression and anxiety on the processing of infant faces. *Journal of Affective Disorders, 133*, 197–203.

Asendorpf, J., & Wallbott, H. G. (1982). Contributions of the German "Expression Psychology" to nonverbal communication research. *Journal of Nonverbal Behavior, 6*, 7, 20–32, 135–147, 199–219.

Asla, N., de Paúl, J., & Pérez-Albéniz, A. (2011). Emotion recognition in fathers and mothers at high risk for child physical abuse. *Child Abuse and Neglect, 35*, 712–721.

Athanasiou, R., & Yoshioka, G. A. (1973). The spatial character of friendship formation. *Environment and Behavior, 5*, 43–65.

Aubanel, V., & Nguyen, N. (2010). Automatic recognition of regional phonological variation in conversational interaction. *Speech Communication, 52*, 577–586.

Aviezer, H., Bentin, S., Dudarev, V., & Hassin, R. R. (2011). The automaticity of emotional face-context integration. *Emotion, 11*, 1406–1414.

Avni-Babad, D. (2011). Routine and feelings of safety, confidence, and well-being. *British Journal of Psychology, 102*, 223–244.

Axtell, R. (1991). *Gestures.* New York, NY: Wiley.

Aznar, A., & Tenenbaum, H. R. (2016). Parent–child positive touch: Gender, age, and task differences. *Journal of Nonverbal Behavior, 40*, 317–333.

Babad, E. (1992). Teacher expectancies and nonverbal behavior. In R. S. Feldman (Ed.), *Applications of nonverbal behavioral theories and research* (pp. 167–190). Hillsdale, NJ: Lawrence Erlbaum.

Bachmann, T., & Nurmoja, M. (2006). Are there affordances of suggestibility in facial appearance? *Journal of Nonverbal Behavior, 30*, 87–92.

Back, M. D., & Nestler, S. (2016). Accuracy of judging personality. In J. A. Hall, M. Schmid Mast, & T. V. West (Eds.), *The social psychology of perceiving others accurately* (pp. 98–124). New York, NY: Cambridge University Press.

Back, M. D., Schmukle, S. C., & Egloff, B. (2010). Why are narcissists so charming at first sight? Decoding the narcissism-popularity link at zero acquaintance. *Journal of Personality and Social Psychology, 98*, 132–145.

Baeck, H., Corthals, P., & Van Borsel, J. (2011). Pitch characteristics of homosexual males. *Journal of Voice, 25*, e211–e214.

Bailenson, J. N., & Yee, N. (2007). Virtual interpersonal touch and digital chameleons. *Journal of Nonverbal Behavior, 31*, 225–242.

Bales, K. L., Witczak, L. R., Simmons, T. C., Savidge, L. E., Rothwell, E. S., Rogers, F. D., del Razo, R. A. (2018). Social touch during development: Long-term effects on brain and behavior. *Neuroscience and Biobehavioral Reviews, 95*, 202–219.

Ball, V. K. (1965). The aesthetics of color: A review of fifty years of experimentation. *Journal of Aesthetics and Art Criticism, 23*, 441–452.

Banse, R., & Scherer, K. R. (1996). Acoustic profiles in vocal emotion expression. *Journal of Personality and Social Psychology, 70*, 614–636.

Barakat, R. (1973). Arabic gestures. *Journal of Popular Culture, 6*, 749–792.

Barash, D. P. (1973). Human ethology: Personal space reiterated. *Environment and Behavior, 5*, 67–73.

Barber, N. (2001). Mustache fashion covaries with a good marriage market for women. *Journal of Nonverbal Behavior, 25*, 261–272.

Bard, K. A., Myowa-Yamakoshi, M., Tomonaga, M., Tanaka, M., Costall, A., & Matsuzawa, T. (2005). Group differences in the mutual gaze of chimpanzees (*Pan Troglodytes*). *Developmental Psychology, 41*, 616–624.

Bareket, O., Shnabel, N., Abeles, D., Gervais, S., & Yuval-Greenberg, S. (2018). Evidence for an association between men's spontaneous objectifying gazing behavior and their endorsement of objectifying attitudes toward women. *Sex Roles.*

Bargh, J. A., & Chartrand, T. L. (1999). The unbearable automaticity of being. *American Psychologist, 54*, 462–479.

Baringer, D. K., & McCroskey, J. C. (2000). Immediacy in the classroom: Student immediacy. *Communication Education, 49*, 178–186.

Barker, T. H., George, R. P., Howarth, G. S., & Whittaker, A. L. (2017). Assessment of housing density, space allocation and social hierarchy of laboratory rats on behavioural measures of welfare. *PLoS ONE, 12*, Article ID e0185135.

Barkow, J. H., Cosmides, L., & Tooby, J. (Eds.). (1992). *The adapted mind: Evolutionary psychology and the generation of culture.* New York, NY: Oxford University Press.

Barlow, J. D. (1969). Pupillary size as an index of preference in political candidates. *Perceptual and Motor Skills, 28,* 587–590.

Barnard, M. (2001). *Fashion as communication* (2nd ed.). New York, NY: Routledge.

Barnlund, D. C. (1975). Communicative styles in two cultures: Japan and the United States. In A. Kendon, R. M. Harris, & M. R. Key (Eds.), *Organization of behavior in face-to-face interaction* (pp. 427–456). The Hague, The Netherlands: Mouton.

Baron, R. A. (1997). The sweet smell of . . . helping: Effects of pleasant ambient fragrance on prosocial behavior in shopping malls. *Personality and Social Psychology Bulletin, 23,* 498–503.

Baron, R. A., & Ransberger, V. M. (1978). Ambient temperature and the occurrence of collective violence: The "long hot summer" revisited. *Journal of Personality and Social Psychology, 36,* 351–360.

Baron-Cohen, S., Wheelwright, S., Hill, J., Raste, Y., & Plumb, I. (2001). The "Reading the mind in the eyes" test revised version: A study with normal adults, and adults with Asperger syndrome or high-functioning autism. *Journal of Child Psychology & Psychiatry & Allied Disciplines, 42,* 241–251.

Baron-Cohen, S., Wheelwright, S., & Jolliffe, T. (1997). Is there a "language of the eyes"? Evidence from normal adults and adults with autism or Asperger syndrome. *Visual Cognition, 4,* 311–331.

Barrett, K. C. (1993). The development of nonverbal communication of emotion: A functionalist perspective. *Journal of Nonverbal Behavior, 17,* 145–169.

Bar-Tal, D., & Saxe, L. (1976). Perceptions of similarly and dissimilarly attractive couples and individuals. *Journal of Personality and Social Psychology, 33,* 772–781.

Bartsch, R. A., Burnett, T., Diller, T. R., & Rankin-Williams, E. (2000). Gender representation in television commercials: Updating an update. *Sex Roles, 43,* 735–743.

Bas, O., & Grabe, M. E. (2016). Personalized news and participatory intent: How emotional displays of everyday citizens promote political involvement. *American Behavioral Scientist, 60,* 1719–1736.

Bates, E., & Dick, F. (2002). Language, gesture, and the developing brain. *Developmental Psychobiology, 40,* 293–310.

Bauldry, S., Shanahan, M. J., Russo, R., Roberts, B. W., & Damian, R. (2016). Attractiveness compensates for low status background in the prediction of educational attainment. *PLoS ONE, 11.*

Baum, A., & Valins, S. (1979). Architectural mediation of residential density and control: Crowding and regulation of social contact. In L. Berkowitz (Ed.), *Advances in experimental social psychology* (Vol. 12). New York, NY: Academic Press.

Baum, K. M., & Nowicki, S., Jr. (1998). Perception of emotion: Measuring decoding accuracy of adult prosodic cues varying in intensity. *Journal of Nonverbal Behavior, 22,* 89–107.

Bavelas, J. B. (1994). Gestures as part of speech: Methodological implications. *Research on Language and Social Interaction, 27,* 201–221.

Bavelas, J. B., Black, A., Chovil, N., Lemery, C. R., & Mullett, J. (1988). Form and function in motor mimicry: Topographic evidence that the primary function is communicative. *Human Communication Research, 14,* 275–299.

Bavelas, J. B., Black, A., Chovil, N., & Mullett, J. (1990). *Equivocal communication.* Newbury Park, CA: SAGE.

Bavelas, J. B., Black, A., Lemery, C. R., & Mullett, J. (1986). "I show how you feel": Motor mimicry as a communicative act. *Journal of Personality and Social Psychology, 50,* 322–329.

Bavelas, J. B., & Chovil, N. (1997). Faces in dialogue. In J. A. Russell & J. M. Fernβndez-Dols (Eds.), *The psychology of facial expression* (Studies in emotion and social interaction, 2nd series; pp. 334–346). Paris, France: Cambridge University Press.

Bavelas, J. B., & Chovil, N. (2006). Nonverbal and verbal communication: Hand gestures and facial displays as part of language use in face-to-face dialogue. In V. Manusov & M. L. Patterson (Eds.), *The SAGE handbook of nonverbal communication* (pp. 97–115). Mahwah, NJ: Lawrence Erlbaum.

Bavelas, J., & Chovil, N. (2018). Some pragmatic functions of conversational facial gestures. *Gesture, 17,* 98–127.

Bavelas, J. B., Chovil, N., Coates, L., & Roe, L. (1995). Gestures specialized for dialogue. *Personality and Social Psychology Bulletin, 21,* 394–305.

Bavelas, J. B., Chovil, N., Lawrie, D. A., & Wade, A. (1992). Interactive gestures. *Discourse Processes, 15,* 469–489.

Bavelas, J. B., Coates, L., & Johnson, T. (2002). Listener responses as a collaborative process: The role of gaze. *Journal of Communication, 52*, 566–580.

Bavelas, J. B., Kenwood, C., Johnson, T., & Phillips, B. (2002). An experimental study of when and how speakers use gestures to communicate. *Gesture, 2*, 1–17.

Beattie, G., & Shovelton, H. (2006). When size really matters: How a single semantic feature is represented in the speech and gesture modalities. *Gesture, 6*, 63–84.

Beattie, G. W. (1978). Sequential temporal patterns of speech and gaze in dialogue. *Semiotica, 23*, 27–52.

Beaulieu, C. M. J. (2004). Intercultural study of personal space: A case study. *Journal of Applied Social Psychology, 34*, 794–805.

Beaver, K. M., Boccio, C., Smith, S., & Ferguson, C. J. (2019). Physical attractiveness and criminal justice processing: Results from a longitudinal sample of youth and young adults. *Psychiatry, Psychology and Law.* Advance online publication.

Beck, L., & Feldman, R. S. (1989). Enhancing children's decoding of facial expression. *Journal of Nonverbal Behavior, 13*, 269–278.

Beck, S. B., Ward-Hull, C. I., & McLear, P. M. (1976). Variables related to women's somatic preferences of the male and female body. *Journal of Personality and Social Psychology, 34*, 1200–1210.

Bell, P. A., Kline, L. M., & Barnard, W. A. (1988). Friendship and freedom of movement as moderators of sex differences in interpersonal spacing. *Journal of Social Psychology, 128*, 305–310.

Belopolsky, A. V., Devue, C., & Theeuwes, J. (2011). Angry faces hold the eyes. *Visual Cognition, 19*, 27–36.

Bensing, J. M., Kerssens, J. J., & van der Pasch, M. (1995). Patient-directed gaze as a tool for discovering and handling psychosocial problems in general practice. *Journal of Nonverbal Behavior, 19*, 223–242.

Bente, G., Leuschner, H., Al Issa, A., & Blascovich, J. J. (2010). The others: Universals and cultural specificities in the perception of status and dominance from nonverbal behavior. *Consciousness and Cognition: An International Journal, 19*, 762–777.

Berenbaum, H., & Rotter, A. (1992). The relationship between spontaneous facial expressions of emotion and voluntary control of facial muscles. *Journal of Nonverbal Behavior, 16*, 179–190.

Berg, R. C. (2004). *Interaction appearance theory and initial interactions.* Unpublished master's thesis, University of Texas, Austin.

Berger, K. W., & Popelka, G. R. (1971). Extra-facial gestures in relation to speech reading. *Journal of Communication Disorders, 3*, 302–308.

Bergeson, T. R., Miller, R. J., & McCune, K. (2006). Mothers' speech to hearing-impaired infants and children with cochlear implants. *Infancy, 10*, 221–240.

Berke, J., & Wilson, V. (1951). *Watch out for the weather.* New York, NY: Viking.

Berkowitz, L. (1989). Frustration-aggression hypothesis: Examination and reformulation. *Psychological Bullentin, 106*, 59–73.

Berman, J. M. J., Chambers, C. G., & Graham, S. A. (2010). Preschoolers' appreciation of speaker vocal affect as a cue to referential intent. *Journal of Experimental Child Psychology, 107*, 87–99.

Bernieri, F. J. (1991). Interpersonal sensitivity in teaching interactions. *Personality and Social Psychology Bulletin, 17*, 98–103.

Bernieri, F. J. (2001). Toward a taxonomy of interpersonal sensitivity. In J. A. Hall & F. J. Bernieri (Eds.), *Interpersonal sensitivity: Theory and measurement* (pp. 3–20). Mahwah, NJ: Lawrence Erlbaum.

Bernieri, F. J., Gillis, J. S., Davis, J. M., & Grahe, J. E. (1996). Dyad rapport and the accuracy of its judgment across situations: A lens model analysis. *Journal of Personality and Social Psychology, 71*, 110–129.

Bernieri, F. J., Reznick, J. S., & Rosenthal, R. (1988). Synchrony, pseudosynchrony, and dissynchrony: Measuring the entrainment process in mother–infant interactions. *Journal of Personality and Social Psychology, 54*, 243–253.

Bernieri, F. J., & Rosenthal, R. (1991). Interpersonal coordination: Behavior matching and interactional synchrony. In R. S. Feldman & B. Rimé (Eds.), *Fundamentals of nonverbal behavior* (pp. 401–432). New York, NY: Cambridge University Press.

Berry, D. S. (1991a). Accuracy in social perception: Contributions of facial and vocal information. *Journal of Personality and Social Psychology, 61*, 298–307.

Berry, D. S. (1992). Vocal types and stereotypes: Joint effects of vocal attractiveness and vocal maturity on person perception. *Journal of Nonverbal Behavior, 16*, 41–54.

Berry, D. S., & Hansen, J. S. (2000). Personality, nonverbal behavior, and interaction quality in female dyads. *Personality and Social Psychology Bulletin, 26*, 278–292.

Berry, D. S., Hansen, J. S., Landry-Pester, J. C., & Meier, J. A. (1994). Vocal determinants of first impressions of young children. *Journal of Nonverbal Behavior, 18*, 187–197.

Berry, D. S., & McArthur, L. Z. (1986). Perceiving character in faces: The impact of age-related craniofacial changes on social perception. *Psychological Bulletin, 100*, 3–18.

Berry, D. S., & Pennebaker, J. W. (1993). Nonverbal and verbal emotional expression and health. *Psychotherapy and Psychosomatics, 59*, 11–19.

Berry, D. S., & Wero, J. L. (1993). Accuracy in face perception: A view from ecological psychology. *Journal of Personality, 61*, 497–520.

Berscheid, E., & Walster, E. H. (1969). *Interpersonal attraction.* Reading, MA: Addison-Wesley.

Bickman, L. (1974a). Social roles and uniforms: Clothes make the person. *Psychology Today, 7*, 48–51.

Bickman, L. (1974b). The social power of a uniform. *Journal of Applied Social Psychology, 4*, 47–61.

Biehl, M., Matsumoto, D., Ekman, P., Hearn, V., Heider, K., Kudoh, T., & Ton, V. (1997). Matsumoto and Ekman's Japanese and Caucasian Facial Expressions of Emotion (JACFEE): Reliability data and cross-national differences. *Journal of Nonverbal Behavior, 21*, 3–21.

Birdwhistell, R. L. (1966). Some relations between American kinesics and spoken American English. In A. G. Smith (Ed.), *Communication and culture* (pp. 182–189). New York, NY: Holt, Rinehart & Winston.

Birdwhistell, R. L. (1970). *Kinesics and content: Essays on the body motion communication.* Oxford, UK: Ballantine.

Bissell, K. L., & Zhou, P. (2004). Must-see TV or ESPN: Entertainment and sports media exposure and body-image distortion in college women. *Journal of Communication, 54*, 5–21.

Biswas, D., Szocs, C., Chacko, R., & Wansink, B. (2017). Shining light on atmospherics: How ambient light influences food choices. *Journal of Marketing Research, 54*, 111–123.

Bjornsdottir, R. T., & Rule, N. O. (2017). The visibility of social class from facial cues. *Journal of Personality and Social Psychology, 113*, 530–546.

Blairy, S., Herrera, P., & Hess, U. (1999). Mimicry and the judgment of emotional facial expressions. *Journal of Nonverbal Behavior, 23*, 5–41.

Blanch-Hartigan, D., Andrzejewski, S. A., & Hill, K. M. (2012). The effectiveness of training to improve person perception accuracy: A meta-analysis. *Basic and Applied Social Psychology, 34*, 483–498.

Blanch-Hartigan, D., & Ruben, M. A. (2013). Training clinicians to accurately perceive their patients: Current state and future directions. *Patient Education and Counseling, 92*, 328–336.

Blanch-Hartigan, D., Ruben, M. A., & Hall, J. A. (2020). Communication skills to engage patients in treatment. In A. Hadler, S. Sutton, & L. Osterberg (Eds.), *The Wiley handbook of healthcare treatment engagement* (pp. 274–296). Hoboken, NJ: John Wiley.

Blanck, P. D. (Ed.). (1993). *Interpersonal expectations: Theory, research, and applications.* New York, NY: Cambridge University Press.

Blanck, P. D., & Rosenthal, R. (1992). Nonverbal behavior in the courtroom. In R. S. Feldman (Ed.), *Applications of nonverbal behavioral theories and research* (pp. 89–115). Hillsdale, NJ: Lawrence Erlbaum.

Bloch, P. H. (1993). Involvement with adornments as leisure behavior: An exploratory study. *Journal of Leisure Research, 25*, 245–262.

Bloom, K., Moore-Schoenmakers, K., & Masataka, N. (1999). Nasality of infant vocalizations determines gender bias in adult favorability ratings. *Journal of Nonverbal Behavior, 23*, 219–236.

Bloom, K., Zajac, D. J., & Titus, J. (1999). The influence of nasality of voice on sex-stereotyped perceptions. *Journal of Nonverbal Behavior, 23*, 271–281.

Böckler, A., Knoblich, G., & Sebanz, N. (2011). Observing shared attention modulates gaze following. *Cognition, 120*, 292–298.

Bogaert, A. F., & McCreary, D. R. (2011). Masculinity and the distortion of self-reported height in men. *Sex Roles, 65*, 548–556.

Bogart, K. R., & Matsumoto, D. (2010). Facial mimicry is not necessary to recognize emotion: Facial expression recognition by people with Moebius syndrome. *Social Neuroscience, 5*, 241–251.

Bolt, R., Cooper, F., Davis, E., Jr., Denes, P., Pickett, J., & Stevens, K. (1973). Speaker identification by speech spectrograms. *Journal of the Acoustical Society of America, 54*, 531–537.

Bonanno, G. A., & Keltner, D. (2004). The coherence of emotion systems: Comparing "on-line" measures of appraisal and facial expressions and self-report. *Cognition and Emotion, 18*, 431–444.

Bond, C. F., Jr., & DePaulo, B. M. (2006). Accuracy of deception judgments. *Personality and Social Psychology Review, 10*, 214–234.

Bond, C. F., Jr., & DePaulo, B. M. (2008). Individual differences in judging deception: Accuracy and bias. *Psychological Bulletin, 134*, 477–492.

Boothroyd, L. G., Cross, C. P., Gray, A. W., Coombes, C., & Gregson-Curtis, K. (2011). Perceiving the facial correlates of sociosexuality: Further evidence. *Personality and Individual Differences, 50*, 422–425.

Boothroyd, L. G., Jones, B. C., Burt, D. M., DeBruine, L. M., & Perrett, D. I. (2008). Facial correlates of sociosexuality. *Evolution and Human Behavior, 29*, 211–218.

Boraston, Z. L., Corden, B., Miles, L. K., Skuse, D. H., & Blakemore, S. (2008). Perception of genuine and posed smiles by individuals with autism. *Journal of Autism and Developmental Disorders, 38*, 574–580.

Borelli, M., & Heidt, P. (1981). *Therapeutic touch: A book of readings*. New York, NY: Springer.

Borkenau, P., & Liebler, A. (1993a). Consensus and self-other agreement for trait inferences from minimal information. *Journal of Personality, 61*, 477–496.

Borkenau, P., & Liebler, A. (1993b). Convergence of stranger ratings of personality and intelligence with self-ratings, partner ratings, and measured intelligence. *Journal of Personality and Social Psychology, 65*, 546–553.

Borkenau, P., & Liebler, A. (1995). Observable attributes as manifestations and cues of personality and intelligence. *Journal of Personality, 63*, 1–25.

Borkowska, B., & Pawlowski, B. (2011). Female voice frequency in the context of dominance and attractiveness perception. *Animal Behaviour, 82*, 55–59.

Borod, J. C., Koff, E., Yecker, S., Santschi, C., & Schmidt, J. M. (1998). Facial asymmetry during emotional expression: Gender, valence, and measurement technique. *Neuropsychologia, 36*, 1209–1215.

Borod, J. C., Yecker, S. A., Brickman, A. M., Moreno, C. R., Sliwinski, M., Foldi, N. S., . . . Welkowitz, J. (2004). Changes in posed facial expression of emotion across the adult life span. *Experimental Aging Research, 30*, 305–331.

Borrill, J., Rosen, B. K., & Summerfield, A. B. (1987). The influence of alcohol on judgment of facial expressions of emotion. *British Journal of Medical Psychology, 60*, 71–77.

Bouchard, T. J., Jr. (1984). Twins reared apart and together: What they tell us about human diversity. In S. W. Fox (Ed.), *Individuality and determinism* (pp. 147–178). New York, NY: Plenum.

Bouchard, T. J., Jr. (1987). Diversity, development and determinism: A report on identical twins reared apart. In M. Amelang (Ed.), *Proceedings of the meetings of the German Psychological Association—1986*. Heidelberg, Germany.

Boucher, J. D., & Carlson, G. E. (1980). Recognition of facial expression in three cultures. *Journal of Cross-Cultural Psychology, 11*, 263–280.

Bouhuys, A. L. (2003). Ethology and depression. In P. Philippot, R. S. Feldman, & E. J. Coats (Eds.), *Nonverbal behavior in clinical settings* (pp. 233–262). Oxford, UK: Oxford University Press.

Boundy, L., Cameron-Faulkner, T., & Theakston, A. (2016). Exploring early communicative behaviours: A fine-grained analysis of infant shows and gives. *Infant Behavior & Development, 44*, 86–97.

Bowers, A. L., Crawcour, S. C., Saltuklaroglu, T., & Kalinowski, J. (2010). Gaze aversion to stuttered speech: A pilot study investigating differential visual attention to stuttered and fluent speech. *International Journal of Language & Communication Disorders, 45*, 133–144.

Bowman, J. M., & Compton, B. L. (2014). Self-presentation, individual differences, and gendered evaluations of nonverbal greeting behaviors among close male friends. *Journal of Men's Studies, 22*, 207–221.

Boyes, A. D., & Latner, J. D. (2009). Weight stigma in existing romantic relationships. *Journal of Sex and Marital Therapy, 35*, 282–293.

Boyle, E. A., Anderson, A. H., & Newlands, A. (1994). The effects of visibility on dialogue and performance in a cooperative problem-solving task. *Language and Speech, 37*, 1–20.

Brannigan, C. R., & Humphries, D. A. (1972). Human nonverbal behavior, a means of communication. In N. Blurton Jones (Ed.), *Ethological studies of child behavior* (pp. 37–64). New York, NY: Cambridge University Press.

Brauer, J., Call, J., & Tomasello, M. (2005). All great ape species follow gaze to distant locations and around barriers. *Journal of Comparative Psychology, 119*, 145–154.

Braun, C., Gruendl, M., Marberger, C., & Scherber, C. (2001). *Beautycheck—ursachen und folgen von attraktivitaet* (Report) [pdf-document]. Retrieved from http://www.beautycheck.de/English/bericht/bericht.htm

Braun, M. F., & Bryan, A. (2006). Female waist-to-hip and male waist-to-shoulder ratios as determinants of romantic partner desirability. *Journal of Social and Personal Relationships, 23*, 805–819.

Brey, E., & Pauker, K. (2019). Teachers' nonverbal behaviors influence children's stereotypic beliefs. *Journal of Experimental Child Psychology, 188*, Article 104671.

Brey, E., & Shutts, K. (2018). Children use nonverbal cues from an adult to evaluate peers. *Journal of Cognition and Development, 19*, 121–136.

Brislin, R. W., & Lewis, S. A. (1968). Dating and physical attractiveness: Replication. *Psychological Reports, 22*, 976.

Briton, N. J., & Hall, J. A. (1995). Beliefs about female and male nonverbal communication. *Sex Roles, 32*, 79–90.

Brittan, D. (1992). Being there: The promise of multimedia communications. *Technology Review, 95*, 42–50.

Brooks, D. C. (2011). Space matters: The impact of formal learning environments on student learning. *British Journal of Educational Technology, 42*, 719–726.

Brown, G., & Robinson, S. L. (2011). Reactions to territorial infringement. *Organization Science, 22*, 210–224.

Brown, P., & Levinson, S. C. (1987). *Politeness: Some universals in language usage.* New York, NY: Cambridge University Press.

Browne, B. A. (1998). Gender stereotypes in advertising on children's television in the 1990s: A cross-national analysis. *Journal of Advertising, 27*, 83–96.

Bruneau, T. J. (1973). Communicative silences: Forms and functions. *Journal of Communication, 23*, 17–46.

Brunner, L. J. (1979). Smiles can be back channels. *Journal of Personality and Social Psychology, 37*, 728–773.

Brunsma, D. L., & Rockquemore, K. A. (1998). Effects of student uniforms on attendance, behavior problems, substance use, and academic achievement. *Journal of Educational Research, 92*, 53–62.

Bryant, G. A., Fessler, D. M. T., Fusaroli, R., Clint, E., Amir, D., Chβvez, B., . . . Zhou, Y. (2018). The perception of spontaneous and volitional laughter across 21 societies. *Psychological Science, 29*, 1515–1525.

Bryant, G. A., Fessler, D. M. T., Fusaroli, R., Clint, E., Aarøe, L., Apicella, C. L., . . . Zhou, Y. (2016). Detecting affiliation in colaughter across 24 societies. *PNAS Proceedings of the National Academy of Sciences of the United States of America, 113*, 4682–4687.

Bryski, B. G., & Frye, J. K. (1979–1980). Nonverbal communication in presidential debates. *Australian Scan, 7–8*, 25–31.

Bucher, A., & Voss, A. (2019). Judging the mood of the crowd: Attention is focused on happy faces. *Emotion, 19*, 1044–1059.

Buck, R. (1975). Nonverbal communication of affect in children. *Journal of Personality and Social Psychology, 31*, 644–653.

Buck, R. (1976). A test of nonverbal receiving ability: Preliminary studies. *Human Communication Research, 2*, 162–171.

Buck, R. (1977). Nonverbal communication of affect in preschool children: Relationships with personality and skin conductance. *Journal of Personality and Social Psychology, 35*, 225–236.

Buck, R. (1979). Measuring individual differences in the nonverbal communication of affect: The slide-viewing paradigm. *Human Communication Research, 6*, 47–57.

Buck, R. (1984). *The communication of emotion.* New York, NY: Guilford.

Buck, R. (1991). Social factors in facial display and communication: A reply to Chovil and others. *Journal of Nonverbal Behavior, 15*, 155–161.

Buck, R. (1993). Emotional communication, emotional competence, and physical illness: A develop-mental-interactionist view. In H. C. Traue & J. W. Pennebaker (Eds.), *Emotion, inhibition, and health* (pp. 32–56). Seattle, WA: Hogrefe & Hubner.

Buck, R., & Duffy, R. (1980). Nonverbal communication of affect in brain-damaged patients. *Cortex, 16*, 351–362.

Buck, R., Miller, R. E., & Caul, W. F. (1974). Sex, personality and physiological variables in the communication of affect via facial expression. *Journal of Personality and Social Psychology, 30*, 587–596.

Buck, R., & Powers, S. R. (2006). The biological foundations of social organization: The dynamic emergence of social structure through nonverbal communication. In V. Manusov & M. L. Patterson (Eds.), *The SAGE handbook of nonverbal communication* (pp. 119–138). Thousand Oaks, CA: SAGE.

Buck, R., Powers, S. R., & Hull, K. S. (2017). Measuring emotional and cognitive empathy using dynamic, naturalistic, and spontaneous emotion displays. *Emotion, 17*, 1120–1136.

Buck, R., Savin, V., Miller, R., & Caul, W. (1972). Communication of affect through facial expressions in humans. *Journal of Personality and Social Psychology, 23*, 362–371.

Buck, R., & VanLear, A. (2002). Verbal and nonverbal communication: Distinguishing symbolic, spontaneous, and pseudo-spontaneous nonverbal behavior. *Journal of Communication, 52*, 522–541.

Budesheim, T. L., & DePaola, S. J. (1994). Beauty or the beast? The effects of appearance, personality, and issue information on evaluations of political candidates. *Personality and Social Psychology Bulletin, 20*, 339–349.

Bugental, D. E. (1974). Interpretations of naturally occurring discrepancies between words and intonation: Modes of inconsistency resolution. *Journal of Personality and Social Psychology, 30*, 125–133.

Bugental, D. E., Kaswan, J. W., & Love, L. R. (1970). Perception of contradictory meanings conveyed by verbal and nonverbal channels. *Journal of Personality and Social Psychology, 16*, 647–655.

Bull, P. E., & Brown, R. (1977). The role of postural change in dyadic conversation. *British Journal of Social and Clinical Psychology, 16*, 29–33.

Bull, P., & Connelly, G. (1985). Body movements and emphasis in speech. *Journal of Nonverbal Behavior, 9*, 169–187.

Burgess, C. A., Kirsch, I., Shane, H., Niederauer, K. L., Graham, S. M., & Bacon, A. (1998). Facilitated communication as an ideomotor response. *Psychological Science, 9*, 71–74.

Burgoon, J. K. (1978). A communication model of personal space violations: Explication and an initial test. *Human Communication Research, 4*, 129–142.

Burgoon, J. K. (1980). Nonverbal communication research in the 1970s: An overview. In D. Nimmo (Ed.), *Communication yearbook 4* (pp. 179–197). New Brunswick, NJ: Transaction.

Burgoon, J. K., Birk, T., & Pfau, M. (1990). Nonverbal behaviors, persuasion, and credibility. *Human Communication Research, 17*, 140–169.

Burgoon, J. K., Buller, D. B., & Woodall, W. G. (1989). *Nonverbal communication: The unspoken dialogue*. New York, NY: Harper & Row.

Burgoon, J. K., & Dunbar, N. E. (2006). Nonverbal expressions of dominance and power in human relationships. In V. Manusov & M. L. Patterson (Eds.), *The SAGE handbook of nonverbal communication* (pp. 279–297). Thousand Oaks, CA: SAGE.

Burgoon, J. K., & Hale, J. L. (1988). Nonverbal expectancy violations: Model elaboration and application to immediacy behaviors. *Communication Monographs, 55*, 58–79.

Burgoon, J. K., & Jones, S. B. (1976). Toward a theory of personal space expectations and their violations. *Human Communication Research, 2*, 131–146.

Burgoon, J. K., Stern, L. A., & Dillman, L. (1995). *Interpersonal adaptation: Dyadic interaction patterns*. New York, NY: Cambridge University Press.

Burley, D. T., Gray, N. S., & Snowden, R. J. (2019). Emotional modulation of the pupil response in psychopathy. *Personality Disorders: Theory, Research, and Treatment, 10*, 365–375.

Burnett, A., & Badzinski, D. M. (2005). Judge nonverbal communication on trial: Do mock jurors notice? *Journal of Communication, 55*, 209–224.

Burtt, H. E., & Clark, J. C. (1923). Facial expression in advertisements. *Journal of Applied Psychology, 7*, 114–125.

Buslig, A. L. S. (1999). "Stop" signs regulating privacy with environmental features. In L. Guerrero, J. A. DeVito, & M. L. Hecht (Eds.), *The nonverbal communication reader* (2nd ed., pp. 241–249). Prospect Heights, IL: Waveland Press.

Buss, D. M. (1994). *The evolution of desire*. New York, NY: Basic Books.

Buss, D. M., & Shackelford, T. K. (2008). Attractive women want it all: Good genes, economic investment, parenting proclivities, and emotional commitment. *Evolutionary Psychology, 6*, 134–146.

Butler, D., & Geis, F. L. (1990). Nonverbal affect responses to male and female leaders: Implications for leadership evaluations. *Journal of Personality and Social Psychology, 58*, 48–59.

Butler, E. A., Egloff, B., Wilhelm, F. H., Smith, N. C., Erickson, E. A., & Gross, J. J. (2003). The social consequences of expressive suppression. *Emotion, 3*, 48–67.

Buttelmann, D., Call, J., & Tomasello, M. (2009). Do great apes use emotional expressions to infer desires? *Developmental Science, 12*, 688–698.

Buunk, A. P., Fernandez, A. M., & Muñoz-Reyes, J. A. (2019). Height as related to self-perceived mate value and attractiveness. *Evolutionary Behavioral Sciences, 13*, 93–100.

Buunk, A. P., Poliet, T. V., Klavina, L., Figueredo, A. J., & Dijkstra, P. (2009). Height among women is curvilinearly related to life history strategy. *Evolutionary Psychology, 7*, 545–559.

Byron, K., Terranova, S., & Nowicki, S., Jr. (2007). Nonverbal emotion recognition and salespersons: Linking ability to perceived and actual success. *Journal of Applied Social Psychology, 37*, 2600–2619.

Calhoun, J. B. (1962). Population density and social pathology. *Scientific American, 206*, 139–148.

Calvo, M. G., & Lundqvist, D. (2008). Facial expressions of emotion (KDEF): Identification under different display-duration conditions. *Behavior Research Methods, 40*, 109–115.

Cameron, G., Oskamp, S., & Sparks, W. (1978). Courtship American style: Newspaper advertisements. *The Family Coordinator, 26*, 27–30.

Cameron, H., & Xu, X. (2011). Representational gesture, pointing gesture, and memory recall of preschool children. *Journal of Nonverbal Behavior, 35*, 156–171.

Camgoz, N., Yener, C., & Guvenc, D. (2004). Effects of hue, saturation, and brightness. Part 2: Attention. *Color Research and Application, 29*, 20–28.

Campbell, D. E. (1979). Interior office design and visitor response. *Journal of Applied Psychology, 64*, 648–653.

Campbell, D. E., & Beets, J. L. (1978). Lunacy and the moon. *Psychological Bulletin, 85*, 1123–1129.

Campbell, J. B., & Hawley, C. W. (1982). Study habits and Eysenck's theory of extraversion-introversion. *Journal of Research in Personality, 16*, 139–148.

Campbell, L. A., & Bryant, R. A. (2007). How time flies: A study of novice skydivers. *Behaviour Research and Therapy, 45*, 1389–1392.

Camps, J., Tuteleers, C., Stouten, J., & Nelissen, J. (2013). A situational touch: How touch affects people's decision behavior. *Social Influence, 8*, 237–250.

Camras, L. A. (1994). Two aspects of emotional development: Expression and elicitation. In P. Ekman & R. J. Davidson (Eds.), *The nature of emotion: Fundamental questions* (pp. 347–351). New York, NY: Oxford University Press.

Camras, L. A., Sullivan, J., & Michel, G. (1993). Do infants express discrete emotions? Adult judgments of facial, vocal, and body actions. *Journal of Nonverbal Behavior, 17*, 171–186.

Canadas, E., & Schmid Mast, M. (2017). Drawn towards what others seem to like: Implicit preference for objects and people looked at with a Duchenne smile. *Motivation and Emotion, 41*, 628–635.

Capaldi, C. A., Passmore, H.-A., Ishii, R., Chistopolskaya, K. A., Vowinckel, J., Nikolaev, E. L., & Semikin, G. I. (2017). Engaging with natural beauty may be related to well-being because it connects people to nature: Evidence from three cultures. *Ecopsychology, 9*, 199–211.

Caplan, M. E., & Goldman, M. (1981). Personal space violations as a function of height. *Journal of Social Psychology, 114*, 167–171.

Caporael, L. R. (1981). The paralanguage of caregiving: Baby talk to the institutionalized aged. *Journal of Personality and Social Psychology, 40*, 876–884.

Capozzi, F., Bayliss, A. P., & Ristic, J. (2018). Gaze following in multiagent contexts: Evidence for a quorum-like principle. *Psychonomic Bulletin & Review, 25*, 2260–2266.

Cappella, J. N. (1981). Mutual influence in expressive behavior: Adult-adult and infant-adult dyadic interaction. *Psychological Bulletin, 89*, 101–132.

Cappella, J. N. (1985). Controlling the floor in conversation. In A. W. Siegman & S. Feldstein (Eds.), *Multichannel integrations of nonverbal behavior* (pp. 69–104). Hillsdale, NJ: Lawrence Erlbaum.

Cappella, J. N., & Greene, J. O. (1982). A discrepancy-arousal explanation of mutual influence in expressive behavior of adult–adult and infant–adult interaction. *Communication Monographs, 49*, 89–114.

Carlsmith, J. M., & Anderson, C. A. (1979). Ambient temperature and the occurrence of collective violence: A new analysis. *Journal of Personality and Social Psychology, 37*, 337–344.

Carney, D. R., Colvin, C. R., & Hall, J. A. (2007). A thin slice perspective on the accuracy of first impressions. *Journal of Research in Personality, 41*, 1054–1072.

Carney, D. R., Hall, J. A., & Smith LeBeau, L. (2005). Beliefs about the nonverbal expression of social power. *Journal of Nonverbal Behavior, 29*, 105–123.

Carpenter, S. M., & Niedenthal, P. M. (2019). Disrupting facial action increases risk taking. *Emotion.* 2020 20(6) 1084–1092.

Carr, S. J., & Dabbs, J. M. (1974). The effect of lighting, distance, and intimacy of topic on verbal and visual behavior. *Sociometry, 37*, 592–600.

Carrard, V., Schmid Mast, M., & Cousin, G. (2016). Beyond "one size fits all": Physician nonverbal adaptability to patients' need for paternalism and its positive consultation outcomes. *Health Communication, 31*, 1327–1333.

Carroll, J. M., & Russell, J. A. (1996). Do facial expressions signal specific emotions? Judging emotion from the face in context. *Journal of Personality and Social Psychology, 70*, 205–218.

Cartei, V., & Reby, D. (2012). Acting gay: Male actors shift the frequency components of their voices towards female values when playing homosexual characters. *Journal of Nonverbal Behavior, 36*, 79–93.

Carter, J. D., & Hall, J. A. (2008). Individual differences in the accuracy of detecting social covariations: Ecological sensitivity. *Journal of Research in Personality, 42*, 439–455.

Cary, M. S. (1978). The role of gaze in the initiation of conversation. *Social Psychology, 41*, 269–271.

Cascio, C. J., Moore, D., & McGlone, F. (2019). Social touch and human development. *Developmental Cognitive Neuroscience, 35*, 5–11.

Cash, T. F., Gillen, B., & Burns, S. (1977). Sexism and "beautism" in personnel consultant decision making. *Journal of Applied Psychology, 62*, 301–310.

Cash, T. F., Winstead, B. A., & Janda, L. H. (1986). The great American shape-up. *Psychology Today, 20*, 30–37.

Castles, D. L., Whitens, A., & Aureli, F. (1999). Social anxiety, relationships and self-directed behaviour among wild female olive baboons. *Animal Behavior, 58*, 1207–1215.

Castro, V. L., Cooke, A. N., Halberstadt, A. G., & Garrett-Peters, P. (2018). Bidirectional linkages between emotion recognition and problem behaviors in elementary school children. *Journal of Nonverbal Behavior, 42*, 155–178.

Castro, V. L., & Isaacowitz, D. M. (2019). The same with age: Evidence for age-related similarities in interpersonal accuracy. *Journal of Experimental Psychology: General, 148*, 1517–1537.

Caudill, W., & Weinstein, H. (1972). Maternal care and infant behavior in Japan and America. In C. Lavatelli & F. Stendler (Eds.), *Readings in child behavior and development* (pp. 78–87). New York, NY: Harcourt.

Cavior, N., & Lombardi, D. H. (1973). Developmental aspects of judgment of physical attractiveness in children. *Developmental Psychology, 8*, 67–71.

Chaiken, S. (1979). Communicator physical attractiveness and persuasion. *Journal of Personality and Social Psychology, 37*, 1387–1397.

Chaiken, S. (1986). Physical appearance and social influence. In G. P. Herman, M. P. Zanna, & E. T. Higgins (Eds.), *Physical appearance, stigma, and social behavior: The Ontario symposium* (Vol. 3, pp. 143–178). Hillsdale, NJ: Lawrence Erlbaum.

Chaikin, A. L., Sigler, E., & Derlega, V. J. (1974). Nonverbal mediators of teacher expectancy effects. *Journal of Personality and Social Psychology, 30*, 144–149.

Chan, R. S., & Thompson, N. S. (2011). Whines, cries, and motherese: Their relative power to distract. *Journal of Social, Evolutionary, and Cultural Psychology, 5*, 131–141.

Chaney, K. E., & Sanchez, D. T. (2018). Gender-inclusive bathrooms signal fairness across identity dimensions. *Social Psychological and Personality Science, 9*, 245–253.

Chapple, E. D. (1949). The interaction chronograph: Its evolution and present application. *Personnel, 25*, 295–307.

Chapple, E. D. (1953). The standard experimental (stress) interview as used in interaction chronograph investigations. *Human Organizations, 12*, 23–32.

Chapple, E. D., & Sayles, L. R. (1961). *The measure of management*. New York, NY: Macmillan.

Charney, E. J. (1966). Postural configurations in psychotherapy. *Psychosomatic Medicine, 28*, 305–315.

Chartrand, T. L., & Bargh, J. A. (1999). The chameleon effect: The perception–behavior link and social interaction. *Journal of Personality and Social Psychology, 76*, 893–910.

Cheek, J. M., & Buss, A. H. (1981). Shyness and sociability. *Journal of Personality and Social Psychology, 41*, 330–339.

Chen, F. S., & Yoon, J. M. (2011). Brief report: Broader autism phenotype predicts spontaneous reciprocity of direct gaze. *Journal of Autism and Development and Disorders, 41*, 1131–1134.

Chen, M., & Bargh, J. A. (1997). Nonconscious behavioral confirmation processes: The self-fulfilling consequences of automatic stereotype activation. *Journal of Experimental Social Psychology, 33*, 541–560.

Chen, N. T. M., Clarke, P. J. F., MacLeod, C., Hickie, I. B., & Guastella, A. J. (2016). Aberrant gaze patterns in social anxiety disorder: An eye movement assessment during public speaking. *Journal of Experimental Psychopathology, 7*, 1–17.

Cheryan, S., Meltzoff, A. N., & Kim, S. (2011). Classrooms matter: The design of virtual classrooms influences gender disparities in computer science classes. *Computers and Education, 57*, 1825–1835.

Cheval, B., Grob, E., Chanal, J., Ghisletta, P., Bianchi-Demicheli, F., & Radel, R. (2016). Homophobia is related to a low interest in sexuality in general: An analysis of pupillometric evoked responses. *Journal of Sexual Medicine, 13*, 1539–1545.

Chevalier-Skolnikoff, S. (1973). Facial expression of emotion in nonhuman primates. In P. Ekman (Ed.), *Darwin and facial expression* (pp. 11–89). New York, NY: Academic Press.

Choi, Y. S., Gray, H. M., & Ambady, N. (2005). The glimpsed world: Unintended communication and unintended perception. In R. R. Hassin, J. S. Uleman, & J. A. Bargh (Eds.), *The new unconscious* (pp. 309–333). New York, NY: Oxford University Press.

Chovil, N. (1991). Social determinants of facial displays. *Journal of Nonverbal Behavior, 15*, 141–115.

Chovil, N. (1991/1992). Discourse-oriented facial displays in conversation. *Research on Language and Social Interaction, 25*, 163–119.

Christenfeld, N. (1995). Does it hurt to say um? *Journal of Nonverbal Behavior, 19*, 171–186.

Chu, M., & Kita, S. (2011). The nature of gestures' beneficial role in spatial problem solving. *Journal of Experimental Psychology: General, 140*, 102–116.

Church, R. B., Garber, P., & Rogalski, K. (2007). The role of gesture in memory and social communication. *Gesture, 7*, 137–158.

Cialdini, R. B. (2007). *Influence: The psychology of persuasion* (Rev. ed.). New York, NY: Collins.

Cialdini, R. B., Kallgren, C. A., & Reno, R. R. (1991). A focus theory of normative conduct: A theoretical refinement and reevaluation of the role of norms in human behavior. *Advances in Experimental Social Psychology, 24*, 210–234.

Cicone, M., Wapner, W., Foldi, N., Zurif, E., & Gardner, H. (1979). The relation between gesture and language in aphasic communication. *Brain and Language, 8*, 324–349.

Clark-Gordon, C. V., Bowman, N. D., Watts, E. R., Banks, J., & Knight, J. M. (2018). "As good as your word": Face-threat mitigation and the use of instructor nonverbal cues on students' perceptions of digital feedback. *Communication Education, 67*, 206–225.

Clark, H. H., & Fox Tree, J. E. (2002). Using uh and um in spontaneous speaking. *Cognition, 84*, 73–111.

Cline, M. (1956). The influence of social context on the perception of faces. *Journal of Personality, 25*, 142–158.

Clore, G. L., Wiggins, N. H., & Itkin, S. (1975a). Gain and loss in attraction: Attributions from nonverbal behavior. *Journal of Personality and Social Psychology, 31*, 706–712.

Clore, G. L., Wiggins, N. H., & Itkin, S. (1975b). Judging attraction from nonverbal behavior: The gain phenomenon. *Journal of Consulting and Clinical Psychology, 43*, A9X–A91.

Cochet, H., & Vauclair, J. (2010). Pointing gestures produced by toddlers from 15 to 30 months: Different functions, hand shapes and laterality patterns. *Infant Behavior and Development, 33*, 431–441.

Cohen, A. A. (1977). The communicative functions of hand illustrators. *Journal of Communication, 27*, 54–63.

Cohen, A. A., & Harrison, R. P. (1973). Intentionality in the use of hand illustrators in face-to-face communication situations. *Journal of Personality and Social Psychology, 28*, 276–279.

Cohn, J. F., & Ekman, P. (2005). Measuring facial action. In J. A. Harrigan, R. Rosenthal, & K. R. Scherer (Eds.), *The new handbook of methods in nonverbal behavior research* (pp. 10–64). Oxford, UK: Oxford University Press.

Colapinto, J. (2000). *As nature made him: The boy who was raised as a girl.* New York, NY: HarperCollins.

Cole, P. M. (1986). Children's spontaneous control of facial expression. *Child Development, 57*, 1309–1321.

Collins, M. A., & Zebrowitz, L. A. (1995). The contributions of appearance to occupational outcomes in civilian and military settings. *Journal of Applied Social Psychology, 25*, 129–163.

Comadena, M. E. (1982). Accuracy in detecting deception: Intimate and friendship relationships. In M. Burgoon (Ed.), *Communication yearbook 6* (pp. 446–472). Newbury Park, CA: SAGE.

Condon, W. S. (1976). An analysis of behavioral organization. *Sign Language Studies, 13*, 285–318.

Condon, W. S., & Ogston, W. D. (1966). Sound film analysis of normal and pathological behavior patterns. *Journal of Nervous and Mental Disease, 143*, 338–347.

Condon, W. S., & Sander, L. W. (1974). Neonate movement is synchronized with adult speech: Interaction participation in language acquisition. *Science, 183*, 99–101.

Cook, M. (1965). Anxiety, speech disturbances, and speech rate. *British Journal of Social and Clinical Psychology, 4*, 1–7.

Cook, M. (1970). Experiments on orientation and proxemics. *Human Relations, 23*, 61–76.

Cook, S. W., Mitchell, Z., & Goldin-Meadow, S. (2008). Gesturing makes learning last. *Cognition, 106*, 1047–1058.

Cook, S. W., Yip, T. K., & Goldin-Meadow, S. (2010). Gesturing makes memories that last. *Journal of Memory and Language, 63*, 465–475.

Cooley, C. H. (1902). *Human nature and the social order.* New York, NY: Charles Scribner's.

Cooperrider, K., Slotta, J., & Núñez, R. (2018). The preference for pointing with the hand is not universal. *Cognitive Science, 42*, 1375–1390.

Copeland, G. A. (1989). Face-ism and prime time television. *Journal of Broadcasting and Electronic Media, 33*, 209–214.

Cordaro, D. T., Keltner, D., Tshering, S., Wangchuk, D., & Flynn, L. M. (2016). The voice conveys emotion in ten globalized cultures and one remote village in Bhutan. *Emotion, 16*, 117–128.

Cortés, J. B., & Gatti, F. M. (1965). Physique and self-description of temperament. *Journal of Consulting Psychology, 29*, 432–439.

Costa, M. (2010). Interpersonal distances in group walking. *Journal of Nonverbal Behavior, 34*, 15–26.

Costanzo, M. (1992). Training students to decode verbal and nonverbal cues: Effects on confidence and performance. *Journal of Educational Psychology, 84*, 308–313.

Costanzo, M., & Archer, D. (1989). Interpreting the expressive behavior of others: The interpersonal perception task. *Journal of Nonverbal Behavior, 13*, 225–245.

Cotter, J., Granger, K., Backx, R., Hobbs, M., Looi, C. Y., & Barnett, J. H. (2018). Social cognitive dysfunction as a clinical marker: A systematic review of meta-analyses across 30 clinical conditions. *Neuroscience and Biobehavioral Reviews, 84*, 92–99.

Coyle, J. M., & Kaschak, M. P. (2012). Female fertility affects men's linguistic choices. *PLoS ONE, 7*, e27971. doi:10.1371/journal.pone.0027971

Craig, B. M., Nelson, N. L., & Dixson, B. J. W. (2019). Sexual selection, agonistic signaling, and the effect of beards on recognition of men's anger displays. *Psychological Science, 30*, 728–738.

Crane, D. R., Dollahite, D. C., Griffin, W., & Taylor, V. L. (1987). Diagnosing relationships with spatial distance: An empirical test of a clinical principle. *Journal of Marital and Family Therapy, 13*, 307–310.

Creel, S. C., & Bregman, M. R. (2011). How talker identity relates to language processing. *Language and Linguistics Compass, 5*, 190–204.

Creider, C. (1977). Toward a description of East African gestures. *Sign Language Studies, 14*, 1–20.

Crivello, C., & Poulin-Dubois, D. (2019). Infants' ability to detect emotional incongruency: Deep or shallow? *Infancy, 24*, 480–500.

Crosby, F., Bromley, S., & Saxe, L. (1980). Recent unobtrusive studies of black and white discrimination and prejudice: A literature review. *Psychological Bulletin, 87*, 546–563.

Crosby, J. R., Monin, B., & Richardson, D. (2008). Where do we look during potentially offensive behavior? *Psychological Science, 19*, 226–228.

Cross, S. E., & Madson, L. (1997). Models of the self: Self-construals and gender. *Psychological Bulletin, 122*, 5–37.

Crusco, A. H., & Wetzel, C. G. (1984). The Midas touch: The effects of interpersonal touch on restaurant tipping. *Personality and Social Psychology Bulletin, 10*, 512–517.

Cui, M., Zhu, M., Lu, X., & Zhu, L. (2019). Implicit perceptions of closeness from the direct eye gaze. *Frontiers in Psychology, 9*.

Cunningham, M. R., Barbee, A. P., & Philhower, G. L. (2002). Dimensions of facial physical attractiveness: The intersection of biology and culture. In G. Rhodes & L. A. Zebrowitz (Eds.), *Facial attractiveness* (pp. 193–238). Westport, CT: Ablex.

Curtis, M. E., & Bharucha, J. J. (2010). The minor third communicates sadness in speech, mirroring its use in music. *Emotion, 10*, 335–348.

Cutler, W. B., Preti, G., Krieger, A., Huggins, G. R., Garcia, G. R., & Lawley, H. J. (1986). Human axillary secretions influence women's menstrual cycles: The role of donor extract from men. *Hormones and Behavior, 20*, 463–473.

Cyr, D., Head, M., & Larios, H. (2010). Colour appeal in website design within and across cultures: A multi-method evaluation. *International Journal of Human-Computer Studies, 68*, 1–21.

Dabbs, J. M., Evans, M. S., Hopper, C. H., & Purvis, J. A. (1980). Self-monitors in conversation: What do they monitor? *Journal of Personality and Social Psychology, 39*, 278–284.

Dael, N., Mortillaro, M., & Scherer, K. R. (2012). Emotion expression in body action and posture. *Emotion, 12*, 1085–1101.

Daigen, V., & Holmes, J. G. (2000). Don't interrupt! A good rule for marriage? *Personal Relationships, 7*, 185–201.

Dailey, M. N., Joyce, C., Lyons, M. J., Kamachi, M., Ishi, H., Gyoba, J., & Cottrell, G. W. (2010). Evidence and a computational explanation of cultural differences in facial expression recognition. *Emotion, 10*, 874–893.

Daly, J. A., Hogg, E., Sacks, D., Smith, M., & Zimring, L. (1983). Sex and relationship affect social self-grooming. *Journal of Nonverbal Behavior, 7*, 183–189.

Damasio, A. R. (1994). *Descartes' error: Emotion, reason and the human brain*. New York, NY: Putnam.

Daniel, T. A., & Camp, A. L. (2018). Emojis affect processing fluency on social media. *Psychology of Popular Media Culture*.

Danziger, K. (1976). *Interpersonal communication*. New York, NY: Pergamon.

Darwin, C. (1998). *The expression of emotion in man and animals* (3rd ed.). New York, NY: Oxford University Press. (Original work published in 1872)

Darwin, C. R. (1872). *The expression of the emotions in man and animals*. London, UK: John Murray.

da Silva Ferreira, G. C., Crippa, J. A. S., & de Lima Osório, F. (2014). Facial emotion processing and recognition among maltreated children: A systematic literature review. *Frontiers in Psychology, 5*, Article ID 1460.

Datta Gupta, N., Etcoff, N. L., & Jaeger, M. M. (2016). Beauty in mind: The effects of physical attractiveness on psychological well-being and distress. *Journal of Happiness Studies, 17*, 1313–1325.

Davis, E. M., & Fingerman, K. L. (2016). Digital dating: Online profile content of older and younger adults. *Journals of Gerontology: Series B: Psychological Sciences and Social Sciences, 71*, 959–967.

Davis, J. I., Senghas, A., Brandt, F., & Ochsner, K. N. (2010). The effects of BOTOX injections on emotional experi-ence. *Emotion, 10*, 433–440.

Davis, M. (1979). The state of the art: Past and present trends in body movement research. In A. Wolfgang (Ed.), *Nonverbal behavior: Applications and cultural implications*. New York, NY: Academic Press.

Davis, M. (1995). Presidential body politics: Movement analysis of debates and press conferences. *Semiotica, 106*, 205–244.

Davis, M., & Dulicai, D. (1992). Hitler's movement signature. *The Drama Review, 36*, 152–172.

Davitz, J. R. (1964). *The communication of emotional meaning*. New York, NY: McGraw-Hill.

Davitz, J. R., & Davitz, L. J. (1959). The communication of feelings by content-free speech. *Journal of Communica-tion, 9*, 6–13.

Deethardt, J. F., & Hines, D. G. (1983). Tactile communication and personality differences. *Journal of Nonverbal Behavior, 8*, 143–156.

de Groot, J. H. B., & Smeets, M. A. M. (2017). Human fear chemosignaling: Evidence from a meta-analysis. *Chemical Senses, 42*, 663–673.

DeGroot, T., & Motowidlo, S. J. (1999). Why visual and vocal interview cues can affect interviewers' judgments and predict job performance. *Journal of Applied Psychology, 84*, 986–993.

DePaulo, B. M. (1992). Nonverbal behavior and self-presentation. *Psychological Bulletin, 111*, 203–243.

DePaulo, B. M., & Friedman, H. S. (1998). Nonverbal communication. In D. T. Gilbert, S. T. Fiske, & G. Lindzey (Eds.), *The handbook of social psychology* (4th ed., Vol. 2, pp. 3–40). New York, NY: McGraw-Hill.

DePaulo, B. M., Kashy, D. A., Kirkendol, S. E., Wyer, M. M., & Epstein, J. A. (1996). Lying in everyday life. *Journal of Personality and Social Psychology, 70*, 979–995.

DePaulo, B. M., Lindsay, J. J., Malone, B. E., Muhlenbruck, L., Charlton, K., & Cooper, H. (2003). Cues to deception. *Journal of Personality and Social Psychology, 129*, 74–118.

Dermer, M., & Thiel, D. L. (1975). When beauty may fail. *Journal of Personality and Social Psychology, 31*, 1168–1176.

de Ruiter, J. P. (2007). Postcards from the mind. *Gesture, 7*, 21–38.

deTurck, M. A. (1991). Training observers to detect spontaneous deception: Effects of gender. *Communication Reports, 4*, 79–89.

deTurck, M. A., Feeley, T. H., & Roman, L. A. (1997). Vocal and visual cue training in behavioral lie detection. *Communication Research Reports, 14*, 249–259.

Devlin, A. S. (2008). Judging a book by its cover: Medical building facades and judgments of care. *Environment and Behavior, 40*, 307–329.

de Waal, F. B. M. (2002). Evolutionary psychology: The wheat and the chaff. *Current Directions in Psychological Science, 11*, 187–191.

DiBiase, R., & Gunnoe, J. (2004). Gender and culture differences in touching behavior. *Journal of Social Psychol-ogy, 144*, 49–62.

Dickey, E. C., & Knower, F. H. (1941). A note on some ethnological differences in recognition of simulated expres-sions of emotions. *American Journal of Sociology, 47*, 190–193.

Diener, E., Sandvik, E., & Larsen, R. (1985). Age and sex effects for emotional intensity. *Developmental Psychology, 21*, 542–546.

Diener, E., Wolsic, B., & Fujita, F. (1995). Physical attractiveness and subjective well-being. *Journal of Personality and Social Psychology, 69*, 120–129.

DiMatteo, M. R., Hays, R. D., & Prince, L. M. (1986). Relationship of physicians' nonverbal communication skill to patient satisfaction, appointment noncompliance, and physician workload. *Health Psychology, 5*, 581–594.

DiMatteo, M. R., Taranta, A., Friedman, H. A., & Prince, L. M. (1980). Predicting patient satisfaction from physicians' nonverbal communication skills. *Medical Care, 18*, 376–387.

Dimberg, U. (1982). Facial reaction to facial expressions. *Psychophysiology, 19*, 643–647.

Dimberg, U., Thunberg, M., & Elmehed, K. (2000). Unconscious facial reactions to emotional facial expressions. *Psychological Science, 11*, 86–89.

Dimitrovsky, L. (1964). The ability to identify the emotional meaning of vocal expressions at successive age levels. In J. R. Davitz (Ed.), *The communication of emotional meaning* (pp. 69–86). New York, NY: McGraw-Hill.

Dindia, K. (1987). The effects of sex of subject and sex of partner on interruptions. *Human Communication Research, 13*, 345–371.

Dinella, L. M. (2017). Halloween costume choices: Reflections of gender development in early childhood. *Journal of Genetic Psychology, 178*, 165–178.

Dion, K. K. (2002). Cultural perspectives on facial attractiveness. In G. Rhodes & L. A. Zebrowitz (Eds.), *Facial attractiveness* (pp. 239–259). Westport, CT: Ablex.

Dion, K. K., Berscheid, E., & Walster, E. (1972). What is beautiful is good. *Journal of Personality and Social Psychology, 24*, 285–290.

Dion, K. K., & Stein, S. (1978). Physical attractiveness and interpersonal influence. *Journal of Experimental Social Psychology, 14*, 97–108.

Dipboye, R. L., Arvey, R. D., & Terpstra, D. E. (1977). Sex and physical attractiveness of raters and applicants as determinants of resume evaluations. *Journal of Applied Psychology, 62*, 288–294.

Dittmann, A. T. (1972). The body movement-speech rhythm relationship as a cue to speech encoding. In A. W. Siegman & B. Pope (Eds.), *Studies in dyadic communication*. New York: Pergamon Press.

Dixson, B. J., Dixson, A. F., Bishop, P. J., & Parish, A. (2010). Human physique and sexual attractiveness in men and women: A New Zealand–U.S. comparative study. *Archives of Sexual Behavior, 39*, 798–806.

Dixson, B. J., Grimshaw, G. M., Linklater, W. L., & Dixson, A. F. (2011). Eye-tracking of men's preferences for waist-to-hip ratio and breast size of women. *Archives of Sexual Behavior, 40*, 43–50.

Dixson, B. J. W., Lee, A. J., Blake, K. R., Jasienska, G., & Marcinkowska, U. M. (2018). Women's preferences for men's beards show no relation to their ovarian cycle phase and sex hormone levels. *Hormones and Behavior, 97*, 137–144.

Dixson, M. D., Greenwell, M. R., Rogers-Stacy, C., Weister, T., & Lauer, S. (2017). Nonverbal immediacy behaviors and online student engagement: Bringing past instructional research into the present virtual classroom. *Communication Education, 66*, 37–53.

Dobrogaev, S. M. (1931). The study of reflex in problems of linguistics (M. Kendon, Trans.). In E. A. Marr (Ed.), *Lazykovedenie i materializm* (Vol. 2).

Dodd, D. K., Harcar, V., Foerch, B. J., & Anderson, H. T. (1989). Face-ism and facial expressions of women in magazine photos. *Psychological Record, 39*, 325–331.

Dodd, D. K., Russell, B. L., & Jenkins, C. (1999). Smiling in school yearbook photos: Gender differences from kindergarten to adulthood. *Psychological Record, 49*, 543–554.

Doherty-Sneddon, G., & Phelps, F. G. (2005). Gaze aversion: A response to cognitive or social difficulty? *Memory and Cognition, 33*, 727–733.

Dolinski, D. (2010). Touch, compliance, and homophobia. *Journal of Nonverbal Behavior, 34*, 179–192.

Doody, J. P., & Bull, P. (2011). Asperger's syndrome and the decoding of boredom, interest, and disagreement from body posture. *Journal of Nonverbal Behavior, 35*, 87–100.

Döring, N., & Pöschl, S. (2009). Nonverbal cues in mobile phone text messages: The effects of chronemics and proxemics. In R. Ling & S. Campbell (Eds.), *The reconstruction of space and time: Mobile communication practices* (pp. 109–135). Piscataway, NJ: Transaction.

Dossinger, K., Wanberg, C. R., Choi, Y., & Leslie, L. M. (2019). The beauty premium: The role of organizational sponsorship in the relationship between physical attractiveness and early career salaries. *Journal of Vocational Behavior, 112*, 109–121.

Dovidio, J. F., & Ellyson, S. L. (1985). Patterns of visual dominance behavior in humans. In S. L. Ellyson & J. F. Dovidio (Eds.), *Power, dominance, and nonverbal behavior* (pp. 129–149). New York, NY: Springer-Verlag.

Dovidio, J. F., Kawakami, K., Johnson, C., Johnson, B., & Howard, A. (1997). On the nature of prejudice: Automatic and controlled processes. *Journal of Experimental Social Psychology, 33*, 510–540.

Drescher, V. M., Gantt, W. H., & Whitehead, W. E. (1980). Heart rate response to touch. *Psychosomatic Medicine, 42*, 559–565.

Droney, J. M., & Brooks, C. I. (1993). Attributions of self-esteem as a function of duration of eye contact. *Journal of Social Psychology, 133*, 715–722.

Dumitrescu, D. (2016). Nonverbal communication in politics: A review of research developments, 2005–2015. *American Behavioral Scientist, 60*, 1656–1675.

Dunbar, N. E., & Abra, G. (2010). Observations of dyadic power in interpersonal interaction. *Communication Monographs, 77*, 657–684.

Duncan, S. (1973). Toward a grammar for dyadic conversation. *Semiotica, 9*, 24–26.

Duncan, S. D., Jr. (1974). On the structure of speaker–auditor interaction during speaking turns. *Language in Society, 2*, 161–180.

Duncan, S. D., Jr. (1975). Interaction units during speaking turns in dyadic face-to-face conversations. In A. Kendon, R. M. Harris, & M. R. Key (Eds.), *Organization of behavior in face-to-face interaction* (pp. 189–213). Chicago, IL: Aldine.

Duncan, S. D., Jr., & Fiske, D. W. (1977). *Face-to-face interaction: Research, methods, and theory*. Hillsdale, NJ: Lawrence Erlbaum.

Dunlap, K. (1927). The role of eye muscles and mouth muscles in the expression of the emotions. *Genetic Psychology Monographs, 2*, 199–233.

Dunn, E. C., Crawford, K. M., Soare, T. W., Button, K. S., Raffeld, M. R., Smith, A. D. A. C., . . . Munafò, M. R. (2018). Exposure to childhood adversity and deficits in emotion recognition: Results from a large, population-based sample. *Journal of Child Psychology and Psychiatry, 59*, 845–854.

Durante, K. M., Griskevicius, V., Hill, S., Perilloux, C., & Li, N. P. (2011). Ovulation, female competition, and product choice: Hormonal influences on consumer behavior. *Journal of Consumer Research, 37*, 921–934.

Durso, F. T., Geldbach, K. M., & Corballis, P. (2012). Detecting confusion using facial electromyography. *Human Factors, 54*, 60–69.

Eagly, A. H. (1987). *Sex differences in social behavior: A social-role interpretation*. Hillsdale, NJ: Lawrence Erlbaum.

Eagly, A. H., Ashmore, R. D., Makhijani, M. G., & Longo, L. C. (1991). What is beautiful is good, but . . . : A meta-analysis of research on the physical attractiveness stereotype. *Psychological Bulletin, 110*, 109–128.

Edinger, J. A., & Patterson, M. L. (1983). Nonverbal involvement and social control. *Psychological Bulletin, 93*, 30–56.

Edvardsson, D. (2009). Balancing between being a person and being a patient—A qualitative study of wearing patient clothing. *International Journal of Nursing Studies, 46*, 4–11.

Edwards, J., Jackson, H. J., & Pattison, P. E. (2002). Emotion recognition via facial expression and affective prosody in schizophrenia: A methodological review. *Clinical Psychology Review, 22*, 789–832.

Effron, D. A., Niedenthal, P. M., Gil, S., & Droit-Volet, S. (2006). Embodied temporal perception of emotion. *Emotion, 6*, 1–9.

Efran, J. S., & Broughton, A. (1966). Effect of expectancies for social approval on visual behavior. *Journal of Personality and Social Psychology, 4*, 103–107.

Efran, M. G. (1974). The effect of physical appearance on the judgment of guilt, interpersonal attraction, and severity of recommended punishment in a simulated jury task. *Journal of Experimental Research in Personality, 8*, 45–54.

Efron, D. (1941). *Gesture and environment*. New York, NY: King's Crown Press. (Republished in 1972 as *Gesture, race and culture*. The Hague, Netherlands: Mouton.)

Efron, D. (1972). *Gesture, race and culture*. The Hague, The Netherlands: Mouton. (Original work published in 1941 as *Gesture and environment*. New York, NY: Kings Crown Press.)

Egland, K. L., Spitzberg, B. H., & Zormeier, M. M. (1996). Flirtation and conversational competence in cross-sex platonic and romantic relationships. *Communication Reports, 9*, 105–117.

Eibl-Eibesfeldt, I. (1971). Ethology of human greeting behavior: II. The greeting behavior and some other patterns of friendly contact by the Waika Indians (Yanoama). *Zeitschrift für Tierpsychologie, 29*, 196–213.

Eibl-Eibesfeldt, I. (1972). Similarities and differences between cultures in expressive movements. In R. Hinde (Ed.), *Non-verbal communication* (pp. 297–314). Cambridge, UK: Cambridge University Press.

Eibl-Eibesfeldt, I. (1973). The expressive behavior of the deaf-and-blind born. In M. von Cranach & I. Vine (Eds.), *Social communication and movement* (pp. 163–194). New York, NY: Academic Press.

Eibl-Eibesfeldt, I. (1975). *Ethology: The biology of behavior* (2nd ed.). New York, NY: Holt, Rinehart & Winston.

Eibl-Eibesfeldt, I. (1988). Social interactions in an ethological, cross-cultural perspective. In F. Poyatos (Ed.), *Cross-cultural perspectives in nonverbal communication* (pp. 107–130). Toronto, Ontario, Canada: Hogrefe.

Einhäuser, W., Koch, C., & Carter, O. L. (2010). Pupil dilation betrays the timing decisions. *Frontiers in Human Neuroscience, 4*, 18. doi:10.3389/fnhum.2010.00018

Eisenbarth, H., & Alpers, G. W. (2011). Happy mouth and sad eyes: Scanning emotional facial expressions. *Emotion, 11*, 860–865.

Eisenberg, M. L., Shindel, A. W., Smith, J. F., Breyer, B. N., & Lipshultz, L. I. (2010). Socioeconomic, anthropomorphic, and demographic predictors of adult sexual activity in the United States: Data from the National Survey of Family Growth. *Journal of Sexual Medicine, 7*, 50–58.

Ekman, P. (1965). Communication through nonverbal behavior: A source of information about an interpersonal relationship. In S. S. Tomkins & C. E. Izard (Eds.), *Affect, cognition and personality* (pp. 390–442). New York, NY: Springer.

Ekman, P. (1972). Universals and cultural differences in facial expressions of emotion. In J. Cole (Ed.), *Nebraska symposium on motivation* (Vol. 19). Lincoln: University of Nebraska Press.

Ekman, P. (Ed.). (1973). *Darwin and facial expression: A century of research in review*. New York, NY: Academic Press.

Ekman, P. (1976). Movements with precise meanings. *Journal of Communication, 26*, 14–26.

Ekman, P. (1977). Biological and cultural contribution to bodily and facial movement. In J. Blacking (Ed.), *The anthropology of the body* (pp. 34–84). London, UK: Academic Press.

Ekman, P. (1979). About brows: Emotional and conversational signals. In V. von Cranach, K. Foppa, W. Lepenies, & D. Ploog (Eds.), *Human ethology* (pp. 169–202). Cambridge, UK: Cambridge University Press.

Ekman, P. (1982). Methods for measuring facial action. In K. R. Scherer & P. Ekman (Eds.), *Handbook of methods in nonverbal behavior research* (pp. 45–90). Cambridge, UK: Cambridge University Press.

Ekman, P. (1992). *Telling lies* (2nd ed.). New York, NY: Norton.

Ekman, P. (1994). Strong evidence for universals in facial expressions: A reply to Russell's mistaken critique. *Psychological Bulletin, 115*, 268–287.

Ekman, P. (1998). After word. Universality of emotional expression? A personal history of the dispute. In C. Darwin (Ed.), *The expression of emotion in man and animals* (3rd ed., pp. 363–393). New York, NY: Oxford University Press.

Ekman, P. (2003). *Emotions revealed*. New York, NY: Times Books.

Ekman, P., Davidson, R. J., & Friesen, W. V. (1990). The Duchenne smile: Emotional expression and brain physiology: II. *Journal of Personality and Social Psychology, 58*, 342–353.

Ekman, P., & Friesen, W. V. (1969a). Nonverbal leakage and clues to deception. *Psychiatry, 32*, 88–106.

Ekman, P., & Friesen, W. V. (1969b). The repertoire of nonverbal behavior: Categories, origins, usage, and coding. *Semiotica, 1*, 49–98.

Ekman, P., & Friesen, W. V. (1971). Constants across cultures in the face and emotion. *Journal of Personality and Social Psychology, 17*, 124–129.

Ekman, P., & Friesen, W. V. (1972). Hand movements. *Journal of Communication, 22*, 353–374.

Ekman, P., & Friesen, W. V. (1974a). Detecting deception from the body or face. *Journal of Personality and Social Psychology, 29*, 288–298.

Ekman, P., & Friesen, W. V. (1974b). Nonverbal behavior and psychopathology. In R. J. Friedman & M. M. Katz (Eds.), *The psychology of depression: Contemporary theory and research* (pp. 203–232). Washington, DC: Winston.

Ekman, P., & Friesen, W. V. (1975). *Unmasking the face*. Englewood Cliffs, NJ: Prentice-Hall.

Ekman, P., & Friesen, W. V. (1978). *The Facial Action Coding System: A technique for the measurement of facial movement*. Palo Alto, CA: Consulting Psychologists Press.

Ekman, P., & Friesen, W. V. (1982). Felt, false, and miserable smiles. *Journal of Nonverbal Behavior, 6*, 238–252.

Ekman, P., Friesen, W. V., & Ancoli, S. (1980). Facial signs of emotional experience. *Journal of Personality and Social Psychology, 39*, 1125–1113.

Ekman, P., Friesen, W. V., & Ellsworth, P. (1972). *Emotion in the human face*. Elmsford, NY: Pergamon Press.

Ekman, P., Friesen, W. V., & Ellsworth, P. (1982). What are the relative contributions of facial behavior and contextual information to the judgment of emotion? In P. Ekman (Ed.), *Emotion in the human face* (2nd ed., pp. 111–127). Cambridge, UK: Cambridge University Press.

Ekman, P., Friesen, W. V., & O'Sullivan, M. (1988). Smiles when lying. *Journal of Personality and Social Psychology, 54*, 414–420.

Ekman, P., Friesen, W. V., O'Sullivan, M., Chan, A., Diacoyanni-Tarlatzis, I., Heider, K., . . . Tzavaras, A. (1987). Universals and cultural differences in the judgments of facial expressions of emotion. *Journal of Personality and Social Psychology, 53*, 712–717.

Ekman, P., Friesen, W. V., & Tomkins, S. S. (1971). Facial Affect Scoring Technique: A first validity study. *Semiotica, 3*, 37–58.

Ekman, P., Hager, J. C., & Friesen, W. V. (1981). The symmetry of emotional and deliberate facial actions. *Psychophysiology, 18*, 101–106.

Ekman, P., Levenson, R. W., & Friesen, W. V. (1983). Autonomic nervous system activity distinguishes between emotions. *Science, 221*, 1208–1210.

Ekman, P., Matsumoto, D., & Friesen, W. V. (1997). Facial expression in affective disorders. In P. Ekman & E. Rosenberg (Eds.), *What the face reveals: Basic and applied studies of spontaneous expression using the Facial Action Coding System (FACS)* (pp. 331–341). New York, NY: Oxford University Press.

Ekman, P., & Oster, H. (1982). Review of research, 1970–1980. In P. Ekman (Ed.), *Emotion in the human face* (2nd ed., pp. 147–173). Cambridge, UK: Cambridge University Press.

Ekman, P., Sorenson, E. R., & Friesen, W. V. (1969). Pan-cultural elements in facial displays of emotions. *Science, 164*, 86–88.

Elfenbein, H. A. (2006). Learning in emotion judgments: Training and the cross-cultural understanding of facial expressions. *Journal of Nonverbal Behavior, 30*, 21–36.

Elfenbein, H. A. (2013). Nonverbal dialects and accents in facial expressions of emotion. *Emotion Review, 5*, 90–96.

Elfenbein, H. A., & Ambady, N. (2002). On the universality and cultural specificity of emotion recognition: A meta-analysis. *Psychological Bulletin, 128*, 203–235.

Elfenbein, H. A., & Ambady, N. (2003). When familiarity breeds accuracy: Cultural exposure and facial emotion recognition. *Journal of Personality and Social Psychology, 85*, 276–290.

Elfenbein, H. A., & Eisenkraft, N. (2010). The relationship between displaying and perceiving nonverbal cues of affect: A meta-analysis to solve an old mystery. *Journal of Personality and Social Psychology, 98*, 301–318.

Elfenbein, H. A., Foo, M. D., White, J., Tan, H. H., & Aik, V. C. (2007). Reading your counterpart: The benefit of emotion recognition accuracy for effectiveness in negotiation. *Journal of Nonverbal Behavior, 31*, 205–223.

Ellgring, H. (1986). Nonverbal expression of psychological states in psychiatric patients. *European Archives of Psychiatric Neurological Science, 236*, 31–34.

Ellgring, H., & Scherer, K. R. (1996). Vocal indicators of mood change in depression. *Journal of Nonverbal Behavior, 20*, 83–110.

Elliot, A. J., & Niesta, D. (2008). Romantic red: Red enhances men's attraction to women. *Journal of Personality and Social Psychology, 95*, 1150–1164.

Elliot, A. J., Niesta Kayser, D., Greitemeyer, T., Lichtenfeld, S., Gramzow, R. H., Maier, M. A., & Liu, H. (2010). Red, rank, and romance in women viewing men. *Journal of Experimental Psychology: General, 139*, 399–417.

Elliott, A. M., Alexander, S. C., Mescher, C. A., Mohan, D., & Barnato, A. E. (2016). Differences in physicians' verbal and nonverbal communication with Black and White patients at the end of life. *Journal of Pain and Symptom Management, 51*, 1–8.

Ellis, C. (1991). Sociological introspection and emotional experience. *Symbolic Interaction, 14*, 23–50.

Ellis, L., Das, S., & Buker, H. (2008). Androgen-promoted psychological traits and criminality: A test of the evolutionary neuroandrogenic theory. *Personality and Individual Differences, 44*, 701–711.

Ellsworth, P. C., Carlsmith, J. M., & Henson, A. (1972). The stare as a stimulus to flight in human subjects: A series of field experiments. *Journal of Personality and Social Psychology, 21*, 302–311.

Ellyson, S. L., Dovidio, J. F., & Fehr, B. J. (1981). Visual behavior and dominance in women and men. In C. Mayo & N. M. Henley (Eds.), *Gender and nonverbal behavior* (pp. 63–81). New York, NY: Springer-Verlag.

Ellyson, S. L., & Dovidio, J. F. (1985). Power, dominance, and nonverbal behavior: Basic concepts and issues. In S. L. Ellyson & J. F. Dovidio (Eds.), *Power, dominance, and nonverbal behavior* (pp. 1–27). New York, NY: Springer-Verlag.

El-Mallakh, R. S., Brar, K., Watkins, C., Nuss, S., O'Connor, S. S., Gao, Y., & Wright, J. H. (2017). Association between low barometric pressure and completed suicides. *American Journal of Psychiatry, 174*, 905.

Emmers, T. M., & Dindia, K. (1995). The effect of relational stage and intimacy on touch: An extension of Guerrero and Andersen. *Personal Relationships, 2*, 225–236.

Engstrom, E. (1994). Effects of nonfluencies on speaker's credibility in newscast settings. *Perceptual and Motor Skills, 78*, 739–743.

Erickson, B., Lind, E. A., Johnson, B. C., & O'Barr, W. M. (1978). Speech style and impression formation in a court setting: The effects of "powerful" and "powerless" speech. *Journal of Nonverbal Behavior, 14*, 266–279.

Erickson, F. (1975). One function of proxemic shifts in face-to-face interaction. In A. Kendon, R. M. Harris, & M. R. Key (Eds.), *Organization of behavior in face-to-face interaction*. Chicago, IL: Aldine.

Erickson, F. (1979). Talking down: Some cultural sources of miscommunication in interracial interviews. In A. Wolfgang (Ed.), *Nonverbal behavior: Applications and cultural implications* (pp. 115–129). New York, NY: Academic Press.

Eritz, H., & Hadjistavropoulos, T. (2011). Do informal caregivers consider nonverbal behavior when they assess pain in people with severe dementia? *Journal of Pain, 12*, 331–339.

Esposito, G., Venuti, P., & Bornstein, M. H. (2011). Assessment of distress in young children: A comparison of autistic disorder, developmental delay, and typical development. *Research in Autism Spectrum Disorders, 5*, 1510–1516.

Etcoff, N. (1999). *Survival of the prettiest*. New York, NY: Random House.

Evans, G. W., Lepore, S. J., & Allen, K. M. (2000). Cross-cultural differences in tolerance for crowding: Fact or fiction? *Journal of Personality and Social Psychology, 79*, 204–210.

Evans, G. W., Ricciuti, H. N., Hope, S., Schoon, I., Bradley, R. H., Corwyn, R. F., & Hazan, C. (2010). Crowding and cognitive development: The mediating role of maternal responsiveness among 36-month-old children. *Environment and Behavior, 42*, 135–148.

Everitt, J., Best, L. A., & Gaudet, D. (2016). Candidate gender, behavioral style, and willingness to vote: Support for female candidates depends on conformity to gender norms. *American Behavioral Scientist, 60*, 1737–1755.

Exline, R. V., & Eldridge, C. (1967). *Effects of two patterns of a speaker's visual behavior upon the perception of the authencity of his verbal message*. Paper presented at a meeting of the Eastern Psychological Association, Boston, MA.

Exline, R. V., Ellyson, S. L., & Long, B. (1975). Visual behavior as an aspect of power relationships. In P. Pliner, L. Kramer, & T. Alloway (Eds.), *Nonverbal communication of aggression*. New York, NY: Plenum.

Exline, R. V., Thibaut, J., Hickey, C. B., & Gumpert, P. (1970). Visual interaction in relation to Machiavellianism and an unethical act. In P. Christie & F. Geis (Eds.), *Studies in Machiavellianism* (pp. 53–75). New York, NY: Academic Press.

Exline, R. V., & Winters, L. (1965). Affective relations and mutual glances in dyads. In S. S. Tomkins & C. E. Izard (Eds.), *Affect, cognition, and personality: Empirical studies*. Oxford, UK: Springer.

Fallon, A., & Rozin, P. (1985). Sex differences in perceptions of desirable body shape. *Journal of Abnormal Psychology, 94*, 102–105.

Farabee, D. J., Holcom, M. L., Ramsey, S. L., & Cole, S. G. (1993). Social anxiety and speaker gaze in a persuasive atmosphere. *Journal of Research in Personality, 27*, 365–376.

Farber, S. L. (1981). *Identical twins reared apart: A reanalysis*. New York, NY: Basic.

Fardouly, J., & Rapee, R. M. (2019). The impact of no-makeup selfies on young women's body image. *Body Image, 28*, 128–134.

Farley, S. (2008). Attaining status at the expense of likability: Pilfering power through conversational interruption. *Journal of Nonverbal Behavior, 32*, 241–260.

Farrenkopf, T., & Roth, V. (1980). The university faculty office as an environment. *Environment and Behavior, 12,* 467–177.

Fast, J. (1970). *Body language.* New York, NY: M. Evans.

Fast, L. A., Reimer, H. M., & Funder, D. C. (2008). The social behavior and reputation of the attributionally complex. *Journal of Research in Personality, 42,* 208–222.

Fehr, B. J., & Exline, R. V. (1987). Social visual interaction: A conceptual and literature review. In A. W. Siegman & S. Feldstein (Eds.), *Nonverbal behavior and communication* (2nd ed., pp. 225–325). Hillsdale, NJ: Lawrence Erlbaum.

Feingold, A. (1992). Good-looking people are not what we think. *Psychological Bulletin, 111,* 304–341.

Feldman, R. (2011). Maternal touch and the developing infant. In M. J. Hertenstein & S. J. Weiss (Eds.), *The handbook of touch: Neuroscience, behavioral, and health perspectives* (pp. 373–407). New York, NY: Springer.

Feldman, R., Singer, M., & Zagoory, O. (2010). Touch attenuates infants' physiological reactivity to stress. *Developmental Science, 13,* 271–278.

Fernβndez-Dols, J. M., Carrera, P., & Crivelli, C. (2011). Facial behavior while experiencing sexual excitement. *Journal of Nonverbal Behavior, 35,* 63–71.

Fernβndez-Dols, J. M., & Carroll, J. M. (1997). Is the meaning perceived in facial expression independent of its context? In J. A. Russell & J. M. Fernβndez-Dols (Eds.), *The psychology of facial expression* (pp. 275–294). Paris, France: Cambridge University Press.

Fernβndez-Dols, J. M., & Ruiz-Belda, M. A. (1995). Are smiles a sign of happiness? Gold medal winners at the Olympic Games. *Journal of Personality and Social Psychology, 69,* 1113–1119.

Fernβndez-Dols, J. M., & Ruiz-Belda, M. A. (1997). Spontaneous facial behavior during intense emotional episodes: Artistic truth and optical truth. In J. A. Russell & J. M. Fernβndez-Dols (Eds.), *The psychology of facial expression* (pp. 255–274). New York, NY: Cambridge University Press.

Ferris, G. R., Treadway, D. C., Kolodinsky, R. W., Hochwarter, W. A., Kacmar, C. J., Douglas, C., & Frink, D. D. (2005). Development and validation of the Political Skill Inventory. *Journal of Management, 31,* 126–152.

Festinger, L., Schachter, S., & Back, K. (1950). *Social pressures in informal groups: A study of human factors in housing.* New York, NY: Harper & Row.

Feyereisen, P., & Havard, I. (1999). Mental imagery and production of hand gestures while speaking in younger and older adults. *Journal of Nonverbal Behavior, 23,* 153–171.

Field, T. (1982). Individual differences in the expressivity of neonates and young infants. In R. S. Feldman (Ed.), *Development of nonverbal behavior in children* (pp. 279–298). New York, NY: Springer-Verlag.

Field, T. (1995). Infants of depressed mothers. *Infant Behavior and Development, 18,* 1–13.

Field, T. (1998). Touch therapy effects on development. *International Journal of Behavioral Development, 22,* 779–797.

Field, T. (2001). *Touch.* Cambridge, MA: MIT Press.

Field, T. (2002). Early interactions between infants and their postpartum depressed mothers. *Infant Behavior & Development, 25,* 25–29.

Field, T. (2010). Touch for socioemotional and physical well-being: A review. *Developmental Review, 30,* 367–383.

Field, T. (2019). Social touch, CT touch and massage therapy: A narrative review. *Developmental Review, 51,* 123–145.

Field, T., Diego, M., & Hernandez-Reif, M. (2007). Massage therapy research. *Developmental Review, 27,* 75–89.

Field, T., Diego, M., Hernandez-Reif, M., Deeds, O., & Figueiredo, B. (2009). Pregnancy massage reduces prematurity, low birthweight and postpartum depression. *Infant Behavior and Development, 32,* 454–460.

Field, T., & Hernandez-Reif, M. (2008). Touch and pain. In M. M. Haith & J. B. Benson (Eds.), *Encyclopedia of infancy and early childhood development* (Vol. 1, pp. 364–368). New York, NY: Academic Press.

Field, T. M., Woodson, R., Greenberg, R., & Cohen, D. (1982). Discrimination and imitation of facial expressions of neonates. *Science, 218,* 179–181.

Finando, S. J. (1973). *The effects of distance norm violation on heart rate and length of verbal response.* Unpublished doctoral dissertation, Florida State University, Tallahassee, FL.

Fiquer, J. T., Moreno, R. A., Brunoni, A. R., Barros, V. B., Fernandes, F., & Gorenstein, C. (2018). What is the non-verbal communication of depression? Assessing expressive differences between depressive patients and healthy volunteers during clinical interviews. *Journal of Affective Disorders, 238*, 636–644.

Fish, K., Rothermich, K., & Pell, M. D. (2017). The sound of (in)sincerity. *Journal of Pragmatics, 121*, 147–161.

Fisher, J. D., & Byrne, D. (1975). Too close for comfort: Sex differences to invasions of personal space. *Journal of Personality and Social Psychology, 32*, 15–21.

Fisher, J. D., Rytting, M., & Heslin, R. (1976). Hands touching hands: Affective and evaluative effects of an interpersonal touch. *Sociometry, 39*, 416–421.

Fitzgerald, C. J., Horgan, T. G., & Himes, S. M. (2016). Shaping men's memory: The effects of a female's waist-to-hip ratio on men's memory for her appearance and biographical information. *Evolution and Human Behavior, 37*, 510–516.

Flaisch, T., Hacker, F., Renner, B., & Schupp, H. T. (2011). Emotion and the processing of symbolic gestures: An event-related brain potential study. *Social Cognitive and Affective Neuroscience, 6*, 109–118.

Flamme, G. A., Stephenson, M. R., Deiters, K., Tatro, A., van Gessel, D., Geda, K., . . . McGregor, K. (2012). Typical noise exposure in daily life. *International Journal of Audiology, 51*, S3–S11.

Fletcher, S. (2013). Touching practice and physical education: Deconstruction of a contemporary moral panic. *Sport, Education and Society, 18*, 694–709.

Floyd, K., & Ray, G. B. (2003). Human affection exchange: IV. Vocalic predictors of perceived affection in initial interactions. *Western Journal of Communication, 67*, 56–73.

Foddy, M. (1978). Patterns of gaze in cooperative and competitive negotiation. *Human Relations, 31*, 925–938.

Forestell, C. A., Humphrey, T. M., & Stewart, S. H. (2004). Involvement of body weight and shape factors in ratings of attractiveness by women: A replication and extension of Tassinary and Hansen (1998). *Personality and Individual Differences, 36*, 295–305.

Fortenberry, J. H., MacLean, J., Morris, P., & O'Connell, M. (1978). Modes of dress as a perceptual cue to deference. *Journal of Personality and Social Psychology, 104*, 139–140.

Foulsham, T., Cheng, J. T., Tracy, J. L., Henrich, J., & Kingstone, A. (2010). Gaze allocation in a dynamic situation: Effects of social status and speaking. *Cognition, 117*, 319–331.

Fowler, K. A., Lilienfeld, S. O., & Patrick, C. J. (2009). Detecting psychopathy from thin slices of behavior. *Psychological Assessment, 21*, 68–78.

Fox, E., Mathews, A., Calder, A. J., & Yiend, J. (2007). Anxiety and sensitivity to gaze direction in emotionally expressive faces. *Emotion, 7*, 478–486.

Fox, N. A., & Davidson, R. J. (1988). Patterns of brain electrical activity during facial signs of emotion in 10-month-old infants. *Developmental Psychology, 14*, 230–236.

Fraccaro, P. J., Jones, B. C., Vukovic, J., Smith, F. G., Watkins, C. D., Feinberg, D. R., . . . DeBruine, L. M. (2011). Experimental evidence that women speak in a higher voice pitch to men they find attractive. *Journal of Evolutionary Psychology, 9*, 57–67.

Framorando, D., George, N., Kerzel, D., & Burra, N. (2016). Straight gaze facilitates face processing but does not cause involuntary attentional capture. *Visual Cognition, 24*, 381–391.

Frank, M. G., & Gilovich, T. (1988). The dark side of self- and social perception: Black uniforms and aggression in professional sports. *Journal of Personality and Social Psychology, 54*, 74–85.

Franklin, R. G., Jr., & Zebrowitz, L. A. (2013). Older adults' trait impressions of faces are sensitive to subtle resemblance to emotions. *Journal of Nonverbal Behavior, 37*, 139–151.

Frederick, D. A., Hadji-Michael, M., Furnham, A., & Swami, V. (2010). The influence of leg-to-body ratio (lbr) on judgments of female physical attractiveness: Assessments of computer-generated images varying in lbr. *Body Image, 7*, 55–55.

Freedman, N. (1972). The analysis of movement behavior during the clinical interview. In A. W. Siegman & B. Pope (Eds.), *Studies in dyadic communication* (pp. 153–175). New York, NY: Pergamon Press.

Freedman, N., Blass, T., Rifkin, A., & Quitkin, F. (1973). Body movements and the verbal encoding of aggressive affect. *Journal of Personality and Social Psychology, 26*, 72–85.

Freedman, N., & Hoffman, S. P. (1967). Kinetic behavior in altered clinical states: Approach to objective analysis of motor behavior during clinical interviews. *Perceptual and Motor Skills, 24*, 527–539.

Fridlund, A. J. (1991). Sociality of solitary smiling: Potentiation by an implicit audience. *Journal of Personality and Social Psychology, 60*, 229–240.

Fridlund, A. J. (1994). *Human facial expression: An evolutionary view*. San Diego, CA: Academic Press.

Fridlund, A. J. (1997). The new ethology of human facial expressions. In J. A. Russell & J. M. Fernβndez-Dols (Eds.), *The psychology of facial expression* (pp. 103–129). Paris, France: Cambridge University Press.

Fridlund, A. J., Ekman, P., & Oster, H. (1987). Facial expressions of emotion: Review of literature, 1970–1983. In A. W. Siegman & S. Feldstein (Eds.), *Nonverbal behavior and communication* (2nd ed., pp. 143–223). Hillsdale, NJ: Lawrence Erlbaum.

Friedman, H. S. (1979a). The concept of skill in nonverbal communication: Implications for understanding social interaction. In R. Rosenthal (Ed.), *Skill in nonverbal communication: Individual differences* (pp. 2–27). Cambridge, MA: Oelgeschlager, Gunn & Hain.

Friedman, H. S. (1979b). The interactive effects of facial expressions of emotion and verbal messages on perceptions of affective meaning. *Journal of Nonverbal Behavior, 15*, 453–469.

Friedman, H. S., & Booth-Kewley, S. (1987). Personality, Type A behavior, and coronary heart disease: The role of emotional expression. *Journal of Personality and Social Psychology, 53*, 783–792.

Friedman, H. S., Hall, J. A., & Harris, M. J. (1985). Type A behavior, nonverbal expressive style, and health. *Journal of Personality and Social Psychology, 48*, 1299–1315.

Friedman, H. S., Prince, L. M., Riggio, R. E., & DiMatteo, M. R. (1980). Understanding and assessing nonverbal expressiveness: The Affective Communication Test. *Journal of Personality and Social Psychology, 39*, 333–351.

Friedman, H. S., & Riggio, R. E. (1981). Effect of individual differences in nonverbal expressiveness on transmission of emotion. *Journal of Nonverbal Behavior, 6*, 96–104.

Friedman, H. S., Riggio, R. E., & Cassella, D. F. (1988). Nonverbal skills, personal charisma, and initial attraction. *Personality and Social Psychology Bulletin, 14*, 203–211.

Friedman, H. S., Riggio, R. E., & Segall, D. O. (1980). Personality and the enactment of emotion. *Journal of Nonverbal Behavior, 5*, 35–48.

Frischen, A., Bayliss, A. P., & Tipper, S. P. (2007). Gaze cueing of attention: Visual attention, social cognition, and individual differences. *Psychological Bulletin, 133*, 694–724.

Fry, A. M., & Willis, F. N. (1971). Invasion of personal space as a function of the age of the invader. *Psychological Record, 21*, 385–389.

Fuller, B., Simmering, M. J., Marler, L. E., Cox, S. S., Bennett, R. J., & Cheramie, R. A. (2011). Exploring touch as a positive workplace behavior. *Human Relations, 64*, 231–256.

Funder, D. C., & Harris, M. J. (1986). On the several facets of personality assessment: The case of social acuity. *Journal of Personality, 54*, 528–550.

Furley, P. (2019). What modern sports competitions can tell us about human nature. *Perspectives on Psychological Science, 14*, 138–155.

Furnham, A., & Lay, A. (2019). The universality of the portrayal of gender in television advertisements: A review of the studies this century. *Psychology of Popular Media Culture, 8*, 109–124.

Galati, D., Miceli, R., & Sini, B. (2001). Judging and coding facial expression of emotions in congenitally blind children. *International Journal of Behavioral Development, 25*, 268–278.

Galati, D., Scherer, K. R., & Ricci-Bitti, P. E. (1997). Voluntary facial expression of emotion: Comparing congenitally blind with normally sighted encoders. *Journal of Personality and Social Psychology, 73*, 1363–1379.

Galati, D., Sini, B., Schmidt, S., & Tinti, C. (2003). Spontaneous facial expressions in congenitally blind and sighted children aged 8–11. *Journal of Visual Impairment & Blindness, 97*, 418–428.

Galbarczyk, A., & Ziomkiewicz, A. (2017). Tattooed men: Healthy bad boys and good-looking competitors. *Personality and Individual Differences, 106*, 122–125.

Gamé, F., Carchon, I., & Vital-Durand, F. (2003). The effect of stimulus attractiveness on visual tracking in 2- to 6-month-old infants. *Infant Behavior and Development, 26*, 135–150.

Ganahl, D. J., Prinsen, T. J., & Netzley, S. B. (2003). A content analysis of prime time commercials: A contextual framework of gender representation. *Sex Roles, 49*, 545–551.

Garber, L. L., Jr., & Hyatt, E. M. (2003). Color as a tool for visual persuasion. In L. M. Scott & R. Batra (Eds.), *Persuasive imagery: A consumer response perspective* (pp. 313–336). Mahwah, NJ: Lawrence Erlbaum.

Garver-Apgar, C. E., Gangestad, S. W., Thornhill, R., Miller, R. D., & Olp, J. J. (2006). Major histocompatibility complex alleles, sexual responsivity, and unfaithfulness in romantic couples. *Psychological Science, 17*, 830–835.

Gatewood, J. B., & Rosenwein, R. (1981). Interactional synchrony: Genuine or spurious? A critique of recent research. *Journal of Nonverbal Behavior, 6*, 12–29.

Gawley, T., Perks, T., & Curtis, J. (2009). Height, gender, and authority status at work: Analyses for a national sample of Canadian workers. *Sex Roles, 60*, 208–222.

Geen, R. G. (1984). Preferred stimulation levels in introverts and extraverts: Effects on arousal and performance. *Journal of Personality and Social Psychology, 46*, 1303–1312.

Geen, R. G., & McCown, E. J. (1984). Effects of noise and attack on aggression and physiological arousal. *Motivation and Emotion, 8*, 231–241.

Geiselman, R. E., Haight, N., & Kimata, L. (1984). Context effects of the perceived physical attractiveness of faces. *Journal of Experimental Social Psychology, 20*, 409–424.

Gentilucci, M., & Dalla Volta, R. (2008). Spoken language and arm gestures are controlled by the same motor control system. *The Quarterly Journal of Experimental Psychology, 61*, 944–957.

Gergle, D., Kraut, R. E., & Fussell, S. R. (2004). Language efficiency and visual technology: Minimizing collaborative effort with visual information. *Journal of Language and Social Psychology, 23*, 491–517.

Gerwing, J., & Bavelas, J. (2004). Linguistic influences on gesture's form. *Gesture, 4*, 157–195.

Gesn, P. R., & Ickes, W. (1999). The development of meaning contexts for empathic accuracy: Channel and sequence effects. *Journal of Personality and Social Psychology, 77*, 746–761.

Gifford, R. (1994). A lens-mapping framework for understanding the encoding and decoding of interpersonal dispositions in nonverbal behavior. *Journal of Personality and Social Psychology, 66*, 398–412.

Gil, S., & Droit-Volet, S. (2011). How do emotional facial expressions influence our perception of time? In S. Masmoudi, D. Yan Dai, & A. Naceur (Eds.), *Attention, representation, and human performance: Integration of cognition, emotion and motivation* (pp. 61–74). London, UK: Psychology Press.

Gilbert, T., Martin, R., & Coulson, M. (2011). Attentional biases using the body in the crowd task: Are angry body postures detected more rapidly? *Cognition and Emotion, 25*, 700–708.

Gildersleeve, K. A., Haselton, M. G., Larson, C. M., & Pillsworth, E. G. (2011). Body odor attractiveness as a cue of impending ovulation in women: Evidence from a study using hormone-confirmed ovulation. *Hormones and Behavior, 61*, 157–166.

Gillath, O., Bahns, A. J., & Burghart, H. A. (2017). Eye movements when looking at potential friends and romantic partners. *Archives of Sexual Behavior, 46*, 2313–2325.

Gillath, O., Bahns, A. J., Ge, F., & Crandall, C. S. (2012). Shoes as a source of first impressions. *Journal of Research in Personality, 46*, 423–430.

Givens, D. B. (1978a). Contrasting nonverbal styles in mother–child interaction: Examples from a study of child abuse. *Semiotica, 24*, 33–37.

Givens, D. B. (1978b). The nonverbal basis of attraction: Flirtation, courtship, and seduction. *Psychiatry, 41*, 346–359.

Givhan, R. (2003, March 28). Torie Clarke's bold hues raise some cries. *The Washington Post*, p. C01.

Glasgow, G. M. (1952). A semantic index of vocal pitch. *Speech Monographs, 19*, 64–68.

Glass, D., & Singer, J. E. (1973). Experimental studies of uncontrollable and unpredictable noise. *Representative Research in Social Psychology, 4*, 165.

Glenberg, A. M., Schroeder, J. L., & Robertson, D. A. (1998). Averting the gaze disengages the environment and facilitates remembering. *Memory & Cognition, 26*, 651–658.

Goffman, E. (1963). *Behavior in public places*. New York, NY: Free Press.

Goffman, E. (1971). *Relations in public*. New York, NY: Basic Books.

Goffman, E. (1979). *Gender advertisements*. Cambridge, MA: Harvard University Press.

Göksun, T., Hirsh-Pasek, K., & Golinkoff, R. M. (2010). How do preschoolers express cause in gesture and speech? *Cognitive Development, 25*, 56–68.

Goldinger, S. D., He, Y., & Papesh, M. H. (2009). Deficits in cross-race face learning: Insights from eye movements and pupilometry. *Journal of Experimental Psychology: Learning, Memory, and Cognition, 35*, 1105–1122.

Goldin-Meadow, S. (2003). *Hearing gesture: How our hands help us think*. Cambridge, MA: Belknap Press of Harvard University Press.

Goldin-Meadow, S. (2018). Taking a hands-on approach to learning. *Policy Insights from the Behavioral and Brain Sciences, 5*, 163–170.

Goldin-Meadow, S., & Iverson, J. M. (2010). Gesturing across the lifespan. In W. F. Overton (Ed.) & R. M. Lerner (Editor-in-chief), *Cognition, biology, and methods across the lifespan. Volume 1 of the handbook of life-span development* (pp. 36–55). Hoboken, NJ: Wiley.

Goldman-Eisler, F. (1961). A comparative study of two hesitation phenomena. *Language and Speech, 4*, 18–26.

Goldman-Eisler, F. (1968). *Psycholinguistics: Experiments in spontaneous speech*. New York, NY: Academic Press.

Goldstein, A. G., & Jeffords, J. (1981). Status and touching behavior. *Bulletin of the Psychonomic Society, 17*, 79–81.

Gong, Z. H., & Bucy, E. P. (2016). When style obscures substance: Visual attention to display appropriateness in the 2012 presidential debates. *Communication Monographs, 83*, 349–372.

Gonzalez, A., & Zimbardo, P. G. (1985). Time in perspective. *Psychology Today, 19*, 21–26.

Goodboy, A. K., Weber, K., & Bolkan, S. (2009). The effects of nonverbal and verbal immediacy on recall and multiple student learning indicators. *Journal of Classroom Interaction, 44*, 4–12.

Goodwin, C. (1986). Gestures as a resource for the organization of mutual orientation. *Semiotica, 62*, 29–49.

Gorawara-Bhat, R., Cook, M. A., & Sachs, G. A. (2007). Nonverbal communication in doctor-elderly patient transactions (NDEPT): Development of a tool. *Patient Education and Counseling, 66*, 223–234.

Gordon, I., Zagoory-Sharon, O., Leckman, J. F., & Feldman, R. (2010). Oxytocin and the development of parenting in humans. *Biological Psychiatry, 68*, 377–382.

Gorham, J., Cohen, S. H., & Morris, T. L. (1999). Fashion in the classroom: III. Effects of instructor attire and immediacy in natural classroom interactions. *Communication Quarterly, 47*, 281–299.

Gortmaker, S. L., Must, A., Perrin, J. N., Sobol, A. M., & Dietz, W. H. (1993). Social and economic consequences of overweight in adolescence and young adulthood. *New England Journal of Medicine, 329*, 1008–1012.

Gosling, S. (2008). *Snoop: What your stuff says about you*. New York, NY: Basic Books.

Gosling, S. D., Gaddis, S., & Vazire, S. (2008). First impressions based on the environments we create and inhabit. In N. Ambady & J. J. Skowronski (Eds.), *First impressions* (pp. 334–356). New York, NY: Guilford.

Gosling, S. D., Ko, S. J., Mannarelli, T., & Morris, M. E. (2002). A room with a cue: Judgments of personality based on offices and bedrooms. *Journal of Personality and Social Psychology, 82*, 379–398.

Gosselin, P., Perron, M., Legault, M., & Campanella, P. (2002). Children's and adults' knowledge of the distinction between enjoyment and nonenjoyment smiles. *Journal of Nonverbal Behavior, 26*, 83–108.

Graham, J. A., & Heywood, S. (1976). The effects of elimination of hand gestures and of verbal codability on speech performance. *European Journal of Social Psychology, 5*, 189–195.

Graham, J. A., & Jouhar, A. J. (1981). The effects of cosmetics on person perception. *International Journal of Cosmetic Science, 3*, 199–210.

Graham, J. A., & Jouhar, A. J. (1982). *The effects of cosmetics on self perception: How we see ourselves*. Unpublished manuscript, University of Pennsylvania, Philadelphia.

Graham, K. A., Blissett, J., Antoniou, E. E., Zeegers, M. P., & McCleery, J. P. (2018). Effects of maternal depression in the Still-Face Paradigm: A meta-analysis. *Infant Behavior & Development, 50*, 154–164.

Graham, S. A., & Kilbreath, C. S. (2007). It's a sign of the kind: Gestures and words guide infants' inductive inferences. *Developmental Psychology, 43*, 1111–1123.

Grammer, K., Kruck, K., Juette, A., & Fink, B. (2000). Nonverbal behavior as courtship signals: The role of control and choice in selecting partners. *Evolution and Behavior, 21*, 371–390.

Grammer, K., & Thornhill, R. (1994). Human (*Homo sapiens*) facial attractiveness and sexual selection: The role of symmetry and averageness. *Journal of Comparative Psychology, 108*, 233–242.

Grandey, A. A., Fisk, G. M., Mattila, A. S., Jansen, K. J., & Sideman, L. A. (2005). Is "service with a smile" enough? Authenticity of positive displays during service encounters. *Organizational Behavior and Human Decision Processes, 96*, 38–55.

Grebelsky-Lichtman, T., & Katz, R. (2019). When a man debates a woman: Trump vs Clinton in the first mixed gender presidential debates. *Journal of Gender Studies, 28*, 699–719.

Greenbaum, P. E., & Rosenfeld, H. M. (1980). Varieties of touching in greetings: Sequential structure and sex-related differences. *Journal of Nonverbal Behavior, 5*, 13–25.

Greene, J. O., & Frandsen, K. D. (1979). Need-fulfillment and consistency theory: Relationships between self-esteem and eye contact. *Western Journal of Speech Communication, 43*, 123–133.

Greene, J. O., & Ravizza, S. M. (1995). Complexity effects on temporal characteristics of speech. *Human Communication Research, 21*, 390–421.

Greenlees, I. A., Eynon, M., & Thelwell, R. C. (2013). Color of soccer goalkeepers' uniforms influences the outcome of penalty kicks. *Perceptual and Motor Skills, 117*, 1–10.

Greitemeyer, T. (2009). Effects of songs with prosocial lyrics on prosocial behavior: Further evidence and a mediating mechanism. *Personality and Social Psychology Bulletin, 35*, 1500–1511.

Greven, C. U., Lionetti, F., Booth, C., Aron, E. N., Fox, E., Schendan, H. E., . . . Homberg, J. (2019). Sensory processing sensitivity in the context of environmental sensitivity: A critical review and development of research agenda. *Neuroscience and Biobehavioral Reviews, 98*, 287–305.

Grieser, D. L., & Kuhl, P. K. (1988). Maternal speech to infants in a tonal language: Support for universal prosodic features in motherese. *Developmental Psychology, 24*, 14–20.

Griffiths, P., & Ashwin, C. (2016). Accuracy in perceiving facial expressions of emotion in psychopathology. In J. A. Hall, M. Schmid Mast, & T. V. West (Eds.), *The social psychology of perceiving others accurately* (pp. 185–205). New York, NY: Cambridge University Press.

Grinspan, D., Hemphill, A., & Nowicki, S., Jr. (2003). Improving the ability of elementary school-age children to identify emotion in facial expression. *Journal of Genetic Psychology, 164*, 88–100.

Grunau, R. V. E., & Craig, K. D. (1990). Facial activity as a measure of neonatal pain perception. In D. C. Tyler & E. J. Krane (Eds.), *Advances in pain research and therapy. Proceedings of the first international symposium on pediatrie pain*. New York, NY: Raven.

Guadagno, R. E., Muscanell, N. L., Okdie, B. M., Burk, N. M., & Ward, T. B. (2011). Even in virtual environments women shop and men build: A social role perspective on second life. *Computers in Human Behavior, 27*, 304–308.

Guastella, A. J., Mitchell, P. B., & Dadds, M. R. (2007). Oxytocin increases gaze to the eye region of human faces. *Biological Psychiatry, 63*, 3–5.

Gudykunst, W. B., & Ting-Toomey, S. (1988). *Culture and interpersonal communication*. Newbury Park, CA: SAGE.

Guellai, B., & Streri, A. (2011). Cues for early social skills: Direct gaze modulates newborns' recognition of talking faces. *PLoS ONE, 6*(4), e18610. doi:10.1371/journal.pone.0018610

Guerrero, L. K. (1997). Nonverbal involvement across interactions with same-sex friends, opposite-sex friends and romantic partners: Consistency or change? *Journal of Social and Personal Relationships, 14*, 31–58.

Guerrero, L. K., & Andersen, P. A. (1991). The waxing and waning of relational intimacy: Touch as a function of relational stage, gender and touch avoidance. *Journal of Social and Personal Relationships, 8*, 147–165.

Guerrero, L. K., & Andersen, P. A. (1994). Patterns of matching and initiation: Touch behavior and touch avoidance across romantic relationship stages. *Journal of Nonverbal Behavior, 18*, 137–153.

Guerrero, L. K., & Floyd, K. (2006). *Nonverbal communication in close relationships*. Mahwah, NJ: Lawrence Erlbaum.

Guerrero, L. K., & Miller, T. A. (1998). Associations between nonverbal behaviors and initial impressions of instructor competence and course content in videotaped distance education courses. *Communication Education, 47*, 30–42.

Gunnery, S. D., Hall, J. A., & Ruben, M. A. (2013). The deliberate Duchenne smile: Individual differences in expressive control. *Journal of Nonverbal Behavior, 37*, 29–41.

Gunnery, S. D., & Ruben, M. A. (2016). Perceptions of Duchenne and non-Duchenne smiles: A meta-analysis. *Cognition and Emotion, 30*, 501–515.

Guyer, J. J., Fabrigar, L. R., & Vaughan-Johnston, T. I. (2019). Speech rate, intonation, and pitch: Investigating the bias and cue effects of vocal confidence on persuasion. *Personality and Social Psychology Bulletin, 45*, 389–405.

Ha, T., Overbeek, G., & Engles, R. C. M. E. (2010). Effects of attractiveness and social status on dating desire in heterosexual adolescents: An experimental study. *Archives of Sexual Behavior, 39*, 1063–1071.

Haber, G. M. (1982). Spatial relations between dominants and marginals. *Social Psychology Quarterly, 45*, 221–228.

Hadar, U. (1989). Two types of gesture and their role in speech production. *Journal of Language and Social Psychology, 8*, 221–228.

Hadar, U., Wenkert-Olenik, D., Krauss, D., & Soroker, N. (1998). Gesture and the processing of speech: Neuropsychological evidence. *Brain and Language, 62*, 107–126.

Hadjikhani, N., & de Gelder, B. (2003). Seeing fearful body expressions activates the fusiform cortex and amygdala. *Current Biology, 13*, 2201–2205.

Haggard, E. A., & Isaacs, F. S. (1966). Micro-momentary facial expressions as indicators of ego mechanisms in psychotherapy. In L. A. Gottschalk & A. H. Auerback (Eds.), *Methods of research in psychotherapy* (pp. 154–165). New York, NY: Appleton-Century-Crofts.

Halberstadt, A. G. (1985). Race, socioeconomic status and nonverbal behavior. In A. W. Siegman & S. Feldstein (Eds.), *Multichannel integrations of nonverbal behavior* (pp. 227–266). Hillsdale, NJ: Lawrence Erlbaum.

Halberstadt, A. G., & Hall, J. A. (1980). Who's getting the message? Children's nonverbal skill and their evaluation by teachers. *Developmental Psychology, 16*, 564–573.

Halberstadt, A. G., & Saitta, M. B. (1987). Gender, nonverbal behavior, and perceived dominance: A test of the theory. *Journal of Personality and Social Psychology, 53*, 257–272.

Halberstadt, J., & Rhodes, G. (2003). It's not just average faces that are attractive: Computer-manipulated averageness makes birds, fish, and automobiles attractive. *Psychonomic Bulletin and Review, 10*, 149–156.

Hall, E. T. (1959). *The silent language*. Garden City, NY: Doubleday.

Hall, E. T. (1966). *The hidden dimension*. Garden City, NY: Doubleday.

Hall, E. T. (1976). *Beyond culture*. Garden City, NY: Doubleday Anchor.

Hall, E. T. (1983). *The dance of life*. Garden City, NY: Anchor.

Hall, J. A. (1978). Gender effects in decoding nonverbal cues. *Psychological Bulletin, 85*, 845–857.

Hall, J. A. (1984). *Nonverbal sex differences: Communication accuracy and expressive style*. Baltimore, MD: Johns Hopkins University Press.

Hall, J. A. (1996). Touch, status, and gender at professional meetings. *Journal of Nonverbal Behavior, 20*, 23–44.

Hall, J. A. (2006). How big are nonverbal sex differences? The case of smiling and sensitivity to nonverbal cues. In K. Dindia & D. J. Canary (Eds.), *Sex differences and similarities in communication* (2nd ed., pp. 59–81). Mahwah, NJ: Lawrence Erlbaum.

Hall, J. A. (2010). Nonverbal behavior in social psychology research: The good, the bad, and the ugly. In C. R. Agnew, D. E. Carlston, W. G. Graziano, & J. R. Kelly (Eds.), *Then a miracle occurs: Focusing on behavior in social psychological theory and research* (pp. 412–437). New York, NY: Oxford University Press.

Hall, J. A. (2011a). Clinicians' accuracy in perceiving patients: Its relevance for clinical practice and a narrative review of methods and correlates. *Patient Education and Counseling, 84*, 319–324.

Hall, J. A. (2011b). Gender and status patterns in social touch. In M. J. Hertenstein & S. J. Weiss (Eds.), *The handbook of touch: Neuroscience, behavioral, and health perspectives* (pp. 329–350). New York, NY: Springer.

Hall, J. A., Andrzejewski, S. A., Murphy, N. A., Schmid Mast, M., & Feinstein, B. (2008). Accuracy of judging others' traits and states: Comparing mean levels across tests. *Journal of Research in Personality, 42*, 1476–1489.

Hall, J. A., Andrzejewski, S. A., & Yopchick, J. E. (2009). Psychosocial correlates of interpersonal sensitivity: A meta-analysis. *Journal of Nonverbal Behavior, 33*, 149–180.

Hall, J. A., & Bernieri, F. J. (Eds.). (2001). *Interpersonal sensitivity: Theory and measurement*. Mahwah, NJ: Lawrence Erlbaum.

Hall, J. A., Bernieri, F. J., & Carney, D. R. (2005). Nonverbal behavior and interpersonal sensitivity. In J. A. Harrigan, R. Rosenthal, & K. R. Scherer (Eds.), *The new handbook of methods in nonverbal behavior research* (pp. 237–281). Oxford, UK: Oxford University Press.

Hall, J. A., & Braunwald, K. G. (1981). Gender cues in conversations. *Journal of Personality and Social Psychology, 40*, 99–110.

Hall, J. A., & Carter, J. D. (1999). Gender-stereotype accuracy as an individual difference. *Journal of Personality and Social Psychology, 77*, 350–359.

Hall, J. A., Coats, E. J., & Smith LeBeau, L. (2005). Nonverbal behavior and the vertical dimension of social relations: A meta-analysis. *Psychological Bulletin, 131*, 898–924.

Hall, J. A., & Friedman, G. B. (1999). Status, gender, and nonverbal behavior: A study of structured interactions between employees of a company. *Personality and Social Psychology Bulletin, 25*, 1082–1091.

Hall, J. A., Gunnery, S. D., & Andrzejewski, S. A. (2011). Nonverbal emotion displays, communication modality, and the judgment of personality. *Journal of Research in Personality, 45*, 77–83.

Hall, J. A., Gunnery, S. D., & Horgan, T. G. (2016). Gender differences in interpersonal accuracy. In J. A. Hall, M. Schmid Mast, & T. V. West (Eds.), *The social psychology of perceiving others accurately* (pp. 309–327). Cambridge, UK: Cambridge University Press.

Hall, J. A., & Halberstadt, A. G. (1986). Smiling and gazing. In J. S. Hyde & M. Linn (Eds.), *The psychology of gender: Advances through meta-analysis* (pp. 136–158). Baltimore, MD: Johns Hopkins University Press.

Hall, J. A., Halberstadt, A. G., & O'Brien, C. E. (1997). "Subordination" and nonverbal sensitivity: A study and synthesis of findings based on trait measures. *Sex Roles, 37*, 295–317.

Hall, J. A., Harrigan, J. A., & Rosenthal, R. (1995). Nonverbal behavior in clinician-patient interaction. *Applied and Preventive Psychology, 4*, 21–37.

Hall, J. A., Horgan, T. G., Stein, T. S., & Roter, D. L. (2002). Liking in the physician–patient relationship. *Patient Education and Counseling, 48*, 69–77.

Hall, J. A., Irish, J. T., Roter, D. L., Ehrlich, C. M., & Miller, L. H. (1994). Gender in medical encounters: An analysis of physician and patient communication in a primary care setting. *Health Psychology, 13*, 384–392.

Hall, J. A., & Knapp, M. L. (Eds.). (2013). *Nonverbal communication* (Vol. 2, Handbooks of communication science). Berlin, Germany: deGruyter Mouton.

Hall, J. A., Murphy, N. A., & Schmid Mast, M. (2006). Recall of nonverbal cues: Exploring a new definition of interpersonal sensitivity. *Journal of Nonverbal Behavior, 30*, 141–155.

Hall, J. A., Murphy, N. A., & Schmid Mast, M. (2007). Nonverbal self-accuracy in interpersonal interaction. *Personality and Social Psychology Bulletin, 33*, 1675–1685.

Hall, J. A., Rosip, J. C., Smith LeBeau, L., Horgan, T. G., & Carter, J. D. (2006). Attributing the sources of accuracy in unequal-power dyadic communication: Who is better and why? *Journal of Experimental Social Psychology, 42*, 18–27.

Hall, J. A., Roter, D. L., Blanch, D. C., & Frankel, R. M. (2009). Nonverbal sensitivity in medical students: Implications for clinical interactions. *Journal of General Internal Medicine, 24*, 1217–1222.

Hall, J. A., Roter, D. L., & Katz, N. R. (1987). Task versus socioemotional behaviors in physicians. *Medical Care, 25*, 399–412.

Hall, J. A., Roter, D. L., & Rand, C. S. (1981). Communication of affect between patient and physician. *Journal of Health and Social Behavior, 22*, 18–30.

Hall, J. A., & Schmid Mast, M. (2007). Sources of accuracy in the empathic accuracy paradigm. *Emotion, 7*, 438–446.

Hall, J. A., Schmid Mast, M., & West, T. V. (Eds.). (2016). *The social psychology of perceiving others accurately*. Cambridge, UK: Cambridge University Press.

Hall, J. A., Ship, A. N., Ruben, M. A., Curtin, E. M., Roter, D. L., Clever, S. L., . . . Pounds, K. (2015). Clinically relevant correlates of accurate perception of patients' thoughts and feelings. *Health Communication, 30*, 423–429.

Hall, J. A., & Veccia, E. M. (1990). More "touching" observations: New insights on men, women, and interpersonal touch. *Journal of Personality and Social Psychology, 59*, 1155–1162.

Hall, J. K., Hutton, S. B., & Morgan, M. J. (2010). Sex differences in scanning faces: Does attention to the eyes explain female superiority in facial expression regnition? *Cognition and Emotion, 24*, 629–637.

Hall, S. S. (2006). *Size matters: How height affects the health, happiness, and success of boys—and the men they become*. Boston, MA: Houghton Mifflin.

Hamermesh, D. S., & Biddle, J. E. (1994). Beauty and the labor market. *American Economic Review, 84*, 1174–1194.

Hancock, J. T., & Toma, C. L. (2009). Putting your best face forward: The accuracy of online dating photographs. *Journal of Communication, 59*, 367–386.

Hanlon, R. E., Brown, J. W., & Gerstman, L. J. (1990). Enhancement of naming in nonfluent aphasia through gesture. *Brain and Language, 38*, 298–314.

Hansen, C. H., & Hansen, R. D. (1988). Finding the face in the crowd: An anger superiority effect. *Journal of Personality and Social Psychology, 54*, 917–924.

Hanzal, A., Segrin, C., & Dorros, S. M. (2008). The role of marital status and age on men's and women's reactions to touch from a relational partner. *Journal of Nonverbal Behavior, 32*, 21–35.

Hare, A., & Bales, R. (1963). Seating position and small group interaction. *Sociometry, 26*, 480–486.

Hargie, O. (Ed.). (2006). *The handbook of communication skills*. New York, NY: Routledge.

Harker, L., & Keltner, D. (2001). Expressions of positive emotion in women's college yearbook pictures and their relationship to personality and life outcomes across adulthood. *Journal of Personality and Social Psychology, 80*, 112–124.

Harkins, S., & Szymanski, K. (1987). Social facilitation and social loafing: New wine in old bottles. In C. Hendrick (Ed.), *Review of personality and social psychology* (Vol. 9, pp. 167–188). Beverly Hills, CA: SAGE.

Harlow, H. F. (1958). The nature of love. *American Psychologist, 13*, 678–685.

Harlow, H. F., & Mears, C. (1978). The nature of complex, unlearned responses. In M. Lewis & L. A. Rosenblum (Eds.), *The development of affect*. New York, NY: Plenum.

Harms, L. S. (1961). Listener judgments of status cues in speech. *Quarterly Journal of Speech, 47*, 164–168.

Harnsberger, J. D., Brown, W. S., Jr., Shrivastav, R., & Rothman, H. (2010). Noise and tremor in the perception of vocal aging in males. *Journal of Voice, 24*, 523–530.

Harrar, V., Piqueras-Fiszman, B., & Spence, C. (2011). There's more to taste in a coloured bowl. *Perception, 40*, 880–882.

Harrigan, J. A. (1984). The effects of task order on children's identification of facial expressions. *Motivation and Emotion, 8*, 157–169.

Harrigan, J. A., Gramata, J. F., Luck, K. S., & Margolis, C. (1989). It's how you say it: Physicians' vocal behavior. *Social Science & Medicine, 28*, 87–92.

Harrigan, J. A., & O'Connell, D. M. (1996). How do you look when feeling anxious? Facial displays of anxiety. *Personality and Individual Differences, 21*, 205–212.

Harrigan, J. A., Suarez, I., & Hartman, J. S. (1994). Effect of speech errors on observers' judgments of anxious and defensive individuals. *Journal of Research in Personality, 28*, 505–529.

Harrigan, J. A., Wilson, K., & Rosenthal, R. (2004). Detecting state and trait anxiety from auditory and visual cues: A meta-analysis. *Personality and Social Psychology Bulletin, 30*, 56–66.

Harris, C. R., & Alvarado, N. (2005). Facial expressions, smile types, and self-report during humour, tickle, and pain. *Cognition and Emotion, 19*, 655–669.

Harris, C. R., & Christenfeld, N. (1999). Can a machine tickle? *Psychonomic Bulletin and Review, 6*, 504–510.

Harris, M. B., Harris, R. J., & Bochner, S. (1982). Fat, four-eyed, and female: Stereotypes of obesity, glasses, and gender. *Journal of Applied Social Psychology, 12*, 503–516.

Harris, M. J., & Rosenthal, R. (1985). Mediation of interpersonal expectancy effects: 31 meta-analyses. *Psychological Bulletin, 97*, 363–386.

Harris, M. J., & Rosenthal, R. (2005). No more teachers' dirty looks: Effects of teacher nonverbal behavior on student outcomes. In R. E. Riggio & R. S. Feldman (Eds.), *Applications of nonverbal communication* (pp. 157–192). Mahwah, NJ: Lawrence Erlbaum.

Harris, P. B., & Sachau, D. (2005). Is cleanliness next to godliness? The role of housekeeping in impression formation. *Environment and Behavior, 37*, 81–101.

Harris, P. L., Bartz, D. T., & Rowe, M. L. (2017). Young children communicate their ignorance and ask questions. *PNAS Proceedings of the National Academy of Sciences of the United States of America, 114*, 7884–7891.

Harrison, A. A., & Saeed, L. (1977). Let's make a deal: An analysis of revelations and stipulations in lonely hearts advertisements. *Journal of Personality and Social Psychology, 35*, 257–274.

Harrison, C., Binetti, N., Coutrot, A., Johnston, A., & Mareschal, I. (2018). Personality traits do not predict how we look at faces. *Perception, 47*, 976–984.

Harrison, N. A., Wilson, C. E., & Critchley, H. D. (2007). Processing of observed pupil size modulates perception of sadness and predicts empathy. *Emotion, 7*, 724–729.

Harrison-Speake, K., & Willis, F. N. (1995). Ratings of the appropriateness of touch among family members. *Journal of Nonverbal Behavior, 19*, 85–100.

Hart, A. J. (1995). Naturally occurring expectation effects. *Journal of Personality and Social Psychology, 68*, 109–115.

Hartwig, M., & Bond, C. F., Jr. (2011). Why do lie-catchers fail? A lens model meta-analysis of human lie judgments. *Psychological Bulletin, 137*, 643–659.

Haselton, M. G., Mortezaie, M., Pillsworth, E. G., Bleske-Rechek, A., & Frederick, D. A. (2007). Ovulatory shifts in human female ornamentation: Near ovulation, women dress to impress. *Hormones and Behavior, 51*, 40–45.

Haskard, K. B., Williams, S. L., DiMatteo, M. R., Heritage, J., & Rosenthal, R. (2008). The provider's voice: Patient satisfaction and the content-filtered speech of nurses and physicians in primary medical care. *Journal of Nonverbal Behavior, 32*, 1–20.

Hassin, R. R., Aviezer, H., & Bentin, S. (2013). Inherently ambiguous: Facial expressions of emotions, in context. *Emotion Review, 5*, 60–65.

Hassin, R., & Trope, Y. (2000). Facing faces: Studies on the cognitive aspects of physiognomy. *Journal of Personality and Social Psychology, 78*, 837–852.

Hâta, T. D. (2004). Inferences about resident's personality in Japanese homes. *North American Journal of Psychology, 6*, 337–348.

Hatfield, E., Cacioppo, J. T., & Rapson, R. L. (1994). *Emotional contagion.* New York, NY: Cambridge University Press.

Hatfield, E., & Sprecher, S. (1986). *Mirror, mirror: The importance of looks in everyday life.* Albany, NY: SUNY Press.

Havas, D. A., Glenberg, A. M., Gutowski, K. A., Lucarelli, M. J., & Davidson, R. J. (2010). Cosmetic use of botulinum toxin-A affects processing of emotional language. *Psychological Science, 21*, 895–900.

Haviland, J. M., & Lelwica, M. (1987). The induced affect response: 10-week-old infants' responses to three emotion expressions. *Developmental Psychology, 23*, 97–104.

Hays, E. R., & Plax, T. G. (1971). Pupillary response to supportive and aversive verbal messages. *Speech Monographs, 38*, 316–320.

Hazlett, R. L., & Hazlett, S. Y. (1999). Emotional response to television commercials: Facial EMG vs. Self-report. *Journal of Advertising Research, 39*, 7–23.

Heaven, L., & McBrayer, D. (2000). External motivators of self-touching behavior. *Perceptual and Motor Skills, 90*, 338–342.

Heaver, B., & Hutton, S. B. (2011). Keeping an eye on the truth? Pupil size changes associated with recognition memory. *Memory, 19*, 398–405.

Hebl, M. R., & Heatherton, T. F. (1998). The stigma of obesity in women: The difference is black and white. *Personality and Social Psychology Bulletin, 24*, 417–426.

Hecht, M. A., & Ambady, N. (1999). Nonverbal communication and psychology: Past and future. *New Jersey Journal of Communication, 7*, 1–14.

Hecker, S., & Stewart, D. W. (Eds.). (1988). *Nonverbal communication in advertising.* Lexington, MA: Lexington.

Heider, K. (1974). *Affect display rules in the Dani.* Paper presented at the annual meeting of the American Anthropological Association, New Orleans, LA.

Hellbernd, N., & Sammler, D. (2018). Neural bases of social communicative intentions in speech. *Social Cognitive and Affective Neuroscience, 13*, 604–615.

Hemsley, G. D., & Doob, A. N. (1978). The effect of looking behavior on perceptions of a communicator's credibility. *Journal of Applied Psychology, 8*, 136–144.

Henley, N. (1977). *Body politics: Power, sex, and nonverbal communication*. Englewood Cliffs, NJ: Prentice-Hall.

Hensley, W. E. (1981). The effects of attire, location, and sex on aiding behavior: A similarity explanation. *Journal of Nonverbal Behavior, 6*, 3–11.

Hensley, W. E. (1990). Pupillary dilation revisited: The constriction of a nonverbal cue. *Journal of Social Behavior and Personality, 5*, 97–104.

Herbert, B. G., & Vorauer, J. D. (2003). Seeing through the screen: Is evaluative feedback communicated more effectively in face-to-face or computer-mediated exchanges? *Computers in Human Behavior, 19*, 25–38.

Herman, C. P., Zanna, M. P., & Higgins, E. T. (Eds.). (1986). *Physical appearance, stigma, and social behavior: The Ontario symposium* (Vol. 3). Hillsdale, NJ: Lawrence Erlbaum.

Hertenstein, M. J. (2011). The communicative functions of touch in adulthood. In M. J. Hertenstein & S. J. Weiss (Eds.), *The handbook of touch: Neuroscience, behavioral, and health perspectives* (pp. 299–327). New York, NY: Springer.

Hertenstein, M. J., Holmes, R., McCullough, M., & Keltner, D. (2009). The communication of emotion via touch. *Emotion, 9*, 566–573.

Hertenstein, M. J., Keltner, D., App, B., Bulleit, B. A., & Jaskolka, A. R. (2006). Touch communicates distinct emotions. *Emotion, 6*, 528–533.

Hertenstein, M. J., Verkamp, J. M., Kerestes, A. M., & Holmes, R. M. (2006). The communicative functions of touch in humans, nonhuman primates, and rats: A review and synthesis of the empirical research. *Genetic, Social, and General Psychology Monographs, 132*, 5–94.

Herzog, H. (2011). The impact of pets on human health and psychological well-being: Fact, fiction, or hypothesis? *Current Directions in Psychological Science, 20*, 236–239.

Heslin, R., & Alper, T. (1983). Touch: A bonding gesture. In J. M. Wiemann & R. P. Harrison (Eds.), *Nonverbal interaction* (pp. 47–75). Beverly Hills, CA: SAGE.

Heslin, R., & Boss, D. (1980). Nonverbal intimacy in airport arrival and departure. *Personality and Social Psychology Bulletin, 6*, 248–252.

Heslin, R., Nguyen, T. D., & Nguyen, M. L. (1983). Meaning of touch: The case of touch from a stranger or same-sex person. *Journal of Nonverbal Behavior, 7*, 147–157.

Heslin, R., & Patterson, M. L. (1982). *Nonverbal behavior and social psychology*. New York, NY: Plenum.

Hess, E. H. (1975a). The role of pupil size in communication. *Scientific American, 233*, 110–112, 116–119.

Hess, E. H. (1975b). *The tell-tale eye*. New York, NY: Van Nostrand Reinhold.

Hess, E. H., & Petrovich, S. B. (1987). Pupillary behavior in communication. In A. W. Siegman & S. Feldstein (Eds.), *Nonverbal behavior and communication* (2nd ed., pp. 329–349). Hillsdale, NJ: Lawrence Erlbaum.

Hess, E. H., & Polt, J. M. (1960). Pupil size as related to interest value of visual stimuli. *Science, 132*, 349–350.

Hess, E. H., Seltzer, A. L., & Shlien, J. M. (1965). Pupil response of hetero- and homosexual males to pictures of men and women: A pilot study. *Journal of Abnormal Psychology, 70*, 165–168.

Hetherington, A. (1998). The use and abuse of touch in therapy and counselling. *Counselling Psychology Quarterly, 11*, 361–364.

Hill, R. A., & Barton, R. A. (2005, May 19). Psychology: Red enhances human performance in contests. *Nature, 435*, 293.

Hilton, I. (2004, March 29). The Buddha's daughter. *The New Yorker*, pp. 42–50.

Hines, T. (1996). *The total package*. New York, NY: Little, Brown.

Hinsz, V. B. (1989). Facial resemblance in engaged and married couples. *Journal of Social and Personal Relationships, 6*, 223–229.

Hinsz, V. B., & Tomhave, J. A. (1991). Smile and (half) the world smiles with you, frown and you frown alone. *Personality and Social Psychology Bulletin, 17*, 586–592.

Hirschman, L. (1994). Female–male differences in conversational interaction. *Language in Society, 23*, 427–142.

Hodgins, H. S., & Belch, C. (2000). Interparental violence and nonverbal abilities. *Journal of Nonverbal Behavior, 24*, 3–24.

Hodgins, H. S., & Koestner, R. (1993). The origins of nonverbal sensitivity. *Personality and Social Psychology Bulletin, 19*, 466–473.

Hofstede, G. (2001). *Culture's consequences* (2nd ed.). Thousand Oaks, CA: SAGE.

Hoicka, E., & Wang, S.-H. (2011). Fifteen-month-old infants match vocal cues to intentional actions. *Journal of Cognition and Development, 12*, 299–314.

Holland, E., Wolf, E. B., Looser, C., & Cuddy, A. (2017). Visual attention to powerful postures: People avert their gaze from nonverbal dominance displays. *Journal of Experimental Social Psychology, 68*, 60–67.

Holler, J., & Beattie, G. (2003). Pragmatic aspects of representational gestures: Do speakers use them to clarify verbal ambiguity for the listener? *Gesture, 3*, 127–154.

Hollien, H. (1990). *The acoustics of crime: The new science of forensic phonetics*. New York, NY: Plenum.

Honeycutt, J. M., & Eidenmuller, M. E. (2001). Communication and attribution: An exploration of the effects of music and mood on intimate couples' verbal and nonverbal conflict resolution behaviors. In V. Manusov & J. H. Harvey (Eds.), *Attribution, communication behavior, and close relationships* (pp. 21–37). New York, NY: Cambridge University Press.

Hopkins, I. M., Gower, M. W., Perez, T. A., Smith, D. S., Amthor, F. R., Wimsatt, F. C., & Biasini, F. J. (2011). Avatar assistant: Improving social skills in students with an ASD through a computer-based intervention. *Journal of Autism and Developmental Disorders, 41*, 1543–1555.

Hopyan-Misakyan, T. M., Gordon, K. A., Dennis, M., & Papsin, B. C. (2009). Recognition of affectivespeech prosody and facial affect in deaf children with unilateral right cochlear implants. *Childneuropsychology, 15*, 136–146.

Horai, J., Naccari, N., & Faloultah, E. (1974). The effects of expertise and physical attractiveness upon opinion agreement and liking. *Sociometry, 37*, 601–606.

Horgan, T. G., McGrath, M. P., Bastien, C., & Wegman, P. (2017). Gender and appearance accuracy: Women's advantage over men is restricted to dress items. *Journal of Social Psychology, 157*, 680–691.

Horgan, T.G. (2020). A New Look at Person Memory. In: Sternberg R., Kostić A.(eds), Social Intelligence and Nonverbal Communication. Palgrave Macmillan, Cham. doi.org/10.1007/978-3-030-34964-6_7

Horgan, T. G., Herzog, N.L., & Dyszlewski, S. (2019). Does your messy office make your mind look cluttered? Office appearance and perceivers' judgments about the owner's personality. *Personality and Individual Differences, 138*, 370–379

Horgan, T. G., Grey, M., Looney, N. L., Long, T., & Lindenmulder, J. (2017). Sex doesn't always sell: The effects of objectifying images on perceivers' judgments of a female speaker. *Psychology of Popular Media Culture. doi.org/10.1037/ppm0000145*

Horgan, T. G., Broadbent, J., McKibbin, W. F., & Duehring, A. J. (2015). Show versus Tell? The effects of mating context on women's memory for a man's physical features and verbal statements. *Journal of Social and Personal Relationships, 32*, 1–18.

Horgan, T. G., Schmid Mast, M., Hall, J. A., & Carter, J. D. (2004). Gender differences in memory for the appearance of others. *Personality and Social Psychology Bulletin, 30*, 185–196.

Hornik, J. (1991). Shopping time and purchasing behavior as a result of in-store tactile stimulation. *Perceptual and Motor Skills, 73*, 969–970.

Hornik, J. (1992). Tactile stimulation and consumer response. *Journal of Consumer Research, 19*, 449–158.

Hostetter, A. B., & Alibali, M. W. (2007). Raise your hand if you're spatial. *Gesture, 7*, 73–95.

Hostetter, A. B., & Skirving, C. J. (2011). The effect of visual vs. verbal stimuli on gesture production. *Journal of Nonverbal Behavior, 35*, 205–223.

Houser, M. L., & Frymier, A. B. (2009). The role of student characteristics and teacher behaviors in students' learner empowerment. *Communication Education, 58*, 35–53.

Howells, L. T., & Becker, S. W. (1962). Seating arrangement and leadership emergence. *Journal of Abnormal and Social Psychology, 64*, 148–150.

Hu, Y., Parde, C. J., Hill, M. Q., Mahmood, N., & O'Toole, A. J. (2018). First impressions of personality traits from body shapes. *Psychological Science, 29*, 1969–1983.

Huang, R.-H., & Shih, Y.-N. (2011). Effects of background music on concentration of workers. *Work: Journal of Prevention, Assessment and Rehabilitation, 38*, 383–387.

Hughes, S. M., Dispenza, F., & Gallup, G. G., Jr. (2004). Ratings of voice attractiveness predict sexual behavior and body configuration. *Evolution and Human Behavior, 25*, 295–304.

Hughes, S. M., Farley, S. D., & Rhodes, B. C. (2010). Vocal and physiological changes in response to the physical attractiveness of conversational partners. *Journal of Nonverbal Behavior, 34*, 155–167.

Hummert, M. L., Mazloff, D., & Henry, C. (1999). Vocal characteristics of older adults and stereotyping. *Journal of Nonverbal Behavior, 23*, 111–132.

Hunger, J. M., Dodd, D. R., & Smith, A. R. (2019). Weight-based discrimination, interpersonal needs, and suicidal ideation. *Stigma and Health.* 2020 5(2) 217–224.

Hurley, C. M., Anker, A. E., Frank, M. G., Matsumoto, D., & Hwang, H. C. (2014). Background factors predicting accuracy and improvement in micro expression recognition. *Motivation and Emotion, 38*, 700–714.

Hurley, C. M., & Frank, M. G. (2011). Executing facial control during deception situations. *Journal of Nonverbal Behavior, 35*, 119–131.

Hutt, C., & Ounsted, C. (1966). The biological significance of gaze aversion with particular reference to the syndrome of infantile autism. *Behavioral Science, 11*, 346–356.

Hwang, H., & Matsumoto, D. (2015). Evidence for the universality of facial expressions of emotion. In M. K. Mandal & A. Awasthi (Eds.), *Understanding facial expressions in communication: Cross-cultural and multidisciplinary perspectives* (pp. 41–56). New York, NY: Springer Science + Business Media.

Hwang, H. C., Matsumoto, D., Yamada, H., Kosti⊠, A., & Granskaya, J. V. (2016). Self-reported expression and experience of triumph across four countries. *Motivation and Emotion, 40*, 731–739.

Iacono, W. G., & Ben-Shakhar, G. (2019). Current status of forensic lie detection with the comparison question technique: An update of the 2003 National Academy of Sciences report on polygraph testing. *Law and Human Behavior, 43*, 86–98.

Ickes, W. (2001). Measuring empathic accuracy. In J. A. Hall & F. J. Bernieri (Eds.), *Interpersonal sensitivity: Theory and measurement* (pp. 219–241). Mahwah, NJ: Lawrence Erlbaum.

Ickes, W. (2003). *Everyday mind reading: Understanding what other people think and feel*. Amherst, NY: Prometheus Books.

Ickes, W., Gesn, P. R., & Graham, T. (2000). Gender differences in empathic accuracy: Differential ability or differential motivation? *Personal Relationships, 7*, 95–109.

Ickes, W., Stinson, L., Bissonnette, V., & Garcia, S. (1990). Naturalistic social cognition: Empathic accuracy in mixed-sex dyads. *Journal of Personality and Social Psychology, 59*, 730–742.

Ilie, A., Ioan, S., Zagrean, L., & Moldovan, M. (2008). Better to be red than blue in virtual competition. *CyberPsychology & Behavior, 11*, 375–377.

Incollingo Rodriguez, A. C., White, M. L., Standen, E. C., Mann, T., Wells, C. R., & Tomiyama, A. J. (2019). Body mass index and educational inequality: An update of Crandall (1995). *Stigma and Health, 4*, 357–363.

Ingersoll, B. (2011). Recent advances in early identification and treatment of autism. *Current Directions in Psychological Science, 20*, 335–339.

Inzlicht, M., Gutsell, J. N., & Legault, L. (2011). Mimicry reduces racial prejudice. *Journal of Experimental Social Psychology, 48*, 361–365.

Irish, J. T., & Hall, J. A. (1995). Interruptive patterns in medical visits: The effects of role, status, and gender. *Social Science & Medicine, 41*, 873–881.

Isaacowitz, D. M., Löckenhoff, C. E., Lane, R. D., Wright, R., Sechrest, L., Riedel, R., & Costa, P. T. (2007). Age differences in recognition of emotion in lexical stimuli and facial expressions. *Psychology and Aging, 22*, 147–159.

Izard, C. E. (1971). *The face of emotion*. New York, NY: Appleton-Century-Crofts.

Izard, C. E. (1977). *Human emotions*. New York, NY: Plenum.

Izard, C. E. (1979). *The maximally discriminative facial movement coding system*. Unpublished manuscript, University of Delaware, Newark, NJ.

Izard, C. E. (1990). Facial expressions and the regulation of emotions. *Journal of Personality and Social Psychology, 58*, 487–498.

Izard, C. E., Fine, S., Schultz, D., Mostow, A., Ackerman, B., & Youngstrom, E. (2001). Emotion knowledge as a predictor of social behavior and academic competence in children at risk. *Psychological Science, 12*, 18–23.

Izard, C. E., & Malatesta, C. (1987). Perspectives on emotional development I: Differential emotions theory of early emotional development. In J. Osofsky (Ed.), *Handbook of infant development* (pp. 494–554). New York, NY: Wiley.

Jachmann, T. K., Drenhaus, H., Staudte, M., & Crocker, M. W. (2019). Influence of speakers' gaze on situated language comprehension: Evidence from event-related potentials. *Brain and Cognition, 135,* Article 103571.

Jackson, D., Engstrom, E., & Emmers-Sommer, T. (2007). Think leader, think male and female: Sex vs. seating arrangement as leadership cues. *Sex Roles, 57*, 713–723.

Jacob, S., McClintock, M. K., Zelano, B., & Ober, C. (2002). Paternally inherited HLA alleles are associated with women's choice of male odor. *Nature Genetics, 30*, 175–179.

Jacobson, J. W., Mulick, J. A., & Schwartz, A. A. (1995). A history of facilitated communication: Science, pseudoscience, and antiscience. *American Psychologist, 50*, 750–765.

Jacobson, R. (1972). Motor signs for yes and no. *Language in Society, 1*, 91–96.

Jaffe, J., Stern, D. N., & Peery, C. (1973). "Conversational" coupling of gaze behavior in prelinguistic human development. *Journal of Psycholinguistic Research, 2*, 321–329.

Jahncke, H., Hygge, S., Halin, N., Green, A. M., & Dimberg, K. (2011). Open-plan office noise: Cognitive performance and restoration. *Journal of Environmental Psychology, 31*, 373–382.

Jakubiak, B. K., & Feeney, B. C. (2017). Affectionate touch to promote relational, psychological, and physical well-being in adulthood: A theoretical model and review of the research. *Personality and Social Psychology Review, 21*, 228–252.

Jamieson, J. P. (2010). The home field advantage in athletics: A meta-analysis. *Journal of Applied Social Psychology, 40*, 1819–1848.

Jamieson, K. H. (1988). *Eloquence in an electronic age.* New York, NY: Oxford University Press.

Janisse, M. P., & Peavler, W. S. (1974). Pupillary research today: Emotion in the eye. *Psychology Today, 7*, 60–63.

Janssen, D., SchoUhorn, W. I., Lubienetzki, J., Foiling, K., Kokenge, H., & Davids, K. (2008). Recognition of emotions in gait patterns by means of artificial neural nets. *Journal of Nonverbal Behavior, 32*, 79–92.

Javaras, K. N., Austin, S. B., & Field, A. E. (2011). Season of birth and disordered eating in a population-based sample of young U.S. females. *International Journal of Eating Disorders, 44*, 630–638.

Jaworski, A. (1993). *The power of silence: Social and pragmatic perspectives.* Newbury Park, CA: SAGE.

Jaywant, A., & Pell, M. D. (2012). Categorical processing of negative emotions from speech prosody. *Speech Communication, 54*, 1–10.

Jensen, J. V. (1973). Communicative functions of silence. *ETC, 30*, 249–257.

Jiang, X., & Pell, M. D. (2017). The sound of confidence and doubt. *Speech Communication, 88*, 106–126.

Johannsen, L., Guzman-Garcia, A., & Wing, A. M. (2009). Interpersonal light touch assists balance in the elderly. *Journal of Motor Behavior, 41*, 397–399.

Johnson, C. (1994). Gender, legitimate authority, and leader–subordinate conversations. *American Sociological Review, 59*, 122–135.

Johnson, H. G., Ekman, P., & Friesen, W. V. (1975). Communicative body movements: American emblems. *Semiotica, 15*, 335–353.

Johnson, K. R. (1972). Black kinesics—some nonverbal communication patterns in the black culture. In L. A. Samovar & R. E. Porter (Eds.), *Intercultural communication: A reader*. Belmont, CA: Wadsworth.

Johnson, P. A., & Staffieri, J. R. (1971). Stereotypic affective properties of personal names and somatotypes in children. *Developmental Psychology, 5*, 176.

Johnson, R. L., Roter, D., Powe, N. R., & Cooper, L. A. (2013). Patient race/ethnicity and quality of patient–physician communication during medical visits. In T. A. LaVeist & L. A. Isaac (Eds.), *Race, ethnicity, and health: A public health reader* (pp. 569–585). San Francisco, CA: Jossey-Bass.

Jones, B. C., Main, J. C., Little, A. C., & DeBruine, L. M. (2011). Further evidence that facial cues of dominance modulate gaze cuing in human observers. *Swiss Journal of Psychology, 70*, 193–197.

Jones, B. T., Jones, B. C., Thomas, A. P., & Piper, J. (2003). Alcohol consumption increases attractiveness ratings of opposite-sex faces: A possible third route to risky sex. *Addiction, 98*, 1069–1075.

Jones, S. (1991). Problems of validity in questionnaire studies of nonverbal behavior: Jourard's tactile body-accessibility scale. *Southern Communication Journal, 56*, 83–95.

Jones, S. E., & Yarbrough, A. E. (1985). A naturalistic study of the meanings of touch. *Communication Monographs, 52*, 19–56.

Joule, R., & Guéguen, N. (2007). Touch, compliance, and awareness of tactile contact. *Perceptual and Motor Skills, 104*, 581–588.

Jourard, S. M. (1966). An exploratory study of body-accessibility. *British Journal of Social and Clinical Psychology, 26*, 235–242.

Judge, P. G., Griffaton, N. S., & Fincke, A. M. (2006). Conflict management by hamadryas baboons (*Papio hamadryas hamadryas*) during crowding: A tension-reduction strategy. *American Journal of Primatology, 68*, 993–1006.

Judge, T. A., & Cable, D. M. (2004). The effects of physical height on workplace success and income: Preliminary test of a theoretical model. *Journal of Applied Psychology, 89*, 428–441.

Juslin, P. N., & Laukka, P. (2003). Communication of emotions in vocal expression and music performance: Different channels, same code? *Psychological Bulletin, 129*, 770–814.

Juslin, P. N., Laukka, P., & Bänziger, T. (2018). The mirror to our soul? Comparisons of spontaneous and posed vocal expression of emotion. *Journal of Nonverbal Behavior, 42*, 1–40.

Juslin, P. N., & Scherer, K. R. (2005). Vocal expression of affect. In J. A. Harrigan, R. Rosenthal, & K. R. Scherer (Eds.), *The new handbook of methods in nonverbal behavior research* (pp. 65–135). Oxford, UK: Oxford University Press.

Jorgenson, D. O. (1978). Nonverbal assessment of attitudinal affect with the smile-return technique. *Journal of Social Psychology, 106*, 173–179.

Judge, P. G. (2000). Coping with crowded conditions. In F. Aureli & F. B. M. de Waal (Eds.), *Natural conflict resolution* (pp. 129–154). Berkeley: University of California Press.

Judge, P. G., & de Waal, F. B. M. (1993). Conflict avoidance among rhesus monkeys: Coping with short-term crowding. *Animal Behaviour, 46*, 221–232.

Judge, P. G., & de Waal, F. B. M. (1997). Rhesus monkey behaviour under diverse population densities: Coping with long-term crowding. *Animal Behaviour, 54*, 643–662.

Kaiser, S., & Wehrle, T. (1992). Automated coding of facial behavior in human–computer interactions with FACS. *Journal of Nonverbal Behavior, 16*, 65–140.

Kaisler, R. E., & Leder, H. (2016). Trusting the looks of others: Gaze effects of faces in social settings. *Perception, 45*, 875–892.

Kalick, S. M., & Hamilton, T. E. (1986). The matching hypothesis reexamined. *Journal of Personality and Social Psychology, 51*, 673–682.

Kalma, A. (1993). Sociable and aggressive dominance: Personality differences in leadership style? *Leadership Quarterly, 4*, 45–64.

Kanazawa, S., & Still, M. C. (2018). Is there really a beauty premium or an ugliness penalty on earnings? *Journal of Business and Psychology, 33*, 249–262.

Kang, M. (1997). The portrayal of women's images in magazine advertisements: Goffman's gender analysis revisited. *Sex Roles, 37*, 979–996.

Kaufman, D., & Mahoney, J. M. (1999). The effect of waitresses' touch on alcohol consumption in dyads. *Journal of Social Psychology, 139*, 261–267.

Kaurin, A., Heil, L., Wessa, M., Egloff, B., & Hirschmüller, S. (2018). Selfies reflect actual personality—Just like photos or short videos in standardized lab conditions. *Journal of Research in Personality, 76*, 154–164.

Kaya, N. (2007). Territoriality: Seat preferences in different types of classroom arrangements. *Environment and Behavior, 39*, 859–876.

Kaya, N., & Weber, M. J. (2003). Territorial behavior in residence halls: A cross-cultural study. *Environment and Behavior, 35*, 400–414.

Keating, C. F. (1985). Human dominance signals: The primate in us. In S. L. Ellyson & J. F. Dovidio (Eds.), *Power, dominance, and nonverbal behavior* (pp. 89–108). New York, NY: Springer-Verlag.

Keating, C. F., Randall, D., & Kendrick, T. (1999). Presidential physiognomies: Altered images, altered perceptions. *Political Psychology, 20*, 593–610.

Keizer, K., Lindenberg, S., & Steg, L. (2008). The spreading of disorder. *Science, 322*, 1681–1685.

Kelling, G., & Coles, C. (1996). *Fixing broken windows: Restoring order and reducing crime in our communities.* New York, NY: Free Press.

Kelly, F., Fröhlich, A., Dellwo, V., Forth, O., Kent, S., & Alexander, A. (2019). Evaluation of VOCALISE under conditions reflecting those of a real forensic voice comparison case (forensic_eval_01). *Speech Communication, 112*, 30–36.

Kelly, S. D., & Goldsmith, L. H. (2004). Gesture and right hemisphere involvement in evaluating lecture material. *Gesture, 4*, 25–42.

Keltner, D. (1995). Signs of appeasement: Evidence for the distinct displays of embarrassment, amusement, and shame. *Journal of Personality and Social Psychology, 68*, 441–454.

Kendler, K. S., Halberstadt, L. J., Butera, F., Myers, J., Bouchard, T., & Ekman, P. (2008). The similarity of facial expressions in response to emotion-inducing films in reared-apart twins. *Psychological Medicine: A Journal of Research in Psychiatry and the Allied Sciences, 38*, 1475–1483.

Kendon, A. (1967). Some functions of gaze direction in social interaction. *Acta Psychologies, 26*, 22–63.

Kendon, A. (1972). Some relationships between body motion and speech: An analysis of an example. In A. Siegman & B. Pope (Eds.), *Studies in dyadic communication* (pp. 177–210). New York, NY: Pergamon Press.

Kendon, A. (1980). Gesticulation and speech: Two aspects of the process of utterance. In M. R. Key (Ed.), *The relationship of verbal and nonverbal communication* (pp. 207–227). The Hague, The Netherlands: Mouton.

Kendon, A. (1981a). Current issues in "nonverbal communication." In A. Kendon (Ed.), *Nonverbal communication, interaction, and gesture* (pp. 1–56). The Hague, The Netherlands: Mouton.

Kendon, A. (1981b). Geography of gesture. *Semiotica, 37*, 129–163.

Kendon, A. (1983). Gesture and speech: How they interact. In J. M. Wiemann & R. P. Harrison (Eds.), *Nonverbal interaction* (pp. 13–45). Beverly Hills, CA: SAGE.

Kendon, A. (1984). Did gesture have the happiness to escape the curse at the confusion of Babel? In A. Wolfgang (Ed.), *Nonverbal behavior: Perspectives, applications, intercultural insights* (pp. 75–114). Toronto, Ontario, Canada: Hogrefe.

Kendon, A. (1987). On gesture: Its complementary relationship with speech. In A. W. Siegman & S. Feldstein (Eds.), *Nonverbal behavior and communication* (2nd ed., pp. 65–97). Hillsdale, NJ: Lawrence Erlbaum.

Kendon, A. (1988). How gestures can become like words. In F. Poyatos (Ed.), *Cross-cultural perspectives in nonverbal communication* (pp. 131–141). Toronto, Ontario, Canada: Hogrefe.

Kendon, A. (1989a). Gesture. In E. Barnouw, G. Gerbner, W. Schramm, T. L. Worth, & L. Gross (Eds.), *International encyclopedia of communications* (Vol. 2, pp. 217–222). New York, NY: Oxford University Press.

Kendon, A. (1989b). Nonverbal communication. In E. Barnouw, G. Gerbner, W. Schramm, T. L. Worth, & L. Gross (Eds.), *International encyclopedia of communications* (Vol. 3). New York, NY: Oxford University Press.

Kendon, A. (2000). Language and gesture: Unity or duality? In D. McNeill (Ed.), *Language and gesture* (pp. 47–63). New York, NY: Cambridge University Press.

Kendon, A. (2002). Some uses of the head shake. *Gesture, 2*, 147–182.

Kendon, A. (2004). *Gesture: Visible action as utterance.* New York, NY: Cambridge University Press.

Kendon, A., & Ferber, A. (1973). A description of some human greetings. In R. P. Michael & J. H. Crook (Eds.), *Comparative ecology and behavior of primates* (pp. 591–668). London, UK: Academic Press.

Kennedy, C. W., & Camden, C. T. (1983). A new look at interruptions. *Western Journal of Speech Communication, 47*, 45–58.

Kennedy, J., Baxter, P., & Belpaeme, T. (2017). Nonverbal immediacy as a characterisation of social behaviour for human–robot interaction. *International Journal of Social Robotics, 9*, 109–128.

Kenner, A. N. (1993). A cross-cultural study of body-focused hand movement. *Journal of Nonverbal Behavior, 17*, 263–279.

Kenrick, D. T., & Johnson, G. A. (1979). Interpersonal attraction in aversive environments: A problem for the classical conditioning paradigm? *Journal of Personality and Social Psychology, 37*, 572–579.

Kenrick, D. T., & MacFarlane, W. W. (1986). Ambient temperature and horn-honking: A field study of the heat/aggression relationship. *Environment and Behavior, 18,* 179–191.

Kerr, C. E., Wasserman, R. H., & Moore, C. I. (2007). Cortical dynamics as a therapeutic mechanism for touch healing. *Journal of Alternative and Complementary Medicine, 13,* 59–66.

Kerstholt, J. H., Jansen, N. J. M., van Amelsvoort, A. G., & Broeders, A. P. A. (2006). Earwitnesses: Effects of accent, retention and telephone. *Applied Cognitive Psychology, 20,* 187–197.

Kesner, L., Grygarovβ, D., Fajnerovβ, I., Lukavský, J., Nekovβřovβ, T., Tintěra, J., . . . Horβček, J. (2018). Perception of direct vs averted gaze in portrait paintings: An fMRI and eye-tracking study. *Brain and Cognition, 125,* 88–99.

Kezuka, E. (1997). The role of touch in facilitated communication. *Journal of Autism and Developmental Disorders, 27,* 571–593.

Khan, S. A., Levine, W. J., Dobson, S. D., & Kralik, J. D. (2011). Red signals dominance in male rhesus macaques. *Psychological Science, 22,* 1001–1003.

Kibler, R. J., & Barker, L. L. (1972). Effects of selected levels of misspelling and mispronunciation on comprehension and retention. *Southern Speech Communication Journal, 37,* 361–374.

Kiesler, S., Siegel, J., & McGuire, T. W. (1984). Social psychological aspects of computer-mediated communication. *American Psychologist, 39,* 1123–1134.

Kiire, S. (2016). Effect of leg-to-body ratio on body shape attractiveness. *Archives of Sexual Behavior, 45,* 901–910.

Kim, K., Lee, Y., Kim, H.-T., & Lee, J.-H. (2019). Detecting deception: Effect of auditory and visual stimuli on pupil dilation. *Social Behavior and Personality: An International Journal, 47,* 1–10.

Kim, E., Ku, J., Kim, J., Lee, H., Han, K., Kim, S. I., & Cho, H.-S. (2009). Nonverbal social behaviors of patients with bipolar mania during interactions with virtual humans. *Journal of Nervous and Mental Disease, 197,* 412–418.

Kimbara, I. (2008). Gesture form convergence in joint description. *Journal of Nonverbal Behavior, 32,* 123–131.

Kimura, D. (1976). The neural basis of language via gesture. In H. Whitaker & H. A. Whitaker (Eds.), *Studies in neurolinguistics* (Vol. 2). New York, NY: Academic Press.

King, M. J. (1966). Interpersonal relations in preschool children and average approach distance. *Journal of Genetic Psychology, 109,* 109–116.

King, P. E., & Behnke, R. R. (1989). The effect of time-compressed speech on comprehensive, interpretive, and short-term listening. *Human Communication Research, 15,* 428–443.

Kita, S. (2009). Cross-cultural variation of speech-accompanying gesture: A review. *Language and Cognitive Processes, 24,* 145–167.

Kitchen, D. M., Cheney, D. L., & Seyfarth, R. M. (2003). Female baboons' responses to male loud calls. *Ethology, 109,* 401–412.

Kleck, R. (1968). Physical stigma and nonverbal cues emitted in face-to-face interaction. *Human Relations, 21,* 19–28.

Kleck, R. E. (1969). Physical stigma and task oriented interaction. *Human Relations, 22,* 51–60.

Kleck, R. E., & Nuessle, W. (1968). Congruence between the indicative and communicative functions of eye contact in interpersonal relations. *British Journal of Social and Clinical Psychology, 7,* 241–246.

Kleck, R. E., Richardson, S. A., & Ronald, L. (1974). Physical appearance cues and interpersonal attraction in children. *Child Development, 45,* 305–310.

Kleck, R. E., & Strenta, A. C. (1985). Physical deviance and the perception of social outcomes. In J. A. Graham & A. M. Kligman (Eds.), *The psychology of cosmetic treatments.* New York, NY: Praeger.

Kleinke, C. L. (1986). Gaze and eye contact: A research review. *Psychological Bulletin, 100,* 78–100.

Kleinke, C. L., Bustos, A. A., Meeker, F. B., & Staneski, R. A. (1973). Effects of self-attributed and other-attributed gaze in interpersonal evaluations between males and females. *Journal of Experimental Social Psychology, 9,* 154–163.

Kleisner, K., Kočnar, T., Rubešovβ, A., & Flegr, J. (2010). Eye color predicts but does not directly influence perceived dominance in men. *Personality and Individual Differences, 49,* 59–64.

Kliemann, D., Dziobek, I., Hatri, A., Steimke, R., & Heekeren, H. R. (2010). Atypical reflexive gaze patterns on emotional faces in autism spectrum disorders. *Journal of Neuroscience, 30*, 12281–12287.

Klinger, H. N. (1959). *The effects of stuttering on audience listening comprehension.* Unpublished doctoral dissertation, New York University, New York, NY.

Knapen, J. E. P., Blaker, N. M., & Pollet, T. V. (2017). Size, skills, and suffrage: Motivated distortions in perceived formidability of political leaders. *PLoS ONE, 12*, Article ID e0188485.

Knapp, M. L. (1983). Dyadic relationship development. In J. M. Wiemann & R. P. Harrison (Eds.), *Nonverbal interaction* (pp. 179–207). Beverly Hills, CA: SAGE.

Knapp, M. L. (1984). The study of nonverbal behavior vis-à-vis human communication theory. In A. Wolfgang (Ed.), *Nonverbal behavior: Perspectives, applications, and intercultural insights* (pp. 15–40). New York, NY: Hogrefe.

Knapp, M. L. (2006). Lying and deception in close relationships. In A. L. Vangelisti & D. Perlman (Eds.), *The Cambridge handbook of personal relationships* (pp. 517–532). New York, NY: Cambridge University Press.

Knapp, M. L. (2008). *Lying and deception in human interaction.* Boston, MA: Pearson Education/Allyn & Bacon.

Knapp, M. L., Cody, M. J., & Reardon, K. K. (1987). Nonverbal signals. In C. R. Berger & S. H. Chaffee (Eds.), *Handbook of communication science* (pp. 385–118). Beverly Hills, CA: SAGE.

Knapp, M. L., Hart, R. P., Friedrich, G. W., & Shulman, G. M. (1975). The rhetoric of goodbye: Verbal and nonverbal correlates of human leave-taking. *Speech Monographs, 40*, 182–198.

Kneidinger, L. M., Maple, T. L., & Tross, S. A. (2001). Touching behavior in sport: Functional components, analysis of sex differences, and ethological considerations. *Journal of Nonverbal Behavior, 25*, 43–62.

Knowles, E. S. (1973). Boundaries around group interaction: The effect of group size and member status on boundary permeability. *Journal of Personality and Social Psychology, 26*, 327–332.

Knutson, B. (1996). Facial expressions of emotion influence interpersonal trait inferences. *Journal of Nonverbal Behavior, 20*, 165–182.

Koch, S. C. (2005). Evaluative affect display toward male and female leaders of task-oriented groups. *Small Group Research, 36*, 678–703.

Koch, S. C., Baehne, C. G., Kruse, L., Zimmermann, F., & Zumbach, J. (2008). *Visual dominance and visual support in groups.* Manuscript submitted for publication.

Koch, S. C., Baehne, C. G., Kruse, L., Zimmermann, F., & Zumbach, J. (2010). Visual dominance and visual egalitarianism: Individual and group-level influences of sex and status in group interactions. *Journal of Nonverbal Behavior, 34*, 137–153.

Koeppel, L. B., Montagne-Miller, Y., O'Hair, D., & Cody, M. J. (1993). Friendly? Flirting? Wrong? In P. J. Kalbfleisch (Ed.), *Interpersonal communication: Evolving interpersonal relationships* (pp. 13–32). Hillsdale, NJ: Lawrence Erlbaum.

Koerner, A. F., & Fitzpatrick, M. A. (2003). Nonverbal communication and marital adjustment and satisfaction: The role of decoding relationship relevant and relationship irrelevant affect. *Communication Monographs, 69*, 33–51.

Kollock, P., Blumstein, P., & Schwartz, P. (1985). Sex and power in interaction: Conversational privileges and duties. *American Sociological Review, 50*, 34–36.

Koneya, M. (1973). *The relationship between verbal interaction and seat location of members of large groups.* Unpublished doctoral dissertation, Denver University, Denver, CO.

Konishi, H., Karsten, A., & Vallotton, C. D. (2018). Toddlers' use of gesture and speech in service of emotion regulation during distressing routines. *Infant Mental Health Journal.*

Koppensteiner, M., Stephan, P., & Jäschke, J. P. M. (2016). Moving speeches: Dominance, trustworthiness and competence in body motion. *Personality and Individual Differences, 94*, 101–106.

Kornreich, C., Foisy, M.-L., Philippot, P., Dan, B., Tecco, J., Noël, X., . . . Verbanck, P. (2003). Impaired emotional facial expression recognition in alcoholics, opiate dependence subjects, methadone maintained subjects and mixed alcohol-opiate antecedents subjects compared with normal controls. *Psychiatry Research, 119*, 251–260.

Kory Westlund, J. M., Dickens, L., Jeong, S., Harris, P. L., DeSteno, D., & Breazeal, C. L. (2017). Children use non-verbal cues to learn new words from robots as well as people. *International Journal of Child–Computer Interaction, 13*, 1–9.

Koudenburg, N., Postmes, T., & Gordijn, E. H. (2011). Disrupting the flow: How brief silences in group conversations affect social needs. *Journal of Experimental Social Psychology, 47*, 512–515.

Koukounas, E., & Itsou, S. (2018). Alcohol, women's clothing, and the perception of sexual intent. *Journal of Substance Use, 23*, 206–210.

Koutlak, R. (1976, November 7). With half a brain, his IQ is 126, and doctors are dumbfounded. *Chicago Tribune*, pp. 1–6.

Kozel, F. A., Johnson, K. A., Grenesko, E. L., Laken, S. J., Kose, S., Lu, X., . . . George, M. S. (2009). Functional MRI detection of deception after committing a mock sabotage crime. *Journal of Forensic Sciences, 54*, 200–231.

Kraft-Todd, G. T., Reinero, D. A., Kelley, J. M., Heberlein, A. S., Baer, L., & Riess, H. (2017). Empathic nonverbal behavior increases ratings of both warmth and competence in a medical context. *PLoS ONE, 12*, Article e0177758.

Kramer, C. (1978). Female and male perceptions of female and male speech. *Language and Speech, 20*, 151–161.

Kraus, S. (1996). Winners of the first 1960 televised presidential debate between Kennedy and Nixon. *Journal of Communication, 46*, 78–94.

Kraus, M. W., & Keltner, D. (2009). Signs of socioeconomic status: A thin-slicing approach. *Psychological Science, 20*, 99–106.

Krauss, R. M., Chen, Y., & Chawla, P. (1996). Nonverbal behavior and nonverbal communication: What do conversational hand gestures tell us? In M. Zanna (Ed.), *Advances in experimental social psychology* (Vol. 28, pp. 389–450). San Diego, CA: Academic Press.

Krauss, R. M., Dushay, R. A., Chen, Y., & Rauscher, F. (1995). The communicative value of conversational hand gestures. *Journal of Experimental Social Psychology, 31*, 533–552.

Krauss, R. M., Freyberg, R., & Morsella, E. (2002). Inferring speakers' physical attributes from their voices. *Journal of Experimental Social Psychology, 38*, 618–625.

Krauss, R. M., & Hadar, U. (1999). The role of speech-related arm/hand gestures in word retrieval. In L. S. Messing & R. Campbell (Eds.), *Gesture, speech, and sign* (pp. 93–116). New York, NY: Oxford University Press.

Kraut, R. E., Fussell, S. R., & Siegel, J. (2003). Visual information as a conversational resource in collaborative physical tasks. *Human–Computer Interaction, 18*, 13–49.

Kraut, R. E., & Johnston, R. E. (1979). Social and emotional messages of smiling: An ethological approach. *Journal of Personality and Social Psychology, 37*, 1539–1553.

Krenn, B. (2015). The effect of uniform color on judging athletes' aggressiveness, fairness, and chance of winning. *Journal of Sport & Exercise Psychology, 37*, 207–212.

Kret, M. E., & De Dreu, C. K. W. (2019). The power of pupil size in establishing trust and reciprocity. *Journal of Experimental Psychology: General, 148*, 1299–1311.

Krieger, D. (1987). *Living the therapeutic touch: Healing as a lifestyle.* New York, NY: Dodd, Mead.

Kring, A. M., & Earnst, K. S. (2003). Nonverbal behavior in schizophrenia. In P. Philippot, R. S. Feldman, & E. J. Coats (Eds.), *Nonverbal behavior in clinical settings* (pp. 263–285). Oxford, UK: Oxford University Press.

Kring, A. M., & Gordon, A. H. (1998). Sex differences in emotion: Expression, experience, and physiology. *Journal of Personality and Social Psychology, 74*, 686–703.

Kring, A. M., & Sloan, D. M. (2007). The Facial Expression Coding System (FACES): Development, validation, and utility. *Psychological Assessment, 19*, 210–224.

Krivonos, P. D., & Knapp, M. L. (1975). Initiating communication: What do you say when you say hello? *Central States Speech Journal, 26*, 115–125.

Kruger, D. J. (2006). Male facial masculinity influences attributions of personality and reproductive strategy. *Personal Relationships, 13*, 451–463.

Kruger, J., Epley, N., Parker, J., & Ng, Z. (2005). Egocentrism over e-mail: Can we communicate as well as we think? *Journal of Personality and Social Psychology, 89*, 925–936.

Krumhuber, E. G., & Manstead, A. S. R. (2009). Can Duchenne smiles be feigned? New evidence on felt and false smiles. *Emotion, 9*, 807–820.

Krumhuber, E. G., Tamarit, L., Roesch, E. B., & Scherer, K. R. (2012). FACSGen 2.0 animation software: Generating three-dimensional FACS-valid facial expressions for emotion research. *Emotion, 12*, 351–362.

Krys, K., Vauclair, C.-M., Capaldi, C. A., Lun, V. M.-C., Bond, M. H., Domínguez-Espinosa, A., . . . Yu, A. A. (2016). Be careful where you smile: Culture shapes judgments of intelligence and honesty of smiling individuals. *Journal of Nonverbal Behavior, 40,* 101–116.

Kucharska-Pietura, K., Nilolaou, V., Masiak, M., & Treasure, J. (2004). The recognition of emotion in the faces and voice of anorexia nervosa. *International Journal of Eating Disorders, 35,* 42–47.

Kuhl, P. K., & Meltzoff, A. N. (1982). The bimodal perception of speech in infancy. *Science, 218,* 1138–1141.

Kuhn, G., & Tipples, J. (2011). Increased gaze following for fearful faces. It depends on what you're looking for! *Psychonomic Bulletin and Review, 18,* 89–95.

Kulczynski, A., Ilicic, J., & Baxter, S. M. (2016). When your source is smiling, consumers may automatically smile with you: Investigating the source expressive display hypothesis. *Psychology & Marketing, 33,* 5–19.

Kulka, R. A., & Kessler, J. B. (1978). Is justice really blind? The influence of litigant physical attractiveness on juridical judgment. *Journal of Applied Social Psychology, 8,* 366–381.

Kumin, L., & Lazar, M. (1974). Gestural communication in preschool children. *Perceptual and Motor Skills, 38,* 708–710.

Kunzmann, U., & Isaacowitz, D. (2017). Emotional aging: Taking the immediate context seriously. *Research in Human Development, 14,* 182–199.

Kurkul, W. W. (2007). Nonverbal communication in one-to-one music performance instruction. *Psychology of Music, 35,* 327–362.

Küster, D. (2018). Social effects of tears and small pupils are mediated by felt sadness: An evolutionary view. *Evolutionary Psychology, 16.*

Kuwabara, M., & Son, J. Y. (2011). Attention to context: U.S. and Japanese children's emotional judgments. *Journal of Cognition and Development, 12,* 502–517.

Kylliäinen, A., & Hietanen, J. K. (2006). Skin conductance responses to another person's gaze in children with autism. *Journal of Autism and Developmental Disorders, 36,* 517–525.

Ladefoged, P., & Ladefoged, J. (1980). The ability of listeners to identify voices. *UCLA Working Papers in Phonetics, 49,* 43–51.

LaFrance, M. (1979). Nonverbal synchrony and rapport: Analysis by the cross-lag panel technique. *Social Psychology Quarterly, 42,* 66–70.

LaFrance, M. (1985). Postural mirroring and inter-group relations. *Personality and Social Psychology Bulletin, 11,* 207–217.

LaFrance, M., & Broadbent, M. (1976). Group rapport: Posture sharing as a nonverbal indicator. *Group and Organization Studies, 1,* 328–333.

LaFrance, M., Hecht, M. A., & Levy Paluck, E. (2003). The contingent smile: A meta-analysis of sex differences in smiling. *Psychological Bulletin, 129,* 305–334.

Laird, J. D. (1974). Self-attribution of emotion: The effects of expressive behavior on the quality of emotional experience. *Journal of Personality and Social Psychology, 24,* 475–486.

Lakin, J. L. (2006). Automatic cognitive processes and nonverbal communication. In V. Manusov & M. L. Patterson (Eds.), *The SAGE handbook of nonverbal communication* (pp. 59–77). Thousand Oaks, CA: SAGE.

Lakin, J. L., & Chartrand, T. L. (2003). Using non-conscious behavioral mimicry to create affiliation and rapport. *Psychological Science, 14,* 334–339.

Lakoff, G., & Johnson, M. (1999). *Philosophy in the flesh: The embodied mind and its challenge to western thought.* New York, NY: Basic Books.

Lakoff, R. (1975). *Language and women's place.* New York, NY: Harper & Row.

Lalljee, M. G. (1971). *Disfluencies in normal English speech.* Unpublished doctoral dissertation, Oxford University, Oxford, UK.

Lalljee, M. G., & Cook, M. (1969). An experimental investigation of the filled pauses in speech. *Language and Speech, 12,* 24–28.

Lamb, T. A. (1981). Nonverbal and para verbal control in dyads and triads: Sex or power differences. *Social Psychology Quarterly, 44,* 49–53.

Lancelot, C., & Nowicki, S., Jr. (1997). The association between receptive nonverbal processing abilities and internalizing/externalizing problems in girls and boys. *Journal of Genetic Psychology, 158*, 297–302.

Langlois, J. H., Kalakanis, L. E., Rubenstein, A. J., Larson, A. D., Hallam, M. J., & Smoot, M. T. (2000). Maxims or myths of beauty: A meta-analysis and theoretical review. *Psychological Bulletin, 126*, 390–423.

Langlois, J. H., Ritter, J. M., Roggman, L. A., & Vaughn, L. S. (1991). Facial diversity and infant preferences for attractive faces. *Developmental Psychology, 27*, 79–84.

Langlois, J. H., & Roggman, L. A. (1990). Attractive faces are only average. *Psychological Science, 1*, 115–121.

Langlois, J. H., Roggman, L. A., Casey, R. J., Ritter, J. M., Rieser-Danner, L. A., & Jenkins, V. Y. (1987). Infant preferences for attractive faces: Rudiments of a stereotype? *Developmental Psychology, 23*, 363–369.

Lanzetta, J. T., & Kleck, R. E. (1970). Encoding and decoding of nonverbal affect in humans. *Journal of Personality and Social Psychology, 16*, 12–19.

Lapakko, D. (1997). Three cheers for language: A closer examination of a widely cited study of nonverbal communication. *Communication Education, 46*, 63–67.

Larsen, R. J., & Shackelford, T. (1996). Gaze avoidance: Personality and social judgments of people who avoid direct face-to-face contact. *Personality and Individual Differences, 21*, 907–917.

Laser, P. S., & Mathie, V. A. (1982). Face facts: An unbidden role for features in communication. *Journal of Nonverbal Behavior, 7*, 3–19.

Lass, N. J., Hughes, K. R., Bowyer, M. D., Waters, L. T., & Broune, V. T. (1976). Speaker sex identification from voiced, whispered and filtered isolated vowels. *Journal of the Acoustical Society of America, 59*, 675–678.

Laukka, P., Linnman, C., Ahs, F., Pissiota, A., Frans, O., Faria, V.,. . . Furmark, T. (2008). In a nervous voice: Analysis and perception of anxiety in social phobies' speech. *Journal of Nonverbal Behavior, 32*, 195–214.

Lavrakas, P. J. (1975). Female preferences for male physiques. *Journal of Research in Personality, 9*, 324–334.

Law, M. K. H., Jackson, S. A., Aidman, E., Geiger, M., Olderbak, S., & Kleitman, S. (2018). It's the deceiver, not the receiver: No individual differences when detecting deception in a foreign and a native language. *PLoS ONE, 13*, Article ID e0196384.

Lawrence, S. G., & Watson, M. (1991). Getting others to help: The effectiveness of professional uniforms in charitable fund-raising. *Journal of Applied Communication Research, 19*, 170–185.

Leaper, C., & Robnett, R. D. (2011). Women are more likely than men to use tentative language, aren't they? A meta-analysis testing for gender differences and moderators. *Psychology of Women Quarterly, 35*, 129–142.

Leathers, D. G. (1979). The impact of multichannel message inconsistency on verbal and nonverbal decoding behaviors. *Communication Monographs, 46*, 88–100.

Ledbetter, A. M., & Vik, T. A. (2012). Parental invasive behaviors and emerging adults' privacy defenses: Instrument development and validation. *Journal of Family Communication, 12*, 227–247.

Lederman, S. J., Klatzky, R. L., Abramowicz, A., Salsman, K., Kitada, R., & Hamilton, C. (2007). Haptic recognition of static and dynamic expressions of emotion in the live face. *Psychological Science, 18*, 158–164.

Lee, L., Loewenstein, G., Ariely, D., Hong, J., & Young, J. (2008). If I'm not hot, are you hot or not? Physical-attractiveness evaluations and dating preferences as a function of one's own attractiveness. *Psychological Science, 19*, 669–677.

Lee, M. S., Pittler, M. H., & Ernst, E. (2008). Effects of reiki in clinical practice: A systematic review of randomised clinical trials. *International Journal of Clinical Practice, 62*, 947–954.

Lee, V., & Wagner, H. (2002). The effect of social presence on the facial and verbal expression of emotion and the interrelations among emotion components. *Journal of Nonverbal Behavior, 26*, 3–25.

Leeb, R. T., & Rejskind, F. G. (2004). Here's looking at you, kid! A longitudinal study of perceived gender differences in mutual gaze behavior in young infants. *Sex Roles, 50*, 1–5.

Leeland, K. B. (Ed.). (2008). *Face recognition: New research*. Hauppauge, NY: Nova Science.

Leffler, A., Gillespie, D. L., & Conaty, J. C. (1982). The effects of status differentiation on nonverbal behavior. *Social Psychology Quarterly, 45*, 153–161.

Lefkowitz, M., Blake, R., & Mouton, J. (1955). Status factors in pedestrian violation of traffic signals. *Journal of Abnormal and Social Psychology, 51*, 704–706.

Lei, X., Holzleitner, I. J., & Perrett, D. I. (2019). The influence of body composition effects on male facial masculinity and attractiveness. *Frontiers in Psychology, 9*, Article 2658.

Leigh, T. W., & Summers, J. O. (2002). An initial evaluation of industrial buyers' impressions of salespersons' nonverbal cues. *Journal of Personal Selling and Sales Management, 22*, 41–53.

Leipold, W. E. (1963). *Psychological distance in a dyadic interview*. Unpublished doctoral dissertation, University of North Dakota, Grand Forks, ND.

Lenneberg, E. (1969). *Biological foundations of language*. New York, NY: Wiley.

Leonard, G. (1978). The rhythms of relationships. In G. Leonard (Ed.), *The silent pulse*. New York, NY: Elsevier-Dutton.

LePoire, B. A., & Burgoon, J. K. (1994). Two contrasting explanations of involvement violations: Expectancy violations theory versus discrepancy arousal theory. *Human Communication Research, 20*, 560–591.

Leppanen, J., Cardi, V., Ng, K. W., Paloyelis, Y., Stein, D., Tchanturia, K., & Treasure, J. (2017). Effects of intranasal oxytocin on the interpretation and expression of emotions in anorexia nervosa. *Journal of Neuroendocrinology, 29*, 1–13.

Leppard, W., Ogletree, S. M., & Wallen, E. (1993). Gender stereotyping in medical advertising: Much ado about something? *Sex Roles, 29*, 829–838.

LeResche, L. (1982). Facial expression in pain: A study of candid photographs. *Journal of Nonverbal Behavior, 7*, 46–56.

LeResche, L., Dworkin, S. F., Wilson, L., & Ehrlich, K. J. (1992). Effect of temporomandibular disorder pain duration on facial expressions and verbal report of pain. *Pain, 51*, 289–295.

Lerner, R. M., & Gellert, E. (1969). Body build identification, preference, and aversion in children. *Developmental Psychology, 1*, 456–462.

Lerner, R. M., & Korn, S. J. (1972). The development of body build stereotypes in males. *Child Development, 43*, 908–920.

Lerner, R. M., & Schroeder, C. (1971). Physique identification, preference, and aversion in kindergarten children. *Developmental Psychology, 5*, 538.

Lerner, R. M., Venning, J., & Knapp, J. R. (1975). Age and sex effects on personal space schemata toward body build in late childhood. *Developmental Psychology, 11*, 855–856.

Lester, P. M. (2006). *Visual communication: Images with messages*. Belmont, CA: Wadsworth.

Letzring, T. D. (2008). The good judge of personality: Characteristics, behaviors, and observer accuracy. *Journal of Research in Personality, 42*, 914–932.

Levav, J., & Argo, J. J. (2010). Physical contact and financial risk taking. *Psychological Science, 21*, 804–810.

Levenson, R. W., Ekman, P., Heider, K., & Friesen, W. V. (1992). Emotion and autonomie nervous system activity in the Minangkabau of West Sumatra. *Journal of Personality and Social Psychology, 62*, 972–988.

Levesque, M. J., & Kenny, D. A. (1993). Accuracy of behavioral predictions at zero acquaintance: A social relations analysis. *Journal of Personality and Social Psychology, 65*, 1178–1187.

Levine, L. R., Bluni, T. D., & Hochman, S. H. (1998). Attire and charitable behavior. *Psychological Reports, 83*, 15–18.

Levine, R., & Wolff, E. (1985). Social time: The heartbeat of a culture. *Psychology Today, 19*, 30.

Lewandowski, G. W., Jr., Aron, A., & Gee, J. (2007). Personality goes a long way: The malleability of opposite-sex physical attractiveness. *Personal Relationships, 14*, 571–585.

Lewis, M. B. (2010). Why are mixed-race people perceived as more attractive? *Perception, 39*, 136–138.

Lewis, M., & Rosenblum, L. A. (Eds.). (1978). *The development of affect*. New York, NY: Plenum.

Lewis, R. J., Derlega, V. J., Nichols, B., Shankar, A., Drury, K. K., & Hawkins, L. (1995). Sex differences in observers' reactions to a nurse's use of touch. *Journal of Nonverbal Behavior, 19*, 101–113.

Lewis, R. J., Derlega, V. J., Shankar, A., Cochard, E., & Finkel, L. (1997). Nonverbal correlates of confederates' touch: Confounds in touch research. *Journal of Social Behavior and Personality, 12*, 821–830.

Lewy, A. J., Bauer, V. K., Cutler, N. L., Sack, R. L., Ahmed, S., Thomas, K. H., . . . Jackson, J. M. (1998). Morning vs. evening light treatment of patients with winter depression. *Archives of General Psychiatry, 55*, 890–896.

Li, J., & Robertson, T. (2011). Physical space and information space: Studies of collaboration in distributed multi-disciplinary medical team meetings. *Behaviour and Information Technology, 30*, 443–454.

Li, N. P., Bailey, J. M., Kenrick, D. T., & Linsenmeier, J. A. W. (2002). *Journal of Personality and Social Psychology, 82*, 947–955.

Lieber, A. L. (1978). *The lunar effect: Biological tides and human emotions*. New York, NY: Anchor/Doubleday.

Lieberman, D. A., Rigo, T. G., & Campain, R. F. (1988). Age-related differences in nonverbal decoding ability. *Communication Quarterly, 36*, 290–297.

Likowski, K. U., Mühlberger, A., Seibt, B., Pauli, P., & Weyers, P. (2008). Modulation of facial mimicry by attitudes. *Journal of Experimental Social Psychology, 44*, 1065–1072.

Lin, L., & McFerran, B. (2016). The (ironic) dove effect: Use of acceptance cues for larger body types increases unhealthy behaviors. *Journal of Public Policy & Marketing, 35*, 76–90.

Lippa, R. (1998). The nonverbal display and judgment of extraversion, masculinity, femininity, and gender diagnosticity: A lens model analysis. *Journal of Research in Personality, 32*, 80–107.

Lippa, R. A., & Dietz, J. K. (2000). The relation of gender, personality, and intelligence to judges' accuracy in judging strangers' personality from brief video segments. *Journal of Nonverbal Behavior, 24*, 25–43.

Lippman, L. G. (1980). Toward a social psychology of flatulence: The interpersonal regulation of natural gas. *Psychology: A Quarterly Journal of Human Behavior, 17*, 41–50.

Little, A. C., Penton-Voak, I. S., Burt, D. M., & Perrett, D. I. (2002). Evolution and individual differences in the perception of attractiveness: How cyclic hormonal changes in self-perceived attractiveness influence female preferences for male faces. In G. Rhodes & L. A. Zebrowitz (Eds.), *Facial attractiveness* (pp. 59–90). Westport, CT: Ablex.

Livant, W. P. (1963). Antagonistic functions of verbal pauses: Filled and unfilled pauses in the solution of additions. *Language and Speech, 6*, 1–4.

Llobera, J., Spanlang, B., Ruffini, G., & Slater, M. (2011). Proxemics with multiple dynamic characters in an immersive virtual environment. *ACM Transactions on Applied Perception, 8*, 1–12.

Lodder, G. M. A., Scholte, R. H. J., Goossens, L., Engels, R. C. M. E., & Verhagen, M. (2016). Loneliness and the social monitoring system: Emotion recognition and eye gaze in a real-life conversation. *British Journal of Psychology, 107*, 135–153.

Loehr, D. (2007). Aspects of rhythm in gesture and speech. *Gesture, 7*, 179–214.

Lohmann, A., Arriaga, X. B., & Goodfriend, W. (2003). Close relationships and placemaking: Do objects in a couple's home reflect couplehood? *Personal Relationships, 10,* 437–449.

Lord, T., & Kasprzak, M. (1989). Identification of self through olfaction. *Perceptual and Motor Skills, 69,* 219–224.

Lövgren, K. (2016). Comfortable and leisurely: Old women on style and dress. *Journal of Women & Aging, 28*, 372–385.

Luce, G. G. (1971). *Biological rhythms in human and animal physiology*. New York, NY: Dover.

Lukaszewski, A. W., Simmons, Z. L., Anderson, C., & Roney, J. R. (2016). The role of physical formidability in human social status allocation. *Journal of Personality and Social Psychology, 110*, 385–406.

Lumsden, J., Miles, L. K., Richardson, M. J., Smith, C. A., & Macrae, C. N. (2011). Who syncs? Social motives and interpersonal coordination. *Journal of Experimental Social Psychology, 48*, 746–751.

Lundberg, J. K., & Sheehan, E. P. (1994). The effects of glasses and weight on perceptions of attractiveness and intelligence. *Journal of Social Behavior and Personality, 9*, 753–760.

Lundqvist, L. O. (1995). Facial EMG reactions to facial expressions: A case of facial emotional contagion? *Scandinavian Journal of Psychology, 36*, 130–141.

Lundström, J. N., & Jones-Gotman, M. (2009). Romantic love modulates women's identification of men's body odors. *Hormones and Behavior, 55*, 280–284.

Lundy, B., Field, T., & Pickens, J. (1996). Newborns of mothers with depressive symptoms are less expressive. *Infant Behavior and Development, 19*, 419–124.

Luo, S., & Zhang, G. (2009). What leads to romantic attraction: Similarity, reciprocity, security, or beauty? Evidence from a speed-dating study. *Journal of Personality, 77*, 933–964.

Lyman, S. M., & Scott, M. B. (1967). Territoriality: A neglected sociological dimension. *Social Problems, 15*, 236–249.

Lynch, R. (2010). It's funny because we think it's true: Laughter is augmented by implicit preferences. *Evolution and Human Behavior, 31*, 141–148.

Lyons, M., Marcinkowska, U., Moisey, V., & Harrison, N. (2016). The effects of resource availability and relationship status on women's preference for facial masculinity in men: An eye-tracking study. *Personality and Individual Differences, 95*, 25–28.

Macintyre, S., & Homel, R. (1997). Danger on the dance floor: A study of interior design, crowding, and aggression in nightclubs. In R. Homel (Ed.), *Policing for prevention: Reducing crime, public intoxication, and injury. Crime prevention studies* (pp. 92–113). Monsey, NY: Criminal Justice Press.

Mackinnon, S. P., Jordan, C. H., & Wilson, A. E. (2011). Birds of a feather sit together: Physical similarity predicts seating choice. *Personality and Social Psychology Bulletin, 37*, 879–892.

Maddux, J. E., & Rogers, R. W. (1980). Effects of source expertness, physical attractiveness, and supporting arguments on persuasion: A case of brains over beauty. *Journal of Personality and Social Psychology, 39*, 235–244.

Madey, S. F., Simo, M., Dillworth, D., & Kemper, D. (1996). They do get more attractive at closing time, but only when you are not in a relationship. *Basic and Applied Social Psychology, 18*, 387–393.

Magen, E., & Konasewich, P. A. (2011). Women support providers are more susceptible than men to emotional contagion following brief supportive interactions. *Psychology of Women Quarterly, 35*, 611–616.

Magnusson, A. K. (2006). Nonverbal conversation-regulating signals of the blind adult. *Communication Studies, 57*, 421–433.

Mahl, G. E., & Schulze, G. (1964). Psychological research in the extralinguistic area. In T. Sebeok, A. S. Hayes, & M. C. Bateson (Eds.), *Approaches to semiotics* (pp. 51–124). The Hague, The Netherlands: Mouton.

Mahl, G. F. (1956). Disturbances and silences in the patient's speech in psychotherapy. *Journal of Abnormal and Social Psychology, 53*, 1–15.

Major, B., Carrington, P. I., & Carnevale, P. J. (1984). Physical attractiveness and self-esteem: Attributions for praise from an other-sex evaluator. *Personality and Social Psychology Bulletin, 10*, 43–50.

Major, B., & Heslin, R. (1982). Perceptions of cross-sex and same-sex nonreciprocal touch: It is better to give than to receive. *Journal of Nonverbal Behavior, 6*, 148–162.

Malatesta, C. Z., Jonas, R., & Izard, C. E. (1987). The relation between low facial expressibility during emotional arousal and somatic symptoms. *British Journal of Medical Psychology, 60*, 169–180.

Mammen, M. A., Moore, G. A., Scaramella, L. V., Reiss, D., Ganiban, J. M., Shaw, D. S., . . . Neiderhiser, J. M. (2015). Infant avoidance during a tactile task predicts autism spectrum behaviors in toddlerhood. *Infant Mental Health Journal, 36*, 575–587.

Mandal, M. K., Pandey, R., & Prasad, A. B. (1998). Facial expressions of emotions and schizophrenia: A review. *Schizophrenia Bulletin, 24*, 399–412.

Mansell, W., Clark, D. M., Ehlers, A., & Chen, Y. (1999). Social anxiety and attention away from emotional faces. *Cognition and Emotion, 13*, 673–690.

Mantis, I., Mercuri, M., Stack, D. M., & Field, T. M. (2019). Depressed and non-depressed mothers' touching during social interactions with their infants. *Developmental Cognitive Neuroscience, 35*, 57–65.

Manusov, V., Floyd, K., & Kerssen-Griep, J. (1997). Yours, mine, and ours: Mutual attributions for nonverbal behaviors in couples' interactions. *Communication Research, 24*, 234–260.

Marche, T. A., & Peterson, C. (1993). The development and sex-related use of interruption behavior. *Human Communication Research, 19*, 388–408.

Marcus, D. K., & Lehman, S. J. (2002). Are there sex differences in interpersonal perception at zero acquaintance? A social relations analysis. *Journal of Research in Personality, 36*, 190–207.

Mares, S. H. W., de Leeuw, R. N. H., Scholte, R. H. J., & Engels, R. C. M. E. (2010). Facial attractiveness and self-esteem in adolescence. *Journal of Clinical Child and Adolescent Psychology, 39*, 627–637.

Marier, P., Evans, C. S., & Hauser, M. D. (1992). Animal signals: Motivational, referential, or both? In H. Papousek, U. Jurgens, & M. Papousek (Eds.), *Nonverbal vocal communication: Comparative and developmental approaches* (pp. 66–86). Paris, France: Cambridge University Press.

Maringer, M., Krumhuber, E. G., Fischer, A. H., & Niedenthal, P. M. (2011). Beyond smile dynamics: Mimicry and beliefs in judgments of smiles. *Emotion, 11*, 181–187.

Markel, N. N., Prebor, L. D., & Brandt, J. F. (1972). Biosocial factors in dyadic communication: Sex and speaking intensity. *Journal of Personality and Social Psychology, 23*, 11–13.

Markham, R., & Adams, K. (1992). The effect of type of task on children's identification of facial expressions. *Journal of Nonverbal Behavior, 16*, 21–39.

Markson, L., & Paterson, K. B. (2009). Effects of gaze-aversion on visual-spatial imagination. *British Journal of Psychology, 100*, 553–563.

Marsh, A. A., & Blair, R. J. R. (2008). Deficits in facial affect recognition among antisocial populations: A meta-analysis. *Neuroscience and Biobehavioral Reviews, 32*, 454–465.

Marsh, A. A., Kozak, M. N., & Ambady, N. (2007). Accurate identification of fear facial expressions predicts prosocial behavior. *Emotion, 7*, 239–251.

Marsh, A. A., Rhoads, S. A., & Ryan, R. M. (2018). A multi-semester classroom demonstration yields evidence in support of the facial feedback effect. *Emotion.* 2019 19(8) 1500–1504.

Martin, B. A. S. (2012). A stranger's touch: Effects of accidental interpersonal touch on consumer evaluations and shopping time. *Journal of Consumer Research, 39*, 174–184.

Martin, J., Rychlowska, M., Wood, A., & Niedenthal, P. (2017). Smiles as multipurpose social signals. *Trends in Cognitive Sciences, 21*, 864–877.

Martineau, J., Hernandez, N., Hiebel, L., Roché, L., Metzger, A., & Bonnet-Brilhault, F. (2011). Can pupil size and pupil responses during visual scanning contribute to the diagnosis of autism spectrum disorder in children? *Journal of Psychiatric Research, 45*, 1077–1082.

Martins, Y., Preti, G., Crabtree, C. R., Runyan, T., Vainius, A. A., & Wysocki, C. (2005). Preference for human body odors is influenced by gender and sexual orientation. *Psychological Science, 16*, 694–701.

Masip, J., Garrido, E., & Herrero, C. (2009). Heuristic versus systematic processing of information in detecting deception: Questioning the truth bias. *Psychological Reports, 105*, 11–36.

Maslow, A. H., & Mintz, N. L. (1956). Effects of esthetic surroundings: I. Initial effects of three esthetic conditions upon perceiving "energy" and "well-being" in faces. *Journal of Psychology, 41*, 247–254.

Mason, M. F., Tatkow, E. P., & Macrae, C. N. (2005). The look of love: Gaze shifts and person perception. *Psychological Science, 16*, 236–239.

Mason, M. J., & Mennis, J. (2010). An exploratory study of the effects of neighborhood characteristics on adolescent substance abuse. *Addiction Research and Theory, 18*, 33–50.

Mast, J. F., & McAndrew, F. T. (2011). Violent lyrics in heavy metal music can increase aggression in males. *North American Journal of Psychology, 13*, 63–64.

Mastro, D., & Figueroa-Caballero, A. (2018). Measuring extremes: A quantitative content analysis of prime time TV depictions of body type. *Journal of Broadcasting & Electronic Media, 62*, 320–336.

Masuda, T., Ellsworth, P. C., Mesquita, B., Leu, J., Tanida, S., & Van de Veerdonk, E. (2008). Placing the face in context: Cultural differences in the perception of facial emotion. *Journal of Personality and Social Psychology, 94*, 365–381.

Matarazzo, J. D., Wiens, A. N., & Saslow, G. (1965). Studies in interview speech behavior. In L. Krasner & U. P. Ullman (Eds.), *Research in behavior modification.* New York, NY: Holt, Rinehart & Winston.

Mathews, A., Fox, E., Yiend, J., & Calder, A. (2003). The face of fear: Effects of eye gaze and emotion on visual attention. *Visual Cognition, 10*, 823–835.

Matsumoto, D. (1987). The role of facial response in the experience of emotion: More methodological problems and a meta-analysis. *Journal of Personality and Social Psychology, 52*, 769–774.

Matsumoto, D. (1991). Cultural influences on facial expressions of emotion. *Southern Communication Journal, 56*, 128–137.

Matsumoto, D., & Hwang, H. S. (2010). Judging faces in context. *Social and Personality Psychology Compass, 4*, 393–402.

Matsumoto, D., Keltner, D., Shiota, M. N., O'Sullivan, M., & Frank, M. (2008). Facial expressions of emotion. In M. Lewis, J. M. Haviland-Jones, & L. Feldman Barrett (Eds.), *Handbook of emotions* (3rd ed., pp. 211–234). New York, NY: Guilford.

Matsumoto, D., LeRoux, J., Wilson-Cohn, C., Raroque, J., Kooken, K., Ekman, P., . . . Goh, A. (2000). A new test to measure emotion recognition ability: Matsumoto and Ekman's Japanese and Caucasian Brief Affect Recognition Test (JACBART). *Journal of Nonverbal Behavior, 24*, 179–209.

Matsumoto, D., & Willingham, B. (2006). The thrill of victory and the agony of defeat: Spontaneous expressions of medal winners of the 2004 Athens Olympic Games. *Journal of Personality and Social Psychology, 91*, 568–581.

Matsumoto, D., Yoo, S. H., & Chung, J. (2010). The expression of anger across cultures. In M. Potegal, G. Stemmler, & C. Spielberger (Eds.), *The international handbook of anger: Constituent and concomitant biological, psychological, and social processes* (pp. 125–137). New York, NY: Springer.

Mattes, K., Spezio, M., Kim, H., Todorov, A., Adolphs, R., & Alvarez, R. M. (2010). Predicting election outcomes from positive and negative trait assessments of candidates images. *Political psychology, 31*, 41–58.

Matthews, G., Zeidner, M., & Roberts, R. D. (Eds.). (2002). *Emotional intelligence: Science & myth*. Cambridge, MA: MIT Press.

Matthews, J. L. (2007). Hidden sexism: Facial prominence and its connections to gender and occupational status in popular print media. *Sex Roles, 57*, 515–525.

Mauss, I. B., & Gross, J. J. (2004). Emotion suppression and cardiovascular disease: Is hiding feelings bad for your heart? In I. Nyklíček, L. Temoshok, & A. Vingerhoets (Eds.), *Emotional expression and health: Advances in theory, assessment and clinical applications* (pp. 61–81). New York, NY: Brunner-Routledge.

Maxwell, L. E. (2003). Home and school density effects on elementary school children: The role of spatial density. *Environment and Behavior, 35*, 566–578.

Maxwell, L. E. (2007). Competency in child care settings: The role of the physical environment. *Environment and Behavior, 39*, 229–245.

McArthur, L. Z., & Baron, R. M. (1983). Toward an ecological theory of social perception. *Psychological Review, 90*, 215–238.

McBride, G., King, M. G., & James, J. W. (1965). Social proximity effects on galvanic skin responses in adult humans. *Journal of Psychology, 61*, 153–157.

McCarthy, A., & Lee, K. (2009). Children's knowledge of deceptive gaze cues and its relation to their actual lying behavior. *Journal of Experimental Child Psychology, 103*, 117–134.

McClave, E. (2000). Linguistic functions of head movements in the context of speech. *Journal of Pragmatics, 32*, 855–878.

McClave, E., Kim, H., Tamer, R., & Mileff, M. (2007). Head movements in the context of speech in Arabic, Bulgarian, Korean, and African-American vernacular English. *Gesture, 7*, 343–390.

McClintock, M. K. (1971). Menstrual synchrony and suppression. *Nature, 229*, 244–245.

McClure, E. B. (2000). A meta-analytic review of sex differences in facial expression processing and their development in infants, children, and adolescents. *Psychological Bulletin, 126*, 424–453.

McClure, E. B., & Nowicki, S., Jr. (2001). Associations between social anxiety and nonverbal processing skill in preadolescent boys and girls. *Journal of Nonverbal Behavior, 25*, 3–19.

McCormick, N. B., & Jones, A. I. (1989). Gender differences in nonverbal flirtation. *Journal of Sex Education and Therapy, 15*, 271–282.

McCornack, S. A., & Parks, M. R. (1986). Deception detection and relationship development: The other side of trust. In M. L. McLaughlin (Ed.), *Communication yearbook 9* (pp. 377–389). Newbury Park, CA: SAGE.

McCroskey, J. C., Larson, C. E., & Knapp, M. L. (1971). *An introduction to interpersonal communication*. Engelwood Cliffs, NJ: Prentice Hall.

McCroskey, J. C., & Richmond, V. P. (1992). Increasing teacher influence through inmediacy. In V. P. Richmond & J. C. McCroskey (Eds.), *Power in the classroom: Communication, control, and concern* (pp. 101–119). Hillsdale, NJ: Lawrence Erlbaum.

McDaniel, E., & Andersen, P. A. (1998). International patterns of interpersonal tactile communication: A field study. *Journal of Nonverbal Behavior, 22*, 59–73.

McDowall, J. J. (1978a). Interactional synchrony: A reappraisal. *Journal of Personality and Social Psychology, 36*, 963–975.

McDowall, J. J. (1978b). Microanalysis of filmed movement: The reliability of boundary detection by observers. *Environmental Psychology and Nonverbal Behavior, 3*, 77–88.

McGee, G., & Morrier, M. (2003). Clinical implications of research in nonverbal behavior of children with autism. In P. Philippot, R. S. Feldman, & E. J. Coats (Eds.), *Nonverbal behavior in clinical settings*. Oxford, UK: Oxford University Press.

McGeehan, P. (2005, May 31). For train riders, middle seat isn't the center of attention. *The New York Times*, pp. Al, C11.

McGehee, F. (1937). The reliability of the identification of the human voice. *Journal of General Psychology, 17*, 249–271.

McGloin, R., & Denes, A. (2018). Too hot to trust: Examining the relationship between attractiveness, trustworthiness, and desire to date in online dating. *New Media & Society, 20*, 919–936.

McKelvie, S. J. (1997). Perception of faces with and without spectacles. *Perceptual and Motor Skills, 84*, 497–498.

McIntosh, D. N., Zajonc, R. B., Vig, P. S., & Emerick, S. W. (1997). Facial movement, breathing, temperature, and affect: Implications of the Vascular Theory of Emotional Efference. *Cognition and Emotion, 11*, 171–195.

McLarney-Vesotski, A. R., Bernieri, F., & Rempala, D. (2006). Personality perception: A developmental study. *Journal of Research in Personality, 40*, 652–674.

McMahan, E. A., & Estes, D. (2015). The effect of contact with natural environments on positive and negative affect: A meta-analysis. *Journal of Positive Psychology, 10*, 507–519.

McNeill, D. (1985). So you think gestures are nonverbal? *Psychological Review, 92*, 350–371.

McNeill, D. (1992). *Hand and mind: What gestures reveal about thought*. Chicago, IL: University of Chicago Press.

McNeill, D. (Ed.). (2000). *Language and gesture*. New York, NY: Cambridge University Press.

McNicholas, J., Gilbey, A., Rennie, A., Ahmedzai, S., Dono, J.-A., & Ormerod, E. (2005). Pet ownership and human health: A brief review of evidence and issues. *BMJ: British Medical Journal, 331*, 1252–1254.

Meer, J. (1985, September). The light touch. *Psychology Today, 19*, 60–67.

Mehrabian, A. (1970). A semantic space for nonverbal behavior. *Journal of Consulting and Clinical Psychology, 35*, 248–257.

Mehrabian, A. (1972b). *Nonverbal communication*. Chicago, IL: Aldine-Atherton.

Mehrabian, A. (1976). *Public places and private spaces*. New York, NY: Basic Books.

Mehrabian, A. (1977). Individual differences in stimulus screening and arousability. *Journal of Personality, 45*, 237–250.

Mehrabian, A. (1981). *Silent messages* (2nd ed.). Belmont, CA: Wadsworth.

Mehrabian, A., & Ferris, S. R. (1967). Inference of attitudes from nonverbal communication in two channels. *Journal of Counseling Psychology, 31*, 248–252.

Mehrabian, A., & Wiener, M. (1967). Decoding of inconsistent communication. *Journal of Personality and Social Psychology, 6*, 109–114.

Mehrabian, A., & Williams, M. (1969). Nonverbal concomitants of perceived and intended persuasiveness. *Journal of Personality and Social Psychology, 13*, 37–58.

Meisels, M., & Dosey, M. (1971). Personal space, anger arousal, and psychological defense. *Journal of Personality, 39*, 333–334.

Meissner, K., & Wittmann, M. (2011). Body signals, cardiac awareness, and the perception of time. *Biological Psychology, 86*, 289–297.

Meissner, M., & Philpott, S. B. (1975). The sign language of sawmill workers in British Columbia. *Sign Language Studies, 9*, 291–308.

Mellor, D., Fuller-Tyszkiewicz, M., McCabe, M. P., & Ricciardelli, L. A. (2010). Body image and self-esteem across age and gender: A short-term longitudinal study. *Sex Roles, 63*, 672–681.

Meltzoff, A. N. (1985). Immediate and deferred imitation in fourteen- and twenty-four-month-old infants. *Child Development, 56*, 62–72.

Meltzoff, A. N. (1988a). Infant imitation after a 1-week delay: Long-term memory for novel acts and multiple stimuli. *Developmental Psychology, 24*, 470–476.

Meltzoff, A. N. (1988b). Infant imitation and memory: Nine-month-olds in immediate and deferred tests. *Child Development, 59*, 217–225.

Meltzoff, A. N., & Gopnik, A. (1989). On linking nonverbal imitation, representation, and language learning in the first two years of life. In G. E. Speidel & K. E. Nelson (Eds.), *The many faces of imitation in language learning* (pp. 23–51). New York, NY: Springer-Verlag.

Meltzoff, A. N., & Moore, M. K. (1977). Imitation of facial and manual gestures by human neonates. *Science, 198*, 75–78.

Meltzoff, A. N., & Moore, M. K. (1983a). Newborn infants imitate adult facial gestures. *Child Development, 54*, 702–709.

Meltzoff, A. N., & Moore, M. K. (1983b). The origins of imitation in infancy: Paradigm, phenomena, and theories. In L. P. Lipsitt (Ed.), *Advances in infancy research* (Vol. 2, pp. 265–301). Norwood, NJ: Ablex.

Menculini, G., Verdolini, N., Murru, A., Pacchiarotti, I., Volpe, U., Cervino, A., . . . Tortorella, A. (2018). Depressive mood and circadian rhythms disturbances as outcomes of seasonal affective disorder treatment: A systematic review. *Journal of Affective Disorders, 241*, 608–626.

Merlo, S., & Barbosa, P. A. (2010). Hesitation phenomena: A dynamical perspective. *Cognitive Processing, 11*, 251–261.

Merten, J. (2005). Culture, gender and the recognition of the basic emotions. *Psychologia, 48*, 306–316.

Messaris, P. (1994). *Visual literacy: Image, mind, and reality*. Boulder, CO: Westview Press.

Michael, G., & Willis, F. N. (1968). The development of gestures as a function of social class, education and sex. *Psychological Record, 18*, 515–519.

Michael, G., & Willis, F. N. (1969). The development of gestures in three subcultural groups. *Journal of Social Psychology, 79*, 35–41.

Middlemist, R. D., Knowles, E. S., & Matter, C. F. (1976). Personal space invasions in the lavatory: Suggestive evidence for arousal. *Journal of Personality and Social Psychology, 33*, 541–546.

Miller, G., Tybur, J. M., & Jordan, B. D. (2007). Ovulatory cycle effects on tip earnings by lap dancers: Economic evidence for human estrus? *Evolution and Human Behavior, 28*, 375–381.

Miller, N., Maruyama, G., Beaber, R. J., & Valone, K. (1976). Speed of speech and persuasion. *Journal of Personality and Social Psychology, 34*, 615–624.

Miller, R. E., Caul, W. F., & Mirsky, I. A. (1967). Communication of affects between feral and socially isolated monkeys. *Journal of Personality and Social Psychology, 7*, 231–239.

Miller, S. L., & Maner, J. K. (2010). Scent of a woman: Men's testosterone responses to olfactory ovulation cues. *Psychological Science, 21*, 276–283.

Mills, J. S., Musto, S., Williams, L., & Tiggemann, M. (2018). "Selfie" harm: Effects on mood and body image in young women. *Body Image, 27*, 86–92.

Milmoe, S., Rosenthal, R., Blane, H. T., Chafetz, M. E., & Wolf, I. (1967). The doctor's voice: Postdictor of successful referral of alcoholic patients. *Journal of Abnormal Psychology, 72*, 78–84.

Min, J., & Min, K. (2018). Outdoor light at night and the prevalence of depressive symptoms and suicidal behaviors: A cross-sectional study in a nationally representative sample of Korean adults. *Journal of Affective Disorders, 227*, 199–205.

Mintz, N. L. (1956). Effects of esthetic surroundings: II. Prolonged and repeated experience in a "beautiful" and "ugly" room. *Journal of Psychology, 41*, 459–466.

Mitchell, W. J. (1992). *The reconfigured eye: Visual truth in the post-photographic era*. Cambridge, MA: MIT Press.

Miwa, Y., & Hanyu, K. (2006). The effects of interior design on communication and impressions of a counselor in a counseling room. *Environment and Behavior, 38*, 484–502.

Mobbs, N. (1968). Eye contact in relation to social introversion/extroversion. *British Journal of Social and Clinical Psychology, 7*, 305–306.

Modigliani, A. (1971). Embarrassment, facework and eye-contact: Testing a theory of embarrassment. *Journal of Personality and Social Psychology, 17*, 15–24.

Mogg, K., Garner, M., & Bradley, B. P. (2007). Anxiety and orienting of gaze to angry and fearful faces. *Biological Psychology, 76*, 163–169.

Mogilski, J. K., & Welling, L. L. M. (2018). The relative contribution of jawbone and cheekbone prominence, eyebrow thickness, eye size, and face length to evaluations of facial masculinity and attractiveness: A conjoint data-driven approach. *Frontiers in Psychology, 9,* Article 2428.

Monk, R. (1994). *The employment of corporate nonverbal status communicators in Western organizations.* Unpublished doctoral dissertation, The Fielding Institute, Santa Barbara, CA.

Montagu, M. F. A. (1971). *Touching: The human significance of the skin.* New York, NY: Columbia University Press.

Monteleone, G. T., Phan, K. L., Nusbaum, H. C., Fitzgerald, D., Irick, J.-S., Fienberg, S. E., & Cacioppo, J. T. (2009). Detection of deception using fMRI: Better than chance, but well below perfection. *Social Neuroscience, 4,* 528–538.

Montepare, J. M., Goldstein, S. B., & Clausen, A. (1987). The identification of emotions from gait information. *Journal of Nonverbal Behavior, 11,* 33–41.

Montepare, J. M., & Zebrowitz, L. A. (1993). A cross-cultural comparison of impressions created by age-related variations in gait. *Journal of Nonverbal Behavior, 17,* 55–68.

Montepare, J. M., & Zebrowitz-McArthur, L. (1988). Impressions of people created by age-related qualities of their gaits. *Journal of Personality and Social Psychology, 55,* 547–556.

Moore, M. M. (1985). Nonverbal courtship patterns in women: Content and consequences. *Ethology and Sociobiology, 6,* 237–247.

Moore, M. M. (2010). Human nonverbal courtship behavior—A brief historical review. *Journal of Sex Research, 47,* 171–180.

Morningstar, M., Dirks, M. A., & Huang, S. (2017). Vocal cues underlying youth and adult portrayals of socio-emotional expressions. *Journal of Nonverbal Behavior, 41,* 155–183.

Morningstar, M., Ly, V. Y., Feldman, L., & Dirks, M. A. (2018). Mid-adolescents' and adults' recognition of vocal cues of emotion and social intent: Differences by expression and speaker age. *Journal of Nonverbal Behavior, 42,* 237–251.

Morrel-Samuels, P., & Krauss, R. M. (1992). Word familiarity predicts temporal asynchrony of hand gestures and speech. *Journal of Experimental Psychology: Learning, Memory and Cognition, 18,* 615–662.

Morris, D. (1971). *Intimate behaviour.* New York, NY: Random House.

Morris, D. (1977). *Manwatching: A field guide to human behavior.* New York, NY: Abrams.

Morris, D. (1994). *Bodytalk: The meaning of human gestures.* New York, NY: Crown.

Morris, D., Collett, P., Marsh, P., & O'Shaughnessy, M. (1979). *Gestures: Their origins and distribution.* London, UK: Jonathon Cape.

Morrison, E. R., Bain, H., Pattison, L., & Whyte-Smith, H. (2018). Something in the way she moves: Biological motion, body shape, and attractiveness in women. *Visual Cognition, 26,* 405–411.

Morton, J. B., & Trehub, S. E. (2001). Children's understanding of emotions in speech. *Child Development, 72,* 834–843.

Moszkowski, R. J., Stack, D. M., & Chiarella, S. S. (2009). Infant touch with gaze and affective behaviors during mother–infant still-face interactions: Co-occurrence and functions of touch. *Infant Behavior and Development, 32,* 392–403.

Mottet, T. P. (2000). Interactive television instructors' perceptions of students' nonverbal responsiveness and their influence on distance teaching. *Communication Education, 49,* 146–164.

Moyer, C. A., Rounds, J., & Hannum, J. W. (2004). A meta-analysis of massage therapy research. *Psychological Bulletin, 130,* 3–18.

Mueser, K. T., Penn, D. L., Blanchard, J. J., & Bellack, A. S. (1997). Affect recognition in schizophrenia: A synthesis of findings across three studies. *Psychiatry, 60,* 301–308.

Mui, P. H. C., Goudbeek, M. B., Swerts, M. G. J., & Hovasapian, A. (2017). Children's nonverbal displays of winning and losing: Effects of social and cultural contexts on smiles. *Journal of Nonverbal Behavior, 41,* 67–82.

Mulac, A. (1976). Assessment and application of the revised speech dialect attitudinal scale. *Communication Monographs, 43,* 238–245.

Mulac, A., Lundell, T. L., & Bradac, J. J. (1986). Male/female language differences and attributional consequences in a public speaking situation: Toward an explanation of the gender-linked language effect. *Communication Monographs, 53*, 115–129.

Muñoz, P., & Farkas, C. (2017). Gestural representation of emotions: A comparative study on Chilean and American women. *Journal of Child and Family Studies, 26*, 2166–2174.

Murphy, J. D., Driscoll, D. M., & Kelly, J. R. (1999). Differences in the nonverbal behavior of men who vary in the likelihood to sexually harass. *Journal of Social Behavior and Personality, 14*, 113–128.

Murphy, N. A. (2005). Using thin slices for behavioral coding. Journal of Nonverbal Behavior, *29*, 235–246.

Murphy, N. A., Hall, J. A., & Colvin, C. R. (2003). Accurate intelligence assessments in social interaction: Mediators and gender effects. *Journal of Personality, 71*, 465–493.

Murphy, N. A., Hall, J. A., Ruben, M. A., Frauendorfer, D., Schmid Mast, M., Johnson, K. E., & Nguyen, L. (2019). Predictive validity of thin-slice nonverbal behavior from social interactions. *Personality and Social Psychology Bulletin, 45*, 983–993.

Murphy, N. A., Hall, J. A., Schmid Mast, M., Ruben, M. A., Frauendorfer, D., Blanch-Hartigan, D., . . . Nguyen, L. (2015). Reliability and validity of nonverbal thin slices in social interactions. *Personality and Social Psychology Bulletin, 41*, 199–213.

Murphy, S. T., & Zajonc, R. B. (1993). Affect, cognition, and awareness: Affective priming with optimal and suboptimal stimulus exposures. *Journal of Personality and Social Psychology, 64*, 723–739.

Murray, D. C., & Deabler, H. L. (1957). Colors and mood-tones. *Journal of Applied Psychology, 41*, 279–283.

Myers, P. N., Jr., & Biocca, F. A. (1992). The elastic body image: The effect of television advertising and programming on body image distortions in young women. *Journal of Communication, 42*, 108–133.

Myrick, R., & Marx, B. S. (1968). *An exploratory study of the relationship between high school building design and student learning*. Washington, DC: U.S. Department of Health, Education and Welfare, Office of Education, Bureau of Research.

Nadig, A., Lee, I., Singh, L., Bosshart, K., & Ozonoff, S. (2010). How does the topic of conversation affect verbal exchange and eye gaze? A comparison between typical development and high-functioning autism. *Neuropsychologia, 48*, 2730–2739.

Nair, S., Sagar, M., Sollers, J., III, Consedine, N., & Broadbent, E. (2015). Do slumped and upright postures affect stress responses? A randomized trial. *Health Psychology, 34*, 632–641.

Nannberg, J. C., & Hansen, C. H. (1994). Post-compliance touch: An incentive for task performance. *Journal of Social Psychology, 134*, 301–307.

Napieralski, L. P., Brooks, C. I., & Droney, J. M. (1995). The effect of duration of eye contact on American college students' attributions of state, trait, and text anxiety. *Journal of Social Psychology, 135*, 273–280.

Naumann, L. P., Vazire, S., Rentfrow, P. J., & Gosling, S. D. (2009). Personality judgments based on physical appearance. *Personality and Social Psychology Bulletin, 35*, 1661–1671.

Nelson, C. A. III, Zeanah, C. H., & Fox, N. A. (2019). How early experience shapes human development: The case of psychosocial deprivation. *Neural Plasticity, 2019*, Article ID 1676285.

Nelson, N. L., & Russell, J. A. (2011). Preschoolers' use of dynamic facial, bodily, and vocal cues to emotion. *Journal of Experimental Child Psychology, 110*, 52–61.

Nephew, B. C., & Bridges, R. S. (2011). Effects of chronic social stress during lactation on maternal behavior and growth in rats. *Stress: The International Journal on the Biology of Stress, 14*, 677–684.

Neumann, R., & Strack, F. (2000). "Mood contagion": The automatic transfer of mood between persons. *Journal of Personality and Social Psychology, 79*, 211–223.

Nevid, J. S. (1984). Sex differences in factors of romantic attraction. *Sex Roles, 2*, 401–411.

Nevill, D. (1974). Experimental manipulation of dependency motivation and its effects on eye contact and measures of field dependency. *Journal of Personality and Social Psychology, 29*, 72–79.

Next army chief may be retired general. (2003). *Austin American Statesman* (1970, October 5). *Newsweek*, p. 106.

Nguyen, M. L., Heslin, R., & Nguyen, T. (1976). The meaning of touch: Sex and marital status differences. *Representative Research in Social Psychology, 7*, 13–18.

Nicholls, M. E. R., Wolfgang, B. J., Clode, D., & Lindell, A. K. (2002). The effect of left and right poses on the expression of facial emotion. *Neuropsychologia, 40*, 1662–1665.

Niedenthal, P., Halberstadt, J. B., Margolin, J., & Innes-Ker, A. H. (2000). Emotional state and the detection of change in facial expression of emotion. *European Journal of Social Psychology, 30*, 211–222.

Niedenthal, P. M., Mermillod, M., Maringer, M., & Hess, U. (2010). The simulation of smiles (SIMS) model: Embodied simulation and the meaning of facial expression. *Behavioral and Brain Sciences, 33*, 417–433.

Nielsen, G. (1962). *Studies in self-confrontation.* Copenhagen, Denmark: Munksgaard.

Niit, T., & Valsiner, J. (1977). Recognition of facial expressions: An experimental investigation of Ekman's model. *Tartu Riikliku Ulikooli Toimetised: Trudy po Psikhologii, 429*, 85–107.

Nilsen, W. J., & Vrana, S. R. (1998). Some touching situations: The relationship between gender and contextual variables in cardiovascular responses to human touch. *Annals of Behavioral Medicine, 20*, 270–276.

Nisbett, R. E., & Wilson, T. D. (1977). Telling more than we can know: Verbal reports on mental processes. *Psychological Review, 84*, 231–259.

Nishitani, S., Miyamura, T., Tagawa, M., Sumi, M., Takase, R., Doi, H., . . . Shinohara, K. (2009). The calming effect of a maternal breast milk odor on the human newborn infant. *Neuroscience Research, 63*, 66–71.

Nohara, M. (1992). Sex differences in interruption: An experimental réévaluation. *Journal of Psycholinguistic Research, 21*, 127–146.

Noller, P. (1980). Misunderstandings in marital communication: A study of couples' nonverbal communication. *Journal of Personality and Social Psychology, 39*, 1135–1148.

Noller, P. (1986). Sex differences in nonverbal communication: Advantage lost or supremacy regained? *Australian Journal of Psychology, 38*, 23–32.

Noller, P., & Gallois, C. (1986). Sending emotional messages in marriage: Non-verbal behaviour, sex and communication clarity. *British Journal of Social Psychology, 25*, 287–297.

North, A. C., Hargreaves, D. J., & McKendrick, J. (1997, November 13). In-store music affects product choice. *Nature*, 132.

North, A. C., Shilcock, A., & Hargreaves, D. J. (2003). The effects of musical style on restaurant customers' spending. *Environment and Behavior, 35*, 712–718.

North, A. C., Tarrant, M., & Hargreaves, D. J. (2004). The effects of music on helping behavior: A field study. *Environment and Behavior, 36*, 266–275.

North, M. S., Todorov, A., & Osherson, D. N. (2012). Accuracy of inferring self- and other-preferences from spontaneous facial expressions. *Journal of Nonverbal Behavior, 36*, 227–233.

Notarius, C. I., & Levenson, R. W. (1979). Expressive tendencies and physiological response to stress. *Journal of Personality and Social Psychology, 37*, 1204–1210.

Nowicki, S., Bliwise, N., & Joinson, C. (2019). The association of children's locus of control orientation and emotion recognition abilities at 8 years of age and teachers' ratings of their personal and social difficulties at 10 years. *Journal of Nonverbal Behavior.*

Nowicki, S., Jr., & Carton, E. (1997). The relation of nonverbal processing ability of faces and voices and children's feelings of depression and competence. *Journal of Genetic Psychology, 158*, 357–363.

Nowicki, S., Jr., & Duke, M. P. (1994). Individual differences in the nonverbal communication of affect: The Diagnostic Analysis of Nonverbal Accuracy Scale. *Journal of Nonverbal Behavior, 18*, 9–35.

Nowicki, S., Jr., & Mitchell, J. (1998). Accuracy in identifying affect in child and adult faces and voices and social competence in preschool children. *Genetic, Social, and General Psychology Monographs, 124*, 39–59.

NU's lacrosse team sparks flip-flop flap at White House. (2005, July). *The Associated Press*. Retrieved from http://www.usatoday.com/news/nation/2005-07-19-flip-flops_x.htm

Obayashi, K., Saeki, K., & Kurumatani, N. (2015). Light exposure at night is associated with subclinical carotid atherosclerosis in the general elderly population: The HEIJO-KYO cohort. *Chronobiology International, 32*, 310–317.

O'Connell, D. C., & Kowal, S. (2005). Uh and um revisited: Are they interjections for signaling delay? *Journal of Psycholinguistic Research, 34*, 555–576.

O'Connor, J. J. M., & Feinberg, D. R. (2012). The influence of facial masculinity and voice pitch on jealousy and perceptions of intrasexual rivalry. *Personality and Individual Differences, 52*, 369–373.

Olivola, C. Y., & Todorov, A. (2010). Elected in 100 milliseconds: Appearance-based trait inferences and voting. *Journal of Nonverbal Behavior, 34*, 83–110.

Olson, M. A., & Fazio, R. H. (2007). Discordant evaluations of Blacks affect nonverbal behavior. *Personality and Social Psychology Bulletin, 33*, 1214–1224.

O'Neal, E. C., Brunalt, M. A., Carifio, M. S., Troutwine, R., & Epstein, J. (1980). Effect of insult upon personal space preferences. *Journal of Nonverbal Behavior, 5*, 56–62.

Oren, C., & Shamay-Tsoory, S. G. (2019). Women's fertility cues affect cooperative behavior: Evidence for the role of the human putative chemosignal estratetraenol. *Psychoneuroendocrinology, 101*, 50–59.

Orr, D. B. (1968). Time compressed speech—A perspective. *Journal of Communication, 18*, 288–292.

Oster, H., & Ekman, P. (1978). Facial behavior in child development. *Minnesota Symposium on Child Psychology, 11*, 231–276.

Oster, H., Hegley, D., & Nagel, L. (1992). Adult judgments and fine-grained analysis of infant facial expressions: Testing the validity of a priori coding formulas. *Developmental Psychology, 28*, 1115–1131.

Ostwald, P. F. (1961). The sounds of emotional disturbance. *Archives of General Psychiatry, 5*, 587–592.

Otero, S. C., Weekes, B. S., & Hutton, S. B. (2011). Pupil size changes during recognition memory. *Psychophysiology, 48*, 1346–1353.

Oveis, C., Gruber, J., Keltner, D., Stamper, J. L., & Boyce, W. T. (2009). Smile intensity and warm touch as thin slices of child and family affective style. *Emotion, 9*, 544–548.

Owen, P. M., & Gillentine, J. (2011). Please touch the children: Appropriate touch in the primary classroom. *Early Child Development and Care, 181*, 857–868.

Ozanne, M., Tews, M. J., & Mattila, A. S. (2019). Are tattoos still a taboo? The effect of employee tattoos on customers' service failure perceptions. *International Journal of Contemporary Hospitality Management, 31*, 874–889.

Ozcaliskan, S., & Goldin-Meadow, S. (2010). Sex differences in language first appear in gesture. *Developmental Science, 13*, 752–760.

Park, H. S., Lee, S. A., Yun, D., & Kim, W. (2009). The impact of instructor decision authority and verbal and nonverbal immediacy on Korean student satisfaction in the US and South Korea. *Communication Education, 58*, 189–212.

Park, Y.-M. M., White, A. J., Jackson, C. L., Weinberg, C. R., & Sandler, D. P. (2019). Association of exposure to artificial light at night while sleeping with risk of obesity in women. *JAMA Internal Medicine, 179*, 1061.

Parr, L. A., & Heintz, M. (2009). Facial expression recognition in rhesus monkeys. *Animal Behaviour, 77*, 1507–1513.

Parr, L. A., Waller, B. M., & Heintz, M. (2008). Facial expression categorization by chimpanzees using standardized stimuli. *Emotion, 8*, 216–231.

Partala, T., & Surakka, V. (2003). Pupil size variation as an indication of affective processing. *International Journal of Human–Computer Studies, 59*, 185–198.

Pascalis, O., & Kelly, D. J. (2009). The origins of face processing in humans: Phylogeny and ontogeny. *Perspectives on Psychological Science, 4*, 200–209.

Patrick, C. J., Craig, K. D., & Prkachin, K. M. (1986). Observer judgments of acute pain: Facial action determinants. *Journal of Personality and Social Psychology, 50*, 1291–1298.

Patterson, M. L. (1968). Spatial factors in social interaction. *Human Relations, 21*, 351–361.

Patterson, M. L. (1976). An arousal model of interpersonal intimacy. *Psychological Review, 83*, 235–245.

Patterson, M. L. (1983). *Nonverbal behavior: A functional perspective*. New York, NY: Springer-Verlag.

Patterson, M. L. (1984). Nonverbal exchange: Past, present, and future. *Journal of Nonverbal Behavior, 8*, 350–359.

Patterson, M. L. (1995). A parallel process model of nonverbal communication. *Journal of Nonverbal Behavior, 19*, 3–29.

Patterson, M. L. (2019). A systems model of dyadic nonverbal interaction. *Journal of Nonverbal Behavior*. Advance online publication.

Patterson, M. L., Churchill, M. E., Burger, G. K., & Powell, J. L. (1992). Verbal and nonverbal modality effects on impressions of political candidates: Analysis from the 1984 presidential debates. *Communication Monographs, 59,* 231–242.

Patterson, M. L., Iizuka, Y., Tubbs, M. E., Ansel, J., Tsutsumi, M., & Anson, J. (2007). Passing encounters East and West: Comparing Japanese and American pedestrian interactions. *Journal of Nonverbal Behavior, 31,* 155–166.

Patterson, M. L., Powell, J. L., & Lenihan, M. G. (1986). Touch, compliance, and interpersonal affect. *Journal of Nonverbal Behavior, 10,* 41–50.

Patterson, M. L., Webb, A., & Schwartz, W. (2002). Passing encounters: Patterns of recognition and avoidance in pedestrians. *Basic and Applied Social Psychology, 24,* 57–66.

Pattison, J. E. (1973). Effects of touch on self-exploration and the therapeutic relationship. *Journal of Consulting and Clinical Psychology, 40,* 170–175.

Paulick, J., Deisenhofer, A.-K., Ramseyer, F., Tschacher, W., Boyle, K., Rubel, J., & Lutz, W. (2018). Nonverbal synchrony: A new approach to better understand psychotherapeutic processes and drop-out. *Journal of Psychotherapy Integration, 28,* 367–384.

Paulmann, S., & Pell, M. D. (2011). Is there an advantage for recognizing multi-modal emotional stimuli? *Motivation and Emotion, 35,* 192–201.

Paulmann, S., Titone, D., & Pell, M. D. (2012). How emotional prosody guides your way: Evidence from eye movements. *Speech Communication, 54,* 92–107.

Pawlowski, B., Dunbar, R. I. M., & Lipowicz, A. (2000). Tall men have more reproductive success. *Nature, 403,* 156.

Pazhoohi, F., Silva, C., Lamas, J., Mouta, S., Santos, J., & Arantes, J. (2018). The effect of height and shoulder-to-hip ratio on interpersonal space in virtual environment. *Psychological Research.*

Pear, T. H. (1931). *Voice and personality.* London, UK: Chapman & Hall.

Pearl, R. L. (2018). Weight bias and stigma: Public health implications and structural solutions. *Social Issues and Policy Review, 12,* 146–182.

Pearson, N. O. (2006, January 22). In Venezuela, beauty's become a national craze, big business. *Austin American Statesman,* p. A20.

Pedersen, N. L., Plomin, R., McClearn, G. E., & Friberg, L. (1988). Neuroticism, extraversion, and related traits in adult twins reared apart and reared together. *Journal of Personality and Social Psychology, 55,* 950–957.

Pell, M. D., Jaywant, A., Monetta, L., & Kotz, S. A. (2011). Emotional speech processing: Disentangling the effects of prosody and semantic cues. *Cognition and Emotion, 25,* 834–853.

Pelligrini, R. F., & Schauss, A. G. (1980). Muscle strength as a function of exposure to hue differences in visual stimuli: An experiential test of Kinesoid theory. *Journal of Orthomolecular Psychiatry, 2,* 144–147.

Perry, A., Nichiporuk, N., & Knight, R. T. (2016). Where does one stand: A biological account of preferred interpersonal distance. *Social Cognitive and Affective Neuroscience, 11,* 317–326.

Pennebaker, J. W., Dyer, M. A., Caulkins, R. S., Litowitz, D. L., Ackerman, P. L., Anderson, D. B., & McGraw, K. M. (1979). Don't the girls' get prettier at closing time: A country and western application to psychology. *Personality and Social Psychology Bulletin, 5,* 122–125.

Penton-Voak, I. S., Pound, N., Little, A. C., & Perrett, D. I. (2006). Personality judgments from natural and composite facial images: More evidence for a "kernel of truth" in social perception. *Social Cognition, 24,* 607–640.

Peperkoorn, L. S., Roberts, S. C., & Pollet, T. V. (2016). Revisiting the red effect on attractiveness and sexual receptivity: No effect of the color red on human mate preferences. *Evolutionary Psychology, 14,* Article 1474704916673841.

Perdue, V. P., & Connor, J. M. (1978). Patterns of touching between preschool children and male and female teachers. *Child Development, 49,* 1258–1262.

Perez, J. E., & Riggio, R. E. (2003). Nonverbal social skills and psychopathology. In P. Philippot, R. S. Feldman, & E. J. Coats (Eds.), *Nonverbal behavior in clinical settings* (pp. 17–44). Oxford, UK: Oxford University Press.

Perper, T. (1985). *Sex signals: The biology of love.* Philadelphia, PA: ISI Press.

Perper, T., & Weis, D. L. (1987). Proceptive and rejective strategies of U.S. and Canadian college women. *Journal of Sex Research, 23,* 455–480.

Pertschuk, M., Trisdorfer, A., & Allison, P. D. (1994). Men's bodies—the survey. *Psychology Today, 27*, 35–36, 39, 72.

Peskin, S. H. (1980). Nonverbal communication in the courtroom. *Trial Diplomacy Journal, 3* (Spring), 8–9; (Summer), 6–7, 55.

Peterson, R. T. (2005). An examination of the relative effectiveness of training in nonverbal communication: Personal selling implications. *Journal of Marketing Education, 27*, 143–150.

Pettigrew, T. F., & Tropp, L. R. (2006). A meta-analytic test of intergroup contact theory. *Journal of Personality and Social Psychology, 90*, 751–783.

Petty, R. E., Cacioppo, J. T., & Schumann, D. (1983). Central and peripheral routes to advertising effectiveness: The moderating role of involvement. *Journal of Consumer Research, 10*, 135–146.

Pfungst, O. (1965). *Clever Hans (the horse of Mr. Von Osten): A contribution to experimental, animal and human psychology* (C. L. Rahn, Trans.). New York, NY: Holt, Rinehart & Winston. (Original work published 1911)

Phelps, F. G., Doherty-Sneddon, G., & Warnock, H. (2006). Helping children think: Gaze aversion and teaching. *British Journal of Development Psychology, 24*, 577–588.

Philippot, P., Feldman, R. S., & McGee, G. (1992). Nonverbal behavioral skills in an educational context: Typical and atypical populations. In R. S. Feldman (Ed.), *Applications of nonverbal behavioral theories and research* (pp. 191–213). Hillsdale, NJ: Lawrence Erlbaum.

Philippot, P., Kornreich, C., & Blairy, S. (2003). Nonverbal deficits and interpersonal regulation in alcoholics. In P. Philippot, R. S. Feldman, & E. J. Coats (Eds.), *Nonverbal behavior in clinical settings* (Chapter 9). Oxford, UK: Oxford University Press.

Phillips, R. D., Wagner, S. H., Fells, C. A., & Lynch, M. (1990). Do infants recognize emotion in facial expressions? Categorical and "metaphorical" evidence. *Infant Behavior and Development, 13*, 71–84.

Phinney, M. (2006, October 11). Mason County Jail is in the pink, and the offenders are offended. *Austin American Statesman*, p. B8.

Pickett, C. L., Gardner, W. L., & Knowles, M. (2004). Getting a cue: The need to belong and enhanced sensitivity to social cues. *Personality and Social Psychology Bulletin, 30*, 1095–1107.

Pika, S., Liebal, K., Call, J., & Tomasello, M. (2005). The gestural communication of apes. *Gesture, 5*, 41–56.

Pika, S., & Mitani, J. (2006). Referential-gestural communication in wild chimpanzees (*Pan troglodytes*). *Current Biology, 16*, R191–R192.

Pika, S., Nicoladis, E., & Marentette, P. (2009). How to order a beer: Cultural differences in the use of conventional gestures for numbers. *Journal of Cross-Cultural Psychology, 40*, 70–80.

Pine, K. J., Bird, H., & Kirk, E. (2007). The effects of prohibiting gestures on children's lexical retrievalability. *Developmental Science, 10*, 747–754.

Pine, K. J., Gurney, D. J., & Fletcher, B. (2010). The semantic specificity hypothesis: When gestures do not depend upon the presence of a listener. *Journal of Nonverbal Behavior, 34*, 169–178.

Ping, R., & Goldin-Meadow, S. (2010). Gesturing saves cognitive resources when talking about nonpresent objects. *Cognitive Science: A Multidisciplinary Journal, 34*, 602–619.

Pinheiro, A. P., Galdo-Álvarez, S., Rauber, A., Sampaio, A., Niznikiewicz, M., & Gonçalves, O. F. (2011). Abnormal processing of emotional prosody in Williams syndrome: An event-related potentials study. *Research in Developmental Disabilities, 32*, 133–147.

Pinker, S. (1994). *The language instinct*. New York, NY: HarperCollins.

Pitcairn, T. K., & Eibl-Eibesfeldt, I. (1976). Concerning the evolution of nonverbal communication in man. In M. E. Hahn & E. C. Simmel (Eds.), *Communicative behavior and evolution* (pp. 81–113). New York, NY: Academic Press.

Pitner, R. O., Yu, M., & Brown, E. (2012). Making neighborhoods safer: Examining predictors of residents' concerns about neighborhood safety. *Journal of Environmental Psychology, 32*, 43–49.

Pittam, J., & Scherer, K. S. (1993). Vocal expression and communication of emotion. In M. Lewis & J. M. Haviland (Eds.), *Handbook of emotions* (pp. 185–197). New York, NY: Guilford.

Pitterman, H., & Nowicki, S., Jr. (2004). A test of the ability to identify emotion in human standing and sitting postures: The Diagnostic Analysis of Nonverbal Accuracy–2 posture test (DANVA2-POS). *Genetic, Social, and General Psychology Monographs, 130*, 146–162.

Place, S. S., Todd, P. M., Penke, L., & Asendorpf, J. B. (2009). The ability to judge the romantic interest of others. *Psychological Science, 20*, 22–26.

Plank, S. B., Bradshaw, C. P., & Young, H. (2009). An application of "broken-windows" and related theories to the study of disorder, fear, and collective efficacy in schools. *American Journal of Education, 115*, 227–247.

Platt, B., Kamboj, S., Morgan, C. J. A., & Curran, H. V. (2010). Processing dynamic facial affect in frequent cannabis-users: Evidence of deficits in the speed of identifying emotional expressions. *Drug and Alcohol Dependence, 112*, 27–32.

Plomin, R. (1989). Environment and genes: Determinants of behavior. *American Psychologist, 44*, 105–111.

Poggi, I. (2002). Symbolic gestures: The case of the Italian gestionary. *Gesture, 2*, 71–98.

Pönkänen, L. M., Alhoniemi, A., Leppänen, J. M., & Hietanen, J. K. (2011). Does it make a difference if I have an eye contact with you or with your picture? An ERP study. *Social Cognitive and Affective Neuroscience, 6*, 486–494.

Pollak, S. D., & Sinha, P. (2002). Effects of early experience on children's recognition of facial displays of emotion. *Developmental Psychology, 38*, 784–791.

Porter, N., & Geis, F. (1981). Women and nonverbal leadership cues: When seeing is not believing. In C. Mayo & N. M. Henley (Eds.), *Gender and nonverbal behavior* (pp. 39–61). New York, NY: Springer-Verlag.

Porter, R. H., Cernoch, J. M., & Balogh, R. D. (1985). Odor signatures and kin recognition. *Physiology and Behavior, 34*, 445–448.

Porter, R. H., Cernoch, J. M., & McLaughlin, F. J. (1983). Maternal recognition of neonates through olfactory cues. *Physiology and Behavior, 30*, 151–154.

Porter, R. H., & Moore, J. D. (1981). Human kin recognition by olfactory cues. *Physiology and Behavior, 27*, 493–495.

Poulin-Dubois, D., Hastings, P. D., Chiarella, S. S., Geangu, E., Hauf, P., Ruel, A., & Johnson, A. (2018). The eyes know it: Toddlers' visual scanning of sad faces is predicted by their theory of mind skills. *PLoS ONE, 13*, Article e0208524.

Poutvaara, P., Jordahl, H., & Berggren, N. (2009). Faces of politicians: Babyfacedness predicts inferredcompetence but not electoral success. *Journal of Experimental Social Psychology, 45*, 1132–1135.

Poyatos, F. (1993). *Paralanguage: A linguistic and interdisciplinary approach to interactive speech and sound.* Amsterdam, The Netherlands: Benjamins.

Preti, G., Wysocki, C. J., Barnhart, K. T., Sondheimer, S. J., & Leyden, J. J. (2003). Male axillary extracts contain hormones that affect pulsatile secretion of luteinizing hormone and mood in women recipients. *Biology of Reproduction, 68*, 2107–2113.

Preuschoft, S. (1995). *"Laughter" and "smiling" in macaques: An evolutionary perspective.* Utrecht, The Netherlands: University of Utrecht.

Prkachin, K. M. (1992). The consistency of facial expressions of pain: A comparison across modalities. *Pain, 51*, 297–306.

Prkachin, K. M., & Craig, K. D. (1995). Expressing pain: The communication and interpretation of facial pain signals. *Journal of Nonverbal Behavior, 19*, 191–205.

Proposed smirking ban raises eyebrows. (2003, April 9). *Reuters.*

Pryor, B., & Buchanan, R. W. (1984). The effects of a defendant's demeanor on juror perceptions of credibility and guilt. *Journal of Communication, 34*, 92–99.

Puccinelli, N. M., Motyka, S., & Grewal, D. (2010). Can you trust a customer's expression? Insight into nonverbal communication in the retail context. *Psychology and Marketing, 27*, 964–988.

Putnam, L. L., & McCallister, L. (1980). Situational effects of task and gender on nonverbal display. In D. Nimmo (Ed.), *Communication yearbook 4* (pp. 679–697). New Brunswick, NJ: Transaction.

Putnam, P., Hermans, E., & van Honk, J. (2006). Anxiety meets fear in perception of dynamic expressive gaze. *Emotion, 6*, 94–102.

Quednow, B. B. (2017). Social cognition and interaction in stimulant use disorders. *Current Opinion in Behavioral Sciences, 13*, 55–62.

Quesque, F., Behrens, F., & Kret, M. E. (2019). Pupils say more than a thousand words: Pupil size reflects how observed actions are interpreted. *Cognition, 190*, 93–98.

Raine, J., Pisanski, K., & Reby, D. (2017). Tennis grunts communicate acoustic cues to sex and contest outcome. *Animal Behaviour, 130*, 47–55.

Ramseyer, F., & Tschacher, W. (2011). Nonverbal synchrony in psychotherapy: Coordinated body movement reflects relationship quality and outcome. *Journal of Consulting and Clinical Psychology, 79*, 284–295.

Rantala, M. J., Pölkki, M., & Rantala, L. M. (2010). Preference for human male body hair changes across the menstrual cycle and menopause. *Behavioral Ecology, 21*, 419–423.

Raskin, A. (2003, December). A face any business can trust. *Business 2.0, 58*, 60.

Rauscher, F. H., Krauss, R. M., & Chen, Y. (1996). Gesture, speech, and lexical access: The role of lexical movements in speech production. *Psychological Science, 7*, 226–231.

Ray, G. B., & Floyd, K. (2006). Nonverbal expressions of liking and disliking in initial interaction: Encoding and decoding perspectives. *Southern Communication Journal, 71*, 45–65.

Re, D. E., & Rule, N. O. (2016). The big man has a big mouth: Mouth width correlates with perceived leadership ability and actual leadership performance. *Journal of Experimental Social Psychology, 63*, 86–93.

Redican, W. K. (1982). An evolutionary perspective on human facial displays. In P. Ekman (Ed.), *Emotion in the human face* (2nd ed., pp. 212–280). Cambridge, MA: Cambridge University Press.

Reed, L. I., Sayette, M. A., & Cohn, J. F. (2007). Impact of depression on response to comedy: A dynamic facial coding analysis. *Journal of Abnormal Psychology, 116*, 804–809.

Regan, P. C., Jerry, D., Narvaez, M., & Johnson, D. (1999). Public displays of affection among Asian and Latino heterosexual couples. *Psychological Reports, 84*, 1201–1202.

Reich, A. R., Moll, K. L., & Curtis, J. F. (1976). Effects of selected vocal disguises upon spectrographic speaker identification. *Journal of the Acoustical Society of America, 60*, 919–925.

Reingen, P. H., & Kernan, J. B. (1993). Social perception and interpersonal influence: Some consequences of the physical attractiveness stereotype in a personal selling setting. *Journal of Consumer Psychology, 2*, 25–38.

Reis, H. T., Maniaci, M. R., Caprariello, P. A., Eastwick, P. W., & Finkel, E. J. (2011). Familiarity does indeed promote attraction in live interaction. *Journal of Personality and Social Psychology, 101*, 557–570.

Reis, H. T., Nezlek, J., & Wheeler, L. (1980). Physical attractiveness in social interaction. *Journal of Personality and Social Psychology, 38*, 604–617.

Reis, H. T., Wheeler, L., Spiegel, N., Kernis, M. H., Nezlek, J., & Perri, M. (1982). Physical attractiveness in social interaction: II. Why does appearance affect social experience? *Journal of Personality and Social Psychology, 43*, 979–996.

Reiss, M., & Rosenfeld, P. (1980). Seating preferences as nonverbal communication: A self-presentational analysis. *Journal of Applied Communication Research, 8*, 22–30.

Remland, M. S., Jones, T. S., & and Brinkman, H. (1991). Proxemic and haptic behavior in three European countries. *Journal of Nonverbal Behavior, IS*, 215–232.

Renninger, L. A., Wade, T. J., & Grammer, K. (2004). Getting that female glance: Patterns and consequences of male nonverbal behavior in courtship contexts. *Evolution and Human Behavior, 25*, 416–431.

Rhodes, G. (2006). The evolutionary psychology of facial beauty. *Annual Review of Psychology, 57*, 199–226.

Rhodes, G., Harwood, K., Yoshikawa, S., Nishitani, M., & McLean, I. (2002). The attractiveness of average faces: Cross-cultural evidence and possible biological basis. In G. Rhodes & L. A. Zebrowitz (Eds.), *Facial attractiveness* (pp. 35–58). Westport, CT: Ablex.

Rhodes, G., Lee, K., Palermo, R., Weiss, M., Yoshikawa, S., Clissa, P., . . . Jeffery, L. (2005). Attractiveness of own-race, other-race, and mixed-race faces. *Perception, 34*, 319–340.

Ricciardelli, R. (2011). Masculinity, consumerism, and appearance: A look at men's hair. *Canadian Review of Sociology, 48*, 181–201.

Richards, J. M., & Gross, J. J. (1999). Composure at any cost? The cognitive consequences of emotional suppression. *Personality and Social Psychology Bulletin, 25*, 1033–1044.

Richeson, J. A., & Shelton, J. N. (2005). Thin slices of racial bias. *Journal of Nonverbal Behavior, 29*, 75–86.

Riding, D., Lonsdale, D., & Brown, B. (2006). The effects of average fundamental frequency and variance of fundamental frequency on male vocal attractiveness to women. *Journal of Nonverbal Behavior, 30*, 55–61.

Rieger, G., Savin-Williams, R. C., Chivers, M. L., & Bailey, J. M. (2016). Sexual arousal and masculinity-femininity of women. *Journal of Personality and Social Psychology, 111*, 265–283.

Riggio, H. R., & Riggio, R. E. (2002). Emotional expressiveness, extraversion, and neuroticism: A meta-analysis. *Journal of Nonverbal Behavior, 26*, 195–218.

Riggio, H. R., & Riggio, R. E. (2010). Appearance-based trait inferences and voting: Evolutionary roots andimplications for leadership. *Journal of Nonverbal Behavior, 34*, 119–125.

Riggio, R. E. (1986). Assessment of basic social skills. *Journal of Personality and Social Psychology, 51*, 649–660.

Riggio, R. E. (2005). Business applications of nonverbal communication. In R. E. Riggio & R. S. Feldman (Eds.), *Applications of nonverbal communication* (pp. 119–138). Mahwah, NJ: Lawrence Erlbaum.

Riggio, R. E., & Friedman, H. S. (1986). Impression formation: The role of expressive behavior. *Journal of Personality and Social Psychology, 50*, 421–427.

Riggio, R. E., Widaman, K. F., & Friedman, H. S. (1985). Actual and perceived emotional sending and personality correlates. *Journal of Nonverbal Behavior, 9*, 69–83.

Riggio, R. E., Widaman, K. F., Tucker, J. S., & Salinas, C. (1991). Beauty is more than skin deep: Components of attractiveness. *Basic and Applied Psychology, 12*, 423–139.

Rimé, B. (1982). The elimination of visible behaviour from social interactions: Effects on verbal, nonverbal and interpersonal behaviour. *European Journal of Social Psychology, 12*, 113–129.

Rimer, S. (1989, November 18). Doors closing as mood on homeless sours. *New York Times*, p. A1.

Rinck, C. M., Willis, F. N., & Dean, L. M. (1980). Interpersonal touch among residents of homes for the elderly. *Journal of Communication, 30*, 44–47.

Rinn, W. E. (1984). The neuropsychology of facial expression: A review of the neurological and psychological mechanisms for producing facial expressions. *Psychological Bulletin, 95*, 52–77.

Riordan, M. A., & Kreuz, R. J. (2010). Emotion encoding and interpretation in computer-mediated communication: Reasons for use. *Computers in Human Behavior, 26*, 1667–1673.

Ritter, K., & Henry, D. (1990). The 1980 Reagan-Carter presidential debate. In R. V. Friedenberg (Ed.), *Rhetorical studies of national political debates: 1960–1988* (pp. 69–93). New York, NY: Praeger.

Roach, K. D. (1997). Effects of graduate teaching assistant attire on student learning, misbehaviors, and ratings of instruction. *Communication Quarterly, 45*, 125–141.

Roberts, A., & Good, E. (2010). Media images and female body dissatisfaction: The moderating effects of the Five-Factor traits. *Eating Behaviors, 11*, 211–216.

Roberts, S. C., Owen, R. C., & Havlicek, J. (2010). Distinguishing between perceiver and wearer effects in clothing color-associated attributions. *Evolutionary Psychology, 8*, 350–364.

Roberts, J. V., & Herman, C. P. (1986). The psychology of height: An empirical review. In C. P. Herman, M. P. Zanna, & E. T. Higgins (Eds.), *Physical appearance, stigma, and social behavior: The Ontario symposium* (Vol. 3, pp. 113–140). Hillsdale, NJ: Lawrence Erlbaum.

Robinson, J. D. (2006). Nonverbal communication and physician–patient interaction: Review and new directions. In V. Manusov & M. L. Patterson (Eds.), *The SAGE handbook of nonverbal communication* (pp. 437–459). Thousand Oaks, CA: SAGE.

Robinson, K. J., Hoplock, L. B., & Cameron, J. J. (2015). When in doubt, reach out: Touch is a covert but effective mode of soliciting and providing social support. *Social Psychological and Personality Science, 6*, 831–839.

Robinson, L. F., & Reis, H. T. (1989). The effects of interruption, gender, and status on interpersonal perceptions. *Journal of Nonverbal Behavior, 13*, 141–153.

Robinson, W. P. (1996). *Deceit, delusion, and detection*. Thousand Oaks, CA: SAGE.

Robson, S. K. A., Kimes, S. E., Becker, F. D., & Evans, G. W. (2011). Consumers' responses to table spacing in restaurants. *Cornell Hospitality Quarterly, 52*, 253–264.

Rochester, S. R. (1973). The significance of pauses in spontaneous speech. *Journal of Psycholinguistic Research, 2*, 51–81.

Rodriguez, J. L., Plax, T. G., & Kearney, P. (1996). Clarifying the relationship between teacher nonverbal immediacy and student cognitive learning: Affective learning as the central causal mediator. *Communication Education, 45*, 293–305.

Roese, N. J., Olson, J. M., Borenstein, M. N., Martin, A., & Shores, A. L. (1992). Same-sex touching behavior: The moderating role of homophobic attitudes. *Journal of Nonverbal Behavior, 16*, 249–259.

Rogers, P. L., Scherer, K. R., & Rosenthal, R. (1971). Content filtering human speech: A simple electronic system. *Behavior Research Methods and Instrumentation, 3*, 16–18.

Rogers, W. T. (1978). The contribution of kinesic illustrators toward the comprehension of verbal behavior within utterances. *Human Communication Research, 5*, 54–62.

Rohles, R. H., Jr. (1980). Temperature or temperament: A psychologist looks at thermal comfort. *ASHRAE Transactions, 86*(1), 541–551.

Rohner, J. (2002). The time-course of visual threat processing: High traitanxious individuals eventually avert their gaze from angry faces. *Cognition & Emotion, 16*, 837–844.

Romantshik, O., Porter, R. H., Tillmann, V., & Varendi, H. (2007). Preliminary evidence of a sensitive period for olfactory learning by human newborns. *Acta Paediatrica, 96*, 372–376.

Roney, J. R., Hanson, K. N., Durante, K. M., & Maestripieri, D. (2006). Reading men's faces: Women's mate attractiveness judgments track men's testosterone and interest in infants. *Proceedings of the Royal Society B, 273*, 2169–2175.

Rosa, E., & Mazur, A. (1979). Incipient status in small groups. *Social Forces, 58*, 18–37.

Roschk, H., Loureiro, S. M. C., & Breitsohl, J. (2017). Calibrating 30 years of experimental research: A meta-analysis of the atmospheric effects of music, scent, and color. *Journal of Retailing, 93*, 228–240.

Rose, S. M., & Zand, D. (2002). Lesbian dating and courtship from young adulthood to midlife. *Journal of Lesbian Studies, 6*, 85–109.

Rosenberg, A., & Kagan, J. (1987). Iris pigmentation and behavioral inhibition. *Developmental Psychobiology, 20*, 377–392.

Rosenbaum, R. (1995, January 15). The posture photo scandal. *New York Times Magazine*, pp. 26–31, 40, 46, 55–56.

Rosenfeld, H. (1965). Effect of approval-seeking induction on interpersonal proximity. *Psychological Reports, 17*, 120–122.

Rosenfeld, H. (1966). Instrumental and affiliative functions of facial and gestural expressions. *Journal of Personality and Social Psychology, 4*, 65–72.

Rosenfeld, H. M. (1981). Whither interactional synchrony? In K. Bloom (Ed.), *Prospective issues in infant research*. Hillsdale, NJ: Lawrence Erlbaum.

Rosenfeld, H. M. (1987). Conversational control functions of nonverbal behavior. In A. W. Siegman & S. Feldstein (Eds.), *Nonverbal behavior and communication* (2nd ed., pp. 563–601). Hillsdale, NJ: Lawrence Erlbaum.

Rosenfeld, H. M., & Hancks, M. (1980). The nonverbal context of verbal listener responses. In M. R. Key (Ed.), *The relationship of verbal and nonverbal communication* (pp. 193–206). The Hague, The Netherlands: Mouton.

Rosenfeld, L. B., Kartus, S., & Ray, C. (1976). Body accessibility revisited. *Journal of Communication, 26*, 27–30.

Rosenthal, N. E. (1993). *Winter blues*. New York, NY: Guilford.

Rosenthal, R. (1966). *Experimenter effects in behavioral research*. New York, NY: Appleton-Century-Crofts.

Rosenthal, R. (1985). Nonverbal cues in the mediation of interpersonal expectancy effects. In A. W. Siegman & S. Feldstein (Eds.), *Multichannel integration of nonverbal behavior* (pp. 105–128). Hillsdale, NJ: Lawrence Erlbaum.

Rosenthal, R., Hall, J. A., DiMatteo, M. R., Rogers, P. L., & Archer, D. (1979). *Sensitivity to nonverbal communication: The PONS test*. Baltimore, MD: Johns Hopkins University Press.

Rosenthal, R., & Jacobson, L. (1968). *Pygmalion in the classroom*. New York, NY: Holt, Rinehart & Winston.

Rosenthal, R., Vanicelli, M., & Blanck, P. (1984). Speaking to and about patients: Predicting therapists' tone of voice. *Journal of Consulting and Clinical Psychology, 52*, 679–686.

Rosip, J. C., & Hall, J. A. (2004). Knowledge of nonverbal cues, gender, and nonverbal decoding accuracy. *Journal of Nonverbal Behavior, 28*, 267–286.

Rosse, R. B., Kendrick, K., Wyatt, R. J., Isaac, A., & Deutsch, S. I. (1994). Gaze discrimination in patients with schizophrenia: Preliminary report. *American Journal of Psychiatry, 151,* 919–921.

Roter, D. L., Hall, J. A., Blanch-Hartigan, D., Larson, S., & Frankel, R. M. (2011). Slicing it thin: New methods for brief sampling analysis using RIAS-coded medical dialogue. *Patient Education and Counseling, 82,* 410–419.

Rotton, J., & Cohn, E. G. (2003). Global warming and U.S. crime rates: An application of activity theory. *Environment and Behavior, 35,* 802–825.

Rotton, J., & Kelly, I. W. (1985). Much ado about the full moon: A meta-analysis of lunar-lunacy research. *Psychological Bulletin, 97,* 286–306.

Rousseau, P. V., Matton, F., Lecuyer, R., & Lahaye, W. (2017). The Moro reaction: More than a reflex, a ritualized behavior of nonverbal communication. *Infant Behavior & Development, 46,* 169–177.

Rowland-Morin, P. A., Burchard, K. W., Garb, J. L., & Coe, N. P. (1991). Influence of effective communication by surgery students on their oral examination scores. *Academic Medicine, 66,* 169–171.

Ruback, R. B., & Kohli, N. (2005). Territoriality at the Magh Mela: The effects of organizational factors and intruder characteristics. *Environment and Behavior, 37,* 178–200.

Ruben, M. A., Blanch-Hartigan, D., & Hall, J. A. (2017). Nonverbal communication as a pain reliever: The impact of physician supportive nonverbal behavior on experimentally induced pain. *Health Communication, 32,* 970–976.

Ruben, M. A., & Hall, J. A. (2016). Healthcare providers' nonverbal behavior can lead patients to show their pain more accurately: An analogue study. *Journal of Nonverbal Behavior, 40,* 221–234.

Rubin, Z. (1970). The measurement of romantic love. *Journal of Personality and Social Psychology, 16,* 265–273.

Ruffman, T., Henry, J. D., Livingstone, V., & Phillips, L. H. (2008). A meta-analytic review of emotion recognition and aging: Implications for neuropsychological models of aging. *Neuroscience and Biobehavioral Reviews, 32,* 863–881.

Ruiz-Belda, M., Fernβndez-Dols, J., Carrera, P., & Barchard, K. (2003). Spontaneous facial expressions of happy bowlers and soccer fans. *Cognition and Emotion, 17,* 315–326.

Rule, N. O., & Ambady, N. (2008a). Brief exposures: Male sexual orientation is accurately perceived at 50 ms. *Journal of Experimental Social Psychology, 44,* 1100–1105.

Rule, N. O., & Ambady, N. (2008b). The face of success: Inferences from chief executive officers' appearance predict company profits. *Psychological Science, 19,* 109–111.

Rumbough, T. (2001). The development and maintenance of interpersonal relationships through computer-mediated communication. *Communication Research Reports, 18,* 223–229.

Russart, K. L. G., & Nelson, R. J. (2018). Light at night as an environmental endocrine disruptor. *Physiology & Behavior, 190,* 82–89.

Russell, M. J. (1976). Human olfactory communication. *Nature, 260,* 520–522.

Russell, J. A. (1994). Is there universal recognition of emotion from facial expression? A review of the cross-cultural studies. *Psychological Bulletin, 115,* 102–141.

Russell, J. A., Bachorowski, J., & Fernβndez-Dols, J. (2003). Facial and vocal expressions of emotion. *Annual Review of Psychology, 54,* 329–349.

Russo, M., Islam, G., & Koyuncu, B. (2017). Non-native accents and stigma: How self-fulfilling prophesies can affect career outcomes. *Human Resource Management Review, 27,* 507–520.

Russo, N. (1967). Connotation of seating arrangement. *Cornell Journal of Social Relations, 2,* 37–44.

Rutherford, M. D., Baron-Cohen, S., & Wheelwright, S. (2002). Reading the mind in the voice: A study with normal adults and adults with Asperger syndrome and high functioning autism. *Journal of Autism & Developmental Disorders, 32,* 189–194.

Rutter, D. R. (1984). *Looking and seeing: The role of visual communication in social interaction.* New York, NY: Wiley.

Rutter, D. R., Stephenson, G. M., & White, P. A. (1978). The timing of looks in dyadic conversation. *British Journal of Social and Clinical Psychology, 17,* 17–21.

Rutter, L. A., Norton, D. J., Brown, B. S., & Brown, T. A. (2019). A double-blind placebo controlled study of intranasal oxytocin's effect on emotion recognition and visual attention in outpatients with emotional disorders. *Cognitive Therapy and Research, 43,* 523–534.

Ryan, S., & Mendel, L. L. (2010). Acoustics in physical education settings: The learning roadblock. *Physical Education and Sport Pedagogy, 15*, 71–83.

Sachs, M. E., Habibi, A., Damasio, A., & Kaplan, J. T. (2018). Decoding the neural signatures of emotions expressed through sound. *NeuroImage, 174*, 1–10.

Sagoe, D., Pallesen, S., & Andreassen, C. S. (2017). Prevalence and correlates of tattooing in Norway: A large-scale cross-sectional study. *Scandinavian Journal of Psychology, 58*, 562–570.

Saitz, R. L., & Cervenka, E. J. (1972). *Handbook of gestures: Colombia and the United States*. The Hague, The Netherlands: Mouton.

Sakkalou, E., & Gattis, M. (2012). Infants infer intentions from prosody. *Cognitive Development, 27*, 1–16.

Saks, M. J. (1976). Social scientists can't rig juries. *Psychology Today, 9*, 48–50, 55–57.

Salovey, P., & Mayer, J. D. (1989). Emotional intelligence. *Imagination, Cognition, and Personality, 9*, 185–211.

Sandalla, E. (1987). Identity symbolism in housing. *Environment and Behavior, 19*, 569–587.

Sandberg, D. E., Bukowski, W. M., Fung, C. M., & Noll, R. B. (2004). Height and social adjustment: Are extremes a cause for concern and action? *Pediatrics, 114*, 744–750.

Sato, W., & Yoshikawa, S. (2007). Spontaneous facial mimicry in response to dynamic facial expressions. *Cognition, 104*, 1–18.

Sauter, D. A. (2017). The nonverbal communication of positive emotions: An emotion family approach. *Emotion Review, 9*, 222–234.

Sauter, D. A., Eisner, F., Calder, A. J., & Scott, S. K. (2010). Perceptual cues in nonverbal vocal expressions of emotion. *The Quarterly Journal of Experimental Psychology, 63*, 2251–2272.

Sauter, D. A., Eisner, F., Ekman, P., & Scott, S. K. (2010). Cross-cultural recognition of basic emotions through nonverbal emotional vocalizations. *PNAS Proceedings of the National Academy of Sciences of the United States of America, 107*, 2408–2412.

Sauter, D. A., & Scott, S. K. (2007). More than one kind of happiness: Can we recognize vocal expressions of different positive states? *Motivation and Emotion, 31*, 192–199.

Savic, I., Berglund, H., & Lindström, P. (2005). Brain response to putative pheromones in homosexual men. *Proceedings of the National Academy of Sciences, 102*, 7356–7361.

Saxton, T. K., DeBruine, L. M., Jones, B. C., Little, A. C., & Roberts, S. C. (2011). A longitudinal study of adolescents' judgments of the attractiveness of facial symmetry, averageness and sexual dimorphism. *Journal of Evolutionary Psychology, 9*, 43–55.

Schachter, S., Christenfeld, N., Ravina, B., & Bilous, F. (1991). Speech disfluency and the structure of knowledge. *Journal of Personality and Social Psychology, 60*, 362–367.

Schachter, S., Rauscher, F., Christenfeld, N., & Crone, K. T. (1994). The vocabularies of academia. *Psychological Science, 5*, 37–41.

Schafer, J. A., Varano, S. P., Jarvis, J. P., & Cancino, J. M. (2010). Bad moon on the rise? Lunar cycles and incidents of crime. *Journal of Criminal Justice, 38*, 359–367.

Scharinger, M., Monahan, P. J., & Idsardi, W. J. (2011). You had me at "Hello": Rapid extraction of dialect information from spoken words. *NeuroImage, 56*, 2329–2338.

Schauss, A. G. (1985). The physiological effect of color on the suppression of human aggression: Research on Baker-Miller Pink. *International Journal of Biosocial Research, 7*, 55–64.

Scheflen, A. E. (1965). Quasi-courtship behavior in psychotherapy. *Psychiatry, 28*, 245–257.

Scheflen, A. E. (1972). *Body language and the social order*. Englewood Cliffs, NJ: Prentice-Hall.

Scheflen, A. (1973). *Communicational structure: Analysis of a psychotherapy transaction*. Bloomington: University of Indiana Press.

Schelde, T., & Hertz, M. (1994). Ethology and psychotherapy. *Ethology and Sociobiology, 15*, 383–392.

Scherer, K. R. (1982). Methods of research on vocal communication: Paradigms and parameters. In K. R. Scherer & P. Ekman (Eds.), *Handbook of methods in nonverbal behavior research* (pp. 136–198). Cambridge, UK: Cambridge University Press.

Scherer, K. R. (1986). Vocal affect expression: A review and a model for future research. *Psychological Bulletin, 99*, 143–165.

Scherer, K. R. (2003). Vocal communication of emotion: A review of research paradigms. *Speech Communication, 40*, 227–256.

Scherer, K. R., Banse, R., & Wallbott, H. G. (2001). Emotion inferences from vocal expression correlate across languages and cultures. *Journal of Cross-Cultural Psychology, 32*, 76–92.

Scherer, K. R., Banse, R., Wallbott, H. G., & Goldbeck, T. (1991). Vocal cues in emotion encoding and decoding. *Motivation and Emotion, 15*, 123–148.

Scherer, K. R., Trznadel, S., Fantini, B., & Sundberg, J. (2017). Recognizing emotions in the singing voice. *Psychomusicology, 27*, 244–255.

Scherer, S. E. (1974). Proxemic behavior of primary school children as a function of their socioeconomic class and subculture. *Journal of Personality and Social Psychology, 29*, 800–805.

Schiavenato, M., Butler-O'Hara, M., & Scovanner, P. (2011). Exploring the association between pain intensity and facial display in term newborns. *Pain Research and Management, 16*, 10–12.

Schick, V. R., Calabrese, S. K., Rima, B. N., & Zucker, A. N. (2010). Genital appearance dissatisfaction: Implications for women's genital image self-consciousness, sexual esteem, sexual satisfaction, and sexual risk. *Psychology of Women Quarterly, 34*, 394–404.

Schiefenhövel, W. (1997). Universals in interpersonal interactions. In U. Segerstråle & P. Molnβr (Eds.), *Nonverbal communication: Where nature meets culture* (pp. 61–85). Mahwah, NJ: Lawrence Erlbaum.

Schiffrin, D. (1974). Handwork as ceremony: The case of the handshake. *Semiotica, 12*, 189–202.

Schiffenbauer, A. (1974). Effect of observer's emotional state on judgments of the emotional state of others. *Journal of Personality and Social Psychology, 30*, 31–35.

Schlegel, K., Fontaine, J. R. J., & Scherer, K. R. (2019). The nomological network of emotion recognition ability: Evidence from the Geneva Emotion Recognition Test. *European Journal of Psychological Assessment, 35*, 352–363.

Schlegel, K., Palese, T., Mast, M. S., Rammsayer, T. H., Hall, J. A., & Murphy, N. A. (2019). A meta-analysis of the relationship between emotion recognition ability and intelligence. *Cognition and Emotion*.

Schlegel, K., & Scherer, K. R. (2017). The nomological network of emotion knowledge and emotion understanding in adults: Evidence from two new performance-based tests. *Cognition and Emotion*.

Schlegel, K., Vicaria, I., Isaacowitz, D., & Hall, J. A. (2017). Effectiveness of a short audiovisual emotion recognition training program in adults. *Motivation and Emotion, 41*, 646–660.

Schlenker, B. R., Phillips, S. T., Boniecki, K. A., & Schlenker, D. R. (1995). Championship pressures: Choking or triumphing in one's own territory? *Journal of Personality and Social Psychology, 68*, 632–643.

Schmid Mast, M. (2002). Dominance as expressed and inferred through speaking time: A meta-analysis. *Human Communication Research, 28*, 420–450.

Schmid Mast, M. (2007). On the importance of nonverbal communication in the physician-patient interaction. *Patient Education and Counseling, 67*, 315–318.

Schmid Mast, M. (2010). Interpersonal behavior and social perception in a hierarchy: The interpersonal power and behavior model. *European Review of Social Psychology, 21*, 1–33.

Schmid Mast, M., & Hall, J. A. (2004). Who is the boss and who is not? Accuracy of judging status. *Journal of Nonverbal Behavior, 28*, 145–165.

Schneider, F. W., Lesko, W. A., & Garrett, W. A. (1980). Helping behavior in hot, comfortable, and cold temperatures: A field study. *Environment and Behavior, 12*, 231–240.

Schoenherr, D., Paulick, J., Strauss, B. M., Deisenhofer, A.-K., Schwartz, B., Rubel, J. A., . . . Altmann, U. (2019). Nonverbal synchrony predicts premature termination of psychotherapy for social anxiety disorder. *Psychotherapy*.

Schroeder, J., Fishbach, A., Schein, C., & Gray, K. (2017). Functional intimacy: Needing—But not wanting—The touch of a stranger. *Journal of Personality and Social Psychology, 113*, 910–924.

Schutte, J. G., & Light, N. M. (1978). The relative importance of proximity and status for friendship choices in social hierarchies. *Social Psychology, 41*, 260–264.

Schwartz, B., & Barsky, S. (1977). The home advantage. *Social Forces, 55*, 641–661.

Schwarz, N., & Kurz, E. (1989). What's in a picture? The impact of face-ism on trait attribution. *European Journal of Social Psychology, 19*, 311–316.

Searcy, M., Duck, S., & Blanck, P. (2005). Communication in the courtroom and the "appearance" of justice. In R. E. Riggio & R. S. Feldman (Eds.), *Applications of nonverbal communication* (pp. 41–61). Mahwah, NJ: Lawrence Erlbaum.

Secord, P. F., Dukes, W. F., & Bevan, W. (1959). Personalities in faces: I. An experiment in social perceiving. *Genetic Psychology Monographs, 49*, 231–279.

Segal, N. L. (1999). *Entwined lives: Twins and what they tell us about human behavior*. New York, NY: Dutton.

Seger, C. R., Smith, E. R., Percy, E. J., & Conrey, F. R. (2014). Reach out and reduce prejudice: The impact of interpersonal touch on intergroup liking. *Basic and Applied Social Psychology, 36*, 51–58.

Sehlstedt, I., Ignell, H., Backlund Wasling, H., Ackerley, R., Olausson, H., & Croy, I. (2016). Gentle touch perception across the lifespan. *Psychology and Aging, 31*, 176–184.

Seiter, J. S., & Dunn, D. (2000). Beauty and believability in sexual harassment cases: Does physical attractiveness affect perceptions of veracity and the likelihood of being harassed? *Communication Research Reports, 17*, 203–209.

Sell, A., Cosmides, L., & Tooby, J. (2014). The human anger face evolved to enhance cues of strength. *Evolution and Human Behavior, 35*, 425–429.

Seltzer, L. J., Prososki, A. R., Ziegler, T. E., & Pollak, S. D. (2012). Instant messages vs. speech: Hormones and why we still need to hear each other. *Evolution and Human Behavior, 33*, 42–45.

Senju, A., Yaguchi, K., Tojo, Y., & Hasegawa, T. (2003). Eye contact does not facilitate detection in children with autism. *Cognition, 89*, B43–B51.

Shackelford, T. K., & Larsen, R. J. (1999). Facial attractiveness and physical health. *Evolution and Human Behavior, 20*, 71–76.

Shannon, M. L., & Stark, C. P. (2003). The influence of physical appearance on personnel selection. *Social Behavior and Personality, 31*, 613–624.

Shariff, A. F., & Tracy, J. L. (2009). Knowing who's boss: Implicit perceptions of status from the nonverbal expression of pride. *Emotion, 9*, 631–639.

Shaw, J., & Wafler, M. (2016). Tipping the scales: How defendant body type may result in eyewitness biases. *Psychiatry, Psychology and Law, 23*, 676–683.

Shawn, T. (1954). *Every little movement: A book about Francois Delsarte*. Pittsfield, MA: Eagle.

Shepherd, S. V., & Platt, M. L. (2008). Spontaneous social orienting and gaze following in ringtailed lemurs (*Lemur catta*). *Animal Cognition, 11*, 13–20.

Sherzer, J. (1974). Verbal and nonverbal deixis: The pointed-lip gesture among the San Bias Cuna. *Language in Society, 2*, 117–131.

Shimoda, K., Argyle, M., & Ricci-Bitti, P. (1978). The intercultural recognition of expressions by three national racial groups: English, Italian, and Japanese. *European Journal of Social Psychology, 8*, 169–179.

Shin, J.-e., Suh, E. M., Li, N. P., Eo, K., Chong, S. C., & Tsai, M.-H. (2019). Darling, get closer to me: Spatial proximity amplifies interpersonal liking. *Personality and Social Psychology Bulletin, 45*, 300–309.

Shuter, R. (1976). Proxemics and tactility in Latin America. *Journal of Communication, 26*, 46–52.

Shuter, R. (1977). A field study of non-verbal communication in Germany, Italy and the United States. *Communication Monographs, 44*, 298–305.

Shreve, E. G., Harrigan, J. A., Kues, J. R., & Kagas, D. K. (1988). Nonverbal expressions of anxiety in physician–patient interactions. *Psychiatry, 51*, 378–384.

Siegman, A. W. (1987). The telltale voice: Nonverbal messages of verbal communication. In A. W. Siegman & S. Feldstein (Eds.), *Nonverbal behavior and communication* (2nd ed., pp. 351–433). Hillsdale, NJ: Lawrence Erlbaum.

Simmons, L. W., Peters, M., & Rhodes, G. (2011). Low-pitched voices are perceived as masculine and attractive but do they predict semen quality in men? *PLoS ONE, 6*(12), e29271. doi:10.1371/journal.pone.0029271

Simpson, D. M., Weissbecker, I., & Sephton, S. E. (2011). Extreme weather-related events: Implications for mental health and well-being. In I. Weissbecker (Ed.), *Climate change and well-being: Global challenges and opportunities* (pp. 57–78). New York, NY: Springer.

Simpson, J. A., Gangestad, S. W., & Nations, C. (1996). Sociosexuality and relationship initiation: An ethological perspective of nonverbal behavior. In G. J. O. Fletcher & J. Fitness (Eds.), *Knowledge structures in close relationships* (pp. 121–146). Mahwah, NJ: Lawrence Erlbaum.

Singh, D. (1993). Adaptive significance of female physical attractiveness: Role of waist-to-hip ratio. *Journal of Personality and Social Psychology, 65*, 293–307.

Singh, D. (1995). Female judgment of male attractiveness and desirability for relationships: Role of waist-to-hip ratio and financial status. *Journal of Personality and Social Psychology, 69*, 1089–1101.

Skinner, M., & Mullen, B. (1991). Facial asymmetry in emotional expression: A meta-analysis of research. *British Journal of Social Psychology, 30*, 113–124.

Slater, A., Halliwell, E., Jarman, H., & Gaskin, E. (2017). More than just child's play? An experimental investigation of the impact of an appearance-focused Internet game on body image and career aspirations of young girls. *Journal of Youth and Adolescence, 46*, 2047–2059.

Slater, A., Von der Schulennurg, C., Brown, E., Badenoch, M., Butterworth, G., Parsons, S., & Samuels, C. (1998). Newborn infants prefer attractive faces. *Infant Behavior and Development, 21*, 345–354.

Smith, D. E., Willis, F. N., & Gier, J. A. (1980). Success and interpersonal touch in a competitive setting. *Journal of Nonverbal Behavior, 5*, 26–34.

Smith, E., Bell, P. A., & Fusco, M. E. (1986). The influence of color and demand characteristics on muscle strength and affective ratings of the environment. *Journal of General Psychology, 113*, 289–297.

Smith, E. W. L., Clance, P. R., & Imes, S. (1998). *Touch in psychotherapy: Theory, research, and practice.* New York, NY: Guilford.

Smith, J. L., Ickes, W., Hall, J. A., & Hodges, S. D. (Eds.). (2014). *Managing interpersonal sensitivity: Knowing when—and when not—to understand others.* New York, NY: Novinka/Nova Science.

Smith, S. M., & Shaffer, D. R. (1991). Celerity and cajolery: Rapid speech may promote or inhibit persuasion through its impact on message elaboration. *Personality and Social Psychology Bulletin, 17*, 663–669.

Smith, W. J., Chase, J., & Lieblich, A. K. (1974). Tongue showing: A facial display of humans and other primate species. *Semiotica, 11*, 201–246.

Smolak, L., & Murnen, S. K. (2011). Gender, self-objectification and pubic hair removal. *Sex Roles, 65*, 506–517.

Smythe, M.-J., & Hess, J. A. (2005). Are student self-reports a valid method for measuring teacher nonverbal immediacy? *Communication Education, 54*, 170–179.

Snodgrass, S. E. (1992). Further effects of role versus gender on interpersonal sensitivity. *Journal of Personality and Social Psychology, 62*, 154–158.

Snodgrass, S. E., Hecht, M. A., & Ploutz-Snyder, R. (1998). Interpersonal sensitivity: Expressivity or perceptivity? *Journal of Personality and Social Psychology, 74*, 238–249.

Snow, C. E., & Ferguson, C. A. (Eds.). (1977). *Talking to children.* Cambridge, UK: Cambridge University Press.

Snowden, R. J., McKinnon, A., Fitoussi, J., & Gray, N. S. (2019). Pupillary responses to static images of men and women: A possible measure of sexual interest? *Journal of Sex Research, 56*, 74–84.

Snyder, M. (1974). Self-monitoring of expressive behavior. *Journal of Personality and Social Psychology, 30*, 526–537.

Snyder, R. A., & Sutker, L. W. (1977). The measurement of the construct of dominance and its relation to nonverbal behavior. *Journal of Psychology, 97*, 227–230.

So, W. C. (2010). Cross-cultural transfer in gesture frequency in Chinese–English bilinguals. *Language and Cognitive Processes, 25*, 1335–1353.

Solomon, H., Solomon, L. Z., Arnone, M. M., Maur, B. J., Reda, R. M., & Roth, E. O. (1981). Anonymity and helping. *Journal of Social Psychology, 113*, 37–43.

Sommer, R. (1961). Leadership and group geography. *Sociometry, 24*, 99–110.

Sommer, R. (1967). Classroom ecology. *Journal of Applied Behavioral Science, 3*, 487–503.

Sommer, R. (1969). *Personal space.* Englewood Cliffs, NJ: Prentice-Hall.

Sommer, R. (1974). *Tight spaces: Hard architecture and how to humanize it.* Englewood Cliffs, NJ: Prentice Hall.

Song, H., Kim, J., & Luo, W. (2016). Teacher–student relationship in online classes: A role of teacher self-disclosure. *Computers in Human Behavior, 54*, 436–443.

Sorokowska, A., Sorokowski, P., & Havlíček, J. (2016). Body odor–based personality judgments: The effect of fragranced cosmetics. *Frontiers in Psychology, 7*, Article 530.

Sorokowska, A., Sorokowski, P., Hilpert, P., Cantarero, K., Frackowiak, T., Ahmadi, K., . . . Pierce, J. D., Jr. (2017). Preferred interpersonal distances: A global comparison. *Journal of Cross-Cultural Psychology, 48*, 577–592.

Soussignan, R. (2002). Duchenne smile, emotional experience, and autonomie reactivity: A test of the facial feedback hypothesis. *Emotion, 2*, 52–74.

Sparhawk, C. M. (1978). Contrastive identificational features of Persian gesture. *Semiotica, 24*, 49–86.

Spezio, M. L., Adolphs, R., Hurley, R. S. E., & Piven, J. (2007). Abnormal use of facial information in high-functioning autism. *Journal of Autism and Developmental Disorders, 37*, 929–939.

Spitz, H. H. (1997). *Nonconscious movements: From mystical messages to facilitated communication*. Mahwah, NJ: Lawrence Erlbaum.

Stack, D. M., & Jean, A. D. L. (2011). Communicating through touch: Touching during parent–infant interactions. In M. J. Hertenstein & S. J. Weiss (Eds.), *The handbook of touch: Neuroscience, behavioral, and health perspectives* (pp. 273–298). New York, NY: Springer.

Staffieri, J. R. (1972). Body build and behavioral expectancies in young females. *Developmental Psychology, 6*, 125–127.

Stafford, L. D., Fernandes, M., & Agobiani, E. (2012). Effects of noise and distraction on alcohol perception. *Food Quality and Preference, 24*, 218–224.

Stamp, G., & Knapp, M. L. (1990). The construct of intent in interpersonal communication. *Quarterly Journal of Speech, 76*, 282–299.

Stass, J. W., & Willis, F. N., Jr. (1967). Eye contact, pupil dilation, and personal preference. *Psychonomic Science, 7*, 375–376.

Steidtmann, D., Ingram, R. E., & Siegle, G. J. (2010). Pupil response to negative emotional information in individuals at risk for depression. *Cognition and Emotion, 24*, 480–496.

Stenberg, C. R., Campos, J. J., & Emde, R. N. (1983). The facial expression of anger in seven-month-old infants. *Child Development, 54*, 178–184.

Stephen, I. D., & McKeegan, A. M. (2010). Lip colour affects perceived sex typicality and attractiveness of human faces. *Perception, 39*, 1104–1110.

Stepper, S., & Strack, F. (1993). Proprioceptive determinants of emotional and nonemotional feelings. *Journal of Personality and Social Psychology, 64*, 211–220.

Stern, K., & McClintock, M. K. (1998). Regulation of ovulation by human pheromones. *Nature, 392*, 177–179.

Sternberg, R., & Kostic, A. (Eds.). (2020). *Social intelligence and nonverbal communication*. London, UK: Palgrave Macmillan.

Stier, D. S., & Hall, J. A. (1984). Gender differences in touch: An empirical and theoretical review. *Journal of Personality and Social Psychology, 47*, 440–459.

Stiff, J. B., Hale, J. L., Garlick, R., & Rogan, R. G. (1990). Effect of cue incongruence and social normative influences on individual judgments of honesty and deceit. *Southern Communication Journal, 55*, 206–229.

Storck, J., & Sproull, L. (1995). Through a glass darkly: What do people learn in videoconferencing? *Human Communication Research, 22*, 197–219.

Stouffer, S. A. (1940). Intervening opportunities: A theory relating mobility and distance. *American Sociological Review, 5*, 845–867.

Strack, F., Martin, L. L., & Stepper, S. (1988). Inhibiting and facilitating conditions of the human smile: A nonobtrusive test of the facial feedback hypothesis. *Journal of Personality and Social Psychology, 54*, 768–777.

Strack, F., & Neumann, R. (2000). Furrowing the brow may undermine perceived fame: The role of facial feedback in judgments of celebrity. *Personality and Social Psychology Bulletin, 26*, 762–768.

Strauss, N. (2005). *The game: Penetrating the secret society of pickup artists*. New York, NY: Regan Books.

Streeck, J. (1993). Gesture as communication: I. Its coordination with gaze and speech. *Communication Monographs, 60*, 275–299.

Streeck, J., & Knapp, M. L. (1992). The interaction of visual and verbal features in human communication. In F. Poyatos (Ed.), *Advances in nonverbal communication* (pp. 3–23). Amsterdam, The Netherlands: John Benjamins.

Street, R. L., Jr., Brady, R. M., & Lee, R. (1984). Evaluative responses to communicators: The effects of speech rate, sex, and interaction context. *Western Journal of Speech Communication, 48*, 14–27.

Streeter, S. A., & McBurney, D. H. (2003). Waist–hip ratio and attractiveness: New evidence and a critique of a "critical test." *Evolution and Human Behavior, 24*, 88–98.

Sturman, E. D. (2011). Involuntary subordination and its relation to personality, mood, and submissive behavior. *Psychological Assessment: A Journal of Consulting and Clinical Psychology*. doi:10.1037/a0021499

Surakka, V., & Hietanen, J. K. (1998). Facial and emotional reactions to Duchenne and non-Duchenne smiles. *International Journal of Psychophysiology, 29*, 23–33.

Surguladze, S. A., Young, A. W., Senior, C., Brébion, G., Travis, M. J., & Phillips, M. L. (2004). Recognition accuracy and response bias to happy and sad facial expressions in patients with major depression. *Neuropsychology, 18*, 212–218.

Swami, V., Einon, D., & Furnham, A. (2006). The leg-to-body ratio as a human aesthetic criterion. *Body Image, 3*, 317–323.

Swami, V., Tran, U. S., Kuhlmann, T., Stieger, S., Gaughan, H., & Voracek, M. (2016). More similar than different: Tattooed adults are only slightly more impulsive and willing to take risks than non-tattooed adults. *Personality and Individual Differences, 88*, 40–44.

Szalma, J. L., & Hancock, P. A. (2011). Noise effects on human performance: A meta-analytic synthesis. *Psychological Bulletin, 137*, 682–707.

Tähkämö, L., Partonen, T., & Pesonen, A.-K. (2019). Systematic review of light exposure impact on human circadian rhythm. *Chronobiology International, 36*, 151–170.

Takeuchi, M. S., Miyaoka, H., Tomoda, A., Suzuki, M., Liu, Q., & Kitamur, T. (2010). The effect of interpersonal touch during childhood on adult attachment and depression: A neglected area of family and developmental psychology? *Journal of Child and Family Studies, 19*, 109–117.

Tassinary, L. G., & Hansen, K. A. (1998). A critical test of the waist-to-hip ratio hypothesis of female physical attractiveness. *Psychological Science, 9*, 150–155.

Taylor, C. R., Mafael, A., Raithel, S., Anthony, C. M., & Stewart, D. W. (2019). Portrayals of minorities and women in super bowl advertising. *Journal of Consumer Affairs*.

Taylor, L. S., Fiore, A. T., Mendelsohn, G. A., & Cheshire, C. (2011). "Out of my league": A real-world test of the matching hypothesis. *Personality and Social Psychology Bulletin, 37*, 942–954.

Taylor, S. E., & Fiske, S. T. (1975). Point of view and perceptions of causality. *Journal of Personality and Social Psychology, 32*, 429–445.

Tcherkassof, A., Bollon, T., Dubois, M., Pansu, P., & Adam, J. (2007). Facial expressions of emotions: A methodological contribution to the study of spontaneous and dynamic emotional faces. *European Journal of Social Psychology, 37*, 1325–1345.

Teen shot while learning to sign. (2000). *Austin American Statesman*.

Termine, N. T., & Izard, C. E. (1988). Infants' responses to their mothers' expressions of joy and sadness. *Developmental Psychology, 24*, 223–229.

Thayer, S. (1969). The effect of interpersonal looking duration on dominance judgments. *Journal of Social Psychology, 79*, 285–286.

Thirer, J., & Rampey, M. S. (1979). Effects of abusive spectators' behavior on performance of home and visiting intercollegiate basketball teams. *Perceptual and Motor Skills, 48*, 1047–1053.

Thompson, E. H., & Hampton, J. A. (2011). The effect of relationship status on communicating emotions through touch. *Cognition and Emotion, 25*, 295–306.

Thompson, T. L. (1982). Gaze toward and avoidance of the handicapped: A field experiment. *Journal of Nonverbal Behavior, 6*, 188–196.

Thorpe, W. H. (1972). The comparison of vocal communication in animals and man. In R. Hinde (Ed.), *Non-verbal communication* (pp. 27–47). Cambridge, MA: Cambridge University Press.

Tickle-Degnen, L., & Rosenthal, R. (1990). The nature of rapport and its nonverbal correlates. *Psychological Inquiry, 1*, 285–293.

Tidd, K., & Lockard, J. (1978). Monetary significance of the affiliative smile: A case of reciprocal altruism. *Bulletin of the Psychonomic Society, 11*, 344–346.

Tiemens, R. K. (1978). Television's portrayal of the 1976 presidential debates: An analysis of visual content. *Communication Monographs, 45*, 362–370.

Tiggemann, M. (2015). Considerations of positive body image across various social identities and special populations. *Body Image, 14*, 168–176.

Tiggemann, M., & Lacey, C. (2009). Shopping for clothes: Body satisfaction, appearance investment, and functions of clothing among female shoppers. *Body Image, 6*, 285–291.

Tiitinen, S., & Ruusuvuori, J. (2012). Engaging parents through gaze: Speaker selection in three-party interactions in maternity clinics. *Patient Education and Counseling, 89*, 38–43.

Timmermann, M., Jeung, H., Schmitt, R., Boll, S., Freitag, C. M., Bertsch, K., & Herpertz, S. C. (2017). Oxytocin improves facial emotion recognition in young adults with antisocial personality disorder. *Psychoneuroendocrinology, 85*, 158–164.

Timming, A. R., Nickson, D., Re, D., & Perrett, D. (2017). What do you think of my ink? Assessing the effects of body art on employment chances. *Human Resource Management, 56*, 133–149.

Tiwari, V., Hashmi, M. F., Keskar, A., & Shivaprakash, N. C. (2019). Speaker identification using multi-modal i-vector approach for varying length speech in voice interactive systems. *Cognitive Systems Research, 57*, 66–77.

Todorov, A., Mandisodza, A. N., Goren, A., & Hall, C. C. (2005). Inferences of competence from faces predict election outcomes. *Science, 308*, 1623–1626.

Toma, C. L., & Hancock, J. T. (2010). Looks and lies: The role of physical attractiveness in online dating self-presentation and deception. *Communication Research, 37*, 335–351.

Toosi, N. R., Babbitt, L. G., Ambady, N., & Sommers, S. R. (2012). Dyadic interracial interactions: A meta-analysis. *Psychological Bulletin, 138*, 1–27.

Touchy topic: What to do when a handshake isn't enough? (2000, February 16). *Boston Globe*, pp. A1, A20.

Tourangeau, R., & Ellsworth, P. C. (1979). The role of facial response in the experience of emotion. *Journal of Personality and Social Psychology, 37*, 1519–1531.

Tracy, J. L., & Robins, R. W. (2004). Show your pride: Evidence for a discrete emotion expression. *Psychological Science, 15*, 194–197.

Tracy, J. L., & Robins, R. W. (2007). The prototypical pride expression: Development of a nonverbal behavior coding system. *Emotion, 7*, 789–801.

Tracy, J. L., & Robins, R. W. (2008). The nonverbal expression of pride: Evidence for cross-cultural recognition. *Journal of Personality and Social Psychology, 94*, 516–530.

Trager, G. L. (1958). Paralanguage: A first approximation. *Studies in Linguistics, 13*, 1–12.

Trainor, L. J., Austin, C. M., & Desjardins, R. N. (2000). Is infant-directed speech prosody a result of the vocal expression of emotion? *Psychological Science, 11*, 188–195.

Trapnell, P. D., & Paulhus, D. L. (2012). Agentic and communal values: Their scope and measurement. *Journal of Personality Assessment, 94*, 39–52.

Trees, A. R. (2000). Nonverbal communication and the support process: Interactional sensitivity in interactions between mothers and young adult children. *Communication Monographs, 67*, 239–261.

Triandis, H. C. (1994). Theoretical and methodological approaches to the study of collectivism and individualism. In U. Kim, H. Triandis, C. Kâgitçibasi, S.-C. Choi, & G. Yoon (Eds.), *Individualism and collectivism: Theory, methods, and applications* (pp. 41–51). Thousand Oaks, CA: SAGE.

Triberti, S., Durosini, I., Aschieri, F., Villani, D., & Riva, G. (2017). Changing avatars, changing selves? The influence of social and contextual expectations on digital rendition of identity. *Cyberpsychology, Behavior, and Social Networking, 20*, 501–507.

Triplett, N. (1898). The dynamogenic factors in pacemaking and competition. *American Journal of Psychology, 9*, 507–533.

Trotter, P. D., McGlone, F., Reniers, R. L. E. P., & Deakin, J. F. W. (2018). Construction and validation of the Touch Experiences and Attitudes Questionnaire (TEAQ): A self-report measure to determine attitudes toward and experiences of positive touch. *Journal of Nonverbal Behavior.*

Trout, D. L., & Rosenfeld, H. M. (1980). The effect of postural lean and body congruence on the judgment of psychotherapeutic rapport. *Journal of Nonverbal Behavior, 4*, 176–190.

Truesdale, D. M., & Pell, M. D. (2018). The sound of passion and indifference. *Speech Communication, 99*, 124–134.

Trupin, C. M. (1976). *Linguistics and gesture: An application of linguistic theory to the study of emblems.* Unpublished doctoral dissertation, University of Michigan, Ann Arbor.

Tskhay, K. O., Clout, J. M., & Rule, N. O. (2017). The impact of health, wealth, and attractiveness on romantic evaluation from photographs of faces. *Archives of Sexual Behavior, 46,* 2365–2376.

Tskhay, K. O., & Rule, N. O. (2013). Accuracy in categorizing perceptually ambiguous groups: A review and meta-analysis. *Personality and Social Psychology Review, 17,* 72–86.

Tskhay, K. O., & Rule, N. O. (2015). Emotions facilitate the communication of ambiguous group memberships. *Emotion, 15,* 812–826.

Tucker, J. S., & Riggio, R. E. (1988). The role of social skills in encoding posed and spontaneous facial expressions. *Journal of Nonverbal Behavior, 12,* 87–97.

Turner, L. H., Dindia, K., & Pearson, J. C. (1995). An investigation of female/male verbal behaviors in same-sex and mixed-sex conversations. *Communication Reports, 8,* 86–96.

Tusing, K. J., & Dillard, J. P. (2000). The sounds of dominance: Vocal precursors of perceived dominance during interpersonal influence. *Human Communication Research, 26,* 148–171.

Udry, J. R., & Eckland, B. K. (1984). Benefits of being attractive: Differential payoffs for men and women. *Psychological Reports, 54,* 47–56.

Uebayashi, K., Tado'oka, Y., Ishii, K., & Murata, K. (2016). The effect of black or white clothing on self-perception of morality. *Japanese Journal of Experimental Social Psychology, 55,* 130–138.

Ulrich, R. S., Bogren, L., Gardiner, S. K., & Lundin, S. (2018). Psychiatric ward design can reduce aggressive behavior. *Journal of Environmental Psychology, 57,* 53–66.

Underdown, A., Barlow, J., & Stewart-Brown, S. (2010). Tactile stimulation in physically healthy infants: Results of a systematic review. *Journal of Reproductive and Infant Psychology, 28,* 11–29.

Utzinger, V. A. (1952). *An experimental study of the effects of verbal fluency upon the listener.* Los Angeles: University of Southern California.

Vagnoni, E., Lewis, J., Tajadura-Jiménez, A., & Cardini, F. (2018). Listening to a conversation with aggressive content expands the interpersonal space. *PLoS ONE, 13,* Article ID e0192753.

Valente, D., Theurel, A., & Gentaz, E. (2018). The role of visual experience in the production of emotional facial expressions by blind people: A review. *Psychonomic Bulletin & Review, 25,* 483–497.

Valla, J. M., Ceci, S. J., & Williams, W. M. (2011). The accuracy of interferences about criminality based on facial appearance. *Journal of Social, Evolutionary, and Cultural Psychology, 5,* 66–91.

Van Baaren, R. B., Horgan, T. G., Chartrand, T. L., & Dijkmans, M. (2004). The forest, the trees, and the chameleon: Context dependency and mimicry. *Journal of Personality and Social Psychology, 86,* 453–459.

van Brummen-Girigori, O., & Buunk, A. (2016). Intrasexual competitiveness and non-verbal seduction strategies to attract males: A study among teenage girls from Curaçao. *Evolution and Human Behavior, 37,* 134–141.

Vancil, D. L., & Pendell, S. D. (1987). The myth of viewer-listener disagreement in the first Kennedy–Nixon debate. *Central States Speech Journal, 38,* 16–27.

Van den Berg, Y. H. M., Segers, E., & Cillessen, A. H. N. (2012). Changing peer perceptions and victimization through classroom arrangements: A field experiment. *Journal of Abnormal Child Psychology: An official publication of the International Society for Research in Child and Adolescent Psychopathology, 40,* 403–412.

van der Schalk, J., Fischer, A., Doosje, B., Wigboldus, D., Hawk, S., Rotteveel, M., & Hess, U. (2011). Convergent and divergent responses to emotional displays of ingroup and outgroup. *Emotion, 11,* 286–298.

van Dulmen, A. M., Verhaak, P. F. M., & Bilo, H. J. G. (1997). Shifts in doctor–patient communication during a series of outpatient consultations in non-insulin-dependent diabetes mellitus. *Patient Education and Counseling, 30,* 227–237.

van Hooff, J. A. R. A. M. (1972). A comparative approach to the phylogeny of laughter and smiling. In R. Hinde (Ed.), *Non-verbal communication* (pp. 209–241). Cambridge, MA: Cambridge University Press.

van Hooff, J. A. R. A. M. (1973). A structural analysis of the social behaviour of a semi-captive group of chimpanzees. In M. von Cranach & I. Vine (Eds.), *Social communication and movement* (pp. 75–162). New York, NY: Academic Press.

Van Lancker, D., Kreiman, J., & Emmorey, K. (1985). Familiar voice recognition: Patterns and parameters—Recognition of backward voices. *Journal of Phonetics, 13*, 19–38.

Van Lancker, D., Kreiman, J., & Wickens, T. D. (1985). Familiar voice recognition: Patterns and parameters: II. Recognition of rate-altered voices. *Journal of Phonetics, 13*, 39–52.

Vannier, S. A., & O'Sullivan, L. F. (2011). Communicating interest in sex: Verbal and nonverbal initiation of sexual activity in young adults' romantic dating relationships. *Archives of Sexual Behavior, 40*, 961–969.

Van Osch, Y., Blanken, I., Meijs, M. H. J., & van Wolferen, J. (2015). A group's physical attractiveness is greater than the average attractiveness of its members: The group attractiveness effect. *Personality and Social Psychology Bulletin, 41*, 559–574.

Van Puyvelde, M., Gorissen, A.-S., Pattyn, N., & McGlone, F. (2019). Does touch matter? The impact of stroking versus non-stroking maternal touch on cardio-respiratory processes in mothers and infants. *Physiology & Behavior, 207*, 55–63.

Van Straaten, I., Holland, R. W., Finkenauer, C., Hollenstein, T., & Engles, R. C. (2010). Gazing behavior during mixed-sex interactions: Sex and attractiveness effects. *Archives of Sexual Behavior, 39*, 1055–1062.

Van Wolkenten, M. L., Davis, J. M., Gong, M. L., & de Waal, F. B. M. (2006). Coping with acute crowding by Cebus apella. *International Journal of Primatology, 27*, 1241–1256.

Varnes, J. R., Stellefson, M. L., Janelle, C. M., Dorman, S. M., Dodd, V., & Miller, M. D. (2013). A systematic review of studies comparing body image concerns among female college athletes and non-athletes, 1997–2012. *Body Image, 10*, 421–432.

Vazire, S., Naumann, L. P., Rentfrow, P. J., & Gosling, S. D. (2008). Portrait of a narcissist: Manifestations of narcissism in physical appearance. *Journal of Research in Personality, 42*, 1439–1447.

Vazire, S., Naumann, L. P., Rentfrow, P. J., & Gosling, S. D. (2009). Smiling reflects different affective states in men and women. *Behavioral and Brain Sciences, 32*, 403–405.

Vendemia, J. M. C., Schillaci, M. J., Buzan, R. F., Green, E. P., & Meek, S. W. (2009). Alternate technologies for the detection of deception. In D. T. Wilcox (Ed.), *The use of the polygraph in assessing, treating and supervising sex offenders: A practitioner's guide* (pp. 266–295). Hoboken, NJ: Wiley-Blackwell.

Verhulst, B., Lodge, M., & Lavine, H. (2010). The attractiveness halo: Why some candidates are perceived more favorably than others. *Journal of Nonverbal Behavior, 34*, 111–117.

Verser, R., & Wicks, R. H. (2006). Managing voter impressions: The use of images on presidential candidate Web sites during the 2000 campaign. *Journal of Communication, 56*, 178–197.

Vernetti, A., Ganea, N., Tucker, L., Charman, T., Johnson, M. H., & Senju, A. (2018). Infant neural sensitivity to eye gaze depends on early experience of gaze communication. *Developmental Cognitive Neuroscience, 34*, 1–6.

Vestman, V., Gowda, D., Sahidullah, M., Alku, P., & Kinnunen, T. (2018). Speaker recognition from whispered speech: A tutorial survey and an application of time-varying linear prediction. *Speech Communication, 99*, 62–79.

Vettin, J., & Todt, D. (2004). Laughter in conversation: Features of occurrence and acoustic structure. *Journal of Nonverbal Behavior, 28*, 93–115.

Vicaria, I. M., & Dickens, L. (2016). Meta-analyses of the intra- and interpersonal outcomes of interpersonal coordination. *Journal of Nonverbal Behavior, 40*, 335–361.

Viken, R. J., Rose, R. J., Kaprio, J., & Koskenvuo, M. (1994). A developmental genetic analysis of adult personality: Extraversion and neuroticism from 18 to 59 years of age. *Journal of Personality and Social Psychology, 66*, 722–730.

Vinall, J., Riddell, R. P., & Greenberg, S. (2011). The influence of culture on maternal soothing behaviours and infant pain expression in the immunization context. *Pain Research and Management, 16*, 234–238.

Vinsel, A., Brown, B. B., Altman, I., & Foss, C. (1980). Privacy regulation, territorial displays, and effectiveness of individual functioning. *Journal of Personality and Social Psychology, 39*, 1104–1115.

Virués-Ortega, J., Pastor-Barriuso, R., Castellote, J. M., Población, A., & de Pedro-Cuesta, J. (2012). Effect of animal-assisted therapy on the psychological and functional status of elderly populations and patients with psychiatric disorders: A meta-analysis. *Health Psychology Review, 6*, 197–221.

Vogel, T., Kutzner, F., Fiedler, K., & Freytag, P. (2010). Exploiting attractiveness in persuasion: Senders' implicit theories about receivers' processing motivation. *Personality and Social Psychology Bulletin, 36*, 830–842.

Vogt, D. S., & Colvin, C. R. (2003). Interpersonal orientation and the accuracy of personality judgements. *Journal of Personality, 71*, 267–295.

Vogt, E. Z., & Hyman, R. (2000). *Water witching U.S.A.* (2nd ed.). Chicago, IL: University of Chicago Press.

von Cranach, M., & Ellgring, J. H. (1973). Problems in the recognition of gaze direction. In M. von Cranach & I. Vine (Eds.), *Social communication and movement* (pp. 419–443). New York, NY: Academic Press.

von Grünau, M., & Anston, C. (1995). The detection of gaze direction: A stare-in-the-crowd effect. *Perception, 24*, 1297–1313.

Vranic, A. (2003). Personal space in physically abused children. *Environment and Behavior, 35*, 550–565.

Vrij, A. (2000). *Detecting lies and deceit.* New York, NY: Wiley.

Vrij, A. (2008). *Detecting lies and deceit: Pitfalls and opportunities* (2nd ed.). New York, NY: John Wiley.

Vrij, A., Edward, K., Roberts, K. P., & Bull, R. (2000). Detecting deceit via analysis of verbal and nonverbal behavior. *Journal of Nonverbal Behavior, 24*, 239–263.

Vrij, A., Granhag, P. A., Mann, S., & Leal, S. (2011). Outsmarting the liars: Toward a cognitive lie detection approach. *Current Directions in Psychological Science, 20*, 28–32.

Vrij, A., Granhag, P. A., & Porter, S. (2010). Pitfalls and opportunities in nonverbal and verbal lie detection. *Psychological Science in the Public Interest, 11*, 89–121.

Vrij, A., Mann, S., Leal, S., & Fisher, R. (2010). "Look into my eyes": Can an instruction to maintain eye contact facilitate lie detection? *Psychology, Crime, and Law, 16*, 327–348.

Vrij, A., van der Steen, J., & Koppelaar, L. (1994). Aggression of police officers as a function of temperature: An experiment with the Fire Arms Training System. *Journal of Community and Applied Social Psychology, 4*, 365–370.

Wagner, H., & Lee, V. (1999). Facial behavior alone and in the presence of others. In P. Philippot, R. S. Feldman, & E. J. Coats (Eds.), *The social context of nonverbal behavior* (pp. 262–286). Cambridge, UK: Cambridge University Press.

Wagner, H., & Lee, V. (2008). Alexithymia and individual differences in emotional expression. *Journal of Research in Personality, 42*, 83–95.

Wagner, H. L., Buck, R., & Winterbotham, M. (1993). Communication of specific emotions: Gender differences in sending accuracy and communication measures. *Journal of Nonverbal Behavior, 17*, 29–53.

Wagner, H. L., & Smith, J. (1991). Facial expressions in the presence of friends and strangers. *Journal of Nonverbal Behavior, 15*, 201–214.

Waitt, G., Lane, R., & Head, L. (2003). The boundaries of nature tourism. *Annals of Tourism Research, 30*, 523–545.

Walker, A. S., Nowicki, S., Jones, J., & Heimann, L. (2011). Errors in identifying and expressing emotion in facial expressions, voices, and postures unique to social anxiety. *Journal of Genetic Psychology: Research and Theory on Human Development, 172*, 293–301.

Walker, M., & Vetter, T. (2016). Changing the personality of a face: Perceived Big Two and Big Five personality factors modeled in real photographs. *Journal of Personality and Social Psychology, 110*, 609–624.

Walker, M. B., & Trimboli, C. (1983). The expressive functions of the eye flash. *Journal of Nonverbal Behavior, 8*, 3–13.

Walker-Andrews, A. S. (1997). Infants' perception of expressive behaviors: Differentiation of multimodal information. *Psychological Bulletin, 121*, 437–456.

Walker-Andrews, A. S., & Lennon, E. (1991). Infants' discrimination of vocal expressions: Contributions of auditory and visual information. *Infant Behavior and Development, 14*, 131–142.

Wallbott, H. G., & Scherer, K. R. (1986). Cues and channels in emotion recognition. *Journal of Personality and Social Psychology, 51*, 690–699.

Walster, E., Aronson, V., Abrahams, D., & Rottmann, L. (1966). Importance of physical attractiveness in dating behavior. *Journal of Personality and Social Psychology, 4*, 508–516.

Walters, A. S., Barrett, R. P., & Feinstein, C. (1990). Social relatedness and autism: Current research, issues, directions. *Research in Developmental Disabilities, 11*, 303–326.

Walther, J. B. (2006). Nonverbal dynamics in computer-mediated communication or: (and the net: 's with you,:) and you :) alone. In V. Manusov & M. L. Patterson (Eds.), *The SAGE handbook of nonverbal communication* (pp. 461–479). Thousand Oaks, CA: SAGE.

Walther, J. B., Slovacek, C., & Tidwell, L. C. (2001). Is a picture worth a thousand words? Photographic images in long-term and short-term virtual teams. *Communication Research, 28*, 105–134.

Walther, J. B., & Tidwell, L. C. (1995). Nonverbal cues in computer-mediated communication, and the effect of chronemics on relational communication. *Journal of Organizational Computing, 5*, 355–378.

Wang, J. T. Y. (2011). Pupil dilation and eye tracking. In M. Schulte-Mecklenbeck, A. Kühberger, & R. Ranyard (Eds.), *A handbook of process tracing methods for decision research: A critical review and user's guide* (pp. 185–204). New York, NY: Psychology Press.

Wang, M. Z., & Hall, J. A. (2019). Political skill and outcomes in social life. *Personality and Individual Differences, 149*, 192–199.

Ward, C. (1968). Seating arrangement and leadership emergence in small discussion groups. *Journal of Social Psychology, 74*, 83–90.

Warner, R. M., Malloy, D., Schneider, K., Knoth, R., & Wilder, B. (1987). Rhythmic organization of social interaction and observer ratings of positive affect and involvement. *Journal of Nonverbal Behavior, 11*, 57–74.

Warren, B. L. (1966). A multiple variable approach to the assortative mating phenomenon. *Eugenics Quarterly, 13*, 285–290.

Warren, G., Schertler, E., & Bull, P. (2009). Detecting deception from emotional and unemotional cues. *Journal of Nonverbal Behavior, 33*, 59–69.

Watson, O. M. (1970). *Proxemic behavior: A cross-cultural study*. The Hague, The Netherlands: Mouton.

Waxer, P. (1976). Nonverbal cues for depth of depression: Set versus no set. *Journal of Consulting and Clinical Psychology, 44*, 493.

Waxer, P. H. (1977). Nonverbal cues for anxiety: An examination of emotional leakage. *Journal of Abnormal Psychology, 86*, 306–314.

Wearne, T., Osborne-Crowley, K., Rosenberg, H., Dethier, M., & McDonald, S. (2019). Emotion recognition depends on subjective emotional experience and not on facial expressivity: Evidence from traumatic brain injury. *Brain Injury, 33*, 12–22.

Weaver, J. C., & Anderson, R. J. (1973). Voice and personality interrelationships. *Southern Speech Communication Journal, 38*, 262–278.

Webb, A., & Peck, J. (2015). Individual differences in interpersonal touch: On the development, validation, and use of the "comfort with interpersonal touch" (CIT) scale. *Journal of Consumer Psychology, 25*, 60–77.

Webster, G. D., Urland, G. R., & Correll, J. (2012). Can uniform color color aggression? Quasi-experimental evidence from professional ice hockey. *Social Psychological and Personality Science, 3*, 274–281.

Wedekind, C., & Füri, S. (1997). Body odour preferences in men and women: Do they aim for specific MHC combinations or simply heterozygosity? *Proceedings, Biological Sciences, 264*, 1471–1479.

Wedekind, C., Seebeck, T., Bettens, F., & Paepke, A. J. (1995). MHC-dependent mate preferences in humans. *Proceedings, Biological Sciences, 260*, 245–249.

Wegner, D. M. (2002). *The illusion of conscious will*. Cambridge, MA: MIT Press.

Wegner, D. M., Fuller, V. A., & Sparrow, B. (2003). Clever hands: Uncontrolled intelligence in facilitated communication. *Journal of Personality and Social Psychology, 85*, 5–19.

Weichbold, V., Holzer, A., Newesely, G., & Stephan, K. (2012). Results from high-frequency hearing screening in 14- to 15-year-old adolescents and their relation to self-reported exposure to loud music. *International Journal of Audiology, 51*, 650–654.

Weinstein, N. D. (1978). Individual differences in reactions to noise: A longitudinal study in a college dormitory. *Journal of Applied Psychology, 63*, 458–166.

Weisbuch, M., & Ambady, N. (2009). Unspoken cultural influence: Exposure to and influence of nonverbal bias. *Journal of Personality and Social Psychology, 96*, 1104–1119.

Weisbuch, M., Pauker, K., & Ambady, N. (2009). The subtle transmission of race bias via televised nonverbal behavior. *Science, 326*, 1711–1714.

Weiss, M. W., Trehub, S. E., Schellenberg, E. G., & Habashi, P. (2016). Pupils dilate for vocal or familiar music. *Journal of Experimental Psychology: Human Perception and Performance, 42*, 1061–1065.

Weiten, W. (1980). The attraction-leniency effect in jury research: An examination of external validity. *Journal of Applied Social Psychology, 10*, 340–347.

Wells, D. (2011). The value of pets for human health. *The Psychologist, 24*, 172–176.

Wells, W., & Siegel, B. (1961). Stereotyped somatotypes. *Psychological Reports, 8*, 77–78.

Wendin, K., Allesen-Holm, B. H., & Bredie, W. L. P. (2011). Do facial reactions add new dimensions to measuring sensory responses to basic tastes? *Food Quality and Preference, 22*, 346–354.

Werner, C. M., & Baxter, L. A. (1994). Temporal qualities of relationships: Organismic, transactional, and dialectical views. In M. L. Knapp & J. R. Miller (Eds.), *Handbook of interpersonal communication* (2nd ed., pp. 59–99). Thousand Oaks, CA: SAGE.

Westfall, J. E., Jasper, J. D., & Zelmanova, Y. (2010). Differences in time perception as a function of strength of handedness. *Personality and Individual Differences, 49*, 629–633.

Wexner, L. B. (1954). The degree to which colors (hues) are associated with mood-tones. *Journal of Applied Psychology, 38*, 432–435.

Wheeless, V. E., Witt, P. L., Maresh, M., Bryand, M. C., & Schrodt, P. (2011). Instructor credibility as a mediator of instructor communication and students' intent to persist in college. *Communication Education, 60*, 314–339.

Whitcher, S. J., & Fisher, J. D. (1979). Multidimensional reaction to therapeutic touch in a hospital setting. *Journal of Personality and Social Psychology, 37*, 87–96.

White, S. E. (1995). A content analytic technique for measuring the sexiness of women's business attire in media presentations. *Communication Research Reports, 12*, 178–185.

Whitty, M. T. (2009). eDating: The five phases of online dating. In C. Romm-Livermore & K. Setzekorn (Eds.), *Social networking communities and eDating services: Concepts and implications* (pp. 278–291). Hershey, NY: IGI Global.

Widen, S. C., Christy, A. M., Hewett, K., & Russell, J. A. (2011). Do proposed facial expressions of contempt, shame, embarrassment, and compassion communicate the predicted emotion? *Cognition and Emotion, 25*, 898–906.

Widgery, R. N. (1974). Sex of receiver and physical attractiveness of source as determinants of initial credibility perceptions. *Western Speech, 38*, 13–17.

Widman, D. R., Bennetti, M. K., & Anglemyer, R. (2019). Gaze patterns of sexually fluid women and men at nude females and males. *Evolutionary Behavioral Sciences*.

Wiemann, J. M. (1977). Explication and test of a model of communicative competence. *Human Communication Research, 3*, 195–213.

Wiemann, J. M., & Knapp, M. L. (1975). Turn-taking in conversations. *Journal of Communication, 25*, 75–92.

Wieser, M. J., & Pauli, P. (2009). Is eye to eye contact really threatening and avoided in social anxiety? An eye-tracking and psychophysiology study. *Journal of Anxiety Disorders, 23*, 93–103.

Wieser, M. J., Pauli, P., Grosseibl, M., Molzow, I., & Mühlberger, A. (2010). Virtual social interactions in social anxiety—The impact of sex, gaze, and interpersonal distance. *Cyberpsychology, Behavior, and Social Networking, 13*, 547–554.

Wiggins, N., & Wiggins, J. S. (1969). A topological analysis of male preferences for female body types. *Multivariate Behavioral Research, 4*, 89–102.

Wilke, W., & Snyder, J. (1941). Attitudes toward American dialects. *Journal of Social Psychology, 14*, 349–362.

Wilkins, R. (2005). The optimal form: Inadequacies and excessiveness within the asiallinen [matter of fact] nonverbal style in public and civic settings in Finland. *Journal of Communication, 55*, 383–400.

Williams, C. E., & Stevens, K. N. (1972). Emotions and speech: Some acoustical correlates. *Journal of the Acoustical Society of America, 52*, 1238–1250.

Willis, F. N., Jr., & Briggs, L. F. (1992). Relationship and touch in public settings. *Journal of Nonverbal Behavior, 16*, 55–63.

Willis, F. N., & Hoffman, G. E. (1975). Development of tactile patterns in relation to age, sex, and race. *Developmental Psychology, 11*, 866.

Willis, F. N., & Rawdon, V. A. (1994). Gender and national differences in attitudes toward same-gender touch. *Perceptual and Motor Skills, 78*, 1027–1034.

Willis, F. N., & Reeves, D. L. (1976). Touch interactions in junior high students in relation to sex and race. *Developmental Psychology, 12*, 91–92.

Willis, M., Blunt-Vinti, H. D., & Jozkowski, K. N. (2019). Associations between internal and external sexual consent in a diverse national sample of women. *Personality and Individual Differences, 149*, 37–45.

Wilson, J. Q., & Kelling, G. L. (1982, March). Broken Windows. *The Atlantic Monthly*, 29–38.

Wilson, T. P., Wiemann, J. M., & Zimmerman, D. H. (1984). Models of turn-taking in conversational interaction. *Journal of Language and Social Psychology, 3*, 159–184.

Wirth, J. H., Sacco, D. F., Hugenberg, K., & Williams, K. D. (2010). Eye gaze as relational evaluation: Averted eye gaze leads to feelings of ostracism and relational devaluation. *Personality and Social Psychology Bulletin, 36*, 869–882.

With a handshake, Rabin's fate was sealed. (1995, November 19). *New York Times*.

Witkower, Z., Tracy, J. L., Cheng, J. T., & Henrich, J. (2019). Two signals of social rank: Prestige and dominance are associated with distinct nonverbal displays. *Journal of Personality and Social Psychology*.

Witt, P. L., Wheeless, L. R., & Allen, M. (2004). A meta-analytical review of the relationship between teacher immediacy and student learning. *Communication Monographs, 71*, 184–207.

Wohlrab, S., Fink, B., Kappeler, P. M., & Brewer, G. (2009). Differences in personality attributions toward tattooed and nontattooed virtual human characters. *Journal of Individual Differences, 30*, 1–5.

Wollin, D. D., & Montagre, M. (1981). College classroom environment: Effects of sterility versus amiability on student and teacher performance. *Environment and Behavior, 13*, 707–716.

Woodall, W. G., & Burgoon, J. K. (1981). The effects of nonverbal synchrony on message comprehension and persuasiveness. *Journal of Nonverbal Behavior, 5*, 207–223.

Woodall, W. G., & Burgoon, J. K. (1983). Talking fast and changing attitudes: A critique and clarification. *Journal of Nonverbal Behavior, 8*, 126–142.

Woodall, W. G., & Folger, J. P. (1981). Encoding specificity and nonverbal cue content: An expansion of episodic memory research. *Communication Monographs, 48*, 39–53.

Woodmansee, J. J. (1970). The pupil response as a measure of social attitudes. In G. F. Summers (Ed.), *Attitude measurement* (pp. 514–533). Chicago, IL: Rand McNally.

Woodward, B. (2004). *Plan of attack*. New York, NY: Simon & Schuster.

Woolbert, C. (1920). The effects of various modes of public reading. *Journal of Applied Psychology, 4*, 162–185.

Woolfolk, A. (1978). Student learning and performance under varying conditions of teacher verbal and nonverbal evaluative communication. *Journal of Educational Psychology, 70*, 87–94.

Woolfolk, A. E., & Brooks, D. M. (1983). Nonverbal communication in teaching. In E. Gordon (Ed.), *Review of research in education* (Vol. 10, pp. 103–150). Washington, DC: American Educational Research Association.

Woolfolk, R. L. (1978). Student learning and performance under varying conditions of teacher verbal and nonverbal evaluative communication. *Journal of Educational Psychology, 70*, 87–94.

Word, C. O., Zanna, M. P., & Cooper, J. (1974). The nonverbal mediation of self-fulfilling prophecies in interracial interaction. *Journal of Experimental Social Psychology, 10*, 109–120.

Wuensch, K. L., & Moore, C. H. (2004). Effects of physical attractiveness on evaluations of a male employee's allegation of sexual harassment by his female employer. *Journal of Social Psychology, 144*, 207–217.

Wyland, C. L., & Forgas, J. P. (2010). Here's looking at you kid: Mood effects on processing eye gaze as a heuristic cue. *Social Cognition, 28*, 133–144.

Wylie, L. (1977). *Beaux gestes: A guide to French body talk*. Cambridge, MA: The Undergraduate Press.

Xu, F., Li, J., Liang, Y., Wang, Z., Hong, X., Ware, R., . . . Owen, N. (2010). Residential density and adolescent overweight in a rapidly urbanizing region of mainland China. *Journal of Epidemiology and Community Health, 64*, 1017–1021.

Yabar, Y., Johnston, L., Miles, L., & Peace, V. (2006). Implicit behavioral mimicry: Investigating the impact of group membership. *Journal of Nonverbal Behavior, 30*, 97–113.

Yardley, L., McDermott, L., Pisarski, S., Duchaine, B., & Nakayama, K. (2008). Psychosocial consequences of developmental prosopagnosia: A problem of recognition. *Journal of Psychosomatic Research, 65*, 445–451.

Yoshie, M., & Sauter, D. A. (2019). Cultural norms influence nonverbal emotion communication: Japanese vocalizations of socially disengaging emotions. *Emotion*.

Young, C. (2002). Brain waves, picture sorts, and branding moments. *Journal of Advertising Research, 42*, 42–53.

Young, C. (2007). The power of touch in psychotherapy. *International Journal of Psychotherapy, 11*, 15–24.

Young, D. R., Alhassan, S., Search, S. A., Camhi, S. M., Camhi, S. M., Ferguson, J. F., . . . Heart Association. (2016, August 15). *Sedentary behavior and cardiovascular morbidity and mortality: A science advisory from the American Heart Association.*

Young, M. (1999). Dressed to commune, dressed to kill: Changing police imagery in England and Wales. In K. K. P. Johnson & S. J. Lennon (Eds.), *Appearance and power* (pp. 33–57). New York, NY: Oxford University Press.

Young, S. G., & Hugenberg, K. (2010). Mere social categorization modulates identification of facial expressions of emotion. *Journal of Personality and Social Psychology, 99*, 964–977.

Yu, C. (2011). The display of frustration in arguments: A multimodal analysis. *Journal of Pragmatics, 43*, 2964–2981.

Zaidel, S., & Mehrabian, A. (1969). The ability to communicate and infer positive and negative attitudes facially and vocally. *Journal of Experimental Research in Personality, 3*, 233–241.

Zajonc, R. B. (1985). Emotion and facial efference: A theory reclaimed. *Science, 228*, 15–21.

Zajonc, R. B., Adelmann, P. K., Murphy, S. T., & Niedenthal, P. M. (1987). Convergence in the physical appearance of spouses. *Motivation and Emotion, 11*, 335–346.

Zanna, M. P., & Pack, S. J. (1975). On the self-fulfilling nature of apparent sex differences in behavior. *Journal of Experimental Social Psychology, 11*, 583–591.

Zebrowitz, L. A. (1997). *Reading faces.* Boulder, CO: Westview Press.

Zebrowitz, L. A., Brownlow, S., & Olson, K. (1992). Baby talk to the babyfaced. *Journal of Nonverbal Behavior, 16*, 143–158.

Zebrowitz, L. A., & Rhodes, G. (2004). Sensitivity to "bad genes" and the anomalous face over-generalization effect: Cue validity, cue utilization, and accuracy in judging intelligence and health. *Journal of Nonverbal Behavior, 28*, 167–185.

Zhang, F., & Parmley, M. (2011). What your best friend sees that I don't see: Comparing female close friends and casual acquaintances on the perception of emotional facial expressions of varying intensities. *Personality and Social Psychology Bulletin, 37*, 28–39.

Zilliacus, E., Meiser, B., Lobb, E., Dudding, T. E., Barlow-Stewart, K., & Tucker, K. (2010). The virtual consultation: Practitioners' experiences of genetic counseling by videoconferencing in Australia. *Telemedicine and e-Health, 16*, 350–357.

Zimbardo, P., & Boyd, J. (1999). Putting time in perspective: A valid, reliable individual-difference metric. *Journal of Personality and Social Psychology, 77*, 1271–1288.

Zotto, M., & Pegna, A. J. (2017). Electrophysiological evidence of perceived sexual attractiveness for human female bodies varying in waist-to-hip ratio. *Cognitive, Affective & Behavioral Neuroscience, 17*, 577–591.

Zuckerman, M. (1986). On the meaning and implications of facial prominence. *Journal of Nonverbal Behavior, 10*, 215–229.

Zuckerman, M., Amidon, M. D., Biship, S. E., & Pomerantz, S. D. (1982). Face and tone of voice in the communication of deception. *Journal of Personality and Social Psychology, 43*, 347–357.

Zuckerman, M., DeFrank, R. S., Hall, J. A., Larrance, D. T., & Rosenthal, R. (1979). Facial and vocal cues of deception and honesty. *Journal of Experimental Social Psychology, 15*, 378–396.

Zuckerman, M., DePaulo, B. M., & Rosenthal, R. (1981). Verbal and nonverbal communication of deception. In L. Berkowitz (Ed.), *Advances in experimental social psychology* (Vol. 14, pp. 1–57). New York, NY: Academic Press.

Zuckerman, M., & Driver, R. E. (1989). What sounds beautiful is good: The vocal attractiveness stereotype. *Journal of Nonverbal Behavior, 13*, 67–82.

Zuckerman, M., Hall, J. A., DeFrank, R. S., & Rosenthal, R. (1976). Encoding and decoding of spontaneous and posed facial expressions. *Journal of Personality and Social Psychology, 34*, 966–977.

Zuckerman, M., Hodgins, H., & Miyake, K. (1990). The vocal attractiveness stereotype: Replication and elaboration. *Journal of Nonverbal Behavior, 14*, 97–112.

Zuckerman, M., & Kieffer, S. C. (1994). Race differences in face-ism: Does facial prominence imply dominance? *Journal of Personality and Social Psychology, 66*, 86–92.

Zuckerman, M., & Larrance, D. T. (1979). Individual differences in perceived encoding and decoding abilities. In R. Rosenthal (Ed.), *Skill in nonverbal communication: Individual differences* (pp. 171–203). Cambridge, MA: Oelgeschlager, Gunn & Hain.

Zuckerman, M., Lipets, M. S., Koivumaki, J. H., & Rosenthal, R. (1975). Encoding and decoding nonverbal cues of emotion. *Journal of Personality and Social Psychology, 32,* 1068–1076.

Zuckerman, M., Miserandino, M., & Bernieri, F. J. (1983). Civil inattention exists—In elevators. *Personality and Social Psychology Bulletin, 9,* 578–586.

Zuckerman, M., & Miyake, K. (1993). The attractive voice: What makes it so? *Journal of Nonverbal Behavior, 17,* 119–135.

Zuckerman, M., Spiegel, N. H., DePaulo, B. M., & Rosenthal, R. (1982). Nonverbal strategies for decoding deception. *Journal of Nonverbal Behavior, 6,* 171–187.

Zwebner, Y., Sellier, A.-L., Rosenfeld, N., Goldenberg, J., & Mayo, R. (2017). We look like our names: The manifestation of name stereotypes in facial appearance. *Journal of Personality and Social Psychology, 112,* 527–554.

Zweigenhaft, R. (1976). Personal space in the faculty office: Desk placement and the student–faculty interaction. *Journal of Applied Psychology, 61,* 529–532.

Zweigenhaft, R. L. (2008). A do re mi encore: A closer look at the personality correlates of music preferences. *Journal of Individual Differences, 29,* 45–55.

NAME INDEX

SUBJECT INDEX